Audit and Control of Information Systems

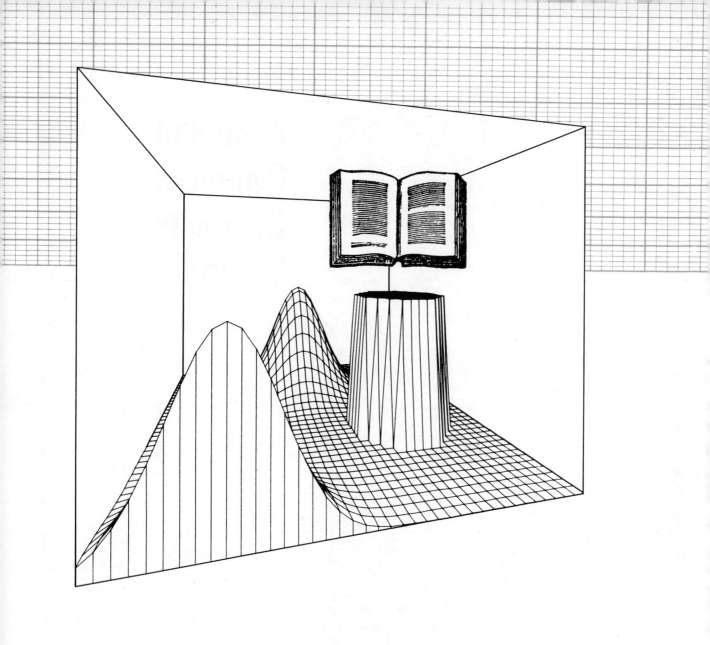

Audit and Control of Information Systems

Frederick Gallegos, CISA, CDE
United States General Accounting Office
Los Angeles, California

Dana R. (Rick) Richardson, CPA, CDP
Partner, Arthur Young & Company
New York, New York

A. Faye Borthick, DBA, CISA, CMA
Assistant Professor
Department of Accounting & Business Law
University of Tennessee, Knoxville

J94

Published by

SOUTH-WESTERN PUBLISHING CO.

CINCINNATI   WEST CHICAGO, IL   DALLAS   LIVERMORE, CA

Contents

Preface

PERSPECTIVE

This book, *Audit and Control of Information Systems,* is designed for those who need to gain a working knowledge of the principles and techniques of computer auditing. Audiences that will find the text particularly relevant include students and professionals in the fields of:

- Business management

- Computer information systems (CIS)

- Accounting, auditing, and finance.

In short, the content of this book should be included in the background of anyone who is, or expects to be, accountable to management for the financial information on the assets of a business organization. To address this multidisciplinary subject area, a team of authors was assembled that represents a wide range of expertise, including computer auditing, government systems, internal audit, public accounting, business management and consulting, and CIS education.

A basic philosophy in the design of the text is that it must serve primarily as a learning experience, not as a manual for performing audit examinations. Thus, emphasis is on principles and techniques, as well as on application through realistic case studies. In addition to cases that are presented within chapter discussions, case projects are included in the chapter assignments. The relevance and usefulness of these cases have been proven in training programs within public and government audit organizations, and in university courses in CIS auditing. Indeed, many of the former students of these courses are employed currently as CIS auditors and have contributed case materials and references.

The endorsement of this text by the Data Processing Management Association-Education Foundation attests to its usefulness as an educational resource. The text is approved for implementation of one of the courses within the DPMA-EF *Model Curriculum for Undergraduate Computer Information Systems Education.* Specifically, the information and assignments in this book meet or exceed the content called for in the suggested outline for CIS-13—EDP Audit and Controls.

CONTENT HIGHLIGHTS

The basic intent of this book is to set computer auditing within the context of today's financial reporting systems, which rely heavily on computer-based information outputs. The presentation is divided into the following major parts:

- Framework

- Concerns and objectives

- Doing computer audits

- Management perspective.

Framework

The first three chapters of the text build a conceptual framework for learning about the principles and techniques of computer auditing. Basic instructional objectives are to establish the need for assuring the reliability of computer-based information systems and to define the role of the computer auditor in addressing that need.

The depth of presentation assumes that students will approach the text from different backgrounds and disciplines. CIS students may have to review principles of accounting and auditing. Students with business and accounting backgrounds may need some further study in the systems field, including technical topics such as microcircuitry and digital communication.

The first three chapters, therefore, aim at establishing common points of departure. Chapter 1 cites some notable cases of computer fraud and abuse, then broadens the perspective to encompass the potentially greater dangers of inefficiency and inadvertent human error, including negligence and faulty systems design. Some students already will be familiar with news accounts detailing computer fraud. However, few of them initially will appreciate the magnitude of other types of threat that do not necessarily stem from malicious intent. Also, students need to be aware that many of today's CIS professionals and business managers do not recognize the extent to which their organizations are exposed to these threats.

Chapter 2 examines the audit function from the perspective of computer-based information technology. Traditional audit approaches are contrasted with the challenges of reviewing massive files of electronic data. Computer technology, in itself, is changing the nature of internal control and the role of the auditor. A major point of emphasis is that, to assure the adequacy of controls, computer auditors should become involved in the systems development process.

Chapter 3 focuses on computer auditing as an emerging professional discipline. The common body of knowledge needed by computer auditors is surveyed. The role of professional organizations and their respective certifications are discussed. Students should begin to see how their backgrounds and academic majors might be supplemented to achieve the necessary levels of understanding and competence for careers as computer auditors. Students who will follow other career paths to management, CIS, or public accounting should begin to appreciate the value of computer auditors as key advisors. Chapter 3 concludes with a survey of legislation that affects the mission of the computer auditor and the responsibility of organizations that maintain computer-based financial information systems.

Concerns and Objectives

The main purpose of the second part of the text is to describe how the mission of computer auditors is defined by their basic responsibilities to organization management.

Chapter 4 surveys overall objectives of control, then follows through to describe the formulation of specific computer audit objectives. With this background, a typical audit scenario is presented.

Types of computer audit activities are covered in Chapter 5, including audits of applications, systems development, and facilities, as well as special studies that are conducted at the request of management.

Chapter 6 presents an overview of CIS controls. Control functions are defined, including prevention, detection, and correction. Then, the implementation of these control functions within computer applications is discussed. This chapter also marks the beginning of in-depth case assignments, which are drawn from the projects in Appendices A–E. The case assignment for Chapter 6 deals with the auditor's overview of controls.

Chapter 7 steps back, in effect, to take a look at general controls, or the environment within which CIS applications are run. Covered topics include organization controls, systems development controls, and operations controls. A case assignment deals with the review of general controls.

The discussion of controls is concluded in Chapter 8 with the evaluation of controls and the design of audit tests. In a suggested case assignment, students design a test deck and select input data according to specific evaluation criteria.

Doing Computer Audits

Chapters in this part of the book focus on typical patterns of computer audit engagements. Chapter 9 explores the involvement of computer auditors in the systems development process. Life-cycle models are reviewed, and a case assignment focuses on specific types of controls that may be designed into a system.

Chapter 10 covers audits of CIS applications. A process-oriented view of the audit is presented and then is applied in an extended case study. Several case assignments introduce students to computer-assisted audit techniques.

In Chapter 11, the implementation of computer-assisted audit procedures is covered in depth. A life-cycle methodology is presented that parallels other types of systems development. A case assignment deals with the implementation of advanced computer-assisted audit procedures.

Chapter 12 is concerned with audits of facilities, including CIS installations and operations. Particular emphasis is placed on identifying exposures and control weaknesses that often are encountered in CIS processing centers. Automated tools for computer performance evaluation and job scheduling are covered. A case assignment deals with a review of operations.

Challenges of auditing new technologies are covered in the next two chapters. Chapter 13 deals with the potential loss of control that can result from proliferation of microcomputers and distribution of information resources. Special concerns are covered for information centers and decision support systems (DSS). The text emphasizes that, for such systems, audit concerns must shift from application controls to general controls. In case assignments, students review control aspects of a distributed DSS and examine corporate policies for use of microcomputers. Chapter 14, then, carries the discussion into the realm of digital communication, with particular emphasis on transmission-oriented controls. An extended case study within the chapter deals with an audit approach that has been tailored to evaluating local area networks. A case assignment requires a review of communication controls within the DSS already studied.

Management Perspective

This last part of the text deals with the techniques and challenges of managing the CIS audit function within an organization. Chapter 15 surveys some specific audit tools, including risk assessment, threat analysis, and cost/benefit analysis. Techniques of quantitative risk assessment (QRA) are covered and then are applied in an extended case study.

Chapter 16 presents concerns, control objectives, and countermeasures in assuring the privacy, integrity, and security of computer-maintained data. Principles of compensating and complementary controls are emphasized. A case assignment asks students to assess the adequacy of security and privacy controls in the DSS already studied.

Chapter 17 describes the charter, organization, staffing, and training of an internal CIS audit department. This overview is from the perspective of a new CIS audit manager who is charged with organizing the function from startup. Professional development and career planning are stressed as ways of retaining and assuring the competency of computer audit staff.

Finally, Chapter 18 explores trends in computer technology and in the profession of CIS auditing. A futuristic scenario highlights evolution toward real-time, on-line, financial reporting systems with embedded audit facilities. Impacts of using microcomputers as audit tools are discussed, as well as the challenges of introducing microtechnology into an audit organization.

SUPPLEMENTARY STUDY AND REFERENCE AIDS

The materials at the end of this book both support its content and suggest directions and resources for further study. These materials include:

- Appendices
- Glossary
- Bibliography.

Appendices

Appendices to this text include:

- Case projects
- Audit standards.

Case projects.   Chapter assignments refer students to case projects, which are found in Appendices A–E. Each of these sections describes a different organization and its CIS. Projects within the sections direct students to review specific aspects of the system described. Solutions and suggested responses to case assignments are included in the accompanying Instructor's Manual. As stated above, these cases have been adapted from materials used successfully in university-level courses in CIS auditing and in training programs within public and government auditing organizations.

Audit standards.   Two appendices are included as reference for accepted standards that apply to CIS auditing. These materials can be especially useful for students who need to review accounting and auditing concepts and practices.

Appendix F reproduces a set of standards that have been promulgated by the Comptroller General of the United States General Accounting Office. Although these standards apply primarily within the public sector, the document can serve as an excellent model for all types of computer audit involvement.

Appendix G summarizes the current position of the public accounting profession on auditing computer-based systems that produce financial information. This document is Statement on Auditing Standards No. 48, "The Effects of Computer Processing on the Examination of Financial Statements," which is an official pronouncement of the Financial Auditing Standards Board (FASB) of the American Institute of Certified Public Accountants (AICPA).

Glossary

The glossary includes key terms that are referenced within this text, as well as other technical terms that should be in the vocabulary of computer auditors. Key terms are shown in *italics* in the text and are defined in context, with full definitions appearing in the glossary. In addition, the glossary includes terms defined in Federal Information Processing (FIPS) Publication 39, *Glossary for Computer Systems Security,* which was released by the National Bureau of Standards in February, 1976.

Bibliography

A list of relevant publications and reference sources is included in the bibliography, which should help students who are interested in CIS auditing to keep up with the rapid changes in this field. This listing also can serve as a guide for building the libraries of CIS managers and audit staff.

References in the bibliography are organized into categories, by sponsoring organization. These organizations include government agencies, professional societies, and commercial publishers. Addresses of the governmental and professional organizations also are included, along with document order numbers, if available.

STUDY/ADMINISTRATION PLAN

Administering the course of study that this text supports can begin with a survey of student backgrounds and majors. Instructors will want to be sure that students who have followed CIS curricula also have sufficient grounding in accounting principles and audit practices. Appendix G (SAS No. 48) should be particularly helpful for this review.

Some familiarity with systems concepts is an essential prerequisite. Accounting and business management students who have taken introductory level CIS courses will need to review systems development life-cycle (SDLC) methodology. An overview of the SDLC process is included in Chapter 5, and the subject is treated in depth in Chapter 9. Specific computer technical knowledge is less important; some review in this area may be needed as background for the discussion of new technologies in Chapters 13 and 14.

Based on this initial survey, the instructor may choose appropriate levels of emphasis for Chapters 1–3. If most students seem well grounded in these concepts, the content of these chapters can be condensed and covered in one or two class presentations. However, it is critical to establish the auditor's attest function and the changes that computer technology has brought in the nature and testing of internal controls.

Discussion questions that can be used to reinforce and expand on the text material are presented at the end of each chapter. These questions can be used to stimulate class discussion or as assignments for individual student essays. Many of these questions are open-ended and have no single, correct answers. Rather, the questions are designed to encourage students to think critically about key issues and audit concerns. Suggested responses are included in the accompanying Instructor's Manual.

A heavy emphasis on cases in the text reflects a strong bias toward the importance of fieldwork in the training of competent computer auditors. In developing sound, professional judgment, no substitute yet has been found for actual experience. Some extended case studies are included in the chapter discussions, and other case narratives are found in Appendices A–E. Beginning with Chapter 6, suggested assignments at the end of each chapter direct students to projects that are based on these narratives. Solutions and suggested responses that have been compiled from using these cases in actual course work are included in appendices to the Instructor's Manual.

Because of wide variations among the computer systems at different institutions, specific, on-line assignments are not given in the text. However, assignments designed around popular microcomputer packages, as well as mainframe audit packages such as DYL-280, have been included in the Instructor's Manual.

If course scheduling permits, assignment of individual student research projects is suggested highly. This type of assignment often involves students in leading-edge technology and computer-assisted audit techniques. Presentation of research papers to the class can stimulate thinking about current issues, evoke peer criticism, and help future management advisers polish important presentation skills.

The authors feel strongly that knowledge of computer audit concerns, objectives, and practices is essential, not only for CIS audit professionals, but also for all practitioners in the disciplines of business management, accounting, finance, and CIS. This book is dedicated to helping create that awareness and, thereby, to promoting the reliability of the systems that increasingly support every aspect of business life.

ACKNOWLEDGMENTS

Some key works provided source material for this text. Portions of this book were drawn from material first written by Frederick Gallegos for Auerbach Publisher's *EDP Auditing* reference publication; copyright Auerbach Publishers, Inc.

Much of the material on the principles of computer auditing is founded on some farsighted work done at Arthur Young & Company in the early 1970s. This work, and particularly the computer auditor's view of controls, is documented in *Computers and Financial Statement Reliability* by Richardson, Samson, and Moore (copyright © 1975 by Arthur Young & Company). In addition, the futuristic scenario in Chapter 18, "It is Saturday morning, January 12, 2002 . . . ," is copyright © 1979 by Arthur Young & Company and is reproduced with the firm's permission. The AY/ASQ™ system also described in Chapter 18 was developed at Arthur Young & Company under the direction of Dana R. Richardson.

Statement on Auditing Standards No. 48, which is found in Appendix G, is copyright © 1984 by the American Institute of Certified Public Accountants, Inc. and is reprinted with permission.

The authors value the cooperation of George E. Grant, Regional Manager, Los Angeles, and Barry Snyder, Group Director, Information Management and Technology Division, U.S. General Accounting Office. Portions of GAO audit guides that were particularly helpful include "Evaluating Internal Controls in Computer-Based Systems" and "Assessing Reliability of Computer Output."

Materials on risk assessment were contributed by Nander Brown, President, Nander Brown & Company, and by Carl Pabst, Partner, Touche Ross

& Company (Los Angeles). Portions of the discussion on risk models were derived from a presentation by R. V. Jacobson at the National Bureau of Standards Workshop, which was held in Florida on March 13, 1985, under the direction of Zella G. Ruthberg.

Material for some of the case studies was provided by: Nicholas W. Horsky, Group Director, Computer Audit Support, Air Force Audit Agency; John Lainhart IV, Director – Office of ADP Audit and Technical Support, Department of Transportation; Robert Parker, Partner, Deloitte, Haskins and Sells (Victoria, B.C.); and Joseph Safier, Principal, Arthur Young & Company (Los Angeles).

Source material also included the following graduate theses by former students of CIS auditing at California State Polytechnic University (Pomona): "Considerations in Auditing Local Area Networks," by Lorne Dear (Audit Manager, EDP Audits, Air Force Audit Agency) and "Developing an Effective EDP Audit Function," by Larry Lam (Computer Audit Specialist, Coopers & Lybrand, San Francisco).

Assistance in compiling the bibliography was obtained from Doug Beiber, EDP Auditor, General Telephone Company (who also served as co-author on part of the Auerbach material); Daniel Ortiz, Technical Information Specialist, U.S. General Accounting Office (Los Angeles Regional Office); and David Wright, Student Assistant, California State Polytechnic University (Pomona).

Others who contributed materials included: Rod Kocot, Senior EDP Auditor, Security Pacific Corp.; David Rhinehart, Senior EDP Auditor, Dataline; Mark Wickham and Cathy Roberts, EDP Auditors, Great Western Savings; Lisa Zanchetti, Computer Audit Specialist, Arthur Andersen and Co.; David Singlyn, Computer Audit Specialist, Arthur Young & Company; Charles Bent, EDP Audit Specialist, Teledyne; Joel Sothern, EDP Audit Manager, Regency Industries, Hong Kong; Ray Gera, and Darryl Damian, Senior EDP Auditors, Hughes Aircraft; Warren Adams, EDP Audit Specialist, Department of Corporations, State of California; Dan Dow and Seth Schneider, EDP Audit, American Savings Corp.; Don Fergus, Senior EDP Auditor, Citicorp; Charles Bogguess, Senior EDP Auditor, Walt Disney Corp.; and Paul King, Manager – Internal Audit, TRW Information Systems.

Other key individuals assisted the authors in developing the book's manuscript and assuring its quality. Benedict Kruse, i/e, inc., collaborated on the development of *Computers and Financial Statement Reliability* (cited above) and helped launch the project that culminated in this book.

Special recognition is given to Gerald E. Jones for consulting and editorial services throughout the project.

To assure the accuracy and completeness of the text, objective reviews were provided by W. Jeff Clark, CSP, Professor, Department of Finance and Information Systems, Western Kentucky University; James A. Hallam, Chairperson, Department of Accounting, Illinois State University (Normal); and Robert T. Keim, Ph.D., CSP, Associate Professor of Information Systems, Department of Decision and Information Systems, College of Business, Arizona State University. The contribution of each of these reviewers is acknowledged with sincere thanks.

In addition to the in-process reviews, final evaluation of the manuscript was provided independently to the DPMA-EF by Barbara R. Farrell, CPA, Assistant Professor of Accounting, Pace University (Pleasantville), whose contribution is hereby acknowledged.

I FRAMEWORK

The first part of this text examines how the audit function has been affected by the widespread application of computer-based techniques to financial record keeping and reporting. The presentations highlight the need for assuring reliability of computer-based information systems and define the role of the computer auditor in addressing that need. Computer auditing is presented as a multidisciplinary field that encompasses the concerns and expertise of business managers, systems professionals, financial managers, accountants, and auditors.

Chapter 1 outlines some of the threats to the integrity and reliability of computer information systems. It is emphasized that unintentional errors and omissions potentially could be more dangerous than outright fraud or abuse. Awareness of the extent of these threats and the need for new audit approaches are stressed.

Chapter 2 focuses on the ways in which computer technology has changed the nature of internal control and the role of the auditor. Trends toward automation indicate that controls should be designed into new systems from the outset, requiring auditors increasingly to become involved in the systems development process.

In Chapter 3, computer auditing is described as a growing profession with its own body of knowledge, specialized skills, and experience requirements. A survey of applicable legislation is presented as evidence of the social and economic forces that are creating new opportunities for computer auditors.

1 The Computer Audit Environment

ABSTRACT

- Cases are cited to indicate that computers have been used with alarming success as vehicles for theft of corporate assets.

- Current protection measures typically are inadequate; the illegal penetration of sophisticated computer networks is relatively easy and commonplace.

- The cost of inefficiency almost always will exceed the cost of dishonesty. Incidents of human error have been, and remain, more costly than crime and abuse.

- Systems controls are the basis for detecting most problems involving either fraud or performance failure. The systems audit function exists to verify the effectiveness of systems controls.

- Professional organizations set new professional standards and guidelines in accounting and other fields. These include certification programs that evaluate systems controls and computer security measures in internal information processing functions.

- Management concerns include the high cost of information systems, as well as the learning process associated with new technologies and the disappearance of the traditional audit trail.

- Differences between computerized and manual financial systems include realignment of functions, changes in custody of files and documents, transfer of responsibilities, and a decline of accountability.

- Auditors may use the computer itself to conduct reliability tests of computerized transactions and operations.

- Legislation affects how computer systems are built and operated, the processing logic of computer application systems, and the care, retention, and protection of data and systems.

- The internal auditor performs an advisory function to management in assessing the impact of existing legislation on computer operations, performing tests to determine whether systems comply, designing controls for systems under development, and auditing operational systems periodically.

- From the auditor's viewpoint, new criteria must be developed and applied to evaluate the impact of control weaknesses in computer systems. The auditor must tailor testing techniques to the nature of the data processing system.

INTRODUCTION

Since the early 1970s, newspaper headlines have brought a continuing stream of major cases of computer fraud to the attention of the general public. To some observers, such abuse was a surprise—a new image for computers, the electronic marvels that helped send people to the moon, aided the design and manufacture of new products, and facilitated the management and growth of organizations of every kind. Although surprising to some people, the headlines realized some of the greatest fears of management, audit, and computer information systems (CIS) professionals. It is proper to note at this point that many organizations have come a long way since the early 1970s in their abilities to apply internal control. This is true especially for computer-based systems.

Major computer-related fraud in big business is always newsworthy, but the introduction of the computer into multimillion-dollar fraud cases represents a dramatic change in the potential scope and effect of such crimes. In short, in cases such as Equity Funding and Union Dime, computers were characterized as burglary tools. It should not be surprising, however, that computers, like so many other powerful tools of technology, hold the potential for abuse and misuse.

The Tip of the Iceberg

The truly shocking aspect of these revelations—to professionals and the general public alike—is the ease with which computers have been turned to malicious purposes. Unfortunately, many instances of abuse have not required a highly skilled, knowledgeable person or an electronic whiz; instead these crimes have been achieved in a far less sophisticated manner than might have been anticipated.

In 1983, testimony before the Civil and Constitutional Rights Subcommittee of the House Judiciary Committee estimated losses from abuse of computers by white-collar criminals at $40 billion annually. The report further stated that current protection measures typically are inadequate; the illegal penetration of sophisticated computer networks is far easier and more common than generally is believed.

As with most cases of fraud, discovery of computer-related crimes has been largely accidental. Some notable cases have included the following:

- Students in Milwaukee known as "The 414s" (named for their telephone area code) gained electronic access to and reprogrammed the computerized radiation therapy records of cancer patients at Sloan-Kettering Cancer Center in Manhattan.

- Using their personal computers and telephone connections, students gained access to the unclassified portions of a computer data file at the Los Alamos research facility in New Mexico.

- Seven employees were dismissed by the Federal Aviation Administration from positions at the technical research center for allegedly misusing the computer.

- Students at the University of California, Los Angeles allegedly gained access to more than 200 computer time-sharing accounts at 14 different locations over a period of three months. According to the district attorney of Los Angeles, a sensitive defense network was entered.

- A former Federal Reserve Board employee, while working for a major stock brokerage firm, tapped into the Board's computer and gained access to a file containing sensitive financial data.

- An 18-year-old computer hacker destroyed part of his high school's computer records in what school officials say was an act of vindictive vandalism.

- In October, 1984, high school students in Irvine, California, had their microcomputers confiscated by the FBI, apparently because they had tapped illegally into the electronic mail system of the General Telephone Telenet Communications Corporation Network based in Vienna, Virginia.

- Two former directors of the computer department at New York Institute of Technology have been charged with illegal use of the school's computer in a data storage scheme that has netted them at least $40,000.

- A study of computer fraud and abuse revealed that people are using computer terminals to steal money from a number of federal public-assistance programs, including food stamps, Social Security, and the Veterans Administration.

- According to computer crime experts, a large number of people are accessing and browsing through computerized files of critical national computer systems without authorization. The extent of this abuse is especially difficult to estimate, since many of the people do not alter or otherwise tamper with the data. A significant problem, as discussed later in this book, is a lack of public awareness that even such seemingly "victimless" acts are serious crimes. Most people would become outraged, for example, if an intruder entered their houses when they were away from home "just to look around."

Management, audit, and CIS professionals have learned to take newspaper accounts regarding fraud, mismanagement, and lawsuits with caution and a degree of skepticism. Some overstatement is likely in such stories. But, the experienced professional knows that the sum of these news accounts can be likened to the tip of an iceberg—highly visible, unquestionably substantial, with greater dangers hidden beneath the surface. These hidden dangers, in fact, may be even more significant and deserve the most careful attention.

Hidden Dangers

Fraud stories are spectacular. Placed within the perspective of the stories just cited, the following statement may seem incredible:

The cost of inefficiency almost always will exceed the cost of dishonesty in organizations. Incidents of human error have been, and remain, more costly than crime and abuse.

Although perhaps incredible, it is generally true that most computer losses do not stem from criminal intent, or even from malice of forethought. Instead, the hidden danger in using complex, computer-based tools is the lack of diligence and experience in understanding the possibilities for error.

The lesson for systems professionals and auditors is not that computer crime is unimportant. Rather, anyone who is concerned with the security, integrity, and reliability of computer systems should understand that most problems—in any organization, involving either fraud or performance failure—will go undetected without appropriate controls.

Today's users of information systems have increasing control over access to computer-based information and its use in making major decisions. The potential dangers of this situation are not limited to large-scale data processing systems. For example, a Dallas-based oil and gas company fired several executives for oversights costing millions of dollars in an acquisition. The errors were traced to faulty financial analysis in a spreadsheet model in a microcomputer-based support system.

This situation is just one example of a widespread, largely underestimated, problem. There is hardly a manager or an executive with a personal computer who is not making some key decisions based on his or her spreadsheet software. There have been several reports about consequences of managers failing to look behind those assuring printouts into the logic and makeup of the spreadsheet and its formulas.

The hidden dangers extend beyond any spreadsheet software. Such problems are representative of some fundamental sources of error, illustrated by the following actual cases:

Logical inconsistency. A spreadsheet formula may be logically inconsistent; that is, the rules applied to one part of the spreadsheet should be applied to another part, but are not. In forecasting revenues, a Georgia manufacturer applied price discounts to one part of a product line, but overlooked them when forecasting sales of complementary products. Actual sales for the complementary lines turned out to be higher than forecast, and bottlenecks resulted when production could not keep up with delivery.

Conceptually flawed. A spreadsheet formula, though logically consistent, may be conceptually flawed. In such cases, bad formulas are reproduced consistently throughout a spreadsheet. A budget analyst with a large savings and loan association submitted five-year forecasts for divisional profits. However, a mistaken formula for compound growth in the spreadsheet program resulted in the figures being overstated for years two through five of the forecast.

Incorrect data format. The data format may be inconsistent or garbled. Typically, such problems occur when different types of data are used side by side in the same or in a parallel spreadsheet. For example, a national retailer, in accounting for staffing requirements, discovered field reports stated variously in persons, worker-hours, worker-days, and worker-months. Evaluation proved impossible until the field reports were rewritten.

Inappropriate tools. The wrong tool may be used for the task. This problem is common and growing, especially for users of microcomputers and other forms of microprocessor technology. An international distributor of industrial goods based its plans for sales to a European country on an analysis of that country's manufacturing capacity. But, the distributor's products were used only in secondary manufacturing, a small part of the country's total production, a distinction that was not made in the spreadsheet. Thus, projections were inaccurate, and sales were far below forecasts. Extra production and inventory costs consumed many thousands of dollars.

In such cases, gross inconsistencies or major problems will stand out. Many times, though, subtle problems will not be detected readily. The root cause is mismanagement—or a complete lack of management—of the computer resource. This text is concerned with the knowledge and discipline that must be acquired and applied, not only to prevent waste and loss of this information resource, but also to maximize the potential of computer automation in support of the goals and objectives of organizations.

THE GREATER EXPOSURE

Many organizations have reached a point in their development at which they are *computer dependent*. That is, there is no effective alternative to the computer-assisted functions. The procedures associated with the computer function simply cannot be replaced, on a moment's notice, should the computer system fail.

At the operational level, the volume and complexity of transactions are too great to be handled practically by other means. At the levels of management information and decision support, information demands are so great and the pace of activity is so swift that there is no other way to derive the necessary information on a large scale.

The demands placed on the information resource function have increased the importance of *systems controls,* or measures for assuring the accuracy, completeness, and reliability of information. The *systems audit* function, therefore, exists to verify the effectiveness of systems controls.

Managers at all levels depend increasingly on computer-based information for planning, evaluating, and controlling activities of their organizations. As organizations have expanded, their need for data communication has increased. Data are being exchanged among previously unrelated management functions and systems. The complexity of organizations with international operations also has made accurate and controlled information a critical need.

Regulatory and Professional Influences

Federal, state, and local regulatory agencies have increased the amount and kinds of information that organizations must collect, process, retain, and report. Security, health and safety programs, affirmative action, equal employment practices, pension funding, and consumer protection laws all have affected computer-based information systems. Organizations frequently must change and enlarge existing systems to remain in compliance with requirements and to avoid penalties for incomplete or inaccurate reporting.

New professional standards and guidelines in accounting and other fields impose significant requirements on information systems. Influential organizations in this area include:

- American Institute of Certified Public Accountants (AICPA)
- Institute of Internal Auditors (IIA)
- Financial Accounting Standards Board (FASB)
- EDP Auditors Association (EDPAA)
- United States General Accounting Office (GAO)
- National Association of Accountants (NAA)
- Certified public accounting (CPA) firms
- U. S. Department of Commerce, National Bureau of Standards (NBS).

These organizations have recognized the need for computer security and increased awareness of computer-based controls. Their efforts have contributed to recognition of the importance of systems controls in day-to-day operations and financial systems. Many of these organizations have established certification programs that evaluate systems controls and computer security measures in internal information processing functions.

This movement is a commendable attempt at dealing with the failure-prone nature of complex systems in which human beings interact with machines. Unfortunately, this same value of security and control is not typical in the design of computerized systems for organizations. In organizational data processing, extensive controls, backup, recovery, and alternative procedures have tended to be considered unnecessary. Some possibilities of failure have been recognized, but provisions for dealing with these threats have been minimal.

With hindsight, it is shocking that so many managers, CIS professionals, and auditors have not provided safeguards against the growing exposure of organizations arising from a dependence on computers. The computer was, in essence, taken for granted. If the programs ran to "end of job," they were assumed to be acceptable. As a result, computing systems swallowed up entire functions so rapidly that the changes went unnoticed. Systems had become so complex, so fast, that conventional approaches and techniques of management control were useless. Optimistic managers became complacent about the perceived effectiveness of traditional controls to cope with the risks of computer-based information systems.

Probably, a lack of knowledge or recognition of potential dangers by managers, auditors, and CIS professionals alike comprises the greatest exposure of all. While computers help to create massive, integrated systems, people still tend to think in terms of their own, isolated responsibilities. For example, managers at middle levels still tend to run their operations as they did when they were, in fact, self-sufficient within their own paperwork systems. Time has run out on these methods, as illustrated above in the examples of fraud, abuse, and human error. The consequences of failing to address the management and control of computer information systems can be catastrophic and must not be underestimated.

ORGANIZATIONAL AWARENESS

The information resource management function has become highly visible recently, partly because of its significant, escalating cost to the organization. Management has learned that hardware costs are only part of the total information systems expense and that the cost of maintaining a capable technical staff can be substantial. The data processing budget continues to rise, even though hardware cost effectiveness is improving constantly. Three or four times the computer "horsepower" at two-thirds the cost does not necessarily equate to lower information systems department costs.

Organizations have become aware of the hidden costs and risks associated with systems change. Systems development projects may take years and external changes may result in missed target dates. Management is beginning to recognize that new applications may become impossible because the entire information systems staff is committed to maintenance and enhancement projects. Top-level managers are now demonstrating an understanding of the fixed and variable costs associated with supporting a computer-based information system.

An additional concern to management is the learning process associated with new technologies and the disappearance of the traditional audit trail. For years, a strong movement has been emerging that is aimed at increasing management's abilities to use, understand, and become involved with the computer information systems. Managers actually have used computers to help them solve problems. But the process of learning the requisite new skills has proved exasperating for many executives who have not equipped themselves to cope with change. As a result, some past efforts aimed at management involvement with computers have proved, in a word, disastrous.

For the 1980s, the picture is different. There is a relatively large population of managers who have acquired hands-on computer experience in the course of their education and training. Thus, management indoctrination is not the block it used to be. Today, as a partial result, managers and information systems departments are creating systems with the involvement of auditors who understand the computer-based environment. The principal reason for this level of audit involvement is the gradual disappearance of traditional audit trails upon which the manager and auditor formerly relied.

Today's "paperless" systems have established their value as decision support and planning tools. With these in-place capabilities, managers have emerged as active users of their organizations' computing capabilities. Thus, today's systems can be characterized as inviting browsers on an open basis. Untold numbers of people can wander through information files or databases without leaving any trace of their presence or their activities. All of these factors combine to make transactions less traceable and systems less auditable.

Erosion of Control Functions

The sweeping adoption of computerized methods has resulted in a fractionalization, or splitting up, of traditional responsibilities and controls. In particular, the following effects have been observed:

- Realignment of functions

- Changes in custody of files and documents

- Transfer of responsibilities

- Decline of accountability.

Realignment of functions. The functions associated with transaction processing have tended to shift between decentralization and centralization of CIS functions. This has been particularly true for the period of the late 1970s and early 1980s. The most obvious example has been the capture and entry of data. Previously, transactions were initiated through the writing of documents by the persons performing the specific services involved. These documents became source media for data capture. Typically, the actual inputs to the system were initiated by a keypunch group or other data capture function not directly associated with providing the services.

The function of control, then, shifted from the people involved in the transaction to the data capture group. Data entry people did not necessarily understand the business functions involved, but they understood the input requirements of the computers that processed the data. In many companies, the net effect has been some loss of functional control.

The mid-1980s saw a shift toward decentralization marked by user-dependent transaction processing applications employing microcomputer technology. The net effect of this trend apparently has been a loss of functional control and an increase in operational dependency on automated inputs. Microcomputers, or microprocessor-based terminals, receive transaction inputs directly from users. Thus, the source of information relies heavily on the user's ability to interact successfully with the system. In applications that use machine-readable inputs, the transition is less apparent.

Changes in custody of files and documents.   The people who create and use data are said to have *ownership* over the data resource. These people retain an overall responsibility that includes the right and duty to establish rules of access to the data. *Custody* of data is a delegated responsibility on behalf of the data owners. Data custodians control physical and electronic access and enforce the authorization rules set up by the owners. Within manual processing systems, custody amounts to physical possession and safeguarding of documents. Within computerized systems, questions of ownership and custody can be elusive.

The use of machine-readable inputs in transaction processing has shifted the nature of source documents from tangible paper to relatively intangible magnetic and optical codes. To the extent that paper documents still exist in organizational systems, the documents themselves tend to be of peripheral value only. Increasingly, information custody rests primarily within the data processing function. Thus, when a computerized file is created, the retention of and reliance on paper documents may constitute a kind of "fool's paradise" for the uninformed. That is, readers of the paper documents may be misled easily; once the file attains a life within the computerized system, the paper record virtually becomes obsolete. Data in electronic form are capable of being changed, updated, and modified at a rate that makes the paper record useless. Thus, paper files cannot be used for verification except through a lengthy audit process.

Managers and auditors must recognize that custody of vital information assets has been transferred to a new entity and environment. Organizations must safeguard these assets with at least as much care as they did prior to their use of computers. For example, it may be common practice to observe a bank teller to be sure the cash drawer is locked every time the teller steps away from the window. This same person may be able to operate a computer terminal and execute transactions of far greater financial consequence with virtually no supervision at all. As another example, a manager may be able to sit at a personal computer and interact with centrally maintained master files and make significant changes to financial information in the corporate database without any authorization whatsoever. Such apparent lack of concern suggests failure to understand the potential risks of access to information.

Transfer of responsibilities. All too frequently, changes in functional and custodial relationships within computer information systems may not include corresponding changes in designated responsibilities. Under a manual system, each person may see one small piece of the total processing cycle. With automation, a programmer, a computer operator, or virtually any user may have access to and control of all functions in the processing cycle. At issue here is the principle of *separation of duties.* A type of control is achieved by partitioning a system so that no one individual can have access to the entire process. The absence of specific controls over access to computer systems jeopardizes separation of duties.

Decline of accountability. One of the problems frequently associated with computer-based information systems has been that *accountability,* or individual responsibility for results, is obscured. In today's environment, the information systems department and the users together may handle and control vital assets of a business without being accountable for what happens to those assets. In these circumstances, company managers and auditors—who will be held accountable in the end—may be taking substantial risks without knowing the reliability of the data upon which they are basing their judgments.

Accountability is concerned with results. Responsibilities relate to functions and identify the people who will be charged with performing certain activities. Also, accountability must deal with a higher level and designate individuals who will be answerable for the results achieved. For example, a company officer who signs checks will be accountable for the distribution of assets, even though others may have been responsible for accumulating the supporting data and actually writing the checks. It must be understood that for a manager to authorize a transaction or payment with a computer terminal is just the same as signing an authorization manually. Accountability does not disappear with electronic access. All users of the system must understand this accountability.

Traditional Auditing Functions—A Crisis of Abdication

Before 1970, the auditing function and its responsibilities were exercised, for the most part, by avoiding the computer system, or working around it. The "around-the-computer" approach consists entirely of tracing data from source documents to the computer output and verifying the information from the output against the source documents. The computer, in effect, was regarded as a *black box,* or a process about which only the inputs and outputs are known. As long as the computer was used merely as an electronic bookkeeper, and if the accounting process remained unchanged, this method was perceived to be adequate.

As more and more computer operations were developed, auditing "through the computer" became the more desirable procedure. This approach regards the computer as a *white box,* or transparent process. Today's auditor uses the computer itself to conduct reliability tests of computerized transactions and operations. Most contemporary information systems, especially automated financial accounting systems, have extremely important control procedures built into them. Thus, auditing "through the computer" is probably the most relevant way to evaluate a major part of an organization's internal controls.

For many years, company managers and auditors chose, by and large, to avoid understanding what processes went on within computer systems. Managers neglected their traditional practices of physical examination of information files and organizational documents. However, these same managers have not substituted alternative methods to assure the reliability of computer output upon which they have based their decisions.

This is not to say that the CIS professional has no responsibilities in the audit area. The design, development, and operation of systems is highly significant in the creation and reporting of operational and financial information. The point, rather, is that management involvement, direction, and support are needed to make such systems viable. Another factor is that the audit professional has matured greatly in this area. For example, the *computer auditor,* a specialist in "through-the-computer" techniques, is a responsible player who can bridge the gaps between management, the user, and the CIS professional.

For most organizations, there is a considerable amount of self evaluation and assessment of operational processes needed. Systems controls are either lacking or inadequate, as the above examples of computer abuse and misuse demonstrate. The value of adequate control and audit of systems is rooted in good business practices and ethics.

PEOPLE IN THE LIMELIGHT

In any human-machine system, the activities of people will be crucial to its success or failure. The accountability for the keys to success or failure of computer systems rests with management, the users, systems designers, operators, and auditors. Perhaps the greatest failing within the full spectrum of organizational data processing is misunderstanding—in short, communications failure. For whatever reason, people have not understood the problems at hand and have not understood one another.

A major obstacle to communication has been the new technology. In too many entities, systems people were viewed as a necessary evil and were not integrated into the mainstream of the organization. Their specialized language abetted this isolation. They were not understood. Critics even said that they did not try to make themselves understood.

Managers and auditors also may have been guilty of not trying to understand. Management may have failed in its responsibility to understand and to make things happen. There was a feeling or hope that results would materialize from a liberal mixture of money and technology. Many bitter experiences have established that the processes of developing and using CIS systems successfully require close management attention. Management and technology must join. Communication is essential.

Some CIS specialists moved from company to company, searching for organizations just beginning CIS development efforts. These specialists feared the personal obsolescence that easily can overtake people working with fast-changing technology. In the CIS field, talent has tended to follow the state of the art. Unfortunately, this desire to keep current and to build experience in the latest techniques has led to many situations in which organizations practiced experimentation for its own sake. In this cycle, the objectives of the CIS function tended to drift away from full support of the organization it served.

The New Specialists

The successful designers, managers, and auditors of advanced computer systems have achieved their goals largely by concentrating on the tasks of human resource development, communications, and management involvement. Through work experience and continuing education programs, a new elite has emerged, establishing new patterns and aspirations for CIS professionals, management, and audit professionals. Evidence of this trend is the fact that there is now a clearly marked career path for computer auditors in government service, internal auditing, and in public accounting.

In general, these new management and audit specialists have built on a background of traditional business education. They have been motivated by a recognition that somebody, some day, must take hold of CIS processes. They have reasoned that the future will be bright for the manager or the auditor who is not bewildered or intimidated by the sight of a computer or a computer-generated report. They have recognized that greater commitment must be made to gaining and maintaining an understanding of CIS processes that continue to increase in significance to their organizations.

Within a well-managed company, the new CIS professional—and the computer auditor, in particular—just may hold the key to the communication dilemma. This person, able to speak the languages of both management and technology, should play a central role in reshaping the approach to systems design so that effective systems mean controlled systems.

The career outlook is exceptionally bright for individuals who understand both management and CIS well enough to manage this critical resource effectively.

THE CHALLENGE

The fundamental commitment needed to support these efforts is for managers to become involved in the CIS function within their own organizations. Management's failure in the past probably derives mostly from a knowledge gap caused by not recognizing, or fearing to get involved in, the fast-changing technology upon which their organization's information systems depend. The cure to present problems—and the prevention of future crises—will include active, coordinated involvement and commitment by everyone associated with the management process: boards of directors, officers, line managers, CIS managers, and internal and external auditors.

The advent of legal cases in which boards of directors and officers have been held accountable for financial misrepresentation has spurred interest in the inevitable relationship between computers and the reliability of financial statements. Prominent evidence of this concern at the board level has been the appointment of *audit committees,* or oversight groups. Increasingly, audit committees have focused on the processes by which systems are developed for computer implementation. It is being recognized that quality cannot be inspected (or audited) into a product: Quality must be built into the production process itself. As a result, emphasis is turning toward the building in of control procedures that assure the reliability of results.

With interest coming from top management levels, the climate is changing against long-standing excuses that controls are merely items of elegance, extra cost, and delay. It is becoming more acceptable to include quality measures within the time schedules and budgets for the development of new CIS systems.

This new emphasis on reliability has helped to transport auditors from a traditional position of looking at historical data to one of evaluating the reliability of controls before new systems are developed or implemented.

Management Concerns

Managers have two primary concerns and accountabilities for the reliability of computer-based information systems:

1. The integrity of results must be assured through reliable controls incorporated into computer systems when the systems are under development. Management must be involved in the early phases of the CIS systems development life cycle to assure the ability of the systems to generate reliable information for decision making.

2. The continuing quality and reliability of computer-based information systems must be tested and verified through programs of audit, evaluation, and revision to correct deficiencies and to accommodate changing conditions.

Audit Involvement

Auditors are finding they must adjust their procedures to the timing and conditions of the systems under examination. Sampling of transactions must take into account any changes in records and policies regarding retention of records in computer-based information systems. The auditor also has two distinct areas of concern:

1. New criteria must be developed and applied to evaluate the impact of control weaknesses in computer systems. In general, the potential impact of control weaknesses will be both greater and more difficult to ascertain in a CIS than in manual processing. The auditor will find it increasingly necessary to be involved at the time of system design to assure that the system has adequate controls and design features that will make the system auditable when it becomes operational.

2. The auditor must tailor testing techniques to the nature of the data processing system. Often it will be advantageous, sometimes mandatory, to use the computer itself in examining computer-maintained data.

The Future

At one time, it may have been possible for a manager, an auditor, or a technician to be considered a success when he or she had mastered a given body of knowledge and thereby acquired a somewhat secure position. Today, more clearly, there is no such thing as a static body of knowledge.

Career professionals in this field should be prepared for a lifetime of learning. Indeed, continuing education is essential for maintaining competency. The challenge is twofold: First, technology is changing so rapidly that it takes a significant effort to keep current. Second, few schools are capable of providing extensive, work-related experience, especially in the emerging field of computer auditing. Therefore, students graduating from CIS curricula with the intent of pursuing careers as computer auditors can count on spending at least 2,000 hours in continuing education and supervised apprenticeship experience before being assigned to lead their first major computer audit.

DISCUSSION QUESTIONS

1. How has the adoption of computerized methods changed the potential for fraud and abuse?

2. Why has detection of computer-related crimes historically been accidental?

3. Why are inefficiency and human error of concern to computer auditors?

4. What has been the impact of professional organizations on the field of CIS auditing?

5. How have traditional control functions changed with the adoption of computerized methods?

6. Why is auditing "through the computer" becoming a mandatory approach?

7. What has been the role of government in the assurance of CIS reliability? How is this role changing?

8. What are the respective concerns of managers and auditors in assuring the reliability of computer information systems?

2 Auditing Concepts in a Computer-Based Environment

ABSTRACT

- As computerized systems have begun to build integrated files, audit involvement in the CIS function has become necessary. Involved professionals include management, internal auditors, external auditors, and CIS audit specialists.

- Functions of auditors, both internal and external, are divided between attesting to the fairness of financial statements and operational auditing to assure the efficiency and effectiveness of computer information systems. A key difference is that the attest function is subject to statutory and professional constraints, whereas there are no legal or licensing requirements for operational audits.

- In systems development, auditors can recommend and evaluate controls that build quality assurance into systems. When CIS applications have been implemented, procedures evaluation is the aspect of operational audit that focuses on tests of controls. Auditors also may be involved in suggesting enhancements to or new applications for a CIS.

- The gradual disappearance of the traditional audit trail represents a progression from handling manual documents, to computerized files, to multiple files, to integrated databases.

- The typical phases of an audit engagement include: preliminary review, application analysis, preliminary evaluation of internal controls, compliance testing, final evaluation of internal controls, substantive testing, and reporting.

- Both audit generalists and computer audit specialists should be involved in the examination of computer information systems.

THE NEED FOR INVOLVEMENT IN CIS

Active involvement by auditors in computer information systems (CIS) is a relatively recent development. During the early years of computer-based information systems, it was common to provide for the auditor's examination of document outputs without requiring actual involvement in the CIS function. That is, computer systems were programmed to generate periodic reports that formed external trails of documentation suitable for use by auditors and managers.

As computerized systems began to build integrated files, it became increasingly apparent that audit involvement in the CIS function itself was necessary. The consolidation of data in centralized, electronic files took custody of information resources away from responsible departments and also obscured conventional, hard-copy audit trails.

Internal, programmed procedures were developed to assure the integrity of these information files; but, someone outside the CIS function needed to verify the adequacy of controls. Also, with increasing frequency, computer-based *management information systems (MIS)* were being used to generate reports that showed exceptions requiring management decisions and intervention in operations. In the case of integrated, computer-based files, audit trail documentation was neither complete nor meaningful. In many cases, available documentation was not sufficient to support audit examinations. In the face of such developments, auditors found it necessary to perform detailed, increasingly technical reviews of computer systems themselves.

MANAGEMENT RESPONSIBILITY

Management bears ultimate responsibility for involving auditors in the CIS function. Financial statements are issued not only by public corporations, but also by private companies and not-for-profit organizations. These statements and all procedures needed to create them are management responsibilities. Thus, management is responsible for the controls incorporated within accounting systems.

Managers engage auditors and other specialists to assist in meeting their responsibilities for assuring the reliability of accounting systems. In doing so, managers seek assistance in a number of areas, including:

- Reviewing computer information systems that are under development. The objective is to assure that adequate, reliable, auditable controls will be built into those systems.

- Determining that specified controls actually are functioning reliably within operational CIS systems.

- Conducting examinations aimed at rendering an opinion on the *fairness,* or conformity with established standards, of financial statements.

Until recently, the requirement for an annual financial audit was virtually nonexistent for federal agencies. The Federal Managers' Financial Integrity Act of 1982 requires annual evaluations to be conducted by each executive agency of its system of controls. Each year, internal control is to be reported to the President and to the Congress of the United States. Similar provisions apply for most state and local governmental agencies. Thus, almost all large organizations, in both the public and private sectors, must have formal methods for the evaluation of systems controls.

Two key players in this evaluation are the internal and external auditors. They have important roles in assuring management of the validity and integrity of financial accounting and reporting systems.

THE INTERNAL AUDITOR

The purpose of the internal audit function is to assure that management-authorized controls are being applied effectively. Internal audit is not a mandatory function within a company. Today, however, most of the country's 10,000 largest businesses do have internal audit departments. The character, mission, and strength of an internal audit group varies widely with the style of top executives and traditions within the company. For many companies, internal audit is a new or emerging function. In even more cases, involvement in CIS is a new dimension for internal audit.

Internal audit is an internal control function, including continual activities for the monitoring and testing of all CIS functions. Of particular concern is the processing of data of financial *relevance*, or materiality. Although it would seem logical, involvement in CIS has not been automatic for most internal auditors.

Top management must be concerned with the reliability of computer-generated information upon which critical organizational decisions are made. In organizations in which management genuinely is concerned about this reliability, internal auditors are growing in stature. As internal auditors extend their capabilities and activities, their efforts become increasingly crucial to the examinations performed by external auditors. Thus, management typically assigns review, consultation, and testing responsibilities to the internal auditor. These responsibilities typically are broader in scope than those of the external auditor.

THE EXTERNAL AUDITOR

The external auditor evaluates the reliability and validity of systems controls, whether manual or automatic. The principal objective in this evaluation is to minimize the amount of substantive auditing, or testing of transactions required to render an opinion on financial statements.

The external auditor can make a positive, cost-effective contribution to systems development by encouraging that controls be built into CIS procedures and programs from the outset. It also is desirable to build in examination procedures at this point. That is, if the auditor is on the scene while systems are being designed and developed, a test methodology can be pre-established that will be applied after the system becomes operational.

Auditor involvement in systems development is the subject of a later chapter. At this point, recognize that external and internal auditor involvement should be full-dimensional in scope. Involvement of external auditors in the systems development process can benefit all parties, especially the internal audit function, with a stake in the reliability of computer-generated information.

The external auditor responsible for testing the reliability of client computer systems should have a special combination of skills and experience. Such an auditor must be thoroughly familiar with the audit *attest* function. The attest function encompasses all activities and responsibilities associated with the rendering of an opinion on the fairness of financial statements. Besides the accounting and auditing skills involved in performing the attest function, these external auditors also must have substantial CIS experience and training.

Increasingly, audit firms also use the services of qualified computer audit specialists. Often, such people have extensive CIS experience before joining the audit firm. They generally work closely with audit staff members, though they may not be involved directly in the non-computerized portions of the audit.

One important service rendered by these specialists is the *CIS operations review,* an evaluation of the efficiency with which a CIS department is being run. In other cases, audit staff members may have identified control weaknesses that are associated with operating practices. The computer audit specialists, then, may be called upon to help develop and implement additional control measures to be incorporated in the operating procedures of the CIS department.

Another important role for a person with these qualifications lies in determining whether the organization is getting an effective return on its CIS investment. Activities include surveys of the appropriateness, timeliness, and utilization levels of reports or inquiry capabilities provided by computer information systems.

COMPUTER AUDIT FUNCTIONS

Computer auditing refers to auditing performed in the environment of computer information systems. Auditing is:

> [A] systematic process of objectively obtaining and evaluating evidence regarding assertions about economic actions and events to ascertain the degree of correspondence between those assertions and established criteria and communicating the results to interested users. [American Accounting Association Committee on Basic Auditing Concepts, 1971.]

A CIS environment can mean any of the following:

- The evidence that the auditor gathers originates or is maintained in a computer system.
- The auditor uses computer-based techniques to gather or evaluate evidence.
- Both of the above.

Assertions about economic events within an organization typically are manifested in statements reporting financial or operational results. Such reports are management's representations, not the auditors'. Established criteria are reporting standards and guidelines for preparation of reports of results.

Communicating the findings of independent auditors to interested parties is known as attestation. The purpose of attestation is to assure the credibility of management's representations for users of reports on financial and operational results. Independence in auditing means that the auditor adheres to the best standards of professional practice with no compromising influence, real or perceived, from the management of the organization being audited. To assure credibility of financial or operating reports through attestation, auditors must be perceived as being independent of the entities they audit.

Auditors, both internal and external, perform functions that can be classified in two broad categories:

- Financial auditing
- Operational auditing.

FINANCIAL AUDITING

Financial auditing encompasses all activities and responsibilities concerned with the rendering of an opinion on the fairness of financial statements. The basic rules governing audit opinions indicate clearly that the scope of an audit encompasses all equipment and procedures used in processing significant data.

Financial auditing, as carried out today by the independent auditor, was spurred by legislation in 1933 and 1934 that created the *Securities and Exchange Commission (SEC)*. This legislation mandated that companies whose securities are sold publicly be audited annually by *certified public accountants (CPAs)*. CPAs, then, were charged with attesting to the fairness of financial statements issued by companies that report to the SEC.

Within the certified public accounting profession, two groups of standards have been developed that affect the preparation of financial statements by publicly held companies and the procedures for their audit examination by CPA firms:

- Generally accepted accounting principles (GAAP)
- Generally accepted auditing standards (GAAS).

Generally Accepted Accounting Principles (GAAP)

Generally accepted accounting principles (GAAP) establish consistent guidelines for financial reporting by corporate managers. As part of the reporting requirement, standards also are established for the keeping of financial records upon which periodic statements are based. An auditor rendering an opinion indicating that financial statements are stated fairly stipulates that the financial statements conform to generally accepted accounting principles. These accounting principles have been formulated and revised periodically by private sector organizations established for this purpose. The present governing body is the *Financial Accounting Standards Board (FASB)*. Implementation of generally accepted accounting principles is the responsibility of management of the reporting entity.

Generally Accepted Auditing Standards

The major national professional organization of CPAs is the American Institute of Certified Public Accountants (AICPA). In 1949, the AICPA adopted standards for audits, known as *generally accepted auditing standards (GAAS)*. These standards cover three categories:

General standards.   *General standards* relate to professional and technical competence, independence, and due professional care.

Field work standards. *Field work standards* encompass planning, study, and evaluation of internal control, and sufficiency of *evidential matter,* or the documentary evidence upon which findings are based.

Reporting standards. *Reporting standards* stipulate compliance with generally accepted auditing standards, consistency with the preceding accounting period, adequacy of disclosure, and, in the event that an opinion cannot be reached, the requirement to state the assertion explicitly.

The standards referred to above provide broad guidelines, but not specific guidance. The profession has supplemented the standards by issuing a series of authoritative pronouncements on auditing. The most authoritative of these pronouncements is the series of *Statements on Auditing Standards (SAS).* The SAS publications provide procedural guidance relating to many aspects of auditing. In 1985, the AICPA released a Codification of the Statements on Auditing Standards Numbers 1 – 49.

The Situation and the Problem

Computers have been in use commercially since 1952. Computer-related crimes were reported as early as 1966. However, it was not until 1973, when the problems at Equity Funding Corporation of America (EFCA) surfaced, that the auditing profession looked seriously at the lack of controls in computer information systems.

When EFCA declared bankruptcy in 1973, the minimum direct losses from illegal activity were reported to be as much as $200 million. Estimates run to as much as $2 billion if indirect costs such as legal fees and stock depreciation are included. These losses were the result of a "computer-assisted fraud" in which a corporation falsified the records of its life insurance subsidiary to indicate the issuance of new policies. In addition to the insurance policies, other assets, such as receivables and marketable securities, were recorded falsely. These fictitious assets should have been revealed as nonexistent during the corporation's regular year-end audits, but were not. Since the computer was used to manipulate files as a means of covering up the fraud, the accounting profession realized that conventional, manual techniques might not be adequate for audit engagements involving computers.

In 1973, the AICPA, in response to the events at Equity Funding, appointed a special committee to study whether the auditing standards of the day were adequate to such situations. The committee was requested to evaluate specific procedures to be used and the general standards to be applied. In 1975, the committee issued its findings. Another critical review of the current auditing standards was begun in 1974, when the AICPA created the

Commission on Auditor's Responsibilities. The Commission reviewed and made recommendations on 11 areas relating to auditing and the auditing profession. In 1977, the Commission published its report. Both of these efforts form the basis of the profession's current position, summarized below.

The Profession's Current Position

The committee charged with the responsibility of reviewing auditing standards as a result of Equity Funding's collapse stated that:

> *. . . Generally accepted auditing standards are adequate and no changes are called for in the procedures commonly used by auditors.*

Indeed, a review of current auditing textbooks concludes that the generally accepted auditing standards are adequate for audits involving the use of the computer. However, the current position of the profession is that there are both similarities and significant differences between the auditing procedures that must be applied.

The following summary is derived from *Auditing: Integrated Concepts and Procedures* by Taylor and Glezen (John Wiley & Sons, Publishers, New York):

Similarities.   No new auditing standards are required for examination of financial statements based on computer-generated records. In general, the standards of field work are the same as those applied to manually generated records. Also, the basic elements of adequate internal control remain the same. The main purposes of the study and evaluation of internal control still are to provide evidence for an opinion and to determine the basis for the scope, timing, and extent of future audit tests.

Differences.   With computer-based financial reporting systems, some new auditing procedures must be developed. There are significant differences in the techniques of maintaining adequate internal control. Also, there is some difference in the manner in which the study and evaluation of internal control is made. A significant difference is that people have been removed from some phases of the system of internal accounting control.

Current Accounting and Auditing Pronouncements

The AICPA Statements of Auditing Standards (SAS) are the professional standards for CPAs. These standards are interpretations of generally accepted auditing standards, and the AICPA requires its members to adhere to the statements or to be prepared to justify any departure from them.

Internal auditors are not required to follow the generally accepted auditing standards in the performance of their audits. However, most internal auditors are familiar with the standards and use them as general guidelines.

Professional associations such as *The Institute of Internal Auditors (IIA)* and the *EDP Auditors Foundation for Education and Research (EDPAF)* have issued their own professional guidelines. In 1978, the IIA issued its *Standards for the Professional Practice of Internal Auditing* and subsequently issued three *Statements on Internal Auditing Standards (SIAS)*. These statements are:

SIAS No. 1   Control: Concepts and Responsibilities (July, 1983)

SIAS No. 2   Communicating Results (July, 1984)

SIAS No. 3   Deterrence, Detection, Investigation, and Reporting of Fraud (May, 1985).

In January, 1984, the EDP Auditors Association issued its "EDP Control Objectives—Update 1984," a set of EDP control standards.

The federal government has not yet issued standards for internal auditors in the private sector. SEC staff personnel, however, have alluded to the importance of the internal auditor's role. The SEC's unofficial position is that having internal auditors review internal control is an important part of an organization's plan to devise and maintain an adequate system of internal control.

One way of evaluating an organization's internal audit function is to measure it against the internal audit standards issued by the *U.S. General Accounting Office (GAO)*. The GAO has issued audit standards that must be followed in audits of federal organizations, programs, activities, and funds received by contractors, nonprofit organizations, and other external organizations (such as companies with federal contracts).

These standards relate to the scope and quality of the audit effort and to the characteristics of professional and meaningful audit reports. The three elements of expanded auditing covered in the standards are: financial and compliance, economy and efficiency, and program results. Appendix 1 of the GAO standards, "Auditing Computer-Based Systems—The Auditor's Role During System Design and Development," presents audit objectives related to achieving adequate internal controls and effective auditability of CIS systems. Also, federal legislation requires that the Inspectors General in federal agencies follow these standards. Because of their importance as guidelines in the conduct of computer audits, excerpts from this publication, *Standards for Audit of Governmental Organizations, Programs, Activities and Functions (1981 revision)*, are included as Appendix F to this book.

AICPA Pronouncements

The accounting profession first addressed the topic of internal control of CIS systems officially in 1974 when the AICPA issued SAS No. 3, "The Effects of EDP on the Auditor's Study and Evaluation of Internal Control." SAS No. 3 was concerned with the evaluation of internal control of clients who processed significant financial records using a computer system. Growing use of computer-based financial systems created a need for auditors to go beyond matters of internal control in audits of financial statements. Consequently, in 1984, the AICPA superseded SAS No. 3 with SAS No. 48, "The Effects of Computer Processing on the Examination of Financial Statements." SAS No. 48 requires auditors to consider the effects of computer processing throughout the whole audit process, not just during the evaluation of internal control. SAS No. 48 amended other SASs to synchronize audit practice with the increased use of computer-based processing in client financial systems.

SAS No. 48 provides the basic framework for the auditing procedures necessary in examining the financial statements of entities that use computer accounting applications. The pronouncement describes the basic procedures and areas of concern with which the auditor should be familiar. The pronouncement specifically covers the following topics:

1. How the audit is affected by:

   a. The extent of computer use in each significant accounting application

   b. The complexity of the organization's computer operations

   c. The organizational structure of CIS activities

   d. The availability of data for audit use

   e. The use of computer-assisted audit techniques to increase the efficiency of audit procedures (AU Sec. 311.09).

2. The need for auditors with specialized expertise in CIS. (AU Sec. 311.10)

3. The influence on internal control procedures of the methods an organization uses to process significant data. Characteristics distinguishing computer processing from manual processing are:

   a. Abbreviated life of transaction trails

   b. Greater uniformity of processing, which decreases processing errors but increases vulnerability to programming errors

   c. Potential for concentration of incompatible functions

   d. Potential for errors and irregularities due to ease of gaining unauthorized access to systems and files

   e. Potential for increased management supervision

    f.   Automatic initiation of processing functions

    g.   Interdependence of manual and automated controls. (AU Sec. 320.33)

4.   The interdependence of control procedures. (AU Sec. 320.57)

5.   The adequacy of general and application controls. General controls relate to several computer-based activities, such as controls over system development. Application controls are application-specific controls. (AU Sec. 320.58)

6.   The need to obtain reasonable assurance for the reliability of the operation of programmed controls. (AU Sec. 320.65–.66)

7.   The need for adequate segregation of incompatible functions. (AU Sec. 320.67–.68)

8.   The unchanging nature of audit objectives, even though evidence collection methods may vary. (AU Sec. 326.12)

For additional information on the implications and implementation of the guidelines and procedures discussed above, see Appendix G. This Appendix contains the entire text of SAS No. 48, which represents the current position of the AICPA on audit of computer-based financial systems.

Another SAS applies in general to CIS auditing. It is SAS No. 16, "The Independent Auditor's Responsibility for the Detection of Errors or Irregularities" (AU Sec. 327). This standard is general in nature and applies to both manual and computerized systems. SAS No. 16 defines the auditor's responsibility for detecting errors and irregularities in an accounting system. AU Sec. 327.05 states:

> . . . *Under generally accepted auditing standards the independent auditor has the responsibility, within the inherent limitations of the auditing process, to search for errors or irregularities that would have a material effect on the financial statements, and to exercise due skill and care in the conduct of that examination.*

A limitation, however, is placed on the auditor's responsibility. Paragraph 13 states:

> . . . *The auditor is not an insurer or guarantor; if his examination was made in accordance with generally accepted auditing standards, he has fulfilled his professional responsibility.*

Other Standards

Guidelines also have been issued by other standards-setting bodies. For example, the IIA, the EDPAF, and the GAO have been quite active in providing audit-related guidelines. Another such organization is the *National Bureau of Standards (NBS)*, a division of the U. S. Department of Commerce. NBS issues the *Federal Information Processing Standards Publication Series (FIPS)*. The Federal Information Processing Standards that focus on computer security are listed in Figure 2-1.

Although the FIPS standards are not considered generally accepted auditing standards by the accounting profession, they do provide valuable guidelines on specific topics not addressed by the AICPA.

OPERATIONAL AUDITING

Operational audits are special engagements or activities under which auditors study and report on the effectiveness and economies of data processing operations in areas beyond the scope of their attest function. In such cases, auditors may advise clients on opportunities or problems that are not related to financial reporting, but which have surfaced in the course of audit examinations. Operational audits are not mandated by professional standards. Thus, operational audits are separate activities from rendering opinions on financial statements and are performed to meet different objectives.

Management is responsible for both specifying and applying controls to accounting systems. Problems arise frequently in establishing that controls specified for given accounting systems actually are being applied. Operational auditing activities are a primary method for making this type of determination.

Operational auditing differs from the attest function in that no legal or licensing qualifications are prescribed. The presence of certified public accountants in this function is not mandated. Operational auditing activities are carried out by several different types of individuals or organizations—except in a few special cases in which regulatory agencies require that reports on internal control be filed by qualified public accountants.

Many corporations have charged their internal audit departments with the responsibility for operational auditing. Conceptually, the internal auditors play much the same role within financial areas as quality control departments do within the manufacturing portions of a business. As with quality control, internal auditors should be independent of the functions or departments they are reviewing or examining. Also, the internal audit department should be staffed by persons who are qualified technically and experienced in the areas under review.

FIPS No.*	Title	Date
FIPS 31	Guidelines for Automatic Data Processing Physical Security and Risk Management	June 1974
FIPS 41	Computer Security Guidelines for Implementing the Privacy Act of 1974	May 1977
FIPS 46	Data Encryption Standard	Jan 1977
FIPS 65	Guideline for Automatic Data Processing Risk Analysis	Aug 1979
FIPS 73	Guidelines for Security of Computer Applications	June 1980
FIPS 74	Guidelines for Implementing and Using the NBS Data Encryption Standard	Apr 1981
FIPS 87	Guidelines for ADP Contingency Planning	Mar 1981
FIPS 88	Guideline on Integrity Assurance and Control in Database Administration	Aug 1981
FIPS 102	Guideline for Computer Security Certification and Accreditation	Oct 1983

These standards are available from the National Technical Information Service, U.S. Department of Commerce, Springfield, VA 22161.

Figure 2-1.

This table presents the Federal Information Processing Standards (FIPS) that relate to computer security.

Traditionally, internal auditors have come from accounting backgrounds and have been responsible for reviews of accounting systems. Strengthening the controls tends to reduce the scope and costs of examinations by external auditors. Basically, however, the internal audit function serves in a management advisory capacity and helps to assure management that information on which decisions are based is reliable.

Ideally, there will be a close working relationship between internal and external auditors. When the function is coordinated effectively, internal auditors, who are on the scene throughout the year, are able to set up examination routines for the external auditors. These examination routines validate internal controls and evaluate the reliability of financial data.

Operational audits of CIS systems typically are highly technical. For this reason, companies frequently use the services of consultants outside the accounting field. These consultants may be employed by the organization directly. For example, technical specialists within the CIS function, or systems analysts within a methods and procedures department, may be deployed on operational review assignments.

Operational auditing engagements also are performed by CPA firms and by technical or management consulting firms that do not provide accounting services. There are many consulting organizations that specialize in the development and implementation of CIS systems.

Development of Control Procedures

The operational auditing function, whether it is applied by internal or external personnel, should be involved closely with CIS systems development. In working with systems development professionals, auditors can recommend and evaluate controls that build quality assurance into CIS systems. Chapter 7 describes control requirements and methods for meeting them.

Technically qualified auditors should be involved in evaluating proposed controls and recommending control measures while systems are still in the developmental stage. Considering the complexity of today's technology, it is possible to develop computerized systems that simply cannot be audited effectively. A company that does not take such precautions runs the risk of extending its audit requirements—and costs—substantially.

Procedures Evaluation

When CIS applications have been implemented, *procedures evaluation* is the aspect of an operational audit that focuses on tests of controls. It is best not to wait until the annual examination by external auditors to find out whether controls designed into the system have been applied, and whether the controls are working as anticipated.

To the extent possible, management should consider assigning responsibility for procedural evaluations to internal audit groups. These evaluations can be performed effectively by qualified internal auditors. Internal auditors are able to apply day-to-day attention in determining whether control measures are being applied actively. The ability of internal audit staff to perform this evaluation function, of course, depends on the availability of qualified staff. Personnel performing these evaluations should have extensive backgrounds in both accounting and CIS areas.

If qualified people are not available within internal audit departments, procedures evaluations frequently are performed as coordinated efforts between internal and external auditors. Typically, computer audit specialists from a CPA firm establish observation and review programs that are carried out on a cooperative basis between qualified computer auditors and members of the internal audit staff.

When internal audit capabilities are not present, procedures evaluation functions frequently are undertaken entirely by the CPA firm. In such cases, the periodic evaluation reviews can be scheduled profitably as interim procedures performed as extensions of annual audit examinations.

CIS Improvements

CIS installations and applications undergo continuing scrutiny and updating. Improvements and enhancements are required for a variety of reasons, including changes in organizational strategy, equipment advancements, new software concepts, new programming languages, mandates from new laws, increased user sophistication, and new insights by CIS personnel.

In most medium- and large-sized CIS departments, there is a staff of systems analysts and technical advisers who spend much of their time considering and implementing changes. However, as in other areas of operations and management, an objective approach by persons with qualified expertise can make a contribution. In the hectic schedules of CIS operations, it is possible for talented and highly qualified people to become so enmeshed in yesterday's developments and today's problems that they lose perspective on future opportunities.

Many independent audit engagements lead to recognition of opportunities for enhancements or improvements of existing CIS installations and applications. In other situations, either internal auditors or qualified outside consultants have been called upon to evaluate new opportunities.

One common instigator of evaluations of the status quo is a conversion or enhancement proposal from a company's equipment supplier or from a prospective, hopeful, new supplier. Typically, managers in medium- and large-sized CIS installations receive several proposals each year for changes to part or all of the installation's equipment, support software, or auxiliary services.

In many other situations, management simply wants to know, from time to time, how the CIS function is performing. There may be nothing wrong. Things may be going exactly as projected. But, either for long-range planning or for operational evaluation purposes, officers or board members may want an independent appraisal of the CIS function. An in-depth discussion of CIS operations reviews is presented in Chapter 12.

PROFESSIONAL PRACTICES

Many of the larger CPA firms in the United States have been conducting research in the area of CIS auditing. This research has not been aimed at creating standards, but has focused on developing techniques for auditing CIS systems. The national accounting firms have done research on CIS auditing for more than two decades. These firms, with some assistance from the private and governmental sectors, have been largely responsible for the development of current CIS audit techniques.

Types of Audit Tests

The underlying principle of audit testing is: If an accounting system includes adequate controls that are applied consistently, that system will generate reliable information. The degree of reliability relates directly to the strength of the controls. That is, the stronger the controls within a system, the more likely it is that its outputs will be reliable. This premise also recognizes that, since accounting systems are implemented by people, a perfectly controlled set of procedures is unlikely. The auditor always will have to perform some tests to become satisfied as to the reliability of an accounting system. However, the more reliance the auditor can place on internal controls, the less extensive must be the additional auditing procedures.

In testing, the auditor usually selects a sample of transactions that have been processed during the reporting period by the system being examined. To validate the reported results, the auditor must verify the validity of source documents and duplicate the processing that was performed. When the auditor's results correspond with those shown in accounting records, there is some assurance of compliance with the stipulated controls. This technique of testing individual transactions, therefore, is known as *compliance testing*. Compliance testing generally is performed on a selective basis following a review and preliminary evaluation of internal control.

Results of compliance testing, in turn, determine the extent of another type of testing used in audit examinations, *substantive tests*. A substantive test verifies summarized, quantitative amounts in financial records—usually through outside references. As an example, an auditor may send *verification request* forms to a company's customers to determine whether accounts receivable are stated fairly. Substantive tests are the most detailed and most costly individual elements of an audit examination. The extent to which substantive testing is used depends, in part, upon the auditor's findings in the review and evaluation of internal controls, as validated by compliance tests.

If internal controls are found to have material weaknesses, substantive tests will be comparatively extensive. Extensive substantive tests are required even if compliance tests indicate that calculations were performed accurately in spite of weaknesses in controls. If internal controls appear reliable but compliance tests show weaknesses, substantive testing will be extended to determine the degree of reliability of financial statements. If both internal control reviews and compliance tests indicate a high level of reliability, substantive testing may be restricted.

The auditor's responsibilities clearly encompass internal controls for all of a company's financially significant accounting systems. Therefore, the auditor also is responsible for reviewing and evaluating both the general and application controls applied to accounting information within a CIS installation. The auditor's responsibilities, under the second field work standard, clearly include controls applied to any processing performed with computers.

There has been some contention about the application of this standard to the computerized portions of accounting systems. Some practitioners have held that it is possible to review and evaluate internal controls on the basis of documentation alone, without computer involvement. However, avoiding the computer may involve risks. Auditable records can disappear within computerized systems that rely on integrated, multi-application databases. If the review and evaluation of internal controls is to conform to the second field work standard, auditors must understand how the computerized portions of the accounting system work.

A BASIS OF UNDERSTANDING

For many years, virtually all double-entry, manual ledger accounting systems looked enough alike so that an auditor was on familiar ground in examining the books of account of just about any company. It did not matter whether records were handwritten or were posted by machine. Everything centered around a general ledger that was structured more or less uniformly.

During a typical examination, an auditor started with the general ledger, selected items for further review, and was led to source journals through posting reference columns on the ledger sheets. The journals, in turn, led the auditor to source transaction documents.

As accounting systems became larger and more complex, auditors began to track and document these accounting relationships through information processing flowcharts that represented graphically the systems under examination. The flowcharts, however, basically did not change anything. They simply acted as road maps of the data paths within accounting systems that were becoming more complex. An auditor examining the financial records of a company still could get right to the heart of the system—the general ledger—with comparatively little delay over concepts and procedures. In effect, the auditor could work from the core of an accounting system outward.

This same degree of standardization and familiarity from system to system has not evolved, and does not appear likely to evolve, for CIS systems.

The auditor examining financial records of a company that relies heavily on CIS for financially significant applications must survey each application and develop individual flowcharts. This can be demonstrated by comparing, for both manual and computerized accounting systems, typical accounting system data flows and their related audit approaches.

Figure 2-2 shows the manual procedures for a portion of a double-entry accounting system in a company's accounts receivable application. This schematic shows the traditional relationships between journals for sales and cash receipts, a subsidiary ledger for accounts receivable, the flow of summary data into a general ledger, the preparation of a trial balance, and the production of financial statements.

In this manual system, there is a clear, documented relationship covering the flow of data. The auditor examining financial records for a company using this approach can track processing in reverse order. That is, the auditor may start with the financial statements, and move back through the general ledger, the subsidiary ledger, the journals, and the source documents. As information flows through the system, internal controls lie in the continuous posting of references when data are summarized. In many cases, control is enhanced by practices under which both journals and subsidiary ledgers are posted through a single clerical action, as occurs with a pegboard-writing or a bookkeeping-machine system.

Figure 2-2 illustrates that, in a traditional, double-entry accounting system, it has been possible for the auditor to go directly to a company's general ledger and work outward, or trace backward, from the financial statements to source data.

MULTIPLE FILE SYSTEMS

While manual approaches are relatively convenient for auditing, they are inefficient for computer processing. Companies no longer could afford a one-to-one relationship between clerical posting functions and entries in accounting records. Since a single business transaction could affect a number of accounting, operating, and management records, it became logical to relegate repetitive entry of data to business machines, then to computers.

In effect, companies using this approach were able to mechanize the journalizing of multiple accounting transactions. For example, a single sales transaction, entered just once into a punched card, could be used under computerized procedures to post to a number of transaction files—sales orders, accounts receivable, inventory, and possibly shipping or transportation records. Instead of requiring separate clerical entries for each journal,

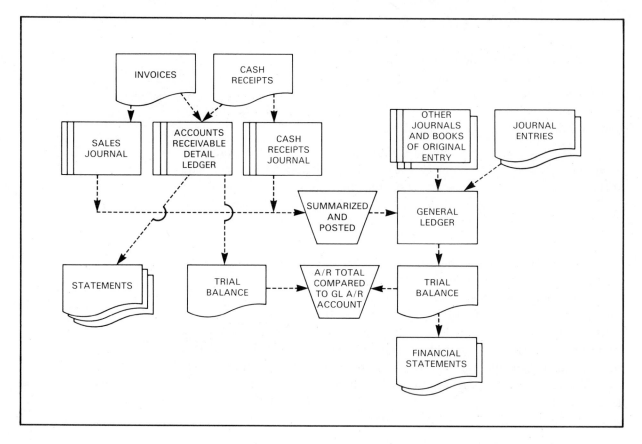

Figure 2-2.

This flowchart traces the data flows within a manual accounting system.

multiple-file computer systems capture and retain individual accounting transactions. A single entry then may be used several times for internal posting.

Figure 2-3 diagrams the effect, in accounting-record terms, of a multiple-file computer system. The diagram shows that, under computerized procedures, individual transactions are posted to multiple files, summarized automatically, and carried forward up to the level of a trial balance. The system diagrammed shows computer-produced trial balances used for manual preparation of a company's financial statements.

An important feature of this transitional step in data processing, from a control and auditing standpoint, is that the general ledger no longer may be the visible hub of the company's accounting. The actual general ledger is invisible, since it may be maintained only in machine-readable form (on magnetic tape in the system illustrated).

Figure 2-3 illustrates a first-level transition into systems within which audit trails lose their visibility. In such cases, the general ledger no longer serves as an automatic starting point for audit examinations.

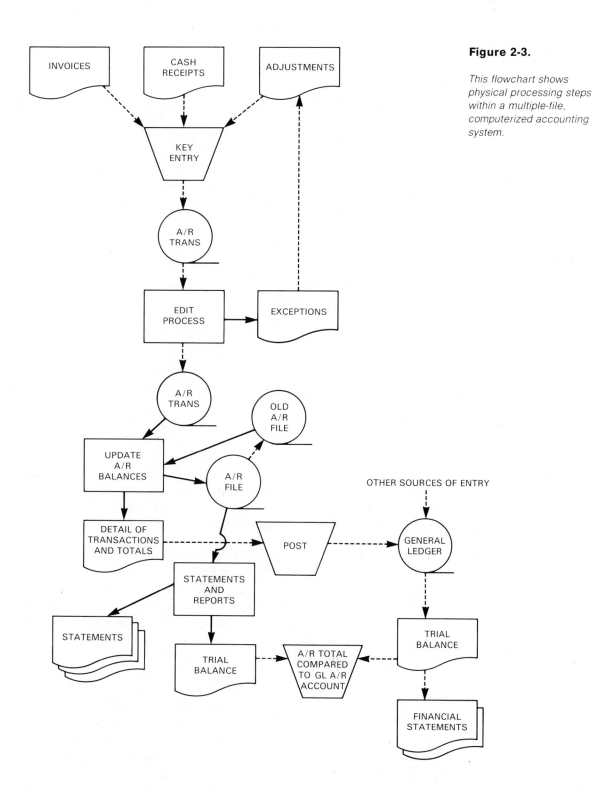

Figure 2-3.

This flowchart shows physical processing steps within a multiple-file, computerized accounting system.

DATABASE SYSTEMS

For purposes of this discussion, a *database system* is a CIS that uses a *database management system (DBMS)* to integrate data storage and access. A significant characteristic of database systems is that data are stored and accessed as individual items, rather than as coherent records and files. From the auditor's viewpoint, the important characteristic is that the DBMS handles all physical access and retrieval. Actual storage structures and locations are not apparent to the user or to the application program. Under a DBMS approach, discrete files composed of records that have data structures derived from physical documents are nonexistent.

As computer systems become more sophisticated, both the actions and the concepts of posting transactions and building account files may be eliminated. When a company moves to an advanced, database computer system, accounting procedures are abridged, as shown schematically in Figure 2-4.

Under this database approach, the conventional concept of posting to journals and ledgers no longer exists. Rather, the process involves converting source transaction data into machine-readable form as early and as efficiently as possible. Often, machine-readable records are created as by-products of source transactions themselves.

In such cases, there is no transcription process comparable with traditional accounting postings. Rather, a computerized database accumulates all of the company's detailed transactions in a structured, massive collection. The process is as though all paperwork associated with a company's operations were thrown into a single, large cabinet and then miraculously could be identified, retrieved, or summarized on command.

Within a database system, transactions are retained in detail form. The computer is capable of reviewing detail items at the rate of hundreds of thousands per second. Detail items, in the process of high-speed reviews, can be identified, sorted, collated, or summarized as necessary. With modern computers, it actually may be more efficient in some applications to accumulate masses of detail than to attempt to summarize and update accounting-type files on a progressive basis.

The resulting database means, however, that the audit trail, in a traditional sense, is even more remote than it is for a multi-file system. With multi-file systems, the equivalent of accounting summaries continue to exist, if not on hard-copy records, at least through integral master and transaction records within computer files. Within a database system, however, summary files generally are transient, created and used only long enough to validate

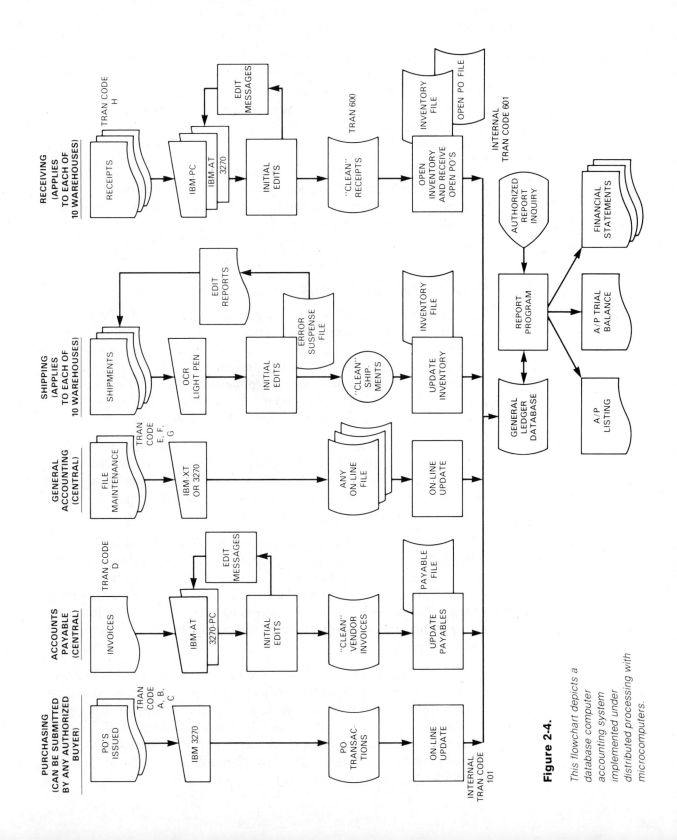

Figure 2-4.

This flowchart depicts a database computer accounting system implemented under distributed processing with microcomputers.

application processing and to produce periodic reports. After that, the summaries are eliminated, or, in data processing terminology, *scratched.* Modern computers are powerful enough so that it often is more efficient to create transient files as needed from permanently retained transaction detail records than to undertake the expense of storing and processing summary files on a continuing basis.

A database system, then, represents extensive discontinuity of the traditional audit trail. For examination purposes, there literally may be nothing to inspect between massive detail files and periodic accounting reports. In such situations, the traditional audit examination approach of beginning with the general ledger and working outward loses its viability.

THE AUDIT PROCESS

The time-honored method of using the general ledger as the starting point for audits does not always work in examinations of modern computer systems. However, the experienced auditor or financial manager recognizes the value of having a consistent, logical, audit or management approach that accommodates both manual and computerized methods. Although auditing computer systems requires changes from the traditional general-ledger approach, any new audit approach should be applicable universally.

Universal approaches that apply equally to manual and computerized systems were formalized for the accounting profession in SAS No. 1. This standard has the effect of mandating a uniform, process-oriented approach to audit engagements. This audit process is diagrammed in Figure 2-5, which summarizes the procedures specified in SAS-1.

The approach depicted is a true process technique. That is, audit engagements follow a series of logical, orderly steps, each designed to accomplish specified end results. In implementation, initial efforts in the audit examination center on gaining a general basis of understanding of the accounting systems. The process continues to increasing depth in the study and examination of the applications that develop financially significant data for inclusion in financial statements.

Although schematic diagrams tend to indicate distinct steps, actual audit processes are less rigid. The phases of auditing activities typically overlap and involve some reassessment and retracing of procedures performed earlier. (The auditing activities described in this chapter and in the two following chapters are based upon the approach shown in Figure 2-5. Accordingly, the relationships and interdependence of the phases illustrated should be studied and understood before continuing.)

The typical phases of an audit engagement identified in Figure 2-5 include:

- Preliminary review
- Application analysis
- Preliminary evaluation of internal controls
- Compliance testing
- Final evaluation of internal controls
- Substantive testing.

Note that the scope of each type of testing depends on the outcome of previous step. This relationship is discussed further below.

The final, necessary phase of each audit engagement is reporting. However, reporting is not affected by the introduction of computers into a client's financial system and, thus, is not treated separately in the discussion below. This chapter discusses the first two phases of the audit engagement in depth to provide an understanding of preliminary work needed to build the audit base. Later chapters discuss the other cited phases in greater depth.

PRELIMINARY REVIEW

The purpose of the preliminary review phase of an audit engagement is to gather information as a basis for formulating an audit plan, which is the end product of the phase. During preliminary review, the auditor will gather general information on the company and its accounting systems, including:

- Nature of business
- Financial history
- Organization structure
- An accounting system overview at sufficient depth to establish which applications are financially significant
- Extent of automation of financial systems.

The auditor conducts this preliminary review at a general level, without examining details of individual applications and the processing they involve. As indicated in Figure 2-5, three separate activities are included in the preliminary review phase:

- General data gathering
- Identifying financial application areas
- Preparing an audit plan.

AUDIT PHASE

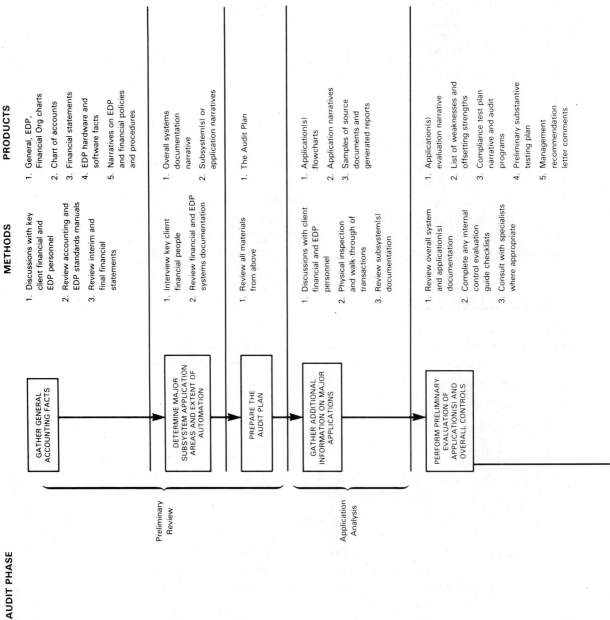

METHODS

PRODUCTS

GATHER GENERAL ACCOUNTING FACTS

Methods:
1. Discussions with key client financial and EDP personnel
2. Review accounting and EDP standards manuals
3. Review interim and final financial statements

Products:
1. General, EDP, Financial Org charts
2. Chart of accounts
3. Financial statements
4. EDP hardware and software facts
5. Narratives on EDP and financial policies and procedures

DETERMINE MAJOR SUBSYSTEM APPLICATION AREAS AND EXTENT OF AUTOMATION

Methods:
1. Interview key client financial people
2. Review financial and EDP systems documentation

Products:
1. Overall systems documentation narrative
2. Subsystem(s) or application narratives

PREPARE THE AUDIT PLAN

Methods:
1. Review all materials from above

Products:
1. The Audit Plan

Preliminary Review

GATHER ADDITIONAL INFORMATION ON MAJOR APPLICATIONS

Methods:
1. Discussions with client financial and EDP personnel
2. Physical inspection and walk-through of transactions
3. Review subsystem(s) documentation

Products:
1. Application(s) flowcharts
2. Application narratives
3. Samples of source documents and generated reports

Application Analysis

PERFORM PRELIMINARY EVALUATION OF APPLICATION(S) AND OVERALL CONTROLS

Methods:
1. Review overall system and application(s) documentation
2. Complete any internal control evaluation guide checklists
3. Consult with specialists where appropriate

Products:
1. Application(s) evaluation narrative
2. List of weaknesses and offsetting strengths
3. Compliance test plan narrative and audit programs
4. Preliminary substantive testing plan
5. Management recommendation letter comments

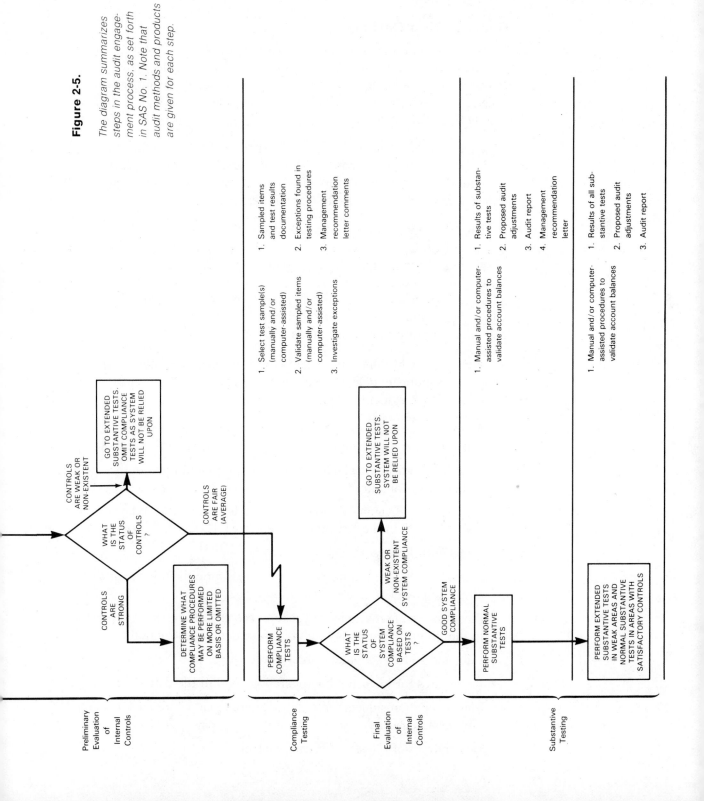

Figure 2-5.

The diagram summarizes steps in the audit engagement process, as set forth in SAS No. 1. Note that audit methods and products are given for each step.

General Data Gathering

The auditor begins the examination process by becoming acquainted, generally, with the company, its line of business, and its financial systems. Typically, an outside auditor would tour the client company's plant and observe general business operations, which bear upon customer service as well as on strictly financial functions.

Given this familiarity, the next level of general data gathering would include the accumulation or preparation of organization charts, particularly those for the accounting and CIS functions. These audit requirements are no different from those for strictly manual systems.

Should adequate organization charts be unavailable, the auditor must develop them. Once drawn, the charts should be reviewed with the client to secure agreement that they represent the actual organization structure. This verification would be done through interviews and discussions with key executives in the accounting and CIS areas. In addition, during these interviews, the auditor would secure copies of the company's chart of accounts and an accounting standards manual, if available.

For systems in which the client company uses computers to process financially significant data, the auditor also would gather a number of other specific items of evidential matter, including:

- An overall narrative or an overview flowchart of the major applications subsystems and their interrelationships, including inputs and outputs

- Descriptions of the make and model of equipment units in the client's computer installation

- Programming languages and data processing standards and procedures manuals used in the computer system

- Data control procedures

- Assurance that an uninterruptible power supply is in place or that an alternate power source is available

- Procedures and provisions for backup, recovery, and restart of operations in the event of equipment failure or accidental destruction of data

- Data and source statement library procedures

- Procedures for job setup and operations within the data center

- The installation's documentation standards manual, or such documentation standards as exist

- Descriptions of physical security controls

- Specifications on insurance for accounting and CIS records and business transactions.

Methods applied in gathering these data are chiefly interviews and reviews of documentation. Physical inspection techniques are used both to gather data and to validate existing documents or representations made during the interviews. For example, a single visit to the computer center can provide both data gathering and validation opportunities for determining equipment configurations, library procedures, operating procedures, physical security controls, and data control procedures.

Many of these procedures are substantially the same regardless of whether the accounting system is computerized. Differences associated with the audit of computerized systems center around changes in controls, in documentation, in audit techniques, and in technical qualifications required by audit staff members.

Identifying Financial Application Areas

Once the auditor has gained a general familiarity with the client's accounting procedures, specific areas of audit interest must be identified. The auditor must decide what applications or subsystems will have to be examined at a more detailed level. As a basis for preparation of the audit plan, the auditor also must determine, in general, how much time will be required; what types of people and skills will be needed to conduct the examination; and, roughly, what the schedule will be.

This requirement applies regardless of whether the client is using a computer. If computers are being used for financially significant applications, the auditor must determine their sophistication and extent of use. This preliminary study goes just deep enough for the auditor to evaluate the complexity and sophistication of the systems and to determine the procedures to be followed in evaluating internal control. During the preliminary review phase of an examination, it is not necessary to go into detailed analysis, such as flowcharting of applications, be they manual or computerized.

Preparing an Audit Plan

The concluding activity in the preliminary review phase of an audit engagement will be the preparation of an audit plan. One form often used is a descriptive audit plan that includes tables and schedules as appropriate. Typical sections for an audit plan might include:

- Description of client organization
- Description of accounting systems and procedures

- Engagement staffing

- Audit scope

- Accounting and auditing problems

- Tax scope and problems

- Work schedules.

APPLICATION ANALYSIS

Emphasis on developing an understanding of client accounting systems is particularly appropriate during the application analysis phase of an audit engagement. It is important for the auditor to understand the relationship of each application to the conduct of the client company's business. Even where a computer plays a critical role, the auditor should avoid having audit activities become too technical and too detailed, too soon.

Another practice to be avoided is the tendency to treat manual and computerized elements of accounting systems as separate, distinct entities. Companies process data manually and on computers in a planned continuum. Manual and mechanized procedures usually are interdependent. The auditor should treat them accordingly. Thus, in walking through applications or subsystems, the auditor should include all the manual and mechanized procedures that go into the preparation and presentation of information in client financial statements.

Where individual applications are concerned, the auditor concentrates on two primary functions:

- Gathering samples of source documents, input forms, and output documents or reports. Documents should include both manually and computer-produced forms and reports.

- Flowcharting each application in continuity. The relationships between manual and automated procedures and identification of control points, where applicable, should be included.

Auditors prepare application flowcharts using standard symbols and techniques. Flowcharts developed during the application analysis phase of an audit engagement are most useful if they distinguish processing according to department, function, or company area.

Flowcharting as an Analysis Tool

For a computer auditor, flowcharts represent a method for identifying and evaluating control weaknesses and strengths within a system under examination. It can be time-consuming to build an understanding of strengths and weaknesses within a system to be audited. However, identification of strengths and weaknesses often is crucial because the entire direction of the remainder of an audit is directed toward substantiating and determining the effect of identified control weaknesses.

As a step toward building the needed understanding of control weaknesses, the audit staff should develop a flow diagram of all information processed. The flow diagrams, or *audit data flow diagrams,* should encompass all information processed, from source documents through to final outputs. Either automated or manual techniques can be used in preparing these audit data flow diagrams. With either approach, the process leads to evaluation of a number of elements of a system, including the following:

- Quality of system documentation

- Adequacy of manual and/or automated controls over documents

- Effectiveness of processing by computer programs (i.e., whether the processing is necessary or redundant, whether the processing sequence is proper, etc.)

- Usefulness of outputs, including reports and stored files.

Steps followed in development of flowcharts and their use as audit evaluation tools include:

- Understanding how data are processed by computers

- Identifying documents and their flow through the system

- Defining critical data

- Developing audit data flow diagrams

- Evaluating the quality of system documentation

- Evaluating controls over documents

- Evaluating the effectiveness of processing under computer programs

- Evaluating the usefulness of reports.

Understanding how data are processed by computers. The auditor should build an understanding of how the system under examination generates its data. This understanding should encompass the entire scope of the system, from preparation of source documents through to final distribution and use of outputs. While learning how the system works, the auditor should identify potential areas for testing, using familiar audit techniques such as:

- Reviewing corporate documentation, including system documentation files, input preparation instructions, and users' manuals

- Interviewing organization personnel, including users, systems analysts, and programmers

- Inspecting, comparing, and analyzing corporate records.

Identifying documents and their flow through the system. To understand document flow, certain background information must be obtained through discussions with corporate officials, from previous audits or evaluations, or from system documentation files. Because this information may not be current or complete, it should be verified with the responsible programmer or analyst. The auditor will have to obtain:

- Name (title) of the computer product

- Purpose of the product

- System name and identification number

- Date the system was implemented

- Type of computer used (manufacturer's model) and location

- Frequency of processing and type of processing (batch, on-line)

- Person(s) responsible for the computer application and database that generates the computer product.

A user or member of the computer center staff may already have a document flow diagram that shows the origin of data and how it flows to and from the computer. *(This diagram should not be confused with either a system flowchart that shows detailed computer processing of data or a program flowchart that describes a computer program.)* More often than not, the auditor will have to develop document flow diagrams in a format that is workable in a given situation, whether it proves to be a narrative description, a block diagram using simple symbols, a flowchart using standard symbols, or some combination. The document flow diagram or narrative description should include:

- Each source document, by title and identification number, with copies of the forms attached

- Point of origin for each source document

- Each operating unit or office through which data are processed

- Destination of each copy of the source document and the action applied to each copy (filed, audited, entered into a computer, etc.)

- Actions taken by each unit or office in which the data are processed (recorded in books of account, unit prices or extensions added, control numbers recorded and checked, etc.)

- Controls over the transfer of source documents between units or offices to assure that no documents are lost, added, or changed (controls include record counts, control totals, arithmetic totals of important data, etc.)

- Recipients of computer outputs.

Document flow descriptions **should not** encompass actual computer processing that takes place within a portion of the system treated as a "black box." Processing details are beyond the scope of reliability assessment. If computer output is the product of more than one input, this condition should be noted clearly in the document flow description.

Document flow in a typical payroll system is shown in Figure 2-6, a block diagram with rectangular symbols. Figure 2-7 shows the same document flow in narrative form.

Defining critical data.   The auditor must build a clear understanding of the data being recorded within the system under study. Therefore, the individual elements of data must be defined. Titles can be deceptive. For example, is a cost amount derived from the current period or is it cumulative? Is the cost accrued or incurred? What are the components of the cost amount? Has the composition of cost changed during the fiscal periods under review?

The organization's data element dictionary is a good source for such definitions. If a data dictionary is not available, a record layout may contain the needed definitions. Figure 2-8 includes a simple record layout.

In many instances, there is no one-to-one relationship between data elements and the data in a computer-processed report or file. Some common differences are shown in Figure 2-9.

Developing audit data flow diagrams.   Inputs from which data flow diagrams are prepared should include copies of the following:

- Narrative descriptions of all major application programs

- All manually prepared source documents that affect application processing, as well as corresponding coding sheets and instructions for data transcription.

ORIGINATING DEPARTMENT   **PAYROLL DEPARTMENT**   **DATA PROCESSING**

```
┌─────────────────────┐
│ TIMEKEEPER PREPARES │
│   BIWEEKLY TIME &   │
│  ATTENDANCE REPORT  │
│        (T&A)        │
└─────────────────────┘
          │
          ▼
┌─────────────────────┐     ┌──────────────────────────────┐
│      EMPLOYEE       │     │  REVIEWS T&A FOR COMPLETENESS │
│  SUPERVISOR REVIEWS │────▶│   AND CHECKS TOTAL HOURS      │
│   AND INITIALS T&A  │     └──────────────────────────────┘
└─────────────────────┘                  │
                                          ▼
                        ┌──────────────────────────────────┐
                        │       PREPARES CONTROL SHEET       │
                        │             INCLUDING:             │
                        │   —TOTAL NUMBER OF T&As            │
                        │   —TOTAL REGULAR HOURS             │
                        │   —TOTAL OVERTIME HOURS            │
                        │   —TOTAL LEAVE WITHOUT PAY HOURS   │
                        └──────────────────────────────────┘
                                          │
                                          ▼
                        ┌──────────────────────────────────┐
                        │    SUBMITS COPIES OF CONTROL       │────┐
                        │    SHEET AND ALL T&As              │    │
                        └──────────────────────────────────┘    │
                                          │                       │
                                          ▼                       │
                        ┌──────────────────────────────────┐    │  ┌──────────────┐
                        │   MAINTAINS COPY OF CONTROL        │    │  │   PROCESS    │
                        │   SHEET AND T&As                   │    │  │     T&As     │
                        └──────────────────────────────────┘    │  └──────────────┘
                                                                  │        │
                        ┌──────────────────────────────────┐    │        │
                        │     RECEIVES PAYROLL LISTING       │◀───────────┘
                        │        OF ALL EMPLOYEES            │
                        └──────────────────────────────────┘
                                          │
                                          ▼
                        ┌──────────────────────────────────┐
                        │    REVIEWS PAYROLL LISTING FOR     │
                        │   ACCURACY AND COMPLETENESS:       │
                        │   —TOTAL NUMBER OF T&As            │
                        │   —TOTAL REGULAR HOURS             │
                        │   —TOTAL OVERTIME HOURS            │
                        │   —TOTAL LEAVE WITHOUT PAY HOURS   │
                        └──────────────────────────────────┘
                                          │
                                          ▼
                        ┌──────────────────────────────────┐    ┌──────────────┐
                        │    IDENTIFIES ANY ERRORS OR        │───▶│ PROCESS ERROR│
                        │  IRREGULARITIES AND INITIATES      │    │  CORRECTIONS │
                        │       CORRECTIVE ACTION            │    └──────────────┘
                        └──────────────────────────────────┘            │
                                          │                               │
                                          ▼                               ▼
                        ┌──────────────────────────────────┐    ┌──────────────┐
┌──────────────────────┐│   MAINTAINS COPY OF PAYROLL        │    │   PROCESS    │
│  EMPLOYEE RECEIVES   │◀─ LISTING FOR 12 MONTHS             │    │  PAYCHECKS   │
│      PAYCHECK        │ └──────────────────────────────────┘    └──────────────┘
└──────────────────────┘
```

Figure 2-6.

This diagram tracks the flow of documents in payroll processing.

NARRATIVE DOCUMENT FLOW OF PAYROLL PROCESS

The following procedures are used to process a biweekly employee payroll:

1. At the end of the pay period, each employee completes a time and attendance (T&A) report.

2. Each employee's supervisor reviews and initials the T&A and submits it to the Payroll Department.

3. A payroll clerk reviews the T&A for completeness and checks total hours reported.

4. When all the T&A reports are received, the payroll clerk prepares a control sheet which shows totals for number of T&A reports, and number of regular hours, overtime hours, and leave-without-pay hours.

5. The payroll clerk keeps the originals and sends a copy of the control sheet and all T&A reports to Data Processing.

6. Data Processing enters the payroll data through an on-line terminal.

7. At the completion of payroll processing, a listing of all employees paid is sent to the payroll clerk.

8. The payroll clerk reviews the listing for completeness and accuracy, which includes a comparison of the number of T&A reports, regular hours, overtime hours, and leave-without-pay hours with the control sheet totals.

9. Any discrepancies are researched and resolved. Errors affecting pay are corrected and resubmitted to Data Processing for immediate action. Errors in leave are corrected in the subsequent pay period.

10. The payroll clerk keeps the payroll listing for 12 months.

11. The payroll process also prints the paycheck and sends it directly to the employee.

Figure 2-7. *This narrative describes the document flow within the payroll process.*

RECORD LAYOUT
DESCRIPTION OF PAYROLL DATA FILE

Data Element	Position in Data File	Data Element Description
SSN	1-9	Social Security Number
Name	10-39	Name—Last, First, Middle Initial
Employee Category	40-41	Payee's Employment Code
Salary	42-47	Yearly Salary
Taxes	48-53	Weekly Tax Deduction
Insurance	54-59	Weekly Insurance Deduction
Bond Code	60	Bond Deduction Code

Bond Code	Bond Amount	Weekly Deduction
1	$ 100	$ 2
2	200	4
3	500	10
4	1,000	20

Data Element	Position in Data File	Data Element Description
Hours	61-64	Hours worked during current pay period. (999V9)

Figure 2-8.

The record layout shown here is included in the file description for payroll data.

EXAMPLES OF DIFFERENCES BETWEEN COMPUTER OUTPUT AND DATA ELEMENTS

Differences	Explanation of the difference
Total deductions on a payroll report might represent an addition of several data elements (taxes + health insurance + bonds + . . .).	The computer program used to produce the report adds the individual deductions and prints the total.
Bond deductions might be represented by a 1-character code on the data file.	The computer program converts the 1-character code to a dollar amount (e.g., 1 = $100 bond, 2 = $200 bond, etc.).
Weekly salary appears on the report and only annual salary is found in the data file.	The computer program converts the yearly salary into a weekly amount through division by weeks.
Average annual salary appears as an individual statistic while annual salaries are recorded in the data file.	The computer program totals all annual salaries in the file and divides the total by the number of records.
A report might show details and summary statistics for first-level supervisors while the database contains payroll information for all employee categories.	The computer program selects only first-level supervisors (category M or above) records for printing and summarization.

Figure 2-9.

This table summarizes principal differences between data elements and outputs for a payroll processing system.

- Record layouts for all major computer input and output records, computer master files, and work files (such as update or file maintenance tapes, computation tapes, etc.)
- All major outputs produced by the automated system
- Lists of standard codes, constants, and tables used by the system.

The documents listed above, along with the information developed in the previous tasks, should enable the audit staff to prepare an audit data flow diagram identifying:

- Point of origin (title or individual) for all source documents
- All transfers of source documents from one person or office to another (make sure that all control points are identified)
- Transcriptions of source documents into machine-readable format
- Computer processing of application data
- All major outputs created from the source documents
- Recipients of all essential outputs.

To illustrate, an example of an audit data flow diagram is shown in Figure 2-10. Note that the symbols used in an audit data flow diagram are the same as those used for preparation of flowcharts under widely accepted standards. A detailed discussion of flowcharting can be found in the publication, *Flowchart Symbols and Their Usage in Information Processing,* issued by the National Bureau of Standards. This is available as Federal Information Processing Standards Publication, FIPS PUB 24, June, 1973. As an immediate reference, Figure 2-11 identifies and summarizes the meaning of the symbols used in Figure 2-10.

Evaluating the quality of system documentation. On the basis of user and CIS staff inputs, as well as on the degree of difficulty experienced in constructing an audit data flow diagram, the auditor should be able to comment upon the quality of system documentation. There are two basic questions to answer:

- Is the documentation accurate?
- Is the documentation complete?

To illustrate, if a federal auditor were examining documentation at a Naval computer facility, he or she might use the documentation standards to be found in the National Bureau of Standards publication, *Guidelines for*

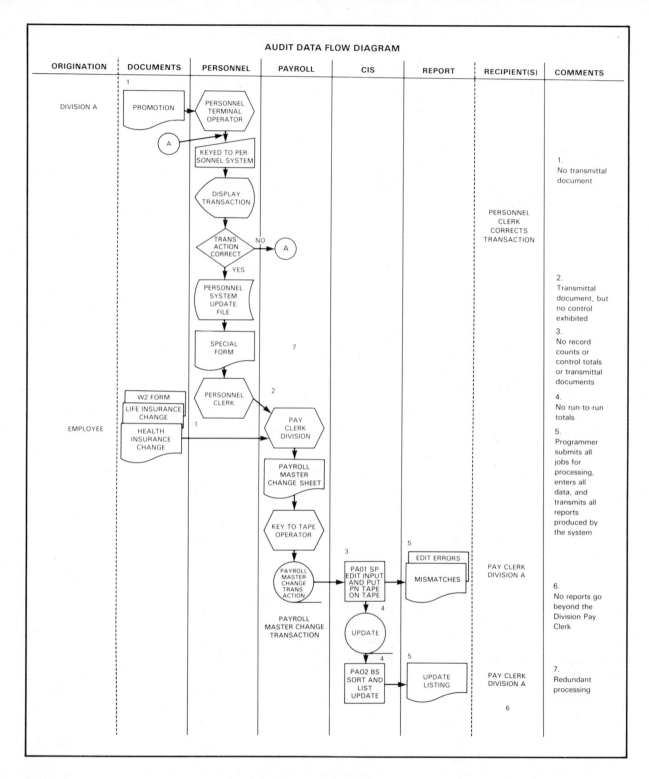

Figure 2-10. *This flowchart depicts the payroll process from an auditor's control-oriented view.*

Symbol		Definition
	DOCUMENT	An I/O function in which the medium is a document.
	DISPLAY	An I/O function in which the information is displayed for human use at the time of processing.
	DECISION	Points in an algorithm where several paths may be possible based on variable conditions.
	MAGNETIC TAPE	I/O function in which the medium is magnetic tape.
	MANUAL INPUT	I/O function in which the information is entered manually at the time of processing.
	ON-LINE STORAGE	Represents an I/O function utilizing mass storage that can be accessed on-line.
	PRE-DEFINED PROCESS	A named process consisting of one or more operations or program steps, specified elsewhere. (Subroutine)
	PREPARATION	A group of instructions which modify, update, correct, or otherwise change the program.
	PROCESS	Represents the process of executing a defined operation or group of operations.
	TERMINAL	A point at which information can enter or leave.

Figure 2-11.

Shown here are flowchart symbols typically used by auditors in analyzing a system of controls.

Documentation of Computer Programs and Automated Data Systems, FIPS PUB 38, February, 1976. This publication would provide a basis for assessing compliance to federal guidelines by the documentation for a system under study.

Evaluating controls over documents.   Control points identified during preparation of the audit data flow diagram, along with information on controls developed in the background segment, should enable the auditor to identify system controls, as shown in Figure 2-10. With a diagram of this type, the auditor can determine whether the following controls are used:

- Turnaround documents [Transmittal documents (manual or automated) should be returned to the originator to make sure that all documents were received and none were added during transmittal.]

- Record counts [Record counts (manual or system-generated) should be maintained for all documents to make sure that none are added or lost.]

- Predetermined control totals [For payroll, predetermined control totals should be developed for important data items, such as hours worked, leave taken, hourly rates, gross pay, and deductions. The purpose is to make sure that records are not altered.]

- Run-to-run totals. [These totals should be maintained to assure that no records are added or lost during steps in the computer processing sequence.]

Evaluating the effectiveness of processing under computer programs.
The audit staff should identify any problem areas in the processing cycle, including but not limited to:

- Redundant processing of data or other forms of duplication

- Bottlenecks that delay processing

- Points in the operating cycle at which clerks do not have enough time to review output reports and make corrections.

Evaluating the usefulness of reports.   The audit staff should review the key or major outputs (such as edit listings, error listings, control of hours listings, etc.) of the application system and determine if the outputs:

- Are accurate

- Can be used as intended.

The auditor should confirm findings by interviewing the users of the output reports. One appropriate technique might be completion of a questionnaire on user satisfaction with output reports.

Appropriateness of Flowcharting Techniques

A distinction should be noted between the use of systems flowcharts in computer auditing and in the broader field of systems analysis. In recent years, systems analysts have begun to favor other methods of modeling and documentation. Data flow diagrams, for example, often are preferred over systems flowcharts for purposes of analysis. The rationale is that data flow diagrams are process-oriented, emphasizing logical flows and transformations of data. By contrast, systems flowcharts emphasize physical processing steps and controls. It is just this type of control-oriented view, however, that is the auditor's primary focus. Thus, though use of systems flowcharting may be declining for systems development purposes, this modeling tool remains important for computer auditors.

This is not to say that systems flowcharting is always the most practical approach for the auditor. Existing documentation—including data flow diagrams, narratives written in structured English, or descriptions of programs in pseudocode—may be used as points of departure. Based on a review of existing documentation, the auditor then can decide what additional modeling is needed to gain adequate understanding of the systems under examination.

The auditor also should be aware of the increasing use of automated tools in preparing flowcharts. Software packages are available, many of which run on mainframes that accept program source code as input and generate finished flowcharts. Also, microcomputer-based software packages now available can aid in documentation or verification of spreadsheets or database applications. Examples include Spreadsheet Auditor, DFlow, and Cambridge Analyzer.

The technique for departmental segregation of processing in the preparation of flowcharts is illustrated in Figure 2-12. Separate vertical columns on the flowchart show processing by function or department. This representation is useful because one of the important controls the auditor evaluates is the segregation of duties within the accounting system. Structuring flowcharts in this way helps both to discipline the auditor's thinking and to identify any incompatible functions that may exist within accounting applications.

During both the preliminary review and application analysis phases, the auditor should be accumulating notes to be considered for later inclusion as comments within a letter of recommendations to client management.

At the conclusion of the preliminary review and application analysis phases of the engagement, the audit team briefs audit firm partners and client managers associated with the audit. All responsible parties should have a

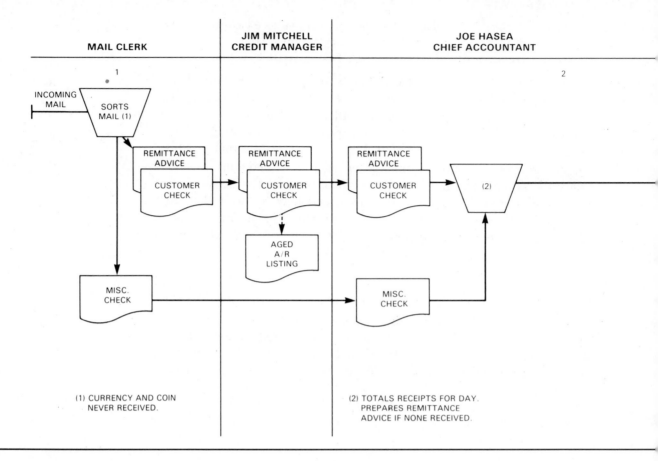

MAIL CLERK	JIM MITCHELL CREDIT MANAGER	JOE HASEA CHIEF ACCOUNTANT

(1) CURRENCY AND COIN NEVER RECEIVED.

(2) TOTALS RECEIPTS FOR DAY. PREPARES REMITTANCE ADVICE IF NONE RECEIVED.

Figure 2-12.

A company's manual cash receipts operation is shown in this flowchart.

clear understanding of the sources and procedures for development of information reflected in the financial statements on which the audit firm will render an opinion.

On completing its preliminary review and application analyses, the audit team should have built an understanding that includes:

- Identification of sources for all financially significant accounting information

- Identification of processing steps, particularly of points within applications at which major changes in accounting information take place

- Identification and understanding of processing results

- The nature and progress of audit trails, to the extent that they exist and can be followed within individual applications.

At the conclusion of the preliminary review and application analysis phases of an engagement, the auditor should have both a basis of understanding and

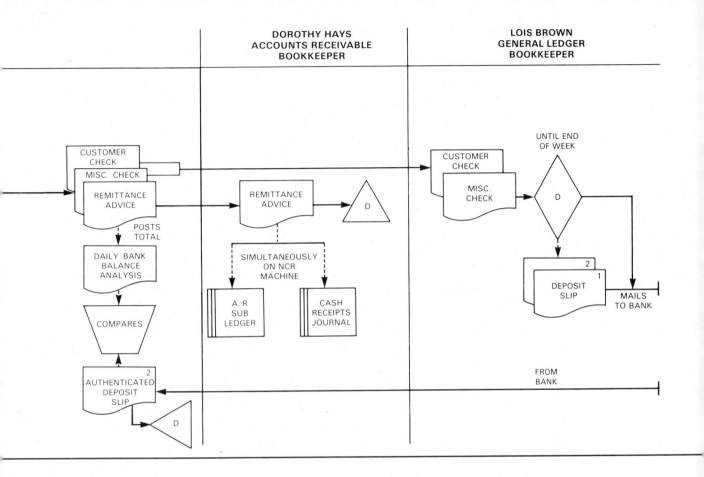

the evidential matter necessary to proceed with preliminary evaluations of internal controls within the client's accounting system.

PROFICIENCY DEMANDS

Adhering to generally accepted auditing standards establishes some specific qualification requirements for audit team members assigned to the examination of computer-inclusive systems:

- All personnel associated with the examination of computer-inclusive procedures should be able to discuss computers and their functions with CIS, accounting, and user-department personnel. Each audit staff member should be able to understand how accounting data are being processed within computer systems. But, every auditor need not be technically expert on the minute details of computer processing, software, and application programming.

- Some staff members associated with the audit team must be competent technically to review programs and functions at a detail level. This includes a requirement for a working familiarity with programming languages. CIS specialists should be available to write and execute programs for implementation of computer-assisted auditing procedures, if appropriate.

In short, all auditors need not be computer experts. Experience has shown that a practical, pragmatic approach to the conduct of audit examinations lies in establishing a balanced, team approach. In some CPA firms, at least one member of the audit team concerned with a computer-inclusive system is a qualified CIS audit specialist. The other staff may be audit generalists who are conversant with CIS functions and procedures. Within this team concept, application of the first field work standard demands that the work of all audit staff members be reviewed by qualified people. Thus, the working papers and findings of a CIS audit specialist usually should be reviewed by a second, qualified specialist. In other firms, the objective is to expand the computer knowledge, skills, and abilities of all staff to a level of competence that qualifies the entire staff for computer audit assignments.

In summary, the special demands of auditing computer-based accounting systems include the following:

- At least some segment of the audit staff must acquire an extensive, in-depth technical knowledge of the computer equipment, software, and the programming languages used in installations of client organizations. The technical backgrounds of these specialists must be advanced, and must be updated continually. The audit staff must possess sufficient technical depth for a full review and evaluation of computer-based control techniques that are far more complex than those encountered in traditional, manual systems.

- Given the technical background to develop an understanding of a computerized system, the reviewer also must have the audit knowledge and experience necessary to perform a review and evaluation of computer-oriented internal controls.

- On the basis of their internal control reviews, auditors determine the types and extent of testing that will be applied to the systems under examination. In a CIS environment, computer-assisted testing techniques often are necessary. Auditors are finding that the computer itself holds great potential as an audit tool.

The special demands associated with auditing in a CIS environment are discussed in the next chapter.

DISCUSSION QUESTIONS

1. Why can it be asserted that traditional audit trails have disappeared with respect to computer information systems?

2. How is the involvement of CIS auditors related to the building of integrated databases?

3. For computer-based systems, what are the respective roles of and relationships between internal and external auditors?

4. What is the current position of the auditing profession on the applicability of GAAS and GAAP to computer-based systems?

5. What are management's responsibilities with respect to the reliability of computer-developed information?

6. How might CIS auditors assist and support management?

7. What is the function of the operational audit and how does this function differ from the auditor's attest function?

8. What are the typical phases of an audit engagement and what changes, if any, might be required if computers were included in the systems under study?

3 Computer Auditing— A Growing Profession

A B S T R A C T

- The computer auditor assesses internal controls within computer information systems and evaluates the efficiency and effectiveness of CIS operations.

- The evolution of computer auditing as a profession is a relatively recent occurrence, spurred by major scandals involving abuse of computerized systems.

- Qualifications of computer auditors should include management and auditing skills, supplemented by a technical grasp of computer information systems and telecommunications, as well as an appreciation of hardware and software capabilities and limitations.

- Concerns of computer auditors include: accidental disclosure; casual, unauthorized access; and deliberate attack.

- Skills and knowledge required of computer auditors in the field of security emphasize the techniques of risk analysis and threat assessment.

- National and international associations concerned with computer auditing include: AICPA, IIA and NAA, CIS professional societies, and EDPAA.

- The role of computer audit specialists in public accounting firms is gaining in importance to match the shift toward computer-based techniques in all aspects of the profession.

- Government legislation and regulatory activities in the field include: FIPS, IRS regulations and guidelines, OSHA, Federal Managers' Financial Integrity Act, privacy legislation, Foreign Corrupt Practices Act of 1977, reporting requirements to the SEC, and Counterfeit Access Device and Computer Fraud and Abuse Act of 1984.

- Trends in higher education are adapting to include the knowledge required to perform computer audits.

THE EMERGENCE OF THE COMPUTER AUDITOR

Most companies with publicly traded securities are processing their financially significant data with computer systems. In general, the larger the organization, the greater its dependence on computers to process financial information.

At current levels of computer technology, traditional methods of financial statement examination by auditors are no longer appropriate to many integrated data processing systems. In addition, operational efficiency, effectiveness, and economy require skilled personnel. Today, computer expertise is almost a prerequisite to professional-quality examinations by auditors.

The accounting and auditing profession has recognized the need for and has committed to accommodating changes mandated by the use of computers. Senior management of audit firms also have evidenced strong commitment by developing staff positions for computer audit specialists and by implementing policies that will nurture and sustain this specialty within the audit practice. Corporate managers and accounting professionals are beginning to recognize CIS impacts and adapt to them, and are determined to enlist the help of computer auditors.

Trends

Given that this specialization has emerged, where is it going? In audit practices of the future, all organizations will have to adapt to environmental pressures. In general, organizations will have to:

- Establish standards of education, experience, and qualification testing for recognized professionals with computer audit credentials.

- Find qualified people, who currently are in short supply. This search probably will generate intense competition among public and private organizations to recruit and develop CIS graduates.

- Give computer audit specialists both recognition and visibility within the audit community.

Among many established organizations, there are attractive career paths for computer audit specialists. These incentives may be expected to include commensurate professional recognition and stature with peers and in the eyes of clients. The largest CPA firms have promoted computer audit specialists to partnership status. This stature is on a par with the recognition given to specialists in taxation, SEC representation, and management consulting.

This chapter looks at the qualifications for computer auditing and the demands that will be placed on the profession in the future. Computer auditors must prepare for and move into a world that literally depends on large, heavily integrated computer information systems. These systems may be characterized by the use of emerging technologies, such as distributed processing, local area networking, microtechnology, firmware, satellite transmission, and others.

COMPUTER AUDITING—WHAT IS IT?

The evaluation of computer information systems by auditors has generated the term *computer auditing.* Computer auditing is the evaluation of computer information systems, practices, and operations to assure the integrity of an entity's information. This evaluation can include the assessment of how efficient, effective, and economical computer-based practices are. This includes the use of the computer as an audit tool. Also, the evaluation should determine the adequacy of internal controls within the CIS environment to assure valid, reliable, and secure information services.

The computer auditor's evaluation of systems, practices, and operations may include one or both of the following:

- Assessment of internal controls within the CIS environment to assure the validity, reliability, and security of information

- Assessment of the efficiency and effectiveness of the CIS environment in economic terms.

There is a growing belief that the roles of auditor, accountant, and internal auditor will converge in the computer auditor of tomorrow. The chairman of a national accounting firm stated that ''. . . The accountant of tomorrow will have to be a computer expert. And 'tomorrow' is already here.'' The corporate director of internal audit at one of the nation's leading banks stated that, of his present staff of 950 auditors, 200 are computer audit specialists. By 1990, all staff within this department are expected to have computer audit competency.

As for the computer auditors of today, their advanced knowledge and skills will progress in two ways. One direction is continued growth and skill in this profession, leading the way in computer audit research and development, and progressing up the external and internal audit career paths. The other direction involves capitalizing on a thorough knowledge of organizational systems and moving into more responsible career areas in general management. Figures 3-1 and 3-2 illustrate the varied opportunities currently available to computer auditors.

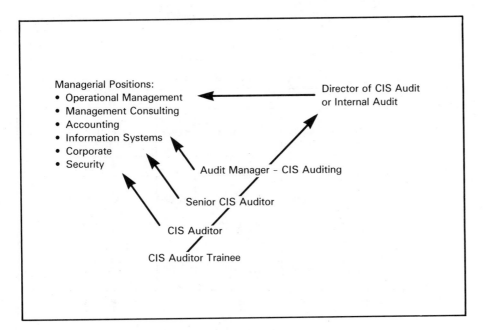

Figure 3-1.

This diagram shows a typical career path for a computer auditor in an internal audit or CIS audit department. Opportunities and job titles will differ from one organization to another. (Adapted from "Planning EDP Audit Career Development," EDP Auditing, 1984.)

Evolution of Computer Auditing

As discussed in previous chapters, computer auditing as it exists today has had an evolutionary development. The profession has had to stay not just current but one step ahead of new technologies and their impacts on computer information systems.

In the late 1950s through the 1960s, traditional audit practices prevailed. During this time, most of the audit work focused on examination of physical controls. It was not until the 1970s that computer auditing came into its own. Government, professional societies, and national accounting firms all were aware of the vulnerabilities of computer-based systems. However, no major scandals involving abuse of these systems had occurred. Then, the Equity Funding scandal made corporate managers aware that such things could occur in their own companies.

The autonomy of CIS departments was never the same after this case. Top management began to ask probing questions and enlisted the help of computer audit specialists. Throughout the 1970s and into the 1980s, as discussed in Chapter 1, the frequency of reported computer-related scandals, abuse, and inefficiencies continued to rise. The result has been that today's managers must demand the audit of all aspects of computer information systems to assure reliability and to protect against fraud.

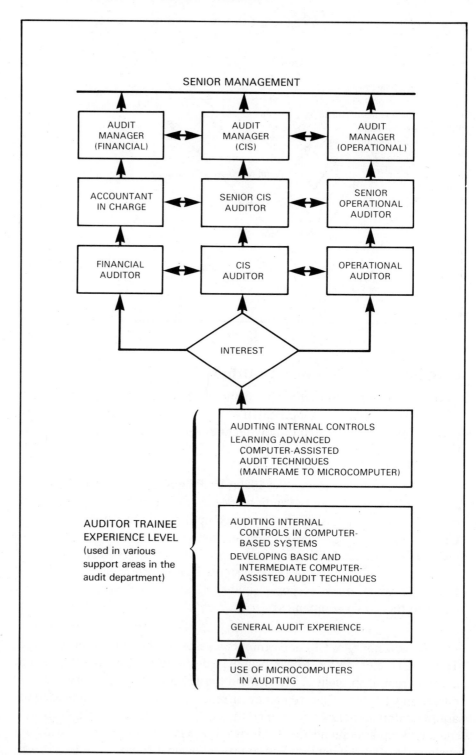

Figure 3-2.

In a departmental career path for computer auditors, a decision point is reached at which the individual may branch into financial, CIS, or operational areas. (Adapted from "Planning EDP Audit Career Development," EDP Auditing, 1984.)

Qualifications of the Computer Auditor

Today's computer auditor possesses a special combination of knowledge, skills and experience. Whether this individual is employed by a CPA firm, government agency, or private company, he or she has attained a degree of skill and competence matched by few other professional groups.

There have been several exhaustive efforts at trying to identify the skills, education, and experience needed to become a qualified computer auditor. The National Bureau of Standards of the U. S. Department of Commerce undertook such a massive effort in 1977 when it gathered more than 75 of the foremost professionals in the field of computer auditing to discuss all aspects of computer audit and security. The outcome of this conference was the National Bureau of Standards Special Publication 500-19, *Audit and Evaluation of Computer Security.*

The AICPA, IIA, EDPAF, and the Canadian Institute of Chartered Accountants (CICA) each has sponsored similar studies and efforts to identify the common body of skills needed to audit computer information systems effectively. Essentially, these studies have concurred: Computer security and audit involve all the controls necessary to assure integrity, accuracy, and reliability of the data in a CIS from a total systems perspective.

Note the emphasis on a "total systems perspective." This perspective encompasses all the controls established over the acquisition, processing, storage, and dissemination of information. The studies tempered their considerations with the qualification that they were unaware of any infallible system of evaluating computer security. The consensus of opinion was that no known system of controls will prevent unauthorized or illegal intervention or penetration of a CIS by sophisticated professionals or technically qualified intruders.

In considering the appropriate level of expertise necessary to conduct these audits, the study groups first attempted to identify the common body of knowledge required. Then, they gave extensive consideration to the complexities of the environment in which the evaluations would be performed. They assumed that the individuals who would conduct these evaluations might have basic education and experience in any generally recognized discipline, including: accounting, business administration, engineering, operations research, computer science, or economics. Each of these disciplines already has a distinct body of knowledge identified or associated with it. Since individuals with varying backgrounds and experience can be expected to conduct computer audit evaluations, several of the study groups felt that it could not be assumed that everyone undertaking this work would be a fully qualified, professional auditor.

Regardless of an individual's basic education and experience, audits of computer systems demand a solid foundation in the concepts and practices of management and auditing. This base must be supplemented by a solid grasp of the fundamentals of computer information systems and telecommunications, including an appreciation of hardware and software capabilities and limitations. Depending on the type, nature, and scope of the audit, the individual will need varying degrees of knowledge and experience in computer operations, software, and performance. An understanding will be needed of the information flows into, through, and out of the automated data processing function. The more complex the system being evaluated, the more comprehensive the technical knowledge required.

Concerns Addressed by Computer Auditors

Consider that an important segment of an audit might be to ascertain the integrity of a computer program or a series of computer programs. In such cases, the auditor, among other things, should be competent to assess the potential or real threats to the system. Concerns might include:

Accidental disclosure.   Accidental disclosure of information might stem from a variety of technical causes, including natural failure of hardware or software, or both. Possibilities for human error also must be considered.

Casual, unauthorized access.   In some cases, a casual, unauthorized intruder, or "browser," might discover flaws in the system. Or, an intruder, having discovered a weakness, might seek to exploit it.

Deliberate attack.   In these situations, a thief might create flaws in the system. Code might be modified to create *trap doors,* or pathways for unauthorized access. The potential for conspiracy or the conduct of a planned attack must be evaluated. The threat of damage or abuse from an individual, irrational employee must be assessed.

Skills and Capabilities of Computer Auditors

Typically, the skills needed to conduct this type of audit do not reside with a single individual. In such situations, *multidisciplinary audit teams* might be used. A multidisciplinary audit team comprises all of the skills and experience needed for a specific audit. The multidisciplinary team approach has been used successfully by many organizations.

In determining the common body of knowledge needed for computer auditors, most of the studies dealt with two basic problems. First, there is the problem of enhancing the basic knowledge and experience of individuals who will conduct the audits. Second, there is the problem of determining the extent of the technical training needed by each individual participating in an audit.

Experience has shown that there are at least three levels of knowledge required for this work:

General background.   A general level of knowledge is required in the disciplines of management and auditing concepts and practices. Individuals graduating from recognized universities or colleges with degrees in business administration or accounting usually will have reached this level of knowledge. However, such individuals may lack a solid foundation in CIS and telecommunications and will have to acquire this knowledge through additional training.

CIS and telecommunications.   The second level of knowledge requires a solid foundation in CIS and telecommunications, including an appreciation of hardware and software capabilities and limitations. A degree from a recognized university or college in a discipline such as computer science or business information systems, often with specialization in programming and systems design, usually indicates this level of competence. However, individuals who have followed this course of study may lack a solid foundation in management and auditing concepts and practices. This knowledge will have to be acquired through additional training and on-the-job experience unless a supplementary business curriculum has provided that background. Today, many accounting majors are taking a fifth year of school, pursuing CIS disciplines as major or minor studies for added depth. Several schools offer advanced education in both areas at the graduate and undergraduate levels. Some even offer specialization in computer auditing.

Comprehensive technical knowledge.   The third level involves the development of a comprehensive technical knowledge and the related experience to audit the more sophisticated aspects of a computer system. For example, this level of knowledge would be required for evaluation of the vulnerability of an operating system (monitor, executive system, etc.) for unauthorized access by a browser or skilled exploiter seeking flaws in the system.

BODY OF KNOWLEDGE FOR COMPUTER AUDITORS

The discussion below summarizes the criteria for a common body of knowledge for the computer auditor, as well as related qualifications and training, as determined by a consensus of the studies mentioned above. The criteria for competence in computer auditing include expertise in the following categories:

- Computer systems, operations, and software
- CIS techniques
- Management concepts and practices
- Security of the CIS function
- Assessment of risks and threats
- Auditing concepts and practices
- Additional qualifications needed to audit and evaluate the security of a CIS.

Computer Systems, Operations, and Software

Under the broad heading of computer systems, operations, and software, computer auditors are expected to have, at minimum, a working knowledge of the following:

- The theory of computer information systems
- Computers
- Data communications.

These categories of knowledge define a broad, theoretical foundation for understanding the interrelationships and interactions of all parts of a CIS. Computer auditors should know how computers operate and must understand the interrelated and essential functions of software. Principles in this category may be applied to any type of system, whether it is standalone, batch, interactive, on-line, or distributed. Study should stress the impact of new technologies on the CIS environment, including the use of multifaceted hardware, or combinations of mainframes, minicomputers, microcomputers, satellite communications, and other new technologies.

CIS Techniques

Dramatic advances in CIS techniques have taken place within the past few decades. Each year brings still faster and more efficient methods for processing data. Programming languages have proliferated, data management has become more efficient, and file processing techniques have made it possible to store and retrieve vast amounts of data. Adapting to this rapid evolution means not only having a basic understanding of CIS techniques, but also making the effort to keep current in this rapidly changing field. Topics in this area of expertise include:

- Information structures
- Programming languages
- Sort and search techniques
- File creation, maintenance, and interrogation methods
- Storage devices
- Data management systems
- Integrated systems
- The dynamics of developing, modifying, and maintaining software.

In view of the speed of development in these areas, keeping current calls for a program of ongoing, or continuing, education.

Management Concepts and Practices

The art and science of management have undergone considerable change since the middle of this century. Mathematical and statistical concepts, computer techniques, and the developing behavorial sciences, to name a few factors, have had a tremendous impact on the concepts and methods of managing.

Authorities differ on the definition of good management. There are no simple formulas or pat answers for managing effectively. Managing is much too complex for that. However, although the authorities differ, they generally agree on the essential areas of study. The topics needed to build expertise for auditing computer systems include:

- Management tasks, responsibilities, practices, and ethics
- Administration
- Principles of organizational structures
- Concepts of general management
- Management of human resources.

In particular, good management of the CIS function is a key element in providing reliable reporting from computer operations. In addition to being responsible for day-to-day operations, CIS managers also must concern themselves with a myriad of details ranging from the physical layout of their operations to the reliability of the software used to process data. The importance of these tasks cannot be overemphasized. The interrelationship of management tasks and their contribution to the ongoing effort of administering CIS services must be understood by the auditor. Areas of expertise within the category of CIS management include:

- Organizational structures
- Personnel selection, training, and management
- Operating and organizational policies and procedures
- Analysis, design, and programming functions
- Security/quality assurance functions.

These topics introduce the computer auditor-in-training to the basic areas of responsibility associated with managing the CIS function. From a management viewpoint, the computer is a processor of information—not a creator or user of information. Thus, a key relationship exists between the computer service function and the creators and users of information. A grasp of these issues includes placing the CIS function into appropriate perspective within the organization as a whole.

Security of the CIS Function

As stated previously, there are no security techniques so foolproof that they absolutely will prevent a determined and technically skilled intruder from penetrating or compromising a computer system. However, specific measures can be taken to discourage security breaches. These safeguards will vary from one installation to another. For example, the implementation of security measures will depend on the sensitivity or classification of data, the clearance levels of personnel, and types of *perimeter control,* or appropriateness of physical access controls.

Computer auditors must be familiar with these security techniques and must be able to assess the sensitivity of the data in a computer system. This expertise is the basis for making reliable evaluations of how adequately the data are being protected. The development of remote access capabilities for computer systems has added to the difficulty of maintaining effective security. Thus, an understanding of the technology of distributed computing, as well as of appropriate control measures, is becoming increasingly important. Coverage of this area should include such topics as security in relation to:

- The computer center
- Remote sites

- Systems, including operating, application, and telecommunication software

- Policies and procedures

- Personnel

- Data handling

- Recovery capabilities

- Testing of systems.

This listing of security issues can be a starting point for directing a course of study. The listing is not exhaustive; rather it outlines a much broader, and generally technical, area.

Assessment of Risks and Threats

To evaluate security techniques and procedures, an individual must be able to assess the extent of damage that could result from a disaster. Thus, a basic understanding is needed of *risk assessment* techniques, which result in realistic evaluations of potential damage.

Managers and individuals evaluating computer operations must be able to recognize the symptoms of potential disaster. *Threat assessment* includes knowing the probability of occurrence of particular types of threats. This type of evaluation is a key to identifying the security procedures that will be most effective against a given type of threat.

Threats may come from any direction. For example, natural hazards, such as flood or fire, are ever present threats to CIS facilities. Or, personnel may accidentally or deliberately interfere with the proper operation of a computer system.

The list of topics for this area of expertise include evaluating risks and threats associated with:

- Physical facilities

- Remote sites

- Application and operating system software

- Information.

These topics encompass a basic understanding of techniques for assessing risks and threats.

Auditing Concepts and Practices

The techniques of auditing and related topics form the foundation for the conduct of audits and evaluations of computer information systems. The basic function of auditing is almost as old as civilization. The common areas of audit action throughout its history have been examining, verifying, and reporting.

The adoption of computer-based techniques has increased the vulnerability of information. Thus, the importance of the audit function has only increased with the advent of the computer.

At a minimum, the computer auditor should be familiar with topics that include:

- Introductory accounting
- Intermediate accounting
- Advanced accounting
- Cost accounting
- Municipal and governmental accounting
- Auditing.

Additional Qualifications

In addition to this common body of knowledge, computer auditors should possess the following qualifications:

- Sufficient experience to be able to plan, direct, and coordinate audits of large complex functions, activities, or programs
- The ability to assign tasks to individuals on the audit team and to identify the specific disciplines and expertise needed to perform the work
- The ability to conduct conferences and to prepare, present, and process the report describing the results of the work.

INFLUENCE ON THE PROFESSION

Trends and influences on the profession of CIS auditing include:

- Professional awareness
- Emergence of a new audit function
- Government influence.

Professional Awareness

National and international professional associations have recognized the need for specialized skills and knowledge in the area of computer auditing.

AICPA. In conjunction with state-affiliated boards of accountancy, the American Institute of Certified Public Accountants and statement boards of account sponsor the Certified Public Accountant (CPA) designation. An increasing number of the questions on the yearly CPA examinations have focused on computer audit and control issues.

IIA and NAA. Certification by The Institute of Internal Auditors (IIA) and the National Association of Accountants (NAA) also requires demonstration of competence in CIS areas. Both organizations sponsor yearly examinations that have begun to emphasize computer audit evaluation and control. Individuals who pass the examination sponsored by the IIA, and who meet an experience requirement, are eligible to become *Certified Internal Auditors (CIA)*. Comparable requirements are set by the National Association of Accountants for the *Certified Management Accountant (CMA)* designation.

CIS professional societies. CIS-oriented professional societies, such as the Data Processing Management Association (DPMA), the Association for Systems Management (ASM), and the Quality Assurance Institute (QAI), wish to assure that their members have adequate knowledge of computer-based controls and audit principles. DPMA initiated the *Certified Data Processor (CDP)* professional designation, a credential that currently is administered by a separate organization, the Institute of Certified Computer Professionals (ICCP). The examination includes a broad range of questions over the field of computer information systems and technology. Two relevant areas deal with internal controls and computer auditing techniques. In addition, in the publication of its Model Curriculum for Undergraduate Computer Information Systems Education, DPMA identified the need for an elective course on EDP Audit and Controls (CIS-13) as part of the curriculum. This text is an implementation of that course.

In addition, a recent accreditation is sponsored by the ASM. This certification is designated as the *Certified Systems Professional (CSP)*. The QAI also sponsors a recent designation, known as the *Certified Quality Assurance Analyst (CQAA)*.

EDP Auditors Association. The EDP Auditors Association was founded in 1969 and grew rapidly into an international organization of more than 10,000 members. Through its foundation, the EDP Auditors Foundation, Inc,

(EDPAF), this organization has developed and maintained professional standards, which are promulgated through its publication, *Control Objectives.* Individuals who meet these standards may be certified as *Certified Information Systems Auditors (CISA).* Certification is awarded based on examination, experience, and continuing education requirements.

Through education, conferences, publications, and funding of research, these organizations have contributed to the evolution and development of the computer auditing profession. Combined with the efforts of national accounting firms and the government, these organizations have helped to build an awareness of the need for CIS controls and specialized audit techniques.

Emergence of a New Audit Function

As computer auditing and other related specializations evolve, a basic change can be expected in function and organization within the audit practice of the typical public accounting firm.

Today, the audit practice within a typical firm encompasses, in effect, dual functions—accounting and auditing. Though often taught as separate disciplines, prevailing practice tends to treat accounting and auditing as a single function. In some firms, the term *accounting and audit department* is used.

Consider the pattern of evolution that has occurred within a typical national accounting firm. This firm has adopted an alternative functional and organizational structure in direct response to the impact of CIS upon the practice. Throughout its offices, the firm has established a department known as the Technical Support Group. This group, operating in a support role, has combined several disciplines of audit specialization, including computer audit specialists, quantitative analysis specialists, and audit test and sampling specialists.

On a regional basis, the Technical Support Group serves as a resource for audit examinations of clients that have large, complex computer systems. In addition, the same group also supports management consultants who have been engaged to assist clients in CIS development for financial systems. In this area, the specialists are responsible for helping to design auditability into new financial information systems.

The establishment of such specialized support functions has justified itself in today's audit and consulting environments. Since a majority of the auditors in the field are not fully conversant with CIS techniques, this kind of task-force approach can move quickly to apply resources and skills as needs arise. Ultimately, however, audit practices will shift increasingly toward computer-based techniques. As the scope of the work of audit specialists increases, groups of specialists actually will perform most of the functions of the audit examination. At this writing, development is under way on fully automated audit methodologies. This prospect further emphasizes the importance of specialized technical expertise in computer areas.

Audit examinations of the future, therefore, may involve a collection of contiguous and overlapping specialties. Thus, today's audit specialist group gradually will evolve into the actual audit examination team of the future.

Government Influence

The federal government has taken significant steps to encourage better CIS controls. Concern has been directed at all aspects of security, integrity, and privacy of information stored in or processed by computers. Many public laws, at both state and federal levels, and standards promulgated by government agencies relate directly to computer auditing. The impacts of this legislation just now are being realized.

Various agencies within the federal government have been active in encouraging the development of computer audit skills. Among the research in this area is a series of 13 special publications on computer audit and security from the National Bureau of Standards (U. S. Department of Commerce). A listing of these publications is included in the bibliography to this text.

Other agencies such as the Congressional Research Service, the General Accounting Office, the Office of Technology Assessment, the Department of Justice, and the Department of Defense have supported efforts aimed at enhancing the role of computer auditing.

The President's Council on Integrity and Efficiency, composed of the Inspectors General (or their equivalents) from more than 20 federal agencies, surveyed known instances of computer-related fraud and abuse during 1978–1982. The study determined that a high proportion of incidents identified were uncovered accidentally. With this finding, the council concluded that federal agencies needed more effective controls over computer systems. Further innovative work of this council has been in the field of computer auditing. For example, the council's guidelines have helped to extend the technique of computer matching, used to detect fraud, to federal and state programs in all 50 states. Also, the council has been active in the area of automated auditing. The use of microtechnology as an audit tool has been proven by the council to be an innovative and effective aid in the audit process.

In September, 1983, the National Bureau of Standards released *Federal Information Processing Standards Publication 102, Guideline For Computer Security Certification and Accreditation.* The primary purpose of this document was to provide a guideline for certifying and accrediting sensitive computer applications. The guideline deals with accreditation both as an institutional program and as a technical process. Subsidiary objectives of the guideline are to:

- Provide the information and insight to permit organizations to adapt or formulate a program and/or process suited to their specific needs.

- Catalyze increased security awareness and help assure more appropriate assignment and assumption of security responsibility.

- Create an awareness of the need for defining security requirements and evaluating compliance with them.

- Help assure that computing resources and sensitive information are protected appropriately.

- Help reduce computer fraud and related crimes.

This guideline is directed primarily toward individuals who are responsible for performing computer security certification and accreditation and for establishing certification and accreditation programs. Titles and job functions of such individuals include:

- Senior executive officers (or department secretaries of government agencies)

- Accrediting officials (senior managers)

- Computer security staff (managers, system/CIS security officers, internal control specialists)

- Application sponsors (users and resource managers)

- Independent reviewers (financial and computer auditors, computer quality assurance personnel, and test and evaluation personnel)

- Suppliers of CIS services (CIS installation managers, database administrators, and communications officers)

- Development staff (analysts, programmers, and designers).

In 1981, the *Standards For Audit of Government Organizations, Programs, Activities, and Functions* was published by the Comptroller General of the U.S. General Accounting Office. In this publication, the Comptroller General identifies the examination and evaluation standards for audits of computer-based systems and prescribes the role of auditors in the review of systems design and development. Federal legislation requires that the Inspectors General of all federal agencies follow these standards.

GOVERNMENT AWARENESS OF COMPUTER-BASED SYSTEMS: A SURVEY OF APPLICABLE LAWS AND REGULATIONS

Current federal regulations dictate certain aspects of many computer system designs and operations. With this influence in the day-to-day operation of both public and private organizations, it can be anticipated that government regulations affecting internal controls, audit trails, and privacy of data will continue. This discussion examines some applicable legislation and presents some additional considerations.

The conversion of an organization's records from hard-copy documents to electronic data stored in computer systems is continuing. Beginning with the 1971 Internal Revenue Service (IRS) Ruling 71-20, which allows computer records to be used as official tax records, the government has taken an increased interest in the use and control of the private sector's computer records. Significant efforts have been made to demonstrate the need for data accuracy and uniformity in retention and audit requirements. Although existing legislation is aimed at preserving data for audit purposes, legislation concerning internal controls will affect systems control methodology and application systems design.

How CIS Functions Are Affected

Federal legislation and guidance affects three aspects of CIS functions:

- How computer systems are built and operated
- The processing logic of computer application systems
- The care, retention, and protection of data and systems.

CIS personnel are concerned primarily about federal guidance that may impact the procedures for building and operating application systems. IRS rulings affect audit trails and data retention. For example, privacy legislation affects the types and use of data retained about individuals. Other legislation specifies standards of accounting control.

The impacts on personnel, processes, and organizations are far-reaching. Where applicable, systems analysts/programmers must adhere to the letter and intent of these regulations in systems design. In certain instances, failure to comply with these regulations can result in both financial penalties and prison sentences. Guidelines aimed at specific functions also must be incorporated into the processing logic of affected applications systems. For example, organizations doing business with the federal government are required to sell products to the government at their lowest prices. To assure comparability of data, billing systems must conform to the applicable federal statutes.

Enforcement Mechanisms

Most federal legislation includes enforcement mechanisms. The government enforces many of its regulations through audits. The federal agency assigned responsibility for the area covered by the legislation usually has field auditors or may contract with an independent CPA firm to verify compliance with federal, state, or organizational standards.

The result of an audit by a federal agency can be:

1. Agreement that the organization is complying with the regulations. (No further action must be taken.)

2. Or, when exceptions are noted, the government acts to:

    *   Require the company to alter procedures to conform with the law.

    *   Assess the organization to pay taxes for unreported revenue.

    *   Assess penalties (in addition to recouping assessments) because of failure to comply with federal regulations.

    *   Possibly imprison individuals who fail to comply with legislation.

Regardless of the end result of the audit, there is a cost to the organization for a government audit. Such costs may involve any or all of the following:

*   Personnel costs to comply with government requests for information

*   Unfavorable publicity

*   Computer costs to obtain the data for the government auditors

*   Delay of scheduled work, including any loss of business or penalties associated with that delay.

Organizations cannot avoid audits. They can, however, prepare for them by determining first if they are in compliance with government regulations. If they are not, they either must change or should be prepared to justify their position. Second, organizations can plan so that audits can be conducted in an orderly, business-like manner. Such plans should identify who will work with the auditors and how.

Internal Audit Involvement

Most federal legislation affecting computer information systems deals with controls and audit trails. The purpose of an audit trail is to enable an auditor to determine how a particular transaction was processed, by tracing that transaction from its inception to the financial records, and from the financial records back to supporting source data. The audit trail established for an organization's own purposes usually will be acceptable for government auditors.

Adherence to government legislation can be a complex process. Internal auditors can assist the CIS manager in two ways:

1. Internal auditors can advise the CIS manager of the impact of existing legislation on computer operations. Internal auditors also can provide the CIS manager with an appreciation of how other organizations comply with regulations, since auditors usually maintain contacts with individuals in other organizations and with external auditors. Frequently, there are wide differences of opinion on how to accomplish compliance. A quick survey of similar organizations by the internal auditors can provide the CIS manager with some perspective and direction.

2. Internal auditors can make tests to determine whether CIS systems comply with government legislation. In the event of an audit by the government, the CIS manager should ask the internal auditors to work with the government auditor. This arrangement offers advantages to both the organization and to the government agency. Government auditors have the advantage of working with individuals who understand their function and can facilitate the performance of their job. Internal auditors may have performed similar audits and can provide the required data quickly and efficiently.

Having internal auditors work with government auditors may limit exposure to liability by focusing attention on relevant areas. Without guidance and direction, the government auditor may investigate many areas through false audit starts. Such a pattern of investigation can lead to unnecessary questioning and additional inquiries. Thus, unnecessary inquiries may be avoided if the organization's auditors assist the government auditor in achieving audit objectives. The amount of time required from CIS personnel also can be reduced substantially because the internal auditors can answer most questions about the systems being investigated.

Key Legislation Affecting CIS

The legislation affecting CIS is extensive. The items discussed here involve common control situations. Government regulations affecting CIS are identified and described in the presentations that follow.

IRS Procedure 64-12.   IRS Procedure 64-12 provides guidelines for record keeping in situations in which part or all of an organization's accounting records are maintained by CIS. This procedure requires the retention of hard-copy documents for audit purposes.

Within this guideline, the IRS states the following requirements for acceptable records:

- *General and subsidiary books of account.* General and subsidiary ledger data should coincide with the data reported on tax returns. The guideline states that both of these ledgers should be written out, or printed in hard-copy form, periodically.

- *Supporting documents and audit trail.* The organization should be able to list supporting data (invoices and vouchers, for example) that underlie the general ledger financial data.

- *Recording or reconstructing data.* The audit trail should trace a transaction from the source document or transaction forward to the final total. From the final total, the audit trail also should lead to the source documents that were used to generate that total.

- *Data storage media.* Organizations must maintain adequate record retention facilities. The Internal Revenue Code of 1954, together with the regulations cited in Program Documentation within this procedure, constitute the requirements for data retention.

- *Program documentation.* A description of the computer-based portion of the accounting system should be available. The statements and illustrations on the scope of operations should be sufficiently detailed to indicate: *(a)* the application being processed, *(b)* the procedures employed in each application (which, for example, might be supported by flowcharts, block diagrams, or other satisfactory descriptions of input and output procedures), and *(c)* the controls used to assure accurate and reliable processing. To preserve an accurate chronological record, important changes, together with their effective dates, should be noted.

Most CIS organizations can comply easily with this procedure. The three most difficult aspects lie in printing the general and subsidiary ledgers routinely, assuring an adequate audit trail with supporting documents, and having adequate documentation of the CIS. The internal auditor can make a significant contribution in all of these areas.

IRS Ruling 71-20 and 72-375.   IRS Ruling 71-20 states requirements for retaining machine-readable records for purposes of tax audit. The ruling requires organizations to retain machine-readable records for computer application systems that process accounting data. One of the key segments of Ruling 71-20 states:

> "It is held that punched cards, magnetic tapes, disks, and other machine-sensible data media used for recording, consolidating, and summarizing accounting transactions and records within a taxpayer's automatic data processing system are records within the meaning of section 6001 of the Code and section 1.6001-1 of the regulations and are required to be retained so long as the contents may become material in the administration of any internal revenue law."

Revenue Ruling 72-375 states that:

> "Evaluation of data processing accounting systems and records to determine which records are to be retained, their retention period, and their adequacy, are not examinations, investigations, or inspections within the meaning of section 7605(b) of the Code."

Because the cost of complying with this ruling can be significant, the IRS will evaluate a company's CIS records and establish specific retention requirements. Without such an evaluation, the organization must decide which records it should maintain to comply with this ruling. IRS agents are interested primarily in two classes of records:

- Original transaction records of data essential to the maintenance and verification of the amounts shown in the general ledger accounts—in other words, the details of the transactions that are summarized into account totals for the year. The agent must be able to separate the account total into its individual transactions and trace those transactions back to source documents or transactions.

- Other data, including internal transactions, that affect federal tax liability and that help substantiate the figures on the tax return.

From a management perspective in an international corporate entity, it is important for the users, corporate officials, and CIS professionals to be aware of these legal aspects in the design, development, and operations of financial systems. For example, certain retention requirements also apply to foreign corporations that are more than 50 percent owned by entities in the United States. The requirements apply if the foreign corporation has a CIS facility overseas, or if it sends data from foreign operations to the U.S. shareholder for processing. In such cases, the U.S. shareholder must retain (or cause to be retained) the electronic data processing records of the controlled foreign corporation. Sufficient data must be retained to determine the amounts of the Subpart F income (income from foreign investments) includable in the domestic shareholder's gross income.

The CIS manager should consult with the internal auditors, the organization's external auditors, and legal counsel on whether to request the IRS to review corporate CIS records and establish specific retention requirements. The advantage to such a review lies in determining specifically that the organization complies with Ruling 71-20. The disadvantage is that, once the essential records have been identified, the fact that the system is changing dynamically may make continued retention of such data impractical. The result would be to force continual evaluations by IRS agents.

In practice, IRS auditors have basically the same needs and objectives as internal auditors. Thus, internal auditors are in a good position to advise which files should be retained for tax purposes and for how long. Many organizations' record retention programs already state these retention periods.

Occupational Safety and Health Act (OSHA).   Under the Occupational Safety and Health Act (OSHA) of 1970, employers have a responsibility to provide a place of employment free from recognized hazards and to comply with the occupational safety and health standards promulgated under the act. Some of the main provisions state that employers must:

- Familiarize themselves with mandatory occupational safety and health standards

- Ensure that employees know about OSHA

- Examine conditions in work places to make sure they conform to applicable safety and health standards

- Ensure that employees have and use safe tools and equipment (including required personal protective gear) that are maintained properly

- Use color codes, posters, labels, or signs to warn employees of potential hazards.

The CIS department is most vulnerable to conflict with OSHA requirements in areas involving the computer operations facility:

- Noise levels from high-speed printers and other data processing equipment might exceed OSHA-permitted levels.

- Chemicals to be used in case of fire or other emergencies might be stored without proper warnings posted.

- Evacuation procedures might not be marked clearly, or the facility might not have a sufficient number of exits.

- Cluttered work areas might pose a potential hazard.

- General fire protection gear might not be properly identified.

All organizations are subject to audits by OSHA personnel, who are empowered to arrive unannounced and make an immediate inspection. These audits may occur at the discretion of OSHA or can be requested by an employee of the organization. If the audit results in a violation, the organization can be charged a substantial penalty.

For this reason, every organization should initiate procedures to follow in the event an OSHA auditor arrives unannounced. These procedures should be part of a general organizational plan, not a CIS plan. The CIS manager, however, should verify whether such a plan actually exists.

From a casual inspection, the CIS manager should be able to observe obvious safety problems. If questions about potential violations arise, the safety department or responsible organizational authority should be consulted to assure adherence to OSHA regulations. Responsible parties within the organization should be aware of OSHA requirements. In addition, any on-the-job injuries must be reported through OSHA reporting mechanisms.

Federal Managers' Financial Integrity Act.   This act (Public Law 97-255, 31 U.S. Code 3512(b)) amended the Accounting and Auditing Act of 1950. The new act's requirements and objectives are similar to those issued earlier in OMB Circular No. A-123, 1981, which established guidelines promulgated by the Office of Management and Budget for internal controls within executive-branch agencies.

In addition, the act requires the Comptroller General to prescribe internal accounting and administrative control standards that apply to federal agencies. Annual evaluations are to be conducted by each executive agency covering its systems of control, in accordance with guidelines established by OMB. Executive agencies also must report to the President and the Congress on the status of the agency's system of internal control. The first report was due December 31, 1983.

Privacy legislation.   Although the Privacy Act of 1974 affects only the public sector, there are many state and federal privacy laws that affect the private sector. As an indication of the public concern in this sensitive area, approximately 30 bills related to privacy in recordkeeping were introduced into Congress prior to the passage of the Act. This still continues today: More than 40 bills were introduced to Congress in the 1981–1985 time frame.

In addition to introducing new privacy legislation, President Carter announced "measures to strengthen safeguards on federal investigations and recordkeeping." According to the President:

"The Federal government holds almost four billion records on individuals, most of them stored in thousands of computers. Federally funded projects have substantial additional files. This information is needed to run the Social Security system, collect taxes, conduct research, measure the economy, and for hundreds of other important purposes. Modern technology, however, makes it possible to turn this storage into a dangerous surveillance system. Reasonable restrictions are needed on the collection and use of this information."

President Carter also ordered the following administrative actions concerning privacy in the public sector:

". . . The practice of comparing computer lists, in so-called matching programs, 'designed to detect fraud in various Government programs, will be conducted (1) only after the public has been notified and given the opportunity to identify privacy problems'; (2) with tight safeguards on access to the data and on disclosure of the names of suspects identified by matching; and (3) only when there are no cost-effective, alternative means of identifying violators."

In a separate section on international privacy issues, President Carter said:

"International information flows . . . are increasingly important to the world's economy. We are, therefore, working with other governments in several international organizations to develop principles to protect personal data crossing international borders and to harmonize each country's rules to avoid needless disruption of international communications. Enactment of the proposals I have outlined will help speed this process by assuring other countries that the U.S. is committed to the protection of personal data."

The cost of privacy legislation will be substantial, including the extra effort required to maintain data, to notify individuals about the use of the data, and to implement procedures to purge unneeded data from both current and historical files. Because of the potential cost, auditors as well as CIS personnel should take a strong interest in any additional privacy legislation.

Internal auditors can help the CIS department develop a method of controlling the use of data. The network of internal controls is a key element in assuring conformity with the proposed privacy law. Control over data is similar to control over any other asset of the organization. Internal auditors should be considered experts in internal control and thus can play a significant role in assuring the CIS manager that data covered by the privacy legislation is safeguarded adequately. The CIS and internal auditing departments can take the following preliminary steps to maintain data in the privacy area:

- Become familiar with the Privacy Act of 1974 and any privacy legislation that has been enacted at the state level.

- Determine what organizational data are personal and thus covered under the law.

- Identify users of those data.

- Develop rules and procedures for purging outdated or unneeded data.

- Determine the accuracy of the data through tests. (One of the main objectives of privacy is to assure that individuals are not harmed by use of inaccurate data.)

By using the information gathered in these steps, an organization can assess how the proposed privacy legislation might affect its operation. This assessment would include identifying the systems that need to be changed, outlining steps to assure data accuracy, describing a system of internal control for data protection, and estimating the cost and effort associated with these controls.

Other acts that apply are the Fair Credit Reporting Act of 1971, the Electronic Funds Transfer Act of 1977, and the Financial Right of Privacy Act of 1978. Today, these acts can serve to augment the Privacy Act of 1974.

The Fair Credit Reporting Act of 1971 protects the right of individuals to access information used by a financial institution or furnished by a credit reporting service during the establishment of credit worthiness. If it is discovered that erroneous information has been reported, action must be taken by the credit reporting service to correct the error and to notify both the individual and the financial institution involved.

The Electronic Funds Transfer Act of 1977 is aimed at providing protection for the consumer. This act requires financial institutions to comply with specific guidelines concerning the use of electronic funds transfer services. It also assigns responsibility to the institutions for the accuracy and integrity of electronic funds transfers.

The Financial Right of Privacy Act states that government agencies can obtain personal financial information only after taking specific legal steps. It contains a provision under which banks, savings and loan associations, credit unions, or other financial institutions must send all of their customers a statement of their rights under the act.

Foreign Corrupt Practices Act of 1977. The Foreign Corrupt Practices Act (FCPA) of 1977 requires public companies to "make and keep books, records, and accounts, which in reasonable detail, accurately and fairly reflect the transactions and dispositions of the assets of the issuer" and to ". . . devise and maintain a system of internal accounting controls sufficient to provide reasonable assurances that:

"(i) transactions are executed in accordance with management's general or specific authorization;

"(ii) transactions are recorded as necessary (a) to permit preparation of financial statements in conformity with generally accepted accounting principles or any other criteria applicable to such statements, and (b) to maintain accountability for assets;

"(iii) access to assets is permitted only in accordance with management's general or specific authorization; and

"(iv) the recorded accountability for assets is compared with the existing assets at reasonable intervals and appropriate action is taken with respect to any differences."

These objectives, categorized as *authorization, accounting,* and *asset safeguarding,* were developed originally to provide broad professional guidance for the external auditor's study and evaluation of internal accounting control. The objectives were cited first in the AICPA *Statement on Auditing Standards No. 1 (1972),* which defines internal control and accounting control. (Auditors test only those controls on which they intend to rely.) CIS management, however, needs to identify and communicate the audit objectives in more specific terms. Thus, the CIS manager first must consider what the term "internal accounting control" means.

According to the Foreign Corrupt Practices Act, a company must have an organizational structure, control procedures, and techniques that help to "safeguard its assets, check the accuracy and reliability of its accounting data, promote operational efficiency, and encourage adherence to prescribed managerial policies." Therefore, management must be concerned about the effectiveness of all organizational controls. However, not all of these controls are internal accounting controls.

Compliance with the act requires an assessment of the internal accounting control environment and of the appropriateness and effectiveness of existing accounting control procedures and techniques, based on an overall knowledge of the company. Those procedures should relate to:

- A re-examination of the accounting control procedures in place and the ongoing process of evaluating them

- A consideration of the need for a shift toward more explicit documentation of those control procedures and the process of evaluating them.

Public reporting on internal accounting control.   The Securities and Exchange Commission (SEC) has specified how SEC-regulated companies should report on the adequacy of their internal accounting control. This program is intended to assure compliance with the internal accounting control provisions of the Foreign Corrupt Practices Act of 1977.

For fiscal years after December 15, 1980, management must include the following information in the organization's annual report and in its 10-K filing with the SEC:

- Statement of its opinion that the company's system of internal controls provides reasonable assurance that the objectives of internal accounting control (outlined in the FCPA) are being met.

- Disclosure of any material weaknesses in internal controls that were uncorrected as of year end.

The external auditor may be asked for an opinion about whether management's assessment of the system of internal control is supportable and whether that assessment is reasonable.

Counterfeit Access Device and Computer Fraud and Abuse Act.   The federal government has become increasingly concerned about computer crimes. In November, 1983, public testimony before the Civil and Constitutional Rights Subcommittee of the House Judiciary Committee estimated that losses due to abuse of computers by white-collar criminals totaled $40 billion annually. This concern resulted in the passage of the Counterfeit Access Device and Computer Fraud and Abuse Act (also known as the Computer Crime Law) in October, 1984. The Act outlaws unauthorized access to the federal government's computers and certain financial databases as protected under the Right to Financial Privacy Act of 1978 and the Fair Credit Reporting Act of 1971.

Punishment under the Computer Fraud and Abuse Act provides for monetary fines and/or for imprisonment, depending on the nature of the crime and whether the offense involves one or multiple occurrences. The monetary fine can range from a minimum of $5,000 to twice the value obtained or the loss created by the offense. Prison sentences may range from one to 20 years, depending on the severity of the computer crime violation.

In addition to the 1984 Computer Crime Law, a number of other initiatives were introduced in the U. S. Congress in 1985. All of these sought to protect the private sector computers not covered by the 1984 law. The content of the bills were similar to the 1984 legislation. Though none of these bills has been enacted at this writing, it can be anticipated that future federal legislation will incorporate all or a good part of the following features:

- Unauthorized access to computers used in interstate commerce, or in financial institutions, would be subject to punishment and/or penalties.

- Unauthorized access to or alteration of individual medical records through a telecommunications device would be penalized.

- Felony and misdemeanor charges would be established for unauthorized access to computers used in interstate commerce if the sum of $5,000 or more is involved.

COMMITMENT IN HIGHER EDUCATION

Colleges and universities increasingly are offering courses and training in subjects related to computer auditing. As cited earlier, the DPMA Model Curriculum for Computer Information Systems Education has had an impact on a number of schools throughout the United States. Many schools offering CIS curricula are adding or developing courses that comply with the DPMA CIS-13, EDP Audit and Control course or with corresponding units within other curricula. A recent survey indicates that, by 1990, one out of four colleges or universities will have a course focusing on computer auditing and security. Thus, schools are taking steps to meet the educational needs of information systems workers and general auditors in this crucial area.

DISCUSSION QUESTIONS

1. As organizations of all types and sizes adopt computer-based methods, what changes may be needed in attitudes and commitment toward computer auditing?

2. Respond to the statement: ". . . The accountant of tomorrow will have to be a computer expert. And 'tomorrow' is already here."

3. What qualifications, including skills and knowledge base, must a computer auditor possess?

4. What are the basic concerns of computer auditors, and how do these concerns relate to areas of expertise in this field?

5. How are risk assessment and threat assessment related to computer audit skills?

6. What specialized skills might be needed by a computer auditor in the areas of project planning? Human resource management? Reporting and making presentations?

7. How can the role of computer auditors be expected to evolve in public accounting firms?

8. What are the concerns of federal agencies in conducting audits, and how are federal regulations and guidelines enforced?

9. What has been the involvement of the federal government in CIS operations, and how might this role change in the future?

II CONCERNS AND OBJECTIVES

In any audit engagement, initial effort centers around establishing audit objectives. The second part of this text parallels that approach by first outlining the concerns and objectives that motivate the auditor's review of computer information systems, then describing the audit process for specific types of engagements. In performing a review, the auditor's basic mission is to assure management that the organization's computer information systems are reliable. Therefore, in a practical sense, Part II deals with internal control issues within computer-based systems. Then, Part III focuses on audit methodologies.

Chapter 4 surveys overall control objectives for computer-based systems, illustrated by a scenario of a typical computer audit.

One of the computer auditor's essential functions involves attesting to the reliability of computer-generated financial statements. However, the auditor's involvement may extend beyond this function to encompass many different roles. Chapter 5 covers specific types of computer audit activities, including audits of applications, systems development, and facilities, as well as special studies for management.

The remainder of the presentation in Part II deals with specific control issues. Chapter 6 covers types of controls and possible weaknesses in computer-based systems. In Chapter 7, general controls are described that may exist in the environment surrounding the system. From this perspective, Chapter 8 then describes how computer auditors design specific audit tests to evaluate the controls they have identified.

4 Computer Audit Concerns and Objectives

A B S T R A C T

- Within a CIS, reasonable assurance must exist that the system is not vulnerable to fraud or embezzlement, faulty design and programming, sabotage, or natural disaster.

- The commitment to the computer audit function requires appropriate involvement for the organization and different factions within it, including: board members, executives, financial managers, managers of using departments, and CIS managers.

- Qualities of computer auditors include: objectivity, the ability to recognize key issues quickly, the ability to communicate effectively, and knowledge of the CIS function.

- The overall objective of computer auditing is the rendering of constructive contributions to the effectiveness of the organization and the validity of its financial and operational reporting through application of computers.

- Formulating an audit plan and staffing audit teams involve seven basic steps, including: defining objectives, building basic understanding, building detailed understanding, evaluating controls, designing audit procedures, testing, and evaluating results.

CONTROL OBJECTIVES

As discussed previously, technological developments, particularly the application of computer-based techniques, have changed the nature of internal control and the traditional audit trail. Since the audit trail can be a management control guide, the management of the accounting function also has undergone significant change. The full extent of these changes has yet to be seen.

In the midst of fundamental change, there may be a tendency to lose sight of basic objectives. In the absence of traditional methods and controls, it may be tempting to apply bandages to symptoms, rather than to look for underlying maladies. Indeed, without a clear articulation of the objectives of controls, it can be difficult to recognize that problems exist at all. This chapter discusses computer audit concerns and objectives within the organization from the perspective of the internal auditor.

A major objective of internal accounting control is founded on the principle of *reasonable assurance.* Reasonable assurance means that there is justifiable, but not absolute, confidence that data (or other assets) are being protected and that financial records are reliable. Protection involves the safeguarding of these information assets from unauthorized use or disposition. Controls also exist to maintain accuracy, completeness, and reliability of information.

The concept of reasonable assurance recognizes that the cost of a system of internal accounting control should not exceed the benefit of protecting the assets. Reasonable assurance also recognizes that the evaluation of these factors necessarily requires estimates and judgment by management.

There are inherent limitations to the potential effectiveness of any system of internal accounting control. In the performance of most control procedures, errors can result from the misunderstanding of instructions, mistakes of judgment, carelessness, or other human factors. Manual control procedures, the effectiveness of which depends partly on the segregation of duties, can be circumvented by *collusion,* or collaborative effort for improper purposes. Similarly, managers can circumvent control procedures to carry out fraudulent recording of transactions, as in the Wells Fargo banking case. Misstatement also may arise from errors in management estimates and judgments required in the preparation of the financial statements.

Another pitfall lies in projecting any evaluation of internal accounting control through future periods. Such projection is subject to the risk that the control procedures may become inadequate because of changes in conditions. Or, the degree of compliance with control procedures may deteriorate over time.

A related issue is that controls established for manual systems may not have been updated for the computer environment. As discussed in Chapters 1 and 3, new technology has severed the time-honored correspondence between source documents and the general ledger of the business. In some cases, the break has been complete. Even though the CIS field is in a period of extensive and dynamic change, controls have remained static in many organizations. Outdated controls in today's electronic environment are equivalent to nonexistent controls.

WHAT IS AT STAKE—
COMPUTER AUDIT CONCERNS

For the main purposes of diagnosis, the computer auditor has three broad categories of concerns:

- Fraud and embezzlement

- Damage due to faulty design and programming

- Disaster due to sabotage and/or natural events.

Fraud and Embezzlement

Based on a number of private and government studies on computer fraud from 1964 through 1984, more than 10,000 cases of computer misuse have been reported in the category of fraud and embezzlement. More than 50 percent of the cases were reported within the last five years of this period. These cases have included monetary fraud or theft, information or property theft, unauthorized use or sale of services, and vandalism. The organizational positions held by embezzlers have included president, officer, bookkeeper, systems analyst, programmer, and others. More recently, individuals have committed theft of information and property, as well as unauthorized use and sale of computer services. It is estimated by some computer experts that less than 15 percent of computer-assisted fraud currently is being detected or discovered accidentally.

Faulty Design and Programming

According to several industry computer security experts, the average computer theft easily exceeds $4 to $5 million. Total fraud and embezzlement in the United States may exceed $40 billion per year. However, losses due to faulty design and programming, and to computer disasters, probably exceed those due to fraud and embezzlement—and are just as likely to lead to financial crises. The damage due to faulty systems development and programming involves some key and complex interfaces.

Accordingly, the systems development process requires above-average control and communication. When large-scale systems efforts get out of control, the damage and cost to an organization are potentially great. There have been several reports of mismanaged or ineffective systems development projects that caused losses, stemming from a single incident, in the multi-millions of dollars.

Disaster

In evaluating the threat of computer disaster, consider the following parallels: Would it be prudent to leave unsecured such physical documents as the corporate general ledger, journals, subsidiary ledgers, and source documents? Would it be standard practice to leave millions of dollars in cash or negotiable securities unprotected, in one room? Would it be common to find supplies, small tools, and high-value inventories unsecured, in one location?

The failure to institute adequate safeguards in each of these cases would be downright negligent. However, in general, information assets are left relatively unsecured in centralized computer facilities. Electronic storage media containing accounting, operational, sales, inventory, and other corporate data thus are exposed to risk unnecessarily. In effect, the "corporate memory" of the organization is being exposed to accidental loss or intentional tampering.

COMMITMENT TO
THE COMPUTER AUDIT FUNCTION

Before computer auditors can deal with the concerns described above, there must be a clear understanding of what the organization expects from the audit function. Computer auditors must understand organizational objectives, priorities, and needs. In turn, the organization must understand and support the audit function.

Close cooperation among the computer audit staff, corporate management, and CIS management is essential for conducting an effective audit program. Both the computer auditor and corporate management receive their authority from the organization's board of directors: Management has the ultimate responsibility for designing and maintaining systems of control. The auditor's responsibility is to evaluate those systems.

The computer audit function depends largely on the nature and size of the CIS installation and the distribution of its services. That is, the audit approach must be tailored to the technical environment, be it a centralized mainframe or distributed processing. Computer auditors also should adapt an approach that is suitable to physical and structural environments of the organization. In fact, any audit—whether internal or external, whether manual and/or CIS-related—must involve all elements of an organization.

An effective audit involves virtually everyone in the organization. The cooperation and professionalism of both management and staff will be needed to deal with key issues. Thus, each person in the organization has a special role to play when an audit is performed. A commitment must exist between the operational and the audit functions to work toward an organization with integrity, an organization that has assurance that serious concerns will not become reality.

ORGANIZATION INVOLVEMENT

Within an organization, CIS services cut across departmental and functional lines. Thus, if computer systems are to be used effectively—and if they are to produce reliable results—managers of all functions that use computer services must be involved. Involvement means taking an interest in and a degree of control over information resources. A transaction processing system, after all, should belong to the users, or owners, of the information held within it.

It is not enough for each line manager whose department uses computer services simply to interact with CIS management. Users also must be involved with one another. In a modern CIS department, there typically are more requests for service than there are resources to develop the systems needed to provide those services. Thus, in deciding which services to implement, some trade-offs are inevitable. When the alternatives involve services to multiple departments, the involvement of all concerned user groups is necessary to establish consensus about how information resources are to be used and shared.

An Illustration of Involvement

Consider a situation that could develop in any medium- to large-sized manufacturing company. A computer has been installed for routine payroll and accounts receivable applications. Because of the nature of these applications, the financial vice president has control of the CIS function. Later, accounting applications become more sophisticated. Under these new applications, the CIS produces invoices, handles accounts payable, and maintains perpetual records for inventories of raw materials and subassemblies.

Suppose now that the vice president of manufacturing returns from a computer convention with a notion that production scheduling might be computerized. The presentation at the convention featured a small computer that could be installed within the production department. The computer vendor has represented that all the necessary hardware and software are available off-the-shelf. Further, the vendor claims that the production department could run this computer with its existing personnel after only a few weeks of training at the vendor's facility.

The proposed solution to the production scheduling problem, at this point, is independent of the existing CIS function within the organization. How the problem is solved represents a case in *information resource management (IRM)*, a coordinated approach to planning for CIS services. Depending on the culture and political climate within the organization, several different scenarios might take place. These scenarios represent varying degrees of coordination and cooperation among user groups in managing information resources.

In one case, the manufacturing vice president might go directly to the company president, receive an approval for a new system, and have a separate CIS under development before the financial vice president, who handles all current information resource functions, even knows about the situation. On the other hand, the financial vice president might learn of the plan and make a counterproposal to the president. The financial vice president might plead that, if the same amount of money were spent to enlarge the existing financial CIS, the expanded department could support the proposed manufacturing functions and also enhance the existing accounting applications.

This case shows a lack of involvement, or vacuum, surrounding the information resource function, isolated in the financial area. Such a vacuum almost invariably will result in turmoil, conflict, and disruption. If the manufacturing vice president is powerful enough, a separate computer installation will be developed for the production scheduling application. When the production installation runs into inevitable problems, all the ingredients for a takeover struggle will be present and ready to explode. The financial department will point to the problems as evidence that all CIS functions should come under its jurisdiction and control.

A decision in the other direction, however, carries no guarantee of success. The president might order the manufacturing vice president to work with the financial vice president. They might cooperate grudgingly, but soon would fall out again over the relative priorities for writing invoices or issuing factory work orders.

In yet another case, a different result is achieved because management groups are involved from the beginning. In this scenario, it has been recognized generally by CIS and user-management groups alike that the accounts receivable application has implications for the sales department. The marketing and financial vice presidents jointly have developed a system that reports on the productivity of salespeople. Also, the purchasing manager is talking about the possibility of issuing purchase orders by computer, tied into the inventory system.

In such an environment, the manufacturing vice president probably would feel more like ''joining the club'' with the production scheduling application than starting a revolt. Either informally or on a regular basis, this company has what amounts to an internal computer users' group. Members of this group are managers who collaborate on decisions involving the commitment of resources and the assignment of priorities to computer applications. Users are involved with one another, and issues are on the table. Managers understand the proportioning of expenditures on a results-oriented basis and know the criteria and ground rules for getting group support.

As such a CIS department grew, it might be spun off as a corporate service group with a broadly based, internal clientele. Thus, doubts about the primary commitment of computer information resources within the financial area would be minimized.

The example easily could have been reversed. That is, there are companies in which manufacturing and production-control applications are so predominant that the computer information resource function is placed under the manufacturing vice president. This predominance, in itself, is no reason why a CIS cannot serve the financial needs of the same company.

Auditors as Users

Particularly where computer-based systems have financial significance, involvement in information resource management should include internal and independent auditors. These groups are responsible for evaluating the quality and reliability of systems after implementation.

The rationale for involvement by auditors is much the same as for user-managers. If a system is developed without consultation of a company's auditors, and if that same system later is found to have control weaknesses, both costly rework and unnecessary friction probably will result. Increasingly, alert executives are realizing that auditors have a stake and an interest in the quality of computer systems that process financial data. As a result, the process of evaluating controls for computer systems can begin with systems design. That is, auditors are participating in design and validation of controls while systems are under development.

Auditors should be able to contribute to the systems design effort to assure the eventual reliability of the system and to minimize the extent of later audit procedures. If a system is large or complex, it may be possible to reduce audit examination time and cost by using computer-assisted techniques in the examination. Further savings and operating benefits may accrue by programming the computer-assisted audit techniques during the development of the accounting system application itself.

SCOPE OF INVOLVEMENT

Given that management involvement is good medicine for preventing organizational information resource ailments, what is the proper dosage? The degrees and areas of involvement for managers and executives affected by computer operations are illustrated in the most general terms in Figure 4-1. The matrix shown has three dimensions: One is a listing of executive and management functions for which involvement should exist. Another dimension indicates the activities that take place during computer systems development and ongoing operations. A third dimension shows types and degrees of involvement: performance, review, approval, or consultation.

Board Members

Involvement of board members in computer information resource matters has been initiated largely on a reactive basis. A few large companies got into trouble because their financial statements, some of which were developed with the aid of computers, did not reflect their respective financial positions accurately. Litigation has held that corporate directors may be liable, at least to some extent, for the content of financial statements. In the wake of these threats, and encouraged by independent CPAs, boards of directors have formed audit committees to oversee the verification of financial statements.

In practice, these audit committees have undertaken activities far beyond the initial, defensive concerns. Corporate directors, it has turned out, are potentially an excellent, objective review group. Audit committees have begun to play significant roles in assessing the practicability and potential value of computer operations in general, and of specific applications in particular.

Such responsibilities, of course, are adjusted to fit individual situations. It hardly would be necessary for board members to become involved personally with a departmental activity calling for minor systems changes. On the other hand, if a company were going into a major, on-line computer application, board members might be inclined to study its feasibility in some depth.

When an organization orders a computer, it is doing more than simply buying another piece of equipment. It may be initiating a fundamental change in the way it conducts some portion of its activities. Therefore, management commitment in the allocation of resources to these efforts should be just as deep, broad, and personal as in other areas of similar magnitude, such as the purchase of manufacturing equipment or facilities.

Executives

As the term is used in Figure 4-1, executives include the president and policy-level officers other than those with financial responsibility. In most medium- and large-sized organizations, CIS and information resource management have come to represent levels of expenditure that merit informed attention from top management.

Involvement at the executive level should include allocation of time for learning computer functions and terms. A company president or other top officer should be able to discuss planned systems with a CIS director or manager in much the same way as a new product might be discussed with a director of research and development.

This expertise encompasses overall understanding rather than technical detail. For example, in discussing a new product, the company president would not be expected to be expert in exotic, new materials. Neither would it be necessary to know about the inner workings of computers. But, today, executives at a company's top levels should be cognizant of what computers do and of cost-performance trade-offs associated with computerization. This background can be gained through selected reading and course work. Given this level of acquaintance, top executives properly may demand that their subordinates present descriptions of planned new systems and current operations in nontechnical terms.

As with board members, the extent of involvement by top executives will vary with the size, scope, and importance to the organization of individual computer-based applications. Involvement of top executives should extend to approval of preliminary designs of new systems. This involvement goes a step beyond the feasibility decisions suggested for board members.

A company's organizational structure is an expression of management philosophy. The placement of computer information resource management within an organization tends to reveal the management commitment and support this function enjoys. If computer technology is to be recognized and used as a valuable management tool, the CIS function must be positioned high enough so that the manager of CIS services or information resource management can deal with user-managers at a level of equality.

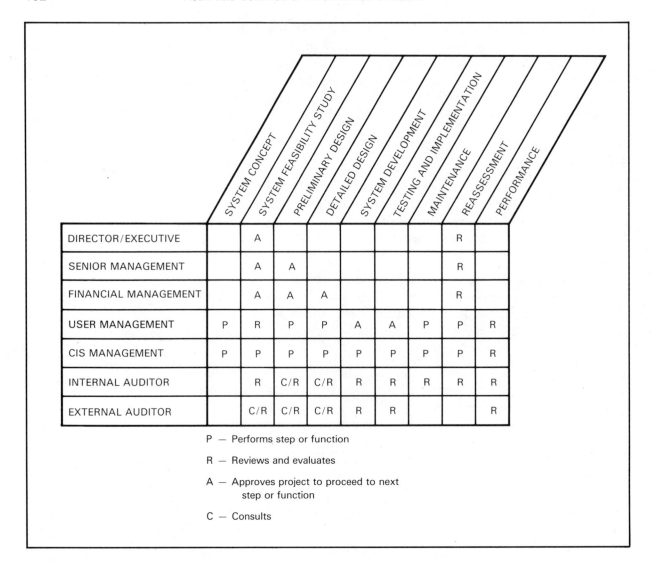

	SYSTEM CONCEPT	SYSTEM FEASIBILITY STUDY	PRELIMINARY DESIGN	DETAILED DESIGN	SYSTEM DEVELOPMENT	TESTING AND IMPLEMENTATION	MAINTENANCE	REASSESSMENT	PERFORMANCE
DIRECTOR/EXECUTIVE		A						R	
SENIOR MANAGEMENT		A	A					R	
FINANCIAL MANAGEMENT		A	A	A				R	
USER MANAGEMENT	P	R	P	P	A	A	P	P	R
CIS MANAGEMENT	P	P	P	P	P	P	P	P	R
INTERNAL AUDITOR		R	C/R	C/R	R	R	R	R	R
EXTERNAL AUDITOR		C/R	C/R	C/R	R	R			R

P — Performs step or function

R — Reviews and evaluates

A — Approves project to proceed to next step or function

C — Consults

Figure 4-1.

This matrix shows the involvement of participants in information resource management.

In an organization that depends on computers, the users and operators of systems, as well as the people who interact with them, are key personnel. Executive commitment requires special measures to develop these needed people and to open career paths that will stimulate and challenge them. This commitment must be extended to include:

- User and line managers who use computer-based capabilities

- Managers within the CIS function

- Computer audit specialists.

Financial Management

The financial vice president or controller (or both) of an organization with a heavy involvement in CIS should be just as conversant with the terminology and capabilities of computers as the manufacturing vice president is with production equipment. Indeed, computers may be viewed as production machines for financial data.

The top financial officer of an organization should be able to work directly with vendors in the information technology trade, including suppliers of hardware, software, communication, and business forms. That is, financial managers should be able to understand vendor presentations. These managers should be able to function as decision makers in the selection of equipment, software, and other elements of computer operations.

Further, financial managers should be at home within the internal computer support shop. They should be able to understand and communicate with the CIS manager. Above all, there must be a thorough understanding of what happens to financially significant data that are entered into, processed by, and stored within a computer system. Financial managers also should be able to assess and deal with matters of data security and reliability of reporting. Managers in these functions should understand and be able to evaluate the controls incorporated into the CIS.

Admittedly, this is a large order. At this writing, most top-level financial executives do not exhibit all aspects of this profile. For the future, however, this caliber of involvement may emerge as a requisite for survival.

Where computer support systems under development have financial implications, Figure 4-1 indicates that the responsibilities of financial managers should extend to approval of detailed designs for systems or applications.

User-Managers

Involvement by managers of departments using computer-based services probably is the most critical unmet requirement. Managers within user departments are in the best positions to understand what data should go into a system and the reasonableness of computer-processed results. For this reason, user-managers are assigned key performance and approval functions in the matrix shown in Figure 4-1.

The user-manager has the most critical approval of all. The final pronouncement that a new computer-based system is acceptable falls to users. User-managers approve the results of testing and implementation. The managers of a concerned group must be satisfied before a computer application system designed to meet its needs becomes operational. Thus, user-managers are key people in the CIS environment. The reason is that computer-based support systems operate for the benefit of users. From this perspective, the financial management group is the user-manager of computerized financial and accounting applications.

Companies should take a long-range view toward building user-managers who are well-grounded in CIS. Such managers are not computer specialists, nor are they potential heads of the CIS functions. Rather, user-managers are qualified people who are attuned thoroughly to the mainstream functions of the organization.

In some instances, such managers must be home-grown. Although today's university graduates are more computer-literate than those of 10 years ago, they are consumed quickly in the job marketplace. Graduates with good education and experience in computing are in high demand. To secure such people, top management usually must provide both the incentives and the opportunities for high-potential candidates to acquire this training and experience. This commitment may involve underwriting tuition at local universities, or encouraging attendance at professional development seminars. Such commitment also will involve a continuing investment in the latest published works on the application of computer techniques to the management discipline.

Interaction with CIS professionals is an important part of this continuing education. For this reason, some companies have adopted programs under which management trainees in noncomputer areas are rotated into CIS assignments, usually for periods of six months to a year. Such assignments include work in programming, systems analysis, and computer operations. With this background, these managers are well equipped for their increasingly important roles as contact persons between CIS functions and the rest of the company.

CIS Management

Involvement by CIS management, obviously, must be total. The major management challenge within the information resource area lies in the extent to which the CIS manager is successful in securing the involvement and commitment of users in their CIS systems. An operational, computer-based system belongs to its users, who must be involved in its development on an active, participatory basis. A user group will not identify as well with a completed system that, in effect, has been handed to it by a CIS department. Rather, users are more likely to support a system they feel they have helped to build and that was developed to their specifications. Thus, the successful CIS manager fosters a service and support perspective of this function, instilling a measure of pride of ownership in managers of user departments with whom systems people work.

This underlying requirement is expressed in Figure 4-1 in the close correspondence between user and CIS performance and responsibilities. These responsibilities culminate in the assignment of approval authority to user-managers for the development, testing, and implementation of new CIS applications. This close interaction between user and CIS managers is critical.

A CIS manager probably will have a technical background. The emphasis in continuing education, however, should include general business and accounting subjects, both external and within the company.

Insofar as is practical, systems analysts and middle-level managers within the CIS function should be rotated to job assignments within user groups. For these people, interaction with users generally is a pattern to be followed throughout their careers.

QUALITIES OF COMPUTER AUDITORS

As discussed previously, to function effectively, the computer auditor must possess certain qualities. Although some of these qualities may be subjective, a basic framework encompasses the following:

Ability to evaluate objectively. This quality involves a working knowledge of accepted CIS standards and the ability to compare existing operations, functions, and procedures with those standards.

Ability to recognize key issues quickly. An important audit function is to identify major strengths, underlying problems, and key deficiencies quickly. For example, the task of distinguishing symptoms from causes requires special diagnostic skills on the part of the computer auditor. The same is true for differentiations involving financial materiality of potential issues.

Ability to communicate effectively. In conducting an audit of a computer-based system, a considerable amount of information must be obtained in a relatively short time from managers, programmers, analysts, operators, and users. Gaining understanding without inducing user apprehension requires strong interpersonal skills. In addition, good writing and communication skills are required to present audit findings and recommendations effectively.

Knowledge of the CIS function. Computer auditors need a general knowledge of the environment surrounding the CIS function. The CIS function involves not only the CIS department, but also its relationships with corporate management, users, and outside resources. Although the computer audit function is concerned with management controls as well as technical controls, computer auditors must be well versed in the concepts of systems design, operation, and maintenance.

By acquiring and improving upon these qualities, the computer auditor can make the job of conducting an audit easier. In particular, expertise in these areas will tend to eliminate the potential for the adversarial relationship that typically has existed between the audit and CIS functions.

Equipped with these qualities, the auditor can work toward major objectives, such as the effectiveness of the CIS department, protection of equipment and data against unauthorized use or access, efficiency of existing and future systems, economic value and practicability of the systems under development, and the management and use of these critical organizational resources.

FORMULATING COMPUTER AUDIT OBJECTIVES

Before an audit can begin, the auditor must establish what is to be accomplished. That is, the auditor must develop objectives for performing the audit function. Though this is a basic and essential starting place, there can be a tendency for auditors to begin without setting objectives. Beginning an audit means first considering what is to be accomplished and then determining the best, most efficient ways to proceed. Having explicit objectives is the only way to determine when an audit is complete or whether it has been effective.

In most organizations, the computer auditor's function is to provide reasonable assurance that assets are safeguarded, that information is timely and reliable, and that all errors and deficiencies are discovered and corrected promptly. Better control, more complete audit trails, and compliance with organizational policies are equally important to the computer auditor. In essence, these also are general objectives for the computer auditor.

The development of organizational goals and objectives is a fundamental process in both business and government. The computer audit function must be drawn into this process. The plans, goals, and objectives for a computer audit function must be congruent with the goals—both short- and long-range—of the entity it supports.

For example, the goal for a computer audit organization might be stated as follows:

Render constructive contributions to the effectiveness of the organization and the validity of its financial and operational reporting through application of computers.

For an organization to achieve this purpose, at least four essential ingredients are required:

- A plan

- Selection of staff

- Ongoing training

- Management support.

In addition, the question of whether to adopt a formal, uniform methodology for computer audit is answered when the choice is made to take a professional approach. A professional staff will need a professional environment in which to operate.

For the computer audit objective stated above, a *computer audit charter* should be drafted to provide management guidance and support for the internal audit function. The charter provides a way to communicate to the entire organization the scope and purposes of the internal audit/computer audit function.

The charter supports the goals of the computer audit function and provides a framework for the computer auditor's mission. This framework encompasses three major CIS support areas that can extend throughout the organization. These support areas include:

- Applications

- Systems development

- CIS facility and environment.

These three areas are discussed in depth in later chapters. An overview of each is presented below.

Applications.   The application area includes all of the business information functions for which computer processing is used. Application systems can involve one or more departments of the organization—frequently on a national or international scale—in addition to computer operations and systems development.

Systems development.   The systems development area encompasses the work of the systems analysts and programmers who design, develop, and enhance application files, computer programs, and other developmental efforts that impact future systems in the organization.

CIS facility and environment.   The information processing facility and environment includes all of the activities actually involving the physical computer equipment, support and contingency arrangements, and files. This area includes, but is not limited to, computer operations, the library of computer files, data entry equipment, remote sites and backup storage facilities, and data distribution and distributed processing.

Computer Audit Plan

A professional computer audit environment supports a professional staff by maximizing the effect of special skills and abilities and by minimizing redundant activity. A key prerequisite for a professional environment is a firm management commitment to discipline and orderly planning.

Under its charter, the computer audit function should formulate both long-range and annual plans. Such plans describe what must be accomplished, include budgets of time and costs, and state priorities according to organizational goals and policies. At a minimum, a computer audit plan should:

- Define scope

- State objectives

- Structure an orderly approach

- Provide for measurement of achievement

- Assure reasonable comprehensiveness

- Provide flexibility in approach.

At this level, the computer audit plan is stated in general terms. The intent is to provide an overall approach within which audit engagements can be conducted. Plans for specific audit engagements, then, are carried to sufficient levels of detail to prepare budgets and actual work assignments. There is, however, another rationale for conceptualizing the computer audit plan at a general level. The reason is that both the systems in development and the state of the art in computer technology are undergoing constant, dynamic change. Detailed plans at the functional level cannot hope to anticipate the pattern of such change. Thus, detailed plans quickly would become obsolete and ineffective.

A computer audit plan partitions the audit of CIS into discrete segments. These segments describe a computer systems audit as a series of manageable audit engagements and steps. At the detailed planning, or engagement, level, these segments will have objectives that are custom-tailored to implement organizational goals and objectives within the circumstances of the audit.

Thus, computer auditing does not call for "canned" approaches. There is no single series of detailed steps that can be outlined once and then repeated in every audit. The computer audit plan, therefore, is an attempt to provide an orderly approach within which flexibility can be exercised.

Using the Plan to Identify Problems

The computer audit objectives, the computer audit charter, and the computer audit plan guide integral processes. The organization and its management must participate in and support this effort fully. Commitment can be gained if participants recognize that a good plan can help pinpoint problems in a highly dynamic, automated CIS environment. Thus, it should be the responsibility of all participants not only to help pinpoint such problems, but also to assist in the measurement and quantification of problems.

Identifying, measuring, and quantifying problems in the CIS area is especially difficult. The CIS field is technologically complex and has a language of its own. Participants in the formulation of the computer audit plan, and particularly the computer auditors themselves, must have sufficient experience and training in technical matters to be able to grasp key concepts and abstractions about systems. For example, abstractions about a CIS might include significant aspects that are susceptible to naming, counting, or conceptualizing. Understanding the systems at this level can lead to the identification of major problem areas. Audit concentration, then, may be directed to the major problem areas most likely to yield significant results.

Based on this identification of problems, the auditor determines what additional data might be required to reach evaluation decisions. The audit process, therefore, must be flexible enough to combine skilled personnel, new technology, and audit techniques in new ways to suit each situation. However, this flexibility of approach requires documentation in planned, directed steps. Systems that are understood poorly (or that have been designed without adequate controls) can result in lost revenues, increased costs, and perhaps disaster or fraud.

Modern management accounting has an obligation in this new environment. Fulfilling this obligation can be addressed in two fundamental steps. First, management must encourage and support the development of professional audit teams. Second, management must assure more vigorous and effective accounting participation in the development and evaluation of systems controls.

BASIC STEPS FOR COMPUTER AUDITORS

There are seven basic steps that can assist an auditor in the review of a computer-based system. These steps are valid regardless of computer environment, audit area, or system complexity. For each audit, the steps must be understood clearly, planned, and coordinated with the organizational objectives set for the audit function.

Define objectives.   The general objective is to verify those processes and controls necessary to make the area being audited free from significant exposures to risk. This objective also encompasses validating adherence of the systems under examination to appropriate standards, e.g. financial accounting should conform to GAAP.

Build a basic understanding of the area being audited.   In this step, the auditor should obtain and review summary-level information and evaluate it in relation to the audit objectives.

Build a detailed understanding of the area being audited.   To complete the understanding, the auditor interviews key personnel to determine policies and practices, and prepares supplemental audit information as required.

Evaluate control strengths and weaknesses.   In this step, the auditor determines which controls are essential to the overall audit objectives.

Design the audit procedures.   In this step, the auditor must prepare an audit program for the area being audited, select the verification techniques applicable to each area, and prepare the instructions for their performance.

Test the critical controls, processes, and apparent exposures.   The auditor performs the necessary testing by using documentary evidence, corroborating interviews, and personal observation.

Evaluate the results.   The last step involves evaluating the results of the work and preparing a report on the findings.

The seven basic steps that comprise the computer auditor's review, the three functional areas, the four qualities of a good computer auditor, the computer auditor's commitment, management's commitment, and the organization's commitment—all form a solid foundation upon which the computer audit function is built.

COMPUTER AUDIT—A SCENARIO

The following scenario illustrates the general preparations, functions, and feedback procedures of a typical computer audit within a CIS facility.

Before the Auditors Arrive

Once the schedule for an audit engagement is established, and before the auditors arrive, there are some specific preparations that a CIS organization can make. These preparations include the following:

- A CIS manager should study any previous audit reports. The audit team already will have done so. The CIS manager should determine if the negative items cited previously have been improved or eliminated. Then, the CIS manager should check positive comments to verify that these conditions have not changed.

- The CIS manager should meet with his or her staff to explain that the auditors are coming and why. The CIS manager should instruct staff members to answer questions to the best of their ability, although staff members should not respond to a question if they are unsure of the answer.

- The CIS manager should schedule CIS staff time so that the appropriate members can spend the necessary time with the audit team while they are on site.

- Finally, the CIS manager should encourage CIS staff to be cooperative and take the audit seriously.

When the Auditors Arrive

Upon arriving, the audit team will meet with the responsible executive officer and the CIS manager. This meeting will lay the groundwork for what the auditors expect to accomplish and will set a length of time for their stay. At this point, key participants will be introduced and audit activities will be outlined.

The activities will begin with extensive interviews, based on the audit work plan, by the audit team leader. This plan is usually in the form of a questionnaire covering every conceivable situation. Since each installation is unique, many of the questions will not be relevant; others will be of marginal value. During this time, there is the opportunity for the CIS manager to establish a rapport with the audit team leader and to set a positive mood for the entire effort.

What Auditors Look For

As an illustration of the audit process, consider an audit team that is interested primarily in an operational audit of the CIS facility and the management of its operations. In this case, some of the specific items to be scrutinized will be:

- Organization charts for both the company and the CIS department

- Equipment inventory, repair records, and contracts

- Systems software description, costs, contracts, and ownership status (This area is of primary concern to users of large-scale systems.)

- Serial numbers compared against billings or purchases, and locations

- Adherence to company rules, regulations, and conventions

- Development and methods of testing for new applications and changes to production programs

- Applications, including the number of programs, size of systems, languages, costs, and primary users

- Input, processing, and output controls

- Standards manuals that pertain to systems development, documentation, operations, emergency procedures, recovery, and alternate operations ability

- Backup procedures for data files

- Fiscal processes including budgets, expenditures, and charge-backs to users

- Plans for new systems, major changes and hardware modifications, proposed personnel additions

- Logs and controls maintained by the CIS and user departments

- Project control procedures, including authorization, budgeting, progress reports, and post-installation reviews

- Analysis of job accounting information and testing of system controls.

As described previously, auditing through the computer involves tracing transactions from documents, through point of entry, then into the computer and its processing (including electronically stored information), then tracing through its outputs, to the eventual disposition of the transactions. Typically, this method is used in single-job or batch processing situations. The purpose of this approach is to establish the existence and quality of controls, through all phases, for handling the organization's data. The audit techniques used include interviews with operations staff, validation and observation on the part of the auditor, and the actual testing of controls through sampling and submission of test data to the CIS.

Validation of the information obtained is prescribed by the auditor's work program. Again, this work program is the organized, written, and preplanned approach to the study of the CIS department. The plan calls for validation in several ways:

- Asking different personnel the same question and comparing the answers

- Asking the same question in different ways at different times

- Comparing checklist answers to work papers, programs, documentation, tests or other verifiable results

- Comparing checklist answers to observations and actual system results

- Conducting mini-studies of critical phases of the operation.

Such an intensive program allows an auditor to become informed about the operation in a short time.

Auditing through the computer involves some additional steps. In addition to the computer audit steps mentioned above, programs are run on the computer to test and authenticate application programs that are run in normal processing. Usually, the audit team will select one of the many generalized audit software (GAS) packages available and determine what changes are necessary to run the software at the installation. The auditor will use this software to do sampling, data extraction, exception reporting, summarize and foot totals, and other tasks.

Such audit packages increasingly are being used by computer audit teams. Many large installations already have GAS installed for their internal auditors. Reasons include the fact that auditors are becoming qualified technically to alter programs and the facility's job control procedures so that packages may run successfully. Also, better, easier to use audit tools are becoming available. However, the auditor must be aware that each installation is unique in its own scheduling and eccentricities. Thus, such customization still is both difficult and time consuming. Also, the installation may have to disrupt its normal processing schedule to accommodate these testing procedures.

Audit Completion

Through the various phases of the audit, the team will make positive comments as well as point out items that could be instituted or improved. At the completion of the audit program, the team manager will review a list of significant items with the CIS manager. These points are not meant to be derogatory, but are suggested improvements for upgrading the operation and protecting the CIS function from fraud or loss.

These suggestions will be discussed more thoroughly in the *exit interview*. The CIS manager will be expected to prepare answers to the items listed. These answers will be in the form of an affirmative plan to correct or eliminate observed deficiencies. The report will include positive comments about things that are done particularly well or that are effective in achieving good control and protection of management interests.

In rare instances, a CIS manager may be given a choice as to whether a formal report must be prepared. However, the report should be prepared in any case. A written report will provide excellent documentation for both the positive and negative points made and will serve as a reference for future audits and improvements.

Post Audit

Upon receipt of the formal report by the CIS department staff, CIS management and affected staff should review the document immediately. Those items not already completed should be handled. Within a relatively short time, then, the fact that all discrepancies have been corrected should be transmitted to the audit staff in a formal manner. These actions are noted in the audit files, and such cooperation reflects favorably in future audits.

COMPUTER AUDITOR'S FUNCTION

Whether the computer audit reviews the CIS facility (as described above) or it examines applications or systems development, the controls applied in these areas need to be verified. The computer auditor's function complements that of the internal auditor by providing reasonable assurance that assets are safeguarded, that information is timely and reliable, and that all errors and deficiencies are discovered and corrected promptly. Equally important objectives of this function are better control, more complete audit trails, and strict compliance with organizational policies.

Today's computer auditor is faced with many concerns about the exposure of computer information systems to a multitude of risks. From these concerns arise the objectives for the audit process and function. Achieving these objectives requires the support and involvement of all the participants described in this chapter.

DISCUSSION QUESTIONS

1. How is the principle of reasonable assurance related to the cost effectiveness of controls?

2. What are some of the inherent limitations to the potential effectiveness of any system of internal accounting control?

3. What are the computer auditor's main areas of concern, and what examples can be given for each?

4. How is an organization's commitment to the computer audit function related to information resource management?

5. What is the basic rationale for involving user-managers and computer auditors in the systems development process?

6. What are the essential qualities of a computer auditor?

7. What are the elements of a computer audit plan?

8. What seven steps can be followed in most computer audit engagements?

5 Types of Computer Audit Activities

A B S T R A C T

- Types of audit engagements in which computer auditors may become involved include reviews of CIS facilities, application systems, systems under development, and special studies requested by top management.

- Within the category of application systems audits, topics covered include audits of production systems, complex systems, program maintenance, as well as production of computer audit routines.

- Some types of complex application systems may require special audit approaches. Such systems may involve real-time processing, on-line file inquiry and updating, database management systems (DBMS), integrated systems, remote source data capture, multiprocessing, multiprogramming, teleprocessing, distributed processing, local area networks (LANs), and microcomputer/mainframe linkage.

- At an overview level, computer-assisted audit procedures encompass the development and implementation of computerized audit programs for systems that are in operational use.

- Audits of systems development projects include participation of computer auditors in systems design, new systems review audits, and development of computer audit routines.

- Audits of CIS facilities are a facet of the overall information resources management function in the organization. Such audits include reviews of management services and computer facilities, feasibility studies of computer equipment, and audits of auxiliary operations.

- Computer auditors also may conduct special studies, cooperative projects, and studies in response to management requests.

AUDITING AND TECHNOLOGICAL CHANGE

As a result of the continuing developments of computer technology, many traditional audit processes never will be the same. Though technology already has had dramatic effects on business and auditing, many changes are yet to be seen.

Each technological advance brings with it new challenges for the audit and accounting profession, as well as for the entire business world. Some problems may well be associated with these rapid changes. Computer audit activities must evolve to keep pace.

Office automation and new computer technology will continue to change the nature of internal control and the management audit trail. Related changes affect CIS, accounting, and audit professionals. In some cases, practitioners are unaware of the changes taking place all around them.

Audit approaches must be modified to meet new challenges and still be effective. The types of computer audits discussed in this chapter are those generally performed in today's computer environment. The degree to which the examination procedures are performed will vary among internal and external audits.

Internal Control Concerns

As cited in prior chapters, the objective of internal accounting control is to provide reasonable—but not absolute—assurance that:

- Organizational assets are secure from loss from unauthorized use or disposition
- Financial records are reliable enough to permit preparation of accurate financial statements.

The concept of reasonable assurance recognizes that the cost of a system of internal accounting control should not exceed the benefits derived. Reasonable assurance also recognizes that evaluation of these factors necessarily requires good management estimates and judgment.

There are inherent limitations in the potential effectiveness of any system of internal accounting control. In the performance of control procedures, for example, errors can result from the misunderstanding of instructions, mistakes of judgment, carelessness, or other personal factors. Control procedures based on the segregation of duties can be circumvented by collusion or fraud. Similarly, other aspects of control procedures can be circumvented intentionally by management or by users. For example, transactions can be recorded or executed inappropriately. Or, estimates and judgments required in the preparation of financial statements can be altered or distorted deliberately.

The presence of good internal accounting control does not mean that control will remain good indefinitely. Uncertainty over the effectiveness of control in the future is a function of changing conditions that may render existing control inadequate and promote possible deterioration in the degree of compliance with controls.

As discussed earlier, computer technology continues to sever the time-honored correlation between source documents and general books of account. In this period of ongoing and extensive change, however, many organizational controls have remained static. Managers and auditors must begin to recognize that outdated controls are nonexistent controls.

The specialized discipline of computer auditing has evolved to meet these fundamental, largely technological, changes. In general, there are four basic types of computer audits:

- Review of application systems
- Review of systems under development
- Review of CIS facilities and information resource management (entailing reviews of general or environmental controls)
- Special studies requested by top management.

REVIEW OF APPLICATION SYSTEMS

Computer auditors generally perform four kinds of reviews of application systems, or *application audits.* These reviews include:

- Production systems audits
- Complex systems audits
- Program maintenance audits
- Computer-assisted audit procedures.

Production Systems Audits

Production systems audits are periodic audits of routine applications, such as payroll, inventory, payments, accounts receivable, accounts payable, fixed assets, or other processing performed in the course of normal organizational activities. It should be noted that such applications depend on sound general controls and that, without sound general controls, some application controls may not be effective. Audits of these systems may incorporate the following techniques:

- Auditing can be performed through the computer by submitting test transactions through all computer processing phases with the assistance of automated testing tools, such as test data generators, or code-generating software for computer-assisted audit procedures.

- Sample data can be entered to yield intermediate outputs or printouts that are followed through to final output as entries to the general ledger or books of account.

- Computerized audit routines such as generalized audit software or specialized computer programming can be used.

- Documentation, balancing, transcribing, and other functions can be reviewed.

- Complete processing cycles, including night, graveyard, and weekend shifts, can be observed.

The application system and the needs of its users must be understood by the auditor before the real audit work can progress. In studying a system, computer auditors must review the program documentation, originator/user interfaces, data processing functions and procedures, and programming. Throughout this examination, the auditor is looking for control strengths and weaknesses.

A complete monitoring of the processing flow and balancing controls must be accomplished. Typical questions might include: Are there bottlenecks? Are the data getting to and from the system in a reasonable manner? That is, are the data timely, accurate, and complete?

The organizational structure, including the relationships among all parties involved with the system, must be reviewed. An organization's structure should be built upon a foundation of effective and efficient operations. In reviewing this organization, the auditor must determine how its structure affects control strengths and weaknesses.

CIS installations should be organized and managed by the same methods that have proven effective in organizational units. Characteristics of good organization include:

- Assignment of individual responsibilities to assure an adequate separation of duties

- Establishment of standard operating practices and procedures

- Implementation of internal control procedures, including management controls and the selection of qualified personnel.

Other actions that should be taken during a production systems audit include the following:

- Evaluate potential for unauthorized manipulation of programs, data files, or data elements.

- Inspect, either manually or automatically, supervisory control printouts, control records, and error listings.

- Confirm work schedules of personnel and computer usage, as well as reliability of usage reports and logs.

- Review any direct or indirect interfaces with other systems.

Although some general principles apply, each production system is an audit unto itself. That is, detailed audit steps must be tailored for each system, after a thorough understanding of the system has been built. A production system audit should be a specific approach to a specific system. Further, computer applications are dynamic. Thus, approaches may vary with changing conditions. Applications that are subject to rapid change should be audited on a repetitive basis.

Complex Systems Audits

Complex systems audits encompass examinations of systems that employ relatively advanced technologies. This type of audit requires considerable groundwork and planning, as well as constant revision and updating of techniques. Therefore, such systems are highly dependent on sound general controls, and some application controls may not be effective. Some techniques associated with complex systems are:

Real-time processing. *Real-time processing* is computer processing in which output occurs fast enough to fit within the normal cycle of the activity being performed. That is, complete processing cycles usually occur quickly enough to effect the outcome of source transactions.

On-line file inquiry and updating. With *on-line file inquiry and updating* techniques, users at terminals can gain immediate access to computer-based information. Inquiry involves retrieval of a desired record or data element, on command. The updating process writes a changed value for the data item back to the master file.

Database management systems (DBMS). *Database management systems (DBMS)* are sets of computer programs that manage integrated databases. DBMS software handles the physical storage of data elements in ways that are transparent, or not readily apparent, to the user or the application program. The user accesses data elements by specifying data relationships. Database management systems typically isolate the data management function from the application program. Thus, all controls related to data and their integrity must be incorporated into the DBMS.

Integrated systems.   An *integrated system* is the automated coordination of multiple computer hardware devices, software programs, and/or information systems. For example, accounts payable and accounts receivable may be interfaced directly to the general ledger. Or, sales order processing may be interfaced directly to accounts receivable and inventory control, then to the general ledger. On a systems level, an example of integration would be a payables system linked to an electronic funds transfer system.

Remote source data capture.   *Remote source data capture* is the recording of data in machine-sensible form at the point of transaction. Banking customers who key in their own transactions at automated teller machines are performing remote source data capture. In another application, point-of-sale terminals in some retail stores are equipped with magnetic or optical wands or scanners that read and enter product identification data directly from encoded price tags.

Multiprocessing.   *Multiprocessing* describes two or more computers (processors) that operate on an integrated basis to share work entered into any of the connected units. Often, one computer interfaces with users and performs file-maintenance housekeeping while another is free for full-time, productive computing. It is possible to have multiple processors of equal stature. Control and audit concerns center around difficulties of determining which computer ran a given job.

Multiprogramming.   *Multiprogramming* is a method for using automatic, operating-system software to control allocation of memory to multiple jobs and to establish processing queues for execution of those jobs. Thus, multiprogramming implements a plan for concurrent processing of multiple applications while multiprocessing can actually perform multiple tasks simultaneously.

Teleprocessing.   *Teleprocessing* describes any system within which communication lines link users and computing facilities. Usually, teleprocessing systems imply a central computer serving remote terminals, work stations, or microcomputers.

Distributed processing. *Distributed processing* is the decentralization and coordination of computer processing and storage capabilities among devices that share a data communication network. For example, an organization may use minicomputers or microcomputers for source data capture and edit functions. Valid data then are transmitted to larger computer resources, usually mainframes, for transaction processing, master file updating, consolidation, and volume reporting. This service implies that computing capabilities are available at remote sites.

Local area network (LAN). A *local area network (LAN)* is implemented through the hard-wiring of multiple microcomputers and peripherals. A LAN is said to be local because of limitations on wiring length and number of devices supported. LANs typically serve a single work group or department at a single site. LANs also may be linked as nodes within larger data communication networks—to corporate mainframes, for example.

Microcomputer/mainframe linkage. *Microcomputer/mainframe linkage* interfaces microcomputers with one or more mainframe systems. Microcomputer users may access the organizational database, then *download* files for local processing and output. Also, locally generated data may be *uploaded* from the microcomputer to the database within the mainframe system.

The audit of complex systems typically includes the examination of:

- Documentation
- Data storage control
- Retrieval and input control
- Transmission control
- Processing control and validation
- Output control.

In the complex systems environment, special emphasis must be placed on controls that are built into the system and its software. This examination entails analysis of:

- Programs (including all types of software and firmware)
- Operational and procedural controls over remote work stations
- Control of access to data
- Control of access to communication terminals

- Privacy of information

- Ability to restart systems and to reconstruct data in the event of disruption or disaster

- Availability of an audit trail, whether manual or mechanized. (For example, transaction log tapes used for system restart and database recovery may constitute a viable audit trail.)

The auditing of complex systems requires a variety of tools and techniques. For example, one technique is the testing of actual transactions on a statistical sampling basis, with confirmation sought for the actual external events. Another audit technique is the comparison of authentic copies of authorized programs with running programs for possible alteration of the original files.

Auditing complex systems is easier if auditors have automated access to data resources. For example, on-line access to the corporate CIS might be provided to internal audit staff through a database management system. Thus, all computer-based data would be available on-line to the computer auditor for random sampling and testing.

Also, computer auditors may wish to use audit routines that are embedded in complex systems. The routines can be invoked upon the auditor's request to produce current samples while data are being processed. Many internal computer audit staffs use video display terminals (VDTs) from which audit programs may be tested and executed; embedded audit routines may be invoked; and data may be drawn from systems for quick, on-line inquiry. Of course, this type of computer auditing demands more technical skills than those required to audit batch or mixed-mode production systems.

Program Maintenance Audits

A *program maintenance audit* is implemented by obtaining control of a copy of the source-code instructions for all production programs from the computer information center, or media library. This tape then represents a "frozen" copy of the programs and is kept in the custody of the computer auditors. At some future time (three to six months, for example), a copy of the current program tape is obtained. The auditor compares the two tapes by using a program, developed by internal computer audit staff, that compares the versions of source code and prints out any differences.

The resulting differences are checked for validity, authorization of changes, and documentation of changes. This type of computer audit is not, in itself, a totally effective tool for detecting unauthorized or inappropriate modification of application programs. Nevertheless, program maintenance audits are a necessary part of computer-based auditing, particularly for internal auditors.

Major changes in programs must meet strict standards of documentation. Items to be checked include request and approval of the change, implementation, the updating of documentation to reflect the change, and feedback or confirmation of the change. These, in addition to testing the actual changes made, are some of the key points to be reviewed by both the audit function and management in assuring the reliability of production programs.

Generally, program maintenance audits protect against the possibility of unauthorized changes that could lead to inappropriate or unauthorized processing, fraudulent practices, or other damage to the integrity of the CIS. Such audits are applied only to systems that have been put into normal production and are considered fully operational. The audit examination usually is done on a surprise basis so that no one has the opportunity to tamper with the programs to conceal unauthorized changes. It should be mentioned that reviewing source code alone does not guarantee that the compiled version of the program in the production library is the same as the source code being audited.

Computer-Assisted Audit Procedures

Computer-assisted audit procedures encompass the development and implementation of computerized audit programs for systems that are in operational use. These computer-assisted audit procedures may have been recommended by an external or internal audit staff in an earlier audit or during systems development.

Once the procedures are installed, auditors must re-evaluate them periodically to assure that the routine is operating properly, that it continues to justify itself in terms of the function performed, and that it continues to solve the basic problem for which it was developed.

The computer-assisted audit procedure also should be reviewed for efficiency and effectiveness. It is important, for example, to assure that the procedure does not degrade the performance of the existing application.

Usually, routines are written in generalized audit software languages, such as Auditape, Culprit, GAMMA, DYL-260, or DYL-280. Examples of special-purpose computer audit software include *IP3* by Computing Productivity, Inc.® and *Ideal* by ADR®. Also, routines for audit purposes could be customized in a higher-level language such as COBOL or RPG (Report Program Generator).

AUDITS OF SYSTEMS DEVELOPMENT ACTIVITIES

The major types of involvement by computer auditors in systems development activities include:

- Participation in new systems design
- New systems review audit
- Development of computer audit routines.

Participation in New Systems Design

Involvement of computer auditors in the design of new systems is perhaps the most difficult and delicate type of computer audit engagement. Participation by computer auditors in the early phases of development, however, also has the most potential for effective contribution to reliable application systems.

A word of caution is in order. This type of audit demands skill, knowledge, expertise, and professionalism. Clearly, tremendous benefits can result if the computer auditor can point out weaknesses in an emerging system and add strength before the system reaches implementation.

This type of computer audit can focus effort at the point of greatest leverage. In most cases, a formal schedule is set up for the auditor's involvement at key points, or benchmarks in the systems development cycle.

All systems result from some development cycle. Structured development methodologies partition project work into distinct phases. Phase completion typically corresponds with major work products and deliverables, as well as with management review and approval for continuing to the next phase. This approval point is often an appropriate time for the computer auditor's involvement. Since there is a scheduled break before beginning work on the next phase, the participation of the computer auditor can be accomplished effectively, without wasted time or major schedule slippage.

A poorly controlled system is a serious liability to an organization. It is much more effective and economical to build controls into the system initially, rather than attempting to retrofit them into an existing system after it is programmed and in production. Because of the impacts on financial reporting, management accounting personnel also must take an active role in the systems development process.

When a primary computer information system encounters trouble, the whole organization may be affected. Many corporate CIS disasters could have been prevented by thorough computer audit analysis, more vigorous management involvement, and the designing of controls into systems early in their development.

To minimize changes after implementation of new systems and to minimize costs in developing new procedures, qualified computer audit personnel should participate in the formulation of proposals for new systems. The objective should be to point out potential weaknesses before the fact, rather than after implementation. User departments must include their most capable people in the design and review processes.

As stated previously, this type of audit engagement requires a high degree of professionalism, communication, and coordination. The auditor typically is not a full-time member of the design team, but must be in contact with the team at critical points throughout the design and development phases. Ongoing contact must be maintained with all parties participating in the design process.

The state of the art in CIS is moving rapidly in the direction of more integrated, comprehensive, complex, and sophisticated systems in the late 1980s and 1990s. Accordingly, the technical challenges of this type of audit also will become increasingly more complex.

New Systems Review Audit

A *new systems review audit* is the examination of a new system after development, but prior to turnover for production. The audit, in effect, is an overall, pre-production appraisal. Further, such audits do not preclude later audits of the system, once it is in production. The key criteria for these reviews are:

- Auditability
- Compliance with documentation standards
- Sound design
- Evidence of effective operating controls
- Evidence of sensitivity to management control.

A good appraisal of a system prior to turnover for production does not mean that every facet of the system has the audit staff's stamp of approval. Upon special request or upon the auditor's noting of a management recommendation, in-depth studies can be initiated. Outside expertise may have to be solicited in some cases.

Development of Computer Audit Routines

In assessing any computer audit routine developed or specified during the systems development process, the auditor asks the following key questions:

- Is the proposed audit routine amenable to computerization?

- Is the audit routine justifiable in terms of the investment in time, money, and resources?

- Can the computer audit routine be used on a repetitive basis? Can portions or modules within the routine be reused in the audit of other, similar applications with similar processing requirements?

- Does the computer audit routine solve a problem with high potential risk and of significant concern to the user and to the auditor?

- Does the computer audit routine increase the efficiency and/or the capability of the audit staff? Does activation of the routine permit auditors to evaluate quickly the operational validity and reliability of specific controls?

- Does use of the computer audit routine require considerable assistance and ongoing support from computer professionals or computer audit personnel? If so, the program may be too costly in staff time, as compared with other audit procedures.

AUDITS OF CIS FACILITIES AND INFORMATION RESOURCE MANAGEMENT

This area of computer auditing encompasses both the assessment of CIS operations and the evaluation of how CIS services are performed throughout the organization. These types of determinations fall under the general heading of information resource management (IRM), or the effective coordination of all types of information assets throughout an organization.

By nature, such audits are primarily operations-oriented. Specific types of audits typically performed by computer auditors for IRM include:

- Management services and computer facilities review
- Computer equipment feasibility study
- Audits of auxiliary operations.

Management Services and Computer Facilities Review

The audit of management services and computer facilities is relatively broad in scope. The review is operational in nature and concentrates on factors, procedures, and controls within the CIS facility and throughout the organization, including organizational relationships and spheres of responsibility. Aspects of this type of audit include the following:

- Facilities
- Organization

- Security controls
- Risk management
- Documentation standards
- Computer center operations, including data transcription and library procedures
- Computer scheduling and production
- Input/output controls
- Disaster recovery procedures
- Training and personnel succession planning
- Budget of CIS function and long-range planning.

In meeting the objectives of this type of audit, the auditor must:

- Assure compliance with policy, standards, and procedures.
- Affirm justification of investment.
- Evaluate efficiency of operation.

As just stated, the scope of such audits is purposely broad. The discussion below focuses on a few of the important concerns in the following areas:

- Utilization and application
- Programming
- Security
- Management services.

Utilization and application.   Computer time is valuable. A sound approach would be to treat computer resources—whether mainframe, minicomputer, microcomputer, or local area network—as just another type of potentially productive industrial equipment. That is, computers cannot be regarded as the special preserve of a particular group of technicians. Accordingly, a critical concern of management is the efficiency of computer use.

Also important is the effective application of computer resources. Seeking this effectiveness sometimes actually may appear to be in conflict with utilization goals. Effective application implies that a sufficient level of resources is being allocated to an identified organizational need. In this context, the term "application" relates to computing capacity—to the capability that is *applied* to the work at hand. Thus, although efficient utilization implies conservation of resources, effective application requires a level of expenditure sufficient to produce the intended results.

To evaluate utilization and application levels properly requires technical specialization on the part of the auditor. When effective utilization measurement and analysis is applied fully, unreported or unnoticed information assets can be identified and converted into tangible cost savings. Possible impacts include:

- The ability to apply savings as additional resources for development activities

- Realization of revenues from the sale of excess computer resources

- More effective management of time-sharing resources

- Reduction or liquidation of unused or antiquated equipment.

Programming. In the programming area, the auditor reviews program authorization procedures and files. A primary focus is on the controls over changes to programs at the critical points of design, testing, and production. In addition, the auditor should review adherence to programming standards, programming languages, etc.

Security. Security controls must be reviewed. Although many practitioners will argue that absolute security is unattainable, following the six steps explained below can provide reasonable assurance that controls are adequate. These steps are diagrammed in Figure 5-1. In order of priority, the steps are:

Identification. Risks must be identified before disaster strikes. An awareness of exposures—on the part of management, operations staff, and auditors alike—is the first step to prevention of loss.

Prevention. Prevention encompasses specific security measures designed to address the risks that have been identified and that prohibit occurrence of offending conditions.

Detection. Detection is the implementation of routine control measures that monitor the systems and report exception conditions. These typically are applied after the fact to detect and report exceptions for follow-up and correction.

Response. When irregularities or exceptions are detected, control measures must be in place for prompt correction of the situation and return to normal, reliable operations.

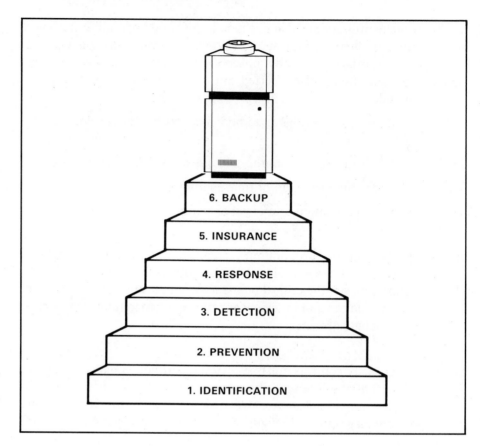

Figure 5-1.

The computer auditor may take six steps to gain reasonable assurance of the security of information systems.

Insurance. Valuable assets must be insured financially against damage or loss. Natural disasters and business interruptions are examples of threats against which insurance is a primary safeguard.

Backup. Copies of program and data files must be made routinely and stored off-site in secure areas. Backup procedures must keep track of the different versions of programs and data files so that clean restarts can be performed in the event of interruption.

The question of computer security involves a trade-off between cost and risk. The judicious use of management decision tools such as *decision tree* analysis may be appropriate. Decision trees are graphic representations of successive alternatives to be addressed in solving a problem or reaching a conclusion. Choices between alternatives, when presented in diagram form, resemble the branches on a tree. An example of decision tree analysis applied to security considerations is shown in Figure 5-2.

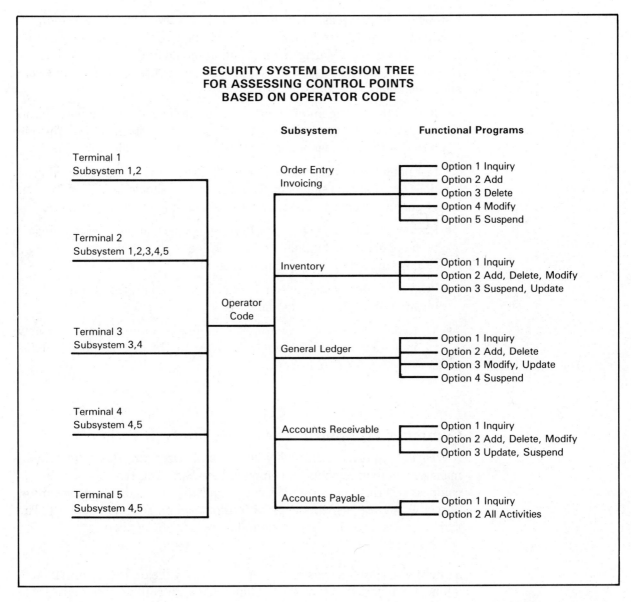

**SECURITY SYSTEM DECISION TREE
FOR ASSESSING CONTROL POINTS
BASED ON OPERATOR CODE**

Subsystem   **Functional Programs**

Terminal 1
Subsystem 1,2

Order Entry
Invoicing
- Option 1 Inquiry
- Option 2 Add
- Option 3 Delete
- Option 4 Modify
- Option 5 Suspend

Terminal 2
Subsystem 1,2,3,4,5

Inventory
- Option 1 Inquiry
- Option 2 Add, Delete, Modify
- Option 3 Suspend, Update

Operator
Code

Terminal 3
Subsystem 3,4

General Ledger
- Option 1 Inquiry
- Option 2 Add, Delete
- Option 3 Modify, Update
- Option 4 Suspend

Terminal 4
Subsystem 4,5

Accounts Receivable
- Option 1 Inquiry
- Option 2 Add, Delete, Modify
- Option 3 Update, Suspend

Terminal 5
Subsystem 4,5

Accounts Payable
- Option 1 Inquiry
- Option 2 All Activities

Figure 5-2.

As shown in this diagram, decision-tree analysis may be applied to security considerations. Each branch of the tree represents a different alternative.

Techniques such as decision tree analysis are useful when specific probabilities and protection costs can be identified. However, care must be taken to apply such analysis with judgment. Risks also should be assessed in light of larger organizational and social considerations. Social attitudes toward rights to privacy and organizational responsibility, as well as vulnerabilities of complex, distributed computer networks, are factors that increase greatly the magnitude of risk and the potential impacts on the organization.

Management services.   For this audit activity, the computer auditor must assure that formal, overall plans exist for productive and profitable use of information resources. Management attention should be directed to potentially profitable opportunities, as well as to cost control or cost reduction. In evaluating such plans, the auditor should:

- Review the statement of objectives and purpose of the computer information systems. Programming and processing efforts must be defined in terms of the organization's short- and long-range goals.

- List potential or proposed computer information systems and applications for future development. This information should be ranked in order of potential benefits, risks, and short- and long-range opportunities.

- Review alternative long-range CIS system plans that must be coordinated with organizational initiatives, staffing goals, proposed hardware acquisitions, and software implementation plans.

- Verify that an effective system of management control exists for each application during the development process.

- Verify that a system of rigorous post-implementation appraisal of new computer applications is performed to assure that the intended benefits actually are being realized.

Computer Equipment Feasibility Study

A *computer equipment feasibility study* emphasizes the determination of management requirements for computer hardware. This type of audit can encompass criteria of performance, cost, acquisition procedures, and terms of purchase or lease, as well as provision for maintenance and support. The auditor poses questions about the following specific concerns:

Timeliness.   Are the existing systems producing the desired information in a timely manner? Is information maintained with sufficient currentness to reflect organizational conditions accurately and to serve as a reliable basis for management decisions? Are on-line or interactive services responsive enough to meet user demand? Does the organization have the information it needs in time to stay competitive and to meet reporting requirements?

Cost.   Are the costs of systems development, operations, and support for a given application justified by the organizational benefits derived? Are costs being monitored and controlled adequately?

Service.   Are maintenance and support adequately matched to the needs of the organization and do they assure continuity and responsiveness of computer service? Have alternative service plans and vendors been investigated fully?

Equipment alternatives.   Is the equipment currently in use outdated? Are extraordinary service costs being incurred because of the age of equipment or the need to maintain obsolete operating systems or application packages? Are price/performance ratios in line with the current state of computer art? Is reliance on a single, turnkey vendor preventing the organization from looking at more innovative or cost-effective approaches?

Processing options.   Is there an appropriate mix between batch and on-line applications within the mainframe facility? Have distributed processing options been investigated? Would off-loading the host system through distributed processing improve service or forestall expensive upgrading of the central facility?

Contract terms.   In vendor contracts for hardware, software, or service, have the most favorable terms for the organization been negotiated? Have such contracts undergone appropriate and timely legal review? Are responsibility for contingencies and liability of the vendor stated clearly in the contract terms? What is the renewal status of existing contracts? What more favorable terms might be obtained by renegotiation? Have lease/purchase options been evaluated for the most favorable impact on the organization's financial position?

System and equipment recommendations.   What proposals exist for acquisition or development of new systems and components? Is a *systems planning* function operating under management direction to set priorities and plan resource expenditures for proposed systems development projects? Are these priorities consistent with the organization's goals and objectives?

The main objective of a computer equipment feasibility study is to report to top management on findings, conclusions, and recommendations about computing resource acquisition and planning. Management thus is provided with another perspective on equipment feasibility. The computer auditor is able to present an opinion as to the most equitable and reasonable solutions that will meet the organization's goals and objectives.

Audits of Auxiliary Operations

Audits of auxiliary operations involve specific, repetitive functions of review surrounding CIS facilities and management services. This is a growing area of specific compliance audits. These audits focus on auxiliary operations that are performed remotely from the central facility, but have significance to overall information resource management. Because of the focus on dispersed locations, audits of operations often involve distributed processing technologies, such as local area networks and microcomputers. Specific audits include:

- Equipment inventory and rental verification

- Monitoring of off-site media storage

- Review of supervisory console printouts

- Review of microcomputer hardware and software use.

This last activity, the review of microcomputer hardware and software use, examines the use of desk-top or portable computing devices throughout the organization. The objectives are to assure that licensing agreements are being complied with, as well as verifying compliance with the organization's computer use standards.

SPECIAL STUDIES, COOPERATIVE PROJECTS, AND MANAGEMENT REQUESTS

The last type of major audit pertains to special situations. Often, computer auditors are called upon to participate in special studies or projects. Because of their special nature, such audits can involve a relatively large scope. Examples of this type of audit engagement include:

- Analysis of computer operations staff overtime

- Analysis of computer processing work load and scheduling

- Development and review of organizational standards and procedures

- Participation on a reconstruction and off-site storage committee

- Consultation with management services and user officials

- Assessment of computer operations at independent subsidiaries or at third-party information processing organizations.

This category of audit usually involves a small percentage of the computer auditor's time. Often, a targeted approach is taken to specific problems and needs. Thus, this type of audit is problem-oriented and requires interdepartmental effort. The basic service performed by the computer auditor is to provide management with independent information or evaluations of specific CIS matters. The auditor's touchstone in such projects is a clear statement of responsibilities and engagement scope.

This chapter provides an overview of the typical engagements conducted by computer auditors. The next chapter explains the types of controls computer auditors examine and test. Emphasis is on principles of control that may be applied generally to all types of information processing systems.

DISCUSSION QUESTIONS

1. How is technological change related to the audit examination procedures required to assure adequate internal control?

2. In what types of application audits might a computer auditor be engaged?

3. What might be the auditor's main focal points in an audit of CIS facilities?

4. How does the use of advanced technologies affect the approach to an application audit?

5. What is the basic method of control used by computer auditors engaged in program maintenance audits?

6. How may computerized audit routines be applied to an operational CIS? To a CIS under development?

7. What criteria should auditors apply in a new systems review audit?

8. What are some types of special projects that may require participation of computer auditors?

6 Computer Information Systems Controls: An Overview

A B S T R A C T

- A key CIS control issue is that there is no single set of generally accepted standards of quality.

- Relationships among controls occur within the dimensions of either organizational patterns or procedures.

- The effectiveness of controls may be determined to be weak, normal, or strong. A control would be operating normally that provided for segregation of duties, authorization, and data validation.

- Basic control functions include preventive, detective, and corrective controls. Preventive controls halt processing when an error or exception is identified. Detective controls, in general, identify errors but do not affect processing directly. Once errors are detected, corrective controls may be applied after the fact to return the system to normal operation.

- Within application controls, there are categories for input, processing, output, and transmission controls.

- Controls within applications must assure completeness of processing, system integrity and data accuracy, authorized and valid data entry, integrity of data transmissions, and auditability.

THE STANDARDS VOID

The following statement is heard frequently by auditors reviewing the extent and quality of controls within computer information systems:

But it works!

Sometimes the words are spoken with relief. Sometimes the speaker is incredulous—wanting to know how anything can be wrong with a system that issued all of this week's paychecks or invoices on time.

The fact that a system may lack adequate controls—or even may hold the potential for disaster—too often is regarded as a noncritical problem for which there simply isn't enough time or money. This attitude can still be found in many medium- and large-size CIS installations.

The triumph of workability over reliability is as understandable as it is lamentable. For the most part, the fact that a system works has been the only measure of quality available. Unfortunately, there are no universal standards governing the reliability and control of CIS applications.

Further, there is no authority, either governmental or quasi-official, in a position to enunciate or to enforce such standards, should they exist. Concerned groups have proposed and publicized standards. Systems manufacturers, government agencies, professional firms, as well as trade and technical associations—all have joined in the effort to advance meaningful standards.

In practice, total standardization of CIS functions and operations would be impossible within a free-enterprise system. CIS systems development practices and computer operations are internal to user organizations. Effective application of computer resources is becoming a critical success factor in organizational strategy. Organizations retain proprietary interests in their computer information systems. Thus, in an increasingly competitive environment, issuance and enforcement of step-by-step standards for all CIS functions and operations is virtually impossible.

Still, publicly held companies must be audited. Auditors must render opinions on the reliability of computer-produced financial information. Therefore, considerable attention has been focused on control standards for CIS reliability. Even in the absence of definitive standards, some authoritative guidelines have emerged. These guidelines constitute judgmental criteria to be applied to individual situations. Further, a specialized body of knowledge relating to control measures and techniques has evolved with the advancing state of computer technology.

CONTROLS AND RELIABILITY

Information reliability is attainable only through application of controls. This chapter identifies and describes controls in a CIS environment. The emphasis is on attainment of controlled conditions within a CIS operation.

The discussion below presents definitions of controls and reliability, and describes, in general terms, how controls work and how they fit into a CIS environment. The discussion in the next chapter covers controls tailored to CIS application life cycles, or from systems development through operations and maintenance. Operational and management controls also are included. These controls are environmental, or apply to all CIS functions, encompassing the relationships between CIS and other departments.

Building on these discussions, Chapter 8 explains the evaluation of CIS controls. Previous discussions of compliance and substantive testing have touched on this subject. Control evaluation is a critical and crucial step in the audit process—especially when the system is automated or combines manual and automated procedures.

Controls Defined

Within information systems, controls are the procedures and organizational patterns that assure reliability. When applied properly, controls should provide assurance or protection that standards will be met and that specified results will be delivered. Control procedures can be applied either manually or electronically—or through a combination of manual and electronic techniques.

Reliability Defined

Reliability is a measure of the extent to which controls actually exist and how well they work within an information system. Reliability is a result, a measure of performance achieved by an application or system. Reliability measurement, then, encompasses the effectiveness of all controls within the application or system under examination.

Reliability is not absolute, but is a matter of extent, or degree. Assurance of reliability is essential in applying judgment to managing or auditing computer-based systems. Reliability attributed to any application or accounting environment becomes the basis for reliance on the system in making organizational decisions.

RELATIONSHIPS AMONG CONTROLS

Within any system, and especially within accounting and financial systems, the impact and evaluation of controls is cumulative. No single control can assure a reliable accounting system. Rather, reliability stems from interrelationships among controls at key processing points within the overall system.

The potential extent and complexity of these interrelationships is illustrated in Figure 6-1, which presents a diagram of internal controls for a large-scale CIS.

To illustrate these concepts on a smaller scale, consider the activities involved in issuing checks within a typical, computerized accounts payable system. Minimal processing, as diagrammed in Figure 6-2, might include the following steps:

1. Prepare accounts payable vouchers or annotate voucher information on invoices received from vendors.

2. Key data into a VDT from invoices or vouchers.

3. Under computer program control, edit and process accounts payable input to produce balancing reports, accounting registers, and actual checks.

4. Sign checks or use an automated signing prestamp.

5. Review checks and their supporting documentation.

6. Mail checks.

Controls are appropriate at each of these key processing points. For example, the person preparing the accounts payable voucher should require that all invoices be authorized for payment. This procedure establishes the first control point in the system. Authorization can be accomplished by matching vouchers to previously issued purchase orders or by requiring authorized signatures on the invoices themselves. This step can be a manual and/or automatic matching process for verification.

Similarly, control may be applied within computerized steps by editing inputs to validate coding, formatting, and account identifications prior to processing runs. As another control, a separate process for signing the checks could include a review of supporting documentation to establish that all disbursements are supported and authorized. Separation of the mailing and signing functions could represent still another control. Again, these controls can be manual and/or automated, depending on the level of sophistication of the organizational processes and procedures.

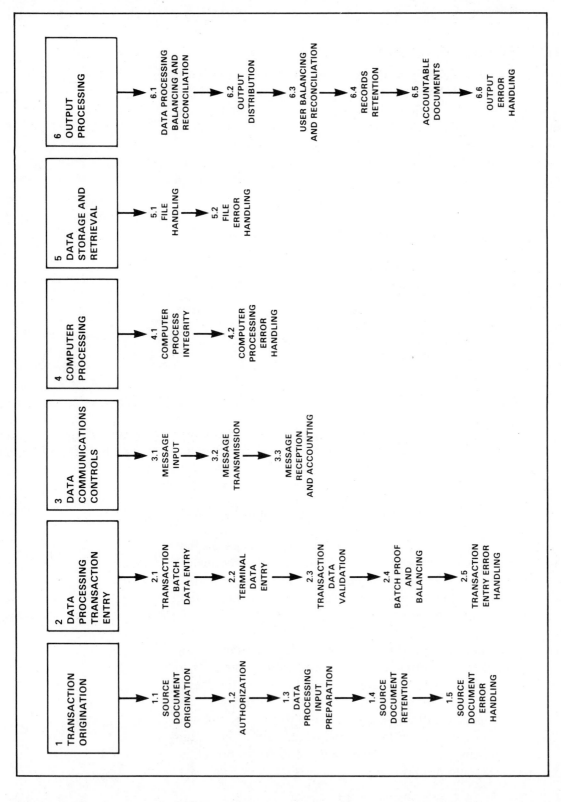

Figure 6-1. *This chart (including the following five pages) shows internal controls for automatic data processing within a large-scale CIS. The chart was prepared by the U. S. Government Accounting Office and is based on "Systems Auditability and Control Study." Stanford Research Institute, January, 1977.*

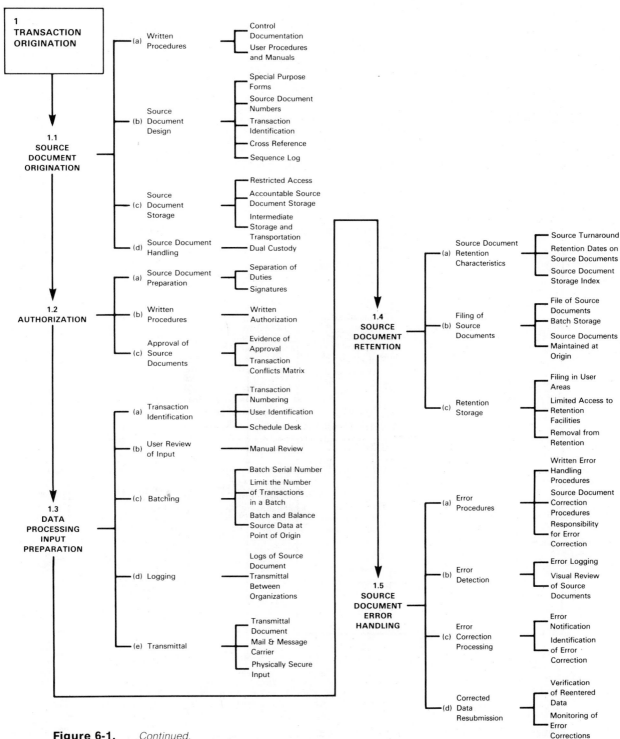

Figure 6-1. *Continued.*

142

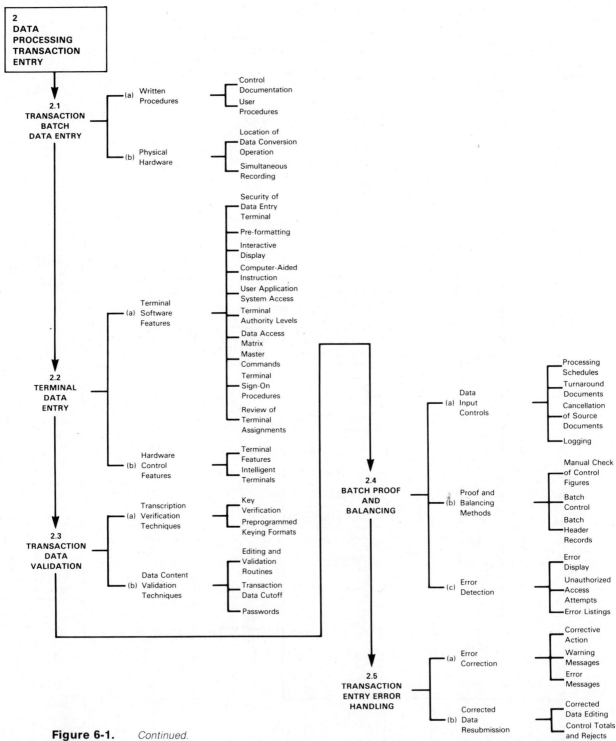

Figure 6-1. *Continued.*

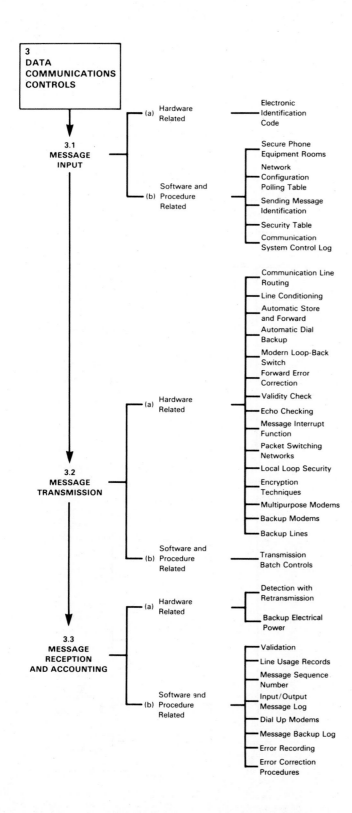

Figure 6-1.   *Continued.*

144

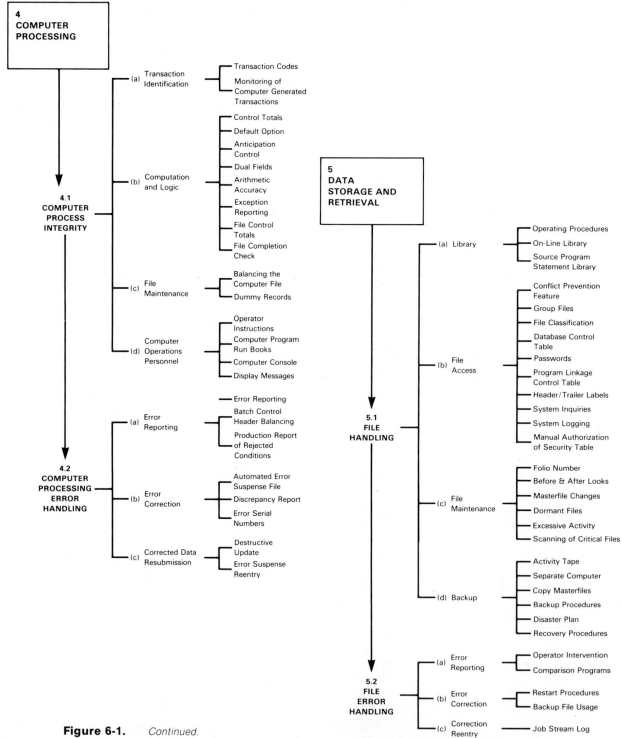

Figure 6-1. *Continued.*

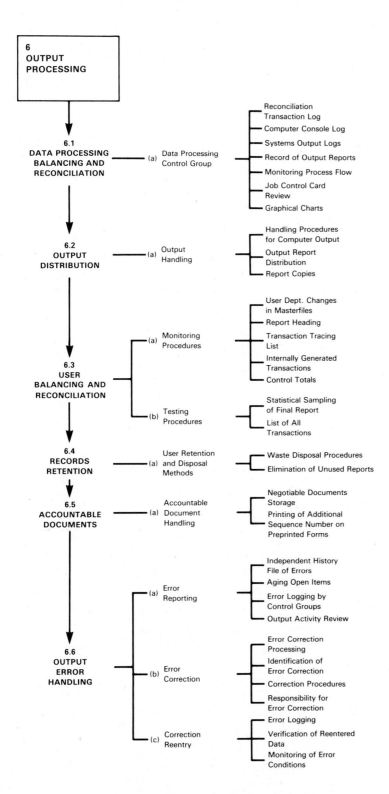

6 OUTPUT PROCESSING

6.1 DATA PROCESSING BALANCING AND RECONCILIATION
- (a) Data Processing Control Group
  - Reconciliation Transaction Log
  - Computer Console Log
  - Systems Output Logs
  - Record of Output Reports
  - Monitoring Process Flow
  - Job Control Card Review
  - Graphical Charts

6.2 OUTPUT DISTRIBUTION
- (a) Output Handling
  - Handling Procedures for Computer Output
  - Output Report Distribution
  - Report Copies

6.3 USER BALANCING AND RECONCILIATION
- (a) Monitoring Procedures
  - User Dept. Changes in Masterfiles
  - Report Heading
  - Transaction Tracing List
  - Internally Generated Transactions
  - Control Totals
- (b) Testing Procedures
  - Statistical Sampling of Final Report
  - List of All Transactions

6.4 RECORDS RETENTION
- (a) User Retention and Disposal Methods
  - Waste Disposal Procedures
  - Elimination of Unused Reports

6.5 ACCOUNTABLE DOCUMENTS
- (a) Accountable Document Handling
  - Negotiable Documents Storage
  - Printing of Additional Sequence Number on Preprinted Forms

6.6 OUTPUT ERROR HANDLING
- (a) Error Reporting
  - Independent History File of Errors
  - Aging Open Items
  - Error Logging by Control Groups
  - Output Activity Review
- (b) Error Correction
  - Error Correction Processing
  - Identification of Error Correction
  - Correction Procedures
  - Responsibility for Error Correction
- (c) Correction Reentry
  - Error Logging
  - Verification of Reentered Data
  - Monitoring of Error Conditions

Figure 6-1. *Concluded.*

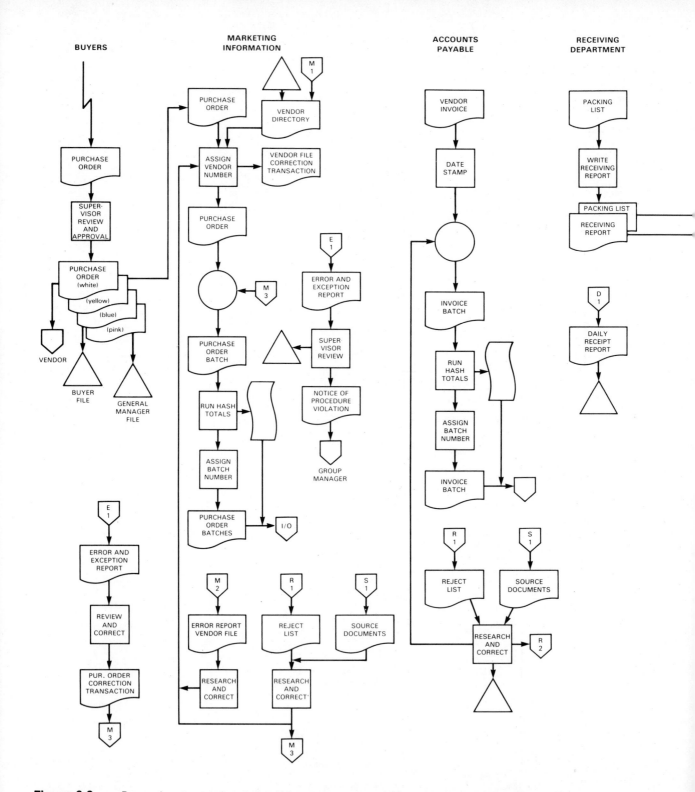

Figure 6-2. *Processing steps and controls within an accounts payable system are documented in this flowchart.*

146

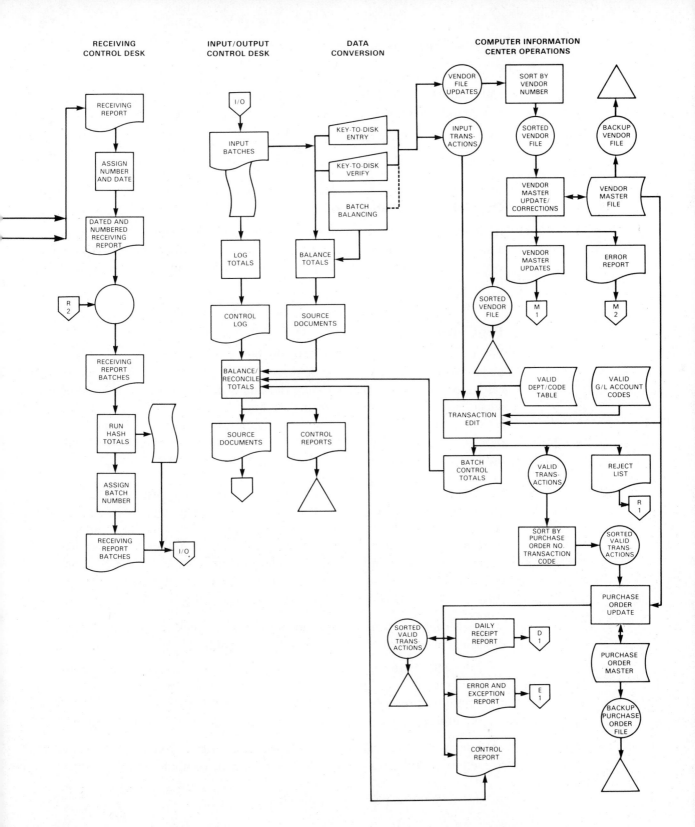

RECEIVING
CONTROL DESK

INPUT/OUTPUT
CONTROL DESK

DATA
CONVERSION

COMPUTER INFORMATION
CENTER OPERATIONS

RECEIVING REPORT

ASSIGN NUMBER AND DATE

DATED AND NUMBERED RECEIVING REPORT

R 2

RECEIVING REPORT BATCHES

RUN HASH TOTALS

ASSIGN BATCH NUMBER

RECEIVING REPORT BATCHES

I/O

I/O

INPUT BATCHES

LOG TOTALS

CONTROL LOG

BALANCE/ RECONCILE TOTALS

SOURCE DOCUMENTS

KEY-TO-DISK ENTRY

KEY-TO-DISK VERIFY

BATCH BALANCING

BALANCE TOTALS

SOURCE DOCUMENTS

CONTROL REPORTS

VENDOR FILE UPDATES

INPUT TRANS- ACTIONS

SORT BY VENDOR NUMBER

SORTED VENDOR FILE

VENDOR MASTER UPDATE/ CORRECTIONS

VENDOR MASTER UPDATES

SORTED VENDOR FILE

BACKUP VENDOR FILE

VENDOR MASTER FILE

ERROR REPORT

M 1

M 2

VALID DEPT/CODE TABLE

VALID G/L ACCOUNT CODES

TRANSACTION EDIT

BATCH CONTROL TOTALS

VALID TRANS- ACTIONS

REJECT LIST

R 1

SORT BY PURCHASE ORDER NO. TRANSACTION CODE

SORTED VALID TRANS- ACTIONS

PURCHASE ORDER UPDATE

SORTED VALID TRANS- ACTIONS

DAILY RECEIPT REPORT

D 1

ERROR AND EXCEPTION REPORT

E 1

CONTROL REPORT

PURCHASE ORDER MASTER

BACKUP PURCHASE ORDER FILE

These controls are interrelated in their impacts on the reliability of the end product—a properly organized check mailed to the correct vendor. Interrelationship occurs within two dimensions of control:

- Organizational patterns

- Procedures.

Organizational Patterns

In the example just cited, controls of an organizational type are implicit in a separation of functions among the preparation of the accounts payable voucher, key entry, computer processing, check signing and review, and finally, mailing.

Procedures

In the example, procedural interrelationships for control exist because each major processing step has specific prerequisites. The check writing process cannot begin, for example, without prior authorization. Either there must be a matching purchase order or the invoice must have been signed by an authorized person. Similarly, computer processing cannot take place unless appropriate vendor and account master files exist. In the next step, a check will not be signed unless there is appropriate supporting documentation.

Systems are more or less reliable, or contain strengths or weaknesses, according to the extent and validity of these interrelationships among controls. Strengths and weaknesses, in turn, are evaluations of existing organizational patterns and procedures, as measured against judgmental standards of what those controls normally should be. The judgments made in establishing degrees of normalcy, strength, or weakness, depend on the skill and experience of the evaluator—the manager or the auditor.

For example, to be considered normal, the check-writing subsystem described above would exhibit the following controls:

- Adequate segregation of duties (an organizational characteristic) would be applied. For example, the functions of voucher writing, keying, computer processing, check signing, and mailing would be performed separately.

- Adequate authorization (a procedural characteristic) would be applied by requiring authorization prior to vouchering, by computer processing that depends upon supporting master files, and by reviews of supporting documentation prior to signing checks.

- Adequate data validation (another procedural characteristic) would be assured by computer editing programs, as well as by manual review of checks and supporting documents associated with check signing.

This set of controls would be considered normal for the check-writing subsystem. Enhancements beyond these controls could indicate strength. Shortcomings in comparison with these controls could indicate weakness.

A strength in such a system might be computer validation of purchase order files as a prerequisite to voucher processing and check writing. A weakness might exist if procedures for mechanical signing of checks were followed by automatic stuffing and mailing, with no review of supporting documents.

Determination of strengths and weaknesses is critical to the evaluation of reliability of financial statements, as well as to selection of audit steps necessary to render an opinion. Within audit examinations, strengths and weaknesses attributed to systems of internal control have a direct bearing on the nature, timing, and extent of the examination procedures.

Because controls interrelate, they may offset or compensate for one another. In principle, it is possible for a strength to overcome or compensate for a weakness—or conversely, for a weakness to degrade an apparent strength. For example, suppose that the above system did not require a purchase order or prior authorization for the preparation of a voucher. By itself, this is a weakness. However, a compensating strength could be applied by requiring two separate manual reviews and two separate signatures on all checks for $100 or more. Such controls, of course, would not be suitable for high-volume applications.

For any given system, then, controls will interrelate. Where strengths and weaknesses are identified, they should be compared to derive a judgmental evaluation of how the system, as a whole, compares with the reliability required to give reasonable assurance that the system is reliable.

CONTROL FUNCTIONS

Three categories of controls that contribute directly to the ultimate reliability of a computer information system include:

- Preventive
- Detective
- Corrective.

Preventive controls halt processing when an error or exception condition is identified. *Detective controls,* in general, do not halt or prevent processing. Rather, such controls identify actual errors or exceptions that already have taken place. Detective controls, then, are applied after the fact. It is appropriate to note at this point that auditors, when they test either preventive or detective controls, must consider both types. While preventive controls are more reliable, they present difficulties for compliance testing because there is little evidence that controls are being applied. Detective controls, on the other hand, have some documentation or evidence that the control is working and that subsequent corrective actions have been taken.

The most sensitive and crucial control is the *corrective control.* Besides having the ability to detect an error, such controls also correct the error or exception so that processing can continue. Corrective controls can be extremely valuable if they are implemented properly.

Examples of Preventive Controls

In general, preventive controls will be applied through one of the following methods:

- Redundancy of clerical operations
- Machine-applied controls.

Redundancy.   A common example of a preventive control applied through *redundancy* of clerical operations is key verification of previously encoded (or captured) data.

Another preventive control approach that uses redundant clerical techniques is the preparation of adding machine tapes that provide *batch control* totals for groups of transactions. In this technique, a computer or other automated equipment applies the actual control. The computer performs batch totaling functions that are redundant with manual processes. Manual- and computer-produced totals are compared. If the two totals do not match, further processing cannot take place until errors or exceptions are resolved.

Machine-applied controls. *Machine-applied controls* generally abort the processing of either individual items or entire transaction streams. Such preventive controls exercised by computers can be applied either to individual transactions or to entire subsystems. For example, order entry data might include customer account numbers or merchandise item numbers. With input editing, any items not verified in comparison with computer-maintained master files would be rejected and treated as exceptions in subsequent processing. The validated items in the batch would proceed to the next processing step. In this case, input editing, a preventive control, is applied to an entire batch of items before subsequent processing.

Another example of machine-applied preventive controls calls for comparison of the identification label on a computer-maintained file with the identification specified in the program being executed. If there is no match, processing is aborted, and the computer operator is alerted.

Examples of Detective Controls

Detective controls also can be applied either by people or by machines. The differences between machine-detected exceptions and those uncovered through human examination center largely on elements of cost and timeliness.

For example, it is a common practice for computers to generate logs of errors or exception transactions. Typically, reports are generated from these machine-maintained logs immediately after the application itself has been run. In many cases, errors and exception records are maintained on a computer file. The file serves as a follow-up control to be sure that errors encountered on input actually are corrected and that the transactions are re-entered.

One characteristic of such machine-initiated detective controls is that human follow-up is almost always necessary to apply correction. Failure to follow up, then, constitutes a weakness of control. Unfortunately, many installations accumulate large, growing files of uncorrected input errors.

Another type of automated detective control is the *flagging,* or segregating, of processed items on the basis of information content. For example, a payroll system might identify and produce an exception report for all records that indicate more than 65 hours of work in any given week. Similarly, an hourly payroll system might identify and report all gross pay amounts of $1,300 or more.

The process of auditing itself—both internal and external—also can be regarded as a detective control. Internal auditors, in particular, perform frequent reviews and analyses of computer-generated reports. Information is traced back through processing to data sources to test the validity of results. This same process is performed, to a different extent, in annual examinations by external auditors. Such procedures are detective, or after-the-fact, controls. Auditors sample the output of a computerized application as one means of establishing a reasonable, normal level of confidence in the quality of the total processing done within the system.

Examples of Corrective Controls

A corrective control assists in both the investigation and correction of the exception that has been detected. Within an automated environment, decision logic always is needed to assist in resolving the cause of the detected error or exception. Such decision logic can be implemented within the application program.

Further, the alarm provided by a detective control is useless if the system is not monitored. Thus, items that cause errors usually are much more difficult to correct in an automated environment that does not rely on human monitoring for correction. To assure that the system is acting appropriately, all items that are corrected automatically, or under program control, should be processed through detective controls. These controls should be the same as—or more stringent than—the controls applied if a person actually were doing the monitoring. Discrepancy reports, transaction trails, error source statistics, automated error correction, and upstream submission—are all examples of corrective controls commonly implemented within application programs.

In short, corrective controls themselves must be monitored by detective controls. Even when the correction is relatively straightforward, the possibility remains that its processing will be inappropriate. For example, an item that should have been subtracted might have been added instead. The use of detective controls to monitor corrective control actions is essential because the correction process itself is prone to error.

Within a data center or computer information processing facility, examples of typical corrective controls applied manually include: recovery plans, file histories, on-site backup, off-site backup, insurance, and uninterruptable power sources.

Cost Considerations and Trade-offs

Typically, preventive controls are both more reliable and more costly than detective or corrective controls. Preventive controls represent a higher investment in staff time to design, develop, and monitor the controls. Higher reliability stems from the fact that preventive controls, by nature, must be applied to the entire set of items being processed.

By comparison, detective controls, also by nature, can be applied on a sampling or exception basis. For example, detective controls could be applied randomly or only to transactions or functions that contain stipulated characteristics. Corrective controls then may be applied to the exceptions for reversing or corrective actions.

The cost to design, develop, and implement detective controls in an automated environment is minimal compared with the cost of corrective controls. One reason is that corrective controls may require complex logic or processing steps to:

- Revise an entry (or portion thereof).

- Post the right amount to the appropriate category.

Preventive controls are inherently more reliable because they actually prohibit the processing of errors. Detective controls, by contrast, typically permit all data, valid and invalid, to pass through application processing. Detective controls then rely on human follow-up or on corrective controls, which are less reliable than total screening.

Levels of reliance that may be placed upon detective and corrective controls will vary with the technique and timing of their application. For example, computer validation of all transactions for high-dollar exceptions would be considered more reliable and less costly than after-the-fact manual reviews of computer output. Further, since manual follow-up is needed with detective controls, timeliness of application can be important. The sooner follow-up occurs, the more reliable the system will be. Timely follow-up is especially crucial when corrective actions have been taken and transactions have been altered on the basis of automated decision logic.

Thus, there would be greater reliability in a system that called for daily— rather than monthly—review and action on errors and exceptions. But, because of the high processing volumes in many installations, this degree of control is not always practical. Most systems contain a combination of preventive, detective, and corrective controls. The mixture of control methods requires careful judgment by system designers and operators in balancing the trade-off between quality and cost.

Emerging Guidelines

The control "standards void" that greeted the introduction and rapid adoption of computer-based methods to accounting applications is being overcome through application of professional guidelines worldwide. Specific concerns center on the application of controls and the assurance of reliability. As cited in Chapter 2, both professional organizations and the federal government have established guidelines.

Figure 6-3 lists some of the major pronouncements that address areas of financial and organizational control concerns.

American Institute of Certified Public Accountants (AICPA)
• Statement on Auditing Standards #48, "The Effects of Computer Processing on Financial Statements," New York, 1984.

Canadian Institute of Chartered Accountants (CICA)
• Computer Audit Guidelines, Toronto, Ontario: Canada, 1975.

Institute of Internal Auditors (IIA)
• Standards for the Professional Practice of Internal Auditing, Altamonte Springs, Fla., 1978.

EDP Auditors Foundation (EDPAF)
• Control Objectives, 1983, Carol Stream, Illinois.

National Bureau of Standards (NBS)
• FIPS 102, "Guideline for Computer Security Certification and Accreditation," October 1983.

U.S. General Accounting Office (GAO)
• Standards for Audit of Governmental Organizations, Programs, Activities, and Functions, 1981.

Figure 6-3.

This table summarizes the existing professional guidelines for management and audit of CIS.

APPLICATION CONTROLS

The term *application control* has specific, limited meaning within a computer auditing context. An application control applies only to a specific information processing system. Application controls thus meet the needs of a specific, individual information system, and are generally applicable to input, processing, or output.

To understand the nature of application controls, consider the distinction between these measures and *general controls.* General controls (or *environmental controls*) are applied to all jobs run in a given CIS facility. Thus, general controls are universal (and pervasive), while application controls are selective, or specific to given jobs.

In looking at application controls that impact the reliability of financial information, there are three prime areas for concentration:

• Recording, classifying, and summarizing authorized transactions

• Updating files

• Reporting the results of processing.

In each area, the objective is to identify the presence—or absence—of organizational patterns and procedures, and to assure that these processes are being performed reliably. As a rule, no two computer applications will be identical. Even where standard, off-the-shelf programs are used, there will be individual variations in manual processing or in CIS procedures within companies. Packaged applications often are adapted further to suit the style and operating requirements of departmental users. Therefore, each application review should be approached with the expectation that its controls will be tailored to specific application requirements.

Reviews of individual CIS applications should be aimed at determining the following:

- The degree to which controls within individual applications meet standards for reliability

- Whether adequate segregation and rotation of duties exist to assure that persons processing data within the application do not have incompatible functions

- The degree to which general controls within the CIS installation contribute to the reliability of the individual application.

Any application review should extend beyond the bounds of the CIS department. Application processing should be evaluated from its source through to its disposition. Review procedures should include user departments, sources of transactions, and intermediaries or service groups that perform processing or control functions. Within the CIS department, review procedures should include the functions performed by supervisory personnel, by the data input section, by any separate data control group that may exist within the CIS department, and by computer operations personnel.

Controls over individual computer applications fall into four broad categories of concentration:

- *Input controls* cover authorization, conversion, completeness of data, and procedures for rejection or reentry of data.

- *Programmed,* or *processing, controls* deal with actual computer processing and are applied by equipment and software.

- *Output controls* deal with completeness and reasonableness of processing results, as well as the distribution of computer output only to authorized users.

- *Transmission controls* deal with the actual transmission of data and information over communication channels. These important controls interface with the three controls identified above. Managers, auditors, and users must have complete assurance in the validity and integrity of such data.

The general principles of control apply both to batch and interactive, or on-line, systems. Remember that all computer systems are based on the same basic information processing cycle: input, processing, output, and storage. Differences between batch and interactive systems are most apparent in the area of transmission controls. Because interactive systems, by nature, depend on highly responsive data communications, their transmission controls may be sophisticated, complex, and interrelated. On the other hand, data communication in batch applications, if used at all, often is relatively straightforward, as are the controls applied.

Perhaps the most striking difference between control considerations for batch and interactive systems centers around the high degree of responsiveness that is possible with on-line techniques. A person attempting to gain unauthorized access to an on-line system receives virtually immediate feedback on the success or failure of the attempt. Without special controls, many attempts might be made in a relatively short time, thereby increasing the chances of successful penetration without detection. Indeed, some persons using microcomputer-based terminals have been able to break into on-line systems by programming the local computer to generate millions of password combinations.

Controls applied to interactive systems, then, may have to be more complex and interdependent than controls over traditional batch systems. Timeliness of detection and correction also becomes critical. Some of the controls that are particularly relevant to interactive systems are presented below in the discussion of transmission controls.

INPUT CONTROLS

Input controls are aimed at preventing the manual entry of erroneous or inappropriate data into a CIS. Three areas for the application of input control techniques include:

- Data preparation
- Data movement
- Data conversion.

Data Preparation

Data preparation controls apply to the creation of source documents or transaction media for use within a CIS. Effective, computerized data preparation controls typically are more precise—and conform to more critical standards—than controls over similar functions or documents within manual systems. For example, in writing an order for manual processing, personnel frequently abbreviate customer names or use initials. When documents are to be processed within a CIS, these shortcuts are not available. Entries on documents must correspond precisely with those in the computer files.

Possibly the most common control enhancement in the data preparation area is the use of standardized forms. Typically, a source-transaction form associated with a CIS will have separate, printed squares for each character, number, or symbol to be entered by clerical personnel. Such forms also may be controlled through preprinting of entry instructions and prenumbering for transaction controls. The primary objective of using standardized forms is to assure completeness and uniformity of input data.

Another reliability enhancement for source transactions is precoding of transaction documents. A common example of this technique is the encoding of checks with magnetic ink character recognition (MICR) symbols that identify the account and bank numbers. This technique reduces clerical effort in capturing data and improves control by reducing the likelihood of erroneous entries.

A more advanced version of the same approach uses *turnaround documents,* or source media generated by computers and reused for input of new transactions. Typical examples include utility company bills encoded by a computer with optical character recognition (OCR) symbols so that a stub returned by the customer can be used as automated input for the crediting of payments.

Underlying all of these data preparation controls, as well as the input controls discussed below, is a need for clear, uniform, complete, and understandable documentation of the clerical procedures to be followed. In practice, the extent of preparation and use of such documentation varies widely among users.

Data Movement

Whenever computer input documents are moved physically from one point to another, they are exposed to error or alteration. From a control standpoint, the movement of data is a highly vulnerable function. This vulnerability lies more in exposure to accident than to malice.

The chief control technique used in such situations is the creation and verification of transmittal control documents. Typically, source documents move from user to CIS departments in manageable batches. Thus, both the totals and the summary documents involved generally are called batch controls. These totals are developed at the point of origination and can be verified when data are input to and accepted for processing by the computer system.

Control totals used for batches can be of several different types. The most obvious control is over dollar amounts or item quantities when these are appropriate to the source documents being handled. Other controls apply to the number of documents or to other numbers associated with the source documents.

For example, a control total may be developed on the serial control numbers on order forms in a batch. The totals are not used in processing; but, if these totals are developed in the user department and validated in computer processing, there is some assurance that all of the data originally created have been entered into the computer. Because totals of this type have no significance other than for input control, they generally are referred to as *hash totals*.

The use of batch controls serves to assure inclusiveness and a high degree of accuracy in transferring data from paper documents to media for computer processing. Within the CIS department, there should be a control log for entry of batch totals to document agreement of input and output control totals for each batch.

The manually maintained log is an input control. Another aspect of input control can be applied at the organizational level by assigning responsibility for maintaining the log to an independent data control group. Both the maintenance of a control log and the assignment of an independent group to this function illustrate a primary principle in CIS control:

There always must be mechanisms to tie outputs of a system back to initial inputs.

Interdependence exists between input, organizational, and output controls. Any individual control, by itself, would not assure reliability. To deliver reliable results, controls must be established at key points within any system and be related to one another. These points occur any time data are processed clerically, converted, sorted, processed, consolidated, or summarized.

Data Conversion

A commonly used control for the data conversion function is *key verification*. This is a technique using at least partial clerical redundancy to validate the accuracy of data entered into machine-sensible form through keyboarding.

Key verification is one of the oldest control techniques in mechanized data processing. One operator performs the initial data conversion, capturing data on magnetic or other media. Through a second set of entries, possibly on a second machine, another operator reenters either all or at least the critical fields of data for each document. The second set of entries is compared with the first. If the entries do not match, the media are coded accordingly; and the differences ultimately are resolved.

One problem associated with key verification is that there tends to be an over-reliance on this technique. In fact, it is possible to pass through a relatively high number of errors in key verification operations. This is true for any data entry system. For example, verifiers, if programmed improperly, may validate bogus or erroneous fields simply because they have passed through the machines continuously and automatically. Thus, in reviewing the general controls within a CIS installation, observation of data conversion operations is a prerequisite to placing reliance upon this function. Further, the frequency and element of surprise associated with observations can increase the reliance placed upon these controls.

Combined Input Controls

Increasingly, users of batch-entry systems are improving controls and reducing input costs by combining the data preparation and data conversion functions. The use of mark-sensing cards by meter readers for utility companies is one example. Persons reading electric or gas meters place marks on columns in a formatted card to correspond with the positions of the dials on usage meters. The cards can be read directly into computer systems either electrostatically or optically.

In such cases, data movement controls are applied by the computer. Movement controls are accomplished through organization of computer files according to meter-reading routes. Computer input functions verify that one input record is present for each meter due to be read in a given cycle. To assure completeness, inputs would include actual meter reading cards or substitute documents to indicate that readings could not be obtained. This automated procedure accomplishes control over data movement by applying controls to batches of input documents.

At a minimum, data conversion controls are applied by computer programs at two levels. At one level, mechanical checking is performed. The marked cards are passed through machines that sense the positions of pencil strokes and capture the data in computer-sensible format, either by punching the cards on which the marking was done or by magnetic recording on tape or disk. In a typical next step, the newly encoded data are compared with the original mark-sensed documents. If there are discrepancies or if markings are unacceptable or out of position, the input documents will be rejected.

Other approaches have been used to consolidate data preparation and data conversion steps. Some machines create human-readable source documents and computer input media simultaneously. Punched tapes, magnetic tapes, or magnetic tape cassettes may be used to encode data at the same time that entries are being printed automatically on source-document forms. Or, entries on forms or adding-machine tapes may be made in OCR type fonts for later sensing by machine.

Perhaps the most common example of these consolidation techniques has been the widespread use of credit card imprinters that capture all data relevant to a sale at a service station, restaurant, or retail establishment on a data-card sales check. The customer's credit card is placed in the imprinter along with a multi-part invoice. Many imprinters make it possible to record both the customer account number and the amount of the sale in OCR fonts that can be read automatically by computer input devices.

The control significance of such applications is that reliability is enhanced in direct proportion to the elimination of clerical procedures in data conversion. In the case of the imprinted sales check, reliability is enhanced further because authorization is built into the procedure: The customer signs the check after it has been imprinted.

PROGRAMMED CONTROLS

Programmed controls are applied by computers. However, these controls are human controls, since the computer follows routines and instructions written by people. Thus, the major quality factor in programmed controls lies in the planning, specification, and writing of the programs themselves.

Programmed controls are important to reliability in the processing of accounting information because they apply the same types of logical verification procedures performed by people under manual systems. The challenge of implementing these controls lies in the constraints of specific, literal processing steps performed within the computer. Although a person can be relied upon, at least in some measure, to use judgment, the computer does exactly what it is programmed to do—and no more. Thus, a person could be relied upon to use judgment in questioning a payroll time card that indicated the employee had worked 120 hours in one week. But, if this type of control is to be applied within computer processing, the potential error must be anticipated; exact instructions must be established for identifying and correcting such errors.

The Computer as Editor

Typically, programmed controls are applied during a separate, dedicated computer operation that precedes the actual processing of data. If processing is done under conventional batch techniques, programmed controls generally are applied in an initial *edit run*. If data entry is done on-line, programmed controls typically are initiated in an *edit loop*, a program module that performs the acceptance edit checks of data before actual processing takes place.

Increasingly, edit functions are being performed on devices that are peripheral to the main computer. In large batch installations, for example, edit controls frequently are applied by a *front-end* computer, or minicomputer that executes programmed controls. The front-end computer does the *housekeeping* associated with getting jobs ready for processing on the large computer, and also handles output functions.

In on-line systems, the concept of distributed processing offers control opportunities. Under this approach, users work at so-called *intelligent terminals*, or terminals with limited electronic processing and memory capabilities. These capabilities are used to apply the programmed controls associated with input and output of data. These controls are performed locally, or without accessing the central computer.

Edit-type controls also are applied during the actual processing cycles performed by computers. The need for such controls stems from the fact that a computer is, in reality, an assemblage of electronic, electrical, and electromechanical devices functioning in coordination. Thus, computers are subject to either functional or coordination failures among any of their components. Such failures can cause data to be lost, recorded incorrectly, or distorted.

To guard against such occurrences, the computer performs the same type of control checks as those discussed above for the data control group within a CIS department. Under this approach, the computer receives and logs input control totals prior to each processing step. The computer system then accumulates its own batch control totals on the basis of processing and, when each processing cycle has been completed, compares the accumulated totals with those received on input. Any mismatch encountered in a control step causes an interruption in processing.

As part of the programmed controls over processing, a computer system also is able to do its own internal housekeeping. For example, most modern computer systems assign use of internal memory and on-line file devices automatically. Computers also have programmed controls that maintain on-line files automatically.

SYSTEM SOFTWARE AND APPLICATION PROGRAM CONTROL FUNCTIONS

	PRIOR TO PROCESSING	DURING PROCESSING	AFTER PROCESSING
SYSTEM SOFTWARE	Validates internal file labels Allocates computer memory and needed storage areas	Maintains control totals on numbers of blocks of data read from or written to data files Monitors memory allocations in multiprogramming environment to assure no loss of program content due to memory overflow from other programs	Closes all files, validates block counts to trailer labels on input files —generates trailer labels on output files Releases allocated memory to other system uses
APPLICATION PROGRAMS		Validates various data elements in files Maintains and compares control totals of logical records to assure all items have been processed	

Figure 6-4.

Software control functions for system software and for application software are presented in this table.

In general, programmed controls applied within computer systems fall into two broad categories, as illustrated in Figure 6-4:

- System software controls
- Application program controls.

System Software Controls

From a control standpoint, system software is essentially a highly specialized set of programs. The main differences between system software and application programs stem from the fact that system software is provided by a manufacturer or highly specialized vendor and usually is written in machine language for the sake of efficient utilization. A frequently overlooked or misunderstood characteristic of system software is that it is composed of computer programs. As with so many other elements of the computer field, system software has been enmeshed in a mystique. This misunderstanding has resulted largely from the highly technical, extremely detailed nature of the programs involved. But, to understand CIS controls, it should be recognized that system software *is* programming.

This programming, however, does perform a specialized function: System software supports computer operations. It provides the operating routines that make the computer workable down to a level at which application programs can be entered into a system and handled reliably. System software programs are resident in the computer and available for the processing of all application programs prepared and/or executed by computer users.

In general, system software controls can be grouped according to three broad categories:

- Label checking
- Library protection controls
- Memory protection controls.

Label checking.   System software has provisions to protect the integrity of files during processing, as well as to assure the accuracy and validity of any new files generated as a result of processing. This assurance is accomplished with several types of separate, individual controls.

One objective of *label checking* is to make sure that the right data file is being processed by the appropriate application program. Under this type of control, processing instructions from a computer user must specify the application data file to be used. The computer then compares the name specified by the user program with a field containing a label code at the head of the data file to be processed. The two designations must match before processing can take place.

As part of the same series of controls, verifications of file integrity are performed during processing. One of the components of file labels in most computer systems, for example, is a count of the blocks of records contained. On large files, there may be intermediately placed labels for interim verification of record-block counts. Virtually all files have machine-sensible labels at the end, or *trailer labels*, that contain control totals compared with current totals developed by the computer in the course of processing. When the computer writes a new file, it routinely counts the number of blocks used and writes the new trailer label accordingly.

Another control applied by the label-checking capabilities of system software is assurance that a data file presented for processing is the current one—that is, the correct version. As processing proceeds, system software updates file labels to identify the generation, iteration, number, and/or date on which a specific version of a data file is created.

This verification of file version is crucial to reliable processing. Within any application program, data files of successive generations will be highly similar in their appearance to the computer system. The only thing that prevents the system from using and updating the wrong file is this generation-control feature of system software.

For example, one popular make of computer uses a control number of zero (0) to identify the most current version of a data file. As the new file is created, the previous version automatically is numbered "-1" (backup), and so on. The user need only specify that processing be done through the use of the "0" file, and the computer will apply controls from within its own internally maintained index. Thus, if a current version of a file were destroyed inadvertently and restart procedures were triggered through the use of the backup version of the file, an instruction would be entered authorizing the computer to use the "-1" version.

Library protection controls. *Library controls* monitor a computer's files automatically to keep track of the application programs stored at any given moment. Further, when a user calls for execution of an application program, system software requires that the user identify the program, including the proper version of that program, to be executed. System software then verifies a match between the user's identification and the program actually on file at that time.

Memory protection controls. *Memory protection controls* govern the allocation of computer memory and storage to application programs. If a user specifies execution of a given program, system software ascertains that there is enough capacity in main memory to hold this program during execution. Most computer systems currently in use are capable of storing and processing data under multiple user programs on a concurrent basis. Recall that this technique is known as multiprogramming. Within a multiprogramming computer system, anywhere between a few to perhaps 100 or more programs may be in various stages of execution at any given moment. System software, in addition to matching data files and programs for every given processing execution, also must allocate and monitor use of computer memory capabilities. Thus, one of the controls applied by system software is to be sure there is room in memory for a program to be brought from the library for execution.

Two main control objectives can be identified here. First, by verifying that there is enough room for the program, system software prevents loss of program content through overflow of available memory space. Second, by building control tables to indicate memory allocation, system software provides assurance that data or instructions generated by user programs do not obliterate existing memory content.

Application Program Controls

Each application or subsystem processed within a computer-inclusive system must contain its own, unique programmed controls. These controls are incorporated in the application programs that control processing of data within the computerized portion of the system.

Identifying, designing, and implementing programmed controls for applications is, of necessity, a relatively complex process. Responsibilities for defining and designing these controls go far beyond the writing of programs. All parties with a stake in the reliability and usability of results delivered by a CIS must be involved. The processes associated with the design and development of computer applications are discussed in depth in the next chapter. It must be recognized that controls built into applications depend on specifications provided by managers of computer user groups, by auditors, by technical specialists, and by others with a stake in system reliability.

The discussion below covers some of the commonly used techniques for applying controls within application programs. The control techniques are covered according to both level of complexity and probability of utilization within application programs. The most commonly encountered controls are covered first.

Data element checks.   *Data elements,* in general, are units of data that have meaning in an application. Fields within records, for example, may be data elements. Examples of data elements are item number, quantity ordered, price, customer name, customer street address, city, state, and ZIP code.

In one type of *data element check,* it is common for each character entered into the system to be checked through hardware controls for *parity,* or validity of bit format. Then, at the application program level, characters or groups of characters that make up data elements are checked to validate their appropriateness for processing under the specific application program.

One type of data element check involves counting the number of characters entered. For example, if the program indicates that a ZIP code has five digits, a four-digit number would be rejected.

Another basic control measure applied to data elements within application programs is the checking of *data type.* Data type refers to whether data are alphabetic, numeric, alphanumeric, integer, real, and so on. Computers assign memory and perform processing for alphabetic data differently from numeric data. For this technical reason—and also to help assure accuracy—it is standard procedure to prevent numeric data from being entered into fields specified as alphabetic, and vice versa.

Limit, range, and reasonableness checks.　There is a saying among veteran systems practitioners that there are very few small mistakes in computerized systems. Many of the errors that occur tend to be of a gross nature. Therefore, it is the common practice to build programmed controls into individual applications to test for and stop processing of obvious, predictable gross errors.

For example, a programmed test might include a range of account numbers from the first to the last assigned. In *range checking,* any transactions presented with account numbers outside this range would be flagged as errors.

When cash disbursements are involved, it is common to check for limits, or reasonableness. In a *reasonableness check,* time reports of more than 70 hours per week for payroll input would trigger exception conditions. A *limit check* might hold that no salaried employee could be issued a check in excess of $1,000 for a single week.

Logical comparisons.　Application program controls frequently make use of the ability of computers to compare two alphabetic or numeric fields of data and react according to the results of the comparison. For example, a payroll or order processing application might call for the comparison of the names of the parties to the transaction with corresponding names in the master file. If such a *logical comparison* does not produce a match, the transaction is rejected.

Basically, numeric comparisons can adjust processing according to three criteria: A given number is either equal to, greater than, or less than another.

Use of this capability as an application program control can be seen in the common payroll procedure that calls for a test to ensure that net pay is less than gross pay.

In general ledger applications, logical comparison controls are used to protect against the posting of transactions to improper accounts. For example, if a transaction is coded as a cash receipt, an application program might incorporate controls to assure that debit postings for this transaction only can go into an appropriate cash account. This can be done by designating a limited series of account numbers to which the posting can occur.

Calculated controls.   The calculation capacity of computers can be used to apply *calculated controls* at the levels of individual data elements or of complete files.

An example of the validation of data elements through calculation controls is the use of self-checking account numbers. Consumer credit cards offer a common example of this technique. A typical credit card might be identified by nine account-number digits and one *check digit*. When the 10-digit account number is entered into the computer, calculations are performed upon all or some of the first nine digits. The result of the calculation should match the check digit. This technique is a highly reliable method for avoiding transposition of numbers during key entry of data into computerized systems. When automated or optical input techniques are used, self-checking calculations guard against the misreading of numbers.

To make this type of control work, the algorithm for the self-checking calculations must be regarded as highly confidential and must be protected accordingly.

As discussed above, label controls, applied by system software, count blocks of records to help assure that hardware errors or power failures have not caused losses of data. In addition, it is a common practice to program calculated controls that are recorded as the last record on a data file, immediately before the trailer label is created by system software. Capabilities used for such applications include actual, detailed counts of individual records (as distinct from blocks) and control totals covering individual fields within records. Depending upon the size of an individual file, such control totals can be used either intermittently or for the file as a whole. To assure integrity and continuity of processing, subsequent application programs can accumulate totals that are balanced against prior totals to validate accuracy of processing.

OUTPUT CONTROLS

In general, output controls are manual procedures designed to provide assurances in three areas:

- Accuracy and completeness of data generated by a CIS

- Distribution of outputs only to authorized recipients

- Logging, follow-up, and accurate reentry of errors reported by a CIS.

Accuracy and Completeness

The primary technique for assuring that data generated by a CIS are accurate and complete involves balancing outputs back to inputs. These processes are similar to those discussed previously for input controls, most of which rely on comparison of control totals.

In addition, output documents should be scanned by qualified persons familiar with the documents' design and specified formats. In scanning the documents, the reviewer should look for incomplete content—omitted columns or fields of data, for example. The reviewer also should check for unmeaningful, or garbled, content in output reports. For many reasons, computers occasionally do issue reports that are, all or in part, gibberish.

The totally meaningless report presents no major danger from a standpoint of financial reliability, even though it may be highly embarrassing to the CIS department that lets it get through. Of greater concern from the standpoint of financial information control is the report in which meaning is distorted through some malfunction within the system. The sources of such errors can be as simple as a sticky printer element that blanks one column of a report or that prints the same digit repeatedly.

Because output is the payoff for computer-based processing, an important control within any CIS lies in the balancing and inspection for reasonableness of the documents generated. Further, this output inspection should concern itself with completeness of both processing and documentation. For example, when a payroll is processed, the check register should be scanned and its validity confirmed with at least spot counts of the actual numbers of checks generated.

Similarly, output inspection should verify that all pages of a report, as numbered by the computer program, are present when the copies are collated. The reviewer also should look for interim totals and final totals specified for inclusion in reports.

In addition to these reviews of report content, the inspection procedure should verify that reports scheduled to be produced actually have been issued. This inspection should cross-check the computer-generated reports with work orders and computer-room schedules. A computer center in a medium- or large-sized company generates so much paperwork that individual documents, sets of documents, or even voluminous reports easily could be lost in the continuing avalanche of paper.

In particular, there is a tendency for computer-room personnel to pay little or no attention to seemingly routine reports of an accounting or system-protection nature. For example, an accounts payable system may call for a report to be generated as a journal of changes to vendor master files. After two or three days, however, the electronic data for these journalized reports probably will be purged completely from the computer system. Thus, if a report of this type is skipped inadvertently, records of transactions processed by the computer in updating the file may be lost entirely. That is, the operations staff must detect the failure of the system to produce a report before the corresponding data retention cycle has passed.

Authorized Distribution

As discussed previously, assets entrusted to the CIS department can be critical to the operating continuity of the company itself. Controls over these assets are exerted largely through the logging and distribution systems applied to the delivery of outputs to authorized parties—and the avoidance of distribution to unauthorized parties.

In addition, distribution control for computer output documents has an added management dimension. The product of data processing is computer-generated output. Delivery of outputs is the visible, tangible fulfillment of the data processing cycle and its customer service function. Therefore, for document outputs, timely, reliable distribution is the final measure of effectiveness and value.

Factors to be considered in conjunction with the degree and extent of control applied to computer outputs include:

- Privacy
- Confidentiality
- Security.

Privacy. Privacy or sensitivity of data must be protected. Managers generally recognize the need for privacy of such records as paychecks and payroll registers. Similarly, a company's pricing information should be available only to authorized persons. As discussed in Chapter 1, a growing body of law also defines responsibilities to the public in this area. Beyond the letter of the law, careless distribution of computer-generated documents can prove embarrassing, can impair morale, and thus can undermine operating efficiency of the organization.

Confidentiality.   Much of the data generated by a well-managed computer system is proprietary, or company-confidential. The sensitivity of pricing information is an example. Obviously, considerable damage could result if competitors received such information. Also confidential are financial projections, product costing data, or current financial statements that have not yet been published.

Security.   Computer systems also generate volumes of negotiable items—such as paychecks, payable checks, and stock certificates or other securities. Such outputs should be protected with the same degree of care appropriate for the actual currency they represent.

The specific techniques used to apply controls over distribution of computer outputs will depend on the sensitivity, security considerations, and monetary values involved. All computer outputs should be controlled on a distribution log. Additional assurances can involve requiring signed receipts for reports, sending outputs via bonded messenger services, or even using armed security personnel.

An underlying consideration is the interrelationships among the control points after the outputs have left the computer center. From the point of dispatch to the points of receipt and authorized use, separation of functions and other appropriate controls must be enforced. For example, the function of an accounts payable clerk responsible for authorizing disbursements to vendors should be separated from the treasurer's function of actually signing and mailing the checks. Negotiable instruments should never come back to the authorization point.

Error Logging and Reentry

Data processing transactions are prone to error. Further, the most error-prone transactions within any CIS are the corrections for errors already committed. Studies show that the probability of further error increases tenfold in the subsequent processing of an error that already has been committed, as compared with the general run of transactions entering the system.

The consequences of breaches in control associated with the logging and reporting of errors are potentially enormous. No system of controls can be considered fully reliable if it does not include assurance that erroneous transactions will be identified, reported, followed up, reentered, and processed correctly.

The most reliable techniques for error control use a combination of computer and manual methods. Under such approaches, the computer creates a log of all errors identified on input. A serial number is assigned to each error record within the computer-maintained file. This numbered record remains active until it is purged as a result of a transaction verifying that a correction has been entered. Should the correction contain an error, a new error-log record is established and numbered. Each time an error status report is printed, all unresolved errors are listed.

Procedures applied to the correction of errors also are important to system reliability. Specifically, a computer operator should never be allowed to make the necessary decision and override or correct an error at the time of occurrence. Similarly, if a data control group within the CIS department were permitted to enter corrections, the segregation of duties implicit in having the user initiate transactions would be either compromised or lost. As a general rule, then, all errors noted on input should be reported back to and be resolved by users. Correction transactions should originate with users and should be processed under all of the procedures and controls appropriate for normal source transactions.

Under more advanced approaches applied to critical applications, it is possible to program the computer so that an end-product report will not be generated until all errors associated with the application have been resolved. For example, in one general ledger system, all input errors are recorded and maintained in a *suspense account,* or temporary account that must be cleared before a trial balance or financial statements can be produced.

At the other end of the spectrum, older and/or smaller systems may rely entirely on manual logging of errors. Evaluations of systems of this type should concentrate on the ascertainment of separation of duties and of maintenance of adequate manual trails to assure follow-up and reentry for all errors. Without the impartiality of computerized controls over error logs, the system becomes more susceptible to either accidental or intentional data manipulation.

TRANSMISSION CONTROLS

Transmission controls focus on protecting or recovering data within a data communication system. Although transmission controls often involve sophisticated technology, effective control also depends upon human interaction and assurances that the controls are functionally sound.

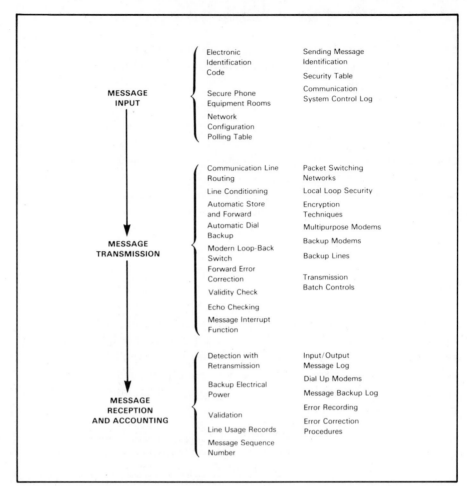

Figure 6-5.

This chart shows transmission controls within a data communication system. Note that these controls form a subset of the overall system of controls presented in Figure 6-1.

Controls within data communication systems are primarily transmission-oriented. That is, protection and recovery measures are applied primarily at the point of origin, which also involves assuring the integrity of communication lines or channels.

In addition to transmission-oriented controls, data entry, computer processing, data storage, and output controls play interlocking roles in the protection and recovery of data. If one of these areas of control is compromised, the vulnerability of the data communication system increases dramatically. Compromise can result from a control that is not functioning properly or from human intervention to override intricate, complementary control processes.

Figure 6-5 presents a set of transmission controls within a typical data communication system. Note that these controls are a subset of the large-system controls shown in Figure 6-1.

An in-depth discussion of technical controls for data communication is beyond the scope of this text. However, from an audit standpoint, key questions on the integrity of data communication include the following:

- Is a unique, hard-wired identification code—that requires *no* human intervention—incorporated into each terminal device?

- Is this identification code checked and validated by the computer to assure that no unauthorized terminals are being used?

- Does the communication system avoid using the general-purpose telephone system, including the internal *private branch exchange (PBX)*, or switchboard? (Routing communications around the PBX reduces the error rate and the exposure to *wiretapping*, or unauthorized interception.)

- Are voice-grade lines used to reduce data transmission errors and to maintain the integrity of transmitted data?

- Are data communication lines *conditioned*, or specially monitored and maintained for low noise and distortion levels, to improve accuracy and physical security?

- Are *encryption*, or scrambling, techniques used in transmitting sensitive data?

- Is an automatic *store-and-forward* capability used to maintain control over messages queued for an inoperative or a busy communication device?

- If leased lines are used, is there a backup capability for assuring that an automatic switchover is accomplished for the duration of any outage?

- Is a *message intercept* function used to receive messages directed to inoperable or unauthorized terminals?

- Are parity checks used to detect errors in transmission of data?

- Are *validity checks* used to compare character signals transmitted with a predefined set of valid characters?

- Is *echo checking* used to verify each character so that erroneous data are detected?

- Are *forward error correction* techniques used for the detection and reporting of data communication errors using sophisticated *redundancy codes?* (Redundancy codes are used in some types of high-speed, synchronous transmissions to perform checks on entire blocks of data.)

- Are techniques available for detecting erroneous retransmissions of data?

- Are modems equipped with *loop-back* switches for fault isolation? (Under a loop-back test, a modem sends a stream of test data to itself. Any discrepancies with the predefined test sequence can be used to trace the source of error.)

These questions address technical control issues in a data communication environment. As data are transferred among different devices, errors usually occur because of distances involved, speeds of transmission, or equipment malfunctions. The inherent complexity of data communication dictates that additional hardware controls be used that are transparent to users. Of the controls listed above, the following are most critical:

- Validity checking of hard-wired terminal identification codes and of data characters being transmitted

- Specially conditioned transmission lines to reduce noise and fading, as well as to minimize amplitude and frequency distortion

- Parity checking of both individual characters and blocks of characters

- Echo checking of characters entered compared with characters received.

Other hardware-oriented controls that can be incorporated in the data communication system include encryption of sensitive data at intermediary points when lines or other devices are inoperative. These controls are designed to make sure that only valid data are entered, transmitted, and received and that no data are lost, accessed, or tampered with along the way.

APPLICATION CONTROL OBJECTIVES

Because computer applications are tailored to suit individual situations, application controls will be designed to accomplish specific, individual purposes. Objectives for application controls, as summarized from several authoritative guidelines, are to assure that:

- All data are processed completely.
- System integrity is maintained and processed data are accurate.
- Data entered into a computerized system are authorized and valid.
- Data transmitted over communication channels are valid and reliable: Integrity of the data has not been compromised.
- Audit or management trails exist in readable form (as documentation) and can be followed or traced to all points within the system.

DISCUSSION QUESTIONS

1. To what extent is the workability of a computer information system related to the degree of reliability that may be placed upon it?

2. In what ways might it not be desirable to have uniform standards of quality that would apply to all computer information systems?

3. How are the existence and interrelationships among controls related to the overall reliability of a CIS?

4. What are the differences among preventive, detective, and corrective controls; and what are the trade-offs associated with each?

5. What is the distinction between general controls and application controls; and how might each be applied?

6. What are the main types of application controls, and what specific controls exist within each of these types?

7. What are the principal objectives of application controls?

CASE ASSIGNMENT

To apply the concepts presented in this chapter, turn to the case study for WhyMe Corporation in Appendix A and work through Project 1, which deals with the auditor's overview of controls.

7 General Controls

ABSTRACT

- General controls encompass organization controls, systems development controls, and operations controls. Organization controls apply to the structuring and management of the CIS function. Systems development controls include the oversight and supervisory functions imposed on development projects. Operations controls are designed to implement the reliability that has been built into computerized systems.

- Specific types of organization controls include segregation of duties, assignment of responsibilities, rotation of duties, and supervision.

- Systems development controls are related to a systems development life-cycle methodology. Controls inherent in the methodology include feasibility studies, development, testing and implementation, documentation, and maintenance.

- Operations controls and operating, or manual processing, controls include physical site controls, operations standards and procedures manuals, library and file controls, as well as backup and restart controls.

NATURE AND TYPES OF GENERAL CONTROLS

General controls apply uniformly to all of an organization's accounting and CIS systems. That is, they are pervasive, or *global,* applying uniformly to every application processed. Thus, general controls affect the strengths and weaknesses of individual applications. General controls impact the reliability of each application and serve as additional strengths (or weaknesses) for the application itself. General control areas include:

- Organization

- Systems development

- Operations.

Organization

The organizational structures associated with the accounting and CIS functions constitute an important control element. With the use of computers, information resources tend to become concentrated in powerful systems. In a conventional, manual accounting system, separation of duties in the processing of transactions is implicit in the multiple steps performed by different people in multiple departments. With large, integrated computer information systems has come greater centralization.

Centralization brings with it increased opportunities for error or irregularities. The very power of such systems to execute relatively concise commands makes them highly vulnerable to intentional or unintentional acts by individuals.

One of the ways of countering this vulnerability is to reimpose controls through organizational structures. A coherent organization plan can help to compensate for the loss of control by dividing tasks among different people, or through the traditional segregation of duties within manual systems.

Organization management controls include documentation and mechanisms that establish relationships between the CIS department and other entities. Also included are the structure and operating principles applied to the CIS department itself.

Systems Development

An important element of financial information reliability lies in building sound application systems and programs, as well as assuring sound operation. Computer application development in most CIS departments is subject to an established life-cycle methodology. That is, distinct phases of effort are identified, which correspond with the delivery of major work products. Management review and approval points coincide with the completion of phases in the life cycle.

An important area of general control is the sponsorship of and adherence to a life-cycle methodology that organizes the development effort into manageable and controllable segments. A management review group, or CIS *steering committee* with oversight responsibility for systems projects, must enforce standards of quality and assure that anticipated organizational benefits are derived from development efforts.

Systems development is an intricate and detail-oriented process that grows increasingly complex as systems become larger and more integrated. A rigorous development methodology also assures a continuity of control as systems efforts increase in scope.

Systems development life cycle (SDLC) controls include policies and standards that apply to the design, development, testing, implementation, and maintenance of application programs and subsystems. These controls also include the standards and procedures for documentation within a CIS installation.

Operations

Operations controls implement the reliability designed into computerized systems during the application development process. Within a CIS installation, operations controls also should exist that implement organizational policy and organization controls.

Other operations controls center around protecting data files and programs, as well as assuring the security of the computer installation itself.

Operating controls, also called *manual processing controls,* are manual procedures within the CIS department aimed at assuring reliability of results from computer processing. Included are physical security measures for the installation itself and the media library, operational separation of duties, and so on.

With this overview, the discussion below explores further each of the general control areas of organization, systems development, and operations.

ORGANIZATION CONTROLS

As cited above, computerization tends to consolidate an organization's data resources. Computerized systems break down or transcend traditional boundaries applied to custody and processing of information within manual systems. This consolidation of custody, in itself, can be a key ingredient in the application of a computer for illicit or accidental loss of control.

For example, in a traditional, manual system, multiple departments and/or different individuals would be involved in the handling of financially significant data. Even a relatively straightforward payroll would involve documentation and procedural continuity among the employee's department, the timekeeper, the payroll department, the accounting department, and the treasurer or controller responsible for executing payroll checks. Within a computerized system, time cards might come directly into a CIS from authorizing supervisors. Processing by computer—within a single department—bridges all the traditional separations up to and including the writing of checks.

Four separate elements can be identified within organization controls:

- Segregation of duties

- Assignment of responsibilities

- Rotation of duties

- Supervision.

Segregation of Duties

Organization controls should be identified and established to provide for adequate segregation of duties within computerized systems. For effective control, segregation of duties requires implementation at two levels. First, there must be separation of duties between the CIS department and the departments that originate or use computer-processed data. These controls must provide assurance that user department personnel do not have access to the CIS area and that, conversely, persons with access to CIS files and records cannot initiate source transactions in the user department. Similarly, persons with access to CIS facilities and files should not have access to company assets, such as stocks of negotiable paper, check signing machines, inventory, or securities.

Within the CIS department itself, there should be an organization plan that assures a clear-cut separation of duties. Functional elements within a CIS plan of organization control should include the following:

- Systems analysis or design personnel should not have access to source programs, to the computer itself, or to data conversion facilities.

- Programmers should not have access to program object media, to data files, or to the computer—except under controlled circumstances associated directly with the development and testing of new programs that have not yet become operational.

- Data control personnel should be identified to serve as an interface with users and other CIS functions. However, these members of the CIS staff should not have access to equipment or files.

- Data conversion personnel should be restricted in their access. They should use their key entry machines or terminals with restricted access capabilities only. They should have no access to computer equipment, other than to special devices dedicated to input creation and balancing.

- CIS operations personnel should not have access to data conversion equipment. Further, access of operations personnel to data files should be limited to authorizing the running of applications only, preferably under control of a library function. Programming documentation never should be available to CIS operations personnel.

- The data library function should be separated from operations. If the installation can support a separate person or persons for this responsibility, the function should be segregated, both physically and organizationally, from operations. If an installation is too small for a full-time librarian, someone who does not have access to the computer should be assigned to this function. In some installations, the data entry supervisor doubles as data librarian.

Assignment of Responsibilities

Work tasks and sequences must be structured so that all tasks within full processing sequences are assigned as specific responsibilities. One of the most common problems within computerized systems stems from failure to determine such responsibilities. Then, when something does go wrong, it can be impossible to tell where it happened or who committed the error or infringement. Computerized systems tend to be involved and complex. A major control potential, therefore, lies in making sure that a specific staff member is responsible for each processing step within the full scope of every application. This control principle applies to both manual and machine functions within the total system.

Rotation of Duties

Another technique for providing general control through the CIS organization plan is the *rotation of duties.* Job assignments of CIS personnel should be rotated to assure that no one person gains a level of cognizance or repetitive exposure to a given application. Otherwise, continued assignment to the same functions can encourage either a high rate of boredom or a temptation to tamper with the system. For example, techniques should be in place that rotate responsibilities for data capture for a given application among data entry operators. Similarly, if a computer installation has more than one operator on duty at a time, job responsibilities should be rotated on an irregular basis.

Supervision

A CIS function must be organized so that there is dual responsibility each time the capability to process transactions is present. Supervision is the controlling element of this dual responsibility. Since a computer is necessary to accomplish any change to information resources, the person operating the computer or terminal represents one element of dual responsibility. The operational supervisor who observes, authorizes, and approves the activity is the other element.

CIS processing consists of three distinct components—equipment, software, and data. Any time equipment is brought together with operating programs and/or data files, responsible supervision must be in place.

Supervision can be applied in either of two ways. First, a responsible supervisor actually can observe or monitor the use of equipment in processing operations. Second, the systems themselves can be set up to produce logs of all significant transactions. These logs then would be reviewed in detail by a responsible supervisor.

Ideally, elements of both types of supervision should be present. That is, if batch processing is being performed, a responsible supervisor should be physically resident in the computer center. If on-line or distributed systems are involved, someone must oversee the activity at remote sites. However, it would be unrealistic to expect a supervisor to note and inspect every operation in detail. Therefore, a log of significant computer transactions always should be created. This log then should be reviewed and approved by a responsible supervisor as a matter of routine.

Almost all computer systems generate such transaction logs. All too frequently, however, the logs are rolled up, wrapped with a rubber band, and placed on a shelf without any meaningful scrutiny. When transaction logs are on magnetic tape, the reels tend to move directly into archival storage.

Supervisory requirements also extend to assuring that all uses of equipment, data files, and software are authorized. Within a CIS organization plan, it is common practice for data files and programs to be maintained in a library separate from the operations center. However, on the day an application is to be run, several data files and application programs typically will be transported in a group to the computer room.

Where adequate controls exist, nothing leaves the data library unless an authorized job ticket is presented. In some shops, the computer generates its own file requisitions, which are printed on a terminal in the data library. Even then, however, exposures to alteration or tampering exist. For example, magnetic media that are transported and handled carelessly are subject to inadvertent alteration. Magnetic fields, such as those produced by running vacuum cleaners or ringing telephones, can corrupt data or program files that are in close proximity.

One control technique that inhibits intentional modification of media is a strict separation between source code programs and object code programs. Generally, operations personnel involved in running active applications will have access only to object programs, that is, to programs coded in machine language. Such programs are much more difficult to alter than source code programs. Carrying this type of control to its next logical level, many organizations have adopted the practice of encoding object programs only in machine-sensible form, usually on tapes or disk packs.

In some instances, segregation of responsibilities can be incorporated in all three elements of the system: equipment, software, and data files. The equipment installation can be segregated physically into separate rooms. In one such installation, tape drives used for application files are in a closed room with the file media. Voice commands are issued over an intercom by a controller, who instructs operators by identifying tapes to be mounted. Identification is by file number and by tape drive. At the conclusion of a run, labels for new tapes are generated automatically by a computer terminal. People working in this area have no access to the computer processing equipment or to input devices. In large computer systems, it is common for tape drive operators to receive mounting directions from a CRT dedicated to that function.

In such a facility, input devices also are segregated from the central processor. Persons bringing in jobs to be run must be cleared for security. The security clearance is based both on the individual's authorization and on the legitimacy of the job itself. That is, each person presenting a job must be cleared for access to both programs and data files.

Within the central processor area of this installation, personnel have no access to input or output media. Further, the operating system software stored within the computer has been either stripped of utility routines or has had such routines moved to controlled libraries. Such utilities would make it possible to alter programs within the on-line object code libraries. Thus, the only way new programs can be introduced in such a system is as original system input. Alteration of existing programs resident in the computer, then, is difficult within normal operating cycles.

SYSTEMS DEVELOPMENT LIFE CYCLE CONTROLS

Controls on the systems development life cycle (SDLC) govern human interactions in the transition from user requirements to system implementation. That is, controls are applied throughout the process of systems development, from the analysis of user needs to the implementation of the systems, elements, and programs for an accounting or other CIS application. Such controls are broader than those that simply guide the writing of code for application programs. Certainly, controls over coding must be included. But, if the data are to be reliable, the entire scope of controlled results must come within the span of these controls. Procedures must exist for involving data users, auditors, top managers, and others with a stake in the reliability of financial data generated by computerized systems.

As shown in Figure 7-1, SDLC controls can be classified in five broad categories:

- Feasibility study
- Development
- Testing and implementation
- Documentation
- Maintenance.

Feasibility Study

Almost without exception, a computerized system that proves unreliable will be one in which a thorough, formal feasibility study was either shortcut or circumvented. The quality of an implemented system reflects the initial planning that preceded its development and implementation.

Discussions in later chapters focus on the structure of feasibility studies and other developmental efforts leading to implementation of a CIS. At this point, remember the importance of investing time and money in a feasibility study. A commitment to study the feasibility of each new system or application is, in itself, a major contribution to a company's overall control and reliability program.

In the process of conducting feasibility studies, it also is important to involve managers who are at a level appropriate to the significance of the data

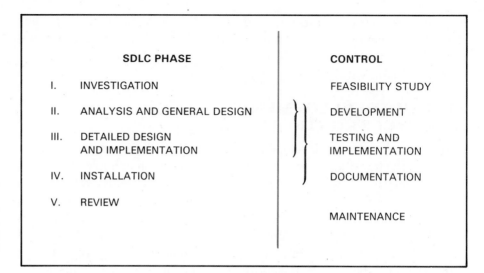

Figure 7-1.

This table shows a five-phase systems development life cycle (SDLC) and the aspects of control applied within each phase.

being processed. A manager who reviews both user specifications and technical implementation plans for systems projects should be at a senior level in the user area. That is, the manager should supervise the person or department that will be using the data. The manager who is responsible for the review also should have an understanding of the data and their value to the organization. Thus, the manager either may be the head of the department for which a system is being developed or may be in a position to make management decisions based on summary data from reports produced by the system.

Feasibility Study Considerations

In general, feasibility studies center around four major considerations:

Economics. Each new application or subsystem should justify its cost. Justification can lie either in savings over existing methods or in the value of newly developed information. In either case, a responsible manager should evaluate the proposed application and affirm that the organization actually will derive sufficient benefits to make the investment worthwhile.

Timeliness. One of the increasingly common reasons for computerizing business applications is that existing, manual methods within an organization just do not deliver information in time for appropriate actions or decisions. Availability of data within time frames important to the overall operation of an organization can be an important justification factor in itself.

Accuracy.   Standards of accuracy demanded for a system under consideration should be appropriate to the business and to the specific job at hand. For example, if a company now is reaching decisions satisfactorily on the basis of approximations, it may be a waste of resources to invest in a computerized system that details transactions minutely. Depending on the situation, it is unwise either to buy more accuracy or to settle for less than is needed.

Flexibility.   In any feasibility study, it should be assumed that the system under consideration will be modified within three to five years. This view reflects the pace of change in organizations. From the outset, users, managers, and auditors should satisfy themselves that the proposed approach will remain adaptable to changing business conditions.

Weighting Feasibility

The feasibility elements described above will carry different emphasis and weighting according to the needs and situations of individual organizations. For example, a wholesaler might put a premium on timeliness in order processing because of such factors as customer service, competition, efficient truck loading, and so on.

Similarly, a bank or savings institution would put a high premium on accuracy. Concerns for accuracy multiply as proposed systems integrate customer and transaction files. Such integration can reach a point at which conventional audit trails disappear.

Economy of individual applications would be critically important to an organization with information-intensive products or services—such as an insurance company. In such cases, the spreading of fixed costs over additional applications and the saving of fractions of pennies on individual transactions can be significant. Conversely, economic considerations are relatively more important to smaller organizations. The smaller the company, the greater the financial impact of the investment in a given application.

Flexibility as a consideration in feasibility studies applies to all sizes and types of organizations. Small organizations need flexibility because their managers frequently plan for growth. In larger entities, constant change is inevitable; readiness for change remains a measure of management effectiveness. This is not to say that small companies are not affected by change. However, the potential cost impact of a given change generally increases in proportion to an organization's size.

Development

From a reliability standpoint, major control considerations in the area of application development lie in:

- Encouraging users and other interested parties to define their requirements for the system.

- Providing assurance that these requirements actually are met by the CIS staff or systems project team.

Problems typically center around communication. Often, it is surprisingly difficult for data users to express themselves clearly to CIS technicians. It may be equally unusual for qualified CIS technicians to explain what they are doing to the satisfaction of users.

To communicate effectively in the systems area, an organization needs a set of CIS standards. These standards should include both terminology and procedures. The people involved must agree and train themselves to use this common ground: The same terms must mean the same things to all participants.

Within the CIS function itself, standards also must apply both to the naming and definition of data. For example, it simply would not be workable for one programmer to use the term "on-hand balance" in an inventory application while another programmer, working with the same data elements, used the term "current balance." In the same company, a third programmer might use the term "inventory quantity" to refer to the same item, and so on. Once a data element enters any system within the organization, there must be mechanisms and procedures in place to assure that it is referred to in the same way—and stored and handled uniformly—throughout all applications.

Similarly, there should be standards governing programming languages used for significant applications. Insofar as possible, applications that relate to one another in a processing continuity or that use common data files should be written in the same programming language. At the least, uniformity of programming language for related applications will assure reliability in review and audit functions. In addition, however, reliability is enhanced when all the programmers within an installation are trained in and familiar with a single, standard language. Language standardization reduces the problems associated with both application incompatibility and personnel turnover within the CIS department.

Control also is enhanced by the practice of establishing milestones, or checkpoints, within any systems development effort. As a general rule, any time an identifiable end product, or deliverable, is created, it should be subjected to review and approval. Deliverables include program modules, documents, decision tables, logic charts, and documentation.

The establishment of milestones will vary from one project to another. Work will have been under way through much of the investigation and analysis phases before specific deliverables can be defined. However, some major deliverables are inherent in life cycle development methodologies. Project phases and activities are structured around types of work products that are encountered in building almost any system. For example, it would be natural to expect that review and approval points would coincide with completion of user specification documents, code walk-throughs, and acceptance tests.

Increasingly, the computer itself is being used to enhance understanding and communication between users and CIS personnel involved in systems development projects. It is becoming fairly common, for example, to find installations that use generalized reporting software to develop samples of reports or documents for review by users. In such situations, data are culled from existing applications, entered into the computer, and output on forms that illustrate exactly what the user will see after the application has been implemented. Thus, the user is in a much better position to determine the value and appropriateness of reporting formats and content. The simulated report provides a much more realistic picture than a layout drawing with letters or numbers that indicate where meaningful data will appear.

Another important element of control associated with systems development lies in ensuring that both internal and external auditors will be involved in design and review processes. Involving auditors in the development process greatly enhances the probability that the resulting application will be reliable.

Testing and Implementation

Almost without exception, new CIS applications are so complex that bugs, or programming errors, are bound to occur. Where significant data are concerned, therefore, procedures for testing a new application and bringing it into useful service must be designed to identify and correct such errors.

In terms of system reliability, implementation is the critical point within the life cycle of a new system. During implementation, reliability either is achieved or is lost. The controls that have been designed into the system prove to be either effective or inadequate. Because of the potential impacts on system reliability, a careful, controlled sequence of activities must be established to govern the testing and implementation portions of a systems development project.

These procedures should anticipate as many points of failure within the new application as is humanly and creatively possible. Then, methods must be established to test the consequences of these anticipated failures. Controls that are built into the system to identify, deal with, and recover from these failures must be exercised thoroughly before the system becomes operational.

The degree of care applied and the quality achieved in testing and implementation activities can determine how well a system is received when it is placed in production. Cooperation and responsiveness of all parties involved are more likely if there is confidence about reliability. Conversely, if a new application is seen as unreliable during its initial months of service, it remains suspect for many more months to come. Suspicion and reluctance may carry over long after the problems have been corrected and reliability actually has been achieved.

Procedures established for quality control during testing and implementation should be applied repeatedly. There should be continual double-checking up to the moment when the system is turned over to its users and to CIS operations personnel. At this point, the development team usually is disbanded, and responsibility for subsequent maintenance is transferred to another group in the CIS department. Testing and implementation controls are applied broadly in three phases:

1. Initial testing

2. System and parallel-run testing

3. Conversion.

Initial Testing

Initial testing concentrates primarily on computer programs and their associated operating procedures. During this phase of development, tests are conducted with collections of data assembled specifically for this purpose. Included in test data should be a meaningful sampling of actual transactions associated with the application at hand. It should be determined that normal data actually are processed as intended.

In addition, however, initial testing should include transactions that represent a sampling of every conceivable error condition or combination of conditions anticipated within the new application.

It is important to understand that initial testing of programs introduces errors and seeks to find points of failure—deliberately. For each program to be incorporated within the new system, as many errors or failures as can be anticipated should be processed to determine the capability of the system to recognize and deal with exception situations.

For the most part, the initial testing function is carried out entirely within the CIS department. Bugs are corrected, and then programs are retested under the same error conditions. Programs should satisfy CIS personnel before the computerized portions of the system are exposed to users and others in the organization. Exposing programs that are not fully debugged to users can undermine confidence in the emerging system.

System Integration and Parallel-Run Testing

After the programs have satisfied CIS management, the new system is tested as an integrated whole. This testing is done under conditions that are as close to normal as possible. This means that user personnel must be involved in normal, functional roles. It also means that live data are processed. Also under test at this point are the written procedures, the training applied to user personnel, the procedures applied to actual operation of the computer—in short, all operational elements of the new application.

When the new system is tested, the old, existing application probably still will be in operation. This seeming dual capability is desirable—in fact, it is essential in most situations. It is a common practice in the implementation of significant CIS applications to run the old and new systems in parallel for a while. Parallel operation continues for a sufficient period to prove the reliability of the new system before discarding the old one.

Under this parallel processing, reliability is established by comparing results of the old and new systems, and then reconciling any differences. This comparison should be done for every processing cycle within the application. Only after the new system has proved reliable for a predetermined number of cycles should the old one be discontinued.

Conversion

The reliability of a new computer-based processing application can be affected strongly by the timing of the actual conversion to the new system. At stake are the integrity of the files that support the application. If the new application impacts the reliability of outputs, the operating continuity of the organization itself can be affected.

Conversion should occur at a logical transition point within each application. For example, a logical time to convert payrolls is at the first of the year. This timing corresponds with the closing out and restarting of with-holding tax and other governmental reporting files. Similarly, a logical time to convert a general ledger application is on the first day of a new fiscal year. If a new application is to account for inventories, conversion should take place as close as possible to the planned completion of a physical inventory count.

To assure reliability of a new processing application, conversion activities have three key requirements:

- The integrity of data files should be maintained while transferring from the old procedures to the new ones. Validation and balancing should be completed before conversion to the new application.

- The audit trail must continue to exist and function properly throughout the activity involving planning for and implementation of conversion. The auditor is responsible for evaluating and determining the degree of reliance that can be placed on internal controls within each financially significant application. Thus, if a significant application were changed in midyear, the auditor would have to evaluate and examine two systems separately. Clearly, such an approach would add to examination costs.

- Control over the personnel training aspects of system conversion is more effective if schedules are tied to the normal operating cycles of the organization. For example, in some entities, operations are geared to create new files and institute new procedures at the beginning of the year. In other cases, fluctuating work loads may be a factor. For instance, department stores simply would not consider installing new transaction processing systems just before Christmas, during their heaviest sales period.

Documentation

Simply stated, documentation *is* the CIS it describes. That is, a viable system does not exist unless it is documented fully. The reliance on documentation may be necessary because people make mistakes. People forget. Also, in the CIS field, people change jobs frequently. Thus, in a well-run CIS department, documentation is the insurance policy that assures continuity of service.

Given this importance, it becomes apparent that documentation should be complete enough so that any qualified person could use it to keep the CIS function and its applications running. To minimize disruption, documentation must be kept current. The system must be represented and described according to the way things actually are done at present.

Unfortunately, attitudes and practices in CIS departments often do not acknowledge the critical role of documentation. As occurs with too many other aspects of control, documentation slips to the end of the list of priorities. In fact, documentation probably is the most neglected control in most CIS shops. Many otherwise professional CIS and user personnel simply fail to update documentation when they change a system. Many who recognize that documentation should be updated underestimate its importance and, therefore, neglect to do so. These people are confident that they know what they are doing. They assume incorrectly that it is sufficient to carry organizationally important information around in their heads.

The problem is compounded by another all-too-common practice. In a typical case, the services of a skilled systems analyst are in great demand. As one systems project nears completion, CIS supervisors are anxious to give the analyst another assignment. Investing the analyst's time in developing complete documentation tends to be regarded as a luxury. The next project often is regarded, understandably in many cases, as more important than the application that already is operational, but undocumented. Thus, working reports may be accepted in place of full documentation, even though such reports are not intended for this purpose and almost always are inadequate.

If documentation does exist, some key criteria can be used to verify its adequacy. These criteria include:

- Adherence to organizational standards for systems work

- Modularity of documentation for ease of updating

- Use of computer-assisted documentation techniques

- Maintainability of documentation.

Standards for systems work.   Standards should exist within the CIS shop for quality in systems work and for the documentation of that work. These standards themselves should exist as documentation that is kept current. The existence of a standards document indicates that organizational and CIS management have made an important commitment. The existence of standards implies that the organization has made a concerted investment in management thought and other resources to enunciate and commit to paper a set of systems policies and philosophies.

If such standards are to represent working control within the CIS department, someone should have specific responsibility for making sure that the standards are enforced. Activities should be monitored to ensure that documentation is updated as appropriate and that revisions conform to standards. A recent trend in some CIS departments is to designate *quality control specialists,* either within project teams or as a separate departmental function that consults with all project teams. *Documentation specialists,* or technicians specifically trained in the writing and organizing of systems documentation, are employed in most large CIS organizations.

Modularity.   Another documentation practice that helps assure control is insistence on documentation that is modular and easily changeable. Documentation should be updated concurrently with changes in computer-based systems. In general, each section—probably each page—of a manual or set of standards should be individually replaceable. Thus, when changes are made, only the affected pages or sections need to be redone. The value of this capability can be seen in considering that up to 50 percent of systems analysis time in CIS installations is expended in changing existing systems.

A related benefit of documentation modularity is the ability to understand quickly what portions of a system have been changed. Version numbers and dates on pages or sections should tell systems analysts, auditors, or anyone attempting to gain an overview of the system what modules within the system have been changed or updated.

Computer-assisted documentation.   Increasingly, documentation can be both protected and updated by applying the computer itself to document the systems or applications it will process. Computer-assisted documentation techniques include automatic flowcharting and/or data flow diagramming, the preparation of diagnostic or descriptive narratives from source programs, and the use of computerized text-editing techniques for storage, revision, and retrieval of manuals or standards.

Maintainability.   Maintainable documentation results from orderly and uniformly applied procedures that encompass classification, retention, and backup. These procedures ordinarily would be included within corporate systems standards. In general, CIS documentation should be cataloged, maintained, and protected at three different levels:

- Department (installation) level

- Application level

- Program level.

This multilevel approach assures that the documentation will reflect the hierarchy, or structure, of the system it describes. Note that proceeding from the departmental level to the program level is inherently top-down, that is, from the general to the specific. Again, the rationale is that methodology reflects the logic and structure of the system, and, hence, leads to ease of understanding and maintainability.

Department (installation) level. Organizational standards for documentation fall under the category of documentation at the departmental, or CIS installation, level. In addition, there should be manuals or guides for computer processing activities common to all applications. For example, there should be a key-entry standards manual, an operations manual, a security manual, a data-control manual, and so on.

Application level. Documentation for CIS applications should include manual, as well as computerized, portions of any given system. Application documentation, in a sense, ties together the activities of source-data, user, and CIS departments. Within the CIS function, application documentation provides connecting threads among the documents or standards for individual application systems. At minimum, documentation of each application should:

- Include a narrative describing the purpose of the system, its objectives, and the actual functions performed.

- Depict processing as application flowcharts or data flow diagrams drawn at a general, systems level. Flowcharts can be drawn manually or prepared with the aid of the computer.

- Illustrate forms and transaction/inquiry screen formats.

- Specify data elements, records, and files.

Within the overall scope of CIS operations, application-level documentation is the common denominator for communication and understanding among systems professionals, operations staff, computer auditors, and management.

Program level. Program-level, or technical, documentation within a CIS installation also should be at a level appropriate to its audience. That is, the format and vocabulary of documents should be commensurate with the technical qualifications and need-to-know of users. For example, there should be a high-level set of program documentation that requires relatively little technical expertise or sophistication for comprehension. The level should be readily understandable to user management and operations personnel. Examples of this level of documentation include narrative descriptions, block-diagram flowcharts showing programming logic, record layouts, and report or form layouts. At this level, programming documentation can be thought of as an interface between sophisticated users and CIS technicians.

Programming, of course, also should be covered by documentation that is universally suitable to technically qualified persons who might be reviewing or modifying programs. Such documentation should include source program listings, computer operating instructions, a program test plan, test data, and results of testing during systems development.

Within the CIS function, documentation is only as good as the degree to which it is used. Thus, part of each installation's controls—and part of the annual audit review—must focus carefully on standards and documentation. There must be assurance that documentation is current and that it actually is being followed in the day-to-day operation of the CIS department and in the user-area processing of computer-related data. Particular attention must be paid to the updating and maintenance of accurate documentation of systems as they actually are being applied.

Maintenance

The cost of a major computerized system is usually in a range that requires approval of an organization's president or board of directors. Yet, the day after a system representing six- or seven-figure expenditures is implemented, the controls applied by management scrutiny may begin to unravel. If adequate maintenance controls are not in place, a production system can be destroyed systematically by relatively low-level staff members.

All too often, it is common practice to apply stringent controls over the development of systems, only to leave their modification and maintenance in the hands of operators, analysts, or anyone else who happens to get involved. Absence or ineffectiveness of maintenance controls must be regarded as a major exposure to defalcation or fraud. Within computer systems, fraud often has been perpetrated through unauthorized modification of systems that originally were designed to be reliable.

Requirements for control—and potential consequences of lapses in control—increase in proportion to the amount of maintenance activity that takes place in a CIS department. As indicated above, it is not uncommon to find installations in which maintenance accounts for 50 percent or more of systems analysis time. It should be assumed that the more maintenance is performed on existing systems, the greater the exposure to either intentional or accidental breaches in control.

Three essential types of controls should be applied to program and application maintenance activities within any sizable CIS operation:

- Authorization
- Program changes
- Testing and documentation.

Authorization. As stated repeatedly in this text, CIS files and programs are major corporate assets that should be protected under measures at least as stringent as those applied to the assets entrusted to a company's treasurer. Within this context, controls over authorizations of changes are the most critical factors in determining whether CIS assets actually are secure.

One control technique over such authorizations is to order changes only with preprinted, prenumbered, multi-part forms. Systems analysts or programmers, then, would not be allowed to access master source programs without such authorization forms, signed by an appropriate manager or executive. When modifications are made to programs, copies of the authorization form must become part of all levels of documentation. One copy should go to a numeric control file. Other copies should update user records, program-level documentation, and, if appropriate, application-level documentation.

Further, authorizations for modifications of existing programs should be secured and documented at two different levels:

- Management should authorize the expenditure of the resources necessary to make the changes. Authorization should be obtained even if a programmer or systems analyst will spend as little as a half day making the change.

- The user of the application should be asked to stipulate that the authorized change does not infringe upon or compromise the reliability of the application or abridge any controls originally specified.

Program changes. Computer programs, in themselves, are mechanisms of control. Unauthorized tampering with programs, therefore, should be guarded against with the same diligence that an organization might expend, for example, in making sure that no unauthorized people work on its burglar-alarm systems.

A starting point, as stated above, is to require authorization before any changes can be made. Additional control measures should be applied to the modification of source code programs. Source programs should be stored in a controlled environment within the data library. The programs should be issued to assigned programmers only on the basis of valid authorizations. These procedures never should be abridged. Even if changes are needed on an emergency basis, a qualified manager must review the situation and approve the modification.

It should be absolutely, irrevocably prohibited for operators or programming personnel to *patch* object programs within a CIS installation. A patch, as the term is used in the industry, is a machine-language instruction entered at the operator's console or through a peripheral device to modify the machine-language version of the program resident in computer memory. (When punched card decks were in common use, a patch also could be made by substituting cards in an object-program deck.)

Patching was a relatively common practice during the late 1950s and early 1960s. Frequently, patching was a daily occurrence—the only way to get a job to run at all. The potential dangers of this practice have become recognized by CIS professionals. At the same time, the magnitude of the exposure has multiplied with the advent of larger, more complex, computers. However, even with this general awareness, some veteran systems practitioners have maintained that patching is a necessary, viable expedient for getting work out. However, if reasonable assurance is to be asserted in the reliability of its systems, a CIS facility cannot afford to waiver on this point:

> *In a controlled CIS department, the act of patching an object program should be grounds for immediate dismissal.*

Because program changes could permit either intentional or accidental misappropriation, the integrity of an installation's programs should be a mandatory, primary concern of both internal and external auditors. One common practice in annual audit examinations is to recompile source programs and then to reprocess application data under the recompiled version. Performing this procedure is straightforward and is a superficial—but telling—method for determining that no major tampering has taken place with the programs.

An example of emerging controls that prohibit program patching can be seen in efforts undertaken by the Inspector General of the U.S. Air Force. As a control measure, the internal auditors of the Air Force insert control algorithms into object programs that are to be run at Air Force installations throughout the world. These algorithms perform calculations upon totals accumulated within the program of its binary switching functions. A random patch by a programmer unfamiliar with the algorithm would cause a variation in the switching functions and, thus, a program halt. To make this control work, the internal auditors, for their part, do not have access to Air Force computers.

Testing and documentation. Following each modification, every application and program should be documented fully, up to installation standards. That is, each change should be documented fully and added to existing records. Further, flowcharts and source programs also should reflect the changes. Each time a program is changed, it should be tested with the same set of data—including erroneous data—that was used for the original application. All of the work, including the tests, should then be incorporated in documentation, as described in the discussion above on documentation controls.

OPERATING, OR MANUAL PROCESSING, CONTROLS

Operating, or manual processing, controls encompass all of the manual procedures, policies, and physical devices (other than the computer equipment itself) that assure functional reliability and, indeed, the very existence of the computer center. These control measures and techniques include:

- Physical site controls
- Operations standards and procedures manuals
- Library and file controls
- Backup/restart and disaster recovery controls.

Physical Site Controls

Physical site controls encompass:

- Physical security measures over access to a computer facility
- Devices that protect against catastrophe, such as sprinkler systems, radiation-proof vaults, and fire-resistant storage facilities.

Physical security measures.   Physical security is, in itself, a complex subject about which entire books have been written. Accordingly, an in-depth discussion of this topic is beyond the scope of this text.

As an investigative technique, a manager or auditor evaluating such controls should try to simulate the thought processes of someone attempting to gain illegal or illicit access to the computer center or its files. The thought processes and patterns of behavior then should be compared with the access controls applied by the physical security system. If this cursory exercise uncovers weaknesses, it can be assumed that a trained person with harmful intent could gain access.

Physical security measures should recognize that commission of fraud through the use of a computer requires four elements: equipment, programs, data files, and documentation. Thus, each of these elements should be individually and separately secured against malicious intent.

Protection devices. Protection devices chiefly are designed to prevent damage to computer resources from fire. A computer facility should have sensitive smoke and heat detection devices that trigger fire extinguishing systems.

Potential threats also include, of course, such natural disasters as earthquakes, floods, and violent storms. Some of the safeguards in these areas are addressed in the design and construction of the physical plant. Most protection equipment for such threats is designed to deal with accompanying disruptions to electrical power. Backup generators, power line conditioners, and power monitors fall into this category.

Disaster prevention plans also should consider that electrical service and computer power supplies create a potential for igniting fires, especially at times when the computer center is unoccupied. Thus, whenever files, documents, or programs are not in use, they should be stored in fire-resistant housing, either in a vault or in an adequate safe. Priorities within a documented protection plan should call for the greatest, most continuous protection for the most critical files, documents, or programs.

Where malice is concerned, any computer system is subject to virtual obliteration at the hands of a person with a magnet. In recognition of this exposure, magnetic detectors are becoming relatively common surveillance equipment at entrances to computer installations. Further, many installations are storing magnetic media in special vaults lined with lead to protect against stray magnetic fields, which can be created by office equipment, air conditioners, radiation devices used in industry, and so on.

Again, in evaluating catastrophe prevention measures, the manager or auditor should attempt to simulate the thought processes of a would-be file destroyer. Also, evidence must be obtained that an uninterruptible power supply system is available to assure uninterrupted processing in the event of natural disaster.

Operations Standards and Procedures Manuals

As stated previously, every computer installation should have specific standards and procedures manuals covering operations. Most operations managers, when confronted with this requirement, will nod and indicate they have these documents—that all is well. The problem, typically, is that the standards and manuals have been prepared neatly, placed on a shelf, and then forgotten.

In other cases, problems arise because procedures manuals have been prepared on the basis of the capabilities of highly experienced, competent operators. These people may feel they do not need to refer to the documentation. Often, they regard their specialized knowledge as a kind of job security. Having these people available can become a rationale for not supplying more detail. However—apart from the inherently poor practice that this attitude represents—situations may arise when these operators are not available for consultation. New hires may have to be trained during peak operational periods; and systems may have to be restarted by less experienced personnel in the event of a major disaster that injures or incapacitates key operations personnel; systems analysts who are unfamiliar with the systems may need to use the manuals to gain an overview understanding. Manuals generally fall far short of guiding people in such situations.

The manager or auditor should regard operating standards and procedures manuals as highly important controls. Accordingly, these controls should be tested periodically. This can be done through observation to determine if the standards and procedures described in the manuals actually are being followed in the day-to-day operation of the computer center.

An important element of any set of standards or manuals should be the requirement that operators maintain logs on which any unusual events or failures are recorded, according to time and in detail. If such logs do not exist or are not kept faithfully, a major control weakness is indicated.

Library and File Controls

In addition to the physical protection measures described above, each computer installation should have a data library and procedures that control access to programs, data files, and documentation.

One important data library control centers around assurance that all file media—card decks, tape reels, disk packs, etc.—are clearly and accurately labeled. That is, external labels must be affixed to or marked upon the data media themselves. For example, with decks of cards, it is common practice to write the name of the file or program across the top of the card deck. On tape reels and disk packs, pressure-sensitive labels usually are affixed to identify both the volume and the file content. Procedures should be in place to assure that all labels are current and that all information they contain is accurate.

Library procedures should assure that only authorized persons receive files, programs, or documents—and that these persons acknowledge their responsibility at the time of each issuance. Each time a file is removed for processing, controls over data files should assure that a new file will be generated and returned to the library. If appropriate to the backup system in place, both the issued and the new files should be returned together, with the prior versions serving as backup.

Control is enhanced by the practice of maintaining an inventory of file media within the data library. That is, an inventory record should exist for each tape reel or disk pack. The record should note each utilization. After a given number of uses, the file medium or device is cleaned and recertified. Further, if any troubles are encountered in reading or writing to the device, maintenance steps are taken and noted.

Ideally, a full-time person independent of computer operations will be assigned as the data librarian. In smaller installations, however, such assignment might not be economically feasible. When an installation cannot afford a full-time librarian, this custodial duty still should be segregated from operations. That is, for adequacy of control, the function of librarian must be assigned as a specific responsibility to someone who does not have access to the computer.

Backup/Restart and Disaster Recovery Controls

Control planning must be based on the assumption that any computer system is subject to several different types of failures. In particular, procedures must exist and must be tested for recovery from failures or losses of equipment, programs, or data files.

In the case of equipment failures, each installation might have a contractual agreement covering the use of an alternate site with a comparable computer configuration, if one is available. In most cases, such agreements will be reciprocal, with two or more computer users agreeing to come to one another's aid in the event of a catastrophe.

Backup and restart capabilities for both programs and data files require specific retention cycles and the storage of backup copies of programs and files at remote, protected locations.

Copies of system documentation, standards, and procedures manuals also should be protected through remote, off-site storage.

DISCUSSION QUESTIONS

1. In what ways do general controls contribute to the reliability of individual CIS applications?

2. How might the centralization of CIS services affect general controls?

3. How are systems development controls related to development methodology?

4. Upon what basic control principles is the segregation of duties founded?

5. What considerations may be included within systems feasibility studies, and why are these important in weighting the feasibility of different alternatives?

6. What is the significance of testing as a general control, and in what phases may testing be applied?

7. What criteria may be used to assess the adequacy of documentation?

8. Why must general controls be applied to system maintenance functions?

9. What is the essential objective of operating controls, and what types of control measures meet this objective?

CASE ASSIGNMENT

To apply the concepts presented in this chapter, turn to the case study for Wedco in Appendix B and work through Project 1, which deals with the review of general controls.

8 Evaluation of Controls and the Design of Audit Tests

A B S T R A C T

- CIS audit activities aimed at evaluating the strengths and weaknesses of controls and applying tests of those controls include: preliminary evaluation of internal controls, compliance testing, final evaluation of internal controls, and substantive testing.

- Techniques for evaluation of controls include: review of documentation, identification and evaluation of compensating controls, and conclusions based on results of compliance tests.

- In the design of audit tests, testing considerations include nature, timing, and extent.

- System considerations include: the auditor's degree of reliance on the system, the nature and extent of the audit trail for each application, as well as the nature and extent of interim changes to the application during the period under examination.

- Compliance testing methods include block, or judgmental, sampling; random attribute sampling; as well as program testing techniques such as test decks, parallel simulation, and integrated test facilities.

- Requirements for corporate financial reporting and related substantive testing techniques include large item selection, statistical item selection, and unusual item selection.

THE AUDIT ENGAGEMENT PROCESS

The initial phases of a computer audit engagement focus on preliminary review and analysis of the applications within the system under study. An overview of this work was presented in previous chapters. In gaining this initial understanding, the computer auditor identifies the existing controls, including controls built into the applications, as well as the general controls applied at the system, departmental, and organizational levels.

Subsequent efforts, then, must evaluate the strengths and weaknesses of existing controls. Tests must be applied to determine whether the controls actually are functioning and effective. This chapter deals with these evaluation and testing phases.

Evaluation and Testing Phases

After the preliminary review and application analyses have been completed, four phases remain in the audit engagement process. The phases are:

- Preliminary evaluation of internal controls
- Compliance testing
- Final evaluation of internal controls
- Substantive testing.

Preliminary evaluation of internal controls. During this phase, the auditor determines the extent to which procedures and organization structure relevant to a given system have sufficient strength to justify audit reliance. If a system appears sufficiently reliable, the auditor proceeds to the next phase and develops compliance tests, or tests for selected strengths and weaknesses. If the system appears not sufficiently reliable, as illustrated in Figure 8-1, compliance testing may be curtailed or omitted in favor of more extensive (and expensive) substantive testing, which probes system outputs.

Compliance testing. Compliance testing, as the term implies, determines whether actual application-processing procedures comply with their specifications. Compliance testing includes the design and application of tests to procedures and transactions. These tests are designed to validate the findings of the preliminary review.

Final evaluation of internal controls. Results of the prior phases—the preliminary evaluation of internal controls and compliance testing—become a basis for judging the degree of reliance that can be placed upon a system. The auditor tempers or modifies the preliminary evaluation on the basis of

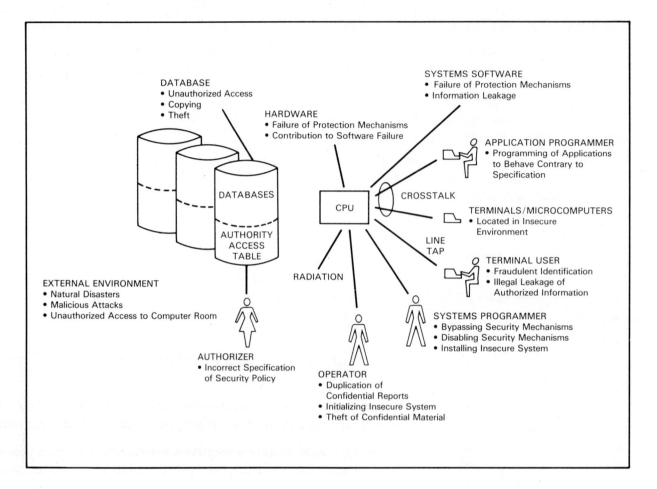

Figure 8-1.

During the preliminary evaluation of internal controls, the auditor may find control weaknesses such as those depicted in this illustration. Such weaknesses can affect seriously the reliability of the system.

the results of compliance tests. Findings during this phase establish the scope of substantive tests, which are performed in the next phase.

Substantive testing. Substantive tests deal with the records, or outputs, from transaction flows that have been validated by compliance tests. Substantive tests are applied against resulting summary information, such as account balances.

These last four phases of the examination process involve, alternately, evaluation and testing functions. For clarity of presentation, however, the discussion below deals with the evaluation phases as a unit, then proceeds to testing activities as a separate topic. The evaluation and design of audit tests then are applied in the next section of the text, which deals with audits of systems development, applications, CIS facilities, and new technologies.

The two audit examination phases concerned with evaluations of internal control mark important crossroads along the route of an audit engagement. These are points at which the auditor gets bearings and decides the nature, timing, and extent of tests that follow the evaluations.

Reliance on Internal Controls

Internal control evaluation is, in perspective, a relatively new professional technique for auditors. Evaluation, testing, and reliance on internal control became necessary with the growth of computer-using organizations. Previously, auditors reviewed total transactions for the period under examination. The examination consisted chiefly of transaction verifications. In effect, all auditing was substantive testing.

With the growth of enterprises and the virtual explosion of transaction volumes, this degree of testing completeness became impossible. The auditor came to rely on principles of statistical sampling.

To be able to use statistical sampling, the auditor first must determine the degree of reliance that can be placed on the system. The preliminary and final evaluations of internal controls, supported with compliance testing, form the basis for this determination.

PRELIMINARY EVALUATION OF INTERNAL CONTROLS

During the preliminary evaluation phase, the auditor evaluates the controls that have been designed into an application. The objective is to determine whether control design is adequate. The auditor looks at work actually being performed to see if specified controls are being exercised. The auditor then rates the effectiveness of systems of internal control. An appropriate scale might rate controls as excellent, fair, poor, or nonexistent. This rating, applied on the basis of the auditor's review and professional evaluation, affects the future course of the examination.

The audit alternatives following the preliminary evaluation of internal controls are outlined below. If controls are rated as excellent, compliance testing may be curtailed. Comprehensive substantive testing may not be necessary for systems with excellent reliability ratings.

In the majority of cases, the auditor will regard internal controls as fair or normal. The auditor then will proceed with what seems to be a normal level of compliance testing, using techniques described later in this chapter.

If the auditor determines that internal controls are poor or nonexistent, no compliance testing is done. The examination proceeds immediately to more extensive substantive testing.

FINAL EVALUATION OF INTERNAL CONTROLS

In the final evaluation of internal controls, the auditor compares the results of compliance testing with the initial review and evaluation of internal controls. If the expectations of reliability have held up as a result of compliance testing, the rest of the audit may proceed as planned. If reliability proves to be greater or less than anticipated, the scope of substantive testing is adjusted accordingly.

In general, the more reliable the system proves to be during compliance testing, the less substantive testing will be necessary. Conversely, the less reliable the system proves to be during compliance testing, the more substantive testing will be required.

At the extreme, the auditor may determine that 100 percent substantive testing is necessary—that all transactions associated with an application must be reviewed individually. Such findings are infrequent, but they can and do happen. For this level of testing to be justified, both of the following conditions must be met:

- The subsystem or application must be judged to have essentially zero reliability.

- The output of the subsystem must be critical to the audit objective.

In some cases, auditors may be inclined to increase substantive testing more often than to decrease substantive testing. That is, since their basic purpose is cautious assurance, auditors tend to be hesitant about reducing the scope of substantive testing, even if compliance testing indicates a high level of reliability. However, in the complex world of large-scale computer information systems, limitation of substantive tests is becoming an increasingly common requirement. Reductions in substantive testing are being encouraged by organization management. These managers have made large investments in systems with built-in, highly automated controls that are designed to increase the reliability of results.

Increasingly, auditors are being expected to understand and interpret the control measures embedded in computer systems and to adjust and limit their own activities accordingly. At the same time, government agencies and the courts are focusing increasing attention upon auditors, particularly in the areas of fraud and defalcation. Thus, in evaluating internal controls, the auditor is forced to strike a sometimes precarious balance between limiting testing to essentials and risking a failure to detect irregularities. New audit methodologies are designed to manage this audit risk, as well as compliance with professional standards.

EVALUATION TECHNIQUES

Broadly, three techniques are commonly used in the actual performance of internal control evaluation:

- Review of documentation
- Identification and evaluation of compensating controls
- Development of judgmental and/or statistical conclusions based on results of compliance tests.

As Figure 8-2 illustrates, the first two techniques are appropriate to both the preliminary and final evaluation phases, though such techniques can be applied more definitively and in greater depth after the results of compliance testing are known. The third technique, development of statistical and/or judgmental conclusions, is appropriate only after the results of compliance testing are known. Therefore, the conclusion process is left to the final evaluation phase.

All three techniques are applied to the evaluation of each significant application. Evaluation can be thought of as identifying the weak and strong links in the chain of control. Then, the chain is tested to see whether it has fallen apart at the weak points and whether identified strengths have withstood the pressure. Pressure is applied through carefully designed tests during the compliance testing phase.

Review of Documentation

During the evaluation phases, the auditor puts to critical use the information gathered or developed during the preliminary review and application analysis phases. For each significant system, the auditor should have in hand all relevant flowcharts, data flow diagrams, narratives, and sample documents, as well as any other evidence to which the auditor's experience and judgment may be applied in arriving at an evaluation.

The auditor looks first for major control attributes in systems under review. Control attributes include segregation of duties, proper authorization, completeness and accuracy of processing, and so on. Taken as a whole, the evaluation of these control attributes determines whether the auditor can rely on the system and to what degree.

Once the extent of probable reliance has been established, the auditor must identify the crucial individual control points within the system. The

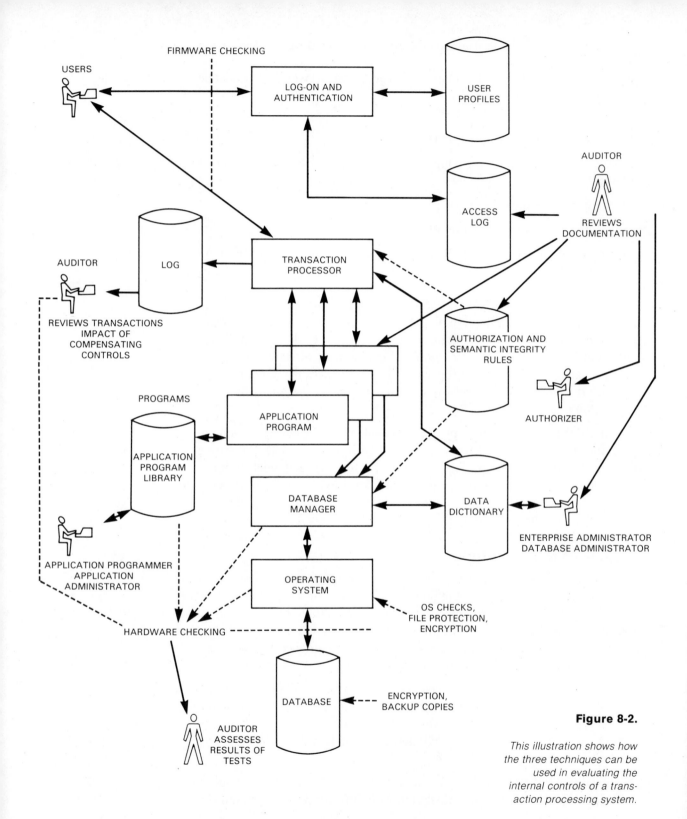

FIRMWARE CHECKING

USERS

LOG-ON AND
AUTHENTICATION

USER
PROFILES

ACCESS
LOG

AUDITOR
REVIEWS
DOCUMENTATION

LOG

AUDITOR

TRANSACTION
PROCESSOR

REVIEWS TRANSACTIONS
IMPACT OF
COMPENSATING
CONTROLS

AUTHORIZATION AND
SEMANTIC INTEGRITY
RULES

PROGRAMS

APPLICATION
PROGRAM

AUTHORIZER

APPLICATION
PROGRAM
LIBRARY

DATABASE
MANAGER

DATA
DICTIONARY

APPLICATION PROGRAMMER
APPLICATION
ADMINISTRATOR

ENTERPRISE ADMINISTRATOR
DATABASE ADMINISTRATOR

OPERATING
SYSTEM

OS CHECKS,
FILE PROTECTION,
ENCRYPTION

HARDWARE CHECKING

DATABASE

AUDITOR
ASSESSES
RESULTS OF
TESTS

ENCRYPTION,
BACKUP COPIES

Figure 8-2.

*This illustration shows how
the three techniques can be
used in evaluating the
internal controls of a transaction processing system.*

208

auditor then must determine which of these controls require compliance testing. The selection of control points for compliance testing depends on one of two factors:

- The control point is crucial to reliance because, based on the evaluation of documentation, it appears to be either strong or normal. Reliance may be high enough so that substantive testing can be restricted.

- A control point appears weak from a design standpoint. If it is judged to be preferable to rely on the system rather than to require extensive substantive testing, the auditor may elect to specify compliance tests that establish a realistic, probable degree of error in spite of the potentially weak control.

In making evaluations based on reviews of documentation, the auditor receives the benefits of having an understanding of the client's system. Such understanding is crucial to effective evaluation of internal controls.

Compensating Controls

During both evaluation phases, it is important to establish and understand relationships among controls. Individual controls should be evaluated for their separate strengths and weaknesses. But, at the overall application level, the auditor should apply judgment in identifying and evaluating compensating circumstances. That is, the strength of one control might serve to offset the weakness of another.

For example, the auditor might note a weakness in the signing out of application tapes to computer operators by an installation's media library. However, such a weakness might be offset by installation software that demands a match between file labels and programs being processed. Further, the weakness in the checking out of tapes might be offset by strong backup and recovery capabilities and by physical security measures within the installation.

A preliminary review of the installation also might have disclosed that irregularities were likely in only two applications—payroll or accounts payable disbursements. A compensating control for the weakness in media control, then, might be the use of prenumbered check forms for which the inventory and signature were controlled strictly by the treasurer's office.

This example also illustrates an important point about the interrelationship of controls within the computer-based processing of significant data. That is, the auditor must recognize the relationships between general, or installation-wide, controls and individual application controls.

As discussed in the previous chapter, general controls comprise a climate, or environment, that impacts the reliability of all work done within a CIS department. If, in a preliminary review, the auditor develops a professional judgment that the department is tightly run and closely controlled, the evaluations concerning the reliability of all applications reviewed will be affected accordingly. Conversely, if the auditor becomes convinced that this is a loosely, or sloppily, controlled environment, all applications reviewed will become proportionately more suspect. Any weaknesses found in applications within a poorly run department would be weighted more heavily than if sound control were characteristic of the CIS function.

As an added example, the auditor would be far more confident about the reliability of all applications in a CIS department if the computer console log was subject to tight controls. For example, the log might be delivered daily to the internal audit group for review. This situation would create a much different overall impression than that of a department in which the logs simply were rolled up, stored, and forgotten. The auditor also would have more confidence if a qualified CIS professional were found on the internal audit staff than if the entire function were staffed by personnel with experience limited to manual systems.

Statistical and/or Judgmental Conclusions

The auditor forms some evaluation conclusions from the results of the compliance tests, be they statistical or judgmental samples. Statistical results normally form the most objective and defensible basis for a conclusion on reliability by the auditor. The reason is that statistical results are more easily quantified and evaluated than are the relatively more subjective judgments on observed controls.

For example, suppose a compliance test used *statistical sampling,* or random selection, based on probability, to choose transactions for examination. Possible attributes to check for compliance are proper signatures on documents and endorsements on checks. Suppose the results of the sample indicated that, for the accounting universe as a whole, the auditor could be 95 percent confident that the error rate for the control attribute tested was not greater than 4 percent. The auditor's evaluation of control, then, hinges on specific questions: Is a 4 percent error rate acceptable? Is a 95 percent confidence level sufficient?

In most situations, compliance testing results will confirm the auditor's preliminary evaluation that controls may be relied upon. Where compliance testing negates the preliminary evaluation conclusion, the auditor probably should accept the results of compliance testing and place no reliance on the controls. In this case, expanded substantive testing is in order.

The auditor may feel that a given sample was not representative of the specific application universe. The auditor's familiarity with the client organization may lead to a conclusion that the sample might not be representative. However, although a nonrepresentative sample is always possible with statistical techniques, the original rationale for sampling argues against extending the sample to disprove an initial sampling conclusion. If 95 percent confidence was used in determining sample size, the probability is 95 in 100 that additional sampling will confirm the initial conclusion. The judgment to extend sampling or to move toward alternative procedures is one the auditor must make and stand by.

Internal control evaluations may be thought of as crossroads activities. Just as a traveler must make a choice at a physical crossroads, the auditor must choose between directions or courses of action. The auditor's professional judgment is required for such choices, in both the preliminary and the final evaluations of internal controls. The auditor will select the specific routes to be followed from among alternatives identified previously. In evaluating internal controls, the auditor is able to determine the degrees of risk and relative economies of alternative testing approaches. The selection, design, and application of these alternative audit testing techniques are covered in the following discussion.

DESIGN OF AUDIT TESTS

Testing involves a series of interrelated auditing activities through which the auditor gathers information and performs verifications to support an opinion. The auditor reviews and evaluates the internal controls within systems under examination to establish the degree of audit reliance that can be placed upon the controls. This preliminary evaluation of controls provides the basis for choosing courses of action (or testing) for the remainder of the engagement.

Compliance testing, which follows the preliminary evaluation of controls, further helps the auditor to decide on the additional examination procedures needed to support an opinion. The results of compliance testing either validate or challenge the auditor's preliminary, subjective findings made on the basis of the review of internal controls.

When compliance testing is complete, the auditor conducts a final evaluation phase. In this phase, the auditor identifies and evaluates the results of compliance testing. The objective is to determine the techniques needed for the substantive testing phase that follows.

Substantive testing, then, comprises the additional examination procedures that satisfy the auditor as to the reliability of the representations in the financial statements of the company under examination. These are fundamental, critical steps toward the formation of the auditor's opinion. Auditing, to a large extent, *is* testing.

TESTING CONSIDERATIONS

Audit tests must be tailored to the characteristics of the system being examined. The makeup of the information processing system itself has much to do with determining the tests to be applied. The auditor's decisions regarding testing have three basic dimensions:

- Nature
- Timing
- Extent.

Nature

The system under examination influences the *nature* of the appropriate audit testing techniques. In general, the nature of audit tests for computer-inclusive information systems are of three broad types:

- Manual examination of audit trail documentation produced by the computer
- A combination of manual examination of computer-generated documents and computer-assisted procedures to select and analyze information system content
- Total reliance on computer-assisted auditing techniques for examination of the computer processing portions of information systems.

All of these techniques apply to both compliance and substantive testing. The nature of audit tests, in turn, is influenced by considerations of timing and extent, as well as by the auditor's preliminary evaluation of the system.

Timing

For a given client organization, *timing* of audit procedures, regardless of whether computers are used, is influenced most by two general factors:

- Data retention cycles
- Reporting requirements.

Data retention cycles.   Retention cycles grow from organizational policies on the length of time that data records are kept in active storage. Legal and governmental record-keeping requirements affect these policies. At the end of a retention cycle, the records are archived, purged, or destroyed, as directed by policy.

Retention cycles, then, are obvious constraints on the auditor. For example, an organization might have a two-month retention cycle on detail source transactions for sales orders, accounts receivable payments, or other significant files. Such relatively short retention cycles are likely to affect the auditor's work schedule. The determining factor is whether testing is required for any of the transactions subject to short retention cycles. If testing is required, the auditor must test transactions at the time when the transaction files actually exist. Or, the auditor must arrange for detail files to be saved on magnetic tapes or disks for later review and examination.

Retention cycle limitations often represent a major difference between the appropriateness of conventional, manual audit procedures and the potential for computer-assisted examination. Traditionally, companies saved their detail source transaction media until the end of the year. Audit examinations then were conducted on a relatively leisurely basis. With computerization, detail records might not be saved for long periods of time or might not be generated at all—at least not in printed form.

Auditors have come to recognize that computerized files lend themselves to computerized review. Shorter retention cycles and economies of scale have changed the timing of some larger audit examinations to an ongoing, or year-round, process. The continuous, or year-round, audit moves closer to reality as the organization's use of the computer becomes more sophisticated and less oriented to paper audit trails.

Contributing to this year-round audit trend is the increasing need for auditors to review and take some degree of responsibility for interim financial representations made to the investment marketplace by client companies.

Another factor weighing in favor of continuous audits is the rate of change of computer information systems themselves. There may be substantial changes made within a CIS during an organization's fiscal year. During such a period, it would not be unusual for a system to undergo a half-dozen changes in processing programs and data file content that could affect the auditor's evaluation. It may be necessary for the auditor to design and execute different testing techniques, each appropriate to the nature of the changing CIS during the year or period under examination.

Reporting requirements. Requirements for reporting either to management or to government authorities are a second important timing consideration. The timing of reporting periods involves constraints upon substantive or end-of-period tests. These constraints may be imposed either by the nature of the system itself or by government regulations.

An example of a constraint on substantive testing arising from the nature of system design may be found in a typical inventory reporting application. A company might take a physical inventory at the end of the month before year-end and then roll the results forward to year-end. In such situations, the auditor must be on hand for substantive testing at the time of the physical inventory count. Auditors also must test the roll-forward of inventory figures following the physical count. In this example, the design of the system places a timing constraint on the auditor. Further, this timing constraint may increase the probability that computer-assisted techniques will have to be used, particularly if the volumes of data and testing are heavy and the time is short.

Timing constraints sometimes are imposed by law, as is the case for companies with publicly traded securities. These companies must deliver certified financial statements to the Securities and Exchange Commission within 90 days after the fiscal year-end. Directors of most such companies put a premium on early reporting of results to the investing public. Therefore, the directors often wish to have results available within 30 to 45 days after the fiscal year-end. These executives are keenly aware that failure to report results promptly could stimulate speculation and uneasiness in the marketplace regarding the prospects for a company's earnings. Prompt reporting is considered by many to be a requirement of competition in the investment marketplace. Since many companies large enough to be affected by these pressures use computers extensively, this situation tends to exert timing pressures on computer-related audit activities. Such situations increase further the likelihood that the auditor will have to use computer-assisted examination techniques.

Extent

Extent is a matter of scope, or depth. The extent of audit testing depends on the reliability of controls within the system itself. The auditor determines the extent of testing principally at two points within the audit engagement. First, on completion of the preliminary review and evaluation of internal controls, the auditor determines the nature and extent of compliance testing. Then, after compliance testing, the auditor performs a final review and evaluation of internal controls. The auditor's findings here, in turn, determine the extent of substantive testing.

The scope, or extent, of testing done is adjusted on the basis of findings during the two internal control reviews. Some basic procedures usually are included in compliance testing for every audit examination. The usual variations as a result of the preliminary review of internal controls are to expand testing in areas of highly critical reliance or to determine the extent of error where controls appear to be weak.

Substantive testing, however, may be contracted as often as it is expanded, based on the auditor's evaluation of the results of compliance testing. If compliance testing indicates that a system has ineffective controls, examination procedures could be extended, in extreme cases, all the way to a complete review of all transactions. Conversely, a system judged to be highly reliable, based on the results of compliance testing, may be subjected to a much more limited extent, or scope, of substantive testing.

SYSTEM CONSIDERATIONS

The nature, timing, and extent of audit procedures, then, depend largely upon the characteristics and activities of the systems under examination (see Figure 8-3). Three characteristics of a CIS can be identified as having the most impact on the design of audit procedures:

- The degree of reliance the auditor places on the system under examination

- The nature and extent of the audit trail available for each application under examination

- The nature and extent of interim changes to the application during the period under examination.

Degree of Reliance

The degree of reliance an auditor places upon a system or application will be conditioned by its materiality to the organization's overall financial or operating reports. For example, a sales application or system almost always will be material because it handles all incoming revenues from goods and/or services sold. A database application also will be material because so many activities of the organization depend on the integrity of the data stored within the system. For such an application, the auditor might look at the impact of controls on specific activities (see Figures 8-4 and 8-5).

If the system or application is material to overall financial or operating reports, the nature and extent of testing will depend directly upon the nature and extent of the transactions involved. For example, a company buying and selling large parcels of real estate might engage in only a few hundred sales transactions during the entire year. In such cases—particularly since all of the transactions are likely to be large—the auditor might elect to review most or all of the transactions individually rather than to test the processing system for reliability.

Activity	Description
1. End user interface to the DBMS	Those individuals and/or programs that need to access data or the attributes of the database structure
2. DBMS operation	The procedures necessary to use the DBMS in an operational environment
3. Database administration	Those activities necessary to design, implement, and monitor the DBMS and to coordinate its use with users
4. Data definition	The documentation of the data elements and database structure
5. Security/access	Those functions which must be performed to protect the integrity of the database from inadvertent or intentional unauthorized access
6. Systems development	Those tasks involved in developing applications to use database technology
7. Backup and recovery	Those functions necessary to modify the database structure and to restore the integrity of the database after a database failure

Figure 8-3.

This table summarizes the kinds of activities within a database environment that would affect the nature, timing, and extent of audit procedures. (Adapted from FIPS 88, "Guideline on Integrity Assurance and Control in Database Administration.")

On the other hand, if the auditor were examining the financial records of a chain of variety stores or supermarkets, it would be impossible to examine all sales transactions individually. In such cases, the auditor *must* place some reliance upon the internal controls of the system. In such situations, the preliminary and final reviews of internal controls will be in relatively greater depth, as will compliance testing.

Audit Trails

The existence of audit trails within computer-inclusive information systems depends largely upon the types of manual functions remaining and their interaction with computerized procedures. If extensive documentation of an audit trail is produced manually, it may not be necessary to use the computer at all in audit examinations. For example, a hospital customarily performs a daily patient census count manually. Even if the hospital used highly computerized procedures, an auditor still might elect to use the daily census figures. One approach would be to extend the census figures by average revenue totals to verify income, rather than to perform detailed tests of all transactions through computer-assisted methods.

ACTIVITY DATABASE CONTROL ISSUES	End User Interface to the DBMS	Operation of the DBMS	Database Adminis- tration	Data Definition	Security/ Access	Systems Develop- ment	Backup/ Recovery/ Reorgani- zation
1. Inadequate assignment of responsibilities			10, 11 14, 16		27	30	
2. Inaccurate or incomplete data in a database	1, 2	4				31, 32	44
3. Losing an update to a single data item		8, 9				31, 34	
4. Inadequate audit trial				21, 22		34, 35 36, 37	41
5. Unauthorized access to data in a database		3			22, 23, 24 25, 26, 27 28, 29		
6. Inadequate service level		4, 5, 6			24, 26	34, 35	42, 45 46
7. Placing data in the wrong calendar period	2			20		36	
8. Failure of DBMS to function as specified		4, 7	13	19, 20		31, 34 35, 36	42
9. Fraud/embezzlement	2	7	16			36	42
10. No independent database audits			16			38, 39	
11. Inadequate documentation	1		12	20, 21		32, 34 35, 36 37	42
12. Continuity of processing	1, 2	4, 5, 6			22, 23 24, 25 26		41, 42 43, 44 45, 46
13. No cost/benefit analysis		7	15			38	
14. Lack of management support	1	7	10, 11, 15		27	30, 33	42

Figure 8-4.

This matrix table references database control issues with specific activities. Controls identified here are described in Figure 8-5. (Adapted from FIPS 88, "Guideline on Integrity Assurance and Control in Database Administration.")

At another level, which probably represents the most prevalent situation today, the auditor may elect to combine computerized and manual examination techniques. A typical example would be a large company with high volumes of accounts payable transactions. The company maintains files of voucher/payment records to support these transactions. However, there usually are too many records for the auditor to examine in detail. Controls, if they are functioning, must provide a basis for audit reliance. Using

Figure 8-5.   *The controls referenced in Figure 8-4 are listed here by activity. (Source: FIPS 88, "Guideline on Integrity Assurance and Control in Database Administration.")*

End-User Interface to DBMS

1. **Program modification and maintenance control.** Assures that the proper change is installed in the proper version.
2. **Adequacy of programmed input validation check.** Programmed routines verify the accuracy, completeness, and authorization of input.

Operation of the DBMS

3. **Access authorization control.** Assures that only authorized individuals gain access to database resources.
4. **Data error handling.** The procedures and timeliness used in examining and correcting detected errors.
5. **Remote data transmission control.** Terminal controls assure that data is not lost at the terminal site.
6. **Central data transmission control.** Assures the accuracy and completeness of the communication system for the entire network.
7. **Processing intent.** Explains the objective of management in processing a specific transaction.
8. **Concurrent data control.** Assures that data elements will not be misprocessed due to two or more users processing the same data element concurrently.
9. **Deadlock detection and resolution.** Breaks a stalemate in processing between two users.

Data administration controls

10. **Assignment of responsibilities.** Makes individuals accountable for their functions.
11. **Segregation of duties.** Splits functions so that no one individual has the responsibility for performing a function and, at the same time, has responsibility for using the results of that function.
12. **Operation documentation.** Details operating procedures.
13. **Output control.** Details the procedures for preparing and disseminating output results.
14. **Rotation of duties.** Limits the amount of time any one individual has day-to-day responsibility for an operating task.
15. **Processing performance standards.** Establishes criteria to measure economy, effectiveness, and efficiency of database technology.
16. **Risk-management team.** A task force comprised of multiple backgrounds identifies the concerns and problems faced when using database technology.

Data definition controls

17. **Centralized coordination of external schema.** Placing the responsibility for coordinating external schema definition in a centralized group.

18. **Data element responsibility**. Making individuals accountable for each data element in a database.

19. **Conceptual data independence**. The organization establishes the data definition as opposed to individual user groups.

20. **Data dictionary system**. An automated documentation tool for data.

21. **Active data dictionary system**. The documentation in the data dictionary is fed automatically into the operating environment.

Security/access controls

22. **Physical barrier**. A physical restraint preventing individuals from accessing database technology.

23. **Surveillance**. The use of guards or electronic equipment to detect penetration.

24. **Database malfunction reporting**. Reports to management identifying the type and severity of problems occurring with database technology.

25. **Natural disaster and environmental protection**. Taking the measures necessary to protect database technology from acts of God and man, such as fire, earthquake, etc.

26. **Maintenance plan**. A predetermined schedule for performing maintenance to correct problems before they occur.

27. **Security officer function**. Appointing one individual accountable for security of database technology.

28. **Security profile**. A matching of user needs to database technology capabilities.

29. **Passwords**. A secret code or word that individuals or programs must know in order to gain access to database technology.

Systems development controls

30. **Database administration function**. A function that establishes interface standards for systems under development and advises systems analysts and programmers on database technology capabilities and interface procedures.

31. **Application system testing**. Methods of assuring that operational systems cannot adversely affect the database.

32. **Formal design process**. The use of structured methods or automated tools and techniques to aid in the design process.

33. **Top management checkpoints**. A series of steps throughout the developmental process at which top management will make a decision regarding performance and continuance of the project.

34. **System implementation standards**. Methods and procedures that must be followed when implementing systems using database technology.

35. **Database standards**. Methods and procedures that must be followed when establishing and operating a database.

36. **Training of personnel**. Providing those courses and materials needed to provide appropriate skills for people using database technology.

37. **System documentation**. Sufficient formal written explanation of the database environment so that its continuity and maintenance can be assured.

38. **Review board**. A group of managers, users, and database personnel who oversee priorities and projects using database technology.

39. **Government reporting requirements**. A formal method of assuring that the use of database technology is in compliance with Federal regulations.

Figure 8-5.

Continued.

40. **Personal privacy requirements.** Methods and procedures of assuring that an individual's privacy has not been compromised through database technology.

Backup/recovery/reorganization controls

41. **Audit trail.** The ability to trace transactions from source document to control totals and back to source documents; and to reconstruct processing should problems occur.

42. **Recovery procedures.** Automated tools and techniques for recovering integrity of database.

43. **Reorganization utilities.** Automated tools and techniques for restructuring and expanding the database.

44. **Database verifier.** An automated tool to assure that all of the data in the database is properly structured and can be located.

45. **Application system failure.** Procedures for users to continue operations in the event their applications are not operational.

46. **Backup databases.** Copies of databases made at specific points in time to use for recovery purposes.

Figure 8-5.

Concluded.

computer-assisted techniques, then, auditors would inspect computer files of accounts payable transactions to select statistical samples of transactions. The sample transactions then would be examined manually.

As discussed previously, changes in information processing are causing audit trails to disappear. Increasingly, auditors are encountering sophisticated computer systems that leave substantial gaps in the audit trail—or no effective audit trail at all. A case in point is a large, consumer credit company that issues credit cards. Transactions are processed in sizable batches on a daily basis. Typically, the only reports generated during computer processing are summaries. The summaries are totals of revenue realized by the credit card plan itself and are based on percentages of dollar volumes and types of transactions submitted by associates in the field. Upon billing, the original charge tickets, or source documents, may be returned to the customers who initiated them. Although many credit card companies maintain microfilm records of these transactions, the volume is so great that manual audit examination simply is not practical. Computer-assisted examination is almost mandatory in such cases.

Interim System Changes

It is common for CIS departments to expend 50 percent or more of their programming and systems analysis resources in maintaining existing computer systems. The probability is high that any major computer system will be modified substantially during the course of any year. During the preliminary review and evaluation of internal controls, the audit team must identify modifications that have been made since the last examination.

In some cases, the auditor may find that the company actually used two or more different CIS systems for a specific application during the period under examination. If so, each system may have to be tested separately to determine its reliability. For the purposes of audit examinations, a substantially modified CIS system actually may have to be considered as a completely new system with regard to the extent of review and evaluation required.

Changes to existing systems can affect the nature, timing, and extent of audit procedures. The nature and extent of testing necessarily will depend upon the nature and extent of the modification and the financial significance of the system or application. Timing is affected because an auditor may have to be present before a major modification is made. The discontinued system may not be available for examination at year-end.

COMPLIANCE TESTING

In compliance testing, the auditor is verifying the system under examination against a preliminary evaluation of the reliability of internal controls. Compliance testing, generally, is a low-volume activity. Its objective is to establish whether reliability is high enough for the system itself to be used later in more voluminous substantive testing. That is, if the system proves reliable during compliance testing, it can be used further in performing substantive tests. On the other hand, if the system proves unreliable in compliance testing, the auditor must seek means and techniques of substantive testing that do not rely on the processing system itself. Because of the incremental nature of evaluation and testing, compliance testing usually is performed on one application or system at a time.

Transactions to be tested in significant computer-processed applications usually are selected through statistical techniques. The reason is that transaction volumes typically are high. For many years, auditors used a technique known as *block sampling*. Under this approach, the auditor tested all transactions that took place during selected periods—specific weeks or months. If the transactions for selected weeks or months were processed accurately, and if the selected periods were representative of the year as a whole, the auditor judged that the system could be considered reliable. This method also is referred to as *judgmental sampling*. Use of the auditor's judgment in the selection of samples has been supplanted in many situations by statistical techniques.

Random Attribute Sampling

More recently, sampling practices have become more objective, sophisticated, and, most practitioners would agree, more reliable. Application of *random attribute sampling* techniques makes it possible to derive results from tests of fewer items than was typical of block, or judgmental, sampling.

Random attribute sampling is a statistical technique that tests for specific, predefined attributes of transactions selected on a random basis from an application file. Attributes for which such testing is done could include signatures, appropriate account distribution, adequate documentary support, and compliance with company policies.

To perform attribute sampling, the auditor must specify three parameters that determine sample size:

- Estimate the *expected rate of error,* or estimated percentage of exception transactions, in specified attributes within the total transaction population. This estimated error rate may vary by the type of attribute to be tested.

- Specify the *required precision,* or degree of accuracy desired, of the sample conclusion to be made. For example, the auditor might estimate that tests performed for attributes on a sample of transactions will show an error rate of 3 percent. The auditor recognizes that it is virtually impossible to reach this conclusion with 100 percent accuracy unless every transaction is examined. Therefore, a tolerance level for accuracy of the conclusion must be set. If a 3 percent error rate is expected, the auditor might accept a tolerance of, say, an additional 2 percent. In effect, the auditor in this case wishes to be assured that the error rate within all transactions is between 1 and 5 percent. Typically, audit attention focuses on the upper limit. That is, the auditor would become more concerned if the sample error rate approaches 5 percent.

- Establish an *acceptable confidence level* for the sampling conclusion. In sampling, confidence level is a statement of probabilities that the conclusion formed is a correct one. For example, the auditor might stipulate a 95 percent confidence level. That is, the auditor wishes to be 95 percent certain that the sample will be descriptive of the entire universe of transactions—within the acceptable tolerances previously specified.

The size of the sample required for any test of transactions will be determined by the combination of these specifications for precision, confidence level, and expected error rate. The more precise the tolerance boundaries of the sample, the greater will be the size of the sample. The required sample size will be smaller to the extent that these tolerances are relaxed.

The confidence level specified will have a smaller impact on sample size than do precision requirements. However, there is a definite relationship between confidence level and sample size. The higher the confidence level, the larger the sample must be; the lower the confidence level, the smaller the sample.

Given these parameters for sampling objectives, the auditor uses a series of statistical tables or formulas to determine sample size. For example, suppose the application under audit involved cash disbursements and accounts payable for a large company. Assume that the universe, for statistical sampling purposes, is large—say, more than 100,000 items. Assume further that the auditor desires a 95 percent confidence level, expects a 3 percent error rate, and will tolerate ± 2 percent precision. Random statistical sampling on an attribute basis would require the examination of 197 items. The auditor then might select the sample by taking any of the following steps:

- Use a random number table and convert manually from random numbers to the actual check or voucher numbers under audit.

- Run a statistical sampling program on, for example, a time-sharing computer service or on a microcomputer that can accommodate a suitable package. The sampling program requires the auditor to enter the beginning and ending numbers of the transaction series and the appropriate statistical parameters. The sampling program then computes the sample size and selects the transactions that should be examined.

- Run a sampling program with the transaction file as input, on the application computer itself or on another computer. Under this approach, the sampling program looks at all records in the file under examination, determines the sample size based on the parameters, and prints out a listing of the relevant data in the computer file for each sampled record.

When the sample size is determined and transactions are selected, the auditor returns to the original documentation. In this example, the auditor would trace accounts payable checks back through vouchers and accounting distribution records. The auditor would keep track of errors according to attributes being tested. This process will result in subtotals of errors, by attribute, for the sample. With this information, the auditor uses additional statistical tables or formulas to determine the range or maximum error rate estimated for the entire file at the specified level of confidence. Based on these results, the auditor forms a conclusion about the adequacy and reliability of the subsystem or application that has been tested.

Tests of Programs

The compliance testing techniques described are tests of the data within applications or systems. Some computerized systems are so voluminous or so complex that tests of data are physically or economically not feasible. In these circumstances, the auditor still can evaluate reliability of the application or system by testing the computer programs that process the transactions.

Program testing may take either of two basic approaches. As one alternative, the auditor can submit to the program a set of test data that will produce known results if the program functions reliably. The test data are processed by the application or system programs, then outputs are compared with pre-established results, as illustrated in Figure 8-6.

The other basic approach is to simulate actual results developed by the programs. The auditor writes a program that simulates, or performs the same processing as, the program under test. Typically, a high-level programming language or report generator is used to create a program that achieves the intended results, though less efficiently than the application program. Selected groups of data that actually have been processed under the application program are then processed under the simulation program and results are compared.

With either type of program testing, comparing the results of test processing with actual or predetermined results provides evidence about the reliability of the production programs. With both techniques, however, a qualified technical specialist must review the coding for the programs involved or otherwise assure the validity of the procedure. If test data are to be processed, the program review helps to establish the nature of the test data. If simulation by an auditor-originated program is to be done, the review of programs determines what processing steps should be performed and assures that the auditor's program implements them correctly.

In choosing test methods, there are many borderline cases. The auditor must exercise judgment in choosing between tests of transactions and program testing in establishing compliance and reliability of applications or systems. Determining whether to use tests of transactions or program testing involves weighing the trade-offs in each audit situation. Advantages of program testing include the following:

- The organization using the CIS does not have to retain detailed data files solely for audit requirements.

- The need to perform detailed manual or computer-assisted testing of data files may be eliminated, or reduced significantly.

- If a program is sufficiently comprehensive and complex to warrant consideration of program testing techniques, the client organization probably has an investment large enough so that changes will not be made frequently or lightly. In these circumstances, a substantial initial investment of audit time may be justified in developing simulation test programs that can be used over several audit periods. In subsequent years,

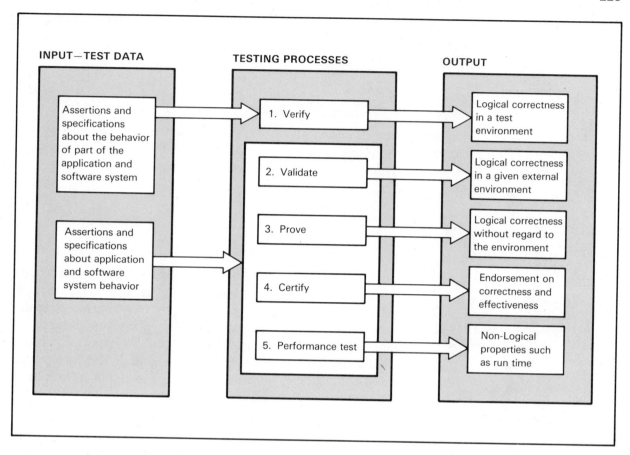

INPUT—TEST DATA

Assertions and specifications about the behavior of part of the application and software system

Assertions and specifications about application and software system behavior

TESTING PROCESSES

1. Verify
2. Validate
3. Prove
4. Certify
5. Performance test

OUTPUT

Logical correctness in a test environment

Logical correctness in a given external environment

Logical correctness without regard to the environment

Endorsement on correctness and effectiveness

Non-Logical properties such as run time

Figure 8-6.

One method of program testing involves test data that are processed by the program under examination.

testing of these applications might be done for a small fraction of initial costs, assuming that changes to the system being tested are not material.

Disadvantages of the program testing approach include:

• Examinations should be performed relatively frequently, or on an interim basis. To be effective, program testing should be done, when possible, on an unannounced, surprise basis. Auditors need to assure that the program being tested is the one actually used in processing during the period under examination.

• Program testing requires a high level of technical skill on the part of the CIS specialist on the audit team.

• If applications or subsystems are subjected to high rates of change, program testing can be costly.

- If program testing uncovers errors, the specific impact of the error or weakness is difficult to determine. The auditor may have to resort to tests of data files, which essentially would be a duplicate effort for reaching the same conclusion.

Program Testing Techniques

Program testing is discussed in depth in later chapters. The presentation here surveys three of the common methods among the wide variety of methods available. Three common program testing methods are:

- Test decks
- Parallel simulation
- Integrated test facilities.

Test decks.   *Test decks* involve techniques for presenting files of test transactions to a computer for processing under existing application programs. In practice, test data are entered from punched cards, magnetic tapes, on-line terminals, and other forms of source data entry. The technique calls for presenting the full spectrum of transactions that could be expected to be encountered by the application program. Both valid and invalid transactions are included in the test data, since the objective is to test how the system processes both correct and erroneous transaction input.

Test-deck techniques often. are used for systems that process large volumes of small-value transactions, such as consumer credit card services. Test transactions entered would include invalid account numbers for cardholders and member-associates, accounts that have been suspended or discontinued, transactions that cause accounts to exceed credit limits, transactions with post-dated or pre-dated transactions, and valid transactions. Since the identity of the invalid transactions is known in advance, testing is performed by comparing output reports with known invalid conditions.

If reliance is to be placed on program testing, some form of *intermittent testing* is essential. That is, test efforts must be timed randomly and spread over a representative period of operations. The objective is to assure that variations in general controls or operating conditions are not influencing test results. Without intermittent testing, or other assurance on organization and operations controls, the auditor could conclude only that the system was reliable at the specific time when the tests were performed.

Parallel simulation.   *Parallel simulation* involves the separate maintenance of two presumably identical sets of programs. The original set of programs is the production copy used in the application under examination. The second set is a copy that was secured by auditors at the same time that the original version was placed in production. As changes or modifications are made to the production programs, the auditors make the same updates to their copies. If no unauthorized alteration has taken place, comparing results from the same version of each set of programs should produce identical results.

Parallel simulation usually is the most expensive of the testing techniques available to the auditor. In selected situations, however, it can be the most effective alternative. In general, parallel simulation will be appropriate to complex systems involving extensive summarizations and/or computations. Conditions must be such that manual tracking or recalculation is either too expensive or ineffective.

Parallel simulation also might be considered for auditing applications in which a program or processing stream has multiple calculations, summarizations, or detail account distributions, yet no intermittent output reports are produced to show the interim results of this multi-step processing.

An example in which parallel simulation was used by auditors involved a government agency providing utility services. In this situation, allocations of costs to customers and product users was central to the system's purpose. Literally hundreds of allocations often were initiated from single accounting transactions. When the system was under development, auditors realized that it would not be practical to track the distribution of transactions manually. In preparation for parallel simulation, the auditors performed extensive examination and testing of the production programs at the time they were written. The auditors kept separate, secured copies of the original programs for audit control. The copies later were used for parallel simulation of transactions. As the production system was changed or updated, identical modifications were made in the auditors' copies, which then were used for parallel processing on a statistical sampling basis. Overall, this approach has both improved audit reliance and reduced audit costs.

Integrated test facilities.   *Integrated test facilities* are built-in test environments within a CIS. This approach is used primarily with large-scale, on-line systems serving multiple locations of a company. The test facility comprises a fictitious corporation or branch, set up in computer files to accept and process test transactions as though they were for an actual operating entity. Throughout the year, auditors devise and submit test transactions to the fictitious entity. Independent auditors may initiate such transactions either on their own or in close coordination with the internal audit function. Reliability is established through the review of processing performed on the test transactions.

Data for the integrated test facility are summarized and reported in the same manner as an actual branch or division. The results, when verified, tend to assure audit reliability because the integrated test facility produces normal operating results as well as reports on exception tests. Data for the fictitious entity are eliminated before preparation of the consolidated reports, such as year-end financial statements, for the organization.

An important requisite for the success of this technique, however, is that the CIS department must not be aware of the presence of the integrated test facility. Files must be established and transactions entered to the test facility independently of the CIS function. As far as the CIS department is concerned, the test facility must be treated as though it were another live branch or division of the parent entity.

Examples of integrated test facilities are found in banks or savings institutions that set up fictitious branches in their computer files. Large utility companies also have used this approach to set up nonexistent operating divisions for audit purposes.

SUBSTANTIVE TESTING

Substantive testing encompasses auditing procedures that determine the validity of summary information, such as account balances, on financial statements. Testing is for both the amount and proper classification of individual balances. The auditor verifies that the amounts shown are stated fairly, that amounts are classified properly according to generally accepted accounting principles, and that the principles have been applied on a basis consistent with prior years.

Corporate Financial Reporting

Corporate financial reporting, today, calls for presentation of three separate statements:

- Income statement
- Balance sheet
- Statement of changes in financial position.

Auditing approaches are necessarily different for items on the income statement and on the balance sheet. Differences stem from the nature of the reported items. Income statement items are periodic—that is, they represent summaries of transactions that occurred during a specified time period. Audit examination activities must provide assurance covering the entire period under examination.

Balance sheet items, on the other hand, represent status at a given point in time—cash on hand at year-end, inventory balance at year-end, and so on. These items can be verified through specific observations and other verifications of their status at year-end.

Substantive Testing Techniques

The underlying purpose of substantive testing techniques is to select specific items for examination that relate to account balances represented in the income statement and in the statement of financial position prepared by corporate management. For the most part, income statement items are audited primarily on an exception basis. Substantial reliance is placed on compliance testing techniques to establish the reliability of the applications or systems that processed transactions during the period under examination. Substantive testing techniques, however, are appropriate to both income statement and balance sheet accounts.

In general, three criteria can be identified for selecting items for substantive testing:

- Large item selection

- Statistical item selection

- Unusual item selection.

Large Item Selection

Large item selection is applied primarily to balance sheet accounts. Definition of large items will vary with the size of the organization. In one company, capital expenditures or dispositions might be considered large at $5,000; in others, the threshold of significance might be $500,000.

Use of this technique is particularly appropriate if transactions are few and relatively large, as is the case with additions or dispositions of capital assets. Large item selection is appropriate in any account—whether income statement or balance sheet—if the auditor can achieve significant examination coverage by verifying relatively few items.

Large item selection generally is performed by establishing size criteria and then examining transactions—either manually or with computer assistance. The objective is to identify transactions that exceed established limits. Frequently, large item selection can be done in conjunction with compliance testing. If a compliance test calls for review of a specific file, the computer program performing the test could be designed to select and report all large transactions along with the results of statistical sampling.

Statistical Item Selection

Compliance testing uses statistical sampling in establishing the reliability of applications or systems that develop amounts appearing in the financial statements. Statistical sampling techniques also may be used to abbreviate the substantive testing process. One common technique for accomplishing substantive auditing objectives is known as *dollar-value estimation.* That is, rather than calling for detailed development of account balances through review of large numbers of transactions, this technique *stratifies* accounting record populations according to dollar-level criteria. Computer programs then count the number of transactions and establish dollar values for each stratum, or level. A series of statistical analyses then is applied to average these figures, calculate standard deviations, and perform other tests that result in the selection of sample transactions from each stratum.

The samples then are audited in any of several conventional and appropriate ways. For example, if the accounting record population covers accounts receivable, customer confirmation techniques would be used. For inventories, physical observation and test counts would be done.

Once the items selected have been audited, the audited value and book value for each item in the statistical sample are entered into an estimation program. In addition, the auditor designates a desired confidence level and the targeted dollar-value precision of the audit conclusion to be made. The estimation program extends the results of the sample to develop and report a *point estimate,* or estimated mean value, for the accounting record population from which the sample was drawn. Also calculated is the dollar-value precision from which the actual population might vary due to possible error in the sample procedure. Both the point estimate and the dollar-precision limits are computed and expressed in relation to the confidence level stipulated by the auditor.

If the account balance reported by management falls within the dollar range resulting from the auditor's sample, the figure probably will be accepted. If the corporate figure is outside the range, reported as a result of the auditor's substantive tests, further testing is necessary; or, an audit adjustment is required.

Dollar-value estimation can be a time-saving and economical audit tool. However, this approach requires technically qualified auditors, both in the statistical sampling and computer disciplines.

Unusual Item Selection

Identification and examination of unusual items plays an important role in any audit examination. This function, however, requires a more disciplined, specific approach when computers are used. With the volumes implicit in computerized systems, it is easier for unusual items to escape detection. Considerable audit attention, therefore, must be devoted to identifying and examining unusual items. Computer-assisted techniques for this purpose include:

- Comparison testing
- Ratio analysis or modeling
- Entry source analysis.

Comparison testing. *Comparison testing* techniques are used to compare items in financial records with corresponding items in prior periods to identify unusual, or exception conditions. One common example occurs in the use of comparison testing to identify potentially obsolete inventory items. If inventory records for a given stock item show no transaction during the current year—or only an insignificant number of transactions—a computer audit program would report this item for audit review. The auditor's concern would center around possible obsolescence and the need for *writedown,* or devaluation, of inventory.

Similarly, current-year inventory balances could be compared with summary figures representing current order backlogs. If a comparison between inventory levels and orders in process appeared out of line, inventory levels might be suspect as being too high.

Ratio analysis or modeling. *Ratio analysis* and *modeling* use specialized computer audit programs that test the relationships of balances to one another. Usually, such techniques are applied to income statement accounts. Current-year items are compared within an income statement, as well as with prior years.

In ratio analysis, commonly used ratios apply relationships between sales figures and a number of other accounts on an income statement. For example, sales commonly are expressed as ratios to net income, to sales expense, to cost of sales, to payroll, and so on. Typically, such ratios developed for the current statement are compared with those of past income statements. Any wide variations are reported and then are subjected to analysis for determining the causes of the variation.

Another approach to achieving the same results is income statement modeling. Under this technique, ratios are developed and compared for a number of past income statements. The current sales figure then is entered into this set of ratios, or model. The result is a model income statement based on the historic financial relationships. The model figures then are compared with the actual income statement amounts. Unusual differences are isolated to analyze the causes of changes in trends. Microcomputer programs have been applied with great success as an audit tool for such tests.

Entry source analysis. *Entry source analysis* is a computerized technique that tests for errors of accounting entries within income statement or balance sheet accounts. The technique frequently can be combined with compliance testing activities. Items posted to a given income statement or balance sheet account normally should be derived from specific sources. For example, a purchasing transaction should come from the purchasing journal. If the entry source is from payroll, something is probably wrong. The high-speed comparison capability of the computer is used to check items posted to significant financial accounts back to their sources. If the sources are different from those specified within the comparison program, the items are reported as exceptions for follow-up. Such techniques are designed to isolate accounting errors, erroneous postings, or unusual items entered through the general journal. These items then should be reviewed and evaluated by the auditor.

SUMMARY OF AUDIT ACTIVITIES

The procedures described in this chapter are familiar territory to experienced auditors, regardless of the orientation to manual or computerized systems. The procedures are proven and relatively common. They are the normal activities that an audit team undertakes in developing support for its expression of opinion as to the fairness of financial statements. What has evolved in computer auditing is a natural integration of computerized tools and techniques with normal audit procedures. The computer has been integrated into the audit engagement process for organizations that make extensive use of computers in processing financially significant data.

In any audit engagement, regardless of the extent of computer use, the examination should follow a pattern of:

- Preliminary review for understanding

- Analysis of significant applications

- Preliminary evaluation of internal controls for the design of compliance tests

- Actual compliance testing

- Final evaluation of internal controls

- Substantive testing.

At the conclusion of this process, the auditor should be able to express an opinion on the fairness of financial statements.

At this point, it is worth noting that substantive testing applies to all auditing (i.e., operational, compliance, and management performance), rather than to purely financial examinations. Financial audits are cited in this chapter primarily because they are the most prevalent and easiest to illustrate. When substantive testing is performed in an operational audit, the purpose is to examine processes and to determine which controls or procedures are actually being applied.

With this overview, this chapter concludes the portion of the text dealing with audit concerns and objectives. Building on this understanding, the four chapters in the next section focus on patterns and procedures for specific types of computer audit engagements.

DISCUSSION QUESTIONS

1. How are phases of evaluation and testing of controls related in a CIS audit engagement?

2. In what ways has the adoption of computer information systems affected the auditor's approach to examination?

3. What is the objective of evaluating internal controls, and what techniques generally are applied in the auditor's evaluation?

4. How does the principle of compensating controls govern the overall reliance that may be placed on a system?

5. How are the considerations of nature, timing, and extent related to the design of audit tests?

6. What characteristics of the system under study can affect the nature, timing, and extent of audit procedures?

7. What are the objectives of compliance testing, and what techniques may be used in tests of compliance?

8. What are the objectives of substantive testing, and what techniques may be used in substantive tests?

CASE ASSIGNMENT

To apply the concepts presented in this chapter, turn to the case study for Wedco in Appendix B and work through Project 2, which deals with the design of audit tests.

III DOING COMPUTER AUDITS

Against the conceptual and theoretical framework that has been built in Parts I and II, this third part of the text describes specific types of computer audits. Particular emphasis is placed on technological considerations that may influence the audit approach.

Chapter 9 describes the auditor's involvement in the systems development process. The auditor must assure that appropriate controls are included in the design of the system, that these controls actually are implemented, and that sufficient testing is performed to assure that the installed controls will operate as planned.

The audit of computer applications is covered in Chapters 10 and 11. Chapter 10 describes the typical audit process and presents an example of its use in an audit of inventories. Chapter 11 deals in greater depth with the implementation of computer-assisted audit procedures, or techniques for using a computer to sample and analyze the content of its own databases.

Chapter 12 describes how auditors can become involved in reviewing CIS centers, encompassing facilities, equipment, and operations. In Chapter 13, consideration shifts to CIS resources that are distributed throughout an organization and perhaps among multiple sites. Special concerns in this area are raised by the potential loss of control through use of semi-autonomous microcomputers and the networking of CIS resources to build sophisticated decision support systems (DSS).

The discussion of networking points up control issues that are inherent in digital communication technology. Chapter 14 covers specific aspects of transmission controls within distributed systems. The chapter concludes with a case study that highlights additional threats to telecommunication links.

9 Auditing Systems Development: Concepts and Practices

A B S T R A C T

- In the involvement of CIS auditors in the systems development process, emphasis is on identifying control needs and designing controls into the new system.

- To avoid barriers to the development process, communication pathways require ongoing, productive relationships between the systems project team and user groups, who eventually must acquire a sense of ownership of the emerging system. From a management standpoint, approvals and resource allocations typically must be sought from a CIS steering committee, or oversight group.

- A generalized systems development life-cycle methodology, viewed from the auditor's perspective, should encompass the following phases: investigation, analysis and general design, detailed design and implementation, installation, and review.

- Internal auditors must be concerned with designs for control procedures, although recent trends indicate that auditors are being drawn increasingly into the analysis and general design phase as well.

- Key opportunities for impacting controls occur during project formulation, preliminary design, detailed design, programming, testing and training, and conversion and operation.

- The rationale for audit involvement in systems development encompasses reasons of economy, continuity, complexity, cost effectiveness, and auditability. Major contributions stem from minimizing the degree of risk to the organization and assuring that all aspects of the project are documented fully, in accordance with organization policy.

- Specific types of new systems reviews include: monitoring audit, design review audit, educational and standards audit, and post-implementation audit.

- Audit participation in systems development should be approached in ways that minimize or avoid compromise of the auditor's independence.

MANAGEMENT AND AUDIT CONCERNS

Both managers and auditors have a stake in the reliability of information generated by computer information systems. Management concerns over information reliability are reflected in the increased recognition and involvement of internal auditors in computer-based financial and operational systems.

Current areas of audit involvement encompass the full spectrum that ranges from systems development through to the continuing operation and maintenance of functional systems. For their part, auditors are recognizing that control requirements are directly proportionate to system complexity; the more complex the system, the greater the need for controls.

Recognition of CIS control needs has paralleled identification of similar control requirements in other areas of business operations. For example, quality control has become an important aspect of manufacturing systems. Quality control experience in manufacturing suggests a premise that bears directly on information system development: Quality cannot be inspected into a product; it must be built in. Indeed, current emphasis is on designing control and reliability into a CIS rather than trying to retrofit them after an unreliable system has been developed and implemented.

THE APPROACH TO SYSTEMS DESIGN

The basic lesson or enlightenment in the area of systems design has been a recognition that a CIS belongs to the departments or managers that use the information it generates. With this recognition of the ownership of information resources have come new definitions of responsibility and authority for systems development.

Before the ownership issue was clarified, existing manual systems were turned over to computer analysts and programmers—who achieved automation through minimal changes to basic functions. In the initial iteration of the system design, there tended to be a one-to-one correspondence between the existing manual system and its automated counterpart. Users had little difficulty understanding a system that merely emulated existing manual processes. When organizational demands led to development of systems that were dissimilar to those they replaced, a comprehension gap grew between users and their systems.

The need to bring systems and their users back together has been an underlying motivation for the evolution of multidisciplinary, team-oriented approaches to CIS development. Another stimulus for a team approach has been the rapid pace of technological change. As computer equipment and software have become more complex, the technical demands of systems development have required the efforts of specialists. In a team approach, technical specialists join the effort as needed to consult with users and systems professionals.

An inevitable difficulty of complex systems design with a team approach has been maintaining communication with users. The intent has been to design systems to user specifications, for user benefits. But, there often have been several layers of technical specialists on a team, each concerned with a different discipline, each speaking a jargon strange to users.

Hurdling the Communication Barriers

To deal with these communication barriers, most organizations have encouraged the development of yet another specialist. This individual operates in the middle ground between the management generalist and the computer professional. This person, a systems analyst or a systems designer, provides the linkage for interpreting user needs to programmers, software specialists, and operations technicians. The systems analyst operates, in effect, with one foot in each world, coordinating and synchronizing system capabilities with user needs.

In addition to satisfying user needs, a systems analyst should be able to identify opportunities for system enhancement and be able to explain these concepts to both users and CIS technicians. Consider a routine payroll application: A systems analyst might see the opportunity to build a comprehensive personnel file instead of the minimal file needed for running payroll. Expanding file content in this way could enhance human resources management capabilities. The analyst might suggest adding fields on training, skills, experience, and education of individual employees. Similarly, a systems analyst might see relationships among invoicing, accounts receivable, and perpetual inventory applications. The analyst will be able to devise ways to use these relationships to eliminate redundant procedures and record keeping. The analyst's responsibilities go beyond mere technical assessment to coordination of the systems design and implementation efforts.

An important part of the analyst's function, therefore, includes visualizing and presenting new dimensions in computer utilization. As far as the auditor is concerned, the systems analyst is in a unique position to identify the points of interaction or interrelationship that pose potential control problems. Thus, the systems analyst is a key person and point of contact for the auditor. The analyst can identify the need for audit advice or assistance aimed at building in quality and reliability during the systems development process.

Increasingly, departments or groups that make heavy use of CIS systems are developing staff who are capable of functioning in the worlds of both the user and the CIS specialist. The same is true of audit organizations. Today, whether internal or external, audit groups require people with multiple skills in management, accounting, auditing, and CIS technology. Other contributors on the systems development team may include a variety of technical specialists: programmers, software technicians, operations managers, data conversion specialists, and data communication specialists.

The Decision Maker

The role of the decision maker tends to be overlooked within systems development projects. Decision making includes the critical responsibilities of allocating resources for systems development, setting priorities among systems under development, and evaluating design trade-offs.

The decision maker is a management representative responsible for the predictability of systems development processes. Whether the role is played by an individual or by a committee, the decision maker should not be involved in the technical aspects of the project. Therefore, the ultimate decision-making role should be assumed by someone other than the team leader or project manager. The decision maker is the individual or group with the authority to commit the organization's resources to the project effort. This position of management involvement in technical oversight facilitates coordination and communication between users and technicians.

Users, systems analysts, and technicians, then, must justify the systems development effort to the decision-making authority to obtain resources. Alternatives and recommendations must be advanced in clear presentations that explain the impact of proposed systems in organizational terms. The decision-making function should apply a structure through which systems projects are undertaken only under terms of clearly stated commitments that stipulate requirements and resource allocations. Where technical understanding is a critical issue—but is still within the scope of the decision-making authority—proven management practices should prevail. In resolving conflicts or choosing alternatives, the decision maker may engage a qualified advisor, either from within the organization or from outside.

Whether the decision-making function is handled by an individual or by a committee (often called a *CIS steering committee*) depends largely on the nature and the resources of the organization. For example, where systems under development impact a number of line departments, many organizations establish an *applications advisory committee*. Such a committee is composed of user department representatives and the head of the CIS function. This type of committee can effect the necessary trade-offs in allocating resources and setting priorities among affected—often competing—departments. If the committee is composed of members at the level of department heads, cooperation by their subordinates in implementing decisions of the group is more likely.

Sometimes it has proven just as workable for decision making to be handled by an individual. This approach is perhaps most successful when an organization has a strong, respected manager with the requisite systems and managerial background. In either case, the main requirement is to recognize and implement the decision-making function.

THE SYSTEMS DEVELOPMENT PROCESS

Figure 9-1 shows the relative participation of users, CIS personnel, and audit staff in systems development. The figure illustrates the interrelationships among development activities for different participants. Development activities correspond with the phases of the systems development life cycle (SDLC). These phases and their related activities are listed and described in the sections that follow.

Investigation

Activities that occur within this phase include:

- Conception
- Project organization
- Review of present system
- Feasibility studies
- Cost-benefit analysis
- Project team formation.

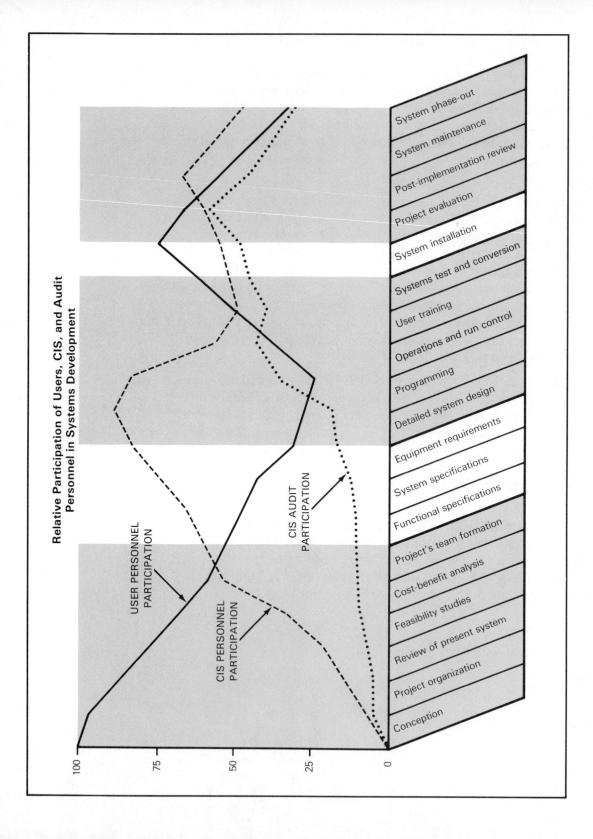

Figure 9-1. This graph shows the relative degrees of involvement of users, CIS professionals, and audit personnel in the systems development process.

The first phase of the SDLC yields a feasibility study to determine whether systems development is warranted in the existing situation. Once a preliminary understanding of the problem has been built, a decision is made whether to carry the project further. The makeup of the team during this phase indicates that responsibility rests primarily with the user. At this point, the user indicates a general intent to buy the services of systems professionals who will design and implement a system that meets a desired objective.

Analysis and General Design

Activities that occur within this phase include:

- Functional specifications

- System specifications

- Equipment requirements.

In analysis and general design, user participation decreases while CIS personnel and audit staff participation increases. The work of this phase analyzes requirements and specifies what the user wants to accomplish. Attention focuses on the user's data analysis and information reporting specifications. That is, the team is not concerned with the means or designs of solution. Rather, emphasis is placed on defining what a proposed system would be required to produce.

Detailed Design and Implementation

Activities that occur within this phase include:

- Detailed system design

- Programming

- Operations and run control

- User training

- Systems test and conversion.

During detailed system design, a high level of CIS involvement continues and audit participation grows. The center of emphasis has shifted and now is squarely over the area occupied by the systems analyst, who is performing at the peak of a catalytic role. The analyst is interpreting and carrying forward the wishes of the user and guiding the programmer. In a coordinated effort, the analyst must interpret and feed back information to both the user and CIS technical groups.

An enlargement and a shifting of commitment takes place during detailed system design. When this phase is complete, the programmer will have made a commitment to the user, and to the decision maker, stipulating in specific terms what the input, processing, and results of the new system will be. The programmer also commits to the levels of time and money that will be required to develop and implement the system as designed.

During this phase, a tightening of commitment and control takes place. For example, experience suggests that, at the conclusion of preliminary design, projections may be accurate to ± 25 percent of anticipated resource and cost requirements. By the time a detailed design has been developed, those making the commitment should be within 10 percent of their estimates of final time and cost requirements. Obviously, the accuracy of the estimates will depend to a great extent upon the skills of the implementers, the complexity of the project, and the state of the art of the techniques being used. It is unrealistic to count on tighter precision in estimating. Unfortunately, examples of gross errors in estimating abound in practice.

Commitment and decision making at the conclusion of the detailed design phase are at their most critical level in the entire systems development process. A decision to go beyond this point calls for commitment of approximately 70 percent of all funds that eventually will be invested. Thus, the decision maker expects that the users, programmers, and analysts involved in the development will have definitive commitments and estimates. The costs of a bad decision may go far beyond the dollars expended on the aborted effort: Other desirable projects may have to be deferred. Also, the emotional wear and tear, as well as the loss of confidence in future commitments, cannot be estimated.

The programming activity encompasses the actual physical design and coding of applications. This work must be structured and controlled so as to assure that the programs developed actually implement the system as designed.

A technical-level testing function is incorporated within programming activities. At this point, the intent is different from system testing, which follows. Rather, individual program modules are tested to assure that they are workable on the limited segments of the total processing that they perform.

An important element of an effective systems development effort—especially from the auditor's viewpoint—is the carrying out of full, integrated testing of the entire application process. Both procedures and results must be tested. The user must be able to determine that the new system can be relied upon. Users must be assured that the results seen during the testing phase are at least as good as those envisioned in the specifications developed during project formulation.

Testing is, in effect, a final developmental control. This is the point at which decision makers determine whether to go ahead with installation, to fall back into the developmental mode for correction, or to take their losses and abandon the effort entirely.

Training facilitates the delivery of the system into the hands of its owners. Training is a preparation for the human side of system testing. It is, in effect, the "programming" of the human-operated portions of a system. Although training is presented as one of the distinct steps on the chart in Figure 9-1, considerable overlapping with the other phases is essential. Clearly, a substantial amount of training must take place before testing can be done. The fine tuning of training programs and the training of all affected members of user and operations staffs cannot take place until the system has been tested and the procedures proven.

Conversion is a point of transition: The existing system is phased out and the new one is brought into being. From the auditor's standpoint, the importance of a thorough conversion must be understood if a reliable system is to result. There are substantial audit and control implications in a system conversion. New controls are installed and rendered operational at this point. An audit trail is either provided or lost in the short period of conversion from one system to another. If a conversion does not run smoothly, the new, ongoing system may be tainted, perhaps unfairly, by the conversion difficulties and, as a result, will be suspect for some time into the future.

Installation

This phase encompasses a single, all-important activity, called system installation.

Divided involvement is shown for this phase in Figure 9-1. At this point, systems professionals are leaving the picture. Installation should encompass primarily the user and operations areas. This limited involvement on the part of systems people is critically important to the systems development process. At a predefined point, development must end and the system must assume a viable, ongoing status. This cutoff is necessary if costs truly are to be controlled and if scarce development staff are to be assigned to a continuing flow of new projects.

One of the requirements for the effective development of any system, therefore, is that there be a predefined point at which development ends. At that point, the systems analyst and programmer have done their work. Routine operations should begin. The programs become a standard part of the installation's library. The team has provided documentation and training materials that help make the user self-sufficient and that put the user and the operations section in business together. Further, unless the analysts and programmers leave the scene, a computer application never really can be secure or reliable.

Review

Activities that occur within this phase include:

- Project evaluation
- Post-implementation review
- System maintenance
- System phase-out.

This phase takes place when the new system is fully operational—after the project team has been disbanded. Typically, two post-implementation reviews are conducted. The first takes place shortly after installation. Its purpose is to evaluate and learn from any mistakes of the project while memories are still fresh in the minds of participants. The second occurs after the system has been in use for some months. It should be aimed at determining how well the initial objectives of the project have been met, particularly through realization of anticipated benefits.

Maintenance is an ongoing requirement. Modification of a system may be required from the moment of installation throughout its useful life. Control is vital in all maintenance activities, particularly to ensure that all changes are duly authorized and documented fully.

At some point after installation, the procedures that have been replaced must be discontinued. Control concerns center on assurances that all functions and checkpoints within the old system are actually carried forward to the new system.

Auditing Systems Development

The audit function, as depicted in Figure 9-1, has application throughout the systems development process. This breadth is necessary to assure that completed systems are auditable. This objective is achieved by involving auditors in the approval of designs for control procedures.

The breadth of audit involvement shown in Figure 9-1 assures that project work is carried forth within approved budget and time allocations, that the allocations are reasonable, and that the benefits derived are both cost-effective and realistic in comparison with original estimates.

Internal audit involvement. Over the years, several industry and professional association surveys have been made to determine the involvement of the internal audit function in systems development projects. A recent estimate is that 40 to 50 percent of internal audit groups are involved in systems development auditing. Further, the studies have shown that the degree of involvement varies widely at different phases, as Figure 9-1 illustrates.

Also according to the studies, internal auditors are becoming more involved in the early phases of analysis and design. The increasing trend within recent years has been to include auditors in the development of requirements and specifications for new systems.

Role of the internal auditor. The auditor should approach the system audit appraisal as an objective consultant. A primary objective should be to develop an understanding of the system at a detailed level. On the basis of this understanding, the auditor should provide as much on-the-spot advice to the systems people as possible with respect to known audit and management requirements.

If the auditor follows this approach effectively and demonstrates a desire and ability to provide the project team with a worthwhile service, both the audit and systems functions will be well served. If the auditor is perceived in this role, every opportunity is likely to be extended to accomplish audit objectives, as well as to assist systems designers in meeting their objectives. After all, the development team and the audit function share a common goal: the design of the best possible information systems. A significant contribution to this goal comes from the auditor's specialized training, experience, and objective viewpoint.

BUILDING CONTROL INTO A CIS

Within most CIS shops, systems development follows a predefined, structured methodology. Such methodologies follow the pattern of life-cycle models and partition CIS development and implementation into discrete phases, activities, tasks, and individual work assignments. An example of a structured methodology is shown in Figure 9-2.

Systems development objectives include the building of efficiency, reliability, and control into each application. In a sense, the fact that a systems development project is structured through a series of logical, interrelated phases and activities constitutes an important control in itself. Control is executed through this structuring, which establishes the allocation of resources and provides a mechanism for determining the status of a project at any given point.

DESIGN PROCESS: LARGE INTERNAL INFORMATION SYSTEMS

MANAGEMENT REVIEWS				
SYSTEM DEVELOPMENT PHASES	Investigation	Analysis and General Design	Analysis and General Design	Detailed Design
PROJECT CHECKPOINTS	1 — Project Selection and Authorization	2 — Completion of Preliminary Study 3 — Completion of Project Plan	4 — Completion of Systems Analysis	5 — Completion of Systems Design
GENERAL TASKS	• Define objectives • Authorize preliminary study • Establish study review date	• Define project scope • Define skills required • Determine Audit Requirements • Develop plan • Develop cost estimate • Develop Hardware/ Software Assumptions • Commit resources for analysis • Perform cost analysis • Commit functional specification	• Data gathering • Define functions • Analyze input and output requirements • Develop alternatives • Select best alternative • Update plan • Update cost analysis • Review Hardware/ Software Assumptions • Define Audit Criteria	• System flow chart • Design outputs • Design inputs • Define files • Processing specifications • System controls • Conversion rqmt's • Design input forms • Commit Hardware/ Software Requirements • Finalize cost analysis
USER-SHARED RESPONSIBILITY	• Define objectives • State anticipated benefits • Cost savings	• Establish total user commitment • Define desired system character • Define information/ audit requirements • Provide user operation cost estimates • Assignment of personnel to task • Benefit measurement criteria	• Support analysis tasks • Update objectives, benefits, cost savings	• Define user procedures • Define system controls • Approve design freeze • Define training requirements

Figure 9-2. *This table indicates the activities of and control points within the systems development process.*

Implementation	Implementation	Installation	Post-Implementation Audit
6 — Completion of Program Design 7 — Completion of Programming and Program Testing	8 — Completion of System Test 9 — Completion of Parallel Test	10 — Implementation Completion	11 — Post-Implementation Audit
• Programming • Define program logic • Develop test plan • Production run plan • Conversion plan • Complete coding • Complete program checkout	• Complete system test • Complete parallel test • Review: parallel test results, production run plan, contingency plan • Finalize program documentation • Finalize operation documentation • Verify Audit Trail	• Review: problems in user area, problems in computer operations • Identify required changes • Verify system operational	• Review performance against: target dates, cost estimates, benefits projected • Review system operation • Identify required improvements • Decide action to be taken
• Review, revise, approve display elements • Organize for testing	• Support analyst in review of plans and results • Train user personnel in the use of the system • Produce user operational documentation	• Formal system acceptance • Identify problems in user area	• User reactions • Measure system results against original requirements and anticipated benefits

Thus, a project structure provides a means of management control. A project's structure also is reflected in its organization. The elements of control are discussed below in relation to the structure of each project phase.

Project Formulation

Recall from the discussion above that projects usually begin with user requests. Within the structure of the project formulation phase, the user's functions and responsibilities are made clear. This is an element of organizational control. In accepting primary initial responsibility, the user undertakes to understand and evaluate the processes that will comprise the new system. The likelihood of effective controls is enhanced by this understanding and assignment of responsibilities early in the design.

Preliminary Design

In preliminary design, this structuring process is carried a step deeper. Typically, preliminary design will specify the content and appearance of source documents, input records, file records, general processing functions (including edits and exception reports), and the primary output records or documents. At this point, broad principles of control can be applied through organization and separation of duties.

Detailed Design:
The Focal Point for Effective Control

As stated previously, the detailed design phase is a focal point for control evaluation. This is the phase during which all of the processing elements of a system take shape at a level sufficiently detailed for evaluation of the planned controls. Also at this point, the reliability of a system can be challenged at a documentation level, as is done in the audit review of internal control for an ongoing system.

The performance of this review—in itself—helps to establish one of the controls over the detailed design phase. If documentation has not been executed to a level that permits this degree of control evaluation, the design effort probably still has deficiencies. These deficiencies should be a clear warning that the design probably has not been refined sufficiently. If such deficiencies exist, the ability to manage the expensive implementation and operations efforts cannot be assured.

For these reasons, managers and auditors both should be involved actively in evaluating the documentation generated during detailed design. Typical detailed design documentation will include all of the paperwork needed to represent a functional system: form and screen layouts, application flowcharts and/or diagrams, decision tables, and program specifications.

Also critically important from an audit standpoint will be descriptions of control and balancing procedures applied wherever data are converted, processed, summarized, or reported.

The detailed design phase is especially important to control because of its positioning within the systems development life cycle. If control weaknesses are not identified and overcome at this point, it is highly likely that weaknesses will be incorporated in the implemented system. The costs to correct these problems later will be much higher than if the problems had been addressed in the design phases.

In the application of advanced, sophisticated techniques involving microcomputers and distributed intelligence networks (discussed in Chapter 13), it is possible to implement systems that are literally unauditable. A totally unauditable system, of course, would be an extreme consequence. Any development effort, however, can benefit from thoughtful attention to controls during detailed design. The penalties of implementing systems with built-in weaknesses are of far greater consequence than the expense and difficulty of applying control at the design stage in systems development.

Programming

Programming is the point at which controls to be applied by computers actually are implemented. Therefore, the documentation of the programming phase is critical. The act of writing and debugging program code usually is the most expensive single cost component in the development of a computerized system. Accordingly, examining program design documentation before actual coding begins is a high-yield control activity. Examination of the logical design, test specifications, and test data for a program under development also can help assure both the cost effectiveness of the completed system and the reliability of the information it will generate.

Testing and Training

Testing, and the training programs that precede actual testing, comprise another significant control element. The purpose of testing is to assure that both processing and controls work as specified.

Control concerns, however, extend further. The purpose of testing is to find bugs. The testing process includes correction and modification of programs and elements of the detailed design. Therefore, the same extent of testing used for preliminary system tests must be applied to any modifications. Again, testing, in a real sense, *is* auditing.

Through the training activity, controls are built into the human element of a system in the same general way that the programming phase establishes controls in the machine element. If the total system is to function reliably, the training process must develop and implement human-applied controls at effective levels.

Conversion and Operation

During conversion and operation, control concerns focus on assuring that measures designed and built into the system actually are being applied. That is, controls must not be forgotten, abridged, or circumvented once personnel develop a familiarity with and confidence in a system that has become routine.

AUDIT CONTRIBUTION
TO SYSTEMS DEVELOPMENT

The role of the auditor in the design of computer information systems has been regarded with some ambivalence. Admittedly, audit involvement in design may not be essential to the attest function in an organization with a well-disciplined systems design function. But this is a view of the audit function in a narrow sense. Audit involvement in systems design is not a luxury. In the current CIS environment, audit participation in systems design should be cost-effective.

The auditor has an important interest in any significant computer information system. Thus, if system users should play a key role in design specification and development of new systems, it follows that the auditor, as an important system user, also should be involved. Within the project implementation team, where the need for involvement by the auditor is recognized, the auditor should have the prime responsibility for evaluating the adequacy of controls designed into the system.

The importance of audit involvement in systems development also has been recognized by the AICPA Auditing Standards Board:

> The attestation skills the certified public accountant acquires through training and experience in auditing financial statements are also useful in evaluating and expressing a conclusion on other types of assertions as well . . . An attester who is sufficiently knowledgeable in the design and operation of information systems and software may, for example, be capable of evaluating and reporting on information about such systems and software. ["Proposed Authoritative Statement Attestation Standards," Exposure Draft prepared by the AICPA Auditing Standards Board, February 15, 1985.]

The Board is considering promulgating standards that would encompass audit involvement in the development of any system that impacts the financial systems within an organization. The exposure draft includes guidelines on this very topic, which, if adopted, will become standards for the profession.

Managers and auditors share common ground in their requirements for reliability of data generated by a CIS. The auditor who participates in systems development from an external, objective vantage point also provides additional assurance of system reliability to the manager who ultimately will use computer-generated information.

It makes sound economic sense, then, for the auditor to be involved at the time of development, rather than after implementation. Increasingly, developers of sophisticated systems are finding it profitable to work with their auditors to structure files and build databases for ease of subsequent auditing. Also, many systems are being designed to include program routines designed specifically for use by the auditor. The ability to develop references or reports specific to the audit examination objectives is being built into increasing numbers of computer systems.

If the auditor gains confidence in the reliability of internal controls during systems development, the economy and cost-effectiveness of subsequent audit involvement are enhanced. In such cases, the auditor can place relatively heavy reliance on internal controls. Testing and verification procedures may be minimized accordingly. For example, if the auditor is satisfied that controls exist in the input and processing routines for a recently developed system, audit concentration might be shifted to examining the reporting and handling of exceptions, as detected by the controls upon which the auditor is relying.

Audit attention also might shift to the recovery and restart routines designed into a computer application. These provisions serve the primary purpose of assuring the auditor that backup files are created and that procedures exist for reconstructing applications from these files, if necessary. In addition, many recovery and restart programs have direct value as audit tools.

Rationale for Audit Involvement

If computer systems are to be designed to produce reliable information, the auditor should be regarded as a valuable member of the systems development team. The auditor is a specialist who can make an important contribution to design and implementation. (See Figures 9-3 and 9-4.)

Figure 9-3.

The participation by the internal audit function in systems development is increasing, as shown by contrasting conventional and contemporary views of this involvement.

**PARTICIPATION OF INTERNAL AUDIT
IN SYSTEMS DEVELOPMENT**

CONVENTIONAL
- Review systems only after the development process is completed.
  Rationale: Independence and objectivity are
              lost through participation.

CONTEMPORARY
- Early participation is the key to ensuring that adequate controls
  are designed into a system.
  Rationale: Too expensive to retrofit/modify system once it is
              completed
              Cannot affect adequacy unless they participate

Figure 9-4.

The rationale for involving internal auditors in systems development is to assure the adequacy of the controls that are designed into an application.

**APPLICATION SYSTEMS
DEVELOPMENT CONTROLS**

CONTROLS OVER THE SYSTEMS DEVELOPMENT PROCESS ARE MANDATORY.

PURPOSE
- Assist in managing costs and schedules.
- Help ensure that appropriate application controls are built in.
- Ensure that application controls are tested before they become
  operational.

RESULTS
- Higher levels of accuracy
- Reliable operation of the application system

In essence, the justification for systems development auditing lies in the following key areas:

- Economy
- Continuity
- Complexity
- Cost effectiveness
- Auditability.

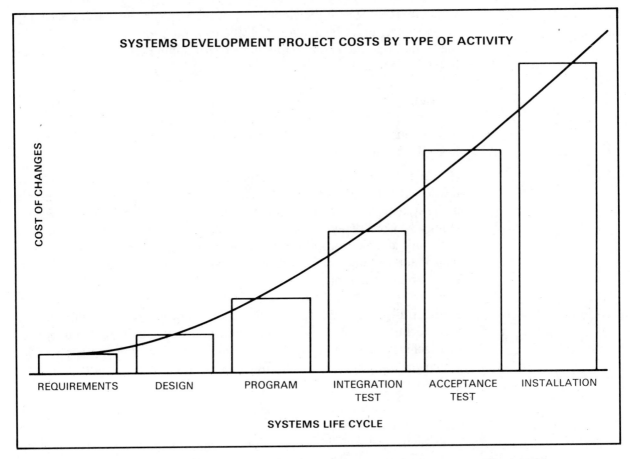

SYSTEMS DEVELOPMENT PROJECT COSTS BY TYPE OF ACTIVITY

COST OF CHANGES

REQUIREMENTS   DESIGN   PROGRAM   INTEGRATION TEST   ACCEPTANCE TEST   INSTALLATION

SYSTEMS LIFE CYCLE

Figure 9-5.

This graph shows that the cost of fixing or changing a system increases greatly in the latter phases of development.

Economy. Veteran CIS practitioners have developed a rule of thumb for the cost impacts of making changes to a system in the latter phases of the development life cycle. The "10-to-100 software rule" holds that any change is likely to range from 10 to 100 times more costly if it is undertaken in the operations phase than if it were addressed during design. This principle is illustrated in Figure 9-5. Software changes are exponentially more expensive as a project advances through its life cycle. In view of the impact on costs, the most economical approach is to involve the auditor in the design phase to identify control opportunities and needed modifications at the earliest possible point.

Continuity. From a logical viewpoint, it always will be less disruptive to the systems design process to receive the auditor's recommendations during early development phases, especially if audit concerns can be addressed in project formulation and preliminary design.

Complexity. Due to the complexity of modern computer-based systems, it is no longer practical to audit after the fact. Auditing the systems development life cycle increases the likelihood of building effective controls into initial system designs.

Cost effectiveness. As stated above, significant savings can be realized from minimizing disruptions to the development process. Also, the efficiency of subsequent audit engagements can be increased by assuring the effectiveness of controls from the outset.

Cost effectiveness also is enhanced by input of audit considerations in the design of the controls themselves. When the auditor is involved directly in the systems design process, controls may be selected and applied most economically. Considerably less latitude of choice will be available if it becomes necessary to make control modifications in an operational system. Gaining the auditor's input at an early date, then, assures maximum control effectiveness at minimum cost.

Auditability. The ability to audit a computerized system is enhanced by audit techniques that are embedded within the system itself. Such embedded techniques require a high degree of integration with the application, which generally is possible only by including them in the original specifications for system design.

An example of this concept is presented in Figure 9-6. The process involves the identification of key control points that management, users, CIS professionals, and auditors agree are critical throughout the life cycle of the system (Figure 9-7). The CIS auditor plays a participatory role in the process of assuring system integrity and adherence to organizational standards.

Risks Inherent in the Development Process

Systems development projects necessarily involve risk and uncertainty. Relatively large capital budgets are required. Coordination and cooperation among multiple departments and disciplines must go into the project effort, yet the participants may have no prior experience with one another. Systems projects are highly visible within the organization. Thus, a major contribution of audit involvement in the systems development process may be to minimize the degree of risk to the organization.

The auditor's special area of expertise is to be aware of and to minimize the potential for risk. Monitoring development budgets and schedules, along with reviews of allocations by the decision maker, assures that the organization will not be subjected to excessive, unanticipated development costs. If schedules are monitored closely and feedback is provided to management and to users, the possibility of disruptions that might result from major project slippage is minimized. Producing needed systems on a timely and predictable basis, therefore, also assures that the organization will not be placed at a competitive disadvantage from lack of timely information or responsiveness of its systems.

A primary area of responsibility for the auditor, of course, is to see that adequate accounting controls are built into automated systems. The auditor's awareness of statutory and regulatory requirements increases the likelihood of full and timely compliance.

A related concern is that effective controls on the operational system will prevent the generation of inadequate or erroneous information. Gross errors, of course, are relatively easy to spot. However, hidden design flaws and logical inconsistencies can result in major errors that are difficult to detect. The potential adverse impacts of management decisions made on the basis of unreliable information are immeasurable.

Besides looking for the possibility of error in normal system operation, the auditor also attempts to minimize the opportunity for fraud and misuse of computer systems.

Sources of Risk

The risks outlined above exist as pitfalls strewn along the development path. Because of specialized training and a relatively objective viewpoint, the auditor is well-equipped to help the project team avoid disaster.

A common problem, for example, is failure to develop adequate or complete specifications. Users may not understand—or may not be able to communicate—the problem they are trying to address. Systems practitioners may misunderstand the problem, may not be communicating effectively, or may be attempting to design an inappropriate solution. In fact, systems people sometimes have a tendency to become overly enthusiastic about a technical challenge or technological innovation, to the extent that the efficiency of the organizational solution actually is impaired. Overly complex approaches, poor designs, and inadequate documentation or training often result in systems that are not maintainable.

Project teams also may make significant errors in budget or schedule estimates. In general, failure to gauge the financial impact of the overall development effort is a major pitfall. Design errors, sometimes the result of poor methodology, can be costly, especially if they are not detected until late in the system testing activities. The auditor also can provide an objective view of the competence levels of technicians and operations personnel. Their skills must be adequate for their roles in the project.

CONTROL POINTS IN AUDITING SYSTEMS DEVELOPMENT

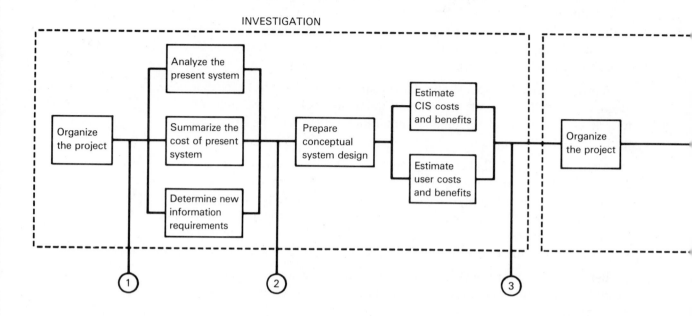

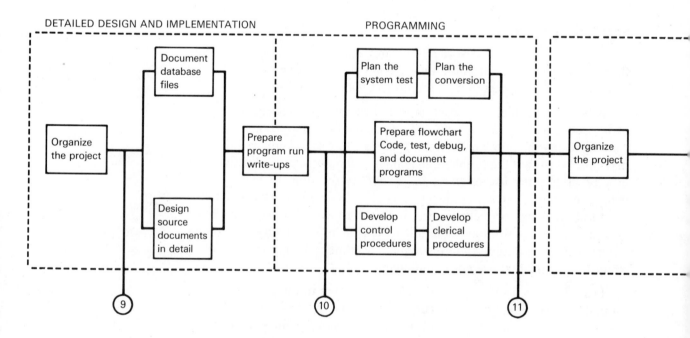

Figure 9-6. *Project phases and their control points are shown in this overview diagram of the SDLC audit. Numbered points correspond with the descriptions of controls in Figure 9-7.*

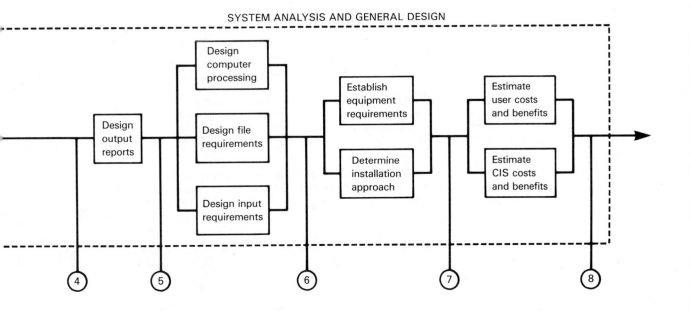

SYSTEM ANALYSIS AND GENERAL DESIGN

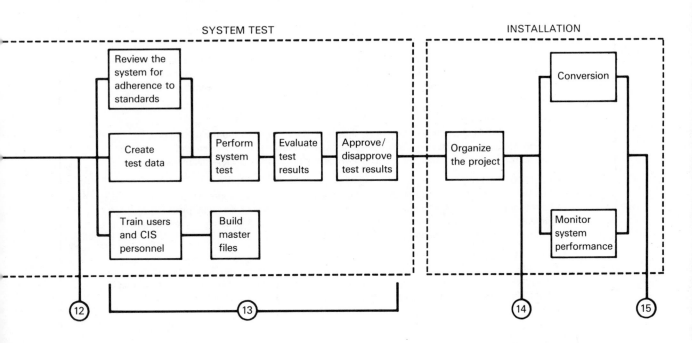

SYSTEM TEST
INSTALLATION

257

Figure 9-7. *Control points within a systems development life cycle are described above. These numbered points are called out on the diagram in Figure 9-6.*

SDLC CONTROL POINTS

- CONTROL POINT 1

  The CIS Auditor, User, and the Project Leader review the project organization, the arrangements with the User for communications, and the plans and work program for the design. This central point helps the project leader to establish a good working relationship with the User to ensure that the system incorporates User requirements.

- CONTROL POINT 2

  The User, CIS Auditor, and Project Leader review the analysis and planned cost for completeness and accuracy. In addition, the project control and communications plan is discussed and changed if necessary. The User plays a major role at this control point in determining if proper analysis has taken place.

- CONTROL POINT 3

  The User, CIS Auditor, and Project Leader review the conceptual design documentation for accuracy, completeness, and any changes that may have occurred. A revised cost-benefit plan is developed, and the CIS Auditor presents the findings to top management.

- CONTROL POINT 4

  The User, CIS Auditor, and Project Leader review the project organization resulting from the first phase, the communication links established between team members, Users, and CIS Auditors, schedules and work plans, and other items relevant to the specific project.

- CONTROL POINT 5

  The CIS Auditor, User, Project Leader, and Design Analysts review the detailed design output reports for completeness and clarity. The CIS Auditor attempts to assure that sufficient design documentation exists to allow a clear understanding by the Test Team and the CIS Audit Staff.

- CONTROL POINT 6

  The User, CIS Auditor, Project Leader, and Design Analysts review the file requirement specifications and the input requirements associated with them. The User checks that the file requirements do not implicitly or explicitly change the original system specifications.

- CONTROL POINT 7

  The User, Project Leader, CIS Auditor and other data processing personnel responsible for hardware planning all review the equipment specifications to assure that they meet the requirements of the designed systems. Completeness of the equipment requirement is important to avoid unanticipated equipment costs at a later date.

- CONTROL POINT 8

  The CIS Auditor, User, and Project Leader review the design from cost, data processing standards, and general management points of view. The Project Leader is interested in assuring that all loose ends from the past two phases are in place before moving into the detailed design phase.

- CONTROL POINT 9

  The CIS Auditor, Project Leader, User, and data processing personnel make a final review of plans, equipment, costs, project organization, and communications channels to assure that all participants have agreed upon the status and direction of the project. The Project Leader is primarily concerned with assuring top management that sufficient systems analysis and design have taken place before the detailed design phase.

- CONTROL POINT 10

  The CIS Auditor, User, and Project Leader review the documentation available describing the file systems, interface data handler programs, and program run documents for compliance to standards, completeness, accuracy, and clarity. The Project Leader is concerned primarily with assuring that the Project Team is providing adequate documentation to meet data processing and User documentation standards.

- CONTROL POINT 11

  The CIS Auditor, Project Team members, Testers, and the User review the detailed system design to assure that it follows from the general system design and still meets the User's requirements. In addition, the test plan is reviewed for completeness, timing, and cost. The conversion plan and associated paperwork are reviewed for reasonableness, completeness, and clarity. As this is the last checkpoint before the test phase, the Project Leader takes special care to assure that the original design requirements are still intact or that a traceable trail exists that explains to top management and Users why the system has changed.

- CONTROL POINT 12

  The CIS Auditor, Testers, User, and Project Leader review the Test Team organization to assure that the proper people are present and that the project test plan is complete and consistent. The Project Leader is primarily concerned with assuring himself that the test plan will test the system completely and, in particular, will test the internal controls designed into the system.

- CONTROL POINT 13

  The CIS Auditor, User, and Testers develop test data, build master files, review test results, and monitor the test plan progress to assure that it is adhered to throughout the test phase.

- CONTROL POINT 14

  The User, CIS Auditor, computer operations personnel, and the Project Leader review the conversion plan for completeness of detail and personnel involved. Plans for communicating the production schedule to top management are discussed as well as other miscellaneous considerations relevant to the specific project.

- CONTROL POINT 15

  The User, CIS Auditor, and Project Leader review all problems not yet resolved, the adequacy of documentation, and any incomplete activities identified. Final reports on the project status then can be written by the CIS Auditor.

Figure 9-7.

Concluded.

Often, problems with a systems development project stem from an overall lack of organization. The auditor is trained to identify the symptoms. Management must be involved at appropriate review points. User and CIS management must validate requirements and approve work in process. Corporate management or a steering committee must conduct phase reviews and provide essential controls over the allocation of major corporate resources.

Finally, a system that has been designed without adequate, effective controls is a temptation for fraud and misuse. The presence of the auditor contributes to a general awareness that control measures will be built-in. Thorough testing and training create further awareness and confidence that, to the extent justified by the potential risks, opportunities and temptations for inappropriate access have been removed.

Documentation

Documentation itself is an essential control on the development process. The auditor's bias often is to begin the building of understanding by reviewing existing documentation. If deficiencies exist in project documentation, the auditor is likely to point them out.

Documentation must be kept current and must be readily available as needed to the project participants. Documentation is an essential communication tool and a common ground for the multiple disciplines within the project team. Without current, dynamic documentation, coordination and quality inevitably will suffer.

The documentation of systems development efforts must be more than a history, or a record of milestones. Documentation must be able to guide and direct the activities of the project team. Tools must be provided for project planning, organization, and control. Reports to users and management must be clear and understandable. Presentations to review bodies must be documented in concise form. Analysts and programmers must have access to tools for modeling, graphic analysis, library and program management, version control, and logging of modifications and updates—all of which should generate ongoing project records.

Once systems are implemented, monitoring is essential to assure a continuity of results. The control measures appropriate for ongoing systems and activities for intermittent reviews to assure that controls remain effective and in place are described in the next chapter.

NEW SYSTEMS REVIEW: TYPES OF AUDITS

New systems review can be subdivided into specific types of audits in support of systems design and implementation efforts. These audits include:

- Monitoring audit
- Design review audit
- Educational and standards audit
- Post-implementation audit.

Monitoring audit. A *monitoring audit* is a systems development audit conducted at specific checkpoints within the systems development life cycle. These audits generally coincide with milestones and reviews that are built into the development methodology. Of particular interest are the outputs for phase reviews by the decision maker or steering committee.

Design review audit. A *design review audit* is an in-process development review conducted at the ends of the preliminary design and detailed design phases. Emphasis is on whether designs implement requirements and on the interfacing of controls.

Educational and standards audit. The *educational and standards audit* examines the compliance of a new system with CIS development, organizational, and operational standards. The educational component of this audit looks at the progress and effectiveness of user training efforts.

Post-implementation audit. A *post-implementation audit* typically is performed three months after implementation of a new system. This audit is a thorough examination of the system and assumes no previous audit participation in development or prior audit examinations.

Selection of Audit Engagements

A fact of life for management of the CIS function is that there are always more requests for new or modified systems than there are resources for development. This situation has given rise to a formal systems planning function in which corporate, CIS, and user managers set priorities for new systems initiatives.

A similar situation exists in the internal audit function. The resources of internal auditors, computer auditors, audit specialists, and technicians typically are in short supply. Just as the cost of implementing controls must be justified by the magnitude of risk, the selection of internal audit engagements also must be weighed against the significance of the systems to be examined.

In making this evaluation, of course, the internal audit function works with and is guided by priorities set by management. Before recommending or selecting a systems development project for audit, a computer auditor (or, more often, the manager of the computer audit function) must weigh the following factors:

- Audit staff usually is limited. The size and makeup of the audit team must be suited to the type of system and to the level of effort required to give an opinion. Moreover, to avoid compromising auditor independence and objectivity, the auditor who performs the post-implementation review should not be the same individual who participates in the systems development process. This condition must be kept in mind when staff assignments are made.

- There are time constraints. Conflicts with other priorities and engagements are bound to arise. As stated previously, further outside pressures may stem from management's desire for prompt reporting of results to outsiders. The need to comply with government regulations also imposes strict time limitations upon many audits.

- The experience level and technical expertise of audit personnel must be considered carefully in making assignments. Outside specialists may have to be recruited and included in the engagement budget. It would be pointless, for example, to attempt to audit an application within a highly distributed computer network without assigning a technical specialist with expertise in data communication controls.

Some additional criteria for evaluation stem from the nature of the project or system itself. These evaluation considerations include:

- Is the technology state-of-the-art? What areas of technical specialization will be involved in gaining adequate understanding of hardware, software, and data communication elements?

- What is the scope of the system's complexity and size? Evidence may be found in the number of lines of code involved; the number of program modules; the sophistication of the programming, tools, or software systems; the degree of distribution; and the complexity of data communications; and so on.

- What is the financial impact of the system on the organization? What is the effect of the application output on decision making?

- Does the application encompass other locations, divisions, or organizations? The scope and magnitude of the audit effort will be affected directly by the number of locations to be covered within the time constraints.

- Does the system or application interact with other systems? This factor bears on complexity, but also raises the possibility that the other systems will have to be examined, thus expanding the scope of the audit.

- In view of these factors, what is the cost of the audit engagement? Is this cost justified by the magnitude of the potential risks to the organization?

- What is the importance of the data asset, or information resource, maintained by the application? How critical is this asset to the business mission or financial viability of the organization?

Systems Development Participation and Independence of the Auditor

Audit participation in the systems development process is aimed at building in controls that, in turn, assure reliability of the finished systems. That's the positive side of the coin. There is also a flip side: Can an auditor participate in the development of a system, and then express an opinion upon its soundness? Is independence compromised?

Clearly, the danger exists, though possibly more in appearance than in reality. Given recognition of this problem, it follows that audit teams must have a way of avoiding either criticism or actual conflict.

In fact, the problem has been recognized and, in most organizations, proven solutions are applied. One effective measure is simply to assign different auditors to systems development projects and to examinations of those projects. Another possibility is to separate responsibilities among auditors. For example, internal auditors may be assigned to systems development while external auditors retain full responsibility for examinations that call for rendering of an opinion.

Also significant is that definitions and implementations of the concepts and standards for independence are spelled out at some length in the publications of all professional societies with a stake in control over CIS systems. These standards must be applied uniformly and with diligence.

These factors, taken together, form a picture of the relative significance of the application or system to the organization. Just as the auditor must decide the controls to be tested within the application, so also the internal audit function must make critical decisions about which applications and systems justify close scrutiny.

The need to be selective in assigning internal audit resources magnifies the importance of involving auditors in systems design. If selective attention can be applied at critical points—as early as possible—the reliance upon the controls that are built-in can be high. Given this degree of reliance, subsequent audit concerns with those systems may focus on examination of exceptions. To paraphrase the analogy to quality control in manufacturing: Quality cannot be inspected into a system; the auditor must see that quality is inherent in the design.

DISCUSSION QUESTIONS

1. How does the issue of system ownership affect the responsibility and authority for systems development?

2. What channels of communication should exist between different interests within the organization and the members of a systems project team?

3. What opportunities for assuring the adequacy of controls might exist at each phase of the systems development life cycle?

4. What is the importance of testing to the auditor's involvement in assuring the adequacy of controls?

5. What should be the role of the internal audit function in systems development?

6. What justifications can be given for involving auditors in systems development?

7. In what ways might a CIS auditor help minimize the risks of systems development to the organization?

8. How does documentation impose control on the systems development process and on the reliability of the emerging system?

9. What types of reviews of new systems might be conducted by CIS auditors?

CASE ASSIGNMENT

To apply the concepts presented in this chapter, turn to the case study for WhyMe Corporation in Appendix A and work through Project 2, which deals with systems development controls.

10 Auditing CIS Applications: Process and Case Study

A B S T R A C T

- An application audit may use computer-assisted techniques to perform some types of audit tests, especially in sampling transactions within large-scale systems.

- Purposes of application audits are outlined in professional standards promulgated by the AICPA, IIA, EDPAA, and IFAC, as well as in relation to policies set by organization management.

- Application audits encompass the basic steps of planning, fieldwork, reporting, and follow-up. Audits may be required by mandates within the scope of the charter of the internal audit function, or auditors may be asked to review a specific application at the request of management.

- Selection criteria for computer-assisted audit tools include the degree of necessity and the function performed, as well as level of audit reliability, economics, and the professional image of auditors and their organizations. Computer-assisted functions can include item selection, mathematics, data analysis, and simulation.

- Typical application areas include: cash, receivables, inventories, investments, accounts payable, equity, income and expense, and income taxes.

INTRODUCTION

Chapter 5 surveys the types of audits typically performed by computer auditors. This chapter covers the audit of computer-based applications, or application audits. Topics covered are:

- Purpose of application audits

- General approach to application audits

- Application of computer-assisted techniques in support of the audit process

- Illustration of an audit involving computer-based applications.

The next chapter completes the discussion of application audits by covering the implementation of specific computer-assisted audit techniques.

PURPOSE OF APPLICATION AUDITS

The purposes of computer application audits stem from responsibilities of the auditor as set forth by:

- American Institute of Certified Public Accountants (AICPA) Statements on Auditing Standards (SAS)

- Institute of Internal Auditors (IIA) Standards for the Professional Practice of Internal Auditing

- EDP Auditors Association Control Objectives (1983)

- International Federation of Accountants International Audit Guidelines

- Organization management.

AICPA Statements on Auditing Standards

SAS No. 48, promulgated by the Auditing Standards Board of the American Institute of Certified Public Accountants, requires auditors to understand the entire financial system and to evaluate accounting controls. SAS No. 48 substantiates the need for examination of computer-based controls that may have financial-statement significance. External auditors of financial statements comply with SAS No. 48 by performing computer application audits in which they identify and evaluate controls. (See Appendix G for a review of SAS No. 48.)

IIA Standards For the Professional Practice of Internal Auditing

Specific purposes for the audit of computer applications have been established by the Institute of Internal Auditors in Audit Standard No. 1, Controls. According to these guidelines, the auditor must assure that:

- Financial and processing controls exist for complete and valid input, accurate data throughout processing, and correct output.

- The system satisfies user needs.

- Development and implementation plans are realistic and provide adequate user training.

- File conversion is controlled properly.

- Operations are controlled during the initial operating cycle.

- System documentation, security, and disaster recovery procedures are established.

EDP Auditors Association Control Objectives

The need for auditability of computer applications is stressed in the publication "Control Objectives, 1983" issued by the EDP Auditors Association. This standard identifies the key types of controls an auditor should evaluate in computer-based applications. This guide also provides an audit checklist designed to guide examinations of computer-based applications.

IFA International Auditing Guidelines

The need for auditability of computer-based applications is not just of concern in the United States, but is a worldwide issue. The International Federation of Accountants has issued two International Auditing Guidelines (IAG) which apply to CIS applications. IAG-15 focuses on "Auditing in an EDP Environment" and IAG-16 addresses "Computer-Assisted Audit Techniques."

Management

An application audit must assure organization management that the systems provide accurate and timely information. Management needs accurate and timely information to make sound decisions that may affect the organization's profits, competitiveness, or viability.

APPLICATION AUDIT PHASES OF ACTIVITY			
PLANNING	FIELDWORK	REPORTING	FOLLOW-UP
• Initiate audit	• Opening conference—meet auditee to coordinate work	• Prepare rough draft	• Wait for auditee to respond
• Prepare engagement letter	• Design tests and gather materials for tests	• Conduct closing conference	• Assess auditee's response
• Gather preliminary information	• Conduct tests and evaluate results	• Prepare final report	• Prepare postaudit follow-up report
• Formulate audit program for guidance in fieldwork	• Record findings in work papers	• Submit final report	• Submit postaudit follow-up report
	• Review audit progress in accordance with audit program		

Figure 10-1.

This chart partitions the application audit functions of planning, fieldwork, reporting, and follow-up into specific tasks.

GENERAL APPROACH TO APPLICATION AUDITS

As shown in Figure 10-1, application audits typically involve four phases of activity. These phases are:

- Planning
- Fieldwork
- Reporting
- Follow-up.

Planning

The planning phase involves initiating the audit, writing an engagement letter, and gathering preliminary information. There are two basic ways to initiate an audit:

- Audit charter

- Management request.

Audit charter. Recall that an audit charter is a formal definition of the internal computer audit function. Because the responsibility to assure the reliability of applications is inherent in the charter, an audit charter mandates application audits. A CIS audit charter generally specifies the following:

- The nature of the CIS audit responsibility

- The coverage expected from the computer audit staff

- Projected staffing level to give this coverage

- The tools needed to execute audit responsibilities properly (for example, software packages, data terminals, etc.)

- Disclaimers.

Disclaimers are critically important and state that the computer audit function is not comprehensive. That is, the computer audit staff cannot examine every application. The process of audit examination is a sampling procedure. There always will be some function, department, or system that will not be audited.

The main reason for being selective about the applications to be audited is to apply limited audit resources effectively. In selecting applications for audit, the computer audit function must weigh the following criteria:

- What is the importance of the application to the daily operations of the organization? Generally, the auditor will want to select applications that are an integral part of the organization's principal business activity.

- What is the sensitivity of the application? Data processed by the application may be of a proprietary or private nature. Auditors will want to focus on situations that might result in disclosure of proprietary information to the public or to competing organizations. Sensitivity would be a critical factor, for example, if unauthorized disclosure of pricing information could put the organization at a competitive disadvantage. Applications that produce outputs to be sent to customers, as in the generation of invoices by a billing system, also would be sensitive.

- What corporate and legal policies bear on the application? Some applications may have to be audited for compliance with corporate directives or governmental requirements. For example, an application that produces reports to be sent to government agencies must be audited for compliance with regulations and for assurance that the information produced is current and accurate.

- What is the impact of the application on the organization's financial statements? An obvious area of concern is with applications that generate financially significant data.

Management request.   The other way to initiate an application audit is by a management request. This simply means that organization management calls upon internal or external auditors to examine a specific system or application. For example, the president of a company might call the director of internal auditing to request an audit of one of the company's divisions. The director then would give this assignment to an audit team. Involvement by external auditors can be by management request. However, external auditors must attest to the reliability of management's financial statements to regulatory agencies such as SEC-mandated financial reporting audits and to the public. Also, external auditors may be engaged for special management advisory engagements.

An application audit, then, may be either selected by the auditor or requested by management. After the audit has been initiated, the auditor conducts an opening conference with the auditee's management. In this conference, the auditor explains the audit, sets the purpose and scope, and elicits information on problems and background.

The auditor then writes an engagement letter informing the auditee of the scope of and the schedule for the examination. After this notice is sent, the auditor gathers data to learn more about the organizational and operational structure of the application to be audited. The subsequent steps of the planning phase of the engagement, then, include:

- Review documentation.

- Conduct interviews with application personnel.

- Formulate an audit program.

Documentation and interviews are sources of data for gaining an overview understanding of the application. On the basis of this preliminary understanding, an audit program is formulated that defines audit tasks for the rest of the engagement.

Review documentation.   To gain a preliminary understanding, the auditor looks at documentation on four distinct levels:

- System overview
- Program detail
- Operations instructions
- User instructions.

System overview.   Documention that supports an overview of system functions includes:

- A narrative description of the application and explanation of its purpose
- A system flowchart showing relationships among input documents, programs, files, reports and input/output displays
- Layouts of input documents and output reports and displays
- Lists of codes.

Program detail.   Documentation that supports each program within the system should include file layouts, programs, processing descriptions, and source listings.

Operations instructions.   Operations documentation should include instructions to tape librarians, data entry clerks, and computer operators.

User instructions.   User manuals should contain instructions for preparing and batching input, entering data into video display terminals (VDTs), correcting and resubmitting errors, and using output.

Conduct interviews.   Another data gathering method is interviewing personnel. Interviews can provide insights into the study area because user and operations personnel are well acquainted with the application and its functions. The auditor may wish to use a questionnaire, such as the sample in Figure 10-2. Such a questionnaire can be used as an instrument for gathering information about the system from department personnel.

A word of caution is in order with respect to interviews. Auditors should understand that people usually have a natural resentment to being audited. Some people even may feel that the auditor is a management spy who is looking for errors. Others believe that the auditor only reports bad news and that the auditees can do nothing to prevent a negative report. As a result, auditees may withhold information, ignore the auditor, or mislead the auditor into improper or unreasonable findings and recommendations.

AUDIT QUESTIONNAIRE

ON-LINE DATA VALIDATION AND EDITING	YES	NO
1. Are preprogrammed keying formats used to make sure that data is recorded in the proper field, format, etc.?	_____	_____
2. Is interactive display used to allow the terminal operator to interact with the system during data entry?	_____	_____
3. Are computer-aided instructions, such as prompting, used with on-line dialog to reduce the number of operator errors?	_____	_____
4. Are intelligent terminals used to allow front-end validation, editing, and control?	_____	_____
5. Is data validation and editing performed as early as possible in the data flow to insure that the application rejects any incorrect transaction before its entry into the system?	_____	_____
6. Is data validation and editing performed for all input data fields even though an error may be detected in an earlier field of the same transaction?	_____	_____

Figure 10-2.

A questionnaire such as this may be used as a basis for interviews of application personnel by the auditor. The area of study in this case is on-line data validation and editing.

To make the best of such situations, the auditor should project a positive, constructive image. The auditor, after all, works for the improvement of the organization. By contrast, it is not the auditor's role to be a police officer, or one who enforces rules and regulations. Of course, there will be times when the auditor must criticize as well as praise. However, these comments always should be framed within the context of seeking the improvement and ultimate benefit of the organization.

From a practical standpoint, the auditor can improve the reliability of data gained in interviews by applying a straightforward investigative technique: To assure that the questionnaire responses are correct, the auditor should ask several people the same questions, pose the same question in different ways, analyze the answers, and observe actual operations to cross-check responses.

Formulate audit program. After the audit has been assigned, the engagement letter written, and the preliminary information gathered, the auditor prepares an audit program for the next phase and the planning phase ends.

APPLICATION SYSTEMS MAINTENANCE   *(PAYROLL SYSTEM)*

1. <u>Authorization and Approval of Systems Changes</u> (authorization objective)
    What techniques are used to provide reasonable assurance that all
    application systems/program changes are authorized and approved by
    appropriate user department and CIS management personnel?

    [✓] User department authorization and ~~written~~ *verbal* approval are required for
    all application systems/program changes.

    [✓] CIS management authorization and ~~written~~ *verbal* approval are required for
    all application systems/program changes.

    [✓] Program library software is used to report all program changes to
    CIS management and user departments.

    [✓] *Verbal* Approved change requests are required for all changes, and a log is
    kept of completed changes and changes in process.

    [✓] Thorough supervision and review of program changes are performed by
    ~~programming supervisors.~~ *controller*

    [✓] Formally approved ~~written~~ standards for program changes and
    documentation exist and are followed.
    Program listings are maintained and updated.

    [ ]

    [ ]

    [ ]

    Control technique exceptions and control and risk evaluation:
    *AUDIT NOTE: Lack of formal guidelines and
    documented audit trail for making program
    changes, very little documentation other
    than annotation on listing.* *KF 1/9/8X*

Figure 10-3.

This checklist is an audit program segment for application systems maintenance. In this case, the application is a payroll system.

The audit program identifies the major areas of the application to be examined and provides the auditor with a systematic guide for performance of the audit. The audit program consists of tasks to be performed by the auditor in the process of examining internal control effectiveness. Based on findings or environmental circumstances, the tasks may be modified continually to meet changing requirements or objectives. Figure 10-3 provides an example of an audit program segment that examines application systems maintenance. Note the remarks made by the auditor.

Fieldwork

The second phase of an application audit is the fieldwork, or the examination and evaluation phase. First, the auditor meets with auditee management to coordinate the fieldwork. Next, the auditor gathers materials and information from the auditee for tests. Then, the auditor develops findings as a result of performing tests of key controls and verifying compliance with procedures and security measures. Taken together, these actions measure the effectiveness of operations.

In performing tests of controls, the auditor may draw on a variety of computer-assisted audit techniques, a sample of which are presented in the table in Figure 10-4. Some of these techniques are discussed in greater depth in this chapter. By way of example, representative techniques are covered below. Some of the principal computer-assisted audit techniques are:

- Use of audit software

- Flowchart generation

- Test decks.

Audit software. Use of audit software makes it possible to perform required functions directly on application files. Audit software can be used to:

- Analyze and compare files

- Count, total, and subtotal file data by category

- Select specific records for examination

- Conduct random samples

- Validate calculations

- Prepare confirmation letters

- Analyze aging of accounts receivable, accounts payable, and similar files.

An audit software package in common use is DYL-280, a *high-level language* that is relatively easy to learn. High-level languages generate program code from powerful, concise commands. DYL-280 can dump file content, manipulate data, conduct tests of random samples, accumulate field counts, and create reports. A source-code listing for a program written in DYL-280 and examples of printed output are shown in Figure 10-5a-c.

A less commonly used package is FOCUS, a *fourth-generation, nonprocedural language.* (A microcomputer-based version is called PC FOCUS.) Fourth-generation languages produce program code based on specifications

TECHNIQUE	CAPABILITY SUPPLIED BY	USED BY	DATA USED	PURPOSE	ADVANTAGES	DISADVANTAGES
Transaction tagging	Vendor or application system designer	Auditors and managers	Live accounting	Compliance and substantive test	Full range of selectivity	Adds to overhead of system, special programming
Real time notification	Systems programmer or vendor	Auditors and managers	Live accounting and system	Compliance test and control	Control and timeliness	Cost
Audit log	System designer	Auditors and control personnel	Live accounting and system	Compliance and substantive test	Specified transactions logged for audit review	Cost
Monitoring	Vendor	Auditors and managers	Live system	Review actual system activity	Shows what has happened	Requires technical knowledge to interpret
Audit software and programs	Vendor and system designer, software house, manufacturer or audit firm	Auditors and managers	Historical and live	Compliance and substantive test. Perform wide variety of audit tests	Retrieves data for audit purposes. Relatively easy to use, not expensive	Requires some programming knowledge by auditor. Presently limited to types of files that can be accessed.
Simulation	Auditors, internal and external, with program copy	Auditors	Historical	Determine accuracy of data processed	Permits comparison with real processing	Extensive use can be large consumer of machine resources
Extended records	Design of client applications	Auditors and managers	Historical	Provide complete trial for audit and management purposes	Provides complete account history	Very costly use of machine resources at present
Integrated test facility	Auditors, mostly internal	Auditors	Dummy	Compliance test	Relatively inexpensive	Must be "backed out" very carefully
Program analysis techniques, i.e. flowchart generation or instrumentation software	Special software, contractor or vendor	Auditors and programmers	Usually dummy	Authentication of program operation. Check of key points in program execution	Gives better understanding of application; gives assurance controls are functioning	Needs auditor knowledge of programming, may be expensive; useful only in certain circumstances.
Test deck	Vendor, system designer, software house, auditor	Auditors and programmers	Dummy and/or live	Authentication of controls	Gives better understanding of application controls, compliance testing	Requires some programming knowledge, limited to range of tests conducted

Figure 10-4.

This table summarizes the characteristics of different computer-assisted audit techniques.

A.

```
DYLAKOR SOFTWARE SYSTEMS INC. DYL-280    3.0              DATE  8/07/85      PAGE    1
1-------------------DYL-280 FREE FORM TEXT-------------------72        -------

** DYL-280 STATEMENTS START HERE ........                                      1
FILE INFILE FB 300 6000                                                        2
  DIVNAM 20 2 CH (DIVISION'NAME)                                               3
  INSTNAME 20 57 CH (INSTITUTION'NAME)                                        4
  TYPE 2 107 CH (PLANT'TYPE)                                                   5
  DATE 4 159 CH (PLANT'DATE)                                                   6
  CASH 6 163 PD 2 A (CASH)                                                     7
  AR 6 175 PD 2 A (ACCOUNTS'RECEIVABLE)                                        8
  WIP 6 187 PD 2 A (WORK IN'PROCESS)                                          9
  AP 6 223 PD 2 A (ACCOUNTS'PAYABLE)                                         10
FILE OUTFILE OUTPUT FROM INFILE FB 300 6000                                  11
READ INFILE                                                                  12
WRITE OUTFILE                                                                13
LIST DIVNAM INSTNAME TYPE DATE CASH AR WIP AP                                14
T1 'SOLUTION TO TERMINAL EXERCISE 1'                                         15
T2 'BASIC DYL-280 CLASS' WITH 4 AFTER                                        16
T1+5 DYLDATE                                                                 17
T1+112 DYLPAGE                                                               18
FIN                                                                          19
                                                                            16.
                                                                            17.
                                                                            18.
                                                                            19.
                                                                            20.
                                                                            21.
                                                                            22.
                                                                            23.
                                                                            24.
                                                                            25.
                                                                            26.
                                                                            27.
                                                                            28.
                                                                            29.
                                                                            30.
                                                                            31.
                                                                            32.
                                                                            33.
                                                                            34.
```

B.

```
DYLAKOR SOFTWARE SYSTEMS INC. *DYL-280   3.0 *           DATE  08/07/85     PAGE    1

        1         2         3         4         5         6         7         8         9
1234567890123456789012345678901234567890123456789012345678901234567890123456789012345678901234567890

DYL-280 CONTROL TOTALS

FILE        RECORD      CHARACTER     BLOCK      DROPPED       REWRITTEN      INSERTED       ERASED
ID          COUNT       COUNT         COUNT      BLOCK COUNT   RECORD COUNT   RECORD COUNT   RECORD COUNT

INFILE      489         146,700
OUTFILE     489         146,700

                 RECORDS                  PAGES

FILE PRINT                                  1

REPORT PRINT                               11

FIXED BLANK COUNT

FIXED DECIMAL DIVIDE

   RETURN CODE-0000

********************************************************************************************
*                                                                                          *
*    DYL-280 IS SOLD OR LEASED ONLY BY DYLAKOR SOFTWARE SYSTEMS.  USE OF THIS PROGRAM       *
*  IS RESTRICTED TO THE FIRM PURCHASING OR RENTING THE SYSTEM FROM DYLAKOR.  PROGRAM TAPES, *
*  MANUALS, FORMS, OR DOCUMENTATION MAY NOT BE REPRODUCED IN WHOLE OR IN PART WITHOUT WRITTEN*
*  CONSENT FROM DYLAKOR.  ALL MANUALS, FORMS, AND MATERIALS ARE PROTECTED BY COPYRIGHTS.     *
*                                                                                          *
********************************************************************************************
```

Figure 10-5. Shown here and on the following page are examples of the high-level language, DYL-280.

A. This printout shows program statements written in DYL-280.

B. This screen shows intermediate results during execution of a DYL-280 program.

C. This printout shows partial output from a DYL-280 program run.

DIVISION NAME	INSTITUTION NAME	PLANT TYPE	PLANT DATE	CASH	ACCOUNTS RECEIVABLE	WORK IN PROCESS	ACCOUNTS PAYABLE
DATA/GRAPHICS DIVISI	ALDERSON	DE	8110	36,293.20	214,206.90	6,423.47	13,845.45
DATA/GRAPHICS DIVISI	ALDERSON	DE	8111	26,602.75	195,548.05	3,022.36	13,062.72
DATA/GRAPHICS DIVISI	ALDERSON	DE	8112	78,850.08	153,179.19	402.51	12,654.55
DATA/GRAPHICS DIVISI	ALDERSON	DE	8201	64,261.15	152,042.76	.00	12,045.85
DATA/GRAPHICS DIVISI	ALDERSON	DE	8202	102,155.18	107,463.33	7,311.72	18,674.25
DATA/GRAPHICS DIVISI	ALDERSON	DE	8203	99,764.98	100,629.24	.00	24,305.79
DATA/GRAPHICS DIVISI	ALDERSON	DE	8204	122,323.87	63,412.58	.00	26,320.24
DATA/GRAPHICS DIVISI	ALDERSON	DE	8205	24,839.44	62,984.97	3,741.43	32,932.93
DATA/GRAPHICS DIVISI	ALDERSON	DE	8206	24,391.37	68,462.77	191.71	41,085.33
DATA/GRAPHICS DIVISI	ALDERSON	DE	8207	17,998.16	55,376.70	2,985.84	47,734.34
DATA/GRAPHICS DIVISI	ALDERSON	DE	8208	19,618.73	60,118.62	1,687.27	50,438.87
DATA/GRAPHICS DIVISI	ALDERSON	DE	8209	1,633.37	43,068.04	.00	46,101.58
DATA/GRAPHICS DIVISI	ENGLEWOOD	DE	8110	83,470.56	27,755.96	120.18	6,190.59
DATA/GRAPHICS DIVISI	ENGLEWOOD	DE	8111	72,730.42	40,819.87	397.14	15,331.30
DATA/GRAPHICS DIVISI	ENGLEWOOD	DE	8112	73,923.08	43,086.40	677.93	16,393.91
DATA/GRAPHICS DIVISI	ENGLEWOOD	DE	8201	94,489.36	19,567.14	1,636.08	20,420.85
DATA/GRAPHICS DIVISI	ENGLEWOOD	DE	8202	77,161.13	27,851.49	1,965.64	18,247.72
DATA/GRAPHICS DIVISI	ENGLEWOOD	DE	8203	69,746.10	23,491.13	1,103.15	15,674.45
DATA/GRAPHICS DIVISI	ENGLEWOOD	DE	8204	62,823.22	25,409.18	1,022.90	17,050.67
DATA/GRAPHICS DIVISI	ENGLEWOOD	DE	8205	47,377.94	29,396.79	2,764.61	16,667.24
DATA/GRAPHICS DIVISI	ENGLEWOOD	DE	8206	39,352.63	29,140.74	1,761.71	17,721.53
DATA/GRAPHICS DIVISI	ENGLEWOOD	DE	8207	27,427.14	34,768.40	.00	19,141.18
DATA/GRAPHICS DIVISI	ENGLEWOOD	DE	8208	42,646.64	11,701.47	449.74	21,466.60
DATA/GRAPHICS DIVISI	ENGLEWOOD	DE	8209	20,728.87	2,220.16	.00	21,058.16
DATA/GRAPHICS DIVISI	FORT WORTH	DE	8110	27,058.90	62,155.33	1,815.96	18,794.03
DATA/GRAPHICS DIVISI	FORT WORTH	DE	8111	10,843.29	76,040.34	4,988.93	21,849.29
DATA/GRAPHICS DIVISI	FORT WORTH	DE	8112	39,294.66	85,784.11	4,014.98	11,857.68
DATA/GRAPHICS DIVISI	FORT WORTH	DE	8201	33,727.48	90,479.50	.00	11,105.04
DATA/GRAPHICS DIVISI	FORT WORTH	DE	8202	29,261.26	89,148.59	.00	12,136.58
DATA/GRAPHICS DIVISI	FORT WORTH	DE	8203	19,134.14	86,626.09	2,849.91	14,101.63
DATA/GRAPHICS DIVISI	FORT WORTH	DE	8204	28,972.17	67,538.13	275.12	10,923.11
DATA/GRAPHICS DIVISI	FORT WORTH	DE	8205	51,148.36	43,823.39	.00	11,304.09
DATA/GRAPHICS DIVISI	FORT WORTH	DE	8206	50,855.51	43,890.26	182.90	12,297.44
DATA/GRAPHICS DIVISI	FORT WORTH	DE	8207	43,497.36	50,694.76	.00	11,964.21
DATA/GRAPHICS DIVISI	FORT WORTH	DE	8208	36,308.67	58,615.64	.00	12,942.59
DATA/GRAPHICS DIVISI	FORT WORTH	DE	8209	37,668.40	26,923.55	3,717.18	12,607.69
DATA/GRAPHICS DIVISI	FORT WORTH	PD	8110	15,269.82	27,983.65	.00	6,965.96
DATA/GRAPHICS DIVISI	FORT WORTH	PD	8111	10,412.80	13,737.00	.00	7,095.75
DATA/GRAPHICS DIVISI	FORT WORTH	PD	8112	4,678.15	20,533.50	.00	7,223.22
DATA/GRAPHICS DIVISI	FORT WORTH	PD	8201	30,068.80	30,625.95	.00	8,308.45
DATA/GRAPHICS DIVISI	FORT WORTH	PD	8202	24,712.00	20,536.85	.00	11,202.95
DATA/GRAPHICS DIVISI	FORT WORTH	PD	8203	18,169.28	30,720.30	.00	6,698.53
DATA/GRAPHICS DIVISI	FORT WORTH	PD	8204	14,619.77	38,313.05	.00	7,799.85
DATA/GRAPHICS DIVISI	FORT WORTH	PD	8205	6,342.23	45,228.80	.00	7,684.81
DATA/GRAPHICS DIVISI	FORT WORTH	PD	8206	30,771.72	24,476.15	.00	7,739.75
DATA/GRAPHICS DIVISI	FORT WORTH	PD	8207	23,636.54	37,698.30	.00	7,866.50
DATA/GRAPHICS DIVISI	FORT WORTH	PD	8208	41,620.84	28,687.10	.00	8,404.95

for inputs and outputs. The language is said to be nonprocedural because a strict, formal syntax is not required. Specifications can be in English-like statements, as shown in Figure 10-6. Thus, FOCUS allows the auditor to think primarily about what information is needed and the output format of the results. For example, the auditor enters English-like phrases that specify the records to be retrieved, the calculations to be performed, how report lines are to be sorted, as well as the format for the report display. Using the generalized packages, programs developed with DYL-280, FOCUS, and PC FOCUS are custom-tailored and generated for each audit job.

Audit software can be an excellent tool for auditing assistance. With a minimum of coding, the auditor can devise tests to check particular fields, as well as to extract and accumulate data from files.

Audit software also has some disadvantages. One disadvantage is that application files must be available to the auditor. For example, to analyze file updating, the auditor needs input and output files associated with the process. If access to the files is not practical, the auditor will have to find another examination technique. Another disadvantage is that audit software is difficult to apply without an in-depth working knowledge of the system under study. If, for example, user or operations personnel do not understand the system correctly, they may misinform the auditor, who then will have difficulty getting the audit package to run properly.

These disadvantages, of course, may be encountered in connection with any audit technique. The real limitation or disadvantage in the use of audit software is that examinations are limited to the results of processing. The actual processing itself is not audited.

Audit software can be expensive—in connection with training, running, and maintaining applications. However, in comparison with other within-the-computer audit techniques, this may be a cost-effective alternative. The price of some typical audit software packages range from about $3,000 to $65,000. Further, some audit software packages generally consume large amounts of computer time. In particular, generation of programs under high-level languages requires extensive interpretation or compilation. Finally, even if these costs appear justified, there is no guarantee that a given package will perform the desired analysis efficiently—or at all. However, they can perform most of the after-the-fact manipulations required by auditors. Examples of typical audit software packages and their vendors are listed in Figure 10-7.

Flowchart generation.   Another computer-assisted audit technique is the use of *flowcharting software,* or utility programs that create system flowcharts for application programs. The flowchart produced shows the input files accessed and the output files created by the program. After the flowchart is

A.   C:AGER.FEX   SIZE=19   LINE=0

```
* * * TOP OF FILE * * *
DEFINE FILE EACCTREC ADD
$BALANCE_DUE/D7.2SBCCR = BALANCE_DUE/100 ;
AGING/A7 = IF INVOICE_DATE LT  850303 THEN 'OVER120' ELSE
IF INVOICE_DATE LT 850402 THEN '91-120' ELSE
IF INVOICE_DATE LT 850502 THEN '61-90' ELSE
IF INVOICE_DATE LT 850601 THEN '31-60' ELSE
IF INVOICE_DATE LT 850631 THEN ' 1-30' ELSE
'C/O_ERR' ;
END
TABLE FILE EACCTREC
SUM $BALANCE_DUE IN +1 AND ROW-TOTAL BY CUSTOMER_NO AS 'CUST#'
ACROSS AGING
AS '  --------------------- DAYS ------------------------ ;
ON TABLE COLUMN-TOTAL
HEADING
   "                         AGING OF"
   "                   ACCOUNTS RECEIVABLE"
   "                   ===================="
END
===>
```

B.   PAGE   1

AGING OF
ACCOUNTS RECEIVABLE
====================

| | | | ------------------------- DAYS ------------------------- | | | |
CUST#	1-30	31-60	61-90	91-120	C/O_ERR	OVER120	TOTAL
10	41.35	405.20	241.35	.	115.50	41.35	844.75
265	464.55	122.00	.	.	.	521.50	1,108.05
449	85.65	205.70	.	.	.	.	291.35
531	80.35	391.00	112.35	.	80.00	542.85	1,206.55
617	.	330.40	.	.	.	.	330.40
1007	93.60	.	.	.	.	.	93.60
1018	141.20	.	.	.	.	.	141.20
1065	34.50	.	.	.	.	.	34.50
1116	608.30	.	.	81.60	.	.	689.90
1168	251.65	.	.	.	.	.	251.65
1204	375.00	215.30	.	245.00	.	.	835.30
1347	191.45	693.10	35.00	108.40	66.10	607.55	1,701.60
1473	.	535.60	.	.	.	.	535.60

Figure 10-6.

A. *Printout shows source code for an audit routine written in PC FOCUS.*

B. *This report was generated by a PC FOCUS routine.*

created, the auditor pinpoints the controls, including the control totals for the number of records read and the number of records written.

Test decks.   Recall that a test deck is a set of input data developed by the auditor. The auditor then runs the test deck against the application program.

SELECTED AUDITING SOFTWARE VENDORS

VENDOR	PACKAGE	EQUIPMENT
Arthur Andersen 33 W. Monroe St. Chicago, IL 60603	Audex 100	IBM 360/370/43XX/ 30XX and PCMs
Coopers & Lybrand 1251 Ave. of the Americas New York, NY 10020	Auditpak II	IBM 360/370 and System 3
Cullinet Software 400 Blue Hill Dr. Westood, MA 02090	EDP-Auditor Culprit	IBM 360/370/43XX/ 30XX and PCMs
Deloitte, Haskins & Sells One World Trade Center New York, NY 10048	Audit tape	IBM 360/370/43XX/ 30XX
Dylakor 17418 Chatsworth St. Granada Hills, CA 91344	DYL-Audit DYL-260 DYL-280	IBM 360/370/43XX/ 30XX and PCMs
Informatics General 21050 Vanowen St. Canoga Park, CA 91304	Mark IV, V	Any IBM or PCM under OS or DOS
Information Builders 1250 Broadway New York, NY 10001	PC-Focus Focus	Any IBM OS/MVS system and PCs (640K)
Pansophic Systems 709 Enterprise Dr. Oak Brook, IL 60521	Panaudit	IBM 360/370/43XX/ 30XX and PCMs
Sage Systems 5161 River Rd. Bethesda, MD 20816	Cars	Burroughs, Control Data, Data General, DEC, Hewlett- Packard, Honeywell, IBM mainframes and PCMs, Systems 34 and 38, ICL, NCR, Prime, Sperry, and Wang
TSI International 50 Washington St. Norwalk, CT 06854	The Audit Analyzer	IBM 360/370/43XX/ 30XX and PCMs

Figure 10-7.

This table lists some of the vendors of auditing software. (Adapted from Snyder, J., "Taking the Angst out of Auditing," Computer Decisions, April, 1983, p. 48.)

There is a key difference between audit software and test decks. Audit software is used to test the validity of certain data in application files. Generalized audit software processes live application data under known procedures. The idea is to derive results that match the live application for the processing of selected data samples. Test decks, on the other hand, exercise the entire, live program under production conditions. Use of test decks by auditors is similar in method and strategy to the testing of programs and program modules by programmers during systems development.

There are two major drawbacks to using test decks. First, the test-deck method can be expensive because a comprehensive test deck is difficult and time-consuming for the auditor to develop. Second, test data must be separated from actual data, which can be rather difficult in practice. To preserve the integrity of application files, separate file copies may have to be made or rebuilt for testing purposes. If the actual application files are large, small dummy files can be created to reduce the time the auditor needs to spend examining the output for the test transactions.

After performing each audit test, the auditor records findings in a set of audit workpapers. At key points, the auditor reviews the workpapers and notes progress. If results are not satisfactory, the auditor gathers additional materials and performs additional tests. When the auditor is satisfied that the examination and evaluation have been carried to sufficient depth, the field-work phase ends.

Reporting

The third phase of an application audit is the reporting phase. First, the auditor prepares a rough draft of the audit report. Then, the auditor conducts a closing conference, in which audit findings are reviewed with the auditee.

In this closing conference, the auditor and auditee should review and consider the following questions:

- What are the audit findings?
- How do the findings differ from expectations and specifications for the application?
- What is the significance of the findings?
- What recommendations are indicated by the findings?

In the closing conference, the auditee has the opportunity to challenge the findings and to correct the auditor if errors are found in the report. This feedback is particularly valuable to the auditor, since it provides an essential check on the accuracy of the audit report.

On the basis of the closing conference, the auditor may revise, edit, and polish the audit report. The report then is rendered formally to auditee and organization management.

Follow-Up

The fourth part of an application audit is the follow-up phase. Normally, a follow-up is needed if there are significant audit findings or if it will be a long time before the next planned audit. After the audit report is submitted, the auditor should allow a reasonable time—perhaps a month—for a response from auditee management. Auditee response generally falls into one of the following categories:

- Implemented per management reply
- Implemented (additional explanation required)
- Resolved
- Unresolved
- Audit findings in error
- Implementation in progress
- Implemented as recommended by audit.

The internal audit function usually will have policies specifying the follow-up actions in each case. The purpose of the follow-up is to determine the degree to which the auditee and its management are being responsive to the audit report. During the follow-up, the auditor may conduct further tests to determine whether the recommendations in the report are being implemented.

After the auditor determines the auditee's response, a postaudit follow-up report is prepared. The follow-up report informs management about the implementation status of the audit recommendations.

The discussion to this point has focused on the process of application audits in computer-based environments. The following presentation explores in greater depth some techniques for using the computer itself to perform much of the examination work.

APPLYING COMPUTER-ASSISTED AUDIT TECHNIQUES

In general, computer-assisted auditing encompasses any procedure or technique in which the computer is used as an audit tool in an audit support function. The terms *audit tool* and *audit support* are indicative of what happens in computer-assisted auditing. The computer does not perform a total audit, nor does it carry out entire examination steps by itself. Rather, the computer provides the professional auditor with specific support in implementing desired analyses and tests. Computer resources can take the form of mainframe, minicomputer, or microcomputer—or a combination of resources.

Computer-assisted auditing can involve a wide variety of techniques. Indeed, computer-assisted auditing comprises different things to different auditors in different situations: The audit approach derives its form and nature from the audit problem itself.

Two elements of the audit situation have the greatest influence on the scope and extent of computer-assisted auditing:

- Degree of necessity
- Function performed.

Degree of Necessity

For many years, it has been common to characterize two choices concerning computerized systems: Auditing could be done through the computer or around the computer. Through the computer meant, simply, that the computer was used as an audit tool. Around-the-computer auditing activities related wholly to the visible audit trail, whether it was produced manually or by computer.

Unfortunately, this latter concept often described a practice of review and testing right up to the front door of the CIS department, then picking up the trail at the back door and developing examination techniques that attempted to test the results of the interim, computer-based processes.

These alternatives oversimplify what really should happen in audits of computer-using entities. Experience has shown that computerized portions of information systems must be audited. The computer used as an audit tool can facilitate reviews and tests. These activities must be based on understanding and evaluation of the computerized, as well as the manual, portions of the system.

Recent cases of computer-associated fraud and abuse have eroded the entrenched, comfortable position of ignoring what happened in the computer room and working around it. Today, audit examination of any significant application that uses computers must include—at a minimum—a review and evaluation of internal controls within the computerized portions of the system.

Thus, the auditor no longer has a choice between going around or through the computer. The computer must be considered in the audit scheme of things. Today, the choice centers around alternatives for auditing computerized systems. The auditor can perform analyses and tests with or without the computer, but the computer cannot be excluded from the picture.

Mandatory or discretionary?   Given that review and evaluation of internal controls built into computerized systems are necessary, the nature of the system itself determines whether the auditor has a choice of using or not using the computer. There are situations in which use of the computer for internal control reviews and tests of financially significant applications is mandatory. There are other cases in which use of the computer is discretionary.

Mandatory situations pretty well identify themselves. The auditor looks for signs indicating that it is impossible to identify or to follow an audit trail. If no visible audit trail exists, the computer probably must be used unless there are some overall tests available. There may be no adequate audit trail if the computerized system does not generate printed copies of master and transaction files on an interim basis. Audit trails also may not exist if files for multiple applications have been incorporated into integrated databases. In other words, if the auditor does not have sufficient evidential matter delivered by the system, the computer must be used to develop or reconstruct needed items.

Another type of mandatory situation may exist when computerized systems are so vast that they defy manual examination of documentation. A company may produce mountains of paper detailing master and transaction files. Thus, the use of computer-assisted audit techniques may be the most economical and efficient means of performing audit tests.

In discretionary situations, the auditor has a choice. The audit may be conducted with or without the computer. Given that sufficient documentation exists, three factors will influence this choice:

- Level of audit reliability
- Economics
- Professional image.

Level of audit reliability.   The importance of increased audit reliability will depend upon the auditor's evaluation of internal controls within a given application. If the reliability of internal controls is evaluated as high, the level of computerized review can be correspondingly reduced. One value of the computer as an examination tool lies in the fact that it is possible, and often relatively cost-effective, to perform a 100-percent review of transactions within any given application. Even though costs might be greater than for manual sampling, the greater reliability inherent in 100-percent examination may justify the incremental costs and lead to a choice of this alternative.

Economics. Economics are an ever-present, though frequently unspoken, influence on the selection of audit techniques. Refer again to the matrix table in Figure 10-4. A major disadvantage listed under many computer-assisted techniques is cost. In most cases, however, it will cost more to perform a computerized examination during the first year. If there are prospects that the same examination programs can be used in two or three succeeding years, the cost picture can change materially.

Professional image. Projecting a professional image can be an important influence for both auditors and organizations. An audit firm, for example, may opt in favor of computerized review, in part, to increase the experience level of its staff in dealing with projected greater use of computers in the future. Similarly, a company's financial vice president might authorize computerized review in a discretionary situation for the impact it will have on directors and government agencies. In the marketplaces for professional services and corporate securities, the influence of professional image considerations is hardly trivial.

Function Performed

A large part of the professional skills required to use computer-assisted auditing lies in understanding and applying the computer to appropriate audit functions. The computer has a broad range of capabilities. By way of illustration, four broad categories of computer auditing functions can be identified:

- Items of audit interest
- Audit mathematics
- Data analysis
- System validation.

The nature and applicability of these functions are described below.

Items of audit interest. The auditor can use the computer to select material items, unusual items, or statistical samples of items from a computer-maintained file. The auditor has alternatives for the application of the computer to selection of items of audit interest; for example, the auditor can:

- Stipulate specific criteria for selection of sample items.
- State relative criteria and let the computer do the selection.

An example of selection by specific criteria might be a specification that the computer identify all transactions of $50,000 or more and prepare a report for audit review. On the other hand, the auditor could take a relative approach and instruct the computer to select the largest transactions that make up 20 percent of the total dollar volume for a given application. A computer-assisted retrieval application is diagrammed in Figure 10-8.

This approach abridges manual audit procedures because the auditor can rely on the computer's selection of items of interest. If the computer were not used, the auditor would have to validate the selection process. Under traditional approaches, for example, it would be common for an auditor to ask client personnel to list all transactions of $50,000 or more. Then, before actual testing of the items could begin, the auditor would have to validate the selection. If it were an accounts-payable application, the auditor would have to go to the cash-disbursements journals to verify that the list, in fact, did include all items of $50,000 or more. With the computer, the auditor can be satisfied that the selection program has looked at the total universe of accounts-payable items. The validation of the selection process is inherent in the auditor's developing and accepting the computer auditing application program.

Audit mathematics. Performing extensions or footings can be a cost-effective payoff area for application of computers in auditing—particularly if the calculations can be performed as a by-product of another audit function. For example, suppose the computer is being used to select significant items from an accounts receivable file. In the process of looking at this file, the computer can be programmed to extend and foot all invoicing transactions. Because of the speed of the computer, these calculations can be performed on 100 percent of the items in a file with no significant addition of time or cost for this processing.

By contrast, extensions and footings are both tedious and costly under conventional, manual examination techniques. Typically, the auditor must limit an examination of any given application to extension and footing of a judgmental sample covering a few short intervals of the period under examination. Clearly, reliance can be far higher when these verification calculations are performed on complete files.

Remember, however, that the computer has limitations in this area. It is an excellent calculation tool. Although it can be programmed to make many logical comparisons and tests, the computer cannot supplant human judgment in examining items to be tested. It might be said that the auditor can delegate footing to the computer, but ticking and hollering should remain human functions.

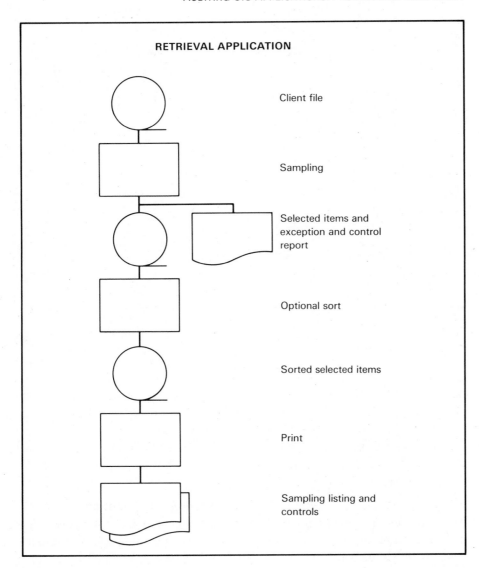

RETRIEVAL APPLICATION

Client file

Sampling

Selected items and exception and control report

Optional sort

Sorted selected items

Print

Sampling listing and controls

Figure 10-8.

This flowchart shows a computer-assisted audit procedure for which the auditor has specified the relative criteria to allow the computer to perform the selection and sorting functions.

Data analysis. Using the computer for analysis of data (Figure 10-9) represents a major opportunity for innovation by the auditor. The computer can compare and summarize data, and can represent data in graphic form under control of special programs. Data analysis programs use such techniques as:

- Histograms
- Modeling
- Comparative analyses.

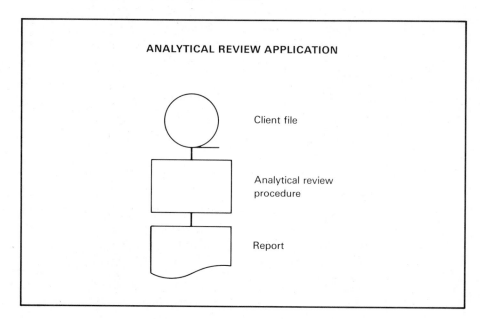

ANALYTICAL REVIEW APPLICATION

Client file

Analytical review
procedure

Report

Figure 10-9.

As shown in this flowchart, the computer may be used in audit procedures that require data analysis, as in comparing data, deriving summaries, or generating graphic output.

Histograms. In an auditing context, *histograms* are bar charts showing graphic relationships among strata of data. In computer-assisted auditing, histograms typically are graphic representations of frequency distributions of records within data files. By picturing these relationships in graphic form, histograms give the auditor an improved perspective on the analysis of financial statements. The histogram is, in effect, a snapshot showing the substance, makeup, and distribution of data within an organization's accounting system.

Figure 10-10 shows a typical histogram representation of an inventory file. With such documentation, the auditor is in a good position to apply judgment in identifying and selecting appropriate testing techniques. By comparison, given a large collection of data about which such distribution data are not known, the auditor performs testing on a relatively blind basis. In such cases, the auditor cannot be sure of the significance of data until after testing is well along. With a histogram, items of significance for testing can be identified in advance, since their relationship to the accounting universe is emphasized graphically.

Modeling. By applying modeling techniques, the auditor can compare current data with a trend or pattern as a basis for evaluating reasonableness. For example, the auditor can develop a model based on several years of financial statements. The model is held within the computer system. Then, the current year's total revenue can be input to the model. The computer can

SAMPLE COMPANY
FILE ANALYSIS
AUDIT DATE

NO	ITEM COUNT	% OF ITEMS	STRATUM VALUE	% OF VALUE	HISTOGRAM
1	17	.69	.00	.00	*
2	58	2.34	341.82	.01	****
3	484	19.56	23,433.56	.51	***
4	217	8.77	31,999.24	.70	***********
5	137	5.54	33,915.69	.74	**********
6	106	4.28	36,569.85	.79	*********
7	79	3.19	35,965.03	.78	*******
8	71	2.87	39,188.12	.85	******
9	80	3.23	52,270.54	1.14	*******
10	61	2.46	45,862.36	1.00	*****
11	55	2.22	46,424.16	1.01	*****
12	58	2.34	55,280.13	1.20	*****
13	393	15.88	543,447.58	12.25	************************************
14	207	8.36	508,060.01	11.04	******************
15	138	5.58	482,005.68	10.48	************
16	70	2.83	306,235.12	6.66	******
17	50	2.02	270,506.16	5.88	****
18	57	2.30	369,117.83	8.02	*****

FILE
TOTALS   2,475   4,600,632.51

LOWEST VALUE ON FILE 00
HIGHEST VALUE ON FILE 57,222.68
HISTOGRAM SCALE PER *   11
COMPUTER RUN DATE 10/25/74

Figure 10-10.   This printout shows a pre-stratification histogram of an inventory file, as produced by a computer-assisted, stratified sampling system.

generate a pro forma financial statement based on past revenue/cost relationships. The pro forma statement is compared with the actual financial statements as a test of reasonableness. Microcomputers have been used by auditors to implement this technique.

Both techniques—histograms and modeling—add new content and dimensions of information to the audit process through use of the computer (mainframe, minicomputer, or microcomputer). With these methods, the auditor is no longer restricted simply to validating data provided by application personnel. With these automated techniques, the auditor generates figures or snapshots of financial data to test the reasonableness of representations under examination.

Comparative analyses.   Another proven, cost-effective application of computers within audit examinations involves the comparison of sets of data to determine relationships that may be of audit interest. For example, the computer may be used to compare the previous and current years' inventory files. Wide variations in year-end balances could lead to reviews for possible obsolescence. A failure to match part numbers from the previous and current years might trigger testing procedures to determine whether old items have been dropped or new ones added. This process is shown in Figure 10-11.

Another example of comparison testing is diagrammed in Figure 10-12. In such tests, shipping and accounts receivable files could be compared to be sure that there is a shipping or delivery transaction to match each sale, and vice versa. In another procedure, the accounts-receivable file could be tested against the cash-receipts file for the month following year-end as a test of subsequent cash collections.

System Validation.   System validation is a method for testing the reliability of programs through simulation with either test data or actual data. With parallel simulation techniques, the auditor may be able to satisfy both compliance and substantive-testing needs in one process. The principles of this technique are covered in Chapter 8.

APPLICATION AREAS

Given the alternatives and functions introduced above, just where, in the audit scheme of things, do computer-assisted techniques fit? One answer is—almost anywhere. Figure 10-13 identifies key areas of audit engagements in which computer-assisted techniques may be appropriate. Applicability of any

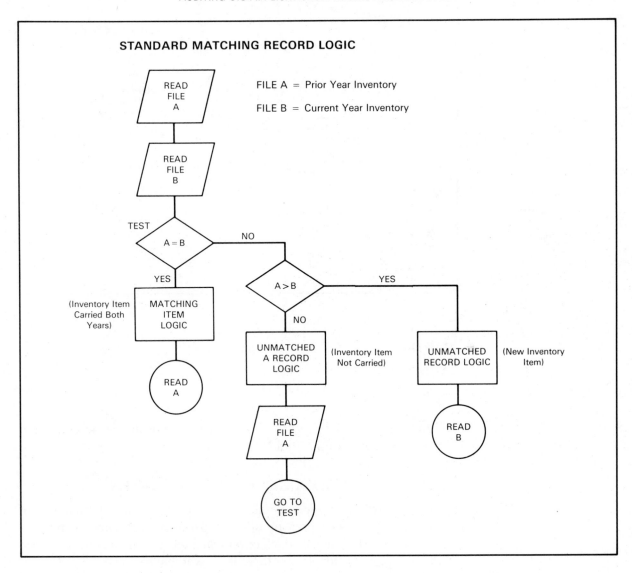

STANDARD MATCHING RECORD LOGIC

FILE A = Prior Year Inventory

FILE B = Current Year Inventory

READ FILE A

READ FILE B

TEST

A = B

NO

YES

(Inventory Item Carried Both Years)

MATCHING ITEM LOGIC

READ A

A > B

YES

NO

(Inventory Item Not Carried)

UNMATCHED A RECORD LOGIC

UNMATCHED RECORD LOGIC

(New Inventory Item)

READ FILE A

READ B

GO TO TEST

Figure 10-11.

This flowchart shows the processing logic applied in matching one data file with another.

of these approaches will be governed by the scope and nature of the systems under examination. The listing is organized according to audit area:

- Cash
- Receivables
- Inventories
- Investments
- Accounts payable

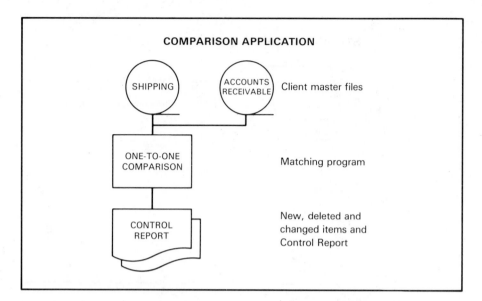

Figure 10-12.

This flowchart shows the overall process of making comparisons by matching one file with another on an item-for-item basis.

- Equity

- Income and expense

- Income taxes.

The following case history presents a description of the use of computer-assisted techniques in the audit of inventories.

APPLICATION EXAMPLE: INVENTORIES

Discount Distributors, Inc., operates two multi-state chains with a total of 120 retail outlets. The stores are of two types—discount markets and auto supply outlets. The chains, which cover a market area spread out across the country, supply all stores from three large warehouses.

The company does have a computer and uses their CIS center for one major application, inventory record keeping. All three warehouses stock the same product lines, and the records of all three are incorporated into an integrated set of files at the service center. Inventory records are processed by computer and updated after shipment. That is, the warehouses process orders and handle their own buying through the use of computer technology. Transaction records captured via OCR or data entry then are transmitted to a central location for data editing and computer processing.

Discount Distributors conducts an annual physical count of all inventories at two separate levels. At the warehouses, item counts are classified

Figure 10-13. *In each audit area shown, specific tasks are listed for which computerized techniques may be applied.*

CASH

- List outstanding checks for review.
- List open bank transfers for follow-up.
- Match checks returned with cutoff statement to files of outstanding checks.

RECEIVABLES

- Select accounts receivable for confirmation.
- Prepare confirmation forms.
- Test aging.
- Analyze accounts by type of receivable or by security.
- Identify large receivables write-offs for verification and evaluation of existing receivables.
- List past-due accounts for follow-up and evaluation.
- Analyze post-year-end accounts receivable receipts. Compare to year-end receivables balances and list large unpaid accounts.
- Verify calculation of unearned finance charge reserve included in receivables.
- Identify the number and amount of loans receivable that have been extended or refinanced prior to year-end.
- Analyze receivables write-offs by type.

INVENTORIES

- Check inventory pricing to master files of prices.
- Verify extension and summarization of inventory amounts.
- Select items for physical counts and price testing.
- Compare inventory test counts to perpetual records and list differences.
- Review perpetual inventory records and list slow-moving items for obsolescence evaluation.
- Analyze accumulation of costs used to value finished goods inventories.
- Test transactions around inventory observation date to verify accurate cutoff of transactions.
- Compare costs of different periods to identify unusual variations.
- Perform lower-of-cost-or-market analysis.
- Project total dollar value of inventory using sampling techniques.

INVESTMENTS

- Test computed interest income on investments to amounts actually received.
- Test dividends declared per published services to amounts actually received.

ACCOUNTS PAYABLE

- Review expense accounts for recurring monthly charges not established as accounts payable at either year-end.
- Perform lengthy or complex year-end calculations of accruals and reserves.
- Perform historical analysis of reserve ratios.
- Identify unrecorded payables included in subsequent payments.

EQUITY

- Calculate average outstanding shares and related earnings-per-share amounts.

INCOME AND EXPENSE

- Analyze income and expense relationships according to trends among years, and within a single year.
- Search for large or unusual items.

INCOME TAXES

- Prepare trial balances in tax-grouping sequence.
- Perform calculation of income-tax provision.
- Review accounts for nonallowable deductions.

Figure 10-13.

Concluded.

according to unique, six-digit stock numbers. Pricing at the warehouse is at cost. Inventory accounting is on a first-in, first-out (FIFO) basis. In the retail stores, inventories are valued at retail price levels and adjusted through application of a multiplier expressing a historical cost-to-retail ratio.

Audit Objectives

Based on a preliminary review of this client's situation, three audit objectives were identified by its external auditors:

- The audit team performed test counts on a sample of inventory items from the warehouses and retail stores. One objective was to match these test counts against physical-inventory records, which were entered into the computer following the count by client personnel.

- The auditors determined that they had to price-test warehouse inventories. It was decided that dollar-value sampling was the most logical technique.

- The auditors determined that they must test the cost-to-retail ratios at which the in-store inventories were valued. By testing the ratio, it was felt, reasonableness of the in-store inventories could be verified.

Available Data Files

A review of the data-center systems revealed that the client had three data files relevant to this examination:

- A warehouse master file was updated through the year to reflect inventory status. Data from this file relevant to the audit examination include merchandise descriptions, costs, the six-digit stock-identification number, the date of last transaction for each item, the retail selling price for each item, and a vendor identification code.

- The warehouse-count file reflected data from the last physical-inventory count. For each item, the file contains the stock-identification number, the warehouse code, and the quantity on hand. The warehouse-count file also contains consecutive numbers of the inventory tags placed on warehouse items during the physical count.

- The retail-count file contains the first two digits of the stock-identification number—indicating the major merchandise category involved, retail price, quantity counted, and a reference showing the page and line number of the in-store inventory count sheet from which the item was taken.

In addition to these client files, the auditors created two data files specifically for their examination:

- A warehouse audit test-count file contains records corresponding with the client's warehouse-count file for the sample of items counted for audit purposes.

- A retail audit test-count file contains information corresponding with the client's retail-count file. In addition, this file also contains the full, six-digit identification number for each item counted by auditors at retail locations.

Audit Approach

Computer-assisted auditing techniques became mandatory, in the opinion of the audit team, when the client data files grew beyond the volume suitable for manual verification. As Discount Distributors has continued to add stores and lines of merchandise, and more sophisticated transaction-capturing devices, the retail-count file alone now contains more than 11 million entries.

The auditors have elected to implement computer-assisted audit techniques incrementally. A plan was devised under which computer-assisted techniques could be phased in over three years to spread the costs of development. Although implementation occurred in one year, subsequent years were needed to refine techniques and integrate with new technology. Through this approach, both the audit firm and the client organization actually began realizing the benefits of cost reductions in examination after the second year, given the savings through reduced inventory counting.

In the situation of Discount Distributors, a four-step approach was used to phase in computerized techniques:

1. Quantity validation was done with computer-assisted techniques.

2. Cost figures were verified with the aid of the computer.

3. Retail sales prices were verified.

4. The cost-to-retail ratio was handled. Since this was the most complex of the operations, two separate computer-assisted techniques were used.

Quantities

At the first level of conversion to computer-assisted techniques, the verification counts were taken manually, as they had been for years before. The chief difference was that the data from audit worksheets were keyed into the computer system, and the comparison was done by the computer instead of manually. Sampling was based on judgments of individual auditors. Samples were taken in each of the three warehouses and in about 25 percent of the stores, which were covered on a rotating basis.

Costs

As a next step, the client's warehouse master file was stratified through dollar-value sampling. Test items were written out by the computer in vendor number sequence. This made it possible for the auditors to refer back to the accounts payable invoice file maintained in vendor-number order to verify cost data.

Verified cost data then were processed under a dollar-value estimation program to project the value of the client's entire warehouse inventory. The figure developed by the computer was compared for reasonableness with the amount reported by the client.

Retail Selling Prices

At this stage, the testing of retail count data was extended. Verification of quantities was the first step in computerization of audit techniques. At this third level, retail pricing figures were included in the computerized verification. This was done by taking the retail test count file generated on the basis of audit observations and processing it with the warehouse master file containing retail price data for each item. This computerized matching verified that retail-price data carried in the master files actually matched the markings on the merchandise at the store locations.

Cost-to-Retail Ratio

Two aspects of the processing of cost-to-retail ratio figures were well suited to use of histogram techniques:

- Retail items were classifiable according to two-digit merchandise classification codes. Thus, development of a histogram profiling patterns of cost/price relationships readily highlighted the percentage figure being used by the client organization for these same merchandise categories.

- To pinpoint the accuracy of ratio figures still further, the warehouse master file was processed according to dollar-value stratification on the basis of selling price. Within each level, a histogram was developed to show cost-to-retail ratios. This provided a cross-check against the merchandise-classification review of cost-to-retail ratio reports.

Data for both these histograms—as well as for another audit verification application—were developed in a single computer processing run. The third dimension for this verification was the development of summary statistics on the cost-to-retail data according to inventory categories. These summary cost-to-retail ratios by inventory category then were processed back against the entire retail count file. Summary cost information was generated by multiplying the summary level cost-to-retail ratio (for the appropriate inventory category) by the extended retail value of each item in the retail count file. Another approach to analyzing summary cost information within this system involved downloading the summary data (depending on the size of file) to a microcomputer, then using graphics/spreadsheet software for repetitive analyses.

Audit Results

Experience showed that the computation of cost-to-retail ratios according to merchandise category and selling-price stratification was both more accurate and more equitable than previous methods the client organization had used. Previously, a single percentage had been applied across the entire spectrum of inventory to establish cost-to-retail relationships. The client organization ultimately refined its cost-to-retail estimating and reporting techniques for interim financial statements.

A major benefit in accounting techniques by the client organization resulted from introduction of dollar-value-sampling methods during the audit examination. Based on audit examination experience, the client converted from physical counts of 100 percent of inventory items to dollar-value sampling techniques for all warehouse inventories. This conversion alone saves the company thousands of dollars each year in inventory counting costs.

The application example given on the previous pages demonstrates the professional and economic benefits that can be derived from computer-assisted auditing techniques. The process of designing, developing, and implementing computer-assisted auditing techniques, however, is neither simple nor automatic. As with the design of any type of audit procedure, the process takes skill and patience. The actual methods appropriate for implementing computer-assisted audit techniques—particularly the selection of software packages and equipment for the performance of computer-assisted auditing—are described in the next chapter.

D I S C U S S I O N   Q U E S T I O N S

1. What professional and organizational standards provide the purposes for audits of CIS applications?

2. What circumstances might require the initiation of an application audit?

3. What steps typically are involved in the planning phase of an application audit?

4. What computer-assisted techniques might be applied in the fieldwork phase of an application audit?

5. What are some typical outcomes of the reporting and follow-up phases of an application audit?

6. What considerations might affect an auditor's choice of computer-assisted techniques for performing audit tests?

7. What general types of audit functions can be performed with computer-assisted techniques?

8. What pitfalls might exist in using a computer, in effect, to audit itself?

9. In the Discount Distributors case, what professional and economic benefits were derived from applying computer-assisted techniques in auditing the inventory application?

C A S E   A S S I G N M E N T S

To apply the concepts presented in this chapter, turn to the case studies for Sleepwell Memorial Hospital, Gotham City, and Honest Bob's Insurance, which are found in Appendix C. Work through Projects 1, 2, 3, and 4, which deal with computer-assisted audit procedures.

11 Auditing CIS Applications: Implementation of Computer-Assisted Techniques

A B S T R A C T

- A general approach for implementing computer-assisted audit techniques can serve as the framework for CIS audit engagements that apply computerized audit routines.

- The general approach is divided into a sequence of steps that include: preliminary evaluation and planning; definition of audit objectives; data gathering and review; selection of hardware and software; selection and design of audit tests; development, testing, and processing of computer programs; review of results; and documentation.

- In the preliminary evaluation and planning step, the relative importance of a given application to all processing activities is assessed.

- Defining audit objectives encompasses identifying specific computerized audit tasks, developing preliminary budgets and schedules, as well as assigning specific work responsibilities.

- The data gathering and review step involves building an understanding of the technical computer environment, including hardware, system software, programming environment, operating considerations, and database format.

- Selection of hardware and software tools also involves identifying the group that actually will do the programming.

- In selecting and designing audit tests, specifications are developed for processing steps and outputs; a system flowchart is prepared; a software approach is selected; budgets and schedules are refined; staff commitments are made; and arrangements are made for obtaining data files.

- During the next step, programs are designed, written, tested, and run.

- The review step includes verifying that results meet audit objectives, that standards of quality are met, and that the expenses of the effort are justified.

- Documentation for such engagements must include a listing of audit objectives, all data gathered during the auditor's initial investigation, copies of end products, evaluation of results, statement of audit conclusions, as well as recommendations for future audits and management review items.

PROJECT STRUCTURE

Each application of computer-assisted auditing involves, at least to some extent, the same control requirements and procedures as are necessary for any other computerized application. That is, the development of systems for computer-assisted auditing presents requirements that parallel closely the development of computerized systems for processing of organizational applications. Procedures and requirements associated with effective systems development are covered in Chapter 9. The application of CIS techniques and tools to the implementation of computer-assisted audit tools throughout a system life cycle is diagrammed in Figure 11-1.

Computer-assisted audit applications represent a classic case of conversion from manual to mechanized procedures. Conversions to computer-assisted auditing are just as subject to cost overruns and breaches of procedure as are conversions to computerized processing applications in organizations. Once a decision has been made to computerize an audit application, particularly since the person involved may have a high level of technical understanding, there is a temptation to abridge or to avoid some of the proper system checkpoints. As with systems development, there is a temptation in computer-assisted auditing to plunge into such details as the coding of programs before the processing logic has been specified and debugged completely.

Experience has shown that it is appropriate to establish a project structure for the development of computer-assisted auditing applications. A

```
                    SOFTWARE SUPPORT AND AUDIT TOOLS

 REQUIREMENT      DESIGN AND       TEST AND VERIFICATION    OPERATIONAL
 ANALYSIS TOOLS   DEVELOPMENT      & VALIDATION             TOOLS
                  TOOLS            TOOLS
```

CONCEPT DEFINITION
SYSTEM REQUIREMENT DEFINITION
SOFTWARE REQUIREMENT DEFINITION
DESIGN
CODING
TEST
INTEGRATION AND TEST
INSTALLATION
OPERATIONAL MODE MAINTENANCE/MODIFICATION/CONVERSION

ORGANIZATIONAL DISCIPLINES	PEOPLE
	PROJECT
	CONFIGURATION
	QUALITY ASSURANCE
METHODOLOGY DISCIPLINES	TECHNOLOGY INTEGRATION
	SOFTWARE ENGINEERING
	PORTABILITY/TRANSFERABILITY
VERIFICATION AND VALIDATION DISCIPLINES	METRICS
	COST
	AUDITABILITY

Figure 11-1.

This chart shows the application of software techniques and tools throughout a systems development life cycle.

project structure for developing computer-assisted auditing applications involves eight steps:

1. Preliminary evaluation and planning

2. Definition of audit objectives

3. Data gathering and review

4. Selection of appropriate hardware and software

5. Selection and design of appropriate audit tests

6. Development, testing, and processing of computer programs

7. Review of results

8. Documentation.

This process is shown as a data flow diagram in Figure 11-2. Steps in the process are described in depth below.

PRELIMINARY EVALUATION AND PLANNING

As in traditional approaches to auditing, determinations of significance and materiality come first in the implementation of computerized approaches. The auditor must establish that a given CIS application and its supporting evidential matter are relevant to audit requirements. Given such a conclusion, the next determination is whether the computerized files for the period under examination are available in computer-processable form. It is not uncommon to see serious consideration given and decisions reached to use computerized techniques only to find that the files necessary to support this method of examination are nonexistent or unavailable.

Relative Importance

Given that the application itself is material and that the files do exist, the next step is to determine realistic priorities. At least initially, the startup of computer-assisted auditing techniques requires extended planning efforts by computer audit staff. In most situations, and on most engagements, selectivity in implementation is necessary. In general, it will not be possible for the auditor to apply computer-assisted auditing techniques to all applications of interest at once. Thus, application significance, measured by a number of criteria, becomes the key to selecting applications. These criteria include the following:

- Would computer-assisted auditing be more efficient once the initial work is completed for the computer audit application?

- Are there potential cost savings? Will the clerical effort within the audit engagement be reduced?

- Will reliability of results be improved? Will the entire audit be more effective?

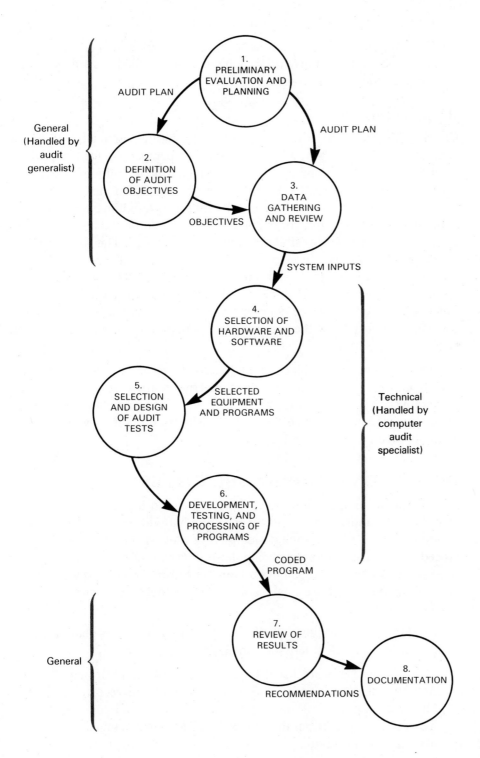

General
(Handled by
audit
generalist)

1.
PRELIMINARY
EVALUATION AND
PLANNING

AUDIT PLAN

AUDIT PLAN

2.
DEFINITION
OF AUDIT
OBJECTIVES

OBJECTIVES

3.
DATA
GATHERING
AND REVIEW

SYSTEM INPUTS

4.
SELECTION OF
HARDWARE AND
SOFTWARE

5.
SELECTION
AND DESIGN
OF AUDIT
TESTS

SELECTED
EQUIPMENT
AND PROGRAMS

Technical
(Handled by
computer
audit
specialist)

6.
DEVELOPMENT,
TESTING, AND
PROCESSING OF
PROGRAMS

CODED
PROGRAM

General

7.
REVIEW OF
RESULTS

8.
DOCUMENTATION

RECOMMENDATIONS

Figure 11-2.

The steps in developing a computer-based audit application are shown in this data flow diagram.

- Do the projected benefits justify the anticipated costs?

- Can computer-assisted auditing techniques be scheduled effectively? Is there enough lead time to do the job this year? If schedules are tight, will any penalties be incurred?

Responsibilities

Clearly, this preliminary review requires the participation of both audit generalists and computer audit specialists. The perspective for this review is vital to success in applying computerized auditing techniques. The audit generalist, who serves as the project leader or manager on the engagement, retains basic responsibilities for contact with organization management and with the auditee, as well as for the professional standards and conduct of the engagement. These responsibilities cannot be delegated. The CIS specialist or computer auditor is a support resource. The CIS specialist can and should provide a degree of guidance and comfort to the generalists. In particular, the resources and schedules of the individual and the audit firm (or internal audit function) as a whole in the computer auditing area should be taken into consideration as part of the preliminary evaluation and planning for each engagement.

There will be situations in which there really is no choice. Some types of computerized systems can be audited effectively only with the use of computers. In such situations, the preliminary evaluation and planning activity resolves itself into one of verifying the feasibility of alternative computer audit approaches and allocating resources.

DEFINITION OF AUDIT OBJECTIVES

Once the areas of application for computer-assisted techniques have been identified, the auditor must specify exactly what will be done. Definitions of audit objectives must include identifying files, specifying examination procedures, and specifying the computer-produced end product. There also must be documented agreement on how the computer-assisted techniques fit into, support, and are cost-justified within the overall audit process for the engagement.

In addition to identifying specific computerized tasks, this phase also encompasses several other activities, including:

- The selected tasks are listed for the benefit of the entire audit team. Activities such as selecting and confirming accounts receivable, inventory footing, payroll extension tests, and so on, are incorporated in task lists along with functions that still will be performed manually within the overall audit program.

- Budgets for computer-assisted auditing tasks are established and evaluated in terms of all resources needed—staff time, computer time, software, and materials.

- Preliminary schedules are established for the computer-assisted functions. The schedules include final deadlines and interim review points, or milestones.

- Specific work responsibilities are assigned as part of the audit program.

DATA GATHERING AND REVIEW

Data gathering begins concurrently with the definition of audit objectives. It is not really possible for a computer audit specialist to commit to objectives and to performance of tasks without having preliminary data such as the type and location of the computers used for the application, their operating system software, data entry methods, and degree of distribution.

This specific phase of computer-assisted auditing marks a change in level of activity from the generalized to the specialized or technical. The computer audit specialist begins to devise the technical solutions that will be used in meeting the audit objectives of the previous phase.

Ideally, data gathering and review should be done by a person who has had extensive experience as an audit generalist and subsequently has acquired CIS expertise. The person performing the data gathering and review function in a computer-assisted audit assignment must begin with an understanding of the full impact and significance of the audit tasks themselves. In gathering technical data and devising technical solutions, this member of the audit team must not lose sight of the fact that auditing is the objective of the application to be developed. Given this orientation, the data gathering and review function requires completion of a number of specific tasks:

- Data must be gathered on the configuration, capacities, and capabilities of the computer hardware used for the application, including specifications on all appropriate peripherals such as tape and disk drives. Mainframe capacities, including memory size, also must be documented.

- Operating systems used within the CIS installation must be identified. This identification includes the version or edition currently in use and any special capabilities or constraints.

- Software specifications must be gathered. These should include data on programming languages, utility programs, or any special packages in use at the CIS installation.

- Operating considerations must be taken into account. The computer audit specialist will need to gather data on scheduling within the CIS installation to determine availability of computer time for audit tasks.

- The computer audit specialist must gather complete information on file formats, including labels. The auditor will be using client/auditee files during the examination and must conform to any constraints or controls that are applied to those files. The auditor must become familiar with the files down to the level of individual data elements (field or record layouts).

In summary, the computer audit specialist performs a detailed review of the organization's CIS installation and applications. Thus, the computer audit specialist gains the exposure necessary to:

- Develop a blueprint, or plan, for the audit examination

- Gain input for advisory comments to management on systems weaknesses and opportunities for improvements in the CIS operations area.

SELECTION OF HARDWARE AND SOFTWARE

For computer-assisted audit purposes, hardware and software are parts of a single set of considerations. Hardware should be considered first because hardware configurations will be controlling factors for the software options open to the auditor.

Hardware

Three computer hardware options are available for computer-assisted auditing:

- The computer system (mainframe, minicomputer, and/or microcomputer) of the client organization or auditee can be used.

- An audit firm may use its own computer resources.

- The audit applications can be run on a computer located in an outside service center.

In general, use of the organization's computer is preferable. Since the applications are in-place, there is no question about configuration compatibility; and costs are relatively fixed. Further, it is easiest to maintain confidentiality of information if data files never leave the installation.

For practical purposes, the organization's computer generally will be used if there is time available to run the audit programs. However, for external audits, if time is not available, the choice between the audit firm's own computer and an outside facility usually will be made based on questions of configuration compatibility.

If the audit firm has a compatible computer and if time is available on this system, its use generally will be preferable to an outside facility. It is easier to maintain control over and confidentiality of files and data within the offices of the audit firm than in an outside facility. However, there may be extenuating circumstances. Most audit firms operate with a single computer installation at one central site. Thus, a firm auditing a California client probably would prefer a local service center over an option of transporting or transmitting all of the client's data to New York for testing.

Compatibility considerations also center around the make and model of computer. In general, it is preferable to run the audit tests on the same make and model of computer as the one that handles the actual production work. However, it is possible, especially if files can be processed under general-purpose software, to process files that are normally handled on one make of computer on another.

Software

Selection of software involves more variables than the choice of hardware. Internal audit functions or outside audit firms, in general, will use one of three approaches in the selection of software for use in their examinations:

- The auditors may use exclusively, or with strong preference, audit packages they have developed or caused to be developed.

- The auditors may use their own packages for some purposes but also may acquire and use packages of commercial vendors and develop special-purpose programs tailored to the specific application.

- The auditors may opt to use software acquired from outside vendors entirely.

No one of these options is best for all situations. In one audit firm, a heavy initial investment was made in developing proprietary general-purpose audit software packages. It became apparent, however, that expanding these software packages to cover the entire scope of audit requirements, as well as keeping the packages current with later models or generations of computers, would involve expenses that exceeded the benefits.

Experience has shown that a single package or set of packages cannot meet all requirements. Further, new introductions of generalized software packages promise powerful audit tools at proportionately smaller investments.

The three general options cited above are all valid and are open to the profession. Different audit departments and firms have taken different approaches. Professionals can derive reliable results from any of these approaches.

Software categories.   In general, one of four software categories will be selected for the performance of audit examinations:

- General-purpose packages
- Existing client/auditee programs
- Custom audit programs
- Commercially available software tools.

General-purpose packages.   Packages either already developed by the auditors or acquired commerically can be used. As described above, general-purpose packages typically involve high-level programming techniques under which relatively few descriptors or parameter statements serve to generate detailed program code. Figure 11-3 presents a list that includes general-purpose audit software packages as well as commercially available software tools (discussed below). Operating environments are coded on this chart as: multisystem, mainframe, minicomputer, and microcomputer.

Existing client/auditee programs.   Existing client/auditee programs can be used after suitable verification. For example, the auditors may have been involved in quality reviews of programs during system development. The auditors then can keep a control copy of the program itself—and update it separately from client/auditee modifications—for use in later examinations. Recall that this technique is known as parallel simulation.

Custom audit programs.   Custom audit programs can be written in programming languages compatible with client/auditee procedures, equipment, and software support.

Commercially available software tools.   Some commercially available software tools are oriented toward design, development, or maintenance but can be used from an audit/review standpoint for specific verifications or tests. Figure 11-3 includes these tools, which can be used for review purposes.

Figure 11-3. *This chart presents some of the commercially available software development tools that have potential for computer-assisted auditing. Functions performed can include analysis and design, coding, testing, and documentation. The environments in which each product can be used are identified as multisystem, mainframe, minicomputer, and microcomputer.*

SOFTWARE TOOLS

VENDOR	PRODUCT	ENVIR	A & D	CODING	TESTING	DOC
AGS Mgt. Systems, Inc.	SDM/Structured Estiplan	Multi/ Micro	X X	X		
Aims Plus, Inc.	Aims	Mini	X	X		
Allen Ashley	Hybrid Dev. Sys.	Micro			X	
	Source Mod. Dev. Util.	Micro		X		
Applied Data Research	Ideal	Main	X	X	X	X
	Metacobol	Main		X		
	ADR/Data Designer	Main	X			
	PC/PTE	Micro	X	X	X	
Aware Company	Active Trace	Micro			X	X
Azrex, Inc.	AZ7	Main		X		
Bristol Info. Systems Inc.	BIS "Data-print"	Mini		X		
Bytel Corp.	Cogen	Micro		X		
	Menupro	Multi		X		
Caine, Faber & Gordon, Inc.	PDL	Multi	X			
Capro Inc.	Pro-IV	Multi	X	X	X	
Cincom Systems Inc.	Mantis	Main		X		
Computer Associates	CA-EZTest	Main			X	
	CA-symbug	Main			X	
	Jobdoc	Main				X
Computing Pro-ductivity Inc.	IP3	Main	X	X	X	X
Cortex Corp.	Application Factory	Mini				
	Application Builder	Mini		X		
Cullinet Software	Ads/Batch	Main	X	X		
	Ads/Online	Main	X	X		
D & V Systems	SYMD Symbolic debugger	Micro			X	X

VENDOR	PRODUCT	ENVIR	A & D	CODING	TESTING	DOC
Datamate Co.	Datamate Ref. Language	Multi		X		
	Genius Screen Gen.	Multi		X		
Digital Research Inc.	BT-80	Micro		X		
	Display Manager	Micro		X		
	Sid & ZS:d	Micro			X	
Dylakor	DYL-260	Main		X		
	DYL-280		X	X		
Dynatech Micro-software Div.	C.O.R.P. Prog. Gen.	Micro	X	X		
	Codewriter Prog. Gen.	Micro	X	X		
	Techwriter Prog. Gen.	Micro	X	X		
Forth Inc.	Polyforth	Mini		X		X
Fox & Geller	Quickcode	Micro		X		X
Generation Sciences Inc.	Gamma	Main	X	X		X
Henco Software Inc.	Info	Multi		X		
Higher Order Software Inc.	Use-It	Multi	X	X	X	X
Informatics General Corp	Mark IV	Main	X	X		
	Mark V		X	X		
Information Builders	Focus	Main		X		
	PC-Focus	Micro		X		
Ken Orr & Associates	Structure(s)	Multi	X	X		X
	DSSD Design Library	Multi	X			
Language Technology	Recoder	Main		X		
M Bryce & Associates	Pride	Main	X			
Mgt & Computer Services	Systemacs	Multi	X			
	Tracmacs	Main			X	
	Datamacs	Main			X	
	Estimacs	Micro	X			X
Manager Software Products	Testmanager	Main			X	
Master Software	Programaster	Main	X	X	X	X
Mathematica Products Group	Ramis II	Main		X		
Micro Focus Inc.	Level II Cobol	Micro		X		
	Animator	Micro			X	
	Sideshow	Micro	X	X		

VENDOR	PRODUCT	ENVIR	A & D	CODING	TESTING	DOC
Micropro Int. Corp	Datastar	Micro		X		
Multiplications Inc.	Accolade	Main	X	X		
National Info Systems	DPL	Main		X		
Netro Inc.	Computer-Aided Programming	Mini		X		
Oxford Software Corp.	UFO	Main	X	X		
Pansophic Systems Inc	Easytrieve	Main		X		
	Pro/Grammar	Main		X	X	
Phoenix Systems Inc	Hercules System-80/2	Micro	X	X		
Progeni Systems Inc	Progeni Tools	Main		X		
Pyramid Data Ltd	Number Cruncher	Micro	X	X		
Quantitative Software Mgt.	Slim	Mini	X			
Relational Data-base Systems, Inc.	Ace	Micro		X		
	Perform	Micro		X		
Softech Micro-systems Inc	Adv. Dev. Kit for P-System	Micro		X	X	X
	Native Code Gen. for P-System	Micro		X		
Softool Corp.	Softool	Mini	X	X	X	
The Software Store	Info-80 App. Dev. Sys.	Micro	X	X		
STSC	APL Plus/80 App. Dev. Sys.	Main		X	X	
Systems & Software Inc	Rex-Tools	Multi		X	X	
System Support Software	Quikjob III	Main		X	X	
	Quickwrite	Main		X		
TOM Software	EZ-Speed	Micro	X	X		
	Speed Utility	Micro	X			
Tominy, Inc	Database-Plus	Multi	X	X		
Triangle Soft-ware	Illustrate	Main				X
	Crosscheck	Main			X	X
	Final Test	Main			X	
TSI International	Data Analyzer	Main		X		
	Pro/Test	Main			X	
Wallsoft Associates	dFlow	Micro			X	X

An important consideration in software selection is the complexity of the task at hand and the auditor's purpose in relation to the audit objectives. In general, the more complex the audit examination, the more inclined the auditor will be to use verified client/auditee programs as a first choice, followed by specially written programs in compiler languages. Conversely, the more straightforward or conventional the computer-assisted audit application, the more the auditor will be inclined to use general-purpose software packages.

Programming resources.   Given that the auditor has a choice among the four approaches described above, the final decision also must consider who actually will do the programming. Resources available to program audit applications include:

- CIS department/client programmers

- CIS specialists on the staff of the audit department or firm

- Outside contract programmers

- The computer audit specialist conducting the examination.

Selection criteria revolve around cost and the complexity of the individual audit task. The more complex the job, the more the computer audit specialist will lean toward development of custom programs. In such cases, it is likely that the auditor will assign the programming task to client/auditee personnel, whose work then is reviewed by audit staff members. If custom audit programs are written—no matter who writes them—the computer audit specialist typically will retain all the elements of control. Control includes the preparation of programming specifications, review of coding before programs are compiled, preparation or supervision of the specifications for program tests, and review of actual testing.

If a decision leans toward use of a general-purpose software package, the likelihood increases that the computer audit specialist will handle the entire job personally. This is largely in the interest of economy, since high-level packages make it more efficient for the specialist to designate and prepare criteria and parameters than to brief somebody else and review the work.

Auditing a given application may present opportunities for use of all three of the tools described above. It should not be assumed that software selection decisions are mutually exclusive. They are not. Two or more approaches may be used in any given examination segment.

SELECTION AND DESIGN OF AUDIT TESTS

In the selection of hardware and software, the computer audit specialist, with appropriate assistance and concurrence, makes the necessary technical decisions. Inherent in this process also is the selection and design of audit tests. The computer audit specialist also develops a detail-level implementation plan for testing. Specific tasks performed include:

- Specifications are developed for processing steps and outputs. This includes definitions of logical rules to be used in the identification of exceptions, selection of specific items, footing requirements, and any special processing logic to be applied.

- A generalized system flowchart is prepared. This flowchart shows the number of programs to be executed, their sequence, and the data files that will be required.

- The software approach to be used for each program is selected and specified.

- Both time and cost budgets are finalized, as is the implementation schedule.

- Concurrence is sought and obtained for the participation of client/auditee personnel and provision of other needed resources. If client/auditee personnel will be doing some or all of the programming, availabilities and schedules have to be confirmed.

- Since data files will have to be copied for use in the computerized examination procedures, arrangements must be made for the copies. Content of these copied files must be specified and agreed upon.

DEVELOPMENT, TESTING, AND PROCESSING OF COMPUTER PROGRAMS

The next phase comprises the actual execution of computer-assisted auditing. Note that these functions are listed sixth among a series of eight phases. Computer-assisted auditing will be as successful and reliable as the preparation that goes into it. All too frequently, as happens in systems development generally, technicians associated with a CIS audit effort are anxious to begin coding programs as soon as possible, if not immediately. Care must be taken to avoid letting a computer-assisted auditing effort become too technical, too soon. Success lies in planning and preparation, not in the writing of code.

At this technical stage in a computer-assisted auditing effort, tasks include the following:

- Program logic specifications are prepared. The specifications include the rules for the actual processing and selection of data fields, records, or file segments.

- File output layouts and report formats are prepared. Concurrence must be obtained to validate their appropriateness for the objectives to be met.

- If they are to be written in programming languages, programs are coded. If software packages are used, parameter specifications are prepared. In either case, the end products are desk-checked, or subjected to manual walk-throughs, for logic or coding errors.

- Program coding or parameters are captured on computer input media.

- A test plan is developed. If required, test data also are developed. If appropriate, portions of actual data files are identified and selected for test purposes.

- Required computer time is scheduled.

- Programs are tested and test results are reviewed. Any necessary adjustments are made. Programs then are retested and results are reviewed again, until the programs are judged reliable for auditing.

- Computer runs are performed, using all appropriate data.

REVIEW OF RESULTS

In assessing the results of the application of computer-assisted audit techniques, audit criteria are paramount. That is, it is possible to have a highly sophisticated, technically elegant computer system that, nonetheless, fails to do a good job of auditing the specific client/auditee representations under examination. Audit criteria, in this case, represent a measure of how well audit objectives were realized.

Results of computer-assisted audit applications should be measured at several levels, including:

- Were specified audit results delivered? Did the outputs of the computerized application satisfy the auditor and the examination objectives?

- What was the level of audit satisfaction? This question has a quality connotation. Can the audit generalist place the same or a greater degree of reliance on results as would have been the case if manual examination techniques had been used?

- Were the projected benefits realized, and do these benefits justify expenses and efforts necessary to deliver them?

As with other postaudit reviews, this task is aimed at evaluating what was done to decide if there should be changes in audit objectives, modifications of other procedures associated with the CIS techniques, or modification of the computer-assisted techniques themselves.

DOCUMENTATION

In computer-assisted auditing, as for auditing generally, thorough, reliable documentation is a necessary by-product. The auditor's working papers must be complete, understandable, and reviewable—whether the work was done with a pencil or a computer.

In a computer-assisted auditing environment, documentation is an especially critical element of control and continuity. Two levels of documentation—application and program—must be present. Both must be reviewed. Both must be defensible and repeatable. Specific documentation for any application of computer-assisted auditing techniques should include:

- A list of the audit objectives for the computer-assisted application.

- Full documentation of materials and information accumulated during the data gathering and review phase.

- Copies of all end products and outputs.

- Evaluation of results in writing, including designation of the person or persons who performed the review, together with their signatures.

- Statement of audit conclusions based on computer-assisted examination documentation.

- Recommendations for changes and improvements in subsequent audits, along with recommendations to be made to the client or auditee management.

This project structure for implementing computer-assisted auditing is a working guide rather than a detailed road map. It applies proven systems management techniques to the development and implementation of computer-assisted auditing applications. The value of these techniques lies in the selectivity with which they are tailored to individual situations. Together with the application of professional judgment in each individual case, these techniques provide the essential ingredients for success in the implementation of computer-assisted auditing.

DISCUSSION QUESTIONS

1. Identify similarities and differences between the implementation of computer-assisted audit techniques and other types of systems development projects.

2. How do the steps for implementing computerized audit routines differ from the phases of a conventional systems development life cycle?

3. What criteria might be used in assessing the relative importance of a particular computer-assisted audit application to an organization's overall scheme of operations?

4. What should be the role of the CIS auditor in evaluating the significance of computer-assisted audit applications?

5. How is the definition of audit objectives for computer-assisted audits related to the function of systems project planning?

6. How might the degree of distribution of CIS resources affect the auditor's perspective on gathering data about the organization's technical environment?

7. What factors might influence the selection of hardware and software tools for implementing computerized audit tests?

8. What difficulties might arise in securing production data files for use in audit tests?

9. What groups within the organization are likely to use the documentation generated by computer-assisted auditing projects?

CASE ASSIGNMENT

To apply the concepts presented in this chapter, turn to the case study for Exotic Electronics in Appendix D and work through the project, which deals with advanced techniques for performing computer-assisted audits.

12 Auditing CIS Installations and Operations

A B S T R A C T

- In the auditor's review of CIS facilities, emphasis is on gaining an overview understanding of CIS center operations, identifying exposures, preparing for and conducting audits, assessing vulnerabilities of systems software, using special audit tools, and auditing microcomputer-based facilities.

- The auditor's overview of a CIS facility encompasses the functions performed within the center's operational life cycle. Key functions, and corresponding areas of audit attention, include planning, operations, and performance evaluation.

- Performance evaluation, in turn, involves the criteria of efficiency, effectiveness, productivity, and profitability.

- Two exposure structures are used to identify and define types of exposures. These structures are known as mutually exclusive exposures and overlapping exposures.

- Typical exposures within the center include erroneous record keeping, unacceptable accounting, processing interruption, erroneous management decisions, fraud and embezzlement, statutory sanctions, excessive costs/deficient revenues, loss or destruction of assets, and competitive disadvantage.

- Causes of exposures lie in specific areas that include applications, systems development, the CIS center itself, advanced systems, computer abuse, as well as accidents and natural events.

- **Essential qualities of CIS facilities include efficient operations; effective management; secure installations and equipment; as well as data integrity, security, and privacy.**

- **Objectives for this type of audit include assuring that assets are safeguarded, verifying accuracy and reliability of information, promoting efficiency and adherence to standards, assuring adequacy of internal control, review of specific internal controls, and assuring the quality of control performance.**

- **Steps in planning the audit of facilities include assignment of staff, review of policies and procedures, and scheduling.**

- **Conduct of the audit carries the review into detailed examination of security, organization, equipment and computer resources, systems and programs, data control, file library, as well as evaluation and testing of systems and programs.**

- **Communication of audit results is achieved principally through the auditor's recommendations to CIS management on the need for modifications or additions to controls.**

- **A number of concerns and issues stem from the vulnerabilities of operating systems. The systems programmer faces many problems in this area, including typical communication problems with management, threats in systems programming, and administration of controls over this critical area of activity. Audit approaches to the systems software area include control over modifications to the operating system.**

- **Audit and quality control software tools include Computer Performance Evaluation (CPE) and Job Accounting Information (JAI) utilities.**

INTRODUCTION

Several approaches have evolved in auditing CIS facilities. Regardless of approach, however, the main objective is to assure a thorough review and examination of internal control, security, efficiency, and accuracy of information support operations. Within this type of audit, topics to be covered include:

- The CIS center itself, its functions and operations, as well as the responsibilities of its personnel

- Types and causes of exposures in the CIS center

- Preparing for and conducting audits of the CIS center

- Concerns and issues related to computer operating systems

- Advanced audit and quality control software tools used in CIS processing center reviews

- Considerations in planning for and control of microcomputers.

OVERVIEW OF CIS CENTER OPERATIONS AND FUNCTIONS

The organization of a typical CIS center is shown in Figure 12-1. Functions within this structure include:

- Planning

- Operations

- Performance evaluation.

These functions comprise the life cycle of a CIS center, as discussed below. Of these functions, the auditor's chief concern lies in evaluating performance of a CIS center. In other words, there is a need to assess the efficiency, effectiveness, and economy of CIS operations.

Planning

CIS plans should identify anticipated services and establish the capabilities to meet expectations. One important planning element is the organizational structure of the CIS center. This structure is essential to effective management control. In filling positions within the structure, staff members need to be screened, hired, and indoctrinated in the policies and procedures pertaining to their functions within the center. In addition, finances and resources need to be identified and allocated. On the basis of this planning, the CIS manager prepares an operating budget.

Operations

For audit purposes, CIS center operations are defined by standard procedures, found typically in a written procedures manual that must be followed. Both in-house and user jobs must be scheduled and resources allocated to achieve a smooth work flow. Effective communications need to be established with other departments within the organization to assure that the CIS center is performing its job in a useful and timely manner.

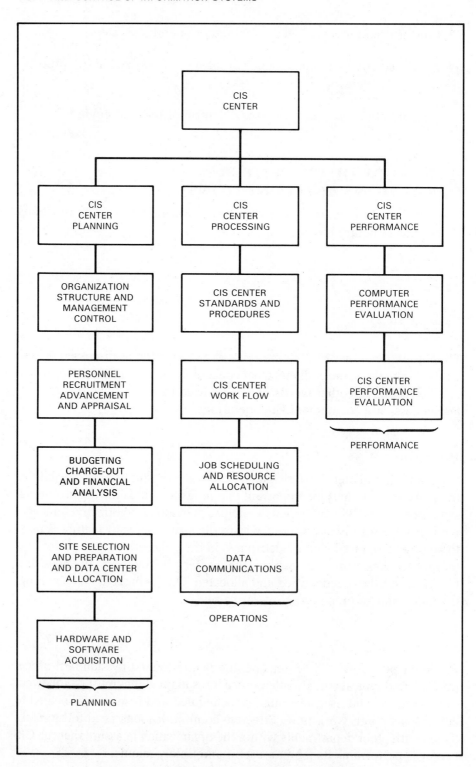

Figure 12-1.

This organization chart shows the hierarchy of functions within a typical CIS operations center.

Performance Evaluation

The performance of all productive elements within the center—including hardware, software, and personnel—must be evaluated periodically within cycled audit examinations. Evaluation criteria include:

- Efficiency
- Effectiveness
- Productivity
- Profitability.

As stated above, these are the areas of primary evaluation emphasis for the auditor. The focus of attention is control and how control measures reduce or prevent *exposures* while enhancing performance. An exposure is a condition or potential event that could allow for violating the integrity of a system. The auditor who succeeds in identifying exposures and improving performance has made a significant contribution to the goals of the organization.

Job Functions and Responsibilities

The typical kinds of job functions in a CIS center are:

- Database administrator
- Security administrator
- VDT operator in the user area
- User providing batch data
- Control clerk
- Computer operator
- Data librarian
- Data entry operator
- Systems analyst/application programmer
- Systems programmer
- User of output
- CIS auditor.

Database administrator (DBA). The *database administrator (DBA)* develops procedures for the operations of organizational databases and their database management systems, or software interface and control over information assets. The DBA is responsible for assuring that access to the database follows established procedures. The DBA also oversees addition of new elements to the database and modifies logical relationships, as necessary. Related to this function are the tasks of developing, maintaining, and controlling the *data dictionary,* which provides correlations among user inquiries and objects within the database.

Security administrator.   The *security administrator* is responsible for assigning, changing, and controlling passwords that permit access to system resources. This person works with user management, or data owners, to determine access limitations for files and corresponding *input screens,* or access controls. The security administrator also assures that data are encrypted, or scrambled, as necessary and that password tables are secure.

VDT operator in the user area.   VDT operators within the user function enter data directly into computer files from source documents or from telephone conversations. Errors in data entry are corrected on-line. If data are entered from transaction source documents, the terminal operator establishes batches and develops control totals.

User providing batch data.   For each batch job, a member of the user staff is responsible for batching documents, developing batch counts and batch totals, and checking these figures against batch balance reports. This user also is responsible for reviewing error reports and correcting input errors.

Control clerk.   The *control clerk* serves as a routing center, or "traffic cop," for the operations group. If the CIS department is responsible for data entry, the control clerk logs the source documents and then turns them over to the data entry section. When the control clerk receives all the output from computer operations, the output is logged; and the clerk verifies run-to-run controls.

Computer operator.   The *computer operator* oversees the actual running of both in-house and user jobs. If the CIS center has a tape management system, the computer operator also may be responsible for pulling and refiling tapes required for processing runs. Unless the computer system has logging facilities, the operator is responsible for logging the time of job starts and completions, as well as operator actions and interventions. In on-line environments, the computer operator monitors system resources to assure reliability and timely response.

Data librarian.   The *data librarian* is the custodian of all data resources within the CIS center. The data librarian pulls and returns all files, checks all external labels, and is responsible for maintaining proper file backup, both on-site and off-site.

Data entry operator. *Data entry operators* key and verify input but, as a control measure, do not verify their own work. Data entry operators also may enter and verify batch totals and batch counts.

Systems analyst/application programmer. *Systems analysts* work with users in identifying and designing new or enhanced applications. *Application programmers* typically do the actual coding of programs from the systems analyst's designs. In some CIS shops, and especially in smaller operations, these job functions are combined in the role of *programmer/analyst.* Technicians within this function also may be charged with maintenance of existing programs, documentation of systems development efforts according to departmental standards, and consultation with users to develop test data. Controls built into programs (or overlooked) by members of this group are the main source of reliability (or vulnerability) of computer applications.

Systems programmer. A *systems programmer* does maintenance and implements enhancements for all systems-level and technical software and utilities, and also makes the appropriate changes to systems documentation. Systems programmers often are called upon to provide assistance in the event of unusual computer system failures.

User of output. The user reviews and approves the design of reports, assists in developing test data, receives and acts upon reports produced by a given application, and logs all reports to verify that they are received.

CIS auditor. The *CIS auditor,* or computer auditor, is responsible for evaluating existing standards for control and audit trails that should be incorporated into system and program designs. This auditor also reviews design documents and completed systems to assure that they adhere to the standards, develops standards for administration and operational controls, and conducts periodic reviews of the CIS operation to verify adherence to standards. The CIS auditor generally is not a part of the CIS department, but reports to an internal audit function.

Separation of the above job functions among different individuals is important to the control of data center operations, helping to assure that exposures do not occur. The important principle of separation of duties is discussed in greater depth later in this chapter.

MUTUALLY EXCLUSIVE EXPOSURES

- Alteration of data
- Destruction of data
- Unauthorized access to data
- Disruption of processing activities

EXPOSURE STRUCTURES

As stated earlier, an exposure is a condition or potential condition that could cause an organization to experience some type of loss. Exposures are either accidental in nature or involve deliberate human intervention. There are two categories, or structures, by which exposures are identified. The first structure is known as mutually exclusive exposures. The exposures falling under this category are listed in Figure 12-2. Generally, these four exposures are technical in nature, relating directly to the type of violation of an information system.

The second structure is known as overlapping exposures. The exposures included within this structure are listed in Figure 12-3. The major difference between the two structures of exposure is apparent: An overlapping exposure includes the cause of exposure and type of loss, as well as the effect of loss, within the definition of the exposure itself; a mutually exclusive exposure is defined only by the type of loss or violation.

The significance of this difference between categories of exposure is felt during an auditor's examination and assessment of exposure possibilities within an organization. The auditor's choice of exposure structure will determine the direction and structure of the auditor's examination. This choice also will affect the risk assessment methodologies and evaluation techniques (covered in Chapter 15) employed by the auditor.

Overlapping exposures are characterized as being management-oriented. That is, this structure of identifying exposures is, in general, more meaningful and relevant to management and its objectives. Thus, this book uses the overlapping exposures structure as its basis in discussing the nature and causes of exposure for the remainder of the text.

OVERLAPPING EXPOSURES

Application Exposures
(exposures related to the operations of application programs)
- Erroneous record keeping
- Unacceptable accounting
- Business interruption
- Erroneous management decisions
- Fraud
- Statutory sanctions
- Excessive costs/deficient revenues
- Loss or destruction of assets
- Competitive disadvantage

Project Exposures
(exposures related to the project development process)
- Erroneous management decisions
- Excessive costs
- Competitive disadvantage
- Business interruption (delay timetable)

Figure 12-3.

The overlapping exposures structure includes the cause of exposure, type of loss, and the effect of loss within the definition of the exposure itself. (Adapted from Touch Ross Co.: Mair, Wood, and Davis, Computer Control & Audit, *The Institute of Internal Auditors, 1976.)*

TYPES OF CIS CENTER EXPOSURES

A number of exposures are associated with CIS activities. Some of the exposures identified in Figure 12-3 are explained more fully in the following discussion.

Erroneous record keeping. Erroneous record keeping is the recording of transactions with errors. Typical errors involve the time of recognition, value, classification, or quantity of items (for example, transposition or inaccurate recording of numbers).

Unacceptable accounting. Unacceptable accounting is the use of accounting principles that are not generally accepted or are inappropriate in the circumstances. Such practices also could lead to further exposures, such as statutory sanctions (discussed below).

Processing interruption. The extent of processing interruptions can range from temporary suspension of operations to permanent termination of the enterprise. For example, at the extreme, a severe processing interruption affects the status of a profit making organization as a "going concern," as defined in generally accepted accounting principles.

Erroneous management decisions.   Erroneous management decisions are objectionable in themselves; but they also can lead to other exposures. Such decisions may result from misleading information, lack of information, or errors in judgment.

Fraud and embezzlement.   Fraud and embezzlement may be perpetrated at different levels—against management or *by* management. Direct misappropriation of funds is only one ramification of fraud. Deliberately misinforming management or investors also is fraudulent, even if the motivation does not involve misuse of assets.

Statutory sanctions.   Statutory sanctions refer to any of the penalties that may be brought by judicial or regulatory authorities with jurisdiction over an organization's operations.

Excessive costs.   Excessive costs include any expenses that could have been avoided readily. A related exposure is the loss of revenues to which the organization is entitled.

Loss or destruction of assets.   Loss or destruction of assets encompasses the unintentional loss of physical assets, monies, or information assets.

Competitive disadvantage.   Competitive disadvantage relates to any inability of an organization to be informed adequately of the demands of the marketplace or to respond effectively to challenges from competing organizations.

CAUSES OF EXPOSURES WITHIN THE CIS CENTER

Usually, exposures are not encountered singly, but are apparent in various combinations. These combinations can indicate the cause of the exposure. The primary responsibility of the computer auditor is, first, to discover what exposures exist and, then, from this evidence, to determine their causes.

The causes of exposures that concern a CIS processing center are rooted in the following areas:

- Applications
- Systems development

APPLICATIONS

Exposures: Erroneous Record Keeping, Unacceptable Accounting, Processing
Interruption, Erroneous Management Decisions, Embezzlement,
Competitive Disadvantage.

CLASSIFICATION	CAUSES
INPUT	LOST
	DUPLICATED
	INACCURATE
	MISSING DATA
	NEVER RECORDED
	BLANKET AUTHORIZATION
	INITIATED INTERNALLY
PROCESSING	WRONG FILE
	WRONG RECORD
	INCOMPLETE
	INCORRECT
	UNTIMELY
	INAPPROPRIATE
	FILE LOST
	PROGRAM LOST
	PEOPLE LOST
OUTPUT	IMPROPER DISTRIBUTION
	LATE OR LOST
	NOT REVIEWED FOR OBVIOUS ERRORS
	ERRONEOUS BUT PLAUSIBLE
	EXCESSIVE ERRORS UNCHECKED
OTHER	UNSUPPORTABLE RESULTS
	SHADOW SYSTEMS
	UNLIMITED ACCESS
	MANAGEMENT OVERRIDE

Figure 12-4.

Causes of exposure for CIS applications are classified here by processing function.

- CIS center

- Advanced systems

- Computer abuse

- Accidents and natural events.

Applications. Exposures stemming from applications occur during the actual processing of in-house or user jobs. Common types of exposure are listed in the table in Figure 12-4. Causes of these exposures are classified according to input, processing, output, and other.

Figure 12-5.

Listed here are some typical causes of exposure arising from systems development activities.

```
SYSTEMS DEVELOPMENT EXPOSURES

INCOMPLETE ECONOMIC EVALUATION
MANAGEMENT ABDICATION
INADEQUATE SPECIFICATIONS
SYSTEM DESIGN ERRORS
INCOMPETENT DESIGN PERSONNEL
TECHNICAL SELF-GRATIFICATION
POOR COMMUNICATIONS
NO PROJECT KILL POINTS
TEMPTATIONS TO COMPUTER ABUSE
UNMAINTAINABLE APPLICATIONS
INCOHERENT DIRECTION
```

Systems development.   Systems-development causes of exposure occur in the development cycle of applications programs or of entire hardware/software systems. Typical causes are listed in Figure 12-5.

CIS center.   Exposures related to the CIS center itself occur during actual day-to-day operations. The causes of these exposures, listed in Figure 12-6, are not related to any specific application. Note that causes are classified according to human error, hardware/software failures, computer abuse, and catastrophe.

Advanced systems.   Advanced systems causes of exposures are related to CIS center operations, but contain additional risks due to technological factors not usually present in daily production. These causes, listed in Figure 12-7, are classified according to remote batch, remote job entry, switching systems, real-time inquiry, real-time update, real-time programming, and databases.

Computer abuse.   Exposure due to computer abuse can happen within any vulnerable computer system, regardless of the size of the computer or the type of installation. Causes of abuse are listed in Figure 12-8. Classifications of causes describe the role of the computer in the abuse—as the target of theft or destruction, as the mechanism of penetration, or as the environment within which abuse is committed.

CIS CENTER

Exposures: **Erroneous Record Keeping, Unacceptable Accounting, Processing Interruption, Erroneous Management Decisions, Embezzlement, Competitive Disadvantage.**

CLASSIFICATION	CAUSES
HUMAN ERROR	DATA ENTRY
	CONSOLE ENTRY
	FILE DAMAGED
HARDWARE/SOFTWARE FAILURES	INTERRUPTED OPERATIONS
	LOSS OF DATA
	LOGIC ERRORS
COMPUTER ABUSE	THEFT
	EMBEZZLEMENT
	FRAUD
	ESPIONAGE
	INVASION OF PRIVACY
	MALICIOUSNESS
	MISCHIEVOUSNESS
CATASTROPHE	FIRE
	WATER
	WIND
	CIVIL DISORDER

Figure 12-6.

Causes of exposure attributable to the CIS processing center can be classified according to human error, hardware/software failures, computer abuse, and catastrophe.

Accidents and natural events.   Accidents and natural causes of exposures generally are unavoidable, though measures may be taken to minimize damage. These exposures can be considered, in effect, a "cost of living" in computer environments. Hazards include fires, water damage, malfunctions of air conditioning systems, electrical disruptions, and natural disasters. (See Figure 12-9.)

AUDITING THE CIS PROCESSING CENTER

Both increasingly powerful microcomputers and large, sophisticated CIS processing centers have caused the auditor's role to change dramatically. The

ADVANCED SYSTEMS

TYPE OF SYSTEM	CAUSES
REMOTE BATCH	LOSS OF DATA DISTORTION OF DATA
REMOTE JOB ENTRY	LOSS OF DATA DISTORTION OF DATA UNLIMITED ACCESS COMPUTER ABUSE
SWITCHING SYSTEMS	LOSS OF DATA DISTORTION OF DATA DELAY OF DATA MISROUTING OF DATA
REAL-TIME INQUIRY	INVASION OF PRIVACY INFORMATION NOT CURRENT DISTORTION OF DATA
REAL-TIME UPDATE	UNLIMITED ACCESS HARDWARE/SOFTWARE FAILURE UNSUPPORTABLE RESULTS HUMAN DATA-ENTRY ERRORS
REAL-TIME PROGRAMMING	UNLIMITED ACCESS HARDWARE/SOFTWARE FAILURE UNSUPPORTABLE RESULTS HUMAN DATA-ENTRY ERRORS COMPUTER ABUSE DESTRUCTION OF PROGRAMS
DATABASES	UNLIMITED ACCESS DESTRUCTION OF FILES SOFTWARE FAILURES SLOW RESPONSE

Figure 12-7.

Causes of exposures arising from advanced systems are classified here by type of system.

environment, simply, is becoming increasingly technical. Whether service is provided by standalone microcomputers or a CIS data center, the following qualities must be present:

- Efficient operations
- Effective management
- Secure installations and equipment
- Data integrity, security, and privacy.

COMPUTER ABUSE

CLASSIFICATION	CAUSES
CIS TARGET	SERVICES THEFT
	INFORMATION THEFT
	HARDWARE THEFT
	MALICIOUS DESTRUCTION
	MISCHIEVOUS DESTRUCTION
MECHANISM—METHOD OF PERPETRATION	DESIGNED ACT
	IMPLEMENTATION ACT
	FRAUD
ENVIRONMENT	EMBEZZLEMENT
	FRAUD
	INVASION OF PRIVACY
	DESTRUCTION OF MEDIA
	UNCORRECTABLE ERRORS

Figure 12-8.

Shown here are some typical causes of exposure from abuse of computer information systems.

The assets of the organization in all types of processing facilities must be safeguarded. The information produced by these services must be consistent, timely, and reliable. Controls must be in place to assure that errors are discovered and corrected in a timely and efficient manner.

The objectives of a computer auditor in performing an audit of a CIS processing center are to:

- Assure management that assets are safeguarded satisfactorily.

- Verify the accuracy and reliability of information on which management decisions are based.

- Promote operational efficiency and adherence to prescribed organizational policies and procedures.

- Help to develop and maintain an adequate system of internal control.

- Review and appraise the soundness, adequacy, and application of all internal control system segments—wherever they exist.

- Appraise the quality of performance in carrying out assigned control responsibilities.

```
ACCIDENTS AND NATURAL EVENTS

Exposures: Processing Interruption,
           Excessive Costs/Deficient Revenues
           Loss or Destruction of Assets

CLASSIFICATION          CAUSES

FIRES                   INTERNAL
                        EXTERNAL

WATER DAMAGE            AUTOMATIC EXTINGUISHER
                        BROKEN PIPE LINES
                        FLOODS

AIR CONDITIONING        TEMPERATURE
                        FILTRATION
                        HUMIDITY

ELECTRICITY             INTERNAL POWER FAILURE
                        EXTERNAL POWER FAILURE

NATURAL DISASTER        WIND
                        TORNADOES
                        HURRICANES
                        FLOODS
                        EARTHQUAKES
```

Figure 12-9.

Causes of exposure from typical kinds of accidents and natural events are listed here by type of disaster.

To achieve these objectives, the computer audit team takes three basic steps: 1. Plan the audit; 2. Conduct the audit; 3. Communicate the findings.

PLANNING THE CIS PROCESSING CENTER AUDIT

An audit of a CIS processing center requires a well planned approach. Approaches will vary, depending on the type of use made of the facility. For example, the approach when resources are used exclusively for internal purposes will be different from an audit of resources used on a contractual basis by outside customers. Some general steps apply, however. Included in any plan will be:

- Assignment of staff to perform the audit

- Preliminary review of policies and procedures (corporate, local, federal, etc.)

- Scheduling.

Assignment of Audit Staff

The assignment of audit staff includes the designation of the auditor responsible for the overall audit. In assigning personnel, the most knowledgeable and experienced staff members for a given situation should be considered. Once assignments are made, all members of the audit team should be briefed on their specific areas of responsibility. Further, team members should be aware that additional responsibilities may be assigned during the course of the audit, as circumstances warrant.

Policy and Procedure Review

All appropriate organizational policies and procedures should be reviewed by each audit team member. All participants should be thoroughly familiar with the requirements or standards established for the CIS processing center. Also, any relevant legal or contractual mandates should be reviewed, including federal laws, contractual limitations, and so on.

Scheduling

In developing a schedule for the audit, consideration should be given to all phases and functions of the CIS processing center. Potential conflicts with operations or processing cycles must be identified, and schedules should be developed for a minimum of disruption to ongoing service. From the auditors' standpoint, careful scheduling assures that sufficient time is allotted for a thorough examination.

CONDUCTING THE AUDIT SEGMENT

When the audit team arrives on site, the initial phase of the examination usually is to conduct a thorough pre-audit survey of the CIS processing center. This critical step highlights areas of weakness in the facility and in operations that will require subsequent, in-depth review. About 30 percent of the total scheduled audit time is devoted to this phase.

The pre-audit survey includes interviews with personnel. This data gathering may use questionnaires or other data collection instruments. The purpose of the interviews is for CIS processing center management and key employees to assist the auditors in identifying the overall organization, assigned duties and responsibilities, and existing internal controls. In addition to interview techniques, the auditor may use personal observation to assess the security of the facility, data, and equipment for further follow-up, as necessary.

During discussions with the CIS manager, an organization chart for the facility or department should be obtained. If such a chart is not available, the auditor should prepare one on the basis of the information supplied. The chart should indicate the position and responsibility of each CIS processing facility employee.

To supplement the organizational view obtained from CIS management, detailed information should be sought in the following areas:

- Overall facility security
- Disaster plans
- Equipment in place
- Applications processed
- Control of data input and output.

Also, particular attention should be given to access to and control over:

- Library files
- Operations scheduling
- Systems and programming documentation
- Computer utilization reports.

Great care should be exercised to assure that all functions and responsibilities are covered and that all internal controls are in effect.

After the discussions with CIS management, all employees within the facility should be interviewed to ascertain their understanding of their own duties and responsibilities. Sometimes, there is a wide variance between the perceptions and directives of the CIS manager and the actual performance of employees.

Conducting these interviews takes the auditor through almost every aspect of CIS operations. The auditor, therefore, should look for opportunities to observe and gather data outside the scope of the individual interview. For example, throughout these interviews, the auditor should be observing the layout of the facility, the security of equipment and facility, safety measures, control of data files, and duties performed by each employee.

A thorough and complete pre-audit survey provides the basis for the audit manager to update or prepare an audit program guide for use during the audit. Based on the findings of the pre-audit survey, this guide will provide for the review and testing of questionable areas, or areas of potential weaknesses, in organization, operations, and internal control. Also, the audit guide includes provisions for further testing of areas that indicated non-compliance with published policies, procedures, and federal or contractual obligations.

Detailed Review of the CIS Processing Center

After completion of the pre-audit survey and the formulation of the audit guide, the detailed review and verification of the total CIS operation can begin. Areas examined during the review should include:

- Security
- Organization
- Equipment and computer resources
- Systems and programs
- Data control
- File library
- Evaluation and testing of systems and programs.

Security. Areas of concern for the security of the CIS facility include:

- Location
- Physical access
- Environment
- Safety rules
- Data security
- Disaster/recovery.

Location. The security of the facility begins with its location. For example, major exposures would arise from the following situations:

- A computer facility might be housed behind a plate-glass wall that displayed the equipment to the public. This arrangement would make the total operation susceptible to destruction by public disorders or riots, as well as by disgruntled ex-employees.

- Computers might be located near production areas. Industrial accidents within the production area could damage the computer equipment or cause interruptions in operations.

- The entire facility might be located in a geographic area in which flood, earthquake, or other violent natural disaster presents a potential exposure to the equipment and operations.

Physical access.   Systems and procedures that protect against access of unauthorized employees to the CIS area, that control the entry of visitors, and that provide control over materials brought into or removed from the processing area are next in priority of review.

Environment.   Systems for the detection, warning, and control of fires and protection from the effects of tornadoes, floods, lightning, etc., should be reviewed for adequacy.

Safety rules.   Another area for review is the set of safety rules followed at the CIS processing facility. Safety rules are reviewed to assure that they are providing the protection necessary for the facility and all of its employees. For example, rules governing smoking and food in the computer area, the location and use of fire extinguishers, as well as provisions for the notification of emergency personnel and agencies, should be reviewed periodically by CIS management and also should be examined by the auditors.

Data security.   A major area for security review is data security. Data security encompasses the control and access to:

- Original data input
- Systems, programs, and data files (data maintained on disk files, diskettes, and tape files)
- Data output.

These areas are reviewed to assure that only authorized personnel have, or can obtain, access to these data resources.

Disaster/recovery.   Any arrangements for the utilization of backup computer resources and the off-site storage of critical data and files should be reviewed by the audit staff to assure that operations will not be interrupted indefinitely in case of emergency or disaster.

A related area of concern and review is disaster plans. All disaster/contingency plans are reviewed to determine the specific assignment of duties and responsibilities in case of an emergency or disaster. These plans should include step-by-step procedures to be followed to assure that the CIS processing facility is back in operation as quickly as possible after a major interruption.

Organization.   A review of the total organization of the CIS facility determines whether the segregation of duties provides an adequate system of internal control. Segregation of the following three duties should be considered essential:

- Custody of assets, including records regarded as assets of the organization
- Custody of records detailing the existence of assets
- Authorizations for execution of transactions, such as the running of production programs.

Also, segregation should exist among such functions as systems and programming, data preparation, data control, computer operations, and the data library. There should not be any overlapping of duties among these functions, nor should individuals assigned to one function have unrestricted access to or responsibility in other functions. For example, computer operators should not have responsibility for the completeness of data input and output. Also, programmers should not have access to programs or master files that are used for the regular processing of data.

Job descriptions and personnel files are reviewed for selected employees. Special note is made of all prior experience and any background checks made prior to hiring, since key factors of security are the loyalty and trustworthiness of each CIS employee.

Equipment and computer resources.   In this major audit segment, the auditor should obtain a listing of all CIS equipment—including data communication equipment and accessories. This listing then should be compared with the listing of equipment authorized for the CIS facility. All overages or shortages of computer resources are noted, and an explanation for each is sought. Equipment overages or shortages may indicate a security problem or unauthorized processing of data. A thorough investigation is required to determine how and why equipment was disposed of, as well as how excess equipment was acquired. The disposition or use of these exception items during the current work schedule is determined.

Systems and programs.   The systems and programs used and operated within the CIS processing center are reviewed for proper authorization and complete documentation in accordance with established standards. This review applies to both applications and systems software used within the processing facility.

All modifications or changes (including temporary patches, if any) should be supported by formal requests and authorizations by responsible individuals. Even operating changes made to systems or programs that do not affect the input or output of data should be communicated formally to the user. From an audit standpoint, it is important to assure that the documentation describes, accurately and in detail, the current operation of the system and programs. The accuracy of the documentation will be verified in a subsequent audit step through actual operational testing by the auditor.

Data control.   The procedures by which data are received and recorded for processing are reviewed in this next major audit segment. The objective is to determine how jobs from the user are controlled—from receipt in the data control area through data entry, computer processing, and delivery of output to users.

In batch applications, data control records should be maintained that indicate the job received, control totals for each, error corrections made, and the re-verification or re-input of rejected data. These records should indicate clearly that the data were received and were processed completely and accurately, with full verification of the number and the value of items received for processing.

Computer logs are internal machine-program controls that record the history of computer jobs processed and programs utilized. These valuable logs—on paper or in machine-readable form—should be reviewed to assure that the proper programs and program versions were used and that the processing had taken place according to predetermined work schedules.

The overall procedures for CIS processing and control should be reviewed for adequacy in preventing disclosure of, or access to, data by unauthorized personnel or means.

File library.   An important responsibility of a CIS processing center is the storage and control of data files and programs. This usually is accomplished by having a limited-access library that is maintained by a full-time librarian or library staff. The librarian is responsible for the identification and security, as well as for the issuance and return, of all data files and programs. In small installations or in isolated, standalone locations, a full-time librarian may not be justified. As a check on the segregation of duties, this function should be reviewed closely if collateral duties are shared.

The procedures for the storage and control of data files and programs are reviewed to assure that they are adequate to prevent access by unauthorized personnel. These procedures should include maintenance of a library register that reflects the current inventory and usage of all programs and master files under the custody of the data librarian. Large CIS installations often use file management systems and access control systems to help manage access to information resources. The auditor must verify the effectiveness of these types of systems.

Evaluation and testing of systems and programs. Many methods are available for evaluating and testing the systems and programs within a CIS processing center. Some of these tools and techniques are discussed later in this chapter. The evaluation and testing process may involve commercial audit packages, audit packages and special programs developed in-house, test decks, simulation/modeling packages, and so on. Used in combination, these tools can help to extract, summarize, and format data as required by the auditor. The results of the auditor's tests are input into the system for the summarizing of final results.

Computer-assisted approaches have been used to test computer-based systems such as inventory/materials control, accounts receivable, payroll, and on-line support—with excellent results. Any method used for testing and evaluation of CIS processing center operations should provide tests for the entire range of conditions that may be encountered in the systems or programs used.

COMMUNICATION OF AUDIT RESULTS

After the audit has been completed, the results should be communicated—both verbally and in writing—to CIS management. The auditor also should provide recommendations to CIS management for dealing with the areas in question. It is important to have these problems well documented so they can be compared with existing documentation of procedures and policies.

If problem areas exist because of a lack of controls, the needed controls should be defined on a cost/benefit basis. CIS management should be shown how the recommended controls can save money for the organization's operations through the reduction of identified exposures. Procedures also need to be defined for the best way of implementing these controls. Supervisors of the affected areas then should be charged with the responsibility of providing a workable plan to incorporate the needed controls within their departments.

After the new controls are in place, the supervisor should report to CIS management on their status and on any problem areas that still exist. CIS management, in turn, can advise the audit department on the implementation of the new controls and on any outstanding problem areas.

The audit department then must be prepared to re-evaluate both the new and the previously existing controls to determine the effectiveness of the total system of controls. This check is needed to assure that new controls intended to enhance the security and integrity of the data center actually do not detract from its performance by degrading existing controls.

Although the audit department is in a necessarily adversarial relationship with the CIS processing center in performing an audit, both functions share the goal of meeting organizational objectives and helping to fulfill the organization's mission. The auditor should keep in mind, therefore, that the implementation of new controls should be justified on a cost/benefit basis. Controls that are installed at the auditor's recommendation should not be more costly to implement and maintain than the exposures they were designed to reduce.

Further, CIS management also should keep in mind that the auditor has the best interests of the organization in mind in recommending added controls. New controls should be seen as a benefit to the affected department or function, not as a burden.

The auditor and CIS management, then, should work toward the common goal of increasing the profitability and integrity of the organization. Lines of communication always should be open and available between the two functions so that there can be a flow of information and ideas between them. With the goal of ultimate benefit to the organization—backed up by sound cost/benefit analysis in view of the exposures—the objectives of both functions, as well as of the organization itself, will be enhanced.

OPERATING SYSTEMS: CONCERNS AND ISSUES

As a critical component of any centralized CIS processing center, the computer's operating system deserves special audit attention. Reasons for concern stem from the fact that an operating system for a large-scale computer installation is both highly technical and highly complex. The difficulty of gaining sufficient overview understanding of all aspects of a given operating system is, in itself, an exposure.

The Role of the Systems Programmer

The caretakers of operating systems are systems programmers. Systems programmers provide an essential service for most CIS installations. These technical specialists maintain the operating system and, where possible, increase computer throughput. Systems programmers also select and install a wide variety of utilities, or systems programs, that are useful and accessible to multiple applications. Technical knowledge of the operating system permits systems programmers to select and install such generally useful programs without degrading system performance.

Of all the job groups within the CIS processing facility, that of the systems programmer is the most technical and computer-oriented. The systems programmer may be called upon to handle almost any data processing problem, especially if the involvement of system software is sufficiently technical. In itself, this multipurpose, or multifunctional, aspect of systems programming creates an area of concern. Because the operating system has pervasive effects on all applications within the installation, the systems programmer necessarily has some ability to affect them all.

A related factor is that, as computer technology has evolved, operating systems on large computers have grown in complexity. For the systems programmer, this means that one person cannot understand the whole operating system. The systems programmer must specialize in areas such as data communication or database management while maintaining a general understanding of the whole.

This situation holds potential for increasing the segregation of duties among systems programmers. Adequate controls should be applied to the systems programming function. These controls can be difficult to devise and apply because systems programming is a highly complex and intricate function. The unavoidable complexity also means that an adequate overview understanding may lie further beyond the reach of computer generalists, management, and computer auditors.

Managers and systems programmers.   For management, the problem is especially acute. There always has existed a communication gap between organizational managers and computer technicians. At the application level, structured systems development methodologies, as well as powerful application generators and tools accessible to users, have helped bridge the gap. At the level of the operating system, however, the gap grows ever wider. The complexity of today's operating systems just gives the systems programmer's job more of a mystical status than before.

Systems programmers and managers typically have not communicated well, largely because of misconceptions by both parties. For example, managers realize, correctly, that the systems programmer plays an important role in keeping the system running. Managers, however, and not systems programmers, have the primary responsibility for maintaining adequate controls. Management, then, must press the technicians to install controls that usually require some trade-off of system performance for increased integrity. Systems programmers may resist controls they feel will introduce unacceptable inefficiencies. Having little technical ability to form an independent judgment, management often has deferred to the systems programmers by default. Management tends to feel that the cost/benefit of introducing a control cannot be worth bringing inefficiency into the computer system. This view is understandable, especially since most large organizations spend considerable sums of money on CIS resources.

This communication gap is compounded by a fundamental organizational problem: Managers and systems programmers do not fit into the organization in the same way. Managers tend to view systems programmers as specialists who cannot communicate well enough to function as managers. Studies and recent articles about systems programmers have reported that, unless the organization provides a management function for systems programming, systems programmers will view themselves as unable to manage effectively.

Ironically, both systems programmers and managers agree that their organizations do not develop management-oriented positions for systems programmers. Application programmers, on the other hand, are viewed as helpmates of management and themselves are assigned the management of systems development projects. Though the pay scales of both types of programmers are highly comparable, systems programmers are regarded—and tend to regard themselves—as an isolated, autonomous group.

These differences between managers and systems programmers may explain why so little attention has been given to placing controls on systems programmers. Although a slow rate of change can be noted, the amount of accounting and data processing literature devoted to controlling operations, data entry, and applications programming outweighs the material written about controlling system programming. Management, however, cannot afford to continue to look the other way. Systems programmers control the smooth functioning of the operating system without which the CIS facility could not function. From the auditor's standpoint, then, controls on systems programming are a mandatory concern.

Threats in systems programming.   A major problem could arise from a systems programmer with intentions adverse to organizational goals. Without controls placed on the systems programmer, this person could steal or destroy assets without detection until it is too late to apply corrective action. A systems programmer also could engage in technical self-gratification, solving complex technical problems not significant to the organization just for the challenge of solving them. Such activity would not accomplish much that the organization could use—at a significant expenditure of both staff and computer time.

Because of the far-reaching scope of the operating system on CIS applications, the impact of a single error by a systems programmer can be significant. Given the systems programmer's level of expertise, the existence of malicious intent multiplies the potential for unauthorized activity. Basically, without adequate controls, it is within the systems programmer's scope of

SYSTEMS PROGRAMMING—THREATS, EXPOSURES AND CONTROLS.

THREATS	EXPOSURES	CONTROLS
Unauthorized changes to the operating system	Severely impaired system performance	Use of time-sharing option. Formal procedures and documentation for system changes.
Unauthorized use of database	Compromise of integrity of the database data	Database control groups to keep the maintenance of data from the maintenance of the database system.
Unauthorized use of application programs	Dollar loss from theft, compromise of sensitive data	System programmers cannot access job command language or any source or object application programs.
Breaking into the telecommunications system	Dollar loss from theft, compromise of sensitive data	Control over all parts to the main computer system. Hardware controls wherever possible work best.
Sabotaging the system	Loss of data, severe interruption of processing	Exit interviews and no two-week notice in event of firing. Understanding system programmer personality. No access to computer room except under close supervision. Restrictions on potentially destructive utilities.
Stealing software	Lawsuits	Log for all microcomputer software. Logbook for system programmer entry and exit. Check for huge bank accounts. Set up possible theft situations to test honesty.
Use of resources for outside	Loss of computer resources	Surprise audits. Terminal monitoring. Check for overtime. Check bank accounts.
Uncontrolled system use or "hacking"	System performance may suffer, bad priority on important jobs	System security checks for abnormal end of job. Written authorization for any system changes. Surprise audits. Maintenance of operating system logs. Supervision on off shifts.

Figure 12-10.

Corresponding threats, exposures, and controls within the systems programming function are shown in this table.

control and expertise both to steal or destroy valuable resources and also to cover up effectively all traces of such activity.

Controls over systems programming. The table in Figure 12-10 summarizes control measures that may be applied against threats in the area of systems programming.

In general, threats in the systems programming area are more likely in CIS facilities with an "exposed" profile. A typical, exposed CIS processing center runs a large volume of financial data, relies on lots of overtime, does not face separation of duties, and may allow an "open shop" philosophy (that is, allow virtually unrestricted access to system resources by staff members).

Historically, controls have been applied primarily in the areas of data entry, operations, and application programming. It has even been asserted that, if controls for application programmers are not applied effectively, systems programmers are more likely to circumvent the system on the application level. However, most systems programmers lack sufficient familiarity with application programs to exploit control weaknesses. It is far more likely that, working with the operating system on a daily basis, systems programmers will use that route.

If controls do not include separation of duties between the operations function and systems programmers, a systems programmer with malicious intent might gain access by using the operator console instead of by making modifications to the operating system. Anyone with access to the operator console has the power to execute a substantial number of operating system utilities. If no controls exist on access to the operator console, it would be difficult to identify who was responsible for execution of system software. In short, in a CIS processing environment where controls are poor, systems programmers can pose the following threats:

- Access might not occur through authorized application programs.

- A logical point of entry is through the operator's console, if access can be gained. Command of system utilities is relatively unrestricted through the console, and responsibility for abnormal situations would be difficult to trace.

- In the presence of strong controls over applications and console operations, the logical method of penetration for systems programmers is through modifications to the operating system.

This last option does not imply that controls and segregation of duties between the applications and systems programming areas are irrelevant. Applications programmers who gain access to system utilities have a valuable tool if they want to circumvent the system.

Security Impact Statement (SIS)

A technique that can help an organization provide increased focus on the programming area is the *security impact statement (SIS)*. The main objective of a security impact statement is to assess control opportunities early in the development of a new system. This is a much more efficient and effective approach than to retrofit controls into an existing system. Under the SIS approach, the system does not suffer from exposure before the new controls finally are activated. Also, the cost of placing controls in a system later will exceed, by far, the costs of implementing the controls in the beginning.

The security impact statement can help resolve the problem of not implementing controls early and of forcing the systems programmer's attention on controls. The SIS should attempt to provide an overall view and rationale for recommended controls. All participants in systems development, then, can understand the potential exposures and the need for controls.

The SIS also can help developers choose among a bewildering number of system utilities and focus on the utilities that control particularly sensitive functions. From the management viewpoint, CIS managers or systems programming supervisors can use the SIS as a benchmark document in helping to assure that systems programmers build controls into emerging systems.

Computer auditors should bear in mind, however, that a coherent SIS does not necessarily assure that controls will be implemented at the operating system level. By definition, an SIS is targeted on a single, emerging application. Emphasis at the systems level probably will be on utilities that must be called, modified, or developed to get the application up and running. Indeed, experience has shown that, as computer technology advances, the involvement of systems programmers in development efforts focuses increasingly on new or modified utilities. To assure the ongoing integrity of the operating system, other audit approaches are required.

Auditing Systems Software

As computer systems become more sophisticated, many former manual operations are automated with system software. (See Figure 12-11.) Typically, this software is provided by outside vendors in packages that fall into the following categories:

- Operating systems
- System utilities
- Program library systems
- File maintenance systems
- Security software
- Data communications systems
- Database management systems.

Often, any one category is a complete system that could require a complete audit. The audit of operating systems is a process for determining overall relationships among the application and the system software and the extent to which system software controls influence accuracy and reliability of the application. Procedures for evaluating specific types of system software are listed in the audit program provided in Figure 12-12.

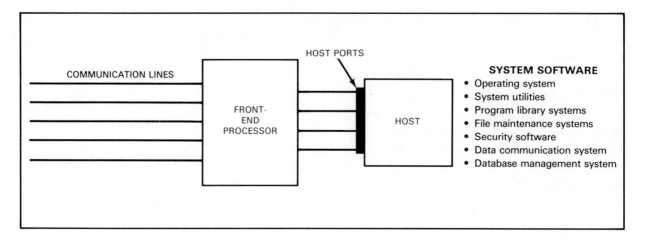

Figure 12-11.

During the first-cut evaluation of systems software controls, the auditor has several areas of concern, including:

- Types and uses of systems software
- Reliance on systems software to perform certain control or critical processing
- Controlling access to systems software
- Controlling changes to systems software.

The depth of evaluation depends on the first two areas because they identify the organization's reliance on systems software.

Types and uses of systems software. Most organizations with third-generation or newer equipment make heavy use of an operating system to:

- Manage the resources of the computer with a minimum of operator intervention.
- Help programmers and operators to control the operations and allocation of peripheral devices and other computer resources.
- Minimize the differences among models in a given manufacturer's line of computers as a way to facilitate the transfer of application programs.

In addition, many system utilities, such as copy programs, sorts, and others are used heavily. To get a better understanding of system software, the auditor should obtain complete technical descriptions and documentation from vendors.

Figure 12-12. *This checklist is a portion of an audit program for evaluating system software.*

SYSTEM SOFTWARE CONTROLS

Many control operations previously performed manually have been automated in "system software," which is defined as any program or system that helps interconnect and/or control the elements of input, output, processing, data, and application programs. System software normally falls into one of the following categories: operating systems, system utilities, program library systems, file maintenance systems, security software, data communications systems, and database management systems. For each of these categories, the auditor should determine:

- Types and uses of system software
- Reliance on system software to perform critical control or critical processes
- Who has access to interworkings of system software
- How well the changes to system software are being controlled.

OPERATING SYSTEMS YES NO

1. Is an operating system used to control the inner workings of the computer hardware? (If "no," skip to question 17.) __ __

2. Has the vendor or developer provided a complete, documented description of the operating system's design and operation? __ __

3. Does the operating system prohibit one application program from accessing memory or data of another application program that is processing simultaneously? __ __

4. Is the operating system "read protected"? (This prohibits an application program from accessing operating system instructions, password tables, and/or other authorization algorithms.) __ __

5. Does the operating system prohibit operators from entering data or changing memory values at the computer console? __ __

6. Is the use of privileged instruction of the operating system strictly controlled? __ __

7. Does the operating system control all input/output functions of data files? __ __

8. Are operating system instructions, password tables, and/or other authorization algorithms protected from unauthorized access when the computer system fails? __ __

9. Has the integrity of the operating system been tested after initial installation? __ __

10. Does the operating system prohibit application programs from overriding or bypassing errors which are detected during processing? __ __

11. Must all application programs or other system software be run only when the operating system is operational? __ __

12. Is an audit trail of all operating system actions maintained either on the automatic console log or the computer system's job accounting data? __ __

13. Is each use of the computer system's "load" button recorded? __ __

14. Is the button physically protected? __ __

15. Is the computer system's internal clock adequately protected from un-authorized access?   —   —

16. Does the operating system adequately and accurately schedule all jobs run on the computer system?   —   —

SYSTEM UTILITIES

17. Are utility programs used to perform frequently repeated functions? (If "no," skip to question 25.)   —   —

18. Has the vendor or developer of the system utilities provided a complete, documented description of their design and operation?   —   —

19. Must the operating system be operational when utility programs are used?   —   —

20. Is there a complete directory of all available utilities?   —   —

21. Is access to system utility documentation denied to computer operators?   —   —

22. Is a supervisory authorization required before installation and use of new versions of utility programs?   —   —

23. Can controls that detect processing errors in system utilities be overridden or bypassed?   —   —

24. Can system utilities be used to override or bypass controls within other system software or application programs?   —   —

PROGRAM LIBRARY SYSTEMS

25. Is a program library system used to control application programs? (If no, skip to question 35.)   —   —

26. Has the vendor or developer of the program library system provided a complete, documented description of the system's design and operation?   —   —

27. Does the program library system:
    a. Restrict access to application programs?   —   —
    b. Control movement of programs from test to production modes?   —   —
    c. Control movement of programs from source code to object code?   —   —
    d. Control changes to application programs?   —   —

28. Are program library system functions adequately supported by proper manual procedures?   —   —

29. Are control functions performed by the program library system protected so they cannot be bypassed?   —   —

30. Does the program library system provide an audit trail of all changes made to application programs?   —   —

31. Does the program library system prevent the existence of more than one version of a source code program?   —   —

32. Does the program library system prevent the existence of more than one version of a source code program?   —   —

33. Are obsolete programs removed regularly from the:
    a. Source code library?   —   —
    b. Object code library?   —   —

34. Are computer operators denied access to all libraries maintained by the program library system?   —   —

Figure 12-12.

Continued.

FILE MAINTENANCE SYSTEMS   YES   NO

35. Is a file maintenance system used to control all tape and disk data sets? (If no, skip to question 43.) — —

36. Has the vendor or developer of the file maintenance system provided a complete documented description of its design and operation? — —

37. Does the file maintenance system:

    a. Restrict access to automated data files? — —
    b. Control the establishment, use and retention of automated data files? — —

38. Are file maintenance system functions adequately supported by proper manual procedures? — —

39. Are control functions performed by the file maintenance system protected so that they cannot be overridden or bypassed? — —

40. Does the file maintenance system provide an audit trail of all uses and accesses of all automated data files? — —

41. Does the file maintenance system prohibit more than one data file from having the same volume serial number? — —

42. Have external labels been removed from all tape data files since the file maintenance system became operational? — —

SECURITY SOFTWARE

43. Is separate security software used to provide additional control over the client's computer resources? — —

44. Has the vendor or developer of the security software provided a complete, documented description of its design and operation? — —

45. Is the security software used to control access to:

    a. Terminals? — —
    b. Remote job entry stations? — —
    c. Individual automated data files? — —
    d. Individual application programs? — —
    e. Other system software? — —

46. Are security software functions adequately supported by proper manual procedures? — —

47. Can the control functions performed by security software be overridden or bypassed? — —

48. Does the security software provide an audit trail of:

    a. All authorized uses of computer resources under control? — —
    b. All unauthorized attempted access? — —

Figure 12-12.

Concluded.

In sophisticated computer centers, systems software is used to control application programs, tape and disk computer files, and other resources that require special security measures because of their critical nature. For example, program library systems, or packages, normally control all application programs, including access, change, and conversion from source to object code. Most of these packages contain a complete audit trail feature that records all changes to application programs, including identification of programmers who make changes. When a program library system is implemented properly, it can help to promote better security and backup of applications programs.

File management systems, or packages, perform similar functions in the area of security and backup for tape and disk files. These packages help to reduce manual library functions, and, in many cases, eliminate the need for external file labels. Audit trails also are normally available within a file management system. The library function records when a particular file was created and used, as well as by whom.

Security software packages are one of the newer methods for automating access controls. Overall, these are designed to control access to the computer system by identifying and verifying persons who try to gain access to protected system resources. Typically, these packages control terminals and remote job entry stations; individual tape, disk, or mass storage data sets; individual application programs; and other systems software, such as operating systems, database management systems, and others. These packages normally provide an audit trail of all accesses, including authorized uses and unauthorized attempts.

For those applications that use on-line terminals, data communications software normally is used to provide an interface between messages to and from terminals, the operating system, data files, or, if present, the DBMS. In addition, data communications software typically performs these added functions:

- Controls access to and use of terminals

- Polls and receives messages from terminals and from other computers

- Addresses and sends messages back to terminals or other computers

- Edits input and output messages

- Handles error situations

- Reroutes messages when a particular terminal or communication line is inoperative

- Performs on-line formatting on video display terminals.

When data resources have been brought under control of a DBMS to reduce redundancy and improve access, the DBMS usually is used to create and update the database, retrieve data, and provide access controls. Thus, a challenge for the auditor lies in using the capabilities built into the DBMS to assure a reasonable level of support to and control over applications that make use of its data resources.

Organizational reliance on systems software. Systems software can affect the levels of reliance placed on controls over application processing within a CIS facility. The auditor should identify, first, the types and uses of systems software that affect the computer-based system being reviewed. Then, the auditor should determine the level of reliance placed on the software within the using organization.

Operating systems, by their very nature, are normally relied upon heavily for general operation of computer hardware. In this role, operating systems warrant further investigation. The auditor should determine whether:

- One application program can access main memory, data storage areas, or files that are in use by another application program

- Important security and accuracy features, such as error handling for invalid data types or formats, are used fully and are not being overridden by application programs or systems programmers

- Access is restricted over use of privileged instructions, such as input/output instructions that would make possible the reading or writing of data from another user's file

- Scheduling functions are self-processing or require extensive operator intervention.

The use of utility software varies greatly among organizations. The most commonly used utilities are copy and sort programs. Regardless of type, the auditor should determine whether:

- Utilities are controlled properly

- Control features within the utilities are used properly

- Utilities can be used to bypass control features of other computer-based systems or systems software packages.

For applications using telecommunications, data communications software can be used to provide the interface between users' terminals and the computer-based system. In most cases, this system software provides additional security and reliability controls. The auditor should determine whether:

- Controls exist to assure that no transactions are lost, added to, or changed during transmission

- All control procedures of the data communications software are being used and cannot be bypassed or overridden

- Only the right people can use the right terminal for the right purposes.

For applications in a database environment, the auditor should determine whether:

- The DBMS can be relied upon to maintain accurate and reliable data with consistency

- Security over different data elements is provided by restricting access only to authorized users

- Proper backup is provided for the database.

Controlling access to systems software. In keeping with the concept of separation of duties, as discussed earlier in this chapter, the responsibility for controlling and maintaining systems software should be separated from comparable responsibilities for applications. A distinction normally is made between systems programmers and application programmers. Thus, access to all systems software should be restricted to systems programmers.

In a database environment, a database administrator (DBA) is the key person who usually has complete access to and control over the DBMS. This person normally is responsible for preserving the integrity of the database, maintaining data definitions, and preventing unauthorized use of or change to the database. DBA activities, like those of the systems programmer, require careful control through increased supervision and cross-checks with database users. For example, a database administrator may initiate DBMS changes that a systems programmer implements. The DBA, however, should be the only person with complete access to the entire database and the only one who changes access levels of other database users.

Controlling changes to systems software. Control procedures over changes to systems software need to be established and followed. For more details, refer to earlier discussions on program change controls in connection with system design, development, and modification controls (Chapter 9). Controls should help to maintain software integrity and prevent unauthorized or inaccurate software changes. Although most changes are initiated as maintenance measures issued by the software vendor, systems software changes should be controlled through use of the following measures:

- Establish formal change procedures and forms that require supervisory authorization before implementation.

- Assure that all changes are tested thoroughly.

- Remove critical files and/or application programs from the computer area while the systems programmer is implementing any change.

AUDIT AND QUALITY CONTROL SOFTWARE TOOLS

An auditor frequently must examine evidence stored on computer media to prove the integrity of file data. As discussed in previous chapters, audit software tools are versatile enough to access and review this information.

Besides these specialized tools, two utilities are especially useful to computer auditors:

- Computer Performance Evaluation (CPE)

- Job Accounting Information (JAI).

Computer Performance Evaluation (CPE)

The main function of Computer Performance Evaluation (CPE) utilities is *performance auditing,* or providing current, raw data and a historical information base on computer resource usage and performance for forecasting and long-range planning. At a technical level, CPE utilities use the system to report on its own efficiency. CPE utilities, then, are tools within the broader function of performance auditing. As a service, performance auditing touches on all areas within the CIS function, as well as on all user areas within the organization. A table that lists some typical CPE tools and utilities is shown in Figure 12-13.

From this service viewpoint, performance auditing is described in terms of the following four steps:

- Specification of objectives

- Measurement bases

- Problem analysis

- Resolution of approaches.

Specification of objectives. Performance evaluation has impacts that extend beyond the CIS area. This function holds potential as an aid to other groups within the organization that make use of or are affected by the performance and quality of CIS services.

A key objective of performance auditing, then, is to develop an awareness of performance criteria and of expectations for performance levels throughout the organization. CPE tools and utilities, such as those listed

COMPUTER PERFORMANCE EVALUATION TOOLS AND UTILITIES

TOOL	COMMERCIAL AVAILABILITY	COST RANGE*	COMPUTER SYSTEM OVERHEAD
1. Accounting data reduction package	Yes**	Low to Medium	Small
2. Software monitor	Yes**	Low to Medium	Small to moderate
3. Program analyzers/ optimizers	Yes	Low	Moderate (program)
4. Hardware monitors:			
Basic	Yes	Low to Medium	None***
Mapping	Yes	Medium to High	None
Intelligent	Yes	High to Very High	Slight***
5. Benchmarks	No	Usually Very High	Usually 100%
6. Simulation:			
Languages	Yes	Medium to High	Small
Packages	Yes	High to Very High	Small

*Costs often change dramatically on these types of products. They are shown here in relative terms for most products in each category solely for comparative purposes. Low = $5,000, Medium = $35,000, High = $100,000.

**These products are widely available for larger IBM systems but on a very limited basis for other systems.

***Hardware monitors producing data that must be reduced after the fact on the subject computer create some overhead at that time. Only intelligent monitors that communicate with the subject computer cause overhead during the monitoring session.

Figure 12-13.

Some of the available tools and utilities for evaluating the performance of computer systems are given in this table.

in Figure 12-11, provide ways of extracting the technical performance data needed to make qualitative evaluations that are meaningful to user groups.

Specific objectives, which are rooted in technical areas within the CIS function, include:

- Hardware
- Operating system
- Application software
- Operations
- System design and physical planning
- Capacity planning.

Hardware. Controls in the hardware area should be on the same level as all system components. That is, hardware performance has a fundamental impact on all other areas. High performance levels in other areas are not achievable if controls on hardware performance are inadequate.

Performance criteria for hardware should be established in terms of minimum and maximum levels of acceptability. Qualitative expectations from users must be translated into quantitative, technical measurements. Measurement methods should be implemented to highlight components that are not operating within these acceptable limits.

Since hardware malfunctions affect system performance directly, hardware failures should be audited routinely. Hardware units of all types with the poorest performance should be identified so that some type of corrective measure (such as repair, enhancement, or replacement) can be taken.

Operating systems. Controls that set maximum and minimum limits of activity should be established for areas within the operating system. Under-utilized system features might be considered for de-activation. Over-utilization, as stated above, may indicate security problems.

A practice that falls into this area of investigation is system *tuning.* System tuning is the modification of system software to enhance overall performance and/or responsiveness. Clearly, potential exposure in this area is great, for reasons stated above. System tuning should be a highly confined activity within the systems programming area and should be restricted to specific, limited objectives in meeting performance commitments and expectations.

Performance auditing measures the operating system's efficiency and helps point out problem areas. Continually measuring a system's performance and attempting to minimize operations overhead helps to increase system performance and to identify bottlenecks.

Application software. Performance auditing allows the evaluation of program products according to economic criteria. CPE utilities analyze routine products such as run reports, *abend* (or *ab*normal *end*ing) reports, device allocation reports, and so on. The end product is an evaluation of the actual costs, in terms of system resources, involved in running a given application.

Operations. The evaluation of operations focuses on the efficiency of resource use on a systemwide basis. CPE utilities analyze multiprogramming levels, on-line availability, and the number of manual interventions that are required to maintain service. Also employed might be benchmark test streams, simulation, or continuous measurement. The computer auditor uses these techniques to arrive at an evaluation of the system's overall operational productivity.

System design and physical planning.   A CPE program also aids in the design of new systems or planned changes to existing ones. For example, performance evaluations would assist in the design of channel configurations for data paths or the placement of a string of devices to provide the most efficient means of transferring data between resources.

Capacity planning.   Performance auditing provides an accurate description of the existing installation. *Capacity planning,* in turn, focuses on meeting projected user demand with available resources. Thus, capacity planning attempts to provide methods of reaching attainable goals within the limits of current configurations. Performance auditing provides the raw data and information base needed for forecasting and subsequent long-range planning. The reports needed for capacity planning include trend analyses extrapolated from data on the actual and potential resources used.

Measurement bases.   Within CIS facilities, the measurement bases for performance evaluation fall into the following broad categories:

- Hardware

- Service

- Work-load statistics and operating system activity.

Hardware.   There are many opinions on the best way to measure the performance of computer hardware. The three data gathering techniques in general use are hardware monitoring, software monitoring, and accounting. An in-depth treatment of these techniques is beyond the scope of this discussion. In broad terms, hardware monitoring focuses on direct measurements of hardware usage and production; and software monitoring attempts to measure hardware performance in terms of system results, or outputs generated by software. Accounting techniques allocate costs to specific computer resources and seek justification in terms of usage volumes and/or significance of the application or service. Usually, some combination of these techniques will be required to gain an accurate picture of how hardware performance is affecting system productivity.

Figure 12-14 is a diagram of some of the critical hardware components usually found in a large-scale computer facility. Measurements must be collected for each critical component: shared data access/storage devices

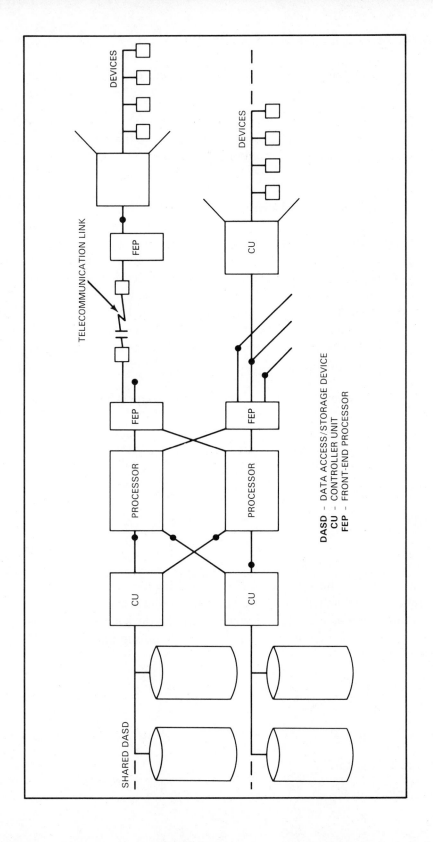

Figure 12-14. Shown in this diagram is a simplified configuration of the hardware components that are critical in evaluating the performance of a large-scale CIS.

(DASD), controller units (CU), processors, front-end processors, and supported devices.

Service. In a technical sense, the term *service* relates to the performance of a CIS network—as measured by monitoring its data communication devices and channels.

In a broader, functional sense, assuring service to users is the reason for measuring performance. In this context, the definition of measures begins with a review of the objectives outlined in the charter of the CIS function. Included in the charter should be the organizational goals and objectives, as well as descriptions of functional areas charged with meeting the objectives. For example, hardware and operations would be considered distinct functional areas within a CIS department. Each functional area turns out a product or performs a process. Since results are of ultimate importance, the measurement of processes must be in terms of the refinement or improvement brought to the product.

Aspects of service also may be considered products in themselves, such as:

- Availability

- Responsiveness

- Turnaround

- Deadline performance

- Quality.

Work-load statistics. The gathering and summarizing of work-load statistics and operating system activity is covered in depth in the discussion below on job accounting approaches. CPE software, however, does have some capabilities in this area. Quantitative measures extracted and summarized by CPE software include:

- CPE activity

- Contention

- Jobs processed

- Total response time

- Transaction rates.

Problem analysis and resolution of approaches. Of the four steps cited above in performance auditing, the first two—specification of objectives and measurement—comprise the process of performance evaluation. Once performance has been assessed, the subsequent steps focus on identifying problem areas and recommending possible corrective actions to improve performance and service levels.

Job Accounting Information (JAI)

The other utility that is especially useful to computer auditors is Job Accounting Information (JAI). The primary function of job-accounting software is to indicate how much it costs to execute a given application and the reasons for the costs. This information permits analysis of the worth of applications and consideration of their possible elimination or improvement.

Job accounting centers on measurements against a pre-established schedule. Scheduling, in turn, is a process of forecasting demands on computer resources and planning the allocation of those resources. The job-accounting process, then, includes the following steps:

- Forecast work-load demands
- Plan resource allocation
- Monitor job processing.

Forecast work-load demands. Trying to determine user demands and their effects on data center resources should not occur just a week or so before jobs are scheduled. For adequate scheduling, work-load demands should be known at least one month in advance. A rough estimate should be prepared one year in advance. In practice, this estimation actually should be done at least two months before the start of a new operating year.

Forecasting work loads is the key to efficient allocation of resources. Emphasis is on forecasting at least a year ahead because time will be needed to make adjustments in schedules, secure user agreements to schedule changes, and step through additional iterations of the scheduling process. The effort always is to anticipate peak and slack periods and to attempt to re-schedule jobs from peak into slack time. The ideal is to achieve a nearly level demand on resources with maximum utilization. Scheduling also must allow for inevitable rush jobs, changes in management priorities, and interruptions in data center or business operations.

Figure 12-15 shows the input to Job Accounting Information needed to prepare a preliminary work-load report for the coming year, and subsequently, for the coming month.

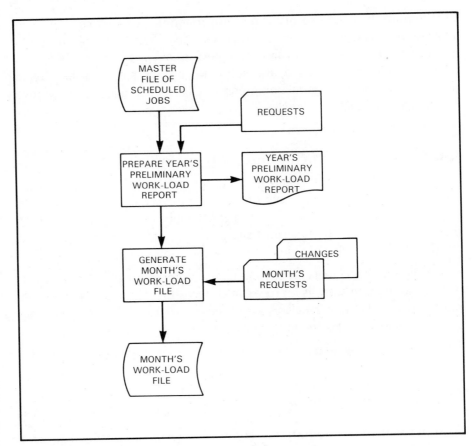

Figure 12-15.

This flowchart shows inputs required for producing a work-load report under Job Accounting Information (JAI) software.

Plan resource allocation. The updated file of scheduled jobs is used to prepare tentative monthly schedules that, as shown in Figure 12-16, are forwarded to the user and programming departments. User and programming personnel then can decide whether the schedule is satisfactory, if any changes are needed, and if any adjustments can be made to relieve overloaded time periods. These changes can be submitted at least one week prior to the end of the month, when a final monthly schedule is printed and distributed. This is the last schedule that the users and programming personnel will receive. Any additional requests after preparation of this schedule must be submitted as unscheduled jobs.

To prepare a tentative schedule and the final monthly schedule, two levels of scheduling should occur: *macroscheduling,* for all data center processing, and *microscheduling,* for only the computer and its resources. Macroscheduling focuses on meeting user commitments and allocating resources so that data center capacities are neither overloaded nor underloaded.

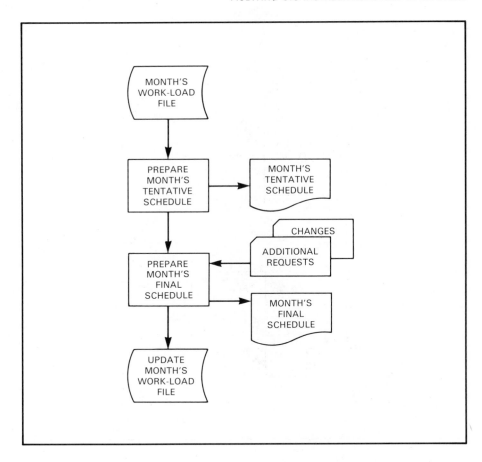

Figure 12-16.

The updating of scheduled-job files under JAI is shown in this flowchart.

Microscheduling focuses on optimizing utilization of computer resources. For example, multiprogramming permits many combinations of jobs to be executed at the same time. Each combination makes different demands on the computer resources; a combination must be found that results in optimum resource utilization.

As shown in Figure 12-17, in the last process of resource allocation, detailed weekly and daily schedules are prepared for each user or work station. Instead of showing each job's due-in and due-out of the data center, dates and times appropriate for each work station are scheduled. Slack time is built into these time requirements to minimize missed deadlines and to permit job completion sooner than scheduled. A job that is expected to require 10 minutes of processing in the data-conversion area, for example, may be scheduled for 15 minutes. This slack allows an extra 5 minutes for delays and disruptions and also permits the inclusion of unscheduled jobs, if necessary.

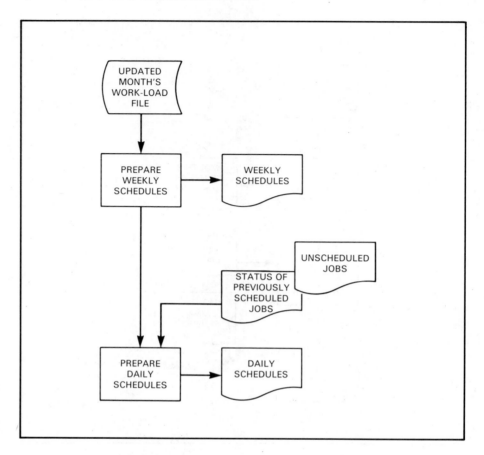

Figure 12-17.

This flowchart depicts the process of computer resource allocation under JAI.

Monitor job processing. Job monitoring produces two basic benefits:

- Control of job processing
- Evaluation.

Control of job processing. Control begins with the existence of schedules, is sustained through awareness of job status and deviations, and is completed when deviations from the schedule can be corrected. A good method of control would be to use control logs at critical work stations: data control, data conversion, computer processing, and postcomputer processing. Under this approach, each of the work stations can inform the scheduler of delayed jobs or disrupted processing. The best method for knowing job status and deviations is on-line access to scheduling information. It is sufficient for each work station to have at least one terminal to display the upcoming jobs and, if desired, a printer to produce a hard copy. The scheduler can respond quickly to job-status inquiries and can display delayed jobs listed by work station.

Evaluation.   The second benefit of monitoring job processing is the ability to evaluate the adequacy of job scheduling. Consider the confusion that would result if no one adhered to schedules and if job processes were not monitored. Without monitoring, user or programming personnel may place pressure on operations staff to change the schedules to accommodate individual priorities.

Besides monitoring adherence to schedules, computer auditors also should observe deficiencies in how jobs are scheduled. The following five situations indicate that a job-scheduling deficiency exists:

- The data center often must purchase outside computer time, although there are other periods when equipment is idle.

- Some computers are in constant use, while others have some periods of no work.

- There is a wide variance in the lateness of jobs. Some are surprisingly early and others are far too late to be of use.

- In the case of multiprogrammed computers, a low percentage of peripheral utilization may indicate a poor job mix.

- The number of jobs waiting to be processed remains relatively the same, while the average throughput time increases.

An overview of the typical mix of applications within a large CIS facility is shown by the bar chart in Figure 12-18.

CASE STUDY: PERFORMANCE REVIEW OF PRODUCTION SOFTWARE

With proper assistance, the auditor can develop a methodology that helps to evaluate the efficiency and effectiveness of production software. These assessments can be made through the aid of computer software tools and techniques.

A number of packaged software and programmer productivity aids have been developed that can allow an auditor to use software to audit software. Also, a number of procedures and methods can be applied through use of software tools to help the auditor to make an assessment of the software's efficiency and effectiveness.

Selecting the Software to Review

The starting point in the process is a review of reports that are generated and used within the information processing facility. A well-run CIS facility will have reports that indicate, by job or computer application, the amount of

PRODUCTIVE TIME BY MAJOR SYSTEMS

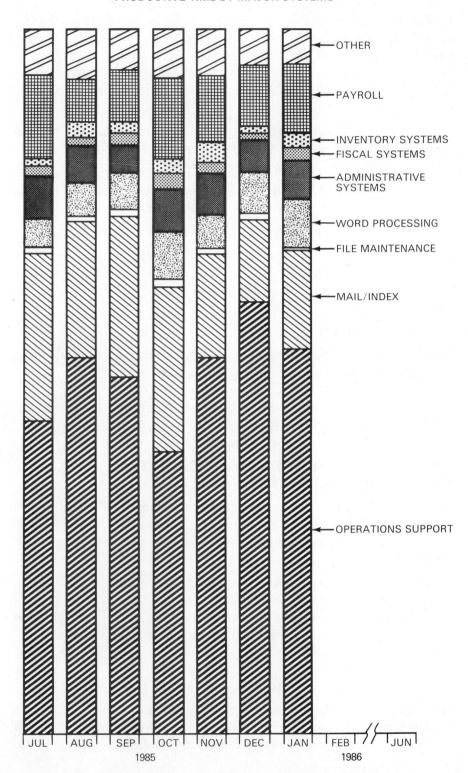

OTHER

PAYROLL

INVENTORY SYSTEMS
FISCAL SYSTEMS

ADMINISTRATIVE
SYSTEMS

WORD PROCESSING

FILE MAINTENANCE

MAIL/INDEX

OPERATIONS SUPPORT

JUL AUG SEP OCT NOV DEC JAN FEB JUN

1985 1986

Figure 12-18.

*This graph shows the mix of
applications, as well as
their relative usage of
resources, within a large
CIS facility.*

computer resources used and the time of occurrence. These reports usually are generated from the computer's internal accounting data.

If these reports do not exist or a formal performance evaluation group is not present to help locate these data, the auditor will probably have to develop this information through use of a generalized audit software package, such as DYL-280, GAMMA, or Focus. Another alternative might be to use a software package that analyzes computer accounting data. Examples include SARA or LOOK. Still another approach would be to write a tailor-made program.

Before implementing a review of production software, the auditor should consult with qualified specialists. These can be found either in a CIS center performance evaluation group or in an outside consulting organization.

An example of a report that can provide an auditor with detail statistics on the characteristics of a computer program is presented in Figure 12-19. This report represents an analysis of the top 50 computer programs (jobs) that were run on an organization's computer. Report items are listed in descending order according to the cost fields of the descriptor lines. The estimated-cost column identifies a quantifiable measurement usable as a basis for assessment. Also important is the fact that this field establishes that the CIS organization has made a quantifiable assessment of the value of using the computer's available resources (such as memory, disk, tape, and other peripherals). The report in Figure 12-19 identifies the five programs that make the greatest use of available resources. These programs, in turn, usually are the best candidates for efficiency and effectiveness review.

Application Program Review Method

After the computer program is selected for a detailed review, the auditor should record the historical run statistics of the selected program on a review worksheet. An example of a suitable worksheet form is shown in Figure 12-20. This type of worksheet, obviously, provides a tool for making before-and-after comparisons. This information can give an auditor some preliminary idea of the average cost to run this program for a year and also can be used to identify cost trends associated with periodic runs. For example, the application selected may be run on a bi-weekly, monthly, quarterly, or annual basis or its high processing costs may occur at those times even though the computer application program is processed more frequently.

The next series of steps is developed to bring the selected program under the auditor's control. A meeting with those responsible for the application software (the programmer analysts and programmers) should be arranged to notify them of the review and to ask them not to make any further program

SYM/NO. 05230/D1027R01   RUN DATE NOV 28, 1985
                                                                                      PAGE

JOB NAME	APP	EST-COST	SEG	STEPS	CPU	DISK	TAPE	HASP	DSK	TP	R-CORE-U	CET	SEC-I/O-%	RUN-HRS
D77HHJX1	D77	1539.56	1	1	1271	393955	50421	4295	35	1	400	392	5.56	4218	.76	3.80
D7500J01	D78	1480.24	1	6	2169	134404		18278	87	5	530	530	3.41	1403	.39	14.27
D7500J01	D78	1468.13	1	6	2156	132047		35771	87	5	530	530	3.40	1396	.39	14.78
D7500J01	D78	1347.61	1	6	2031	113701		15753	69	5	530	530	3.06	1187	.36	14.02
D8900J33	D89	1235.24	1	5	4311	332	121688	1935	37	21	180	164	4.53	382	.08	3.29

Figure 12-19.

This printout gives resource usage for each job.

changes or modifications to the software during the review. Also, any program documentation for the application program should be obtained by the audit staff. Audits of computer software are technically different, but not conceptually different, from management compliance audits. When CIS auditors apply this concept, it is typical for the programming supervisor to indicate that the program is already operating as efficiently and effectively as possible, with no further improvements to be made.

An auditor tests manual systems by verifying input, processing, and output operations. Computer software can be evaluated in the same way. Under this approach, the auditor should hold the input files that impact the application program to evaluate the efficiency and effectiveness of the processing steps and of the outputs.

In the next phase of the evaluation, two copies of the initial source program are made. This allows the auditor to make program improvements to one of the copies and to compare this with the original version of the application. Again, note that copies of the original program are made for evaluation purposes. Working with the actual application program rather than a copy entails great risks for interrupting operations and violating application controls.

After copies of the source program have been made, the auditor should review the portions of the facility standards that deal with efficient programming techniques and methods. Given the availability of the operational program documentation, a review of the program code can be undertaken by the auditor. In this process, the auditor should look for inefficient or ineffective programming practices. These could include:

- Inefficient use of table searching techniques such as iterative subscript, serial, binary, and partition scan

APPLICATION PROGRAM STATISTICS WORKSHEET | DATE   12/1/85

PROGRAM NAME
HOSPITAL INVENTORY UPDATE (D77HHJX1)   CONTROL NO.

☐ Before Review   ☐ After Review

CORE REQUIREMENTS (DECIMAL) WITHOUT BUFFERS   WITH DOUBLE BUFFERS
   400 K

PRODUCTION CYCLE

ELEMENT	1ST	2ND	3RD
EST. COST	1539.56	636.66	1606.55
CPU SEC	1271	609	1309
ELAPSED TIME	3.8 hrs.	2.3 hrs.	5.1 hrs.
I/O SECONDS	4218	2400	5245
MEMORY USED	392 K	370 K	395 K
MEMORY REQUESTED	400 K	400 K	400 K

INPUT RECORDS

FILE 1 Disk	1,400,000	556,676	1,978,007
FILE 2 Tape	104,404	50,666	122,245
FILE 3			
FILE 4			
DATE	11/6/85	10/22/85	10/15/85
PREPARED BY			

REVIEWED BY: R. Reviewer   START DATE 12/1/85   FINISH DATE 12/15/85

COMMENTS:
1) Historical data compiled by C. Compiler, CPE Group
2) P. Nelson, programmer/analyst, notified 12/1/85 of review.

Figure 12-20.

Shown in this worksheet are key historical data for a specific job.

- Ineffective and inefficient use of vendor-unique extensions that do not comply with installation programming standards and that can cause problems in future conversions

- Use of ineffective and inefficient programming logic, such as is used in complicated and cumbersome branching instructions

- Inefficient access of automated logical or physical records.

In processing transactions manually, use of improper techniques or procedures may result in incorrect payments or file posting. The same is true for the maintenance of documentation for application programs; any shortcuts or unauthorized techniques can deliver unacceptable results.

A number of software tools and technologies are available to assist the auditor in code review. For example, a software optimization tool can be used for scanning COBOL program code and to indicate where coding inefficiencies can be improved. Also, a microcomputer can be used to download code and conduct extensive review through use of software tools. Such packages also are available for FORTRAN code and for other high-level languages.

Other available software tools can be used to analyze existing application programs. For example, during a recent examination, auditors used such tools to monitor the performance of the computer programs under review. The tool identifed areas within the program code that took up most of the program's processing time.

At one facility, package tools were used to analyze the logic of a COBOL program. The application program processed an input file of 27,000 records and created the required output records. The analyzer's output results pointed to one area of programming code that was executed 1.3 million times. Further, the auditors' examination identified poor programming logic and inefficient table-searching techniques as the primary causes for the problems.

In other cases, a program analyzer was used by auditors to determine whether all logic paths within the program were executed by the test data specified for the program. For example, only 30 percent of the programming code was executed by the test data. This indicated a weakness in software test processing capabilities within the installation.

After analyzing the results from these review tools and coding review, a list of suggested improvements is prepared. This list is discussed with the programming supervisor and internal auditors as a basis for modifying the source program and retesting the application with the same benchmark runs. In the situation referenced above, a run-time improvement of 88 percent was realized.

Finally, once the parallel run is completed and the efficiency and effectiveness of processing are verified, the auditor should develop meaningful comparative before-and-after data.

DISCUSSION QUESTIONS

1. What should be the auditor's concerns in assessing the functions of planning, operations, and performance in a CIS facility?

2. What types of exposures typically are associated with CIS activities?

3. Causes of exposures in a CIS center can be traced to what areas of activity? Give at least one example in each area.

4. What are the objectives of a CIS auditor in performing an audit of a CIS processing center?

5. What types of detailed examinations might be included in the audit of CIS facilities and operations?

6. What types of recommendations might be included in an auditor's report to CIS management as a result of auditing the CIS center?

7. What characteristics of the systems programming function make it a primary area of concern to CIS auditors?

8. What typical difficulties of communication may exist between systems programmers and their managers?

9. What types of controls may be placed on the systems programming function?

10. What software tools can assist the CIS auditor in evaluating the performance and efficiency of CIS operations?

11. What types of inefficient or ineffective programming practices might an auditor look for in the evaluation of program performance?

CASE ASSIGNMENT

To apply the concepts presented in this chapter, turn to the case study for Abcor in Appendix E and work through Project 1, which deals with the review of operations.

13 Auditing New Technologies: Microcomputers and Distributed Information Resources

A B S T R A C T

- New technologies that can affect the auditor's approach to examining information systems include microcomputers, information centers, decision support systems, new audit tools, and data communication.

- The microcomputer environment can lack audit trails, have inadequate controls, introduce additional exposures through networking, be vulnerable to unauthorized penetration, and lack separation of duties.

- Principles of microcircuitry include the implementation of computer instructions in firmware and the corresponding difficulty of inspecting such instructions directly.

- Audits of microcomputer-based applications can be subdivided into the evaluation of risks and the evaluation of controls. Within the evaluation of risks, areas of concern include the type of application and the degree of sophistication of the microcomputer system. Within the evaluation of controls, issues include segregation of duties, input controls, process integrity, physical security, backup requirements, activity logs, and organizational policies and procedures.

- Planning for and controlling microcomputers may be documented in an organizational plan for advanced office systems (AOS). Planning issues covered include involvement of top managers, the need for centralized planning, the importance of user training, political considerations, control considerations, prime exposures, policy, physical controls, backup and recovery, and documentation.

- Information centers are viewed as extending the exposures of microcomputers through networking with corporate resources. Criteria for auditing microcomputer systems within such networks include the ability to modify significant data and the impact of the system on corporate operations.

- Information-center controls include assigning responsibilities for shared data, developing and enforcing standards for databases, controlling access to and usage of data, establishing error-recovery procedures, and managing data as an organizational resource.

- A decision support system (DSS) may be either model-oriented or data-oriented in generating decision objectives or criteria, alternatives or strategies, and consequences of decisions.

- Model-oriented DSS include accounting models, representation models, optimization models, and suggestion models. Data-oriented DSS types include file-drawer systems, data analysis systems, and analysis information systems.

- DSS risks include failure to identify significant information, failure to interpret the meaning and value of information, and failure to communicate information to responsible managers.

- The auditor's role in reviewing a DSS can be implemented with the aid of a nine-phase audit methodology, the information system audit approach.

- DSS controls can be applied in the areas of documentation, operation, separation of duties, audit trails, and security measures.

- New audit tools include hardware tools, software tools, and trends in use of fourth-generation languages.

TRENDS

Advances in microcomputer and telecommunication technology have served to increase demands for information system services. Desk-top computers and communication networks have extended information access to potentially anyone in the organization. Unit costs of computing are decreasing, the pace of business continues to increase, and demand for information services is rising accordingly.

The main risk of increased access to information resources, as discussed in previous chapters, is that information access will be extended first and control added as an afterthought, if at all. The charter of the CIS audit function mandates careful attention to critical control issues before new systems are implemented and before information can be accessed and modified.

As microcomputers facilitate access to information resources, some of the traditional controls within CIS data centers can lose their effectiveness. One response to the perceived loss of control is a *security safeguard evaluation,* a review of the degree to which an organization's assets are being protected from unauthorized access.

For the public sector, the National Bureau of Standards published *Guidelines for Computer Security Certification and Accreditation* (FIPS 102) within the federal government. These guidelines stipulate a process of certification and accreditation of computer use within the government through CIS auditing and security safeguard evaluations. Although issued specifically for the public sector, the provisions of FIPS 102 have applicability to the private sector as well.

To assure the viability of security controls, CIS audits are being broadened to cover all computer applications used to manage an organization's information resources. Further, security safeguard evaluations increasingly consider exposures, such as an organization's embarrassment or competitive disadvantage, that formerly were not of primary concern to auditors. The distinction between these important functions is that CIS audits are broader in scope and will remain a review function external to the application. On the other hand, security safeguard evaluations are a review function internal to the service provider in the organization.

The increasing importance of the CIS audit function is one aspect of a broader scope for auditors in general. The audit department of the past was a relatively independent function versed in the review of controls surrounding financial statements. The advent of distributed data processing (DDP), decision support systems (DSS), and advanced office systems (AOS) has thrust auditors into an expanded role as evaluators of all types of *information systems (IS).* In this more technical realm, the auditor has a mandate from management to assure the safeguarding of all information assets. Auditors have been given this role because of their independence and their expertise in the analysis of controls.

The audit of new technologies—encompassing all types of information systems—involves complex issues that extend beyond familiar areas. Increasingly, computer auditors must be able to deal with microcircuitry, telecommunications, data security, and law. Each of these areas requires specialized education and training, as well as the use of new audit tools and techniques. Areas of particular challenge to the computer auditor include:

- Microcomputers
- Information centers
- Decision support systems

- New audit tools

- Data communication.

Most of these topics are covered in this chapter. Because of its considerable breadth, however, the discussion of data communication occurs in the next chapter, along with case studies that highlight some network exposures.

THE MICROCOMPUTER ENVIRONMENT

In a recent two-year period, the number of microcomputers in use by U. S. businesses soared from 2.6 million to 4.6 million. It is estimated that within a few years the number could reach 13 million. A 1984 survey of CIS managers primarily employed in large, industrial companies indicated that an average of one microcomputer currently is installed per five staff members. On the average, these organizations planned to increase use of microcomputers to a level of one computer for three staff members. As microcomputers become faster and less expensive, these trends are certain to continue.

What accounts for this explosion in microcomputing? Many users evidently see the microcomputer as the answer to their suppressed needs. Personal computer use can reduce dependency on the CIS department. User perceptions of the CIS function may include long response times, poorly designed systems, and long application backlogs. There is often a feeling that microcomputers permit users to operate independently of other groups. Access is to their own machines, their own applications. Also, microcomputer users often rely on vendors for packaged solutions rather than dealing with the CIS department.

Users are finding that buying personal microcomputers with packaged software and then developing applications on their own can be less expensive than other development alternatives. In view of the relatively low cost of a microcomputer, the reduction in time-sharing expenditures often can justify the purchase expense.

What perhaps started out with word processing has ballooned into electronic mail, spreadsheet analysis, and internal and external database access. The microcomputer has become the indispensable work station that can integrate certain day-to-day office tasks: communication, time management, budget preparation, forecasting, and analysis. Links to mainframes, or *gateways*, extend the processing capabilities of the central processing facility to local microcomputers. Local area networks (LANs) permit microcomputers to be included in processing networks in which data and resources are shared among microcomputer users. Most of these new microcomputer applications

have cut costs and have increased worker efficiency and productivity—
benefits contributing to an enhanced office environment.

In spite of the benefits, microcomputer use creates a dilemma for the
auditor. Auditors who are working at establishing controls in microcomputer-
based applications are encountering problems that include the following:

- Microcomputer software packages may not have adequate accounting
  procedures or audit trails.

- The small business with one microcomputer cannot afford the time or
  money for controls.

- Auditors are concerned not only with what controls to establish for
  standalone microcomputing, but also with the exposures of increasingly
  sophisticated microcomputer-based networks.

- Networking involves a more comprehensive, technical threat: unauthorized interception or penetration of data communications.

- Because fewer people are required to run a microcomputer than to perform traditional CIS procedures, some organizations have combined job
  responsibilities and thus have eliminated the control inherent in separation of duties.

Microcircuitry

Microcircuitry, as implemented in microchips, is the technological heart of
both microcomputers and much of the newer aspects of telecommunications.
Some significant challenges to auditing microcomputer-based applications
stem from the implementation of instructions in hardware, making instruction code resident on microchips. Microcircuits that implement code are
called *firmware* and usually reside in *read-only memory (ROM)*.

The increased migration of software-based CIS applications and algorithms into microchip packages has reduced processing costs and time, and
also has created the need for a new approach to integrity testing. In a software environment, the computer auditor can insert integrated test facilities
(ITFs) directly into applications. The auditor also can scan source code for
trap doors, or unauthorized program "hooks." Security modifications, if
necessary, also can be made directly to the software.

The auditor cannot rely on these techniques to assure reliability of the
operations of the logic on a chip. Even though the advent of new circuit technology may allow self-diagnostic tests, these processes, too, may be implemented in ROM and must be verified.

An example of an algorithm typically implemented in microcircuitry is the National Bureau of Standards' Data Encryption Standard (DES). This algorithm is the heart of many federal agencies' data and communication security. The DES algorithm scrambles data according to an encryption key, or *cipher*. Clearly, this scrambling could cause indeterminable damage if the hardware that implements the cipher process were to fail. For the computer auditor, determining the integrity of the firmware implementation of the DES algorithm would be difficult. In effect, no methods of direct inspection exist. In the case of the DES, the auditor's main comfort stems from the fact that unauthorized modification to the microcircuitry of the DES encryption machine would be improbable.

As an alternative to direct inspection, the computer auditor might regard the DES device as a black box, or unknown process, for purposes of testing. Auditors can gain assurance about the accuracy of the output by frequent tests and redundancy controls. Redundant DES devices may be used, and outputs may be compared before encrypted data can be transmitted or stored. Known test patterns can be used periodically. Independent devices may be used before critical data are stored in encrypted form for a long time. Such approaches represent a small sample of those available to assure the integrity of the algorithm.

In the instance of other microchip-implemented applications, the firmware may contain an ROM algorithm that performs frequent examinations on the input-output features of the chip. Such tests also may be implemented from a software-controlled program that feeds the microcircuit predetermined inputs and compares the results with known outputs. The type of data passed through this testing method may be designed to check every circuit on the chip for possible interface errors.

In addition, most microchip-resident programs require software interfaces to manipulate and control the operations of these algorithms. The integrity of this software may be assured through typical software control procedures—that is, comparison of the working software with a copy held at a secure location, input-output tests, and so on.

AUDITING MICROCOMPUTER-BASED APPLICATIONS

The process of auditing microcomputer-based applications follows a pattern similar to the audit process presented in Chapter 2. Some important differences of emphasis, however, arise from the use of microcomputer technology and sophisticated data communication techniques.

AREAS OF SPECIAL CONCERN	AUDIT STEP	OBJECTIVE
	• Set audit objectives	Establish scope of work
	• Conduct preliminary survey	Gain the background information needed to conduct the audit
EMPHASIS ON MICROCOMPUTER-RELATED RISKS	• Identify audit risks	Determine areas of potential loss
EMPHASIS ON GENERAL CONTROLS	• Evaluate general controls	Determine if reliance can be placed on the general controls
	• Evaluate application controls	Determine if reliance can be placed on application controls
	• Conduct audit tests	Evaluate functioning of the controls and integrity of the data
	• Develop audit findings and recommendations	Analyze audit data and report audit results

Figure 13-1.

This table presents audit objectives for seven key steps in reviewing microcomputer-based applications. Note that areas of special concern include risks arising specifically from microcomputer technology, as well as general controls over such highly distributed systems.

In attempting to audit microcomputer-based applications, the auditor must begin with an assessment of risks. The auditor then will identify and evaluate the adequacy of the controls—both general controls and application controls—designed to reduce the risks. On the basis of this evaluation, the auditor conducts appropriate tests.

This process is illustrated in Figure 13-1. As shown in the illustration, differences stemming from the microcomputer environment lie mainly in the following audit steps:

- Evaluation of risks
- Evaluation of controls.

Evaluation of Risks

The exposures associated with microcomputers can be broken down into two main areas of concern:

- Type of application
- Sophistication of the microcomputer system.

Type of application.   As with other audit involvements, concern depends on the financial significance of the applications being processed. The degree of risk is related directly to the value of the resources controlled by the microcomputer. Payroll and receivables are examples of high-risk applications that may be implemented on microcomputers.

Sophistication of the microcomputer system.   The degree of sophistication of a microcomputer increases with the size and scope of the network within which it may be integrated. If the microcomputer is limited to its own computational and storage/retrieval capacities—without access to external devices—there probably will be minimal audit involvement. If, on the other hand, the microcomputer is linked to mainframes or to other distributed environments, its complexity and capabilities increase—along with the required audit involvement.

The relationship of the degree of microcomputer sophistication to audit involvement is diagrammed in Figure 13-2. Of all the risks in this area, those encountered in sophisticated microcomputer systems are most likely to confound and challenge the auditor.

Evaluation of Controls

The proliferation of microcomputers in sophisticated data communication networks creates a dilemma for the auditor. In such situations, the auditor is faced with the power of large, mainframe systems extended to the work areas of individual microcomputer users.

This environment may be informal and overly casual. In such environments, traditional, mainframe-type processing controls are not available. Data can be destroyed more easily. Users may not be trained adequately. Documentation may be weak.

These issues, however, deal only with the problems. Just as important to auditors and users alike are the opportunities afforded by new technologies. The microcomputer holds the promise of new and better solutions that can be discovered through creative experimentation with computing. If traditional, mainframe-type controls are imposed on users of personal computers, the controls might negate the cost and productivity benefits for which the

Figure 13-2.

The degree of audit involvement spans a continuum from unsophisticated to sophisticated uses of microcomputers. Relatively little attention may be given to standalone microcomputers that produce adequate hard-copy evidence. Heavy audit involvement may be needed to review microcomputers within advanced networks that rely primarily on electronic evidence.

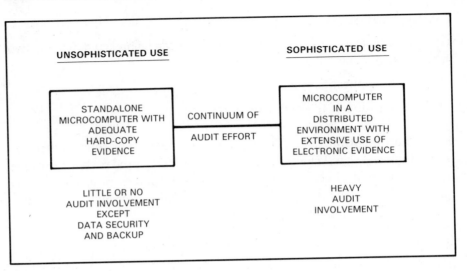

microcomputers were purchased in the first place. That is, traditional controls applied to microcomputer environments easily could act as a straightjacket to the creative freedom of personal computing. The challenge for the organization—and for the auditor—is to achieve a balance between the benefits and the exposures.

A key difference in the implementation of controls in microcomputer-based environments lies in the ability of individuals to control entire processing cycles. Thus, traditional control based on segregation of duties may not be applicable or enforceable. Further, when microcomputer operations are under the direct control of just a few individuals, there is ample opportunity to circumvent most application controls. In most situations, therefore, the primary methods of control for microcomputers will be through general controls. This difference of emphasis, then, must be reflected in the auditor's approach to the engagement, as shown in Figure 13-1.

As microcomputer use increases and diversifies, the auditor will encounter additional causes of exposures. Although controls must be tailored to the system and application being audited, some general control issues usually apply. Also, the auditor will find that the general controls in an unsophisticated microcomputer system will vary in degree from those appropriate for a sophisticated system. Control issues include:

- Segregation of duties

- Input controls

- Process integrity

- Physical security
- Backup requirements
- Activity logs
- Organizational standards, policies, and procedures.

Segregation of duties. Though extensive segregation of duties is not typical of microcomputer controls, individual responsibilities for each system, type of use, and application should be specified as a matter of policy. Especially important are limitations that may be placed on individual responsibilities, including custody of resources and access privileges. Within most microcomputer networks, separate responsibilities may be identified for programming or application generation, backup, system maintenance, data communications (especially batch transmissions to mainframes), and other user support functions.

Input controls. Within microcomputer-based networks, input controls typically focus on user identification and authorization for access requests to organizational resources. The problem of assuring the accuracy of inputs, even locally, must be addressed. These considerations are made more complex by the use of telecommunication links to mainframe and organizational resources.

Process integrity. The integrity of processing performed with microcomputers centers on the question: Are the applications doing what they are supposed to accomplish? In some situations, the microcomputer may be an inappropriate tool for the application.

Physical security. The need for physical security stems from the relative portability of microcomputers and their storage media. Physical security concerns also increase as microcomputers are dispersed onto desk tops throughout the office. Exposures clearly are greater than when all equipment is housed within a single, central facility.

Backup requirements. Provisions should be made against the loss or interruption of key resources, including hardware, software, data, and personnel. These provisions should be set forth in documented plans that have the force of organizational policy.

Activity logs. A record should be kept of each use or access of microcomputers to network resources. To enforce this control, the record should be inspected periodically.

Organizational standards, policies, and procedures.   Standards, policies, and procedures should be established to provide guidelines for acquiring and operating microcomputers. Permissible and prohibited activities should be outlined. The guidelines should be developed under the sponsorship and authority of top management, with authority to implement vested in specific support groups. The effectiveness of such plans as control measures is discussed later in this chapter.

For the most part, the power and freedom of personal computing lies in an essential decentralization of control. Within limits, users are given the resources to solve their own problems. However, centralized control must govern the selection and acquisition of hardware and software, as well as in-house development of software. This aspect of organizational policy and planning is critical to assuring hardware and software compatibility with existing and planned computer systems and networks. In the future, attempting to build an integrated network using different machines will involve needless technical complications.

A central group of both users and technical experts can identify desired systems that could meet the individual user's needs, as well as overall organizational objectives. The central group also can coordinate software development, avoiding the cost of duplicating development efforts at the user level.

PLANNING FOR AND CONTROLLING MICROCOMPUTERS

As noted in previous chapters, the proliferation of microcomputers in business organizations may have occurred in a haphazard manner. The impact on the audit of CIS facilities is that microcomputer proliferation tends to blur the boundaries between information users and providers. As complete processing cycles become possible on individual desk tops, the security of a single remote work station can become as critical as physical access controls to the main computer room.

Networks of microcomputers in information applications often are referred to as *advanced office systems,* or *AOS.* For microcomputers to be integrated successfully with such systems, sufficient resources must be allocated for the development of organization-wide policies and procedures for microcomputer implementation and use. These policies and procedures comprise an *AOS plan.*

In the audit of CIS facilities that include dispersed, microcomputer-based work stations, the starting point must be the AOS plan. If the policies and procedures address control issues adequately, some degree of organization-wide integrity may be achievable. A primary motivation for such a plan, of course, is to build organization and network resources systematically to support expanding microcomputer use. From a management and control standpoint, however, effective controls and auditability are impossible without a comprehensive set of policies and procedures.

From the auditor's standpoint, the discussion below highlights key points to be checked in an AOS plan.

Top Management Involvement

An AOS plan requires the direct involvement of top management. A main reason is both financial and practical: It just is not possible to build up a network of perhaps thousands of work stations over a period of years without a plan that allocates resources in logical, justifiable phases and steps. Although the expenditure for a single microcomputer and peripherals may not be significant, the expenses of building networks, setting up support staff, and conducting large-scale training efforts involve major capital commitments. Without the understanding and commitment of top management, the necessary resources and coordination will not be applied.

A second reason—just as important—is rooted in management's responsibility for the reliability and integrity of the organization's information resources. Without sufficient controls, widespread use of microcomputers represents, in itself, a threat to organizational information assets. Given user demand for these services, management, at the highest levels, cannot afford to delegate responsibility for these planning and control issues.

A third reason for the involvement of top management may seem less urgent, but is absolutely fundamental: Microcomputer technology is making possible major changes in the ways people perform their work and organizations conduct business. Survival in competitive markets may depend on adapting to new work methods. At the same time, any change is disruptive. Such fundamental change, if it is not managed properly, could cause significant business disruptions, employee disorientation, and obstacles to basic organizational goals. Therefore, the human dimension, encompassing training and support in new work methods, must be an integral part of the AOS plan, with the full support of top management.

With this degree of involvement, top management must have an understanding and appreciation of microcomputer capabilities. Also, no executive who has a part in drafting an AOS plan can afford to ignore the nature and magnitude of the exposures inherent in widespread microcomputer use. With the assistance and counsel of systems professionals, AOS planners, and computer auditors, management must identify areas of application for microcomputers. Though technology is moving rapidly and future needs never will be anticipated totally, an attempt must be made. Although the planning process is iterative, or refined continually with experience, there must be a starting point.

Management must be able to identify microcomputer applications that might make significant contributions to the organization's mission. Based on this analysis, individual, departmental, and organizational networks may be built up in stages according to priorities in the plan. Phases and steps within the plan, in general, should proceed as determined by a balancing of costs and benefits at each level of service or integration.

Figure 13-3 shows the magnitude of an AOS implementation effort and the need for a phased approach. The organization in this case has a target of 800 microcomputer work stations within five years. Based on the projected staffing level of 2,400, there will be one work station for every three employees. A trend line connecting a starting point at zero and the five-year target shows the level of resource commitment that will be needed for each year in the planning period. Given a ratio of one support staff member for each 40 work stations, the size of the growing support function can be projected. The magnitude of the training effort also can be derived from staffing levels and projected work-station utilization for specific applications.

Such coordinated planning can minimize the disruptions and disorientations of change. Timing of the implementation is of utmost importance. Employees are most likely to be receptive to new work methods if implementation is carried out in a steady, unimposing manner.

The essential question management must ask is: How will the use of microcomputers affect the nature of the organization? There are no easy answers. Management must develop a rational microcomputer strategy based on the best information available. As stated above, the potential impacts on the organization and its mission are fundamental. A concerted planning effort is needed to derive maximum benefits from new technology without creating unnecessary disruptions or exposures to information assets.

Centralized Approach

Although microcomputer use is, almost by definition, highly distributed throughout the organization, an AOS plan restores elements of centralized control. That is, adherence to a uniform set of policies and procedures for microcomputer implementation and use helps to impose centralized control on otherwise uncoordinated or dispersed activities.

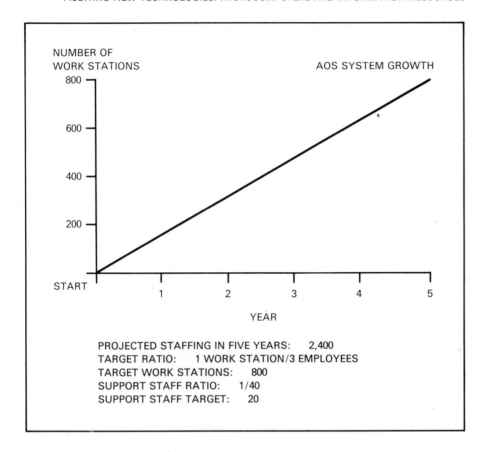

NUMBER OF
WORK STATIONS

AOS SYSTEM GROWTH

PROJECTED STAFFING IN FIVE YEARS: 2,400
TARGET RATIO: 1 WORK STATION/3 EMPLOYEES
TARGET WORK STATIONS: 800
SUPPORT STAFF RATIO: 1/40
SUPPORT STAFF TARGET: 20

Figure 13-3.

Growth of work station population is projected forward to meet a target. Resource planning must work backward from this goal to build infrastructure and support resources.

A major problem in connecting microcomputers to networks has been the lack of compatibility between different makes and models of hardware. In the absence of generally accepted standards or industry guidelines, manufacturers in the microcomputer marketplace have tended to pursue proprietary designs that restrict the exchange of data among different machines.

Although this situation is changing, many organizations have permitted decisions on microcomputer acquisitions to be made on individual or departmental levels, with little regard for compatibility issues. For example, the marketing department of an organization might maintain projected sales data on an IBM microcomputer. Subsequently, the need may arise for the production department to develop a production forecast, which it can run readily on its own Apple microcomputer. The task would be straightforward if the production department could access the sales projections in marketing. However, compatibility problems between the two computers and software packages might make access impractical.

The result, in this case, would be needless duplication of effort and expense. The data resources are an organizational asset that cannot be used to their full potential if they reside in incompatible devices. Such a situation is the direct result of different parts of an organization pursuing independent microcomputer procurement programs.

Also, consideration must be given to the advances in technology that will favor computers that are highly compatible. The technology to develop local area networks (LANs) from individual microcomputers has grown rapidly. LANs have the capability to tap many unused microcomputer resources that already may be in place. But, integration through a LAN is based on the assumption of compatible microcomputers. Organizations that have a haphazard assortment of devices and software packages may miss the benefits of this type of integration. These organizations—for the short term, anyway—may pass up the opportunity, not because they are unaware of the benefits, but because connecting highly incompatible machines or replacing large numbers of microcomputers probably will cost more than the expected benefits will be worth.

A centralized approach to the procurement of microcomputers is needed to alleviate the problems associated with uncoordinated microcomputer proliferation within an organization. Within an AOS plan, such an approach can take the form of minimum integration standards for hardware acquisitions, centralized approval and purchasing, and centralized user support in both resource selection and training.

From a control and integration standpoint, it is highly desirable to have all purchases of microcomputers within an organization processed through a central location or support function. Using a centralized procurement approach will allow the organization to adhere to a well-coordinated AOS plan and to provide for the orderly growth of network and support services.

A word of caution is in order: Although coordination is desirable, a pitfall would be to create a rigid, bureaucratic, and unresponsive centralized structure. Many of the creative and productive applications of microcomputers, after all, are the products of individual initiative and the freedom—within limits—to try new approaches. Centralized coordination that restricts or complicates this freedom needlessly is apt to drive users away and may close off some of the more significant organizational benefits of microcomputer use.

User Training

User education is paramount to the success of a microcomputer usage plan. The effectiveness of microcomputer resources depends directly on the ease and willingness with which people are able to apply the new tools. Too often, users are given inadequate training in the operation of microcomputers, use of software packages and development tools, data communication capabilities, and data storage practices and safeguards. Inadequate training, in turn, leads to user frustration, and ultimately could result in lack of understanding or respect for crucial control policies and procedures.

Users must have hands-on training in the operation of their microcomputers. Training must be tailored specifically to the user's environment and needs. Also, careful consideration must be given to the selection of software. Software packages with self-paced tutorials are especially effective. Users should become aware of the variety of tools that are available and must become comfortable using those tools to solve business problems. Technical assistance and support should be available readily and, for routine applications, should not be subject to elaborate request procedures.

At the same time, users must understand organizational restrictions on program development and database access. As a matter of policy, users of microcomputers should not be allowed to develop programs that modify organizationally significant data. When such development cannot be handled directly by the organization's systems development function, close oversight by systems professionals and by the audit function must be mandatory.

As part of their training, users must learn that internal control considerations also apply to microcomputers. Users must develop an appreciation of the value of the resources they handle and of their responsibilities in safeguarding them. Controls in this area include data backup and archiving, responsible use of shared network resources, physical security of individual work stations and data storage media, restrictions on use of output, access control for sensitive and proprietary information, password and encryption controls, and so on. Training should emphasize the correlation between these controls and sound business practice. If this background is not provided or is not understood completely, it is almost certain that serious exposures will result.

Political Considerations

Depending on the support organization described in the AOS plan, the use of microcomputers can be politically sensitive. If, for example, management decides to administer the microcomputer plan through the office administration function or through a separate AOS support function, conflicts may develop with the existing CIS department. Many entrenched CIS departments view microcomputers as a threat. Clearly, rivalries and lack of cooperation are to be avoided.

Some steps may be taken to alleviate potential conflicts. For example, organizational and reporting relationships may be structured so that the director of the AOS support function and the director of the CIS department both report to the same top executive. This structure allows the proper, separate consideration of user-driven computing and the CIS department and also provides a common ground for resolution of any problems. Respective responsibilities and areas of authority and custody must be defined clearly within the charters of each function. Political conflicts must not be allowed to detract from the potential productivity increases that the microcomputer offers.

Control Considerations

Information processed and stored on microcomputers becomes much more vulnerable than similar information processed and stored in a mainframe environment. The computer auditor must be aware of the controls over microcomputers that are needed to avoid compromising information. Figure 13-4 contrasts graphically the vulnerability of a mainframe computer with the vulnerability of a microcomputer. The base line of the chart depicts the relative increase in the vulnerability of computers. The vertical axis shows the relative skills needed to commit an impropriety and is contrasted with zones representing the following types of abuse:

- Sabotage
- Data entry fraud
- System fraud.

Sabotage.   *Sabotage,* in this context, means the abuse, destruction, or theft of equipment.

Data entry fraud.   *Data entry fraud* is the destruction, alteration, or disclosure of information entering the system.

System fraud.   *System fraud* is unauthorized system use, including the destruction, alteration, or disclosure of application programs, system programs, or databases.

The increased vulnerability of the microcomputer environment is the result of many factors, including the growing number of microcomputers and the increased sophistication of users. Building on the corporate AOS plan, the challenge is for the computer auditor to develop a comprehensive program for the practical control of microcomputers. The following discussion explains important planning issues.

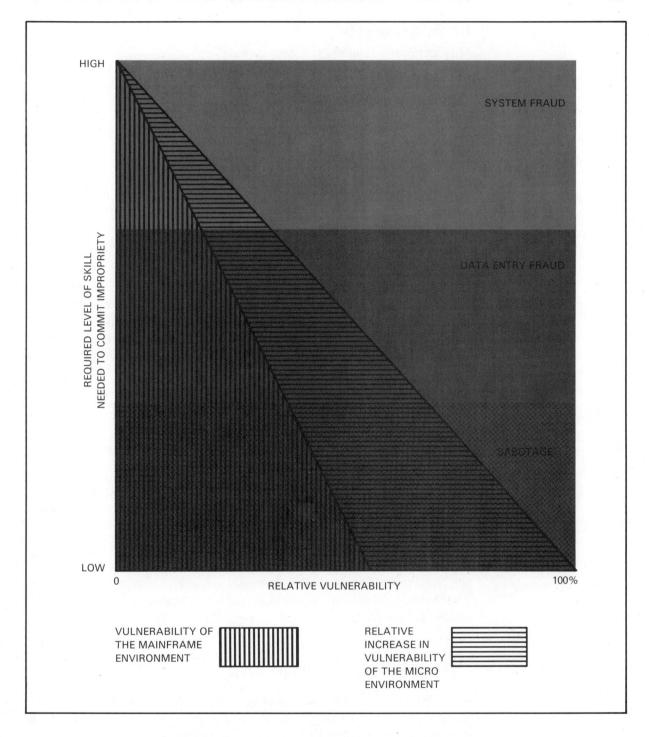

Figure 13-4. *This graph compares the relative vulnerabilities of mainframe and microcomputer environments.*

Prime Exposures

Microcomputer-related exposures include:

- Data security
- Data integrity
- Efficiency of use.

Data security.   Because microcomputers are highly dispersed, centralized control of data access may not be possible. As more people gain access to organizational information through microcomputers, the ability to monitor individual use on widely scattered machines diminishes. If the microcomputer is involved in a telecommunication link, the task of securing data on myriad desk tops grows exponentially.

Data integrity.   The integrity of information resident in a microcomputer system depends on the assumption that the data are input accurately and maintained properly. As mentioned previously, separation of duties, a major control used for maintaining data integrity in mainframe systems, is not practical in microcomputer use. Other controls must be developed to maintain data integrity.

Efficiency of use.   Although microcomputers are thought primarily to be a productivity tool, productivity gains come only with adequate controls. Microcomputers used improperly or inappropriately actually can create more problems than they solve.

It is highly wasteful of the organization's resources, for example, for microcomputers to be regarded as status symbols. Many managers procure microcomputers only to let them sit on their desks untouched. This occurrence ties up organizational assets and does not increase productivity.

Also, many users insist on developing their own applications. This practice is an inefficient use of microcomputer resources. Every effort should be made to encourage the use of packaged software. There are two main reasons to use packages:

- Cost
- Reliability and auditability.

Cost.   Microcomputer software packages are so readily available for all types of applications that developing a custom approach is difficult to justify, both in terms of money and staff time. Even for specialized uses, software often can be found in-house that can be adapted for the new application. As the number of microcomputer users in the organization increases, so does the likelihood that someone has tried to solve a similar problem.

Reliability and auditability. Microcomputer users typically do not have professional systems development skills. Accordingly, if users develop their own applications without close supervision, minimum standards of quality and reliability may not be applied. A related risk is that unstructured source code written by end users may not be auditable or can contain bugs and even intentional trap doors.

On the other hand, commercial packages and program or report generators, once reviewed and evaluated by a systems support function, offer far greater assurance of quality. New applications still must be tested, especially if financially significant data are processed, but involvement of support staff and computer auditors may be limited to the review function.

An issue related to efficiency is that users of microcomputers sometimes attempt to solve problems at an individual level that really should be addressed at the departmental or higher levels. There may be a natural tendency to avoid involving the CIS function, but such problems are its responsibility. Addressing a problem at the appropriate level is necessary to assure that adequate controls will be implemented.

The tendency to tackle the wrong problem argues in favor of strong support and careful monitoring of microcomputer-based software application development. Users may be unaware of the scope or magnitude of the problem they have identified. At the same time, the internal systems function may not be aware of the problem or may have assigned it a low priority. Also, microcomputer users probably will not have the technical expertise to judge what system resources and technical facilities will be needed for an ambitious project.

Policy

As cited above, because of the dispersed use of microcomputers, one of the most effective control measures is the development of an organizational policy for AOS implementation. Policies must state clearly who has access to what resources and under what circumstances. Policies also must be administered by a visible support function, and users must be accountable to that group for their adherence to policy.

A microcomputer policy, or an AOS plan, does not provide absolute assurance or control. Rather, the plan establishes expectations and responsibilities for key participants. Such a general control is exemplary rather than specific or individual. Because control cannot be exercised at all times on all users, punishment for the violation of policy must be severe enough to discourage improper behavior. In addition to the general principles outlined above, the following specific control measures can be included in AOS policy:

- Restrict the use of the microcomputers to organizational purposes. Personal use should be a grounds for disciplinary action.

- Each user should be responsible for the physical security of hardware, software, and other resources under his or her direct control.

- Users should be responsible for the integrity of the data to which they have access. Specific controls must exist over the ability to modify elements in organizational databases. In many organizations, microcomputer users are only allowed to download information from the host computer and have no update capability for audited information files. If needed, microcomputer applications that update elements in organizational databases should be subject to close monitoring and periodic audits.

- All information generated from a microcomputer must have an associated label indicating the source of the data.

- All users should be accountable for the security of the information they control.

- Software license violations should not be tolerated. Infringements represent a needless legal and financial exposure to the organization. Since the organization may be held liable if a user copies licensed software, the punishment for breaching software copyrights must be severe enough to discourage unauthorized copying or software piracy.

Managers and systems people need to be reminded that, though policies for control of microcomputers are essential, there can be a tendency to overregulate. Needlessly complex or bureaucratic procedures can cause productivity gains to remain elusive. Policies must be strict enough to assure the integrity of resources, yet must not discourage possibly innovative uses. That is, there is a fine line between having the needed controls on microcomputers and putting the user in what might be perceived as an unacceptably restrictive environment.

Physical Controls

Because of the size and transportability of microcomputers and their data storage media, physical security plays a major role in any plan of control. In a mainframe facility, physical security of the computer and data storage media is straightforward. It is not possible for an individual to walk into the computer center and steal a mainframe computer or a disk drive. For removable media, including tapes and disk packs, controls within the data library function usually are sufficient to prevent theft. Thus, the physical size of the mainframe and the isolated security of the computer room and data library act as basic controls.

In a microcomputer work area, on the other hand, it is relatively easy for a person to steal diskettes containing important information or even to steal the entire microcomputer (with perhaps an internal hard disk containing many megabytes of data). In fact, this type of theft is becoming a common occurrence in organizations that use many microcomputers.

The problem of theft of microcomputers and portable storage media only can be controlled with proper physical security measures. Such measures can include the following:

- Keep diskettes in a locked and secure place when they are not being used.

- Use mechanical locks on microcomputers that prevent the opening of the computer or the actuation of the power switch without a key. Without locks, it is easy for a person to open a microcomputer and remove internal parts such as memory expansion boards and graphics cards. More expensive than the loss of these components may be proprietary programs resident in ROM or data stored on a Winchester-type hard disk.

- Keep an accurate inventory of microcomputers and related peripherals, including internal options and spares such as memory and communication cards.

- Try to place microcomputers in areas with limited access. This will stop a potential thief from "slipping out the back door" undetected.

- Follow a formal log-out procedure for temporary equipment relocations, such as users taking microcomputers home for work purposes.

Physical security measures also provide some degree of control over unauthorized use. Thus, physical security measures must not be compromised if an organization wishes to minimize the potential for loss by theft or destruction.

Backup and Recovery

Backup considerations are critical in the control of data generated by microcomputers. Most microcomputers store data either on diskette or on fixed disk. Diskettes, however, have not proven to be a durable storage medium. Therefore, it is important that data stored on diskette be backed up frequently. The relatively low cost of diskettes makes it feasible and economical to back up data often.

Fixed disks also must be backed up frequently. Although fixed-disk media are exceptionally durable, the drive mechanism is prone to failure. Backing up fixed disks to diskettes, however, may not be practical. Because of the limited storage capacities of diskettes, backing up an entire fixed disk can require many diskettes and significant operator time. Tape, on the other hand, offers both high capacity and low cost. For these reasons, data on high-volume fixed disks usually are backed up to tapes.

In addition to backup procedures, measures should be taken to prevent storage device failure. A regular microcomputer maintenance program is desirable to decrease the occurrence of such failures. Also, it is good practice to install electrical surge protectors and backup power supplies in office areas with high concentrations of microcomputers.

Documentation

Adequate documentation of all user-derived applications (such as spreadsheet models) is essential. The documentation must describe how an application works and what it is supposed to accomplish.

From the organization's standpoint, if the application is not documented, it might as well not exist. If only one individual is aware of an application used to make important decisions, the organization runs the risk of being without the information if the individual were to leave or be terminated.

Many such occurrences could lead to the unwanted creation of an informal, or ad hoc, information system that is completely undocumented. Once this happens, it is difficult to regain control of the system because many sources of important information are unknown.

THE INFORMATION CENTER

Centralized control of microcomputer use has a decidedly different character from that of traditional CIS service. When systems development required major capital investments, there was a need to be highly selective about the types of projects undertaken and the applications addressed. The availability of relatively inexpensive, microcomputer-based tools, however, has changed this situation. Users can implement individualized solutions, provided that data with organizational significance are not misused or altered without authorization. With respect to the microcomputer, therefore, central coordination takes on new meaning.

Such centralized control has matured into the concept of the *information center*. An information center is a means of providing users of individual microcomputers or work stations with controlled access to organizational information resources. As an extension of microcomputer sophistication, this concept provides insights into some audit problems and approaches that arise from microcomputer and telecommunication technologies.

On a functional level, the information center is a support group. The information center generally recommends a limited selection of microcomputer hardware and software to users. The information center also serves a technical consulting role in responding to and coordinating user requests. Specific responsibilities include serving as a *help desk* to which users can go for advice and assistance on computing problems. Service also is designed to allow users rapid and flexible access to resources without having to submit requests to the CIS department.

User access to internal or external data resources is a primary benefit of centralized support through information centers. For example, many microcomputer applications involve spreadsheet analysis. Users typically want access to organizational data such as sales histories, current prices, summaries by corporate reporting categories, and so on. External resources may be consulted for current stock prices, monetary exchange rates, tax tables, etc. Over the links provided through the information center, users can obtain the desired data in computer-accessible form for input directly into locally maintained spreadsheets. From the users' point of view, the information center creates a degree of transparency so that detailed technical knowledge is not required to obtain the desired resources. From the corporate viewpoint, the information center acts as a safeguard and control point to assure that access is appropriate and consistent with a need to know.

Information Center Audit Implications

Microcomputer users will continue to create application systems. The auditor must have some means of determining what systems have been and are being implemented. Coordination with the information center or user support function is essential. The auditor then must be able to decide whether to audit any of these systems. Given the sheer number of applications, the auditor will have less opportunity to audit all the systems. Criteria for deciding which microcomputer system to audit include:

- Does the microcomputer system have the ability to modify significant organizational data?

- What is the impact of the information produced by the system on the user's operations?

When micro-to-mainframe links or other devices are added to a microcomputer system, both its capability and its exposures are increased significantly. On-line data access can become possible. The microcomputer user can access centrally controlled files containing significant data. A microcomputer user also might be able to access files of other microcomputer users. Modification of such data could occur accidentally or deliberately. Erroneous data could be passed from one update to another. If adequate safeguards do not exist, such erroneous data could corrupt the organizational database. Therefore, the accuracy, availability, and protection of data become key considerations in an information center that serves as a clearing house for data users.

Controls

Prior to the advent of microcomputers, CIS departments could establish controls over the integrity of data. In general, all data within the CIS were under the oversight and custody of the department. Physically, all data to be processed on a mainframe were concentrated in one location. With microcomputers, however, a user may maintain a local database of departmental information. As networks expand and as the accessibility of this information to other users increases, accuracy and integrity issues become increasingly critical. Custodial responsibilities shift or are extended from the information center to individual users.

The auditor must assure, therefore, that proper testing procedures are in place and are followed to protect the integrity of organizational data resources. Controls to provide necessary safeguards over information center data include the following:

- Assign responsibility for assuring the accurate and consistent use of shared data.
- Develop and enforce standards for databases.
- Control access to and usage of data.
- Establish adequate procedures to recover data from errors.
- Manage data as a valuable organizational resource.

As partial implementation of these objectives, procedures that may help to minimize the risk to information center data include:

- Use a password system to limit access to master files and central mainframe databases to authorized personnel. Passwords should be used to restrict access from specific microcomputers to designated files and programs. Access during nonbusiness hours should be prohibited unless special authorization is obtained.

- Use read-only access controls to prevent data in the central system from being modified improperly. That is, microcomputer users can be allowed to download information but cannot write to or update data elements within the organizational database.

- Install an electronic recording system to log accesses to the central system. The log should show the identity of the person gaining access, the time and location of access, and the exact information retrieved. Provide for regular monitoring of the log, including prompt follow-up on deviations from established procedures.

The element of centralized control inherent in the information center concept addresses some of the risks and problems that are of concern to auditors of sophisticated microcomputer systems.

The microcomputer is revolutionizing organizational activities. Microcomputer technology will continue to merge with information systems of increasing capability, complexity, and sophistication. Clearly, the magnitude and complexity of audit concerns also will increase. As in any computerized system, it will be imperative to establish adequate security and control measures. But, it is just as necessary to temper these measures with judgment to realize microcomputer-related benefits.

DECISION SUPPORT SYSTEMS

A *decision support system (DSS)* is a database creation and manipulation capability that assists managers and executives in identifying and selecting decision alternatives on the basis of quantitative evaluations. A DSS typically derives its underlying database from an organization's operational results, as reported by data processing (DP) systems, and from *management information systems (MIS)* that summarize those results. A DSS also may obtain inputs from outside information sources, such as information utilities and time-sharing service bureaus. Elements of a DSS also may include data that represent assumptions or projections for future conditions. A DSS, then, aims at forecasting the future and providing analysis for management decisions rather than reporting on operations.

From the computer auditor's standpoint, a DSS represents a further sophistication of computer use. In their information-gathering capabilities, DSS and information centers pose similar challenges. That is, a DSS has potentially far-reaching scope in being capable of accessing data from virtually anywhere in organizational databases and also from external sources.

The processing capabilities of a DSS also represent relatively high levels of sophistication. Analysis and projection tasks often involve high-level mathematics, report generation, and graphics. Accordingly, a DSS typically is a complex system of modules, programs, and databases.

The challenge of auditing a DSS also is related to some of the problems and pitfalls of evaluating microcomputer-based systems. Access to a DSS usually must be provided from a user's desk top. Users often are top managers who may have limited computer capabilities. The interface to a DSS, therefore, must be suitable for users without extensive computer training. The user's work station usually is an intelligent terminal or a general-purpose microcomputer with data communication capability.

Such desk-top access by nontechnical users shares many of the exposures encountered with microcomputer-based work stations. Custodial responsibilities for data may be unclear. Network links that provide access to organizational databases increase the risk of unauthorized system penetration and use.

DSS configurations have become possible through relatively recent technological advancements, some of which are listed in the table in Figure 13-5. Major elements, for example, include microcomputer-based work stations, distributed processing through mini- and microcomputer controllers, advanced telecommunication, database management systems (DBMS), and high-level languages suitable for modeling and forecasting.

The configuration of a DSS typically is composed of a database, a model (*schema*), a report generator, and a DSS operating system. These elements are illustrated in Figure 13-6. The database obtains its input data from CIS files and from external data sources. The DSS operating system is the interface between the decision maker and the DSS. Through such a system, a decision maker corresponds with the DSS and poses a series of hypothetical situations, as expressed by sets of parameters for future conditions. The system returns results from each set of parameters. These results are projections based on different sets of assumptions. The decision maker poses questions repetitively with different assumptions until a pattern emerges upon which a final decision can be made.

Auditing Decision Support Systems

A successful audit always involves assessing and identifying risks and associated controls. Nowhere will this skill be needed more than in auditing a DSS.

A DSS can have far-reaching effects on the well-being of an organization and its people. Enhanced ability to project the impacts of current decisions can become a powerful management tool. The more information that managers have about the consequences of their decisions, the better their

BUILDING BLOCKS	FUNCTIONS PERFORMED
1. Hardware	
Intelligent terminals, including video	Display information in a way relevant to decision makers; process limited amount of data
Minicomputers and microcomputers	Act as an independent CPU or as a front-end processor; make distributed systems possible
Time-sharing systems	Permit multiple users to access the CPU and files, and reduce users' cost
Telecommunication networks	Transmit messages between remotely located DP centers and make distributed systems possible
2. Software	
Database management systems	Centralize data files
Model-oriented languages	Facilitate model construction and modification of decision support systems
Application packages	Permit immediate in-house installation of the DSS supporting software
3. Human Resources	
Systems software engineers	Coordinate decision makers' needs and the DSS for building an individualized DSS
Staff members	Act as the intermediary between decision makers and DSSs during the execution of the DSS

Figure 13-5.

This table presents the available technological building blocks for decision support systems (DSSs), as well as the functions performed by each element of hardware or software.

ability will be to guide the organization. A DSS, in effect, capitalizes on the value of storing and correlating information in computer-based systems.

With this power comes correspondingly high risks. The use of personal microcomputers and information-center access methods helps to compound the problems. Further, the information produced by a DSS usually is sensitive or proprietary. The organization's strategic planning function, its financial position, and its competitive advantages all depend on decisions at top management levels that may be based heavily on the products of a DSS.

A DSS, therefore, represents a powerful system that may be vulnerable to unauthorized penetration. Because of the exceptional value of the information that can be obtained, a DSS also makes an attractive target. Computer auditors should consider the audit of a DSS as a specialized area deserving careful attention. The discussion below includes an audit methodology tailored to the special risks inherent in a DSS.

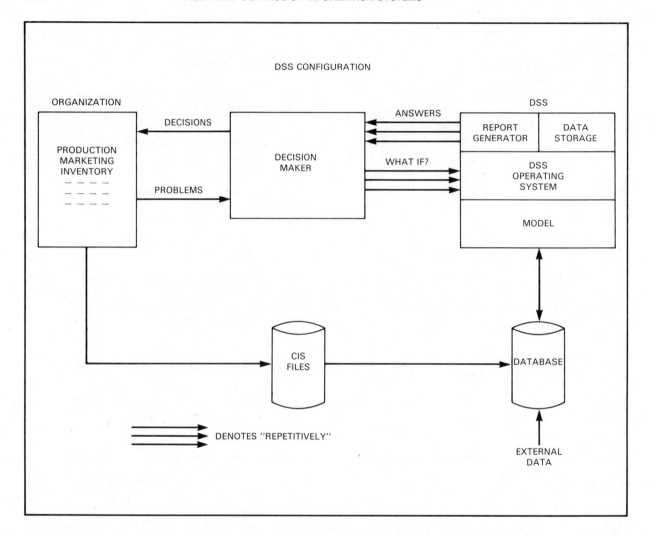

Figure 13-6.

The configuration of hardware and software elements within a typical DSS is depicted in this diagram.

Types of DSS

As mentioned previously, a DSS assists managers in assessing the future impact of current decisions. The system provides this support by returning results based on "What if?" questions, or assumptions about future conditions. Through an iterative process, a DSS can provide the following types of information to decision makers:

- Decision objectives or criteria

- Decision alternatives or strategies

- Consequences of decision alternatives.

In deriving these results, the process may be either *model-oriented* or *data-oriented*. Model-oriented processes make comparisons and perform analyses based on an objective model. The model is a coordinated set of parameters or conditions and their relationships. Models usually are derived from analysis of historical data and trends. Data-oriented processes focus on responses for specific inquiries. While models deal with sets of conditions, data inquiries are concerned with specific questions.

Model-oriented DSS. Types of model-oriented decision support systems include:

- Accounting models

- Representation models

- Optimization models

- Suggestion models.

Accounting models. These models are used for short-term planning for the functional departments of an organization. A model used for budgeting would be an accounting model.

Representation models. These models are strategic in nature and focus on corporate or divisional goals. An example of representation modeling would be risk analysis.

Optimization models. These models provide objectives for a functional operation based on economic constraints. An optimization model, for example, might be used to determine the most cost-effective alternatives for a series of decisions.

Suggestion models. These models pose options for the decision maker. An example would be giving a manager a required rate of return based on a calculated risk.

Data-oriented DSS. Types of data-oriented decision support systems include:

- Interactive database inquiry systems

- Data analysis systems

- Analysis information systems.

Interactive database inquiry systems. These are on-line data retrieval systems that interpret inquiries to gather and present data for use as a decision support tool. Database inquiry systems are based on the *file-drawer* principle: Specific data are retrieved from a database in response to an inquiry, just as a particular file folder can be removed from a file drawer containing many individual files. An example of the file-drawer principle is found in electronic funds transfer systems, as account balances must be maintained on-line for interactive inquiry and update. Another example would be a point-of-sale system that reads inventory tags and retrieves descriptions and current price information from a central database. Systems of this latter type also are known as *transaction control systems.*

Data analysis systems. These are on-line systems designed to answer questions dealing with cost controls. A typical application might be to compare actual costs with standard costs.

Analysis information systems. These are models that can simulate policy or forecast the future. Developing a methodology for making sales forecasts would be one of the possible applications.

DSS Risks

DSS techniques offer exceptional power, accompanied by some unique risks. Successful application of these techniques involves understanding the risks and addressing them in implementing the system. A notable example is a DSS developed by Hunt-Wesson Foods, a major packager and distributor of prepared foods. The company has used a DSS since 1971 to guide the development and expansion of its distribution network. As a result of enhanced decision support, Hunt-Wesson estimates that it has achieved an ongoing annual savings of $3 million. Undoubtedly, this success can be attributed to having understood and prevented the major risks.

One of the greatest risks associated with a DSS is the possibility of information leaks that would permit outsiders to assess the present state and characteristics of an organization. The other major area of concern is that managers may fail to use properly the information available through a DSS. The apparent reasons for such neglect include:

- Failure to identify significant information

- Failure to interpret the meaning and value of the acquired information

- Failure to communicate information to the responsible manager, or *chief decision maker (CDM).*

Any one of these failures can affect the value of a DSS adversely and can bring damage to the organization. To cite a famous example, on December 7, 1941, delays in communicating known information concerning Pearl Harbor to the CDMs resulted in an alert being given hours after the Japanese had executed a devastating air raid on that naval base. The magnitude of this disaster could have been decreased greatly by the proper use of controls and timely reporting for critical decision making. Similarly, a company that underestimates the risks involved in using an automated DSS stands to lose money through missed opportunities, deflated stock prices, loss of competitive position, and so on.

The key to realizing the benefits of a DSS, then, is to keep the probability of exposure extremely low. This objective can be achieved by involving computer auditors who understand when and how to use DSS controls.

The Auditor's Role

Decision support systems have dominated conversation at recent conferences of computer and audit professionals. Concern has been focused on the technological building blocks for a DSS. Particular exposures can result from the rapid proliferation of personal microcomputers and the corresponding erosion of organizational controls. The proliferation of microcomputers also can create, in effect, many "independent systems" within an organization. Stand-alone microcomputers equipped with data communication capabilities and sophisticated software have given DSS users on-line access to potentially sensitive data, as well as the autonomous capability to modify those data.

In light of the major risks, the greatest need for the involvement of auditors will be throughout DSS development. During development, the auditor can help to assure adequate controls and compliance with design standards. The auditor's role is to minimize the probability of exposure. As seen in the Pearl Harbor example, it certainly is more effective to prevent exposures than to correct them.

The responsible, effective auditor should approach any audit with a predetermined audit methodology. Because of the power and complexity of decision support systems, an appropriate methodology is especially important.

A Methodology for DSS Audit

As with any audit, the approach to evaluating a DSS begins with obtaining full knowledge of audit objectives. Setting these objectives means that the auditor has obtained management commitment and also has grasped all audit constraints.

INFORMATION SYSTEM AUDIT APPROACH

	AUDIT STEP	OBJECTIVE OF AUDIT STEP	RECOMMENDED AUDIT METHOD
1	Scope the enviroment	Evaluate the technical complexity of the audit and need for new audit methods	Entrance conference, interviews, checklists, and worksheets
2	Understand the information system	Acquire sufficient background to conduct the audit	Data flow diagram, interviews, documentation
3	Identify the audit risks	Determine where to utilize audit records	Risk analysis
4	Identify audit evidence	Establish the base for conducting tests	Worksheet record layouts, interviews, documentation
5	Identify key control points	Determine points in system at which risk is greatest	Control flowchart
6	Identify control weaknesses	Determine what to test	Control matrix
7	Verify the integrity of computer files	Establish the base for relying on computer files	Computer-assisted audit techniques
8	Conduct audit tests	Verify integrity of computer transactions	Computer-assisted audit techniques
9	Conclude the audit	Analyze tests and develop findings and recommendations	Exit conference, Audit report

Figure 13-7.

As shown in this table, an information system audit approach may consist of nine steps. Audit objectives and recommended audit tools are given for each step.

A step-by-step approach, based on a 1974 report by the AICPA, has been developed by the EDP Auditors Foundation (EDPAF). This approach is a guide for the auditor's use in setting audit objectives. As shown in Figure 13-7, this audit, called the *information system audit approach,* has nine phases. In view of the advanced nature of decision support systems, such a thorough approach is essential if the auditor is to be able to support findings adequately.

Identifying key control points is a major phase in this approach. The discussion below highlights the minimum controls that must be present in a DSS if major exposures are to be avoided.

DSS CONTROLS

Controls can be applied to a DSS in the following areas:

- Documentation
- Operation

- Separation of duties

- Audit trails

- Security measures.

Documentation

Documentation of a DSS, as with other sophisticated systems, consists of descriptions of procedures, instructions to personnel, flowcharts, data flow diagrams, display or report layouts, and other materials that can describe an overall system.

At one level, documentation provides management with an understanding of system objectives and concepts. Without good, comprehensive documentation, adherence to organization policies would be impossible. From an audit standpoint, documentation is a primary basis for review by either internal or external auditors. Documentation for an operational DSS should exist at three levels:

- System documentation

- Program documentation

- Operating documentation.

System documentation. System documentation should include a narrative stating both the objectives and applications of the system and subsystems.

Program documentation. Programs and modules within the DSS must be documented as a basis for identifying system weaknesses and as a point of reference for system modifications.

Operating documentation. Operating documentation is needed to provide instructions for data input and output.

As with microcomputer systems, documentation for a DSS provides a measure of organizational, or general, control. Documentation helps implement organizational policies for appropriate use and fixes individual responsibilities for control measures and system safeguards. In situations involving highly distributed processing, organizational policies, as set forth in user documentation, provide some degree of centralization of control.

Operation

Operation controls are concerned primarily with input, processing, and output. A particular risk is that, within a DSS, fraudulent data may be indistinguishable from legitimate data. Therefore, controls over the input function must anticipate the impacts of inappropriate entries. For example, a strategic management decision might involve the possible closing of a plant. If fraudulent or inappropriate data were entered into a DSS, the result might be that hundreds of people would be put out of work needlessly.

Because a DSS usually must access organizational databases, much of the processing may be centralized, performed by the organization's mainframe. Postprocessing on intelligent terminals may involve generation of graphs or reports. Within the mainframe center, conventional controls may be applied to assure reasonableness and accuracy, including: sequence checks, reasonableness and limit tests, completeness checks, and digit checks. When errors are detected at this level, controls must be present in the form of established procedures for follow-up and correction. Centralized processing within a DSS, therefore, is subject to conventional DP controls. However, because inputs often are of a hypothetical nature, it becomes much more difficult to distinguish inappropriate items from legitimate data.

Output controls must aim at assuring validity and controlling custody. In a DSS, the most important output control is to assure proper distribution of the information. If outputs are produced centrally, conventional controls, such as a security officer and distribution logs, may be appropriate. If output is distributed over a data communication network, control emphasis shifts to access controls for individual work stations.

Separation of Duties

If a DSS involves centralized processing, separation of duties is a crucial control that may be implemented within the data center. No individual should have the access necessary in the normal course of duties both to initiate and to conceal errors or irregularities. If it is possible to restrict access to system elements, the exposure to fraud can be reduced.

As discussed previously, microcomputer-based environments pose different vulnerabilities. Since an individual at a distributed work station may be capable of performing complete processing cycles, a traditional separation of duties may be impractical. It would be particularly difficult to partition portions of the organizational databases from a top-level manager who has broad responsibilities. In such environments, emphasis is on general controls (as set forth in organizational policies) and on access controls (discussed below).

Audit Trails

Audit trails trace the status and content of an individual transaction anywhere within a processing cycle. If computer auditors are involved in DSS development, the system can be designed to build and maintain audit trails in routine operation. Logs can be kept of access by work station, by individual, by program, and by specific files. Through such logs, security personnel and auditors can monitor access to and use of sensitive information.

Security Measures

As indicated above, there is an exceptional need within a DSS to provide controls over the security of sensitive information. Controls must apply wherever a user has contact with data—either through computerized equipment or through manual procedures. Methods for assuring the security of a DSS need to focus on controlling access to the organizational databases and controlling the use of data. Also, controls must exist to detect and report possible security violations.

A critical area of security for a DSS, as noted above, is access controls. To gain access to the system, users should be required to authenticate their identities. Specific measures include assigning password codes, using magnetically coded badges, or applying voice-print analysis.

In a DSS, great care must be given to defining which individuals are to be permitted access to specified levels of information. Once established, access privileges can be enforced by varying the identification schemes, as in changing user passwords on a random basis.

Another kind of access protection may be applied at the file level. Procedures should exist to authenticate which users will have read-only, write-only, or read-and-write access to the DSS. The threat of wiretapping, or unauthorized interception of transmissions, may be countered by encryption, or data scrambling techniques. Encryption may be applied both to file content and to data transmissions. Such methods decrease the threat of wiretapping because an unauthorized user would have to know how to break the code before the data would become useful.

To enforce the above controls, there must be constant monitoring of successful and unsuccessful accesses to the DSS. Controls also must be tested periodically. Figure 13-8 lists security policies and procedures by methods of identification, authorization, encryption, and audit.

NEW AUDIT TOOLS AND TECHNIQUES

The use of the computer for the storage and processing of large amounts of financial data has created the need to analyze such information within its

METHODS FOR DATABASE SECURITY

Method	Threat Addressed	Procedures	Policies
Identification, authorization	All	Identification assignment Password assignment	Definition of legitimate database user
Authorization	All	Grant, revoke privileges	Definition of need to know use
Encryption	Disclosure	Select algorithm	Definition of sensitive data, processing
Audit	Modification	Verify selected data Verify database structure	Determine time and scope of audit

Figure 13-8.

Applicable procedures and policies are given in this table for each type of database security method and the types of threat addressed by each.

own electronic environment. For example, statistical sampling of computer-resident accounts is feasible only with computer-based techniques.

Hardware Tools

The rapid deployment of an on-line, real-time CIS (as opposed to batch processing) reduces the auditor's control over audit applications and files that may be exposed to alteration by an organization's personnel. Especially in distributed or microcomputer-based environments, incompatibilities of hardware devices within a single organization can create serious obstacles for the auditor. In such situations, auditors frequently must adapt audit programs to the specifications of different vendors and multiple computers—ranging from microcomputers, to minicomputers, to mainframes.

A solution to these difficulties has been the introduction of an *audit work station,* a secure microcomputer facility that permits the CIS auditor to download the data to be tested. Related advantages of this approach are a decrease in costs, reduced training time, maintenance of a relatively limited audit software library, and increased security. Several public accounting firms have developed such tools, which offer the same advantages as auditing on a mainframe, but also deliver an additional measure of independence. Extensive use of such a system, however, does not imply that the CIS auditor should avoid completely the use of an organization's CIS facilities. Discrepancies may be encountered that would be impossible to verify through the use of file dumps, or downloaded data. Typical hardware components of an audit work station would include a microcomputer, a printer, a hard disk drive, a floppy disk drive, and a modem. A useful adjunct to the audit work station is a portable or lap-top microcomputer that gives an auditor mobile computer capabilities.

Software Tools

Audit software tools, many of which are available for microcomputers, fall into general categories that include:

- Test support software
- Software analysis tools.

Test support software. *Test support software* includes programs designed for specific audit tasks. Packages have been developed for generation of test data, data reduction, statistical data collection, and so on.

Software analysis tools. *Software analysis tools* are utilities that apply to many different audit tasks. These tools make comparisons, measure complexity, measure coverage, analyze path flow, and even perform formal verifications.

Trends in Use of Fourth-Generation Languages

Previous chapters highlight some features of fourth-generation languages for production of computer-assisted audit programs. As part of this discussion of new techniques, trends in the application of these tools should be noted.

From the CIS auditor's standpoint, the use of fourth-generation languages can reduce the time needed to audit large amounts of data or large programs. In general, a fourth-generation language produces executable code from relatively free-form, or high-level, statements. In computer-assisted auditing, the auditor describes the required tests or data manipulations in such statements; the software package interprets the statements and generates the corresponding code in the correct syntax.

Thus, use of high-level tools sacrifices a degree of flexibility. The trade-offs of convenience for flexibility and control can be illustrated as a pyramid (see Figure 13-9). In terms of programming power, low-level languages (such as assembly language) offer the greatest flexibility and control. Third-generation languages (such as COBOL and Pascal) offer greater convenience and program clarity, but are more restrictive in structure. Fourth-generation languages (such as Focus) are relatively inflexible, but their use speeds application development.

It is unlikely that fourth-generation languages will replace all other programming languages. A more probable scenario would find each tool used

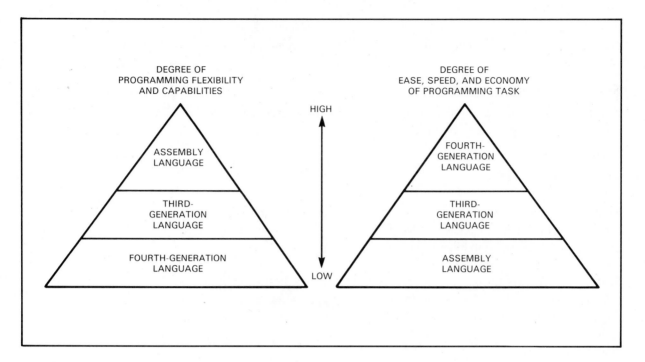

Figure 13-9.

Trade-offs of different computer programming languages may be represented by pyramids that correspond with the degree of flexibility and the ease of programming.

at an appropriate level. Assembly language still will be used for precise coding and achieving maximum efficiency in systems integration and in firmware implementations. Third-generation languages will be used by systems professionals to write structured, maintainable code while reserving some control. Fourth-generation tools will be most appropriate at the end-user level, where English-like description promotes understanding and where efficiency of execution may be less critical.

New technologies that support the computer auditor include innovative hardware, fourth-generation languages, and generalized audit software. In Figure 13-10, these tools are shown in layers. For example, it is most likely that the CIS auditor will use a fourth-generation language to audit systems written in third-generation languages, rather than assembly language. Third-generation languages, in turn, may be used in instances requiring increased flexibility. At the bottom of the hierarchy, as the object of the audit, are the data. As a general rule, auditors would use the highest level tool with the required capabilities to develop audit applications in the least amount of time, with least expense.

This entire audit structure is maintained through other controls besides coding and data analysis. Control points may include CIS and user cooperation and communication, authorization of fourth-generation language

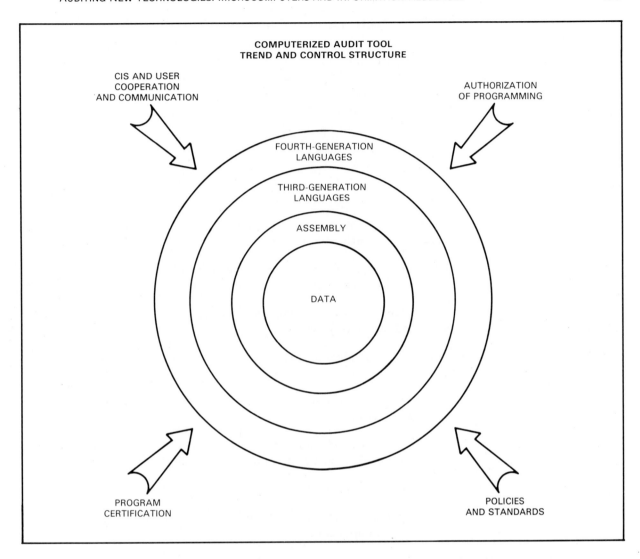

**COMPUTERIZED AUDIT TOOL
TREND AND CONTROL STRUCTURE**

CIS AND USER
COOPERATION
AND COMMUNICATION

AUTHORIZATION
OF PROGRAMMING

FOURTH-GENERATION
LANGUAGES

THIRD-GENERATION
LANGUAGES

ASSEMBLY

DATA

PROGRAM
CERTIFICATION

POLICIES
AND STANDARDS

Figure 13-10.

This diagram presents a conceptual view of trends affecting computerized audit tools. This view can serve as a framework for deciding which tools may be appropriate for implementing a given audit task.

programming, program certification, and the existence of management policies and standards.

These tools and techniques possess great potential in other areas of CIS auditing. It has been suggested, for example, that the systems design process may be planned and programmed through the use of fourth-generation languages, instead of conventional programming languages such as COBOL. This approach would affect the approach to an audit significantly. In one respect, the cost, time, and complexity of the systems development life cycle (SDLC) might be reduced dramatically by allowing end users to create some applications. On the other hand, less control over the environment in which users create their own applications may make auditing more difficult. It may become increasingly difficult to determine the integrity of the input and output, and of the application itself. Maintaining control and auditability will require the combined efforts of CIS staff, end users, and auditors in creating levels of authorization and certification for increasing numbers of application systems.

DISCUSSION QUESTIONS

1. What characteristics of microcomputer-based networks can create significant exposures to information assets?

2. What might be some of the CIS auditor's specific concerns in evaluating the risks and controls within microcomputer-based applications?

3. What might be the control implications of an organizational plan for advanced office systems?

4. Why is user training an especially critical area of control for microcomputer-based systems?

5. What are some prime vulnerabilities that relate to microcomputers, and what might be the consequences of each?

6. What are some of the audit implications of microcomputer systems that are within or connected to corporate information centers?

7. What types of risks are inherent in the use of decision support systems?

8. What types of microcomputer-based tools are available for computer-assisted audit applications?

CASE ASSIGNMENTS

To apply the concepts presented in this chapter, complete the following assignments:

1. Turn to the case study for Abcor in Appendix E and work through Project 2, which deals with the review of policies and procedures for use of microcomputers.

2. Turn to the case study for WhyMe Corporation in Appendix A and work through Project 3, which deals with the audit of a decision support system.

14 Auditing New Technologies: Digital Communication and Case Study

ABSTRACT

• Audit concerns in the review of systems that incorporate digital communication technology include monitoring data flow, assuring security, providing authorization, securing on-line systems with access controls, and safeguarding systems against transmission line failures.

• Significant developments in this area include satellite communication, fiber optics, and electronic funds transfer.

• Risks associated with data transfer include both passive and active wiretapping. The use of message authentication codes as a safeguard against active wiretapping is discussed.

• Transmission-oriented controls include validity checking of identification codes and data characters, conditioning of transmission lines, parity checks on both characters and blocks, and echo checking of characters.

• Telecommunication controls include limiting the direction of data access, multilevel password schemes, file access passwords, partitioning of sensitive data, and automated logging of all telecommunication activity.

• Control issues in auditing data communication with service bureaus include user responsibilities, shared responsibilities, and vendor responsibilities.

• Procedural controls within service-bureau environments include organizational security policy, training and education, system logs, documentation, handling of unusual transactions, control of system modifications, as well as real-time validation and editing.

• Controls administered by service bureaus include controls on network access, data integrity, restart and recovery, and output. These elements are illustrated with a scenario of an actual unauthorized penetration of a CIS facility via the public service telephone network.

DATA COMMUNICATION TECHNOLOGIES

Advances in microcircuitry and in data communication technology have expanded the scope of electronic access to information. As these trends continue, emerging legal issues and data security concerns make the process of auditing much more complex. Data communication technologies are the glue, in effect, that holds together sophisticated systems, such as micro-computer networks, information centers, and decision support systems. To develop new audit tools and techniques for dealing with these entities, the computer auditor must become familiar with some of the technical aspects of data communication.

Some data communication systems may be dedicated to a single application in which each device on the network performs a portion of a larger task. Distributed data processing (DDP) is based on this concept. Other types of networks, such as public data networks and information utilities, provide any home or business computer with access to a wide range of databases or special programs for occasional use. Such multi-user networks may be national or international in scope and may be accessed by virtually anyone dialing up over a telephone network.

Challenges for the auditor center around complexity. In DDP situations, such as those found in international banking and finance, multiple main-frame systems in dispersed geographic locations may be linked. High degrees of integration may make it difficult for the auditor to determine which device within the network executed a given job or task. Within information utilities, programs and databases may be relatively specialized and narrow in scope, yet may be accessible by potentially millions of users.

For such complex systems, the auditor's concerns should focus upon the ability to create an audit trail and to recognize points of risk. The auditor's objectives include the following:

- Assure a capability for monitoring data flow.

- Determine the security of transmission lines.

- Evaluate or require creation of a user authorization system.

- Guarantee the security of on-line access software.

- Plan for contingencies in the event of transmission line failure.

In assuring the reliability of data communication controls, the auditor's ultimate objective is to enhance the stability of systems that may be critical to the daily existence of the using organization.

Although data communication systems are becoming increasingly critical to daily business operations, most organizations do not have the resources to assure the reliability of these systems. Rapid advances in microcircuitry and telecommunication technology have led to a shortage of technical experts who can control the new systems. The computer auditor has no choice but to become involved in these technical areas. Thus, topics such as network architecture, communication protocols, and error-checking techniques are just as important to the computer auditor as the more traditional areas of internal accounting controls.

As background for dealing with new data communication systems, computer auditors must become familiar with emerging technologies that include:

- Satellite communication

- Fiber optics

- Electronic funds transfer.

Satellite Communication

Some observers speculate that within a few years all computers—even small ones—will be connected to a communication network, at least part of the time. Providing these links on a worldwide scale should involve the public service telephone network, with major links provided by communication satellites. To accommodate this growth, the number of satellites serving North America (currently 25) is expected to expand by a factor of six.

Corporate communication via satellite has several advantages:

- Reliability

- Security

- Distant communication.

Reliability.   Communications over satellite channels generally are not subject to geographic obstacles or to changing weather conditions. However, solar flares, or storms on the surface of the sun, can cause disruptions.

Security.   The sheer volume of traffic handled by a satellite makes it difficult to locate the exact channel on which an organization is sending data. Further, each channel usually carries messages from multiple sources concurrently. Multiple messages are transmitted as interleaved, short bursts, or *packets,* using a technique called *time-division multiplexing (TDM).* Multiplexing further complicates the task of isolating a single transmission from all the traffic on a given channel. If, however, the channel being used is disclosed or otherwise compromised, security could be breached. For this reason, an additional level of security usually is provided for satellite transmissions by encrypting the data.

Distant communication.   Both land-based and satellite transmissions are carried at *microwave* radio frequencies. A characteristic of microwave transmissions is that they must follow the *line of sight,* or a straight line between transmitters. Long-distance, land-based communication must allow for the curvature of the earth. Such transmissions, therefore, use multiple nodes, or *repeaters,* that relay the signals.

Most communication satellites are in *geosynchronous* orbits. That is, the satellite remains in a fixed position in the sky. Microwave transmissions are beamed directly to the satellite, which acts as a repeater in relaying the message back to a distant earth node, or *ground station.* Though relatively large distances through space are involved, the number of repeaters is reduced. Such a scheme can increase both the quality and the reliability of the transmission.

Fiber Optics

Fiber optics use light as a transmission carrier. Pulses of light corresponding with data signals are conducted in thin, glass filaments, or fibers. Fiber-optic cables can carry much more information than cables of copper wire. Fiber-optic cables are being used to replace copper wires in many telecommunication networks to permit higher volumes of traffic in the same physical space. For example, when worldwide television coverage was planned for the 1984 Olympic games in Los Angeles, it was discovered that existing copper-wire telephone cables would not be able to handle the anticipated traffic from television broadcasts. Multiple events at locations all over Southern California had to be transmitted over the telecommunication network to a central studio and then relayed to broadcast networks all over the world via satellite. To solve this problem, large sections of the area's telephone cable system were replaced with fiber optics just for televising the games.

Accommodating more traffic in less space gives fiber-optic transmission methods superior cost/performance characteristics over conventional copper wire. Another distinct advantage is that fiber-optic links are not susceptible to *radio frequency interference (RFI)* or *electromagnetic interference (EMI).* RFI may be caused by electrical disturbances or by radio and television transmissions. EMI can be generated by electric motors and magnetic devices.

Further, unlike electrical signals carried in copper wires, light pulses carried over fiber optic links do not generate RFI. Since interception of stray RFI is a primary method of wiretapping, fiber optics provide some protection against this type of penetration.

In many offices, fiber-optic cables are being used increasingly to carry voice telephone traffic, as well as to provide links among devices in local area networks (LANs).

A drawback of fiber-optic technology is that it is relatively difficult to splice broken cables or to expand existing transmission lines.

Electronic Funds Transfer

Electronic funds transfer (EFT) is redefining the conceptual view of money. Point-of-sale (POS) systems, automated teller machines (ATM), home banking, and automated payment systems are handling increasingly larger proportions of routine business transactions. In such applications, bits of data actually represent cash assets. The implications for the audit of financial systems are far-reaching.

An EFT system has its own operating and control characteristics that include the following:

- Reduction in float, or the time lag between a transaction and the debiting of a cash account, can change money management strategies.
- Federal laws govern branch banking and funds transfers.
- Use of communication services provided by multiple carriers may open exposure to transmission errors. Detection and correction of errors can be more difficult than in systems using a single carrier.

Auditors' awareness and ability to recognize problems in EFT systems could help to prevent and detect fraud or error.

Risks of Data Transfer

Methods for exchanging data range from physical transfer to long-distance, microwave transmission. Physical transfer would occur, for example, when one microcomputer user handed a diskette to another, or when a tape is retrieved from remote archival storage and transported to its data center for processing. At the other extreme, data packets may be sent at high speed over microwave links that include communication satellites.

Within this spectrum of possibilities, encryption, or scrambling of data, is perhaps the best single control measure. In providing a safeguard for data transfers, encryption discourages interception by wiretapping. Wiretapping, or unauthorized interception of transmissions, is a twofold threat. Its components are:

- Passive
- Active.

Passive wiretapping.   *Passive wiretapping* involves the illegal scanning or reproduction of data. Intruders may be thwarted through the use of an encryption algorithm involving a secret key. The key is used to encode the transmitted data and render it unreadable. Decoding requires knowledge of the encryption key. In addition, the use of shielded cables or fiber optics can reduce the ability of a passive wiretapper to obtain information by intercepting and analyzing RFI generated by transmissions.

Active wiretapping.   *Active wiretapping* encompasses the unauthorized deletion, addition, or alteration of intercepted data. Active wiretapping involves a greater risk to data security and requires detection of any data alteration that may have occurred between the point of origin and the destination.

As a detective control on active wiretapping, a *message authentication code (MAC)* may be created using encryption technology. The MAC is a known value that is encrypted prior to transmission. The MAC is separate from the message, which need not be encrypted; but both the MAC and the message are carried in the same transmission. If decoding of the MAC at the destination does not yield the known value, it can be assumed that the message has been manipulated during transmission.

In view of these exposures, the auditor should be cautious when sensitive data are obtained from the organization's main facility over a telephone line. In such instances, encryption should be considered as a proper control; the encryption algorithm must be installed at the sending and receiving stations.

AUDITING DATA COMMUNICATION SYSTEMS

A number of data communication controls have been developed and applied with success. These controls focus on protecting and recovering data and are designed to minimize the loss and/or destruction of data.

Though data communication systems may be automated to a high degree, the controls on those systems depend upon human interaction and assurances that the controls are sound. Controls within a data communication system are primarily transmission-oriented. That is, control measures are applied at the point of origin. Control measures also must be applied to communication lines or channels.

Transmission-oriented controls must complement controls in other areas. Controls in data entry, computer processing, data storage, and output functions also relate to data communication. These controls have interlocking relationships in the protection and recovery of data. If controls in one area are not functioning properly, the entire system is exposed. Exposure also can result if human intervention is able to override complementary control processes. Figure 14-1 is an illustration of some data communication controls found in many computer information systems.

The controls listed in Figure 14-1 are categorized as entry-oriented, transmission-oriented, or processing- and file-oriented. Within these categories, controls may be preventive, detective, or corrective—or a combination.

Audit Concerns

The discussion in Chapter 6 presents a list of questions that the auditor may ask in the evaluation of data communication controls. These questions, in effect, form an audit checklist for transmission-oriented controls. These controls are necessary safeguards against the intentional interception of transmissions or the accidental alteration of data during the transmission process. Errors in data communication usually occur because of the distances involved, speeds of transmission, or equipment malfunctions. Of the controls listed in Chapter 6, some measures implemented in hardware are transparent to users and can provide a basic, minimum level of protection:

- Perform validity checking of hard-wired terminal identification codes and data characters being transmitted.

- Use specially conditioned transmission lines to reduce noise and fading, as well as to minimize amplitude and frequency distortion.

- Perform parity checking of both individual characters and blocks of characters.

- Perform echo checking of characters entered against characters received.

Other hardware-oriented controls that can be incorporated in the data communication system include encryption of sensitive data to reduce the effectiveness of wiretapping, and automatically storing data at intermediary points when lines or other devices are inoperative. These controls are designed to make sure that only valid data are entered, transmitted, and received and that no data are lost, accessed, or tampered with along the way.

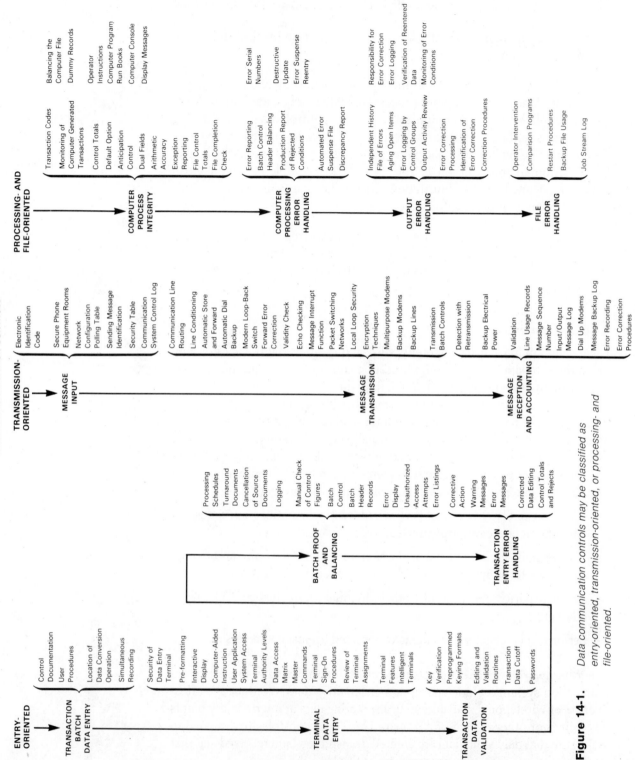

Figure 14-1. Data communication controls may be classified as entry-oriented, transmission-oriented, or processing- and file-oriented.

Telecommunication Controls

If a microcomputer is connected to a mainframe over a telecommunication link, many additional exposures are introduced. Access controls are effective in reducing exposures resulting from micro-to-mainframe links. Such controls include the following:

- Limit the direction of data access. For example, a user might be allowed only to upload data.

- Create multilevel password schemes to lock out unauthorized users selectively from the system. Password levels can be made to correspond with security clearances and the need to know.

- Use file access passwords to screen users from specific types of information and prevent unauthorized manipulation of data.

- Establish separation and protection of sensitive data from nonsensitive data. In a large mainframe environment, it is possible to store sensitive data on one system and all "public" information on another. If the system storing the sensitive information does not have any telecommunication links, controlled access to information is assured.

- Maintain a full log of telecommunication activity. Software to handle this type of logging is available readily. Characteristics such as user identification and files accessed should be shown in the log. This information is of particular interest to the computer auditor.

Another consideration in a telecommunication link is the control of data downloaded to users. If the data are sensitive, the transmission should be encrypted at the point of origin. Thus, access is restricted to users who have knowledge of the encryption key. If a diskette with encrypted data should find its way to an unauthorized user, the security of the data will not be breached. A good general rule is that if the information is extremely sensitive, it should not be available in any form through a telecommunication link.

AUDITING DATA COMMUNICATIONS WITH SERVICE BUREAUS

Service bureaus are outside resources for the processing and storage of information. Since the vendor is not under the direct control of the organization and since access to service bureaus usually is over telecommunication links, this type of service poses special problems for the CIS auditor.

Data held at service bureaus can include inventory records, accounts payable, accounts receivable, customer lists, new product specifications, work in progress, compensation rates, personnel records, payroll records, and so on. The data for each client organization will differ in terms of significance, need, and quantity. As a prerequisite for establishing controls, client managers must determine which data must be secure. Given this determination, the purpose of data security is to prevent any unauthorized disclosure of those business data to unauthorized sources.

Control Issues

From a control standpoint, the transmission medium and the elapsed time for a data transfer are irrelevant. The critical objective is to maintain the integrity of the data, regardless of transmission method or speed.

From a practical standpoint, however, transmission method and speed are economic considerations. Managers are concerned with both the cost and the timeliness of data transfer. Communication methods used between client organizations and service bureaus range from manual deliveries by messengers to on-line, direct transmission over telecommunication links. Regardless of the medium or method of communication used, controls must be present to assure that data are received in the form the sender intended.

The service bureau, or service center, presents a unique set of control challenges for the auditor. The center is a distinct and separate outside entity that becomes an integral part of a client's data processing and internal control system. But, because the center is a separate entity, the client's internal control system has no direct control over it.

Effective control measures over data sent to service bureaus depend on cooperation, planning, understanding, and agreement between the client organization and the outside center. Ultimately, the service center will have to administer the controls established over input, processing, and output.

The role of a service bureau may vary from simply operating a program prepared by the user to providing a complete data processing service. The latter arrangement has been popular because it requires relatively little technical involvement from the user. In such cases, the service organization would design the system and accept full responsibility for programming, data communication, and operation.

User responsibilities. If the responsibility of the user is delegated to the service organization, the user must acquire sufficient knowledge of the system to provide the necessary input, to react to exceptions and differences in reporting, and to understand the outputs and use them appropriately.

The user should be concerned with the specific security measures taken by the service organization to protect user data. Further, the user also should be concerned with the general controls within the service bureau. These controls can affect the integrity of the user's data.

A specific area of concern is the data communication network used to input data to the center and to receive processed output. A typical interface between a user system and an outside service bureau is shown in Figure 14-2. Some areas within the service center facility have access to the center's main computer but are not involved in the processing of user data. These areas include the training room, offices, and on-line test system. The service organization's controls over these areas, including access controls, are an important concern to the user. In the absence of such controls, unauthorized access to user data could be accomplished from these locations. Exposure to abuses by systems programmers are of particular concern. Controls that partition one user organization's system from another also must be examined.

Shared responsibilities.   To provide adequate controls over an on-line network, the service center needs to concern itself with preventive, detective, and corrective controls. The center also must apply these types of controls to the different areas of a data communication system that could access any portion of the user's system or data. These measures, which are subject to verification by the user's auditors, are discussed below.

The responsibility for some control measures cannot be fixed entirely with either party. These controls amount to shared responsibilities between the user and the service organization. This area of shared responsibility—if it is not defined clearly—can be a major source of trouble.

A key area of shared responsibility is input/output controls. These controls are applied at the boundary, in effect, between the user's system and the service bureau. Although overall responsibility is shared, some interrelating functions can be defined for each party. For example, the user's functions in this area include:

- Prepare and submit data for processing.
- Administer procedures controlling data entry personnel.
- Control physical access to terminals within the user facility.
- Verify the accuracy of outputs.
- Control the distribution of outputs.

The service center, on the other hand, should be responsible for the following functions:

- Specify the type of hardware allowed on the data communication system.

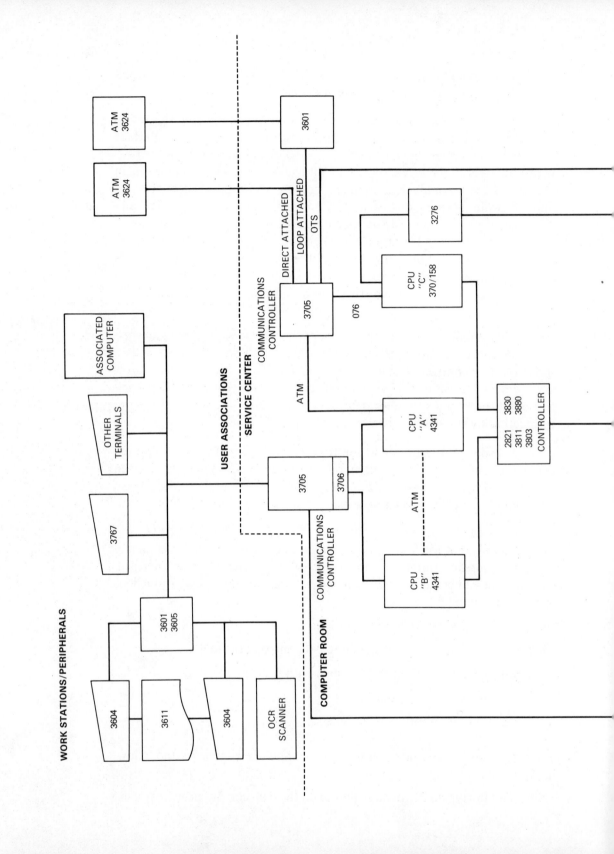

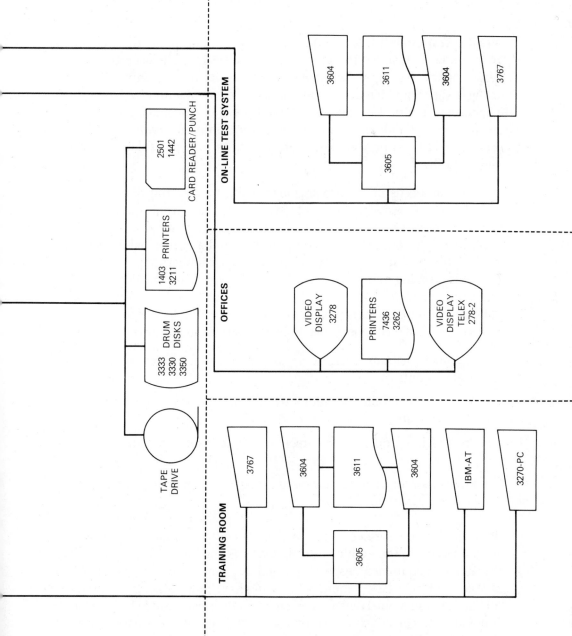

Figure 14-2.

This diagram shows a typical network hardware configuration for data communication with an outside service center.

- Provide training in the procedures to be used by data entry personnel.

- Perform checks to assure that physical access to input terminals by unauthorized users is prevented.

Vendor responsibilities.   The service center should specify the type of terminal and terminal features acceptable to the system. The user, then, has a responsibility to comply. Terminals, work stations, or other input devices at the user site should have keyboard locks to prevent unauthorized use during nonbusiness hours. Terminals also should have buzzers or alarms to indicate malfunctions. Guidelines should be set for minimum *mean time between failures (MTBF)*, or projected up-time, and mean time to fix data communication hardware.

Modem speeds should be variable to enable the lowering of transmission rates in case of excessive errors. Modems should have front-panel indicators that show proper operation. Also, modems with alternate voice capabilities facilitate quick troubleshooting between sites. In the case of dial-up modems, special controls can include changing telephone numbers at predetermined intervals, keeping numbers confidential, using voice verification instead of automatic connections, and using *call-back* systems. Upon user identification, call-back systems terminate incoming calls and reinitiate the connection to known terminal locations, preventing access from unauthorized terminals.

The above actions, then, serve to implement the following data communication controls:

- Assure compatibility of user hardware with the rest of the data communication system.

- Provide for proper error detection and correction during data transmission.

- Prevent or discourage use of terminal equipment by unauthorized persons.

To verify that the service bureau has implemented a reliable data communication system, the auditor also should look for the existence of backup transmission equipment, especially where the user's need for information is critical. All transmission equipment should have indicators for proper operation or malfunction. Transmission equipment should be able to detect and, if possible, to correct transmission errors. If passwords are used, terminal displays should have secured video (suppressed display of input on screen) so that the password cannot be read from the screen. If data encryption devices are used, automatic key changes can be made at predetermined times during the day. Systems are available that permit this changeover without human intervention.

Procedural Controls

Procedural controls are administered primarily by the user organization; but, in many ways, the user's procedural controls must be designed to validate the effectiveness of controls administered by the service bureau. Control areas of concern to the auditor include:

- Organizational security policy

- Training and education

- System logs

- Documentation

- Handling of unusual transactions

- System modifications

- Real-time validation and editing.

Organizational security policy.   A critical procedural control is an overall organizational security policy for the data communication system. Emphasis should be placed on security and privacy of information. All other controls should be integrated with this policy. Operational procedures should cover such areas as security violations; network malfunctions; storage, modification, and use of sensitive communication programs; preventive maintenance; corrective maintenance; trouble reporting; and personnel staffing and evaluation. These procedures should be reviewed periodically by user management and by the internal audit function.

Training and education.   Procedural controls also encompass the training and education of user organization personnel. Accurate data entry, recovery of data from errors, and administration of security measures all depend on adequate training. Use of data communication hardware and software often involves some degree of technical training.

System logs.   Procedural controls should include spot checking of ongoing system logs by supervisory personnel. For example, a *systems communication log* should record all connections to the network. Supervisors should look for any unusual occurrences such as *enable* or *disable* messages, a change in frequency of lines, or a message indicating that an attempt to log in was denied. Such occurrences could indicate unauthorized line manipulation. User training methods should be evaluated continually to assure that operators are familiar with these procedures. Procedures also should state the actions to be taken in case of malfunctions of programs, hardware, or the data communication system.

Documentation.   Another critical area is documentation of a data communication system. Documentation of such a system needs to be both accurate and understandable to user personnel. A full description of the system in terms of physical layout and functional operation should be included. Documentation also should cover the prevention, identification, and recovery from problems.

Handling of unusual transactions.   Special procedural controls directed at terminal users should be applied if high-level security is required or if unusual transactions are being made. Such procedural controls can be implemented in software so that transactions are not accepted until the appropriate supervisor enters a code authorizing it.

Situations requiring such procedures may include *lock-out holds* that restrict processing of specific, controlled accounts. In banking and financial systems, this type of control is necessary for legal or formal account holds, for the processing of loan payments against accounts subject to foreclosure proceedings, and for legal holds or payoffs pending transactions that are active. *Available balance holds* restrict the processing of withdrawals from accounts with insufficient funds. Such situations also may require supervisory action. Another situation in which a supervisor's action should be required would be in the event of *teller alert messages* triggered by the flagging of an account due to a lost passbook or the requirement of two signatures.

System modifications.   Procedural controls are especially necessary to restrict the modification of any element of data communication hardware, software, or firmware. All changes should be approved by appropriate levels of management before installation. Tests should be run in a strictly controlled environment. The updated file or modified component should be put on-line only after thorough checks and approvals have been made. The purpose of stringent controls in this area is to prevent the unauthorized changing of programs. Such intervention could result in personal gain or could compromise the integrity of the system.

Real-time validation and editing.   All procedural controls are intended to direct personnel in the efficient and effective performance of their duties while minimizing the effects of possible network exposures. The very responsiveness of data communication systems can create major exposures. If user/operators are permitted real-time update capability, validation and input editing become critical. In such situations, the auditor must pose questions that include:

- Are data validation and editing performed as early as possible in the data flow to assure that the application rejects any incorrect transaction before master files are updated?

- Are data validation and editing performed for all data fields, even though an error may be detected in an earlier field of the transaction?

- Are special routines used that validate and edit input transaction dates automatically against a table of cutoff dates?

- Do the programs that include tables of values have a control mechanism to assure accuracy of those values?

- Are all persons prevented from overriding or bypassing data validation and editing problems?

In addition to resolving the questions above, the auditor also should assure that the following items are checked for validity on input of each transaction:

- Individual and supervisor authorization or approval codes
- Check digits at the end of numeric data strings not subjected to balancing
- Other transaction codes
- Characters
- Fields and combinations of fields
- Transactions
- Calculations
- Missing data
- Extraneous data
- Amounts
- Units
- Composition
- Logic decisions
- Limit or reasonableness checks
- Signs
- Record matches
- Record mismatches

- Sequence
- Balancing of quantitative data
- Crossfooting of quantitative data.

Controls Administered by the Service Bureau

A sound data communication system for a service bureau will have embedded within its software many preventive and detective controls. Control areas within the service bureau that should be investigated by the auditor include:

- Network access controls
- Data integrity
- Restart and recovery
- Output.

Network access controls. Most preventive controls implemented in software deal with access and are aimed at restricting terminal use to authorized personnel. Any attempt to use a terminal without proper authorization should result in a log-in denial.

Several other controls are desirable at the network level. Each terminal in a network should be assigned a unique number, or identifier. As an added control, each terminal also should be assigned specific associations. That is, a list of authorized personnel and/or applications will be maintained for each terminal. Maintaining such associations makes possible validation of all messages to and from a specific terminal. Any new terminals to be added to the network must:

- Have appropriate approvals.
- Meet specifications stipulated by the service center.
- Be placed into the telecommunication software programs before access can be granted.

As an additional control, telecommunication lines also should be declared properly in the network programs before they can be put into use.

To assure that these controls are in place and operating, an auditor might pose the following questions:

- Is there a logging capability (audit trail) in the data communication system to assist in reconstructing data files?
- Can messages and data be traced back to the user or point of origin?

- Does the application protect against concurrent file updates? That is, does initial access of a record lock out that record so that additional access attempts cannot be made until the initial processing has been completed?

- Are the date and time of each transaction stamped for logging purposes?

- Does data communication software prevent the acceptance of data from foreign terminals?

- Does the data communication system have a history log that is printed on both a line printer and at the console?

- Does this log include:
  Hardware failure messages?
  Software failure messages?
  Processing halts?
  Abnormal terminations of jobs?
  Operator interventions?
  Error messages?
  Unusual occurrences?
  Terminal failure messages?
  Terminal shutdown?
  All input communication messages?
  All output communication messages?

Access to the system can be controlled by the use of passwords and security codes. Users should have personal passwords of five characters or more in length. These passwords should be kept secret. It must be the responsibility of the individual to report any compromise of such secrecy. In addition to the password, user security codes should be assigned to prevent a person with an authorized password from gaining access to areas he or she is not authorized to manipulate. Any attempt to gain access without proper authorization should result in:

- Access denial at the terminal

- Message logs of the terminal, times, and attempts

- Display of the same information at the telecommunication command console.

Once the appropriate passwords, security codes, and user terminal identifications are matched, a terminal can be granted access to the system. Subsequently, all messages to and from the terminal should be recorded in a terminal communication file. Should a terminal be logged on but unused for a predetermined length of time, it should be logged out automatically. This control will prevent access to the system on a terminal that was left in a logged-in condition, either accidentally or purposely. Again, this action must be recorded in the terminal communication log.

Another control that helps to prevent unauthorized access to the network is *poll list reconfiguration.* A poll list is the set of terminals authorized to access the network at a given time. Reconfiguring the poll list has the effect of authorizing specific terminals for access at specific times during the day. This control is designed to allow the entry of specific types of transactions at specific times.

One last control concerned with authorized use is the assignment of only one terminal to transactions of a high-security nature. Thus, maximum control—including strict physical controls—can be exercised over the device.

Data integrity. Many control methods are available to help assure data integrity. Data communication software should provide all necessary data checks as verification of proper transmission to the service center. Such data checks include:

- Vertical parity checks
- Longitudinal parity checks
- Check-digit verification.

Vertical parity checks are applied to all individual bytes of data. Each byte has one bit identified as a *check bit,* or *parity bit.* The system counts the number of bits in each byte and checks for an odd or even value, or parity. The parity bit, then, is assigned a 0 or 1 value to create an odd or even parity in combination with the *data bits* in each byte. This method checks the validity of the coding in each byte.

Longitudinal parity checks are applied against the channels, or tracks, of a group of bytes. The odd or even counts are made against the bits in a given channel position, to verify either an odd or an even value. Under this system, entire bytes are used for validity checking. Vertical and longitudinal parity checking are illustrated in Figure 14-3.

Check-digit verification is another method of checking accuracy. This method is explained in Chapter 6 under the discussion on application program controls.

Should any error be detected using these data checking methods, the system should re-try the transmission until successful or until the *re-try count,* a running total, has been exhausted. Any terminal with an excessive number of transmission failure attempts should be removed automatically from service by the telecommunication software.

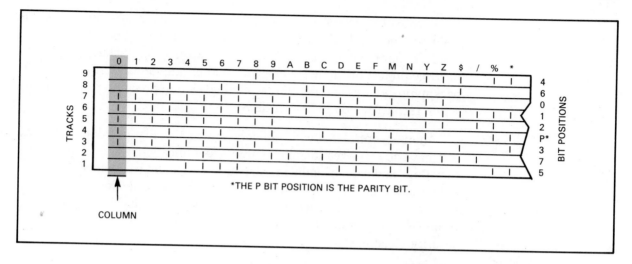

Figure 14-3.

Vertical parity checking is applied to individual bytes. Longitudinal parity checking is applied to the same bit position within a sequence of bytes.

Parity checking and check-digit verification can be considered the first level of data checking. A second level of checking has to do with data content rather than with data form. Examples of such *edited data checks* include:

- Alpha/numeric test

- Limit test

- Validity checks

- Range checks

- Master file checks

- Account number validation

- Field test.

These types of edits are specific to each individual application program and can be used as control needs dictate.

Restart and recovery. Software controls should include adequate restart and recovery procedures in case of system failure. Upon restart, users should be able to continue work from the point of the last transaction. As a general rule, a user's data never should be lost completely. Further, controls should enable individual terminal users to restart processing without affecting other users. Again, the user should be able to continue at the point of the last transaction. The use of terminals should be monitored through software controls, and both excessive and unusually light use should be flagged.

In case of a system crash, controls must provide for reactivation of the system at the point at which the failure occurred. To be able to restore the system to this point, controls should assure adequate file backup, transaction message protection, audit trail logging, and backup of user programs. Such backup procedures and file storage methods are necessary for file or transaction reconstruction in case of disaster.

Another control that will help in reconstructing files or a day's activities is to have all messages contain the user's identification, terminal identification, time, and date. In addition, each message should be numbered sequentially so that the order of occurrence can be maintained. Not only will this logging aid in reconstruction activities, but it also is highly useful for troubleshooting problems, checking on lost transactions, and investigating security violations.

Output.   One other area of audit concern is the output from a service center's data communication system. Output can be returned over telecommunication lines to terminals and printers, or it can be printed at the service center and delivered to the user. In any case, output should be understandable and complete. Any output sent over the data communication system should be subject to the same controls as inputs. Once the output reaches its destination, its security will become the responsibility of the user.

In summary, the audit of data communication controls in a service center environment must assure the integrity and security of data entrusted to the service by the user. The controls used to minimize exposures of the system are preventive, detective, and corrective in nature; they cover data communication procedures, data input, message transmission and reception, and output. These controls are especially important to users because the service center, although a separate and distinct entity, is still an integral part of the user organization's CIS. The client's information resource is only as secure as the weakest control placed on the data communication system.

CASE STUDY: A BREAK-IN BY THE 414s

The case below is an account of the actual penetration of a major computer system by a group of Milwaukee youths who called themselves "the 414s," a name derived from their telephone area code. Using personal computers and telephone dial-up access routes, this group penetrated dozens of commercial and federal computer systems. The case is included here because many of the technical issues relate to discussions in this chapter and the previous one on advanced systems and data communication.

Background

Relevant areas of the computer environment at the company in this case study include:

- Computer configuration
- Communication links
- Security procedures.

Computer configuration.   The company's processing environment was primarily a large IBM shop, but it also used three Digital Equipment Corporation VAX computers for systems development and some production applications. The VAX computers will be referred to as machines A, B, and C. Machine C, the initial object of the penetration, was used for systems development and for collection of overseas transactions through Telenet, a packet switching service provided by General Telephone and Electronics (GTE). Machines A and B were used for production processing. At the time of the break-in, the facility was involved in a transition, migrating to higher-level DEC machines, as well as upgrading the operating system. A diagram of this configuration is shown in Figure 14-4.

Communication links.   In addition to communication via Telenet, Machine C also permitted dial-up access from external sources, although this was not a factor in the penetration. There also was a link between the production and test machines via DECNet, a communication networking facility maintained by the computer manufacturer.

Security procedures.   The internal data security function at the company knew little about the security features of the DEC machines, and thus apparently did little to enforce security. Passwords were relatively easy to obtain and, once assigned, were not rotated.

The internal auditors had reviewed security procedures and had found them to be inadequate for the following reasons:

- Password controls were poor.
- The link between the production and test machines constituted an exposure for which there was no control.

A task force recently had been established within the data processing function to address these security issues, but this group was making slow progress. In fact, the internal auditors were performing a pre-implementation review of the new security system when the break-in began.

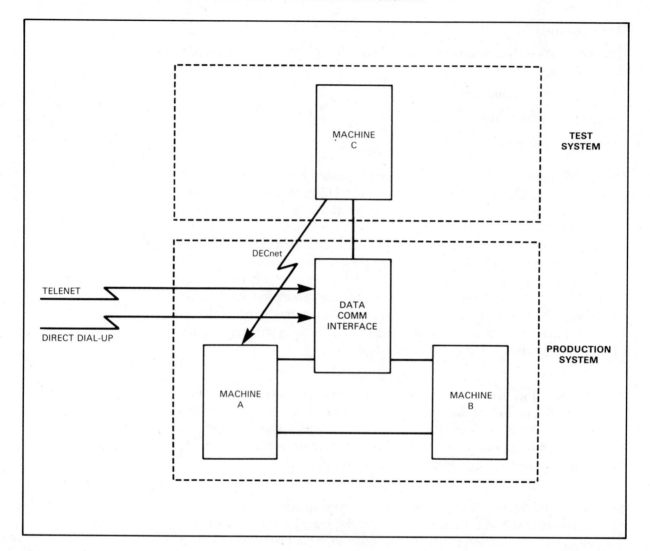

Figure 14-4.

This diagram shows the hardware configuration of the computer system that was penetrated by the 414s, as described in the case study.

Sequence of Break-in Events

The following sequence of events describes how the initial penetration was detected, as well as what steps were taken by the internal audit function to identify the perpetrators and their methods.

1. In late June of 1983, during their pre-implementation review of the new system controls, the internal auditors were informed that there had been a problem with the test system (Machine C) over the previous weekend. System logs showed a high level of activity. At one point, the system had been crashed and brought up from an external source via Telenet. After

further investigation, the internal auditors determined that the penetration had been initiated from an external location. Because the penetration had been initiated by telephone dial-up from outside the company, the investigators suspected that it was the work of a "hacker." The situation became increasingly suspicious when it was learned that this anonymous user was searching for a program called EXECUTIVE PAYROLL.

2. The company then contacted security officers at Telenet, who indicated that they were experiencing problems from hackers in the Milwaukee area. The FBI also was notified but was slow to respond because of a jurisdictional question; at this point, there was no clear evidence that the penetration involved interstate activity. Such evidence would be needed to draw federal authorities into the case. After notifying the authorities, company investigators issued a message via Telenet requesting the person who had crashed and re-booted the system to contact them. A call was received from an individual in New York who said he had done it. Investigators at the company surmised that this person was associated with the 414s.

3. Penetrations continued as hackers presumably attempted to "explore" the system. The hackers then advanced from the test system to the production system (Machines A and B) through the DECNet communication link. In this manner, they were able to disable the job accounting system. This action obliterated the audit trail of computer usage.

4. At this point, the company "pulled the plug." All external access—from DECNet, Telenet, and direct dial-up—was disabled. Data from the company's overseas operations were transmitted verbally over the telephone and recorded manually. The company then installed another VAX machine as an attractive target for the perpetrators. The new machine, which was isolated from other DP operations, contained copies of some programs, data files, and computer games. The machine was equipped for external access through Telenet and direct dial-up, and access was monitored with a data scope that recorded all transmissions over the connecting lines. This machine was operational for approximately two weeks.

5. During this time, the hackers penetrated the target system and used it to play games. They also made copies of some files and renamed them. Based on this pattern of usage, the company concluded that the perpetrators were minors whose primary motive was their own amusement.

6. Having determined the nature of the abuse, the company took down the target machine.

7. In subsequent discussions with company investigators, FBI agents indicated that they were investigating hackers from the Milwaukee area who were minors. These hackers knew the local Telenet number and apparently tried random telephone numbers until they obtained a computer dial-tone. The FBI did not believe that the hackers knew the identity or the nature of the systems they had penetrated. The systems they were able to access had been installed recently and still contained vendor-supplied user identifications and passwords such as SYSTEM/SYSTEM and TEST/TEST. The FBI believed that these were the access codes used to penetrate the computer systems.

The Outcome

As company investigators assessed the damage, they realized that they had been relatively fortunate. To the best of their knowledge, they had lost no data, nor were any programs damaged permanently. As a result of the incident, the total cost for auditing, data security, and systems personnel, as well as for computer time, was estimated at $50,000.

In response to the computer break-in, the company has enhanced significantly its entire password security system for the VAX computer. Also, the link between the production and test machines has been eliminated. The company systems now include a security feature that logs-off, or disconnects, any individual making repeated, unauthorized access attempts. As a further security measure, randomly generated passwords now are issued by the security officer, instead of by systems programmers. Dial-up access also is subject to new restrictions.

A factor that may have contributed to the break-in in this case is the popularity of the DEC VAX machine in many university computer facilities. As a result, students are likely to be proficient in the use of VAX operating systems and software. Also, the challenge of trying to "break" the system as part of related research or experimentation often plays a role in such computer abuses.

In summary, the valuable lesson learned by this company, and to be heeded by all computer auditors, is to:

- Determine the risks of unauthorized access to the organization's computer systems and information resources.

- Implement appropriate security measures, such as dial-up controls and password security, to prevent unauthorized access.

As an organization's information resources increasingly are linked to one another—and to the outside world—through telecommunications, the exposures represented in this case become more likely in the absence of adequate controls.

DISCUSSION QUESTIONS

1. What might be an auditor's primary objectives in reviewing a data communication system?

2. What types of wiretapping pose threats to data transfers, and what control measures may be used to counter these threats?

3. What control measures might be seen as providing a minimum level of protection against unauthorized penetration of a data communication network?

4. What specific controls may be applied within networks that link microcomputers to mainframe computer systems?

5. What special audit concerns arise if the auditee's system is interfaced with an outside service bureau?

6. What is the importance of procedural controls in assuring the integrity of systems that encompass outside service bureaus?

7. How are the exposures represented by the 414 break-in case related to the vulnerabilities of system software?

CASE ASSIGNMENT

To apply the concepts presented in this chapter, turn to the case study for WhyMe Corporation in Appendix A and work through Project 4, which deals with the analysis of data communication controls.

IV MANAGEMENT PERSPECTIVE

This last part of the text deals with the techniques and challenges of managing the CIS audit function within an organization. Management concerns include the need to weigh the cost of controls against the monetary value of assets, the responsibility to prevent unauthorized disclosure or use of information resources, and the need to build an internal audit organization and to develop its staff.

Chapter 15 treats computer auditing as an aspect of management science. Quantitative techniques are covered that can be used to analyze, assess, and manage risks.

Crucial issues in assuring the privacy, integrity, and security of computer information systems are covered in Chapter 16. Legal and social issues considered include custody over private, confidential, and proprietary information. Special concerns are raised about the ability to monitor and control the use of microcomputers.

Chapter 17 deals with the challenge of managing an ongoing, autonomous CIS audit function, including development of CIS audit career paths.

The discussion concludes by extrapolating technological trends to possible future impacts on the profession of CIS auditing. A futuristic scenario is presented in Chapter 18 that speculates about the emergence of real-time, on-line, financial reporting systems with embedded audit facilities. More immediate impacts include the widespread use of microcomputers as audit tools.

15 A Systematic Approach to Auditing

ABSTRACT

- Audit programs should be structured to enhance efficiency and loss control.

- Appropriate techniques include weighing the cost of audit efforts against expected benefits. Specifically, quantitative risk assessment (QRA) provides a way of identifying and evaluating threats and vulnerabilities of assets.

- Alternative risk assessment methodologies include audit judgment and intuition, dollar risk assessment using the risk formula, identifying and assigning weights to risk attributes, and use of risk assessment software packages.

- IST/RAMP is an example of a computer software model for quantitative risk assessment.

- A four-step audit risk prioritization scheme encompasses identification of risk dimensions, identification of risk characteristics, analysis of audit risk characteristics, and assessment of audit risk.

- The first of two case studies covers the General Risk Analysis (GRA) model used by the internal audit function at the Federal Home Loan Mortgage Corporation.

- A second case study describes a methodology in use at Los Alamos National Laboratory for conducting vulnerability analyses of computer systems that fall under the supervision of the Nuclear Regulatory Commission.

IMPACTS OF CIS AUDITS

During computer audits, auditors review controls and safeguards, and also make recommendations for corrective actions. The auditors probably feel that the amounts spent on these efforts are too low. CIS managers, on the other hand, probably feel that the expenditures are too high.

A legitimate question, therefore, is: What is the optimum amount of expenditure for CIS audits? The answer to this question first must involve the recognition that audits generally have two meaningful targets:

- Compliance with regulations
- Efficiency and loss control.

Compliance with Regulations

An organization may be required by law or regulation to conduct audits. If this were the only function of audits, an organization would want to spend the minimum amount required to satisfy the regulations. However, the importance of having adequate controls means that there must be more to auditing than merely assuring compliance with regulations.

Efficiency and Loss Control

The broader mission of the audit function is to have a favorable influence on efficiency and loss control. A well-conducted audit of a significant part of operations can uncover inefficiencies, material exposures to loss, and—in some cases—evidence of actual losses. Typically, an audit report will present observations, findings and conclusions, and will recommend corrective actions.

This chapter focuses on this second topic, the enhancement of efficiency and loss control. In doing so, the discussion also considers the structuring of an audit program to achieve favorable results.

THE COSTS AND BENEFITS OF AUDITING

The audit process itself requires technical knowledge and adherence to high professional standards. The management of audit activities, however, is neither primarily technical nor subject to professional audit standards. Management of an audit examination involves the selection of the functions to be audited and the frequency of those audits. Once compliance requirements have been satisfied, the determination of which audit recommendations to adopt is entirely a management decision to be based on weighing costs and benefits.

The issue to resolve is: How should the audit examination be structured to result in a net improvement in operations? Neither the audit program itself nor adoption of the resulting recommendations can be considered apart from their costs. Regardless of the scope of the current audit program or the level of controls or safeguards already in place, organization management has the responsibility to decide what level of expenditure is appropriate. The key management issue, then, can be stated as follows:

> Which audit program and which recommendations will be optimum for the organization?

A level of expenditure that is too high will be needlessly expensive and inefficient. A level that is too low could result in dangerously inadequate controls over valuable assets.

In some situations, relatively low-cost audit activities, controls, and safeguards may be entirely appropriate. Formal justification may not be necessary. However, if the costs are significant—and if the benefits are not obvious—a formal selection process is needed.

Elements of Quantitative Risk Assessment

The process of identifying risks and their characteristics is called *risk analysis*. Once specific risks and their characteristics are known, the extent of exposure is determined through *risk assessment*. An approach that yields monetary values for exposures is *quantitative risk assessment (QRA)*.

QRA may be used as a basis for selecting controls and security measures. This approach involves constructing an accurate model of risk with which to estimate future losses. Such a model has three basic elements:

- Threats
- Assets
- Vulnerabilities.

Threats.   In this context, threats are events that can trigger losses.

Assets.   For purposes of quantitative risk assessment, assets are the sources of loss.

Vulnerabilities.   Vulnerabilities are the connecting links between threats and assets.

Estimates for each of these elements are input to the risk model. The results show what reasonably can be expected if the estimates prove to be correct.

A manager then can compare the estimate of loss under existing conditions with an estimate based on implementing the recommended controls. The difference between the levels of loss is the estimated payback of the controls. To justify the expenditure, this payback should compare favorably with the cost of the controls. Managers need and want this sort of analysis to guide their resource allocation decisions.

RISK ASSESSMENT AND RISK MANAGEMENT

Risk assessment (RA) is the cornerstone of the CIS *risk management (RM)* process for computer centers and applications. RA can be used to estimate residual risk to operational systems, but it is most useful when applied prior to the definition of requirements within the systems development life cycle. Conducting RA at this point in the life cycle permits the resulting estimates of potential loss to be used to define computer security requirements for the system being developed. Within the design and implementation phases, RA also can form the basis for cost/benefit analysis in the selection of specific safeguards.

The risk management process has all of the above aspects, but extends the process to encompass:

- Threats and frequencies of threats

- Targets, resources, and assets (of a threat)

- Vulnerabilities (to a threat)

- Outcome or consequence (of a threat)

- Frequency of an outcome (how often)

- Impact of an outcome (financial loss, delay, loss of life, etc.)

- Risk and estimate of potential loss

- Safeguards (to protect, detect, or mitigate)

- Cost of safeguards

- Cost/benefit analysis

- Subset of safeguards to be implemented.

Risk assessment methodologies are systematic approaches applied by auditors in evaluating the *audit risk* within a CIS. An audit risk is the probable unfavorable monetary effect associated with the occurrence of an undesirable event. Recall that the occurrence or condition of potential occurrence of such an event is known as an exposure (Chapter 12). Thus, an audit risk makes a monetary evaluation of a particular exposure or cause of exposure.

The process of assessing the audit risk evaluates that exposure's potential impact within the overall system. Audit risk evaluation serves two purposes:

- Determines the need for and amount of audit resources that should be assigned to a CIS under development

- Points the auditor toward those system characteristics most susceptible to vulnerabilities.

Auditors traditionally use audit risk analysis and risk assessment methodologies to identify areas for investigation and to allocate audit resources. Approaches to audit risk assessment vary in perspective from one organization to another. However, audit risk assessment within an organization usually makes a predictable progression through four distinct phases. A given audit group may be using any of these approaches. The approaches include:

- Audit judgment and intuition

- Dollar risk estimation using the risk formula

- Identifying and weighting risk attributes

- Use of risk assessment software packages.

Approach 1: Audit Judgment and Intuition

The use of intuitive, professional judgment has been—and still is—the most prominently used method of audit risk assessment. Under this approach, the auditor calls upon his or her personal, professional experience. This experience base is combined with other learning experiences and a knowledge of the subject organization's mission and external mandates.

With this combined background, the auditor attempts to draw parallels to the CIS under review. That is, the auditor tries to associate the CIS under review with past experience and knowledge to determine comparable characteristics. The objective is to estimate the magnitude of the audit risk and to select specific system characteristics for investigation. Although this method can be effective, it is not a transferable skill. Rather, intuitive judgment is acquired through years of experience and is unique to each practitioner.

Figure 15-1 shows a table in which microcomputer-related causes of exposure are rated intuitively. For each cause of exposure and system configuration, the auditor has rated the level of risk as high (H), moderate (M), low (L), or not applicable (N/A).

Microcomputer Risk Assessment

H = High, M = Moderate, L = Low, N/A = Not Applicable

CAUSES OF EXPOSURE	STAND-ALONE	MULTI-USER	MICRO/MAINFRAME
I. GENERAL			
A. Unsophisticated Users	H	M	M
B. Sophisticated Users	L	M	H
C. Undocumented Systems	H	H	M
D. Informal Policies/Practices			
Acquisition of Microcomputers	H	N/A	N/A
Use of Microcomputers	H	H	H
E. Informal Maintenance Agreements	L	M	M
II. PHYSICAL CONTROLS			
A. Accessibility to Unauthorized Personnel (Lack of physical locks, covers, cabinets, etc.)	H	M	M
B. Uncontrolled Access to Storage Media (diskettes)	H	M	M
C. Unauthorized Removal of Micro Resources From Company Premises	H	L	L
D. Inability to Differentiate Company-Owned and Individual Microcomputing Resources	H	L	M
E. Damage to Hardware (I/O Devices, Internal Boards)	H	H	M
F. Use of Company Resources for Non-Company Use	H	M	L
III. ENVIRONMENTAL CONTROLS			
A. Inadequate Fire Suppression Equipment	L	M	M
B. Lack of Electrical Line Filters, Surge Suppressors	L	M	M
C. Potential Water Damage	L	L	L
D. Inadequate Temperature, Humidity and Air Filtering Systems	L	M	M
E. Uncontrolled Static Electricity	L	M	M
IV. DATA SECURITY			
A. Accidental or Intentional Unauthorized Use, Destruction, Alteration of Company Data	M	H	H
B. Unauthorized Access to Company Data	L	M	H
C. Misuse of Company Data for Personal Use	H	H	H
D. Unauthorized Distribution of Confidential Data	M	M	H
E. Lost Data Due to Inadequate Backup/Recovery Procedures	H	H	L
F. Inadequate Audit Trails	H	M	H
G. Unreliable Data Integrity	H	M	M

Figure 15-1. *In this matrix, degrees of risk are assessed for standalone, multi-user, and microcomputer/mainframe systems. Ratings correspond with the auditor's professional judgment about the degree of exposure within each of the areas shown.*

Approach 2: Dollar Risk Estimation
Using the Risk Formula

Recall that risk is defined as the probability of loss. The probability, or risk, can be expressed as a formula:

Frequency of occurrence times loss per occurrence equals annualized loss expectancy.

The term *frequency of occurrence* refers to the frequency with which a particular vulnerability (flaw in the system) may combine with a possible threat (a human or natural exploitation of the vulnerability). Another term for frequency of occurrence is *occurrence rate*. The term *loss per occurrence* thus is the negative impact of the pairing of a threat and a vulnerability. The average dollar value of losses per year is the *annualized loss expectancy (ALE)*. Thus, audit risk based on this formula can be expressed in monetary terms. Using the risk formula to project monetary loss can have the advantage of presenting results in terms readily understandable by nontechnicians.

As mentioned in Chapter 3 within the discussion of federal standards, the National Bureau of Standards (NBS) published Federal Information Processing Standard 65 (FIPS 65), which described a quantitative method for performing risk assessment. This method was not promulgated as an official NBS standard, but was regarded as a suggested approach. The method, however, does not specify a comprehensive approach for dealing with a wide range of causes of exposure. Thus, the method described in FIPS 65 would not be applicable throughout a more comprehensive RM process. (A typical range of causes of exposure encompassed by RM is shown in Figure 15-1.)

FIPS 65 does describe how an estimate of risk, or annualized loss expectancy, can be obtained for each application data file. To implement this approach, estimates are input to the risk formula. For each application data file, the auditor must:

- Estimate the frequency of occurrence of events that could result in the destruction, modification, disclosure or unavailability of the data file. These estimates are possible outcomes.

- Estimate the loss per occurrence—the potential impact, in dollars, of each outcome.

Historically, there has been a lack of empirical data on the frequency of occurrence of events and their related impacts. Recognizing this, the drafters of FIPS 65 suggested an "order of magnitude" approach to estimation. That is, estimates are deemed to be accurate within a factor of 10. However, some practitioners have tended to ignore the possible variances in such estimates.

Input data to the method described in FIPS 65 should not be regarded as precise, nor should the results be considered exact.

In the years following the publication of FIPS 65, NBS searched for a candidate Risk Management Standard. It was concluded that, in view of the available methods and approaches, no single method or combination of methods was appropriate. The reasons for not settling on a candidate approach for RM included the following:

- Alternatives were either not developed fully or not in wide use. Some methods were still in experimental stages.

- The human interfaces of the available approaches left much to be desired. Typically, data entry and report generation were inadequate.

- RM concepts and terms in the approaches examined were addressed in varying degrees of detail or incompletely.

At this writing, use of the risk formula calls for projecting risks in dollars, based on the method described in FIPS 65. However, the formula has the effect of multiplying the inaccuracies in each of the component factors. That is, the result only can be regarded as accurate within a factor of 100. Because it is so difficult to estimate frequency of occurrence and loss per occurrence, the reliability of the formula hinges on the estimates. A pitfall is that using a formula that yields a specific dollar figure can imply a higher degree of precision than is realistic.

Approach 3: Identifying and Weighting Risk Attributes

Many of the attributes that cause exposure have been identified. Relationships among these attributes can be specified through weighting. Under this third approach, an auditor can determine which of the attributes are present in the CIS under review. The auditor then assigns a numeric weight, or score, to each attribute. The basis of this assignment can be intuitive, or statistical analysis techniques may be used. Based on the accumulation of scores, the auditor can rank CIS applications according to relative audit risk.

Approach 4: Use of Risk Assessment Software Packages

The second and third approaches described above have been implemented as software packages that are available from commercial vendors. For example, a package for calculating dollar risk has been marketed by Pansophic as PANRISK®. A package that applies the attributes method to project risk is ESTIMACS® from Management and Computer Services.

The major advantages of these automated approaches are ease of use and opportunity to try "What if?" strategies. Such computerized tools permit the variation of one or more of the risk characteristics for execution of multiple computations with minimal effort. Other such packages are discussed later in this chapter.

Evaluation of Approaches

There is no ideal audit risk assessment method. No current approach can guarantee the completely correct prediction of audit risk. However, approaches 2, 3, and 4 represent transferrable skills. Also, because they have been formalized, the performance of these methods can be evaluated.

One characteristic that appears to be extremely important is ease of use. The more difficult a method is to use, the less likely it becomes that an auditor will apply it. Lacking a convenient, structured method, the auditor will revert to approach 1 and rely on intuition and judgment.

QUANTITATIVE RISK ASSESSMENT MODEL: IST/RAMP

A number of risk assessment models have been constructed during the past few years. Some do not produce quantitative results, and thus cannot support cost/benefit analysis. Other models generate security recommendations by correlating responses input to a security checklist. However, these models do not attempt to evaluate the monetary impacts of potential losses.

One quantitative model is called IST/RAMP. This computerized package has been in use for several years at more than 40 sites in the United States and Canada. This field use, combined with independent evaluations, has validated IST/RAMP as a practical quantitative risk assessment tool.

Underlying Concepts

Every organization can expect to experience losses: many small ones, occasionally a moderate loss, and at longer intervals, large losses. This irregular stream of future losses often is referred to as *expected loss.* If the expected loss is expressed at an average rate (in dollars per year, for example) the term *annualized loss expectancy (ALE)* is used. The process of quantitative risk assessment estimates ALE two ways:

- On an "as-is" basis for the system being assessed

- Under the assumption that security recommendations for the system have been adopted.

The difference between these two estimates is the anticipated *reduction in future losses.* The difference also can be used as a measure of the benefit of the security recommendations.

Risk losses result from the impact of threat events on the assets and operations of the organization. For the purposes of risk assessment, each asset is characterized by the worst-case loss that can be triggered by a corresponding threat to the asset. This value is called the *loss potential* of the asset. To determine loss potential, the auditor asks:

- If the threat occurred and impacted the asset, how would the organization respond?
- What would that response cost?

These are key questions. The critical issue is how the audit and security program can affect future costs. For example, the loss potential of a database is not influenced in any way by the cost of assembling the data. That is, this historical cost cannot be affected by a future security program. Rather, the only loss potential that has meaning to the audit and security program is a future loss that can be prevented or mitigated.

Recall that each threat is characterized by its occurrence rate, or the number of times it reasonably can be expected to occur over some future period. Each threat-asset pair is characterized further by a *vulnerability factor*. The vulnerability factor is the ratio of the actual loss from a single occurrence to the total loss potential of the asset. That is, the impact of a threat on an asset is apt to be something less than a worst-case loss. Thus, the vulnerability factor is a number between 0.0 and 1.0.

The ALE resulting from the impact of a threat on an asset is given by:

Occurrence Rate × Loss Potential × Vulnerability Factor = ALE

The total ALE for the organization is the sum of individual ALEs for specific pairs of threats and assets. Basing the ALE estimate on these three factors is an important element of the IST/RAMP model. Separating each of these factors makes it easier to define each one and to evaluate it independently of the other two.

Classification of Threats and Losses

The IST/RAMP model can describe five different kinds of losses:

- Delay losses experienced by end users and resulting from service interruptions
- Fraud resulting from manipulation of processing systems (both manual and automated)
- Unauthorized disclosure of information

- Physical theft of property
- Physical damage to property.

IST/RAMP software permits the auditor to define as many as 59 delay-damage threats. This comparatively detailed classification of threats is highly useful because it parallels actual experience. As a result, the determination of loss potential is relatively straightforward; and occurrence rates can be easy to estimate. With such a breakdown, the auditor can cite specific circumstances to frame such questions as: How will we respond? How much will it cost?

Other models use more abstract loss classifications. Also, other approaches tend to combine the factors of vulnerability and loss potential into a single quantity, as in the risk formula described above in connection with FIPS 65.

For example, consider the analysis of the sabotage of a computer system's direct-access hardware. For such a threat, IST/RAMP evaluates two different losses:

- The service interruption, or delay, loss resulting from the need to repair or replace the hardware
- The loss due to physical damage.

Remember that there is absolutely no connection between these two types of loss. The loss from service interruption depends solely on the time urgency of the processing tasks. The physical damage depends solely on the repair/replacement cost of the sabotaged hardware. If there were no back-up files, the replacement cost also would have to include the cost of re-encoding the lost files. In separating these two types of loss, IST/RAMP makes it much easier for the auditor to develop the needed input data.

Features and Advantages of the Model

IST/RAMP is fully computerized, and, therefore, accurate algorithms may be applied for each of the five loss models. For example, consider a situation in which two processing systems have the same delay loss potential; but, one system runs daily and the other runs monthly. The monthly system will have a much lower ALE, since it will be unaffected by most service interruptions. IST/RAMP uses numerical integration to take this effect of scheduling into account. Computerization of the methodology has several other important benefits stemming from:

- Iteration

- Input validation
- Evaluation of alternatives
- Flexibility.

Iteration. Initially, the auditor can use approximate, quickly gathered input data. Preliminary results then can show the auditor how to refine the parameters being used and the type of data being input for the assessment process.

Input validation. IST/RAMP includes features that help the auditor validate the reasonableness and completeness of inputs.

Evaluation of alternatives. With such a fully automated model, "What if?" questions can be posed readily.

Flexibility. With this package, there is no need to freeze the analysis prematurely. Changes, particularly in response to questions from senior management, can be made right up to the last moment. This feature in particular leads to acceptance of the results as a reasonable basis for management action, the ultimate goal of every QRA project.

Reliability of Estimation

Critics of QRA have noted that it may be difficult to estimate the occurrence rates of some threats, particularly of relatively rare threats. This is true, but it does not mean that QRA is of no value. Rather, the results of QRA must be interpreted with an understanding of the reliability of estimation.

The *single occurrence loss (SOL)* that a threat causes depends solely on asset loss potential and vulnerability factors, both of which usually can be estimated with high reliability. Thus, for a given threat, it is possible to have both an unreliable estimate for ALE and a reliable estimate for SOL.

To deal with possible variances in reliability of estimates, the auditor should classify the results of QRA into three groups:

- Low ALE with low SOL
- Unreliable ALE with high SOL
- High ALE based on a reliable estimate of occurrence rate.

Low ALE and low SOL. If both ALE and SOL are estimated to be well below the level of materiality, the corresponding threats can be disregarded safely.

Unreliable ALE with high SOL.   In such cases, the SOL is estimated to be material, but it is not possible to develop a reliable estimate of the occurrence rate. If the SOL is material, senior management must determine how much risk is acceptable without the support of a reliable cost/benefit study.

High ALE based on a reliable estimate of occurrence rate.   For threats in this category, the ALE is estimated to be material; the estimate of the occurrence rate can be considered reliable, or is credible. Controls for these threats can be selected by analyzing the *return on investment (ROI)*, as described below.

Analyzing Return on Investment from Controls

The auditor can select (or reject) controls for the third group of threats (high ALE, reliably estimated) by projecting the reduction in ALE that each control can be expected to yield over its useful life.

The ALE reduction from a given control or security measure can be thought of as a stream of future "payments," which are received as long as the control or security measure is in place. Of course, the organization does not actually receive a steady stream of benefit payments. Instead, each time an adopted security measure averts or decreases a loss, the organization receives a benefit. The assumption in QRA is that the estimate of ALE for a modified system is a reasonable approximation of this irregular stream of benefits. The greater the number of threats included in the analysis, the more valid this assumption will be.

Cost/benefit analysis may be applied to project the return on investment from a proposed set of controls. This analysis compares the *present cost* of a control with its *present value*. The present cost of a control or security measure is defined as the cost to install it, plus the present cost of the future stream of maintenance and operating costs, minus the present value of any salvage value at the end of its useful life. The ROI is the ratio of the present value to the present cost.

The relationships are represented in the following formulas, in which PV stands for present value, and PC for present cost. (All values must be expressed in present dollars.)

PV of Security Measure = ALE Reduction

PC of Security Measure = Cost to install + Cost to maintain − Salvage value

$$\text{ROI of Security Measure} = \frac{\text{ALE Reduction}}{\text{PC of Security Measure}} \times 100 - 100\%$$

Generally, values for ROI will fall into three ranges. Assuming the cost of money to be 12 percent, the point estimates and recommendations for each are:

ROI = -95%. Payback in this range is uneconomical. The proposed security measures should not be implemented.

ROI = +85%. An ROI in this range is extremely attractive. The proposed security measures should be implemented as soon as possible.

ROI = +15%. Results in this range are of marginal value. The estimates involved in the analysis should be reviewed carefully before any decisions are made.

Individual controls or security measures cannot be guaranteed to yield the forecasted ROI. However, collectively and over the long term, the projected ALE reduction will be realized if the input data prove to be accurate projections. Since the future never can be known with certainty, this type of estimation is the best that the auditor can hope to do. If the QRA has been performed carefully and action is taken based on the results, management will have exhibited due care and prudence in addressing risks.

Management of Audits and Selection of Controls

An organization's audit program must be constructed to include a reasonable breadth of coverage. A coordinated approach must assure, for example, that no potential embezzler will be tempted to decide that a target system will never be audited or that inadequate controls will go unnoticed indefinitely. In some cases, there will be additional concerns for life safety. In almost all cases, there must be compliance with applicable regulations.

Once a basic audit program has been established, the key management questions are:

- What systems or aspects of systems should be audited intensively?
- How often should audits be conducted?
- What depth is appropriate for each audit?

QRA can help answer these questions in the following ways:

- The results of QRA will rank the assets and processing systems in descending order of ALE and SOL. All other things being equal, the bigger the ALE and SOL estimates, the more likely it becomes that the audit recommendations can have an impact on operating results. Conversely, if a system appears to be nearly loss-free, there probably is little room for improvement.

- The magnitude of the ALE estimate will suggest a reasonable level of audit effort. For example, it would not be efficient to spend $20,000 to audit a system with an ALE estimate of $5,000 per year.

Audit recommendations sometimes are criticized as lacking cost justification. Managers faced with implementing recommendations of doubtful or unknown utility may feel that the proposed measures have been included solely as a self-protective action by the auditor. However, objections and reluctance can be overcome by projecting ROI based on QRA results. This approach brings quantifiable alternatives into the decision-making process. Auditors and managers alike should understand that the performance of a security measure is not necessarily a valid basis for its selection. Also, the mere assertion that a proposed control will reduce the exposure to fraud is not a meaningful basis for a decision to adopt the control. Apart from life safety and compliance with regulations, the only valid criterion for making a decision is the impact of the control on the financial strength of the organization.

In some situations, senior managers may have to act on incomplete information or to take risks. However, insofar as possible, management wishes to have specific options for consideration, as well as some guidance in choosing among them. Often, auditors forget that managers have little concern for the technical characteristics of proposed audit programs or recommended controls. Rather, a responsible manager wants to know two basic things:

- What are the available options?
- What are the costs and benefits of each option?

These questions apply to all business decisions—not just to setting audit priorities. There is strong reason to believe that lack of meaningful, ROI-supported options—rather than lack of funds—is the most common reason that senior managers cut back on auditing and security budgets. Further, an extremely tight budget provides added motivation for taking a systematic approach to setting audit priorities.

ALLOCATING INTERNAL AUDIT RESOURCES

The internal audit function has limited resources with which to perform its mission. Good audit practices dictate that those resources be assigned to activities that offer the greatest return to the organization.

In 1977, The Institute of Internal Auditors issued a research project report *Systems Auditability and Control.* A major conclusion was that the most fruitful use of internal audit time would be to participate in the systems development process. Based on this research report, the General Accounting Office issued a standard (which in the 1981 revision was changed to a guideline) regarding auditor participation in systems development. Today, there is a general consensus that auditor participation during the systems development life cycle (SDLC) is vital to assuring secure and auditable systems.

As stated above, the internal audit function must work with organization management in setting audit priorities. Major decisions are concerned with which systems (or aspects of systems) are to be audited, at what frequency, and to what depth. To answer these challenges, a scheme of prioritizing audit risks can be used.

AUDIT RISK PRIORITIZATION SCHEME: A CONCEPTUAL APPROACH

An effective *audit risk prioritization scheme* can be composed of the following steps:

1. Identify risk dimensions.

2. Identify risk characteristics.

3. Analyze audit risk characteristics.

4. Assess audit risk.

Step 1: Identify Risk Dimensions

Risk dimensions are factors such as project size, experience with technology, and project structure. The objective of identifying risk dimensions is to categorize audit risk by the *determinant,* or causal factor, for that risk. Audit risk characteristics within a dimension or determinant are more closely related than the characteristics between dimensions. There are some common characteristics among determinants—project size, for example. Identification of risk dimensions provides input for:

- Management of audit risk within the CIS function

- Selection of specific characteristics for investigation by the audit function.

Step 2: Identify Risk Characteristics

Risk characteristics are the attributes of a CIS that are known to create exposures. The presence or absence of these attributes in the system under study can be used to predict system behavior.

An analogy would be predicting the probability of a heart attack by correlating risk characteristics that include an individual's blood pressure, weight, family health history, smoking and dietary habits, and so on. The presence or absence of these characteristics can be used to predict whether a specific person might have a heart attack.

Note that the concept of risk does not necessarily imply that the undesirable event actually will occur. Rather, the aggregate effect of all the risk characteristics is a quantifiable probability of occurrence. One of the objectives of an audit risk prioritization scheme is to derive a numeric value for this probability.

Step 3: Analyze Audit Risk Characteristics

For each identified audit risk characteristic, analysis is performed by measuring:

- Degree of importance
- Applicability to systems under study.

Degree of importance.   In making this measurement, the auditor must determine the degree of importance of each characteristic in representing the magnitude of audit risk. This analysis assigns weights to characteristics among the population of characteristics.

Applicability to systems under study.   For this measurement, the auditor must determine the applicability of a given characteristic to a specific CIS being assessed. The objective is to determine whether the characteristic is present or absent in a manner that could cause an unfavorable event to occur. For example, if an individual is overweight, a risk characteristic is present for heart attack.

The approaches used for measuring applicability of a given characteristic include:

- Relational considerations
- Factors relating to risk
- Dollar risk
- Audit analysis
- Regression analysis.

Relational considerations.   Under this approach, the auditor divides application systems into three risk categories: high, medium, and low. Then the auditor determines which category applies to the specific system under study.

For example, a National Bureau of Standards study has shown that the difficulty of implementation increases with the size of computer programs. In choosing a relational perspective, the auditor would determine how the size of the program for the system being assessed compares with the other systems in the CIS department. In terms of size, the program will be relatively large, average, or relatively small. Programs that fall into the largest third as compared with other programs would be considered to have the highest audit risk.

Factors relating to risk.   This approach attempts to relate specific factors to an expected outcome. That is, the auditor tries to determine which factors apply to the system being assessed. Risk factors would be apparent as the absence of specific controls or safeguards. The greater the number of risk factors, the higher the degree of overall audit risk.

For example, a risk characteristic would be the presence or absence of data validation controls. Low risk might be indicated by the presence of extensive data validation measures, including range checking, alphabetic tests, check digit verification, and relationship tests. A high-risk system might apply only alphanumeric tests.

Dollar risk.   The dollar value associated with each risk characteristic can be used to determine the magnitude of risk for that characteristic. Recall that this dollar risk, or annual loss exposure, can be calculated from the risk formula by multiplying frequency of occurrence by loss (in dollars) per occurrence.

Audit analysis.   Audit analysis requires the auditor to conduct sufficient study to determine potential vulnerability. The most common approach is an assessment of the system of internal controls to identify vulnerabilities associated with the characteristic in question. Again, if the characteristic were data validation, audit review could determine the effectiveness of the data validation controls in reducing the specific audit risks known to be reducible by such controls.

Regression analysis.   Over a period of time, the audit group can record system characteristics and actual operational behavior. Regression analysis can correlate information about risk characteristics with actual performance.

Although this approach is highly reliable statistically, the process of collecting actual performance data is both time-consuming and costly.

Of the approaches presented above, audit practitioners tend to favor the first two—applying relational considerations and identifying risk factors.

Step 4: Assess Audit Risk

The objective of the audit risk prioritization scheme is to assist the internal auditor in using limited resources effectively. The last step in the process is to interpret and apply the risk assessment that results from the first three steps.

As noted above, an audit risk prioritization scheme can be used by both CIS and audit personnel. CIS managers and professionals can use the scheme to identify attributes that may cause a system to be unsuccessful. With this information, developmental approaches may be changed to manage the risks.

Auditors can use the scheme to identify audit risk characteristics for a given system, as well as the magnitude or degree of applicability of those characteristics. This information can help the auditor to:

- Develop an audit risk score.

- Create an audit risk profile.

- Modify the characteristics contributing to audit risk.

- Allocate audit resources.

- Build a database of risk characteristics.

Develop an audit risk score. An *audit risk score* is the sum of assigned point values corresponding with the magnitude of risk for each identified characteristic. The most common scoring method is to divide a risk characteristic into specific subcategories, as shown in the data validation example above. For example, if the application being assessed falls into the high-risk category, it would be assigned three points. Applications in the medium-risk category would receive two points. Low-risk applications would be assigned one point.

If a more sophisticated scoring method is wanted, individual characteristics can be weighted. For example, one characteristic can be considered to be twice as important as another. Thus, the score for that characteristic would be multiplied by two to yield its weighted value. The resulting audit risk score for the application normally is compared with other scores developed for the same CIS department. Thus, risk scoring is used primarily to determine relative risks among applications. That is, a single score has no meaning by itself and should not be regarded as an absolute measurement.

Create an audit risk profile. An *audit risk profile* is a graphic representation of the different risk characteristics measured. By contrast, an audit risk score is a summary of risk for an entire CIS. A risk profile shows the relations among component risk characteristics. That is, the profile shows what characteristics contribute to the total audit risk, and in what proportion.

Modify the characteristics contributing to audit risk.   Both the auditor and the systems analyst can use the audit risk prioritization scheme to identify those characteristics that might cause a CIS to be less successful than proposed. For example, if key members of the systems development project team do not understand the computer technology being used, potential misunderstandings become a risk characteristic; a successful system thus is less likely. Once the characteristics that could cause the system to be less successful than desired are known, those characteristics can be altered to maximize the probability of success. If, for example, project personnel do not understand the proposed technology, a more familiar technology might be substituted to increase the probability of success.

Allocate audit resources.   The information gathered during audit risk analysis can be used as a basis for allocating audit resources. Priorties can be derived for auditors to review application systems and/or to review specific aspects of those systems. For example, high-risk applications might receive extensive review. Medium-risk applications would get cursory review, and low-risk applications would need no review. Further, for those systems reviewed, the specific area of review can be selected based on high-risk characteristics. For example, if computer technology is a high-risk characteristic, the auditors may want to determine whether the project team understands the technology and is applying it effectively.

Build a database of risk characteristics.   The information gathered during the audit risk prioritization process should be saved and used for two purposes. Under this approach, internal auditors can:

- Improve the audit risk prioritization scheme to make it more predictive of audit risk.

- Assist CIS management in structuring and planning projects to maximize the probability of success.

CASE STUDY 1: AUTOMATED GRA AT FEDERAL HOME LOAN MORTGAGE CORPORATION

The internal audit function of the Federal Home Loan Mortgage Corporation has developed a methodology called General Risk Analysis (GRA). The GRA process involves the prioritization of operational and financial risk. The results of the GRA process are used to prepare the annual audit plan for the internal audit department.

The method of collecting data for the GRA is through interviews with corporate managers and the board of directors. Audit management develops a questionnaire that is followed by each auditor throughout the interview process. The results of all the interviews then are correlated to help audit management ascertain the risks at the Federal Home Loan Mortgage Corporation. Under the GRA, the identified risks are evaluated; an audit priority is assigned to each risk.

The GRA methodology has been implemented as a microcomputer software package. Data are entered systematically into the microcomputer, which performs the calculation and prioritization functions.

Description

The two major components in the internal audit department's GRA calculations are:

- Specific risk (SR)
- Pervasive risk (PR).

Specific risk (SR). *Specific risks (SR)* are identified for each activity or audit entity. This is done during the GRA interviews and the review of appropriate work papers. Examples of specific risks include:

- Improper authorization
- Inefficient operation
- Loss of income.

The automated system will accept up to three specific risks per activity/ audit entity. Audit management assigns each SR a rating of from 1 to 10. A rating of 1 or 2 is very low and 10 is very high. For each activity, the auditor then ranks the three identified risks in order of significance. The SR of highest significance is assigned a weight of 2. The second highest SR receives a weight of 1.5. The lowest SR in the ranking is assigned a weight of 1.

For example, specific risks identified for a given activity might be loss of income, lack of management control, and inefficient operation. Audit management might assign ratings of 8, 6, and 2, respectively. The auditor places them in the order highest (Risk 1), second highest (Risk 2), and lowest risk (Risk 3). This ranking corresponds with weights of 2, 1.5, and 1. For each SR, its rating then is multiplied by its weight. The calculation is:

$$2(8) \ + \ 1.5(6) \ + \ 1(2) \ = \ 27$$

The formula for this calculation is shown in Figure 15-2.

Figure 15-2.

Within the GRA model, this formula may be used to calculate a specific risk (SR) rating.

Specific Risk Rating $= 2(\text{Risk } 1) + 1.5(\text{Risk } 2) + 1(\text{Risk } 3)$

Pervasive risk (PR).   Within the GRA methodology, *pervasive risk (PR)* encompasses general risks that apply to all corporate activities. In turn, there are five subcomponents of PR:

- Performance sensitivity (PS)
- General integrity (GI)
- Security impact (SI)
- Audit interval (AI)
- Audit comfort (AC).

The above subcomponents represent operational and financial risks that are assessed for each systems activity. These subcomponents are described and discussed in the following sections. Each subcomponent is assigned a rating from 1 to 10. A rating of 10 means that the likelihood of an adverse impact on the corporation is very high, or that the results of an impact would be very serious. A rating of 1 indicates that the likelihood of an adverse impact is very low, or that the results of an impact would be minimal.

The calculation of pervasive risk from these subcomponents is shown in Figure 15-3.

Performance Sensitivity

Performance sensitivity (PS) will consist of any one of five elements:

- Liquidity
- Relative materiality index (RMI)
- Susceptibility to misappropriation or loss
- Dollar volume
- Type of system.

PERVASIVE RISK $= (PS \times GI) + 0.7(SI \times AI) + AC$

PS = Performance Sensitivity
GI = General Integrity
SI = Security Impact
AI = Audit Interval
AC = Audit Comfort

Figure 15-3.

This formula may be used to calculate pervasive risk (PR) under the General Risk Assessment (GRA) model.

Liquidity. *Liquidity* is a measure of the speed with which an asset can be put to use for an unauthorized purpose. There are two factors in determining liquidity:

• Speed with which the asset can be converted into cash

• Usefulness of the asset to an individual or organization to gain unfair competitive advantage.

To quantify these factors for input to the model, weights are assigned that correspond with predetermined time frames. A table of weights and time frames is presented in Figure 15-4.

Relative materiality index (RMI). The *relative materiality index,* or *RMI,* is a way of indicating the significance of an activity/cycle in relation to overall corporate performance. An example would be the relationship between the budget for a single department as compared with the total corporate budget. To develop inputs to the model, the auditor would determine the ranking of a department's budget based on its percentage of the overall budget. The largest relative budget would be rated as 10, and the smallest would be rated as 1.

Susceptibility to misappropriation or loss. The *susceptibility to misappropriation or loss* is a measure of loss potential by area of activity. For example, an account with a small dollar balance would have a low risk, and a large dollar balance would have a high risk. Or, if no fraud or loss has been detected, the risk is low; an area that has a history of fraud or loss would have a high risk.

In evaluating the level of risk for susceptibility to misappropriation, the following factors should be considered:

• Work in progress, account activity, interdepartmental differences, and bank reconciliation exception activity

WEIGHT	LIQUIDITY	TIME FRAME
10	Immediate conversion	24 hours or less
8	Rapid conversion	Within one week
6	Moderate conversion speed	Within one month
4	Slow to convert	Within one year
2	Very difficult to convert	One year or more

- Potential for fraud or prior fraudulent activity
- Extent of litigation that the area has been or is involved in
- Liquidity and negotiability of assets, funds, or value
- Percentage of jobs in the area classified as high risk or medium risk.

Dollar volume.   Another factor in performance sensitivity is the *dollar volume* of all transactions processed on an average day. Weights and ranges for this factor are shown in Figure 15-5. As shown in the table, weights also are assigned to average closing balances for the general ledger. In applying the procedure for determining dollar volume, the auditor must assess the impact of a loss or failure within each area or activity.

Type of system.   *Type of system* is a set of categories that are used to indicate in which systems, historically, the greatest chance of fraud exists. This determination, however, does not imply that any one type of system is more important than another.

Within the GRA model, a system falls into one of the following categories:

- Financial system
- Feeder system
- Management information system
- Information system.

Financial system.   A *financial system* is defined as a CIS that either creates the company's financial records or posts information directly to those records.

Feeder system.   A *feeder system* is a CIS that supplies information to financial systems but is not connected directly to the company's financial records.

DAILY TRANSACTION VOLUME:

AMOUNT (DOLLARS)	RISK	WEIGHT
Over 1,000,000,000	Very High	10
250,000,001 - 1,000,000,000	High	8
50,000,001 - 250,000,000	Moderate	6
5,000,001 - 50,000,000	Low	4
less than 5,000,000	Very Low	2

AVERAGE CLOSING BALANCES OF GENERAL LEDGER:

AMOUNT (DOLLARS)	RISK	WEIGHT
Over 10,000,000,000	Very High	10
5,000,000,001 - 10,000,000,000	High	8
1,000,000,001 - 5,000,000,000	Moderate	6
50,000,001 - 1,000,000,000	Low	4
less than 50,000,000	Very Low	2

Figure 15-5.

These tables give weights for daily transaction volume and for dollar volume, which become inputs to the GRA model.

Management information system. In this context, a *management information system* is a CIS that supplies information for the use of the company as a whole.

Information system. For purposes of the GRA model, an *information system* is a CIS that supplies information for use by a department, branch, or function.

Ratings assigned to each type of system for purposes of input to the GRA model are shown in Figure 15-6.

General Integrity

General integrity (GI) is a factor that measures the overall environment of integrity, as well as the general attitude within the organization toward security and internal controls. Appropriate elements to be assessed are:

- Management commitment to controls
- Knowledge, skill, experience, and length of time on the job of key personnel
- Complexity of the organization and extent of personnel changes

Figure 15-6.

The type of system is another factor that must be assigned a weight for input to the GRA model.

```
TYPE OF SYSTEM RATING POINTS

10 = FINANCIAL
 8 = FEEDER
 6 = MANAGEMENT INFORMATION
 4 = INFORMATION
```

- Speed with which data and/or assets can be converted to cash or used to the disadvantage of the organization

- Recent developments such as a new automated system or external audit reports that have come to the attention of the internal audit department.

To assess the GI factor, the auditor evaluates the office, function, cycle, or entity based on one or more of the above elements. A high perceived risk would be rated as 10.0, and a low risk would be rated as 1. The table in Figure 15-7 presents additional guidelines for assessing general integrity.

Security Impact

Security impact (SI) measures the potential impact of specific activities or cycles that are or could be detrimental to the corporation. In turn, SI is based on two factors:

- Overall corporate environment

- People-oriented tasks.

Overall corporate environment. The *overall corporate environment* refers to the type of work being performed, such as:

- Sales

- Treasury

- Administration.

LEVEL	WEIGHT	DEFINITION
UNACCEPTABLE	10	• Any system in which significant changes in operation have occurred. • Any system in which, at last audit, significant risk existed due to a lack of controls. Recommendations were made to management but were not seriously accepted.
NEEDS TO BE STRENGTHENED	8	• Any system in which significant changes in key personnel have occurred. • Any system in which, at last audit, significant risk existed due to under-control. Recommendations were made to management; and many, if not all, were accepted.
NEEDS TO BE REVIEWED	6	• Any system that has undergone minor changes in key personnel or operation. • Any system with a history of shortlived controls. • Any system in which, at last audit, moderate risk existed due to under-control. Recommendations were made to management and accepted.
ACCEPTABLE	4	• Risk of loss was minimized due to a well controlled environment. A few areas are under-controlled, but risk was deemed acceptable.
EXCELLENT	2	• Risk of loss is negligible due to a well-controlled environment. System does not have a history of short-lived controls.

Figure 15-7.

Within the GRA model, weights for general integrity (GI) may be correlated with the levels of acceptability and the qualitative definitions given in this table.

However, assessment of the corporate environment also must include more specific factors, such as:

- Office procedure
- Accounting cycle
- Application program.

People-oriented tasks. *People-oriented tasks* include the number of programming enhancements, troubleshooting fixes, and manual procedural changes. The effect of this factor can be diminished by the number of people involved and the quality of documentation. That is, tasks for which many people are involved or that are documented extensively carry reduced levels of risk. The combination of business environment, the number of enhancements and fixes, and the number of employees involved in control also will help determine the security rating.

The impacts of people-oriented tasks range from "fatal" to "inconvenient." For example, if the computer system had no backup, the impact

LEVEL OF IMPACT	WEIGHT	SURVIVAL PERIOD	OPERATIONAL IMPACT
FATAL	10	1-7 days	Operations are no longer capable of continuing.
DISASTROUS	8	8-30 days	Operations are jeopardized. Condition could become fatal if the situation is not rapidly corrected.
DISRUPTIVE	6	31-90 days	Operations are seriously affected, but they can continue at a significantly diminished level.
IMPAIRING	4	91-365 days	Operations are moderately affected but can continue. Productivity or profitability will be inhibited to some degree.
INCONVENIENT	2	Indefinite	It will have a minor effect on operations and may be accepted without a change of current practices.

Figure 15-8.

People-oriented tasks are weighted for input to the GRA model by correlating operational impact with level of impact.

would be fatal, or a rating of 10. By contrast, an activity that might experience delay in manual processing due to personnel problems might be merely inconvenient, for a rating of 2.

As another example, the treasury cycle may have had 10 applications implemented, nine crashes of production jobs, and numerous changes to manual procedures. If only one person is familiar with all these changes, a rating of 10 would be justified.

At the other extreme, there may have been three changes in the administration cycle since the last audit. If all three changes were approved formally and documented adequately, a rating of 2 might be assigned.

The table in Figure 15-8 shows levels of impact, weights, survival periods, and operational impacts for assessing people-oriented tasks.

Audit Interval

Audit interval (AI) measures two factors:

- Length of time between audits
- Number and importance of prior audit recommendations.

AUDIT INTERVAL	WEIGHT	DEFINITION
More than 3 years	10	Unaudited
25–36 months	8	Results are out of date. A re-audit is required.
13–24 months	6	Results are no longer current. Start planning for a re-audit.
7–12 months	4	Results are current. Start planning for a follow-up.
0–6 months	2	Results are current and relevant.

Figure 15-9.

For input to the GRA model, audit intervals (AI) are weighted in terms of time distributions.

If the entity under assessment is an application program, the involvement of internal auditors within the SDLC should be considered. If the time between audits is more than three years, and/or if there were major recommendations, the rating would be 10.0. On the other hand, if the last audit were performed less than six months ago, and if there were no major recommendations, the rating would be 2. Time distributions and weights for audit intervals are shown in the table in Figure 15-9.

Audit Comfort

Audit comfort (AC) is the auditor's subjective evaluation of the activity/entity. The auditor can use prior knowledge of the activity, information gained from other sources, or professional intuition. The auditor must document the reason for the rating assigned. Ratings range from 1 (very low) to 10 (very high).

Final Risk Score Calculation

The *final risk score (FRS)* is the output from the GRA model. The FRS per operating unit is calculated by multiplying specific risk (SR) by pervasive risk (PR) and dividing by 100. This total then is added to PR. This algorithm is presented in Figure 15-10. In this example, the GRA deals with 261 operating units within the corporation. A maximum FRS thus was derived for all the units by multiplying 261 and the FRS per operating unit. Accordingly, the FRS for each unit can be normalized by dividing the total FRS by 261.

Figures 15-11 through 15-17 present a representative set of inputs and outputs for applying the GRA model in calculating the FRS for a cycle review and for a corporate function. The process can be implemented on a microcomputer or a mainframe.

Calculation of Final Risk Score:

$$FRS = PR + [PR \times (SR/100)]$$

The maximum scores possible for a corporation with 261 operating units are:

$$PR = 180$$
$$SR = 45$$
$$MAX\ FRS = 261 \times [180 + (180 \times .45)]$$
$$NORM = FRS/261$$

CASE STUDY 2: LOS ALAMOS VULNERABILITY ANALYSIS

Recently, the National Bureau of Standards (NBS) has been working with the Nuclear Regulatory Commission (NRC) in doing risk analyses of NRC computer systems. NRC selected the Los Alamos Vulnerability Analysis (LAVA) prototype "expert system" software for this task. In its present stage of development, LAVA provides a series of 60 *vulnerability area* raw scores, which indicate the relative proportion of safeguards present in each area under study. The underlying assumption is that a missing safeguard can be viewed as a system vulnerability.

NBS created a model in which security requirements for a system can be expressed by the negative potential impact of three factors. These security factors are:

- Sensitivity

- Integrity

- Criticality.

Sensitivity. In this context, *sensitivity* refers to the potential impacts from disclosure of system information.

Integrity. In specific terms within the LAVA model, *integrity* is assessed in relation to the impacts from intentional or other modification of system information.

Criticality. Within the LAVA model, *criticality* is a measure of the permissible delay in processing for a given system.

CENTRAL RISK ASSESSMENT
DATA ENTRY FORM
FOR CAPTURING INFORMATION

ACTIVITY: GENERAL CONTROLS   **AUDITOR:** Rick Gonzalez

PERVASIVE RISKS   **RATING**

PERFORMANCE SENSITIVITY (PS)	10
GENERAL INTEGRITY (GI)	10
SECURITY IMPACT (SI)	10
AUDIT INTERVAL (AI)	8
AUDIT COMFORT (AC)	8

SPECIFIC RISKS

Ranking No.	"SR" Code		Rating
#1.	48	Lack of coordination--System Changes	9
#2.	12	Inefficient operations	8
#3.	45	Lack of auditability	6

ESTIMATED DOLLAR VALUE IS: $_____

The Pervasive Risks are based on the interview and your notes should identify each. Specific Risk ratings are predetermined. *You* and the *Interviewee* should select and rank the SR. The rating has *already* been determined by audit Management. Estimated Dollar Value is merely to give audit management an idea of the dollar value. it can be the value of fixed assets, total expenditures of an entry/activity, total sales, total commitments, etc. After all the blocks are filled in, you are ready for data entry. The GRA software will make all the calculations.

AUDIT TYPE: (E) EDP; (I) INTERNAL; (S) SELLER/SERVICER   E

AUDIT SCOPE: (O) OPER: (S) SYSTEM DEV; (F) FINANCIAL;
(C) COMPLIANCE; (I) INTERNAL CONTROLS;
(T) TRANS FLOW ANAL   I

EST STAFF DAYS: 40

INTERVIEWER(S):

INTERVIEWEE(S):

REMARKS: The information pertaining to this activity was compiled from several activities that were combined. These include: Data Administration, Technical Support, Standards & Procedures, and Quality Assurance.

Figure 15-11.   *Key inputs to the GRA model may be collected on this data entry form.*

GENERAL RISK ASSESSMENT
RISK ANALYSIS

ACTIVITY:	PERVASIVE RISKS

PS PERFORMANCE SENSITIVITY (PS): The General Controls Review is a review of controls pertaining to the Corporation's EDO Environment. These controls impact all systems in operation at Freddie Mac.

GI GENERAL INTEGRITY (GI): Systems at Freddie Mac are relatively new. A significant amount of new systems development work is underway. Many new staff have been hired. The complexity of the EDP environment has increased.

SI SECURITY IMPACT (SI): The overall corporate EDP environment is complex. Many control functions are dependent upon key personnel regularly performing required tasks.

AI AUDIT INTERVAL (AI): The last audit of general controls was performed in 1984. Because of the many organizational changes and additional software, the results of that audit are no longer valid.

AC AUDIT COMFORT (AC): The Corporation has not decided upon a formal SDM. There remains some outstanding issures in the area of organizational controls. New staff persons (management and technical) have been hired.

List below all Specific Risk identified in this activity.

NR	SPECIFIC RISK	RANKING
12	Inefficient operations	2
13	Lack of management control	
36	Erroneous processing	
38	Lack of continuity of operations	
43	Lack of coordination--overall	
45	Lack of auditability	1
48	Lack of coordination--system changes	3

Figure 15-12.   *In providing inputs to the GRA model, this form is used to rank specific risks.*

GENERAL RISK ANALYSIS

RISK CALCULATIONS

AVAILABLE STAFF DAYS: 0

ACTIVITY NAME	PERV RISK	SPEC RISK	FINAL RISK	NORM	AC	TYPE AUDIT	SCOPE	STAFF DAYS	ACCUM STAFF DAYS
TELEPHONE SYS	180	33	239.40	.917	10	I	O	50	
GENERAL CONTROLS	164	36	223.04	.855	8	E	I	40	
ADP FACTORS	164	32.5	217.30	.833	8	E	S	30	
MICRO MF COMMO	138	34	184.92	.709	10	E	S	25	
MICRO PROCESSOR	134	35	180.90	.693	10	E	S	50	
COMPUTER CENTER	121	32.5	160.33	.614	5	E	I	25	
INTERPERS	116.8	34	156.51	.600	6	E	S	25	
PMI	115.4	35	155.79	.597	6	E	I	50	
PML / CLASS	110	34	147.40	.565	4	E	S	30	
DEMOGRAPHIC	90	36	122.40	.469	5	S	I	15	
CORP SOURCE DOC	92	22	112.24	.430	7	I	O	10	
LOAN & INVESTOR	86.4	28	110.59	.424	7	S	F	30	
CPTR SECURITY	79.6	38	109.85	.421	6	E	I	50	
INFO CENTER	79	38	109.02	.418	7	E	S	30	
SYSTEM TESTING	83	30.5	108.32	.415	8	E	O	15	
CORP FIN SYSTEM	85.8	19	102.10	.391	5	E	S	25	
CUST NETWORK	81	24	100.44	.385	6	E	S	20	
MIS SYSTEM	76	30.5	99.18	.380	2	E	S	30	
SW PRODUCTIVITY	79.25	21	95.89	.367	5	E	O	15	
OFFICE AUTOMAT	52.4	36.5	71.53	.274	6	E	S	25	
TREAS EDP WORK	57.2	14.5	65.49	.251	2	E	I	10	
TRAINING EDP	14.2	32	18.74	.072	1	I	O	5	

Figure 15-13.

In this output from the GRA model, risk calculations are shown for the activities listed on the right.

The system owner assigns scalar values (0 to 10) to each of these factors according to his or her view of the potential impacts on operations. In applying the model, each of the 60 LAVA vulnerability areas is assigned scalar weights (0 to 2) to signify the relative impacts of missing safeguards upon each of the three security factors. The model was developed using microcomputer spreadsheet software that derives four ranking values for each of the three security factors. This analysis is performed using a matrix principle. After the derivation of the four values, a single average value is computed for the three security factors.

The four overall value rankings are called *risk significance values,* and give a relative measure of risk when they are converted to *linguistic* variables

GENERAL RISK ANALYSIS

AUDIT PRIORITIZATION   **AVAILABLE STAFF DAYS: 420**

ACTIVITY NAME	PERV RISK	SPEC RISK	FINAL RISK	NORM	AC	TYPE AUDIT	SCOPE	STAFF DAYS	ACCUM STAFF DAYS
TELEPHONE SYS	0	0	0.00	.917	10	I	O	50	50
GENERAL CONTROLS	0	0	0.00	.855	8	E	I	40	90
ADP FACTORS	0	0	0.00	.833	8	E	S	30	120
MICRO MF COMMO	0	0	0.00	.709	10	E	S	25	145
MICRO PROCESSOR	0	0	0.00	.693	10	E	S	50	195
COMPUTER CENTER	0	0	0.00	.614	5	E	I	25	220
INTERPERS	0	0	0.00	.600	6	E	S	25	245
PMI	0	0	0.00	.597	6	E	I	50	295
PML / CLASS	0	0	0.00	.565	4	E	S	30	325
DEMOGRAPHIC	0	0	0.00	.469	5	S	I	15	340
CORP SOURCE DOC	0	0	0.00	.430	7	I	O	10	350
LOAN & INVESTOR	0	0	0.00	.424	7	S	F	30	380
CPTR SECURITY	0	0	0.00	.421	6	E	I	50	430
INFO CENTER	0	0	0.00	.418	7	E	S	30	460
SYSTEM TESTING	0	0	0.00	.415	8	E	O	15	475
CORP FIN SYSTEM	0	0	0.00	.391	5	E	S	25	500
CUST NETWORK	0	0	0.00	.385	6	E	S	20	520
MIS SYSTEM	0	0	0.00	.380	2	E	S	30	550
SW PRODUCTIVITY	0	0	0.00	.367	5	E	O	15	565
OFFICE AUTOMAT	0	0	0.00	.274	6	E	S	25	590
TREAS EDP WORK	0	0	0.00	.251	2	E	I	10	600
TRAINING EDP	0	0	0.00	.072	1	I	O	5	605

Accum staff days = Available staff days

Figure 15-14.

This output from the GRA model shows accumulated staff-days for each type of activity.

(zero, low, medium, high). The four risk significance values, therefore, indicate the system's security posture relative to the owner's stated requirements. The spreadsheet program also sorts the 60 individual vulnerability area ratings derived by the model to determine those ratings that contribute most to the four risk significance values.

LAVA output reports then can be used to identify the specific missing safeguards associated with the areas of concern for vulnerability. By a process of iteration with LAVA and the spreadsheet model, "What if?" scenarios can be investigated to determine how much the system's risk level would be reduced if proposed safeguards were applied.

```
CALCULATION FORMULAS:
Pervasive Risk   = (PS x GI) + 7(SI x AI) + AC
Specific Risk    = 2(RISK-1) + 1.5(RISK-2) + 1(RISK-3)
Final Risk Score = PR + [PR x (SR / 100)]
Norm FRS         = (FINAL RISK SCORE / TOTAL NO. UNITS)


AUDIT TYPE:
(E) - EDP;    (I) - INTERNAL;    (S) - SELLER/SERVICER;    (R) - REGION


AUDIT SCOPE:
(O) - OPER;    (S) - SYSTEM DEV;    (F) - FINANCIAL
(C) - COMPLIANCE;    (I) - INTERNAL CONTROLS;    (T) - TFA


GENERAL RISK ANALYSIS:

DATE:  02-28-198X        TIME:  09:05:53

Program Name = GRACALC
Input File   = RISKCALC.GRA
Output File  = RISKCAL2.GRA
```

Figure 15-15. *This illustration recaps the main components of the GRA program and its application data files.*

FILE - RISKFILE.GRA
LIST OF SPECIFIC RISKS

TYP	NUM	NAME	RATE	DESC
S	11	IMPROPER AUTHORIZATIONS	5	—
S	12	INEFFICIENT OPERATION	8	—
S	13	LACK OF MANAGEMENT CONTROL	7	—
S	14	LOSS OF CORPORATE KNOWLEDGE BASE	6	—
S	15	LOSS OF INCOME	7	—
S	16	LACK OF STANDARDIZATION	8	—
S	17	LOW EMPLOYEE MORALE	6	—
S	18	INDUSTRY LOSS OF CONFIDENCE	6	—
S	19	LOSS OF COMPETITIVE EDGE	6	—
S	20	INEFFECTIVE REPORTING TO MANAGEMENT	7	—
S	21	CONFLICTS OF INTEREST	2	—
S	22	INABILITY TO MEET GOALS/OBJECTIVES	7	—
S	23	IMPROPER SEGREGATION OF DUTIES	4	—
S	24	INADEQUATE COMMUNICATIONS	7	—
S	25	LEGAL VIOLATION	5	—
S	26	POTENTIAL FOR LAWSUITS	3	—

Figure 15-16.

This is a partial listing of the specific risks that are rated under GRA and are held in the application data file, RISKFILE.GRA.

S	27	INEFFECTIVE MONITORING	5	—
S	28	IMPROPER FINANCIAL DECISIONS	4	—
S	29	OPPORTUNITY LOSS	3	—
S	30	MISSTATEMENT OF FINANCIAL DATA	3	—
S	31	INABILITY TO FUND	2	—
S	32	INEFFECTIVE BUSINESS STRATEGY	2	—
S	33	IMPROPER EXPENDITURES	5	—
S	34	INADEQUATE SUPPORT	6	—
S	35	POTENTIAL FOR FRAUD	3	—
S	36	ERRONEOUS PROCESSING	6	—
S	37	DESTRUCTION OF DATA	5	—
S	38	LOSS OF CONTINUITY OF OPERATIONS	4	—
S	39	INABILITY TO MEET CORP PROC REQMTS	7	—
S	40	CONTROL OVER END-USE COMPUTING	9	—
S	41	INTEGRITY OF INFORMATION	8	—
S	42	INADEQUATE PLANNING	7	—
S	43	LACK OF COORDINATION – OVERALL	8	—
S	44	LACK OF SYSTEM DEV METHODOLOGY	9	—
S	45	LACK OF AUDITABILITY	6	—
S	46	LACK OF PHYSICAL SECURITY	8	—
S	47	RELIANCE ON MANUAL PROCESSING	7	—
S	48	LACK OF COORDINATION – SYS CHANGES	9	—
S	49	CONTINUITY OF OPERS – USER AREAS	10	—

Figure 15-16.

Concluded.

02-26-1985   **File – RISKCALC.GRA**
PARTIAL LISTING OF FILE: RISKCALC.GRA

Record 1		Record 2	
TYPE	SYS	TYPE	SYS
UNIT NAME	TELEPHONE SYS	UNIT NAME	GENERAL CONTROLS
PERF-SEN	10	PERF-SEN	10
GEN-INT	10	GEN-INT	10
SECURITY	10	SECURITY	10
AUD-INTV	10	AUD-INTV	8
AUD-COMF	10	AUD-COMF	8
SR1-NR	22	SR1-NR	48
SR1-RTG	7	SR1-RTG	9
SR2-NR	12	SR2-NR	12
SR2-RTG	8	SR2-RTG	8
SR3-NR	13	SR3-NR	45
SR3-RTG	7	SR3-RTG	6
SCORE	. 917	SCORE	. 855
AUDIT TYPE	I	AUDIT TYPE	E
SCOPE	O	SCOPE	I
MD	50	MD	40

Figure 15-17.

This listing recaps some of the risk calculations performed under GRA. These data are held in the input file, RISKCALC.GRA.

```
                        Record 3
            TYPE              SYS
            UNIT NAME         ADP FACTORS
            PERF-SEN          10
            GEN-INT           10
            SECURITY          8
            AUD-INTV          10
            AUD-COMF          8
            SR1-NR            41
            SR1-RTG           8
            SR2-NR            22
            SR2-RTG           7
            SR3-NR            18
            SR3-RTG           6
            SCORE             . 833
            AUDIT TYPE        E
            SCOPE             S
            MD                30
```

Figure 15-17.

Concluded.

DISCUSSION QUESTIONS

1. What is the auditor's mission in attempting to enhance efficiency and loss control?

2. What assumptions underlie the methodology of quantitative risk assessment (QRA)?

3. What are some specific methodologies for risk assessment, and what might be the relative merits of each?

4. Within the IST/RAMP model, what factors contribute to the total annualized loss expectancy (ALE) for the organization?

5. What are some advantages of computerized risk assessment models such as IST/RAMP?

6. How might an audit risk prioritization scheme be related to the management of the internal audit function?

7. What uncertainties might be inherent in the General Risk Analysis (GRA) model described in the first case study in this chapter?

8. Within the Los Alamos Vulnerability Analysis (LAVA) model described in the second case study, what factors contribute to security needs?

16 Privacy, Integrity, and Security

A B S T R A C T

- The security of computer information systems encompasses measures for assuring the integrity of data held within a CIS and, as a result, protecting the privacy of individuals or entities described by those data.

- Discernible trends affecting the issues of privacy, integrity, and security include growing volume and complexity of activities, growth of the service sector, emergence of an information sector, and competition for resources.

- Privacy is a fundamental right of individuals to expect that information kept about them will be put to authorized uses only and that the information will be accurate. A working guideline in government has been that data must be gathered selectively, according to the purposes of the collection activity. All-encompassing, indiscriminate data collection practices, perhaps aided by computerized techniques, threaten the ability to assure privacy. New and emerging technologies pose further threats and point up the need for increased security and control of access to computer-based information.

- The responsibility of assuring integrity of computer-based information involves the monitoring of controls throughout the processes of design, implementation, and operation of computer information systems. System logs may be maintained that assist the auditor and operations staff in monitoring the effectiveness of controls.

- Aspects of security may be physical, procedural, or technical. Physical security relates to CIS facilities; procedural security encompasses the rules that govern CIS operations; and technical security refers to software, firmware, and hardware controls within specific systems.

- Specific security measures and techniques include passwords, physical identification, possession, and encryption.

- **Overall factors in security implementation include authorization, logging of processes, operating system, data and database security, and technological threats.**

- **FIPS 102, a federal guideline for computer security certification and accreditation, can serve as a model for evaluating the adequacy of computer security.**

- **A case study examines the security evaluation of a local area network according to the guidelines within FIPS 102.**

- **Exposures and control issues that arise from widespread use of microcomputers include protection of hardware, training, documentation, transaction trails, access controls, deliberate changing of data, segregation of duties, authorization, backup and recovery, and involvement of CIS auditors.**

- **A case study describes how a CIS auditor might review a microcomputer-based accounting system in a small business.**

TRENDS TOWARD A COMPUTER-BASED INFORMATION SOCIETY

Trends in business and government organizations are pushing society toward increased reliance on computer-based information. These trends include:

- Growing volume and complexity of organizational activities
- Growth of the service sector of the economy
- Emergence of the information sector
- Economic competition and scarcity of resources.

Volume and Complexity of Organizational Activities

The tasks being undertaken by large organizations that serve society are growing in volume and complexity. For example, the air traffic control system handles more than 20 million flights yearly. Also, every year financial systems clear more than 50 billion checks; the U.S. Postal Service delivers more than 150 billion pieces of mail; and the Internal Revenue Service receives more than 200 million tax returns. The use of computer information systems has been the primary means of coping with this vast, complex information flow.

The Service Sector

In a related trend, the service sector of the economy is growing at a faster rate than the industrial and agricultural sectors. Many services, such as medicine, law, education, and government, involve the transfer of large amounts of information. Resistance to productivity improvements (including automation) in this large sector of the economy has impeded overall productivity growth. Greater application of information technology has been proposed in a vast number of professional studies, including the Grace Commission Report to the federal government. For these reasons, it is highly likely that the service sector increasingly will depend on the use of computer information systems.

The Information Sector

Another trend is that some form of information production, handling, and analysis is performed by more than half of the workers in the United States. This set of activities, in effect, constitutes an "information sector" of the economy. Major shifts in the economy have occurred during the last century. Principal economic activities have undergone transitions from agriculture, to manufacturing, to service and information.

The emerging information sector includes those organizations that generate and sell information as well as those that produce information technology. Included in this category are typewriter and word processor manufacturers, newspaper publishers, and producers of films and stage and television shows, all of whom are rapidly incorporating computer-based information systems into their operations. The information sector also covers information services and products used by any organization for its own internal purposes. Examples are: internal accounting and production management and inventory control systems, many of which are already highly automated.

Competition and Resources

A major trend is increased international economic competition, coupled with decreasing availability of basic resources. Faced with these circumstances, organizations must improve and speed up their decision-making capabilities. Decisions about design, marketing, financing, and resource allocation all require more sophisticated approaches to collection and use of information. Computer information systems are the principal tools for this purpose.

With this background, the discussion below covers the implications of privacy, integrity, and security of computer information systems from the standpoint of the computer auditor.

PRIVACY AND CIS

Privacy as it relates to computers has a more specific meaning than the general usage of the term. In connection with computer maintained files,

SIGNIFICANT DEVELOPMENTS IN
THE COMPUTERIZED RECORD KEEPING ISSUE

1964 Proposal for a National Statistical Center and the resulting public debate on privacy and government data systems—culminating in a series of congressional hearings.

1967 Alan Westin's influential book, *Privacy and Freedom* (New York Atheneum, 1967).

1970 Fair Credit Reporting Act (15 U.S.C. 1681)—provisions regarding credit records on individuals.

1971 Arther R. Miller's book, *The Assault on Privacy: Computers, Data Banks, and Dossiers* (Ann Arbor: University of Michigan Press, 1971).

1972 National Academy of Sciences report: *Databanks in a Free Society,* by Alan Westin and Michael Baker (New York: Quadrangle/New York Times Book Co., 1972).

1973 Health, Education, and Welfare Secretary's Advisory Committee on Automated Personal Data Systems report: *Records, Computers, and the Rights of Citizens* (Department of Health, Education, and Welfare, Washington, D.C., 1973).

1974 Family Educational Rights and Privacy Act (Public Law 93-568)—controlling access to educational records.

1974 Privacy Act of 1974 (Public Law 93-579) enacted.

1977 Privacy Protection Study Commission report: *Personal Privacy in an Information Society,* Washington, D.C., 1977.

1978 Right to Financial Privacy Act of 1978 (Public Law 95-630) enacted to provide controls on release of bank information.

1978 Electronic Funds Transfer Act.

1980 Paperwork Reduction Act.

1983 Hearings before the House Judiciary Committee/Subcommittee on civil and constitutional rights on computer abuse.

1984 Counterfeit Access Device and Computer Fraud and Abuse Act.

Figure 16-1.

This table summarizes some of the significant milestones in the development of the record-keeping issue.

privacy is the right of individuals to expect that any information kept about them will be put to authorized use only and to know about and challenge the appropriateness and accuracy of the information.

Public debate in this area has been concerned with computerized information about individuals, the collection of the information, and the uses made of it. A chronology of major events in the development of government policy on record keeping practices is shown in Figure 16-1. In addition, some congressional hearings, records, and reports have been influential in this area.

Congressional Involvement

Record keeping has not been the only area of privacy that has concerned Congress. Over the last three decades, hearings also have dealt with wiretapping, psychological testing of government employees, and the use of polygraphs, or lie detectors. Privacy issues have been raised by members of Congress and congressional committees concerned with information systems run by federal agencies, including the Federal Bureau of Investigation, the Internal Revenue Service, the Social Security Administration, and the Bureau of the Census. A major concern recently has been the vulnerability of computer information systems to intrusion by people not authorized to use them.

Privacy-related issues will remain on the congressional agenda over the coming years for a number of reasons:

- New computer and communication technologies will create new problems and will change the nature of old ones.

- Public awareness of and sensitivity to privacy issues concerning large-scale databases should continue to grow.

- The federal government has chosen deliberately to react to privacy issues associated with record keeping on a case-by-case, rather than on a general, basis.

Relevance

In an attempt to reduce the amount of data collected by government agencies, Congress specified in the Privacy Act of 1974 that data collected must be relevant to the purposes of collection. The Privacy Protection Study Commission, which followed up on this legislation, reported finding a slight decrease in data collection as a result.

However, the criterion of relevance is both ambiguous and difficult to enforce. The small reduction in data collection was a one-time phenomenon. Record keeping is increasing, both in the government and in the private sector. Furthermore, as transactions in the private sector increasingly become automated, data that normally would not have been collected or retained will be drawn into computer systems—and thus may be subject to inappropriate collection and use.

Relevance also is a weak criterion with respect to the timeliness and currentness of data. The Privacy Commission found that federal agencies generally did not cull their files, or purge outdated information. As the cost of electronic memory continues to drop and large information systems become easier to operate, even existing economic and managerial incentives to clear databases of old and useless information are likely to diminish. This situation gives rise to the danger that outdated, irrelevant, and inaccurate information may be held in computer-maintained files.

The Vacuum-Cleaner Approach

Data collection by accessing computer-based files can be likened to the action of a vacuum cleaner. That is, both relevant and nonrelevant data are apt to be gathered in the process. One of the problems inherent in electronic data gathering is that the technology itself promotes such an all-encompassing, potentially indiscriminate, approach.

As an example, in 1980, a dispute arose between Prudential Insurance and the Department of Labor (DOL) over access to magnetic tapes containing personnel data. The DOL wished to investigate possible discrimination in hiring. The approach was to request the complete set of computer files in this area held by Prudential. Apart from the merits of the case, it still can be observed that the existence of all the files on magnetic tape encouraged this approach. If the records had not been totally machine-readable, such a sweeping request would have been unlikely; the task of analyzing the manual records would have been too burdensome and costly.

Computer technology thus makes the task of analyzing the tape files relatively easy. Although technology appears to have contributed to the problem in this case, it just as easily could point to a solution. Similar file processing techniques could be used to create new tapes containing only the information that the DOL and Prudential mutually agreed were pertinent to the investigation.

The Data Collection Transaction

A fundamental assumption underlying much of the privacy debate in the 1970s was that collecting personal information is in the nature of a transaction: An individual yields personal information in exchange for some benefit. Thus, much of the "fair practice doctrine" in the Privacy Act centers on the requirement that the record keeper abide by obligations implicit in that transaction.

However, individuals increasingly will be encountering computerized systems that collect and store information about them without their knowledge or consent. At this writing, few laws exist pertaining to the ownership or disposition of such information, even when its use may be contrary to an individual's perception of his or her best interests.

Computer-maintained mailing lists were among the involuntary systems studied in depth by the Privacy Commission. Individuals usually have no idea of whether or how information about them is being collected from mailing lists. At the time of the study, the commission deemed mail solicitation to be a socially benign activity; therefore, it did not consider this type of record keeping to be of serious concern.

Pressure from users of such systems for greater selectivity in their mailing lists has led to the eventual collection of more personal data on individuals. Political solicitation lists, for example, may contain information about a person's organizational affiliations, religious beliefs, charitable contributions, income, and history of support for various causes. This type of information can be used to predict whether that person might support a particular candidate or political cause and thus is useful in preparing mailing lists targeted to specific interest groups.

Such personal information often is collected without the consent of the subject through the exchange or purchase of mailing lists or through access to other open sources of information. The resulting record might be vulnerable to misuse because it can assume the character of a political dossier. Controls should be applied both over the use of such systems for purposes beyond compiling mailing lists and over the original collection of data. However, existing controls probably are not adequate to keep pace with the technologies involved in collecting and correlating such data.

Prospects

With increasing efficiency and speed, computer technology in the near future will facilitate the collection of personal data and virtually instantaneous distribution of those data nationwide, or even worldwide. Point-of-sale systems are an example of this trend. A sale made at a store and recorded through a card- and tag-reading terminal will collect a variety of information about the customer, such as a description of the item purchased, the exact time and location of the transaction, and possibly the customer's financial status. This information probably will be recorded at a bank, and thus will fall under the bank's privacy rules. However, the same data also may be retained by the store's management for its own use or even may be sold to third parties.

Rules of Access

Current privacy legislation contains controls over access to data held by government agencies. The requirement for access under these controls is referred to as the *use rule*. That is, with some exceptions, data only can be given to third parties for purposes compatible with those for which the data were collected originally. Such routine uses must be made known to the subject described in the data. This disclosure must be made either directly when the data are solicited or constructively through publication in the *Federal Register*.

The Privacy Protection Study Commission found this rule to be relatively ineffective. The term "compatible" is vague and subject to a variety of interpretations. In addition, there are many exceptions, both within the privacy act and in other laws governing the exchange of information among government agencies. Also, the provisions of notice were found to be equally ineffective. Finally, privacy rules conflict with freedom of information laws. For example, the Iowa Attorney General ruled recently that the state's open record laws supersede any rights to user privacy with respect to library records.

Given these drawbacks, applying such a use rule in the private sector would have limited effectiveness, even if the ambiguities were clarified. The use rule assumes a voluntary relationship between the primary data collector and the subject. The rule also assumes that the individual has yielded personal information willingly. If such an agreement does not exist, the subject of the data is not the owner of the information.

Data collectors argue, usually correctly, that the information being collected is already in the public domain. The central issue, then, may be: Can a compilation of information in the public domain, along with the statistical inferences drawn from it, become so comprehensive as to constitute an intolerable invasion of an individual's privacy? Clearly, the question is a difficult one. To address this problem, some states are considering bills to restrict access to public records—to auto licensing data in particular.

A relevant study has been conducted by the FBI's National Crime Information Center/Computerized Criminal History Records System. This study documents the difficulty of enforcing access rules for a large-scale, distributed information system that serves many users and that contains information of value to a variety of people. The study found that no controls within the system could keep data, once extracted by an authorized user, from being used improperly. The risk would remain even if tight security measures could solve the difficulty and problem of stopping access by unauthorized persons. Similar risks can be seen in the cases in which computer hackers have penetrated sensitive databases throughout the United States.

The current situation involves an overlap of different authorities, as well as differences among each authority's rules and procedures for access. Under these circumstances, it would be exceptionally difficult to establish a single, consistent policy for accessing and using computer-maintained data.

Similar problems exist in the private sector. Sellers of personal data, such as credit service bureaus or providers of mailing lists, have no control over how the information they sell is used. Problems of control also exist within large corporate CIS facilities in which many employees or even outside users have authorized access to data. Control in such situations is a twofold issue:

- Adequate security must be provided over the internal system against unauthorized use.

- Authorized access, as well as the uses made of the data, must be controlled.

Many new information systems are characterized by their wide distribution and easy accessibility over communication lines. Indeed, these can be primary benefits and design features of such systems. In these complex environments, multiple databases may be accessed by multiple users virtually from anywhere in the nation or in the world. Accordingly, procedural control of data use within such systems is impossible.

A final access problem is the impact on privacy of computerization of government files that traditionally have been open to the public. Such files include lists of property transfers, licenses, births, deaths, and so on. Although access to this information has been virtually unrestricted, the difficulty and inconvenience of physical access to manual files has created a practical barrier. At this point, these types of information have not been absorbed readily into privately held databases. However, as computerized files make access easier, and as markets for such information develop, the potential for misuse will increase.

Microprocessors and Surveillance

The possibility now exists for the development and marketing of a wide range of devices either specifically designed or capable of being used for surveillance of individuals without their consent. One reason is that microprocessor technology is progressing to a point at which it will be common for computer logic and data storage capability to be built into inexpensive consumer goods of all kinds.

For example, pocket-sized lie detectors are being sold that sense stress in a subject's voice. Although the reliability of these devices is questionable, they are increasing in popularity. Within a few years, units the size of wristwatches will be available. The state of Pennsylvania has a law requiring subject consent for the use of such devices. However, enforcement would be difficult or practically impossible if units were small and could be hidden readily.

Currently available security systems based on magnetic cards and microprocessor-actuated locks allow an employer or building manager to keep detailed records of the whereabouts of anyone in a building. Devices called *pin registers* provide a similar capability for monitoring telephone traffic. Voice recognition and picture processing technologies undoubtedly will provide other forms of inexpensive, automated surveillance.

Abuse of such technology is becoming a serious problem. However, seemingly legitimate applications—such as surveillance of customers or employees in retail stores—also may cause concern if there are obvious abuses. Arguments for socially sanctioned uses will raise new versions of old controversies, including civil rights versus both law enforcement and the rights of employers to monitor their employees. In this debate, new information technology is placing more powerful tools in the hands of those who argue for greater social control.

INTEGRITY AND AUDITING

A system of security safeguards is effective only if:

- It is designed and implemented correctly.
- It operates correctly thereafter.
- It is monitored constantly.

A major source of vulnerabilities in resource-sharing systems is operating system software, which may contain hundreds of program modules and hundreds of thousands of instructions. It is impossible to design and implement such systems without risking many design flaws and implementation errors. Although a vast majority of such flaws and anomalies will be removed in the debugging phases, many will remain undetected for seemingly long periods; indeed, errors still can be found in operating systems and applications that have been in use as long as five to 10 years. Some of these flaws may provide a way for disabling or circumventing the security system by knowledgeable penetrators and, therefore, are of special concern.

Certainly, software and firmware shortcomings are a general problem in producing reliable systems. However, today's security requirements add a new dimension. Not only should programs perform correctly all tasks and algorithms they are designed for, but they should not do anything that they are not intended to do. Verifying that a program satisfies such a stringent requirement is difficult, and may be possible only after formal *correctness proof.* There has been some recent progress in developing practical program-proving techniques for exhaustive testing and verification. The National Bureau of Standards has published several Federal Information Processing

Standards to help federal agencies deal with these issues. Among these are: FIPS 101, "Guideline for Life Cycle Validation, Verification, and Testing of Computer Software," June 6, 1983, and FIPS 106, "Guideline on Software Maintenance," June 15, 1984.

In the absence of totally effective security safeguards, various auditing procedures are used to discourage those who might be tempted toward abuse or misuse. Typically, chronological logs are maintained for:

- All jobs processed in the system

- All log-ons at all on-line terminals

- Accesses to files

- Exception conditions detected by the system.

If an audit log is designed properly, it can permit the tracing of anomalous user actions. Accountability for these actions thus can be established. Also, active and dynamic audits during system use actually can intercept a penetration attempt in progress. However, the capability for logging all user action typically is not available for microcomputers that are used as terminals with dial-up telephone access through modems. In this case, however, you still can log the user-identification/password. Information stored on such devices remains open to the knowledgeable user and perpetrator.

In some systems, real-time monitoring of threats has been implemented. For example, counts are made of the number of consecutive times a user fails to provide a correct password. If a preset threshold is exceeded, the user is disconnected automatically.

More sophisticated threat monitoring can involve the following automated measures:

- Characterize security violation in terms of measurable system variables.

- Distinguish penetration attempts from other unusual, but legitimate, processing activities.

- Add instrumentation to the system to collect needed information without unacceptable increases in system overhead.

Integrity is an essential characteristic of computer information systems. People use the information generated to make critical decisions. The quality and completeness of the information are measures of system integrity. To assure system integrity, the auditor must rely on procedural audit functions.

SECURITY OVER CIS

Computers have handled sensitive programs and data for many years; however, it is only recently that the need to secure them has become a serious concern to system designers and operators. During the social unrest of the 1960s, concern arose over the physical security of computer systems. The systems were expensive and visible corporate assets and, consequently, might have been attractive targets for sabotage. Later, concerns over privacy and awareness of increasing incidents of computer crime motivated managers to take a more sophisticated look at protecting systems and data. More recently, unauthorized penetrations into computerized databases of banks and financial institutions have raised additional security concerns.

Classifications of Computer Security

Most security experts distinguish among three types of security:

- Physical
- Procedural
- Technical.

Physical. *Physical security* refers to techniques that isolate computer systems physically from access by unauthorized persons. This area of security also is concerned with protection of a CIS facility from external dangers such as earthquake, fire, flood, or power failure.

Procedural. *Procedural security* is the set of rules by which a system operator manages system personnel and the flow of work in an organization. Procedures in this category can include pre-employment screening of staff, work assignments that minimize the opportunities to act in inappropriate ways, auditing procedures, and control over the flow of work throughout the system.

Technical. *Technical security* refers to the software, firmware, and hardware controls set up within a system. Techniques used to provide security may include cryptographic encoding of data, complex access and identification procedures, and hardware or firmware dedicated to the auditing function.

Many security experts claim that too much attention to technical solutions has distracted system operators from more traditional, but effective, measures. However, the proliferation of small systems and microtechnology, as well as trends toward communication-based systems, are making technical security measures more important.

The techniques of physical and procedural security are relatively well understood and can be translated readily from the noncomputer world into the realm of the system operator. Technical security, a newer area of research, is less understood, but is related directly to the problems of system design.

The Nature of Security

Computer scientists have proven theoretically that it is impossible to achieve perfect security within the bounds of any given system. That is, no specific combination of hardware, firmware, and programming can be shown to be invulnerable to some new, unexpected type of attack.

Improving the security of a computer system, therefore, involves balancing the costs of protection against the expectations of losses resulting from threats and vulnerabilities. Although there are no guarantees of complete success, research and development in the field of computer security hold prospects for decreasing protection costs substantially.

As discussed in the previous chapter, risk assessment, or the process of weighing all these factors in a decision model, is a difficult job. The precise factors are unknown, and it is difficult to determine whether all possible alternatives have been covered. Current research is aimed at developing techniques for performing risk assessment with greater precision. In government and private industry alike, there are ongoing research and standards activities in this area. While most of these standards are directed at federal systems, emerging guidelines will have application in the private sector.

Technical Security Goals

Technological instruments for security fall into three major categories, according to the intent of the designer:

- Prevention
- Detection
- Auditing.

Prevention. In this context, *prevention* means keeping unauthorized persons from gaining access to the system and keeping authorized persons from using the system wrongly.

Detection. Within the technical security area, *detection* means catching an unauthorized procedure when it is attempted and preventing its completion.

Auditing.   *Auditing,* in this sense, is the process of determining whether unauthorized acts have occurred.

A particular security technique usually is directed toward one of these goals.

SECURITY TECHNIQUES

The first objective of security is to assure that only authorized personnel can access the system. Generally, permitting access is a two-step process that begins with user *identification* and proceeds to *authentication.* Identification is the process of establishing a claim of access to the system. For example, in keying in a name or account number at a terminal, a user is identifying himself or herself to the system and claiming a right of access. Authentication is the process of verifying the claim. In the case of an identification code entered at a terminal, authentication would involve matching the code to a predetermined list of authorized users as a condition to permitting access. Techniques for user identification and authentication include:

- Passwords
- Physical identification
- Possession
- Encryption.

Passwords

A straightforward, time-honored, access procedure is the use of a password, or alphanumeric access code, that is known only to the individual authorized to use the system. The personal identification numbers assigned to bank customers for use with automated teller machines are examples of such codes.

Within large-scale systems, access controls using passwords often are implemented at multiple levels. That is, separate codes might be used at the terminal, system, application, and file levels.

The security provided by password schemes is limited, although more elaborate versions offering some improvements have been developed recently. An unavoidable risk is that the security of any password scheme depends fundamentally on the ability and the willingness of the user to keep the code secret.

Physical Identification

Physical identification techniques depend on measuring specific types of physical characteristics or personal attributes of individuals. To be useful, any such systems not only must be able to discriminate among persons, but also must be insensitive to changes in the characteristics of a particular individual over time.

In selecting an authentication technology, the systems operator must balance two types of errors. Reliable authentication measures should not:

- Classify a fraudulent identity as correct.

- Classify a proper user as fraudulent.

The first type of error can result if the system is not sufficiently sensitive or accurate to detect impostors. The second type of error often is the result of normal variances in physical characteristics in the same individual. These two types of errors have costs associated with them, and usually are at the opposite ends of a trade-off. In many cases, the occasional rejection of a legitimate user will be tolerated in favor of relatively strict controls against access by unauthorized persons. In some systems, alternate or redundant access controls are used to minimize the likelihood that a specific type of physical variance will result in denial of access to an authorized user.

Widely varying technologies accompany the use of physical identification for security purposes. Some specific techniques include:

- Fingerprints

- Hand geometry

- Voice recognition

- Signature verification

- Retinal scanning.

Fingerprints.   The technology exists today for the reading and encoding of fingerprints as a way of identifying authorized users accurately. However, equipment for authenticating a given fingerprint with a minimum of delay is relatively expensive.

Although fingerprint patterns are complex, the number of features needed for accurate matching can be encoded in less than 100 characters of data. The resulting storage efficiency means that a complete set of fingerprints for every person in the United States could be stored in one of the larger mainframe computer systems.

The cost of reading fingerprints directly, however, suggests that this method will not become widely used for authentication in the near future. Its use will be restricted to systems with exceptionally high security requirements. Also, fingerprint identification might be feasible in applications for which the fingerprints themselves were significant elements of the database, as within a system used for police work.

Hand geometry. A new and surprisingly effective form of physical identification is the geometry of the hand. For example, individual finger lengths vary from one person to another. Such variances are distinctive enough to characterize an individual uniquely. Input devices for this purpose use high-intensity light shining on the hand above a pattern of photocells. Such a device is sensitive both to external geometry and to the translucence of the flesh near the fingertips. Thus, it is quite difficult to deceive it with replicas, special gloves, or other artificial means that might be used by an impostor.

Voice recognition. Research in the field of *voice recognition* has resulted in methods for distinguishing individuals by their patterns of speech. With these techniques, a random list of words is shown to an individual, who then speaks them into a microphone. The microphone input is digitized and processed for matching with known speech patterns. The computer generates a new list of words for each access attempt so that unauthorized access cannot be gained by impostors using tape recordings of authorized users.

Although such systems are highly successful at distinguishing among individuals, variances in the performance of the same individual can create problems. For example, the system may reject authorized persons who are suffering from colds, hoarseness, or even emotional stress.

Voice recognition systems are available commercially and are showing great potential in other fields, including education and medicine. Further, information collection of this type is relatively inexpensive and requires only a standard microphone, amplification, and signal conversion hardware. The limitations of the technology lie mainly in the problems of accurate authentication despite intrapersonal variances. However, there have been major software advancements in this area. As the cost of computer hardware continues to decline, voice recognition should become a popular, low-cost authentication technique.

Signature verification. An emerging technology is the capturing of written signatures as an identification technique. Input devices for this purpose actually sense complex sequences of muscle pressure involved in the writing process. Although no two signatures of the same individual are exactly alike, these patterns of muscle actions are consistent and not easily faked. Under these techniques, forgeries are more likely to be detected than with other signature systems that rely on visual comparison or optical scanning.

Retinal scanning. Another emerging technology is *retinal scanning*, or the sensing of patterns of blood vessels in the retina of the eye. Like signature verification systems, retinal verification systems are capable of tracking and adapting to individual variances over time.

Possession

Possession-oriented security measures depend on the user carrying a physical medium of identification, as in carrying a physical key that opens a lock. Computer security measures based on possession include the following:

- Magnetic card
- Laser card
- Microprocessor card.

Magnetic card.   *Magnetic cards* are plastic identification cards coated with a magnetic stripe. Consumer credit cards and employee identification badges often use this technique. Identification codes are recorded on the magnetic stripe, which can be read by sensors that actuate physical or electronic access controls. A disadvantage of magnetic cards is that their codes can be forged with little difficulty.

Laser card.   *Laser cards* are similar in appearance to magnetic cards but use optical patterns to hold machine-readable identification information. Optical storage methods increase greatly the amount of information that can be stored on a card, which might be as much as a megabyte of data. With this storage capacity, a laser card could hold an entire user profile. Optical recording patterns also are more difficult to forge than magnetic codes.

Microprocessor card.   A *microprocessor card,* also called a "smart" card, is a plastic card composed of multiple layers in which microcircuitry is embedded. A typical card today has a microprocessor, ROM, and RAM sandwiched among seven layers. Such a device can hold a considerable amount of information, which can be processed within the card itself based on commands from control systems into which it is inserted. A disadvantage is that these cards are much more expensive than magnetic or laser cards.

All possession-oriented techniques, of course, share the disadvantage that the cards are subject to loss or theft. Also, each type of card is capable of being forged, although with varying degrees of difficulty.

Use of such identification cards usually is supported by some other type of redundant control. The additional control acts as a cross-check to assure that an unauthorized person has not gained possession of a valid card. For example, a user might have to insert a magnetic card into an access control system and also enter a numeric code on a keypad. To assure the integrity of the second authentication method, its code should not be found anywhere on the access card—not even within its machine-readable information. Also, as with passwords, the redundant code should be changed periodically.

Encryption

Recall that encryption is the scrambling of data to prevent use by unauthorized persons. This technique is an outgrowth of the field of *cryptography,* or the study of secret codes. In the past, cryptography was principally a tool for military and diplomatic communication. Now, however, modern data communication systems increasingly are transmitting private information of high value; the need to protect these communications from interception and manipulation has prompted an explosion of interest in encryption.

Two techniques commonly employed for the purpose of encryption are:

- Data Encryption Standard (DES)
- Public key encryption.

Data Encryption Standard (DES).   A standard algorithm for encryption is the Data Encryption Standard, or DES, which has been established by the National Bureau of Standards for use by the federal government. This standard and its amendments (FIPS 74, FIPS 81, and FIPS 113) also are being adopted widely in the private sector, since several commercial manufacturers are producing devices based on it.

The DES algorithm applies a user-defined, 64-bit encryption key. A key of this length results in 7.2×10^{16} possible combinations, which is a large enough number to discourage the generation of all possible codes in an attempt to derive the key. Some experts, however, have questioned the degree of protection afforded by the DES. This technique remains a low-cost alternative that probably is suitable for all but extremely high-security applications.

Public key encryption.   A coding method that is gaining in popularity is *public key encryption.* Under this method, all users in a network have two unique keys: A *public key* is not secret and is known to all users on the network. The other key is a *private key,* which is secret and known only to the user. Each data transmission requires that the message be encrypted twice—first with the sender's private key, then with the recipient's public key. Upon receipt, the message is decrypted twice—first with the sender's public key, then with the recipient's private key. (See Figure 16-2.)

The concepts for this coding scheme arose from basic research in computational complexity, a field of computer science dealing with the possible theoretical limits in the ability of even the most powerful computers to derive certain mathematical solutions. Because of the computational complexity built into this coding method, knowledge of the public encryption key is no help in deciphering or deriving the private decryption key—although the

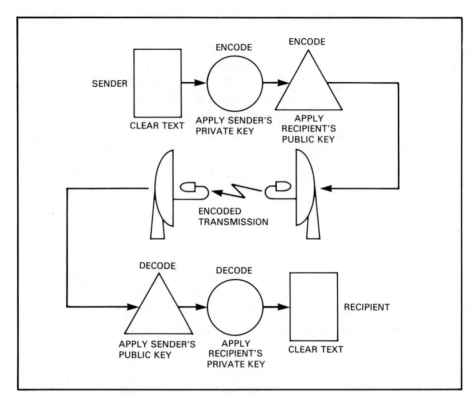

Figure 16-2.

Under public key encryption, each user has a public key as well as a private key. All users on the network know the public keys; each individual has sole knowledge of his or her private key.

mathematical relationship between public and private keys is not secret. Thus, the security of the code does not depend on the security of the public encoding key or of the secrecy of mathematical relationships. Since one of the major problems in the use of cryptography is control of the key itself, a system in which the decryption key need not be known to the sender (nor even to the data center) is promising for many applications.

Public key encryption also promises to be useful in electronic message systems, since private keys can be used for the authentication of messages in the absence of signatures. Several such applications have been developed. However, public key encryption is in its initial stages; it is not known whether unanticipated problems will arise as the technique is implemented further.

Encryption has uses other than merely securing communications. Encrypted files can be used to isolate sets of data from unauthorized users. Encryption also can be used to permit users to enter data but not to read the files directly. Encryption even makes it possible to partition the activities of multiple, connected computer processors.

Encryption software.   In some cases, particularly in microcomputer applications, encryption is implemented in software. When reviewing and evaluating software packages for performing encryption, the auditor should look for the following important functions:

- Authentication
- Encryption key
- Verification
- File destruct.

Authentication.   In this context, authentication refers to a software option that creates a string of bits unique to an encrypted file. If it is determined that these authentication data have been altered at any time (e. g., during transmission or decryption), it may be assumed that the data in the file have been corrupted.

Encryption key.   In the case of the DES, an option should be available that permits the user to create a key containing any of the 256 ASCII characters, rather than being limited to a keyboard's 128 possibilities. This wider range of characters greatly increases the number of possible keys that can be generated and, hence, adds to the difficulty of breaking the code.

Verification.   This feature compares the *cipher text,* or encrypted message, with the *plain text,* or original message. This checking assures that the encrypted version is correct prior to destroying the original, unprotected data.

File destruct.   When a file is deleted by a conventional microcomputer operating system, the name of the file merely is removed from the storage device directory; but the data remain on the device until overwritten or erased explicitly. Through a straightforward utility, it usually is possible to reconstruct the file by restoring the directory entry and its link to the file location. To prevent this, a file destruct capability not only removes the directory entry but also fills the space that the deleted file originally occupied with null values.

In a mainframe setting, performing encryption in software would be impractical due to the potentially large amounts of data to be handled. For such purposes, firmware implementations of encryption algorithms are available. These microchips solve the problem of creating massive amounts of cipher text in a short period of time. Typically, the basic algorithm resides in the chip, and software is used to pass encryption/decryption keys and to perform integrity testing of the microcircuitry. The National Bureau of Standards has mandated the use of hardware implementations of the DES algorithm within all federal computer systems. The reason for this requirement is that microchips are inherently more secure than software.

OVERALL FACTORS IN SECURITY IMPLEMENTATION

Overall factors that apply to the implementation of security measures, regardless of the specific identification and authentication techniques used, include:

- Authorization

- Logging of processes

- Operating systems

- Data and database security

- Technological threats.

Authorization

Most large-scale information systems are designed to serve multiple users concurrently. Databases within such systems often contain clusters of information that serve multiple needs. It becomes necessary, then, to partition authorized system users from specific data areas or files. For each user, the system must keep track of which classifications of data can be accessed and manipulated. Forms of access for each classification also must be specified: read/write, read only, or write only.

A related issue in authorization is the permission given from one user to another to read or access a private file. Under some circumstances, authorization may have to be extended to another user, even if only temporarily. The system may have to provide for such permissions, although this complicates enormously the problems of access control. Researchers are developing ways to model these assignments, or permissions, mathematically in an effort to avoid unexpected loopholes in system access controls.

The continued growth in the size of information systems and the numbers of people allowed to access them will continue to put pressure on systems designers by complicating the authorization process.

Logging of Processes

Logging, in a security context, is the process of auditing the accesses made to a database by all users. Systems for keeping a complete or partial record of all accesses to data have received more attention since privacy has become an issue.

For example, a system operator might need to account for all accesses made to files of personnel data. Since the log itself is a file that contains potentially sensitive personnel information, the need to protect it may be even greater than that for the original database. For this reason, some experts suggest the use of a separate, small machine to monitor accesses to the database.

The system operator should examine the log for unusual patterns of file access or other significant actions that might indicate unauthorized use. In some cases, it is possible to code unusual patterns of use; the logging system can be programmed to react automatically to such events. If the pattern is sensed, the logging system either will send a warning to the system operator or call a special surveillance routine that collects as much detailed information as possible about the transaction.

Operating Systems

The operating system of a computer is a fundamental piece of control software upon which all application programs depend. This relationship holds for microcomputers as well as for mainframes. Consequently, the integrity of the operating system is a prerequisite for any software-based security measures to prevail.

Although no system can be designed to be perfectly secure, there is much that can be done to construct a highly secure system. Research and development is ongoing in this area, and results will be incorporated slowly into existing systems. However, progress will be hindered by the difficulty in adapting current operating systems to the latest high-level languages.

Some computer installations still use operating systems that were written 10 to 20 years ago. Computer operators fear the disruption that might result from adopting radically different operating systems. Manufacturers resist compromising an investment amounting to billions of dollars in existing operating systems. Thus, operating systems based on older software technology probably will remain as barriers to using some of the more advanced software tools; and the most acceptable new techniques over the short term will be those that can be adapted to existing operating systems. However, the size, complexity, and growth history of current operating systems will tend to promote the persistence of illogical holes and flaws through which determined outsiders might gain access.

Data and Database Security

As databases grow larger and are designed to serve multiple purposes, the likelihood increases that system operators will want to grant access selectively. This problem is difficult. One of the major problems is that of authorization, as discussed above. A related issue is how to structure the data so as to permit manipulation while preserving effective control. The question of which controls are even possible is, in itself, a complicated one.

There has been much research in the design of data structures that support control objectives. Many new techniques are evolving that probably will be adopted rapidly as new database systems come into the market. One of the areas of increased importance and new development is that of microcomputer database systems (discussed below).

Encryption is one technique that will be used increasingly for situations in which different groups of data and their users can be partitioned easily. As a technique for access control, encryption will be less useful if the data are highly integrated, or if it is not known during the design stage where boundaries eventually will be drawn.

A particularly challenging situation is the use of sensitive personnel data for statistical research. Although there is no need to know the identities of the data subjects, it is difficult to partition this information from the study, since personal identity usually serves as the primary key or index to the data. A proposed solution has been the use of *aggregated files*, in which identifiers are stripped away and data relevant to the study are placed in statistical data clusters. It has been shown, however, that aggregating data statistically does not always assure that the clever inquirer cannot reverse the process and derive substantial personal information. Also, merely stripping the identifiers from personnel records may not preserve the integrity of the data, since a surprisingly small amount of descriptive information can serve to identify an individual uniquely. Research and development are being conducted on ways to transform databases collected for social research purposes so that information is completely obscure in identifying individuals, but is still usable for making statistically relevant calculations.

Microcomputer data security.   Increasing processing power and memory capabilities of microcomputers—combined with declining costs—have produced distributed concentrations of data in some organizations. Many large organizations with microcomputers do not even know how many they own, much less have specified accountability for specific files and applications. Especially for microcomputers that use removable disks, mainframe security techniques based on shared resources do not apply. For these microcomputers, other control alternatives must be implemented, including policies and procedures for:

- Labeling of floppy disks
- Controlled creation of backup files
- ''Library-style'' distribution.

The reference to library distribution methods means that data media are loaned to users, in effect, and are controlled by manual logs that record usage information, such as date, name of user, name of volume, name of file, application or business reason, and so on. Maintaining such logs may reduce the probability of accidental or intentional destruction of data.

Some software vendors have produced security packages for microcomputers with fixed, hard disks. This software maintains a system of password authorization and selective restriction of functions. For example, under these controls, one user may be authorized to create reports from an electronic spreadsheet program, whereas another user may be permitted only to enter data for processing by the program. A package for this purpose is PC Lock II for the IBM PC/XT and AT. This package utilizes a pass-key system, as well as encryption/decryption techniques. Under this package, the entire microcomputer system and its users are controlled by a ''super user'' who has the authority to alter the status of the other users. (The concept of a super user also is found in some mainframe authorization/permission systems.)

Technological Threats

An example of the growing threats of technology to data security may be seen in the exposures of corporate espionage and intentional data destruction. If the physical environment of the computer system is not relatively safe from unauthorized intrusion, the integrity of the data may be threatened. These threats need not necessarily result from physical intrusion into the CIS center. Equally dangerous threats are corporate espionage through ''bugged'' facilities, electronic wiretaps, or radio frequency (RF) analysis of emissions from computer equipment.

Such problems may be overcome by conducting an *electronic sweep* of the facility. A sweep can detect bugs and other forms of electronic eavesdropping. However, the cost of a single sweep through a computer center is currently prohibitive (about $10,000) for all but highly sensitive applications. Electronic eavesdropping through RF analysis also can be prevented by building computer rooms that are surrounded by RF-shielding material. RF shielding prevents persons outside the computer facility from scrambling data through interference or from monitoring processing or transmissions. Some banks and defense contractors, for example, have found it necessary to adopt these measures.

Determining Security Requirements

In both formulating and evaluating security requirements for data and applications, the auditor should consider two classes of needs:

- Policy needs
- Situational needs.

Policy needs.   *Policy needs* derive from the principles and required practices that the application is obligated to pursue, such as government laws, regulations, professional standards, and organization policies.

Situational needs.   *Situational needs* are those deriving from the application's characteristics and environment. The determination of situational needs is an aspect of risk analysis and assessment. Recall that risk analysis and assessment encompass five areas, listed below. Fundamental questions for determining situational security needs in each area include:

Assets.   What should be protected?

Threats.   What are assets being protected against?

Exposures.   What might happen to assets if a threat were realized?

Controls.   How effective are security safeguards in reducing exposures?

Cost.   Given the above concepts, does the cost of control outweigh the benefits?

FEDERAL GUIDELINE FOR COMPUTER SECURITY CERTIFICATION AND ACCREDITATION (FIPS 102)

In September, 1983, the National Bureau of Standards published the Federal Information Processing Standard *Guide For Computer Security Certification and Accreditation* (FIPS 102). As defined in this document, *security certification* is a technical evaluation, based on security requirements, for the purpose of *accreditation*. Accreditation is management's approval for operation of a CIS.

Approval is based on technical evaluation under the guideline and other management considerations.

Computer security certification and accreditation is a form of quality control for the security of sensitive applications. Critical decisions regarding the adequacy of security safeguards in sensitive applications must be made by authorized managers who have been briefed with reliable technical information.

For this purpose, FIPS 102 provides guidance to organizations on how to:

• Establish a program for computer security certification and accreditation.

• Perform certifications and accreditations.

Of particular importance to computer auditors, the guideline notes that computer security certification and accreditation are one aspect of a general certification and accreditation activity that should be performed to assure that a computer application satisfies all of its requirements.

CASE STUDY: EVALUATING COMPUTER SECURITY

The case below applies concepts covered in this chapter, including the guidelines promulgated in FIPS 102. The case describes how a CIS auditor might approach the security evaluation of a local area network (LAN) at the stages of planning and operations.

Planning for LAN Security

Local area networks provide techniques for data communication and resource sharing among microcomputers. LANs present some special challenges to assuring the integrity of data. The need for planning for the security of such networks is urgent because of the number of installations anticipated. Industry statistics show that 20,000 LANs were installed in the United States during 1983 and 1984. Further, one government report predicts that private networks will grow 500 percent over the next few years.

At this writing, no single, generally accepted approach to LAN security has emerged in the marketplace. Most vendors still are trying to establish the viability and capability of their own network architectures and equipment. In general, planning for data security is left up to user organizations. In their haste to realize cost savings or increased productivity, however, many users may not be placing enough emphasis on security.

The case summarized here presents a model for LAN security planning developed by a group of CIS auditors within the federal government. The model is a structured approach to planning for LAN security, as shown in Figure 16-3. This structured planning process includes eight basic steps. Each step encompasses multiple tasks that should be performed during initial planning. Many of the steps also should be repeated as network requirements, operating environment, or security policies change throughout the network life cycle. The case described below concentrates on the first four steps in the model and describes briefly the remaining four steps.

Initial Network Study

The first step for any LAN development should be to perform a study. The length of the study will vary, depending upon the size and projected use of the LAN. However, several tasks within the study should be performed regardless of the size or scope of the project. These tasks include:

- Establish planning team.
- Obtain top management support.
- Plan for security from the start.

Establish planning team.   A team effort is important to assure that all persons potentially affected by the network have a voice in its development. This involvement will reduce resistance once the LAN is in place and also should increase the potential benefits. Team members should include:

- Potential users
- Management personnel
- Information resource manager
- Systems analysts.

In addition, consultants and technical specialists should be brought in as needed.

Obtain top management support.   The team's mission and role should be established in writing. Then, top management should sign off on this description.

The support of top management is critical to the project. As mentioned above, a management representative should be a member of the network team. The representative should not necessarily lead the team, but should participate as an equal member. This role involves both giving management

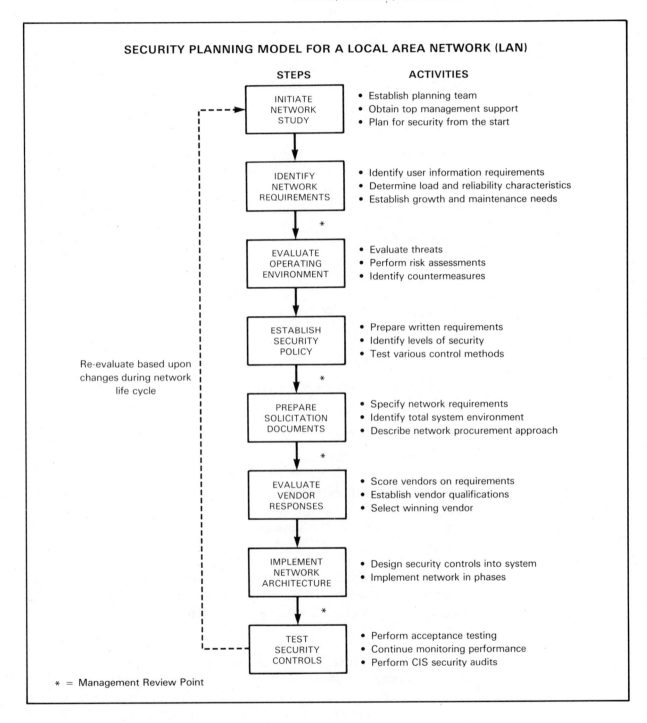

SECURITY PLANNING MODEL FOR A LOCAL AREA NETWORK (LAN)

STEPS   ACTIVITIES

INITIATE NETWORK STUDY
- Establish planning team
- Obtain top management support
- Plan for security from the start

IDENTIFY NETWORK REQUIREMENTS
- Identify user information requirements
- Determine load and reliability characteristics
- Establish growth and maintenance needs

EVALUATE OPERATING ENVIRONMENT
- Evaluate threats
- Perform risk assessments
- Identify countermeasures

ESTABLISH SECURITY POLICY
- Prepare written requirements
- Identify levels of security
- Test various control methods

PREPARE SOLICITATION DOCUMENTS
- Specify network requirements
- Identify total system environment
- Describe network procurement approach

EVALUATE VENDOR RESPONSES
- Score vendors on requirements
- Establish vendor qualifications
- Select winning vendor

IMPLEMENT NETWORK ARCHITECTURE
- Design security controls into system
- Implement network in phases

TEST SECURITY CONTROLS
- Perform acceptance testing
- Continue monitoring performance
- Perform CIS security audits

Re-evaluate based upon changes during network life cycle

* = Management Review Point

Figure 16-3. *This diagram presents the steps within a planning model for assuring the security of a local area network (LAN).*

opinions and—perhaps more important—being a conduit for keeping top management informed.

Top management should support network efforts and should approve the team's reports and/or recommendations as they proceed. Management support will help achieve project and organization goals in as short a time as possible.

Plan for security from the start.   Both top management and the planning team should be concerned about data security from the outset of the study. Planning a LAN with security in mind increases the level of control designed into each component and, therefore, the security of the total network. Further, as with other types of CIS development, attempting to build security into a LAN after development can be costly and may not be completely successful. Thus, planning for security from the outset not only will result in better control but also should prove less costly.

Once it is established, the planning team should conduct a survey of commercially available LANs. Such a survey will provide background on the technical characteristics and other features of network alternatives. Specifically, the survey should cover at least the following areas:

- Available applications and services
- Topology
- Protocol architecture
- Transmission medium.

Available applications and services.   The objective of this portion of the study is to determine, for each alternative, the types of information that can be processed and the transmission, storage, and processing operations supported.

Topology.   The structure and manner in which switching nodes, user devices, and transmission links are interconnected is called the *topology* of the LAN. Topologies typical of current LAN offerings include star, ring, bus, and mesh.

Protocol architecture.   The International Standards Organization (ISO) has promulgated a protocol model for LAN architecture that is composed of seven layers, as shown in Figure 16-4. This architecture, for purposes of the study, can represent an ideal against which alternatives are evaluated. For each alternative identified, the project team should determine which of the seven layers in the ISO model are supported.

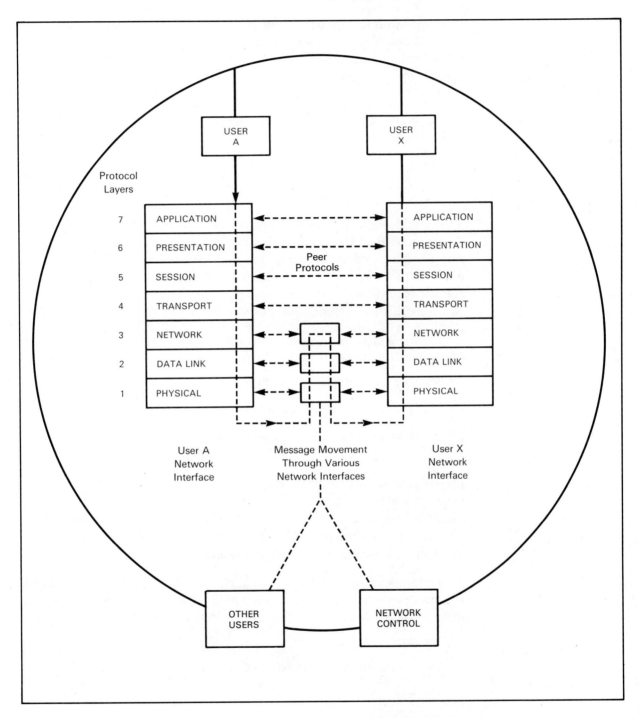

Figure 16-4. *This diagram shows a seven-layer model, as promulgated by the International Standards Organization (ISO), for data communication within CIS networks.*

Transmission medium.   In this context, the transmission medium is the physical connection between the network nodes. Transmission media for LANs include twisted-pair wire, baseband and broadband coaxial cable, optical fiber, and microwave.

Results of the survey should give the team a working knowledge of available LAN capabilities, including security. This information then can be used as background for the identification of network requirements.

Identify Network Requirements

The identification of network requirements is a critical step in the development of a secure LAN. Network requirements help define the scope of necessary planning and will provide direction for the remaining development effort. In turn, this information serves as input to subsequent steps in which specific security measures are planned. As with any systems development effort, specific requirements must be stated to assure that user needs are met.

Clearly stated requirements and performance expectations are built as the planning team performs the following tasks:

- Identify user information requirements.

- Determine load and reliability characteristics.

- Establish growth and maintenance needs.

Identify user information requirements.   User information requirements should include specific applications and network services. Data on applications can be collected through a review of documentation (including information currently processed and reports generated) and existing equipment, as well as conducting interviews and/or issuing a questionnaire.

Performance specifications, such as response times, should be quantified. For example, a precise specification would be the need for response within three seconds, 95 percent of the time. Additional requirements include:

- Interfaces

- Types of information transmitted

- Support equipment

- Network services

- Location.

Interfaces. Factors to be included in identifying interface requirements would be input/output characteristics, synchronous or asynchronous transmission modes, and local or long-haul network distances.

Types of information transmitted. Information types include data, voice, live video, images, graphics, etc.

Support equipment. Needs in this category include terminals, computers, printers, file storage units, and so on.

Network services. Services may include database access, information processing, electronic mail, bulk transfer traffic, graphics, teleconferencing, word processing, scheduling, directory service, modeling, and others.

Location. The locations to which service must be provided need to be identified. Planners should determine the location of buildings, allowable space, and the placement of equipment.

Determine load and reliability characteristics. Traffic volume and data arrival rates determine many aspects of network design. Specific determinations are needed for:

- Throughput
- Tolerable delays
- Interconnectivity between nodes
- Required backup or redundancies
- Acceptable error rates
- Node failures.

Throughput. Volumes and speeds should be determined for peak load conditions, and maximum transmission rates should be derived for equipment and telecommunication links.

Tolerable delays. Acceptable limits should be set for factors such as transmission delays and system time allocated to the processing of protocols.

Interconnectivity between nodes. Data flows, as represented in data flow diagrams, should be determined for traffic, query/response modes, and message streaming.

Required backup or redundancies.   Critical elements and equipment units within the network should be identified. Based on projected mean time between failures (MTBF) for each unit and on the service expectations, the need for extra equipment can be determined.

Acceptable error rates.   Limits should be set for file transfers. Criteria might include delivery with no loss of data, packet sequences in order, and degree of data accuracy.

Node failures.   The probability of node failures should be anticipated and quantified in both number and duration. Since the impact of a node failure varies with the type of architecture, this factor will have to be considered in achieving the desired levels of reliability and performance.

Establish growth and maintenance needs.   A growth factor for the network must be estimated to determine requirements for capacity and protocol architecture. Future requirements that might affect network growth might be the need for additional nodes, new types of traffic, changes to existing traffic, and modifications within the network. For example, digital voice transmission may be added; new applications will be developed; and equipment may have to be moved due to organizational changes.

Maintenance will represent perhaps the single largest cost over the life cycle of the network. Network monitoring equipment may be added as a means of controlling these costs. Also, hardware and software components might be specified to be compatible with standards so that replacements can be obtained off-the-shelf.

During the identification of network requirements, the planning team should be alert for possible security and privacy needs. Access controls for the partitioning of multiple user groups, for example, may be required to enforce data integrity and protection. Such findings provide input to the next planning step.

Evaluate Operating Environment

Once network requirements are identified, potential security and privacy exposures in the operating environment must be evaluated. LANs pose additional exposures over centralized CIS operations because of the telecommunication links that connect network nodes. Although physical security, access controls, and other measures used for centralized CIS facilities still may apply to LANs, additional security measures are needed.

To select specific security measures, the planning team should complete the following tasks:

- Evaluate the potential threats in the network environment.

- Perform risk analysis.

- Identify countermeasures.

Evaluate threats.   Recall that threat evaluation involves the identification of potential persons or environmental factors that may cause a loss or exposure to the network. The evaluation also should anticipate how such a loss or exposure might occur.

Specific threats to LANs by authorized or unauthorized users can be classified into five areas, as shown in the table in Figure 16-5. Note that modes of attack have been classified as:

- Passive

- Active.

Passive.   In a passive attack, an intruder might observe a message as it flows along the network. For example, both release of message content and traffic analysis involve passive modes of attack. Similarly, an intruder might examine the lengths of messages, frequency of transmissions, or sources and destinations to gain knowledge of traffic flow.

Active.   An intruder also might perform active attacks on a network by attempting processing activities. The intruder may try to modify, duplicate or alter messages—by modifying the message stream, for example. Attempts might be made to possibly delete or delay messages, thus denying services to the users. Finally, the intruder might attempt either to violate identification security at terminals or other equipment or to violate time-integrity checks on the connection. These attacks can be classified as *spurious connection initiation.*

Environmental threats, such as natural disasters, also must be considered, especially since some telecommunication links may extend outdoors—for example, between buildings, across a campus, or through a town. Additional exposures to accidental or purposeful threats need to be considered and identified.

Perform risk analysis.   Risk analysis involves the ranking of potential threats that would compromise the security of a LAN and the information

```
┌─────────────────────────────────────────────────────────────────────┐
│                                                                       │
│                    POTENTIAL THREATS TO LANS                          │
│                                                                       │
│                                                                       │
│      THREAT            MODE      CHARACTERISTICS    COUNTERMEASURES    │
│                                                                       │
│      Release of message  Passive   Cannot Detect    Encryption;       │
│        content                                       Node protection  │
│                                                                       │
│      Traffic analysis    Passive   Cannot Detect    Encryption;       │
│                                                      Masking frequency,│
│                                                      length, and origin/destina- │
│                                                      tion patterns     │
│                                                                       │
│      Message stream      Active     Can Detect       Encryption;       │
│        modification                                  Communications protocol │
│                                                      for reliability   │
│                                                                       │
│      Denial of message   Active     Can Detect       Request and response │
│        service                                       protocols         │
│                                                                       │
│      Spurious connection Active     Can Detect       Encryption key    │
│        initiation                                    distribution      │
│                                                                       │
└─────────────────────────────────────────────────────────────────────┘
```

Figure 16-5.

This table correlates potential threats and countermeasures within local area networks.

stored and processed within it. Potential threats, as well as the vulnerabilities of the particular LAN alternative to each threat, are ranked to determine their relative impacts. The seriousness of the risk depends upon both the potential impact of a threat and the probability of its occurrence.

Based upon the relative weight of each threat, the planning team should classify threats as acceptable or unacceptable. For those threats that are unacceptable, security countermeasures need to be implemented.

Identify countermeasures. Countermeasures must be specified to minimize the exposures identified in previous planning steps. For purposes of this study, it is assumed that appropriate physical security and administrative controls already are in place. Such security measures are similar to those implemented within centralized CIS facilities, and include such controls as personnel screening, building or terminal access controls, fire protection, controls over theft or destruction of media, and so on.

Physical and administrative controls are extremely important, especially since a LAN has multiple locations to protect. This study, however, concentrates on internal controls necessary within a LAN due to the telecommunication links between nodes. As indicated in Figure 16-5, encryption of data and/or protocol controls are countermeasures that can be used to offset such threats.

Current standards do not exist, however, for guiding planners and designers in the placement of countermeasures within the network. Security controls can be placed at different layers of the seven-layer ISO model shown in Figure 16-4. However, at this writing, the ISO has not taken a position on specific controls. The ISO does recommend that encryption take place at protocol Layer 6 (Presentation) but also states that encryption can occur at Layers 3 (Network) and 4 (Transport). Further, the standard suggests that additional security controls can be placed at Layer 2 (Data Link).

Similarly, the National Bureau of Standards has not established any specific security control requirements for protocol layers in its recent standard, FIPS 107, "Local Area Networks," November, 1984. Although NBS developed the Data Encryption Standard for use on selected applications by federal agencies, it has not identified which ISO protocol layer should be used for such encryption. NBS has left open the possibility to use Layers 2, 3, 4, or 6, singly or in any combination.

Despite the lack of standards, a prudent approach would be to place security controls in each of the following layers:

- Layer 6 (Presentation)

- Layer 4 (Transport)

- Layer 3 (Network)

- Layer 2 (Data Link).

Layer 6 (Presentation).   Within the *presentation layer,* data are transformed to be readable or accessible by the user. For example, instructions in this layer may interpret the meaning of exchanged data, manage the entry and display of data, or control the structure of data. Because of the interpretation and data-control features, the presentation layer may be an appropriate place to include security controls. Controls over what data can be interpreted and/or displayed, for example, may be activated depending on user identification.

Layer 4 (Transport).   The *transport layer* provides "end-to-end" transfer of messages from one network node to another. Instructions include breaking down a message into packets, as well as addressing and forwarding the packets across the network. On the receiving end, the packets are acknowledged and reassembled into the original message. The transport layer may be the best location for controls, since routing thus could be protected from source to destination. Access controls could authorize the connections based upon security constraints, and accounting controls could maintain a record of transactions. Encryption and decryption could protect the message and sender/receiver addresses. Finally, acknowledgment could verify the security level of the recipient.

Layer 3 (Network).   The *network layer* controls the routing and switching of packets within the network (as well as to any other networks, if applicable). Controls over network connections, logical channels, segmenting, sequencing, and data flow could be placed in this layer. Additional security controls could be added as necessary.

Layer 2 (Data Link).   The *data link layer* provides node-to-node (or link-to-link) control of the data flowing across the circuit. Approximately 70 percent of all error-handling occurs in this layer. Data transfers are controlled by frame sequencing, flow synchronization, abnormal condition recovery, and/or identification exchange. Encryption could be used to protect the message as it flows between network nodes. Each node would decrypt the message received and then re-encrypt it for transmission to the next node. Multiple node encryption/decryption should conceal the source and destination as well as the message; however, subversion of any one node might result in substantial exposure of messages.

In addition to encryption and protocol security, other countermeasures may be used to increase the security of data in a LAN. Messages may be broken down into packets and the packets sent via several different communication lines. Thus, compromise of any one packet would not necessarily jeopardize the entire message. In addition, *frequency division multiplexing,* a broadband technique for the carrying of multiple messages, may be used where the packets would not pick up the entire message. A combination of these two methods (with or without encryption) would provide an even higher level of security.

The concept of *key management* also is an important countermeasure if data encryption is used. Key management is a method of maintaining a secure connection between nodes. Cryptographic keys are maintained on a separate microcomputer tied to the network, and users are authenticated by request. A sender may request that the receiver be verified and a one-time connection be established for message processing. This control prevents unauthorized users from entering and maintaining access to a link.

Once the security countermeasures are identified, they should be matched to the identified risks. Then, the countermeasures that bring risks down to acceptable levels are selected. The next step is to put the security requirements in writing.

Establish Security Policy

Once the security requirements have been identified and evaluated, they must be documented. Clearly stated requirements with precise definitions are needed because security terms can encompass a wide range of meanings. For example, FIPS 39, *Glossary For Computer System Security,* does not define computer security. Instead, it contains 11 separate definitions for types of security: ADP systems security, administrative security, data security, and so on.

Within a network security policy, protection requirements should be defined in terms of specific threats, risks, and countermeasures. This type of precise definition states security objectives clearly. The result will be a network security policy that can be reviewed and agreed to by the users. Such a policy also can provide important information to potential vendors who must build the system.

Specific planning steps documented in the network security policy should include the following:

- State security requirements clearly, in well-defined terms.

- Identify levels of security requirements and the controls associated with each.

- Test the proposed implementation of the controls for feasibility.

State security requirements.   Security requirements must identify *subjects* (users) and *objects* (system resources). A set of rules for the network should exist to determine whether a specific subject can access a given object. Every object must have an *access control label* that identifies its security class and modes of access. Individual subjects must be identified and authorized for specific accesses. Further, accesses should be logged and protected for separate accountability and/or audit. The hardware and software that perform the security control functions should be capable of independent evaluation. Finally, the security control functions should be protected from tampering and/or unauthorized change.

Identify security levels and controls.   Levels of security processing must be identified, although the specific names of classification levels may vary. For example, private industry sometimes classifies information as: unclassified, internal use only, confidential, or "eyes only." The federal government, on the other hand, uses the categories: unclassified, confidential, secret, or top secret. Regardless of the name of each level, specific security controls required for each should be identified in the policy statement.

Test controls for feasibility.   Once the specific security requirements, as well as the associated controls related to each level of classification, have been identified, an implementation scheme should be prepared. The implementation scheme then should be tested to assure that the proposed security methods are feasible. Modeling software may be of assistance in such a test. Control methods thus could be tested for possible weaknesses, such as overlap or exclusion, before the policy is made final.

Once the planning process is complete and documented fully, a sound structure of network security should be in place. Combined with the previously established network requirements, the planning team is ready to proceed with network development.

Prepare Solicitation Documents

The preparation of solicitation documents is the next step toward the development of a LAN. Solicitation documents include *requests for quotation (RFQ)* from vendors and should include specific statements of network requirements in terms of services, traffic, reliability, growth and maintainability. Performance specifications should be stated in quantified, measurable terms, such as: mean time between failure (MTBF), percentage availability of node equipment, and applicable standards (FIPS, etc). A clear description of the system environment should be included. That is, there should be a description of what the LAN does and how it fits into the total organization. These descriptions should be supported with configuration diagrams. Finally, the method of ranking vendor responses and follow-up steps to the procurement should be described to avoid confusion later in the planning and development effort.

Evaluate Vendor Responses

Following receipt of vendor proposals and bids, the planning team needs to evaluate the responses. The team may be broken into separate groups, with the addition of consultants, such as technical specialists, as required. For each bid, a quantitative analysis of the vendor's ability to meet the stated requirements should be made. The requirements could be weighted on the basis of their significance and the vendor responses scored accordingly. In addition, vendor experience, qualifications, and ability to deliver should be evaluated. Finally, a technical performance and cost evaluation should be performed. The planning team also may decide to conduct benchmark tests of the proposed LANs for the purpose of evaluating, among other areas, security controls and performance.

Implement Network Architecture

After vendor selections have been made on the basis of the above evaluations, the LAN should be designed and implemented. The planning team should review vendor progress and pay particular attention to security controls. The team may wish to involve CIS auditors to review available documentation in comparison with the emerging system. Such reviews should continue through implementation. The implementation should occur in phases, not all at once, thus providing more control and allowing for gradual changeover by users.

Test Security Controls

The testing of security controls should be a continual step. First, extensive acceptance testing of security controls should be performed. Attempts to "break" the system should be made to test all aspects of security. Further, performance monitoring of the LAN should be continued throughout the network life cycle. Also, CIS security audits are essential for assuring the continued integrity of the data.

The planning process does not stop here. The network life cycle will continue for many years. During that time, many changes may occur. Operations will continue to be refined, and the LAN may be expanded or upgraded. A need to reevaluate the network security will continue to exist. Thus, the model may have to be repeated in whole or part as the LAN passes through its life cycle.

MICROCOMPUTER EXPOSURES AND CONTROLS

Controls should be a primary concern in any computer system, large or small. The differences between controls for mainframes and for microcomputers lie in considerations of scale and cost/benefits.

Cost/benefit is an important factor in the choice of controls for the microcomputer user. A microcomputer system often is chosen because of its economy. The most effective controls in theory may be impractical because the system would need expensive upgrading that would negate its cost-effectiveness.

Protection of the Hardware

The physical environment can affect the operation of a microcomputer adversely. Many novice microcomputer owners treat the system as if it were another office machine like a typewriter or calculator. However, when a failure is experienced with any computer, valuable data may be destroyed. There are also extra expenses in the loss of productive time and the time needed to reconstruct lost or corrupted files. Thus, the computer is more than just an expensive calculator. Maintaining valuable data in a microcomputer system requires special procedures apart from routine, manual office operations.

Adverse conditions for the computer include airborne particles of dust and smoke. The equipment should be segregated from the general flow of foot traffic in the office by placing it in a protected area. To keep the area as dust-free as possible, dusting should be done with tacky cloths that capture the dust particles instead of stirring them around. If smoking is allowed in the area, adequate ventilation should be provided to keep the smoke away from the disk drives and operating unit. Dust covers should be used when the system is not in use.

High temperatures and humidity can cause warping of plastic parts and disks. The temperature should be regulated to keep the work area from becoming overheated. Humidifiers and water-evaporator coolers should be used with caution.

Another deceptive culprit in the loss of data is static electricity. Data are recorded onto disks using electrical charges. Anything that creates an electrical or magnetic field contrary to the charges recorded on the disk may scramble or destroy the data.

All microcomputer systems should be protected with power surge control at the electrical outlet that will intercept electrical disturbances from the outside. Consideration must be given also to the small but lethal static electricity arising from the environment, such as from walking across carpeted areas. This threat can be controlled by using *antistatic mats* on the floor around the operating unit. These mats consist of conductive material that shunts the static charge away from the individual to an electrical ground.

Training of Personnel

Data can be lost or misused due to an operator's inexperience with hardware. Adequate protection involves recognizing potential problems before they occur. Thus, it is not enough to train personnel in only the portion of the job they are doing. They must have some knowledge of the equipment and measures that prevent equipment failures and loss of data.

Ideally, training classes should be provided by the computer dealer or vendor, with follow-up on the job. In any event, all resources for instructional material should be gathered into a training manual. Included should be descriptive brochures on the equipment, the manufacturer's specifications and recommendations for care, the instructions for software usage, and documentation of the procedures to be used.

Training time on the job for a specified number of hours per week should be required of anyone who will be using a microcomputer. This time can be used to familiarize the operator with the applications currently in use and any other parts of the software that are not being used presently. Practice must be provided with test data, along with the opportunity to experience the unused potential of the system. From this experience should come suggestions for improvement, as well as demands for greater capacity that point toward future expansion of the system.

Documentation

The importance of documentation cannot be stressed too much. Documentation of the system for training purposes is discussed in general terms above. The additional benefits of such documentation will be appreciated at the time the system is updated or expanded. For future use, notes should be made carefully of any changes or discoveries during application operations.

Much of the documentation that comes with software is vague and inadequate. There are many books on the market that go into detail on how to use a specific software to greater advantage. For example, guides for programmers often include more advanced commands and uses than are covered in the owner's manual that comes with the software. This type of resource should not be ignored. The investment in a good "how-to" manual will pay off in increased efficiencies and better use of the present software.

Flowcharts or outlines of the procedures used in the applications should be prepared. With increased use of the system and continued research into more efficiencies, changes will be made in the procedures actually followed by the operators. It is important that a periodic review be made of the procedures in current use. The documentation then should be updated accordingly.

Transaction Trails

Running accounting applications on microcomputers presents unique opportunities for the generation of transaction trails. One of the characteristics of a computerized accounting system is that transactions can be completed, accounts posted, and changes made without any physical evidence. A transaction trail could be provided by printing hard copies of all transactions.

Making hard copies of all transactions usually would not be recommended as an efficient control for a mainframe system because the resulting volume of paper would be too cumbersome to review. Within large-scale systems, other edit checks are used in the place of hard copies.

In a small microcomputer environment, reliance is placed on purchased software. Edit checks in these applications are minimal, thus making transaction trails a more attractive control.

If the hard copies are selective, the volume of paper generated for such documentation need not be any more cumbersome than the old manual accounting system. Absolutely essential, however, would be printouts of the monthly transaction summaries by account number, including beginning balances, changes, and ending balances. A reference code for the changes could be used as a guide to the source. Correspondingly, a printout would be needed of the journal entries coded to match those used in the transaction summaries.

These records would allow the reconstruction of any unusual change or the gathering of more detailed information needed for reports and tax returns.

Batch Totals and Balancing

No matter how experienced or careful the operator is, errors and omissions are always possible at the point of entering original data. Within microcomputer-based accounting systems, the use of batch controls can prevent many of these errors.

Accounts payable entries, for example, lend themselves to batching. The accounts payable clerk could gather all the invoices for the day into a group and assign them a unique batch number. The total of the amount due and the vendor numbers would be entered on a transmittal form in duplicate. One copy then would go with the batch to the computer operator, and one copy would be retained by the accounts payable clerk.

When the data are entered, the total amounts and vendor numbers would be compared with the totals on the transmittal form. Any discrepancy would be apparent. Thus, errors in the two most critical fields—amount and vendor—would be detected.

Limiting Access to Sensitive Data

In a microcomputer environment, anyone with access to the computer has access to the data maintained within the system.

Some systems will allow the segregation of data by user number, but these codes are relatively easy to break and sometimes can be found in the directory listings for storage devices.

One of the most secure ways to prevent unauthorized use of microcomputer-based data is to select floppy disks over the use of a hard disk for sensitive applications. The diskettes can be removed from the work area and locked in a secured vault. For example, fireproof safes are available that are constructed specifically to protect floppy disks.

A person who does not have access to the computer should be assigned as a librarian. This person would have custody of the disks and release them only to individuals who are authorized specifically to use them.

Deliberate Changing of Data

Utility functions that come with standard microcomputer software make it possible to access a file and change the data without a trace. Thus, anyone with access to the documentation of the software and the data file might be able to manipulate payroll or credit authorizations to gain personal advantage.

To avoid this, only the applications needed for a particular job should be on the application disk used. The critical files that make changes possible can be erased from the working copy of the application. The original disk should be safeguarded by the librarian.

Segregation of Duties

In a small computerized system, the operator handles the recording of many assets, and also has access to those assets because of the ability to transfer and multiply them. This situation violates any segregation of duties that might apply within a comparable manual system.

To establish some degree of segregation, there should be at least two people with the ability to function as operator. Duties should be rotated periodically. Not only will this limit the amount of abusive activity, it also will assure that someone will be available if one operator becomes ill or leaves the organization.

Management should be alert to anyone who appears to use the computer excessively, especially if work is done during lunchtime or after hours.

Authorization

Transactions over a certain dollar amount should be authorized by a supervisor for better control over assets. One way of providing some assurance that a transaction cannot be entered without authorization is to limit the length of the data field and to require a separate field for an authorization code.

If the software application does not allow for such a field, a visual check of the transaction summaries will have to be substituted. Any transaction over the limit should be traced to the original document and inspected for evidence of authorization.

Backup and Recovery

Disks in active use are subject to damage and accidental erasure. To assure that the loss of data will not interfere with regular activities, backup disks should be made routinely. This task sometimes is regarded by operators as a waste of time and disks. (Tape cartridge backup subsystems can be added to increase backup capacity economically.) However, a backup routine can save time and money if it is completed at optimum times. The interval between backups should be such that backups are not redundant but are performed soon enough to be effective.

Involvement of CIS Auditors

When accounting systems are converted to microcomputers without professional consultation, internal controls in the prior systems may be circumvented; new areas of exposure can result. Careful consideration must be given to the location at which the computer will be installed, who will operate it, and what degree of access should be given to each person. These measures, of course, should apply to all systems, regardless of size.

Security practices are only as effective as the people who place them into operation. Management must promulgate standards designed to protect both computers and applications and then must carry through with reviews and follow-ups. Employees will not take standard practices seriously if management treats them lightly.

Periodic reviews should be made either by the external auditor or by a CIS consultant to provide an objective viewpoint and to assure that all controls are operating adequately.

CASE STUDY: MICROCOMPUTER SECURITY

The following case describes how a CIS auditor might apply the above concepts to a review of a microcomputer-based accounting system in a small business.

Background

Many business owners and controllers first are exposed to computers when they acquire a personal computer for home use or become interested in the abundant advertising of microcomputer dealers. In many cases, when a decision is made to replace manual accounting systems with microcomputer applications, the main intention of these businesspeople is to increase accounting capacities without increasing the payroll. Seldom is professional assistance sought in implementing these systems, which usually are built from packaged hardware and software alternatives.

When they talk to these businesspeople about potential security problems, auditors often encounter responses such as: "I don't need all that fancy stuff. It's only a micro."

The following case of a recently computerized operation is based upon a composite of observations by a certified public accountant during two years of experience with such client systems.

Offan-Runnan, Inc.

The company began as a small, family-owned business 20 years ago. As a successful retail operation, it has a winning combination of shop design and customer service. Stores now are located in Los Angeles, San Francisco, and Phoenix. Plans for establishing a multi-state franchise operation are being realized.

As the company grew, all of the accounting functions continued to be handled in the Los Angeles office, with support staff in the other divisions. The controller has been with the company for several years in the main office. Faced with time lags among the divisions, he was open to any suggestion that would make his job simpler. The answer came to him when he observed his daughter using a personal computer to communicate over the telephone line with an electronic bulletin board for computer hobbyists.

With the assistance of a local computer dealership, Offan-Runnan acquired a microcomputer in each division. Modems were used to connect the computers to telephone lines for sending accounting data to the main office. A separate microcomputer was installed in the main office to process all of the payrolls.

One of the newer accounting clerks was chosen to be the computer operator for the intercompany network. Her qualifications were based on a previously completed computer class in college. After the assignment, she attended a seminar offered by the computer dealer. As for the payroll clerk, he was trained to operate the payroll computer without any prior experience.

The external auditor was not aware of these changes until it was time for the annual audit. At this point, the manual system had been discarded completely in favor of packaged software used for the data communication, accounting, and payroll.

The auditor examined all available documentation and made a thorough study of internal control. Due to the lack of controls in many areas, substantive testing was extended and the audit fee was raised.

Management Letter Items

At the conclusion of the annual audit, the report of the external auditor to management included the following items:

- Data had been lost due to equipment and disk failures.

- Computer operators showed a lack of adequate training for the applications they were performing.

- There were no formal standards documented for processing data on the microcomputers.

- Many entries in the accounts could not be traced to the original documents.

- Accounts payable did not agree with the voucher details.

- Sensitive information was available readily to anyone with access to the computer.

- The payroll clerk had access to all of the time cards and also controlled the cutting of paychecks.

- Some customers were given credit over the established limit without authorization.

- There were no backup procedures for data retrieval in case of a disk failure.

DISCUSSION QUESTIONS

1. From the viewpoint of a CIS auditor, what are some of the implications of the emergence of an information sector within the world economy?

2. What principles have governed the collection of data in the past, and why might these controls be insufficient to assure privacy in the future?

3. How is the integrity of a CIS related to physical, procedural, and technical security?

4. What types of threats might compromise a password security system, and what countermeasures might be used for each?

5. What trade-offs are inherent in security measures that depend on identification of individuals by physical characteristics?

6. What are the most likely threats to possession-oriented security measures?

7. In what ways might encryption schemes provide reasonable assurance that data transmissions are secure?

8. What attributes of microcomputer-based information systems might create exposures?

CASE ASSIGNMENT

To apply the concepts presented in this chapter, turn to the case study for WhyMe Corporation in Appendix A and work through Project 5, which deals with security and privacy issues.

17 Management of the CIS Audit Function

A B S T R A C T

- The planning, organization, and control functions involved in administering a CIS audit department are covered through a case study that outlines the evolution of the internal CIS audit function at Abcor Data Services Company.

- The Abcor case study describes the planning and start-up of the internal CIS audit function, including its audit charter.

- The organization of the new CIS audit department at Abcor includes job descriptions for CIS Auditor Trainee, Assistant CIS Auditor, CIS Auditor, Senior CIS Auditor, Manager of CIS Auditing, and Director of CIS Auditing. The importance of this organization in providing well-defined career paths and professional development is discussed.

- Specific elements within a coordinated career development plan include planning with management support; definition of required knowledge, skills, and abilities; performance measurement; performance counseling; training; and professional development.

- Operational aspects of administering the CIS audit function include staffing, directing, and controlling the department.

THE MANAGEMENT DISCIPLINE

In some of its aspects, the management of the CIS audit function requires competencies shared by all management disciplines. These competencies include:

- Planning
- Organizing
- Staffing
- Directing
- Controlling.

This chapter surveys challenges in each of these areas by relating them to the management of the internal CIS audit function at a fictional company called Abcor Data Services.

The Complexities of Management

The complexities of a manager's job stem from the challenges of coordinating human skills and talents productively and effectively. In a recent text by Dr. Peter P. Dawson, *Fundamentals of Organizational Behavior: An Experiential Approach* (Prentice-Hall, 1985), he identifies some of the characteristics of the management discipline that contribute to this complexity. According to Dawson, managers need to:

- Possess self-awareness, which is essential to good management and the ability to gather and use feedback properly.
- Understand that each individual is a unique person with unique needs.
- Apply mature "perception-checking" skills to avoid faulty human judgment.
- Work constructively with personalities that are unique to each individual and are subject to change at any time.
- Work continuously to improve and maintain good communications.
- Be able to address any given situation appropriately by dealing with the right set of variables at the right time. In each situation, there are a multitude of human and task variables over which the manager has only partial control.
- Utilize productively the inevitable factors of power, status, conflict, and stress. This ability is essential to the manager of a team effort, and particularly to the leader of an audit team.

Again, CIS auditors and managers of the CIS audit function share these challenges with other types of managers in business. However, the CIS audit function is in a special position at a focal point of the organization. Typically, the CIS auditor must deal with the flow of information in every aspect of operations and management. In this role, the auditor must cope with all the dynamics of the organization. Further, this function—so essential to the viability of the organization and its information assets—is visible constantly to top management. Not only is this responsibility a serious one, it brings with it concerns and pressures that are shared with managers at the highest levels.

PLANNING

Recall from previous chapters that the planning of the CIS audit function begins with the drafting of an audit charter. Once the audit charter is established, more extensive, in-depth planning can take place.

The audit charter articulates—in management's terms—the scope and responsibility of the CIS audit function. That is, with this crucial document, management agrees to the purpose of the audit function, vests the function with authority, and provides for its support.

To illustrate, consider a hypothetic example of this process and of the role of management in CIS auditing:

The Abcor Data Services Company recently established an internal CIS audit function and appointed James Nicotera its manager. Nicotera was appointed to this position by the company's president and the board of directors.

Nicotera's reporting relationships are shown in the organization chart in Figure 17-1. Note that he reports directly to the board of directors and also has access to the president and the chief financial officer.

Nicotera's first responsibility was to establish a charter. To gain background for this task, he did some research on the company and its management. The overview of the company that grew from Nicotera's research is presented below.

Company Background

The Abcor Data Services Company (ADSC) is located in San Diego, California, and was founded in April, 1966. The company began to offer on-line, real-time processing services in June, 1967. ADSC is a partnership between

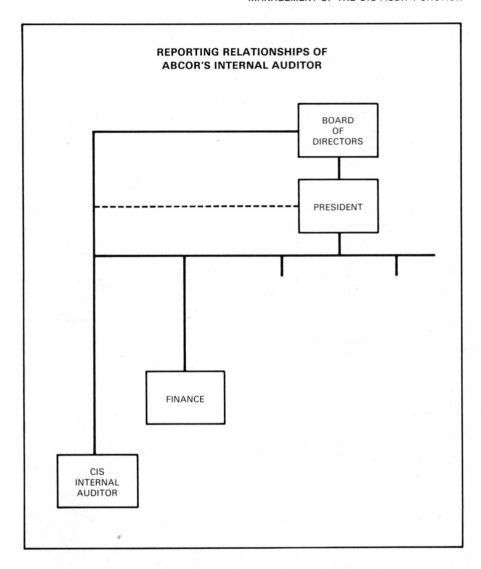

**REPORTING RELATIONSHIPS OF
ABCOR'S INTERNAL AUDITOR**

BOARD
OF
DIRECTORS

PRESIDENT

FINANCE

CIS
INTERNAL
AUDITOR

Figure 17-1.

*This shows the
reporting relationships
between the internal CIS
audit functions and the
senior management
of Abcor.*

a savings bank and a savings and loan association. Today, the scope of the
company's operations and holdings is indicated by the following statistics:

- 4,800,000 accounts served
- 5,700 terminals supported
- 765 branch offices served
- 120 associations in California, Arizona, and Nevada
- $35 billion in combined assets.

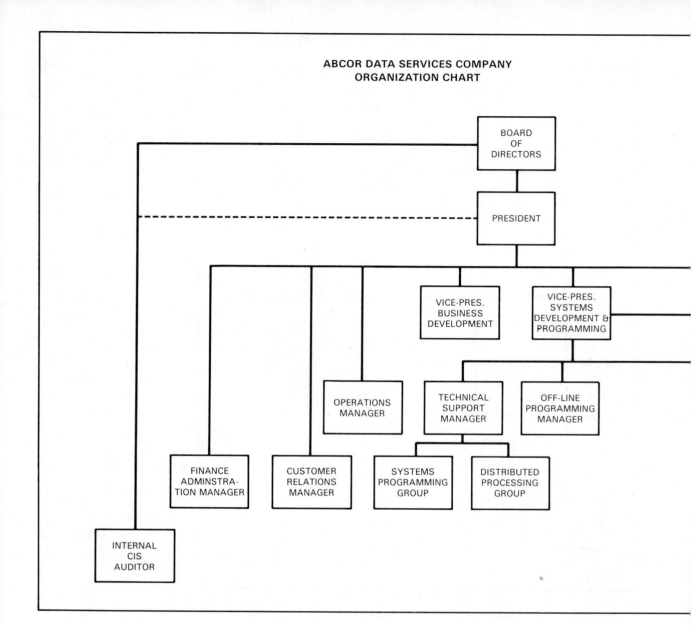

**ABCOR DATA SERVICES COMPANY
ORGANIZATION CHART**

Organization

ADSC employs a staff of more than 200. Company management is organized according to the chart shown in Figure 17-2. Note that the principal functional areas on the organization chart are:

- Systems development
- Operations
- On-line programming

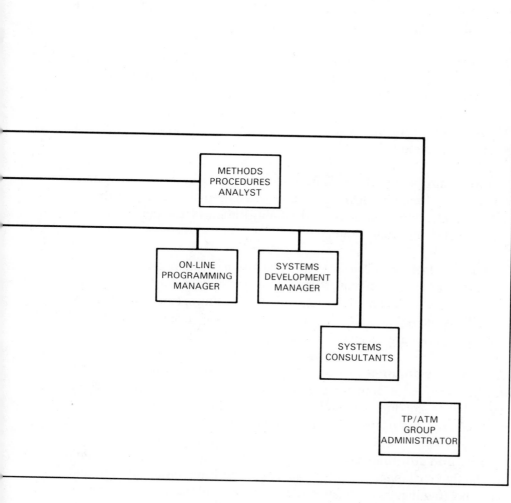

Figure 17-2.

This organization chart shows the reporting relationships among top managers at Abcor Data Services Company.

- Off-line programming

- Technical support

- Customer relations

- Business development

- Finance and administration.

Systems development. The systems development group is responsible for systems analysis and application development.

Operations. Operations encompasses computer operations and supervision, ATMs, telecommunications, data control, data library, output distribution, and security.

On-line programming. Programming functions are divided between on-line and off-line applications. Programmers in the on-line group also support all remote terminals and ATMs.

Off-line programming. Off-line applications include savings collection, general ledger, and loans.

Technical support. The technical support group includes the systems programming function for the company. The group also is responsible for system architecture, planning, and administration of the company's distributed data processing strategy.

Customer relations. The customer relations department deals with ongoing customer inquiry, job request review, review of regulatory requirements, coordination of user committee activities and meetings, conversions of new associations and new systems, training related to users, maintenance of users' manuals, and interfaces among company departments.

Business development. The business development group has contact with prospective customers, represents Abcor in professional organizations and activities, conducts research and planning of products, publishes technical research and users' manuals, and maintains the reference library.

Finance and administration. This department handles Abcor's accounting and financial management, personnel supervision, office management, personnel training, special management projects, internal audit supervision, and food service.

CIS Audit Charter

Based on Nicotera's research and discussions with Abcor's management, a charter for the internal CIS audit function was drafted. The charter was reviewed by management and the external CPA firm that audits the company's financial statements. After their reviews and comments, as well as input from the top management teams of Abcor, the charter that follows was produced.

Objectives. The purpose of establishing this Charter is to lay a solid foundation for professional audit reviews by the Internal CIS Auditor (referred to in this charter as Auditor) that provide Abcor's management and Board of Directors with information that is objective and thorough. Objectivity and practical independence are prime ingredients for a credible and reliable internal audit function.

The objective of the audit function is to assist management by preparing analyses, appraisals, and recommendations to correct deficiencies or to suggest operational improvements.

Authority. The Auditor is authorized to direct a broad, comprehensive program of internal CIS auditing within Abcor. Internal CIS auditing examines and evaluates the adequacy and effectiveness of management control in computer information systems. Internal auditing determines for management that policies and procedures are followed by all affected departments to realize the most efficient use of time and resources.

In accomplishing these objectives, the Auditor is authorized to have full, free, immediate, and unrestricted access to information, records, program and systems documentation, and personnel involved in the computer application or activity under review.

To promote independence and objectivity in the audit function at Abcor, the Auditor should maintain the ability to perform objective audits and should report fully and without reservation to the Board of Directors. Independence is enhanced when the Board concurs in the appointment or removal of the Auditor.

Responsibility. The Auditor shall report to the Board of Directors on a quarterly basis. Any critical system weakness or unusual matter that comes to the Auditor's attention should be reported to the Board monthly. Reporting of daily operational activities shall be made to the Manager of Finance and Administration. Recommendations to implement CIS controls shall be made to the President or Management Council. The Auditor is responsible for assuring to Management that:

- Computerized applications are reviewed, in a timely fashion, to assess the adequacy of controls; to assure that the data are accurate, complete, authorized, and secure; and to assure that computerized applications are developed according to Abcor policies, procedures, standards, and guidelines.

- The operating environment in the processing of information is reviewed to verify the effective execution of standard operating procedures to assure that:

  Computer hardware controls exist within the equipment and computer facility.

  Operating system software program routines process application programs in a safe and secure manner.

  Security of the facility and network is maintained, and recovery methods are available for hardware and software resources.

- The results of audit reviews are made available to all parties affected by audit findings: Abcor programming, systems development, and operations management, user auditors or management, external auditors and other interested senior management or department personnel.

- Technical support and/or training in CIS controls are provided to internal/external auditors, Abcor customer relations, programming, systems development, and operations personnel.

Abcor Management is responsible for responding in writing to all audit findings and for making satisfactory disposition of any approved recommendation resulting from a CIS audit within a reasonable period of time. For this purpose, responses to critical systems weaknesses shall be given within 30 days—to other system weaknesses within 60 days. If corrective action cannot be made within such time periods, a written plan of action shall be outlined.

A critical system weakness is defined as one that affects directly Abcor user associations or their customers and that causes considerable exposure, risk, or cost to their operations. The Auditor may suggest the nature of a weakness, and the President will make the final determination of the potential impact of the weakness. Users will be notified immediately so they can implement appropriate controls to compensate for the weakness while it is being corrected.

Organization of the CIS Audit Function

Once the charter was adopted, Nicotera had to organize his department formally before he could develop strategic and operational plans.

The board of directors authorized four staff positions for the audit function during its first three years. This allocation was based on Nicotera's preliminary plans, as documented in his CIS Audit Time Budget Plan. (See Figure 17-3.) Nicotera developed this plan based on meetings with management to discuss corporate plans, reviews of management projects in process, and his own review of the involvement of external auditors.

In addition to preparing the time budget plan, Nicotera also drafted a forecast of the kinds of skills his staff would need (industry, technical, and audit). For each type of audit, he indicated the level of skill needed in each of these areas. These skill level combinations are summarized in the table in Figure 17-4. Industry refers to skills related directly to the application or industry being audited, such as payroll systems or mortgage loans. Technical refers to skills working with computers and other technologies, such as programming, microcircuitry, and telecommunications. Audit encompasses skills that relate to the performance of an audit.

With this preliminary planning done, Nicotera was able to draft position descriptions for individual staff members. Descriptions are shown in Figure 17-5 for the following positions within the CIS audit function:

- CIS Auditor Trainee
- Assistant CIS Auditor
- CIS Auditor
- Senior CIS Auditor
- Manager of CIS Auditing
- Director of CIS Auditing.

Having outlined these resource requirements, Nicotera then prepared a forecasted first-year budget for the CIS audit function. The budget he submitted is shown in Figure 17-6.

The planning process, therefore, included the estimation of all resource needs: people, travel, computer time, software, and so on.

ORGANIZING

Preliminary work for the organization of the CIS audit function is derived directly from the planning process. With this beginning, Nicotera was ready to define the organization of his department in terms of CIS audit career development, or the career paths that would be available to CIS audit staff.

A *career development plan* is essential to developing and retaining CIS auditing expertise. This aspect of organization considers both the needs of

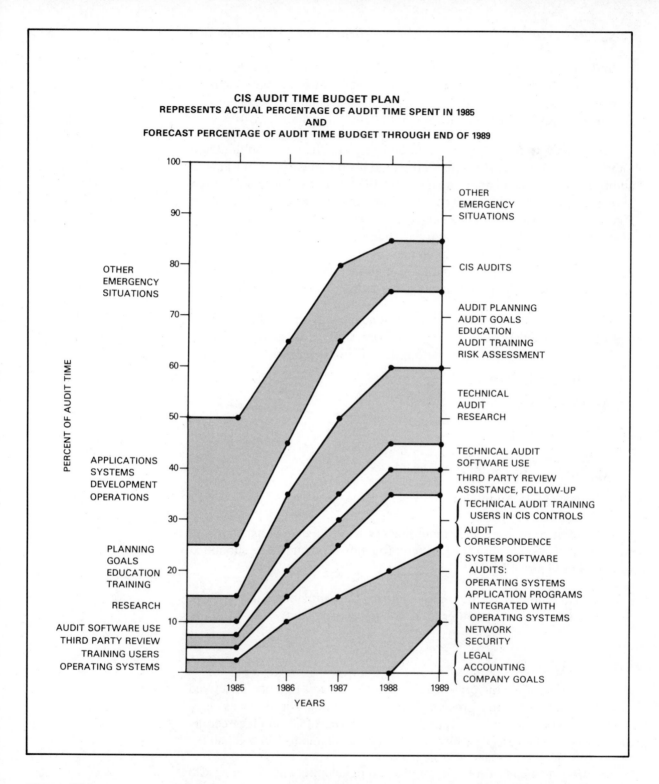

Figure 17-3. *In this graph, CIS audit time is budgeted by type of involvement, as projected over a five-year period.*

SKILL LEVELS NEEDED TO PERFORM CIS AUDITS

Type of Audit	Industry	Technical	Audit
Administrative controls ⎱ alternating	L	H	H
Data Center Review ⎰	L	M	H
Computer Application Audits			
Interest Computation (full)			
First Time	H	H	H
Recurring	H	H	H
Consumer Loans	M	M	M
Mortgage Loans	H	M	M
General Ledger	L	L	M
Fixed Assets	L	L	L
Loan Payment Processing	M	L	L
Operating System	L	H	L
Payroll System	L	M	M
Savings System	H	H	M
New Systems			
Mortgage Loans	H	M	M
Cost Accounting	M	L	L
Other	M	M	M
New Data Center Security	L	M	M
Mini and Micro Computers (at branch)			
First Time	H	H	H
Recurring	H	H	H
Performance Measurement	H	H	L
Audit Test Facility	H	H	H
Miscellaneous Loan Systems	M	M	M
Depreciation/Amortization	M	M	L
Accounts Payable	L	L	L

SKILL LEVELS:
  H = High
  M = Medium
  L = Low

Figure 17-4.   *In this chart, each type of audit is rated in terms of the levels of skill required to complete the engagement successfully. Skills are rated in areas of industry experience, technical expertise, and auditing skill.*

Figure 17-5 A–F.   *Position descriptions are given for each member of the internal CIS audit department. Positions range from CIS Auditor Trainee to the Director of CIS Auditing. Requirements given include job function, results, knowledge and skills, duties, and training.*

JOB TITLE: CIS AUDITOR TRAINEE

FUNCTION

Assist in basic reviews and CIS audits to learn and apply judgment of the effectiveness of controls in computerized and related manual systems in operational areas.

RESULTS

In accordance with current operational plans:

1. Complete all audit tasks assigned by the CIS auditor.
2. Review and appraise the soundness, adequacy, and applications of accounting, financial, and other operating controls.
3. When assigned, assist regular audit staff members in the effective discharge of their responsibilities.

KNOWLEDGE AND SKILLS

The knowledge and skills required for this function include:

1. Hold a college degree or equivalent, at minimum. A major in accounting and/or CIS or business is preferred.
2. Complete successfully required CIS courses, offered either as in-house training programs or from outside institutions.
3. Optionally, have one year of programming and/or systems analysis experience.
4. Possess some knowledge of corporate policies and procedures.
5. Demonstrate the ability to communicate effectively, both verbally and in writing.

TRAINING

The training for this position will deal with communication skills, audit techniques, and corporate policy.

Communication. Communication skills will be developed through presentation of reports to different audit groups. The trainee will prepare these reports in support of the work of CIS auditors.

Audit. The trainee will attend classes dealing with basic audit techniques and procedures for operational audits, as well as for some audits of applications. Training also may be provided through self-directed instruction with in-house training materials (such as videotapes), or courses may be taken at outside institutions. On-the-job training will be used extensively.

Corporate policy. Instruction for trainees in the area of corporate policy will include surveys of corporate structure and line responsibilities. Most of this training will deal with the function of the CIS audit department in relation to organizational goals and objectives.

JOB TITLE: ASSISTANT CIS AUDITOR

FUNCTION

Assist in systems review and CIS audits to evaluate the effectiveness of controls in computerized and related manual systems that are in either developmental or operational stages.

A.

RESULTS

In accordance with current operational plans:

1. Complete all audit tasks assigned by the CIS audit manager or the senior CIS auditor.
2. Review and appraise the soundness, adequacy, and application of accounting, financial, and other operating controls, as well as recommend effective controls at reasonable cost for computer information systems.
3. Determine the company's exposure regarding computer-based information resources.
4. When assigned, assist regular audit staff members in the effective discharge of their responsibilities in fulfilling CIS audit objectives.

KNOWLEDGE AND SKILLS

The knowledge and skills required for this function include:

1. Hold a college degree or equivalent, at minimum. A major in accounting and/or CIS or business is preferred.
2. Complete successfully required CIS courses, offered either as in-house training programs or from outside institutions or professional seminars.
3. Have one year of programming and/or systems analysis experience. Or, have one year of internal auditing experience. Possess a working knowledge of the programming languages in use at the company.
4. Possess a working knowledge of corporate policies and procedures.
5. Demonstrate the ability to function in a diversified environment.
6. Demonstrate the ability to communicate effectively, both verbally and in writing.

DUTIES

The duties of the assistant CIS auditor are:

1. Assist in CIS audits that will:
   A. Appraise the soundness, adequacy, and application of accounting, financial, and operating controls.
   B. Ascertain the extent of compliance with established company policy, plans, and procedures.
   C. Ascertain the extent to which the company's assets are accounted for and the degree of exposures involved.
2. Evaluate data compiled during assigned CIS audits and draft reports of findings and recommendations.
3. Write audit programs and computer extracts necessary to fulfill the audit objectives as approved by the CIS audit manager.

TRAINING

The training for this position will deal with communication skills, audit skills, and corporate policy.

Communication. The training for the assistant CIS auditor in communication will involve a great deal of report writing and oral presentation. Some of this training will be made available as materials for self-directed instruction.

Audit. The auditor will be given training in audit techniques for audits of applications, as well as some training in database concepts. Exposure in application programs will be heavily discussed in training classes.

Corporate policy. Training in corporate policy will involve the cash flows through the organization and general goals and objective setting techniques.

JOB TITLE: CIS AUDITOR

FUNCTION

Conduct systems review and CIS audits to evaluate the effectiveness of controls in computerized and related manual systems that are in either developmental or operational stages.

B.

RESULTS

In accordance with the current operational plans:
1. Complete all audit tasks assigned by the CIS audit manager or the senior CIS auditor.
2. Determine the reliability of computer information systems examined and their outputs.
3. Determine if computerized systems comply with statutory regulations, generally accepted accounting principles, adequate financial controls, and established corporate plans and procedures.
4. As a participant in the systems development effort, propose CIS controls that will report irregularities to management and deter fraud.
5. Determine degrees of exposure regarding the systems examined.

KNOWLEDGE AND SKILLS

The knowledge and skills required for this function include:
1. College degree, or equivalent; a major in accounting and/or CIS or business preferred.
2. Have one year of programming and/or systems analysis experience and two years of CIS auditing experience.
3. Demonstrate the ability to write programs in programming languages and for the operating systems in use at the company.
4. Be able to evaluate the technical aspects and requirements of a CIS.
5. Have thorough knowledge of corporate policies and procedures.
6. Demonstrate the ability to function in a diversified environment, to exercise effective CIS audit techniques, and to display the qualities of a competent, professional CIS auditor.
7. Demonstrate the ability to work with only limited supervision.
8. Communicate effectively, both orally and in writing.
9. Strive toward achieving professional certification, such as: CPA, CISA, CIA, CMA, CDP, or CSP.

DUTIES

The duties of the CIS auditor are:
1. Write audit programs and computer extracts necessary to fulfill audit objectives, as approved by the CIS audit manager.
2. Perform complex CIS audits as assigned. These audits will test for exposures, controls, regulatory compliance, compliance with corporate policy, and fraud.
3. Evaluate data compiled during assigned audits and prepare reports of findings and recommendations.
4. Conduct a survey for each new operating function assigned for review. Recommend audit procedures for operational and post-implementation audits of the related systems.

TRAINING

Training will build on prior work in communication skills, audit skills, and corporate policy.

Communication. Skills will be developed through the preparation and presentation of audit reports.

Audit. Audit skills will be enhanced through professional membership in auditing organizations, seminars given at off-site locations, and reading of professional journals.

Corporate policy. The CIS auditor will be instructed in the basic tasks and responsibilities in the company and the goals and objectives of individual departments. Political factors in the organization will be studied.

JOB TITLE: SENIOR CIS AUDITOR

FUNCTION

Accept responsibility for evaluating the effectiveness of controls in computerized and related manual systems in either developmental or operational stages. Conduct CIS audit training of staff within the CIS audit unit, as well as of auditors assigned temporarily from the regular audit staff.

c.

RESULTS

In accordance with current operational plans:

1. Assure the timely completion of all audit tasks assigned by the CIS audit manager.
2. Assess the reliability of computer information systems examined and their outputs.
3. Assure that all computerized systems examined comply with statutory regulations and generally accepted accounting principles.
4. Ascertain the extent to which company assets are accounted for and safeguarded from losses of all kinds.
5. Provide technical assistance to the regular audit staff members in the effective discharge of their responsibilities in fulfilling CIS audit objectives.

KNOWLEDGE AND SKILLS

The knowledge and skills required for this function include:

1. A college degree or equivalent, at minimum. A major in accounting and/or CIS or business is preferred.
2. Preferably, have two years of programming and systems analysis experience. As a requirement, have three years CIS audit experience with the company.
3. Demonstrate the ability to write programs in the programming languages and for the operating systems in use at the company.
4. Be able to evaluate the technical aspects and requirements of a CIS.
5. Possess thorough knowledge of corporate policies and procedures.
6. Demonstrate the ability to work with little direct supervision.
7. Communicate effectively, both verbally and in writing.
8. Achieve professional certification, such as: CPA, CISA, CDP, CMA, CIA, or CSP.

DUTIES

The duties of the senior CIS auditor include:

1. Develop audit objectives for reviewing computerized systems.
2. Prepare CIS audit procedures and supervise work performed by staff.
3. Write audit programs and computer extracts necessary to fulfill CIS audit objectives, as approved by the CIS audit manager.
4. Conduct complex CIS audits, as assigned.
5. Assist in the development of and be responsible for a training program for assistant CIS auditors, as assigned.
6. Coordinate audits with external auditors and provide any computer extracts, as authorized by management.
7. Perform post-implementation CIS audits as directed by CIS audit managers.

TRAINING

Training will follow through in the areas of communication skills, audit skills, and corporate policy.

Communication. The senior CIS auditor will do extensive report preparation and presentation to both internal and external personnel (such as external auditors). Techniques and training material for increasing the readability of complex information by management will be learned.

Audit. Specialized skills will be acquired in areas such as telecommunications, database, and on-line systems. Learning opportunities in these areas will be made available through external classes and on-the-job training. Use of special audit languages will be examined for possible application to work in the department.

Corporate policy. Proper channels and methods of information flow for reporting will be stressed. Management training also will be conducted.

D.

JOB TITLE: MANAGER OF CIS AUDITING

FUNCTION

Accept primary responsibility for assisting the general auditor in assuring that adequate controls of company assets are maintained. Carry out this charge by developing procedures for auditing computer information systems and by using the computer as a vehicle to improve regular audits. Supervise internal auditing assignments of the CIS audit staff to assure that controls over company assets are maintained, that operations are functioning efficiently, and that the company units are operating in accordance with established procedures.

DUTIES

The duties for the manager of CIS auditing include:

1. Assist the general auditor in developing the annual audit program. Assist in coordinating the corporate auditing effort with the public accounting firm and internal auditors of other units to provide audit coverage without duplication of effort.
2. Initiate follow-up action and review responses to audit reports, including those prepared by the public accountants to assure that appropriate action is being taken on all recommendations.
3. Review workpapers and audit reports prepared by auditors to assure that there is adequate documentation to support the work.
4. Review recommendations to assure that they are reasonable.
5. Act as a CIS audit consultant in matters of concern to other corporate managers.

KNOWLEDGE AND SKILLS

The skills and knowledge required for this position include:

1. Hold an MBA or MS degree in business, accounting, and/or CIS.
2. Possess thorough knowledge of the company, and its policies and procedures.
3. Possess specific knowledge in the areas of budgeting and management by objectives.
4. Demonstrate excellent verbal and written communication skills.
5. Have in-depth knowledge of the workings of the CIS audit department and its charter.
6. Have over five years of combined experience in the areas of CIS auditing, programming, and systems analysis.
7. Have attained professional certification, such as: CPA, CIA, CDP, CISA, CSP, or CMA.

TRAINING

Training is in the advanced aspects of communication skills, audit skills, and corporate policy.

Communication. The manager of CIS auditing is expected to make extensive written and oral presentations to all levels of management, as required by the responsibilities of the position.

Audit. Extensive class attendance is required on topics concerning new developments and applications of audit techniques. General trends and costs for audit departments, as well as control over audits, will be learned.

Corporate policy. Skills and procedures necessary at the levels of corporate managers and directors are learned. Training is received on budgeting and staffing for audits.

JOB TITLE: DIRECTOR OF CIS AUDITING

FUNCTION

Accept responsibility for the entire CIS audit department. The primary concern of this position is the direction and control of the department according to annual plans and budgets. The director is responsible to the board of directors or the president of the company for CIS audits. In this function, the director is the principal information resource for corporate directors regarding CIS audits. Most of the director's time will be spent on setting departmental goals and objectives and on preparing annual plans and budgets.

E.

DUTIES

The duties of the director of CIS auditing include:

1. Set goals and objectives for the department on an annual basis. This function includes both operational and strategic planning.
2. Develop budgets and staffing requirements for the department on an annual basis.
3. Meet with the outside CPA firm and serve as the primary contact with its partner in charge when dealing with CIS audit issues.
4. Attend all meetings of the board of directors and monitor changes in corporate structure that could be affected by CIS exposures.
5. Produce status reports to the president and the board of directors concerning the CIS audit functions.
6. Direct the CIS audit manager and assist in planning at that level, if necessary.

KNOWLEDGE AND SKILLS

The knowledge and skills required for this position include:

1. Possess a strong background in management. Three to four years experience is preferred.
2. Demonstrate strong, persuasive verbal and written skills.
3. Possess a good working knowledge of budgets and staffing requirements.
4. Have thorough knowledge of the policies and procedures of the corporation.
5. Hold a graduate-level college degree in business or accounting.
6. Possess a good working knowledge of the company's computer information systems.
7. Have at least five years experience as a CIS auditor or manager.
8. Hold at least two certifications in any CIS/Accounting/Auditing discipline (CPA, CISA, CDP, IIA, CSP, CMA, etc.).

TRAINING

The training of the director will be aimed at policy, budgets, and staffing requirements of the CIS audit department. Courses will be undertaken that develop management skills. Communication skills to all levels of management will be stressed.

F.

the individual and the goals of the company. Career progression within the company thus is provided for through a directed path of training and on-the-job experience.

Career Development Issues

A CIS auditor's career development is important both to the individual and to the company that commits its resources to training and development. If a clear career path and development program do not exist, the chances of poor performance and turnover of personnel are high. In charting career paths, organizations should recognize that CIS auditors represent a valuable resource for potential positions as corporate, financial, and operational managers. These qualifications can result from the proper mix of training (both formal and on-the-job), development of designated skills, and increased levels of knowledge and abilities through work experience.

```
                    FIRST YEAR CIS AUDIT BUDGET
                            (Forecast)


Total funds budgeted for the CIS Audit Division                    $335,000

To be allocated as follows:

1. Lease commitments for audit software:

   DYL-280 ................................................  $20,000
   CARS-3 .................................................    5,000      $25,000

2. Professional salaries and expenses, audit:

   Experienced CIS Audit Manager ..........................   60,000
   Experienced Senior CIS Auditor .........................   45,000
   Experienced CIS Auditor ................................   35,000
   CIS Auditor Trainee ....................................   20,000
   CIS Auditor Trainee ....................................   20,000     $180,000

   Travel Expense .........................................   50,000      $50,000

Total salaries, travel, and lease commitments ..............               $255,000

3. Allocation for miscellaneous fringe benefits for employees .........   30,000

4. Allocation for training of staff ............................   40,000

5. Reserve for Imprest Fund .....................................   10,000      $80,000

Grand Total ................................................                $335,000
                                                                         = = = = =
                             Remaining unallocated funds                    - 0 -
                                                                         = = = = =
```

Figure 17-6.

Shown here is the forecast budget for the first-year operations of an internal CIS audit department.

Prospects for career advancement also are among the most effective incentives for professional people. In recent surveys, some professionals ranked career advancement higher than monetary rewards. Many of the professionals who go into CIS auditing do so because its visibility can enhance their potential as corporate managers.

In today's environment, career development planning for CIS audit staff is insufficient in many organizations. This situation is due largely to pressures of time and job performance. Many times, an individual suffers in his or her career development by not receiving the appropriate mix of training and experiences. Also, a career path with discernible options may not be apparent. This combination of factors often results in turnover and losses of key staff members to outside organizations.

The surveys cited above sampled at least 100 CIS audit professionals from different organizations, in both government and private industry. Approximately 45 percent of the respondents indicated that their organizations did not have an established career path for CIS auditors. Further, most of the respondents stated that they had considerable problems hiring and retaining CIS auditors.

How does an audit or corporate manager design, develop, and implement a career development plan? Although the process of matching individual career paths with organizational objectives is not easy, the benefits of such planning must not be overlooked. Its key component is a defined career path within which options, training, expected knowledge, skills, and abilities are specified for each level advancement.

Establishing a Career Development Plan

A functional and fully successful career development plan has at least six major elements that must be integrated into an established process within the organization. These elements include:

- Career path planning with management support

- Definition of knowledge, skills, and abilities

- Performance measurement

- Performance counseling

- Training

- Professional development.

Career path planning with management support. To be effective, a career development plan must reflect a viable, workable concept that has management's full support. Without support, a plan is little more than a sales pitch to potential employees or—worse—a false promise to the CIS audit staff. Clearly, employee motivation and trust will suffer if it is discovered that the plan as presented is not coming into reality. In such cases, the loss of credibility for corporate and CIS audit managers alike could damage the basic mission of the department. Also, without established goals for advancement, CIS professionals eventually will seek opportunities outside the organization that offer more well-defined rewards.

An organization that has not established a career path for CIS auditors is confronted with a serious question: Can it continue to bring new staff into these critical positions, train them, and develop them—all to lose them to opportunities outside the organization? With a good career development plan, management is building valuable resources: CIS auditors are knowledgeable about the systems that are vital to the organization; and they have strong skills in CIS technologies and auditing methods, as well as excellent communication and administrative skills. Such people are ideal candidates for managing and integrating new technologies into the operating environment of an organization. As technology shapes the information age of the future, being able to adapt to new technologies increasingly will become a critical success factor for the organization.

Definition of knowledge, skills, and abilities. Specific knowledge, skills, and abilities must be defined for each level or step on the career development path. These requirements set the organization's expectations for an employee's performance in specified areas of responsibility and duty. Inherent in these requirements are the levels of skill needed for satisfactory performance. Nicotera's job descriptions for his department identify these critical elements. (See Figure 17-5.)

Job descriptions should be reviewed periodically. Without such attention, the descriptions might stagnate and might not adequately reflect any changes in responsibilities or technological impacts on the positions. Therefore, job descriptions should be reassessed on at least an annual basis to assure that they are relevant to performance measurement.

As part of a career development plan, the employee must be given specific goals and objectives from which both job performance and acquistion of knowledge and abilities can be measured. The plan should attempt to integrate both goals for yearly performance and long-term career aspirations. With such specific criteria, the employee can take an active role in his or her own career progress.

Performance measurement.   Performance measurement is the process by which criteria for individual career paths are matched to organizational goals and objectives. Employees need to understand how the measurement of their performance relates to their progress both within the CIS audit function and within the organization as a whole. It may not be apparent to them that advancing along the CIS audit career path does not necessarily guarantee horizontal or vertical movement within the organization.

A diagram presented in Chapter 3 is reproduced in Figure 17-7 to clarify this point. This diagram shows how interests, skills, and accomplishments are factors in the advancement of CIS auditors into the ranks of audit management, and on to senior management. To advance, a CIS auditor must demonstrate effectively—through strong performance, as well as the successful attainment of knowledge, skills, and abilities—the traits needed to make the desired transitions.

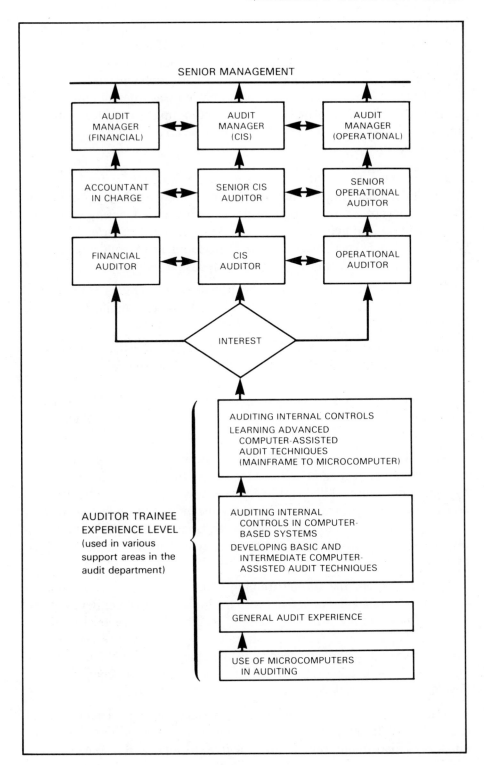

Figure 17-7.

As shown in this diagram, a departmental career path for CIS auditors includes a decision point at which individuals may enter the areas of finance, CIS, or operations.

Performance counseling. Management feedback is another important component of the career development process. Interim feedback on a quarterly or semi-annual basis—in addition to annual reviews—can be given in performance counseling that can address both problems and opportunities in time to make an impact on performance measurement and achievement. Feedback and informal reviews can point up the need for additional training or experience, and supervisors may be able to adjust work assignments accordingly.

Training. One of the main reasons given by CIS auditors for leaving an organization is that they did not receive the training originally promised to them. A relevant training program should be integrated closely with work assignments and individual career objectives. Also, the program should be phased so that it keeps pace with the development of both new and experienced auditors. A training plan should exist at two levels:

- A general curriculum should be prepared that covers training and education that must be administered to give all CIS auditors an opportunity to become fully qualified in their profession.

- Individualized plans should be prepared that are tailored to chosen career paths, as well as to individual strengths and weaknesses.

A general curriculum for CIS auditors is shown in Figure 17-8. This matrix shows the entry level and the competencies through which auditors must progress for each level of career advancement.

Note that the program is modular to allow expansion, substitution, and ease in updating. In general, training focuses on the areas of audit methodology, communication skills, and technical knowledge. If an individual has equivalent training or expertise—in prior education or through related work experience, for example—other courses can be substituted in his or her individual training program, or the training requirement can be identified as already met.

To supplement the formal training plan, specific on-the-job training should be identified and integrated with the individual's career development plan. Formal training thus may be applied directly to practical work experience. For example, training courses designed for audit managers and supervisors will be at an advanced level to prepare them for changes in technology, for new CIS audit methodologies, or to help them concentrate on developing managerial skills.

Care must be taken to prevent the pressures of work deadlines from crowding out training efforts. Management should consider the consequences of inadequate training upon field performance. If a course applies

	AUDIT-ORIENTED COURSES		CIS TECHNOLOGY-ORIENTED COURSES			
CIS AUDIT MANAGER	ADVANCED SUPERVISION	PROGRAM EVALUATION	AUDITING TELECOMMUNI-CATIONS	AUDITING SYSTEM SOFTWARE	AUDITING DATABASE MANAGEMENT SYSTEMS	
SENIOR CIS AUDITOR	ELEMENTS OF SUPERVISION	PRODUCING ORGANIZED WRITING AND EFFECTIVE REVIEWING	ADVANCED CIS CONCEPTS	INTRO TO COMPUTER PERFORMANCE EVALUATION	AUDITING CIS ACQUISITIONS	COMPUTER-ASSISTED AUDIT TECHNIQUES II
CIS AUDITOR	AUDITING AND JOB MANAGEMENT	SKILLS FOR PERFORMANCE AND CAREER DEVELOPMENT	COMPUTER SECURITY AND PRIVACY	INTERNAL CONTROLS IN AUTOMATED SYSTEMS	COMPUTER-ASSISTED AUDIT TECHNIQUES I	SYSTEMS ANALYSIS
CIS AUDITOR TRAINEE (LEVEL II)	CONDUCTING PROGRAM RESULTS REVIEWS	INTERMEDIATE WRITING	BASE LEVEL CIS-II	SYSTEM DESIGN AND DEVELOPMENT	CIS MANAGEMENT AND OPERATIONS	MICRO APPLICATIONS
CIS AUDITOR TRAINEE (LEVEL I)	ENTRY LEVEL TRAINING	ORIENTATION	BASE LEVEL CIS-I	USE OF MODELS AND OPS RESEARCH TECHNIQUES	INTRO TO SPSS AND S.A.S.	STATISTICAL SAMPLING AND MICRO-TECHNOLOGY

↑ ENTRY

Figure 17-8.

A general curriculum for CIS auditors is shown in this matrix for an integrated training program.

directly to ongoing work or adds to a staff member's knowledge base for assignments already planned, there can be a significant impact on the quality and reliability of the audit effort. Before an audit team ever starts an assignment and sets its milestones, management should plan for these developmental interruptions and should allow for both on-the-job and formal training in the work schedules. A training chart, as shown in Figure 17-9, can help managers to identify training needs for each individual and minimize potential conflicts with work assignments.

Professional development. A career development plan should provide for the progress of the CIS auditor within the professional community. As discussed in previous chapters, a number of professional organizations support the professional interests of the CIS auditor. Many of these organizations support professional certification as a method of establishing measures of professional competence for specific disciplines. Certification programs sponsored by different professional organizations are listed in Figure 17-10.

CIS auditors should be encouraged to continue their professional development and to seek certification as appropriate. This can be a specific

COMPUTER AUDITOR DEVELOPMENT PLAN _____

CATEGORY	COURSE #	COURSE TITLE	MONTH J F M A M J J A S O N D	PREREQUISITES	ACCEPTED
BASIC					
INTERMEDIATE					
ADVANCED					

Figure 17-9.

Such forms may be used to chart an individual course of training for a CIS auditor.

developmental goal set between management and the individual. Also, it can become a performance goal that, once achieved, can justify organizational recognition in the form of a bonus or a quality step increase to present salary.

Besides certification, a worthy goal is to pursue continued education beyond a bachelor's degree. Many colleges and universities offer post-bachelor certificate programs or advanced degrees at the masters or doctorate levels in business administration, accountancy, computer information systems, and so on. Also, some universities are beginning to offer training courses and curriculums in CIS auditing.

Training-related goals should be regarded as part of a performance contract between the individual and management. In effect, the individual and the organization agree to a developmental program that is in their mutual best interests. Once a plan is established and agreed upon, the individual is accountable to the organization for his or her own achievements in the fulfillment of its goals.

548

DESIGNATION	TITLE	PROFESSIONAL AFFILIATE
CPA	Certified Public Accountant	American Institute of Certified Public Accountants
CDP	Certified Data Processor	Data Processing Management Association
CIA	Certified Internal Auditor	Institute of Internal Auditors
CMA	Certified Management Accountant	National Association of Accountants
CISA	Certified Information Systems Auditor	EDP Auditors Foundation for Education and Research
CDE	Certified Data Educator	Society of Data Educators
CBA	Certified Bank Auditor	Bank Administration Institute
CSP	Certified Systems Professional	Association for Systems Management

Figure 17-10.

This table presents the certification programs sponsored by different professional organizations in the field of CIS auditing.

Participation in professional associations is another measure of professional development. A career development plan should take advantage of opportunities in professional associations to build management skills and professional contacts. Professional peer groups stimulate exchanges of information that is of mutual concern to the supporting organizations. CIS auditors who are duly recognized by external professional organizations for professionalism and expertise transfer that intangible benefit to their employers.

STAFFING, DIRECTING, AND CONTROLLING

Staffing, directing, and controlling are necessary, integrated steps in carrying out the management functions associated with the operational aspects of CIS auditing. Indeed, the actual results of the work performed must be assessed continually against short- and long-range departmental and corporate plans.

In the Abcor case, Nicotera established a proposed short-range plan for the internal CIS audit function. (See Figure 17-11.) As part of this planning process, Nicotera identified specific areas and applications in need of audit review. Estimates for work hours and levels of experience required in each area are summarized in the table in Figure 17-12.

In addition to these plans, Nicotera instituted a reporting procedure to keep track of ongoing projects. He proposed to use it as a communication vehicle to keep management informed of ongoing audit work. Figure 17-13 shows a monthly report used by the audit manager. Data from this report for

Proposed CIS Audit Plans
Abcor Data Services Company

Total Possible Audit Hours Per Year = 1,900 hrs.
(Excluding Vacation, Holiday and Sick Days)

AUDIT AREA	DESCRIPTION	NUMBER OF HOURS PLANNED FOR		LEVEL OF EXPERIENCE AND KNOWLEDGE NECESSARY TO EFFECTIVELY AUDIT OR PARTICIPATE IN THESE AREAS		
		198X	198Y	SAVINGS & LOAN INDUSTRY	TECH. SKILLS AUDIT MGMT.	AUDITING SKILLS
ATM Security Procedures (completed)	Review internal procedures and participate with ATM Task Group on enhancements.	20		Low	High	Med
Audit Confirmations/Tapes (ongoing)	Interface with External Audit firms in coordinating preparation of confirmations and master file tapes, answer questions.	80	100	Med	Med	Low
Audit Planning & Research (ongoing)	Planning of audit scope and objectives, determination of areas needing review. Research of technical areas using audit publications, IBM and user manuals, vendor publications.	500	650	Low	High	Med
Audit Sub-Committee (ongoing)	Participate with the Committee in suggesting new audit procedures, programs, discuss Third Party Review concerns.	30	30	High	Low	Med
Audit Training/Education (ongoing)	Attend in-house training sessions, audit conferences, seminars, read CIS audit publications.	80	120	Low	Med	Med
Control Standards Committee (ongoing)	Assist the Committee in making recommendations to Management Council on areas needing controls at Abcor.	40	40	Low	High	Med

Task	Description	Hours	Hours			
CIS Audit Software (ongoing)	Program and set-up software to assist and verify findings (IBM utilities, BAL programs, Easytrieve, PANVALET).	30	40	Low	High	Med
Emergency Situations (ongoing)	Research time, review and work papers for unplanned items.	400	200	Med	High	High
Out-of-Balance Conditions (ongoing)	Report and follow-up on out-of-balance conditions, system problems and errors.	150	200	Med	High	High
Project Development (in progress)	Review staff resource usage, planning processes, user involvement, coordination and implementation of projects, phases where CIS audit can effectively assist.	100		Med	High	High
System Enhancements (ongoing)	Review Interest Withholding, Line of Credit Negative Amort., Tiered MMF, ATM Access, and various system enhancements.	100	200	High	High	High
Tape Library Procedures (in progress)	Review control over tape inventory, movement in Library of production tapes, tape backup and retention procedures.	50		Low	Med	High
Third Party Review (ongoing)	External auditor assistance, work papers, follow-up with mgmt., FHLB and external audit questions.	320	320	Med	High	High
TOTAL AUDIT HOURS		**1,900**	**1,900**			

Figure 17-11. *This table recaps the proposed CIS audit plans for the internal function at Abcor.*

Potential Areas Needing Audit Review
Abcor Data Services Company

AUDIT AREA	DESCRIPTION	NUMBER OF HOURS REQUIRED TO ADEQUATELY AUDIT THE AREAS	LEVEL OF EXPERIENCE AND KNOWLEDGE NECESSARY TO EFFECTIVELY AUDIT OR PARTICIPATE IN THESE AREAS		
			SAVINGS & LOAN INDUSTRY	TECH. SKILLS AUDIT MGMT.	AUDITING SKILLS
ATM Network	ATM transfer transactions, multiple account links, future shared networks, review for adequate controls.	500	Med	High	High
Commercial Checking/ Lending Mortgage Banking	Audit implementation of these systems, review processing controls, changes to existing reports, new reports for customers, balancing procedures.	100 / 100	High	High	High
Distributed Data Processing	Mini and Micro computers hooked up to Abcor increases the variety of access to our system. Audit review may be needed to help assure that adequate controls are in place.	1,000	Low	High	Med
Operating Systems	Audit change control procedures, documentation, determine if adequate control options are implemented, operator instructions are provided. IBM's DOS/VSE (existing), IBM's MVS (new), Phoenix's CONDOR and CAMLIB (new).	700	Low	High	High
Teleprocessing Network	Review management and control of our T.P. network, its individual programs, security and access.	700	Low	High	High
TOTAL AUDIT HOURS		3,100			

Figure 17-12. *Potential areas at Abcor needing audit review are summarized in this table.*

CIS AUDIT PROJECTS (Report of September 198X through August 198Y):

The following CIS audit reports have been submitted to Abcor Management on the dates indicated:

	Project #	Date
INFOLINE & VM Controls		9/26/8X
G18 Audit Report—VOP Usage		11/14/8X
4700 ABCS (Advanced Branch Controller System)		11/16/8X
Abcor Terminal Network Controls		12/05/8X
Computer Run Instructions		12/06/8X
IBM System/36 MiniComputer Access	#84S3601	1/19/8Y
Third Party Review—Prior Period Recs.	#84TPR02	2/15/8Y
Third Party Replies (from Management)		3/28/8Y
Project Tracking	#84PRJ03	6/08/8Y
Third Party Review Status	#84TPR05	8/03/8Y
Computer Room Access Procedure	#84CRA06	7/30/8Y

CIS AUDIT ACTIVITIES:

CIS auditing has been involved in the following areas during the period of September 198X through August 198Y:

CONDOR	(Online programming tool, preliminary report #84CON04 was issued to Mgmt., July 198Y)
Audit Committee	(User auditors meet with CIS auditor and Cust. Rep. every other month)
Control Standards Committee	(Abcor management met with CIS auditor every month, committee dissolved since hiring of Methods & Procedures Analyst)
ATM Network and Attala Procedures	(Preliminary gathering of information on ATM network changes, assisted Systems Development Dept. in establishing a secure communication key for data transmission between Abcor and QUICK Teller)
System Enhancements	(Review of selected system write-ups from Systems Development Dept.)
CIS Audit Training	(On-the-job training of new CIS auditor since May 198Y)
CIS Audit Education	(Auditors attended an IBM Project Mgmt. class and IBM Data Security Seminar)

Figure 17-13. *This is an example of a CIS audit manager's monthly report.*

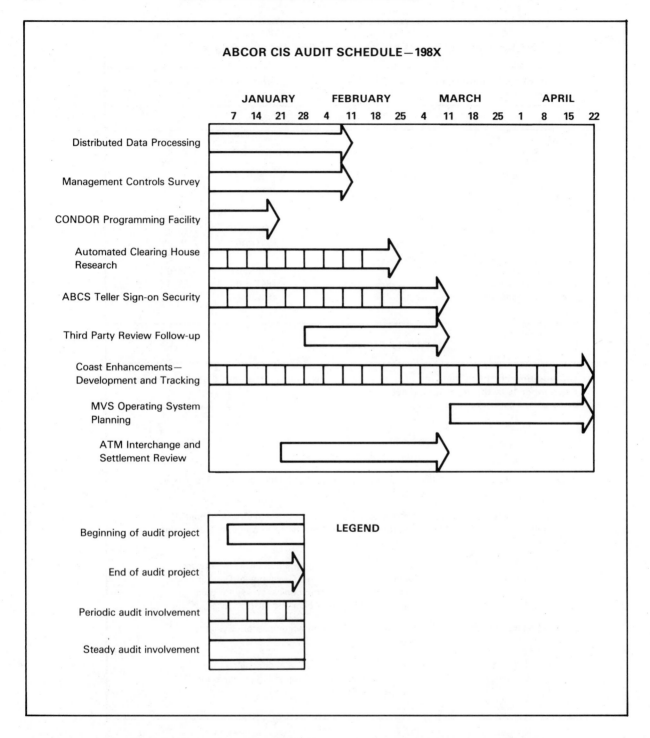

Figure 17-14. *A Gantt chart such as this may be used to plot a CIS audit schedule and work in progress.*

ATM INTERCHANGE SETTLEMENT
Audit Plan
1/16/8Y

PURPOSE

Determine what controls are currently in the ATM Interchange system to ensure that data are valid and complete and to detect out-of-balance conditions. Determine what procedures are documented to recover from out-of-balance conditions.

SCOPE

Review and assess the entire ATM Interchange settlement procedure, including reports and balancing.

BENEFITS

- Assure that the ATM Interchange Settlement reports balance with QUICK Teller reports.
- Assure that a procedure to handle out-of-balance conditions is documented.

PLAN

1. Define purpose and objectives of audit.
2. Gather background information.
3. Interview key personnel for input.
4. Gather detailed information.
5. Evaluate controls and procedures and determine exposures.
6. List observations and findings.
7. Publish preliminary report for comments by February 22.
8. Review comments and follow up with revisions.
9. Draft and review recommendations with key personnel.
10. Issue Final Report by March 8.
11. Present to Management Council on March 13.

Figure 17-15.

This is an example of a CIS audit plan. This particular plan is for a review of settlement procedures for automatic teller machines (ATMs) within the banking systems that Abcor serves.

specific projects are posted to a wall chart in the audit manager's office to help communicate progress to others. This chart is shown in Figure 17-14.

Under Nicotera's procedures, each audit manager is responsible for individual audit plans for specific projects. These plans must be reviewed to assure that purpose, scope, anticipated benefits, and approach are intended to meet the audit mandate. A sample audit plan is shown in Figure 17-15. A critical function involves supervisory review of the audit plan, as well as the work performed and assurances that the working purpose supports both the audit methodology and findings derived.

In essence, the CIS audit management function is a complex process that involves not only traditional management competencies but also special concerns that are unique to CIS auditing. A CIS audit manager, like other business managers, is involved in planning, organizing, staffing, directing, and controlling the department and its work. In addition, the manager of the CIS audit function must deal with environmental influences that affect the audit activity. Human resource development—including career and professional development for CIS auditors—and systems project management are disciplines that are particularly important within the CIS audit function.

D I S C U S S I O N   Q U E S T I O N S

1. **In your opinion, what qualities and skills make a good manager?**

2. **What unique characteristics of CIS auditing might pose special challenges to CIS audit managers?**

3. **What is the importance of a CIS audit charter in planning and organizing a CIS audit group?**

4. **What is the relationship of formal job descriptions to overall career development plans?**

5. **Why might professional development be of particular concern to CIS auditors?**

6. **In managing the CIS audit function, how is the organization of the department related to the ability to control its activities?**

7. **What is the nature and purpose of a formal audit plan for a specific project?**

18 CIS Auditing: A Future Outlook

A B S T R A C T

- The future of the audit profession well may depend on how well auditors, including CIS auditors, adapt to rapidly changing computer and telecommunication technologies.

- As background for examining trends in CIS auditing, a future scenario describes the application of advanced technology to the review of financial statements.

- Trends in technology that may affect the audit profession include the growing use of personal computers, expansion of digital communication networks, growing use of information services, competition for information markets, higher levels of CIS integration, and persistence of a software "bottleneck."

- Training of future CIS auditors is an important area of emphasis. Such training must keep pace with trends in telecommunication and teleprocessing, as well as firmware, microcircuitry, and embedded technology.

- Legal responsibilities of the CIS auditor will become increasingly complex. The CIS auditor will need to understand security and protection legislation to be able to fulfill these responsibilities in evaluating automated systems.

- Sharing of information across professional boundaries may become increasingly crucial in the CIS field. In particular, organizations that can work together include the AICPA, IIA, EDP Auditors Association, NAA, DPMA, ASM, and ACM.

- Challenges of microcomputer-assisted auditing are presented in a case study. Benefits of microtechnology to the audit profession have been analyzed in studies by public accounting firms and the federal government. Preparing an audit organization for the introduction of microtechnology requires careful attention to planning, the pace of introduction, and consideration of organizational impacts.

CHANGE OR PERISH?

The scenario below is the product of imagination, a glimpse of tomorrow's technology as envisioned by some of the professionals at a major public accounting firm. However, the scenario is not a forecast of professional standards in general or of the emerging policies of any particular public accounting firm.

The scenario presents a look at advanced systems technology applied to audit and review of computer-generated financial statements. As sophisticated electronic systems evolve, corporate and audit management will have to look to professionals who have made deliberate efforts to stay ahead of technological advances. That is, auditors and the auditing profession must either change or perish. (The following material is copyrighted © 1979 by Arthur Young & Company and is reproduced here with the firm's permission.)

It is Saturday morning, January 12, 2002 . . .

An Arthur Young partner is completing review of the audit documentation before signing the firm's audit opinion, which will be included in the client's annual financial report to the SEC.

When he first started with the firm in 1981, partner reviews of audit workpapers were conducted by reviewing the key audit judgments and manually prepared workpapers.

Today, this partner is totally comfortable reviewing the audit documentation on his microcomputer. The documentation was prepared through holography—a technique that utilizes three-dimensional laser-photographic and data-reduction processes. This is the same technique many of his clients use for storing, in archival format, various printed records for financial support or legal requirements.

Back in 1981, computer output microfiche (COM) was a commonplace storage medium to replace large volumes of printed reports from computers. As the state of the art advanced, holography provided the capability to squeeze up to two-and-one-half million bits of machine-readable information into one square inch located horizontally across the top of this same microfiche. The recording of this information, in 2002, is accomplished with a digitized format capable of being retrieved and read by computers, not just by humans; thus, the term "human readable/ machine readable (HR/MR) card."

The partner submits a request from his remote computer to search and retrieve specific portions of audit documentation from the firm's central computer facility for audit file record retention. Within ten seconds, the central computer facility obtains the appropriate HR/MR card and provides to his remote computer any data requested from this portion of the audit documentation.

The client company is called Life Line, Inc. It produces a special chemical liquid, for which it holds the exclusive patent, that can be used as an emergency replacement for human blood. It can function for up to eight hours and is normally used either to provide emergency transfusions to accident victims or as a supplement for rare blood types during open-heart surgery. During its ten years of operations, Life Line has been able to establish a worldwide market with strategically located warehouses and distribution facilities to provide speedy dissemination of the product.

As a high-technology company, Life Line, Inc. has developed one of the more sophisticated business support systems available in 2002. Most of the Company's data processing is handled by its central processing and data storage facility, which makes extensive use of supercold (cryogenic) processing and storage technology.

Data is stored on cryogenic storage wafers at a temperature of −450°F. Each wafer measures approximately one-quarter inch by one-quarter inch. Thirty wafers stacked one on top of another would fit vertically between two lines on a human thumbprint. Each wafer can store up to ten thousand characters of data. The Company currently maintains five thousand wafers in its storage facility.

Because of the extremely high cost of maintaining such cold temperatures on earth, the Company has leased one-third of a commercial data processing satellite. This satellite processor and storage facility communicates with the Company's communications computer and archival storage systems on earth. The Company has substantially improved the response time of its communications to its various worldwide locations by communicating directly between its data-processing satellite and standard earth-orbiting communications satellites.

The use of the Company's product in emergencies dictates that its manufacturing facilities operate on a twenty-four-hour-a-day, seven-day-a-week basis. The production, material movement, and inventory control systems are almost totally automated, so that the Company can man its main five-acre production facility with just eleven people. They specialize in production control, hygienic maintenance, and overall plant control and equipment-monitoring.

Life Line, Inc. operates seven major EDP systems, the communications for which are all handled through a sophisticated, often interlocking, electronic network. The newest of these systems is the Stockholder/Investor Reporting System—SIRS. The management at Life Line, Inc. felt that it was just as important to provide timely information to its investors as to provide timely product to its customers. Thus, the Company maintains its financial records in such a manner that a stockholder may utilize his or her home computer to call Life Line's central processing facility and request unaudited financial statements that are no more than forty-eight hours old, or audited financials as of the last month-end. It is this last characteristic of the Company's approach to business that brought Life Line to Arthur Young & Company.

Life Line's month-end financial statements, transmitted back to the investor or stockholder, include the firm's audit opinion. A recent example read as follows:

"To the stockholders of Life Line, Inc.:

We have audited the Company's financial statements through the month ended November 30, 2001 in accordance with professional standards. This examination included on-site visits to the Company's various facilities, and analyses of material financial accounts and those management judgments which have financial impact; it also included regular remote monitoring of transactions performed through audit software under our control which is embedded in the Company's financial and management information systems.

In our opinion, the accompanying financial statements present the financial position of Life Line, Inc. as of the month ended November 30, 2001 and the results of operations for the eleven months then ended in conformity with generally accepted accounting principles.

(Signed) Arthur Young & Company

December 3, 2001."

To provide this client service, Arthur Young & Company was involved during the entire process of systems development at Life Line, Inc. Various audit routines for transaction monitoring and account analysis were encoded into the Company's information systems. The monitoring of the financial transactions is done through remote audit computers located in the Arthur Young office that services Life Line.

The results of these automated audit tests, along with in-person interviews, account analyses, and various evaluative observations made by

Arthur Young personnel, form the substance of the holographic audit documentation our audit partner is reviewing on his remote computer. After he finalizes his review, he keys in a special ciphering code which serves as the firm's "electronic signature" and is required before the Company can transmit its annual financial report to the SEC.

If this scenario typifies tomorrow's business methods, most managers and employees will have to know how to use many different types of computer information systems, including advanced office systems, computer graphics, and management analysis systems. Business people in the future will need a basic understanding of CIS technology, database management, telecommunications, and other fast-developing technologies. With such movement and dynamic change, the auditor of tomorrow also will change or perish. As illustrated in the diagram in Figure 18-1, management competency is being driven by technology.

TRENDS IN CIS TECHNOLOGY

Factors and trends that are shaping the evolution of CIS technology include:

- Growing use of personal computers
- Expansion of digital communication networks
- Trends toward information services
- Competition for information markets
- Higher levels of integration
- The software bottleneck.

Growing Use of Personal Computers

Desk-top microcomputers, or personal computers, are becoming commonplace, both in the office and at home. Despite their small size, these systems are highly capable; some are equivalent in many ways to machines in the 1950s that sold for as much as a million dollars.

In addition, microprocessors are being incorporated into all kinds of devices, including video games, television sets, and telephones, as well as in microwave ovens, washing machines, and automobiles. Thus, more and more aspects of everyday life are being influenced by computers and digital control methods.

These trends should stimulate more widespread computer literacy, reinforced by the consequent increase in the number of people able to program and use computers. The first generation to grow up with computers now is reaching maturity. These computer-literate young adults accept computers

MANAGEMENT PROFICIENCIES	1980's TECHNOLOGY APPLIED
Planning (short-term and strategic)	• Forecasting tools, expert systems, and information systems • Human participation in setting goals • Automated systems that extrapolate past performance • Humanized systems such as planning retreats and brainstorming • Microcomputers that develop planning aids such as charts and graphs • CIS and telecommunications which make products of planning and results accessible • Computer simulations that allow managers to assess options quickly
Organizing (facilitating change)	• Critical Path Method (CPM) and Program Evaluation Review Technique (PERT) to analyze aspects of the organization • Electronic mail to simultaneously announce and track reorganization • Database management simulations and models of "best" organization components • Behavioral theory to "unfreeze" and "refreeze" attitudes about change • Management theory on organizational structures • Socio/technical interaction and group dynamics skills
Staffing (providing right people, right place, right time)	• Aids to the process of assigning staff to jobs (Myers-Briggs Type Indicator, e.g.) • Equipment to screen applicants rapidly • Programmed learning and computer-assisted instruction to speed training • Videotape feedback for improved interviewer skills
Directing (facilitating communication among people)	• Electronic mail and computer controlled in-boxes • Reader-controlled responses at computer keyboard • Computer storage of procedures and directions • Automatic calendaring and automated spreadsheets • Data management and menu capabilities
Controlling (Providing managers more opportunities for monitoring conditions)	• Computer recorded transactions • Instant summaries of results to supervisors • Automated control systems to signal deviations from standards • Voice-activated technology

Figure 18-1.

This table lists the technologies that may be applied to different areas of management proficiency.

as a natural part of their world. Computer design and use are being taught in schools and as a part of adult education. Acceptance and knowledge of this technology will enhance an already thriving market for specialized application programs designed for personal computers.

Expansion of Digital Communication Networks

Commercial digital communication networks are evolving that promise to be efficient, economic, and convenient to use in linking information systems and users. Within a few years, most computers, even small ones, will be connected to a communication network at least part of the time. In some cases, and particularly within business systems, the communication system may be dedicated to a single application under which all machines on the network perform portions of a larger task. Another type of distribution is found within public data networks, which can provide any home or business computer with access to a wide range of databases or special programs for occasional use.

Such multiuser, national (or even global) networks can be expected to grow in both size and number. Accordingly, the number of users should grow at a phenomenal rate.

Trends Toward Information Services

The computer industry traditionally has been concerned with the selling of hardware, including mini- and mainframe computers, and peripherals. However, current trends in both pricing and the structure of the market are aimed at providing computer-based information services, such as bibliographic and database services, electronic publishing, electronic banking, electronic mail, and so on.

To access some of these services, users will have to possess a computer. However, other services will be available over digital communication lines through an "intelligent" telephone or television set. Examples include two-way cable television, videotex, and electronic telephone directories. Eventually, information services of all kinds will dominate the computer information processing market in terms of dollar volume. An example of the progress in this field is the use of voice-activated computer systems by the handicapped.

Competition for Information Markets

With the growth of information services, there should be intense economic competition among giant corporations. For example, IBM, AT&T, Exxon, GTE, and others are preparing to offer a wide variety of digital communication services. These corporations have access to the capital required to install the necessary large-scale technological bases, such as communication satellite systems and fiber-optic transmission networks.

A series of recent rulings by the Federal Communications Commission, some still under challenge at this writing, are intended to clear the way for open competition in providing information services of all kinds over telecommunication lines. Resolution of the pending challenges by the courts or by Congress will have significant implications over the long term for the digital communication and information services industry.

At the same time, an examination of the computer industry shows that small entrepreneurs frequently have been innovators. Certainly, valuable, fundamental advances have originated from the research laboratories of large companies such as AT&T and IBM. However, creative new systems and innovative services often come from relatively small, new enterprises—and often from totally new entrants into the market. Faced with the emerging dominance of this field by large corporations, these small organizations and their supporters are likely to press for public policy that will guarantee their access to and ability to compete within digital communication networks.

Higher Levels of Integration

Many individual networks dedicated to specific corporate and governmental needs will continue to be built. Some of these networks, in turn, will become integrated with one another. For example, most airlines, car rental agencies, and large hotel chains have their own reservation systems. It is now feasible technically to build an integrated system that would provide travel agents access to all of these reservation systems through one desk-top terminal.

Similar integrated information systems evolve in the fields of insurance, banking, entertainment, law enforcement, trading in stocks and commodities, and many other sectors that now use several, separate information systems. In some cases, factors such as system incompatibility, antitrust considerations, or competitive problems may hamper attempts to integrate the systems.

The Software Bottleneck

In all these changes, the cost of software may prove to be the pace-setting factor. Progress has been slow in the development of new techniques for reducing the cost of programming. Some experts see the software problem as a major obstacle to the development of new computer applications and to full utilization of increasing hardware capabilities.

Problems stem from the fact that the productivity of programmers in general is not increasing. Efficiencies are needed in the management of complex systems projects. Also, the installed base of existing applications creates a demand for maintenance and enhancement projects. These urgent needs compete with new applications for the limited availability of programmers.

For some popular applications, programming costs can be written off over a relatively large user base. However, for a number of large, specialized applications, the costs of programming, maintenance, and operation will remain high. For the foreseeable future, at least, the cost of competent, sophisticated programming efforts will limit progress.

Computer programming has been relatively resistant to productivity improvement, especially when compared to corresponding improvements in hardware performance. Programming, by nature, is labor-intensive. Costs are rising due to the increased programming requirements of new, sophisticated hardware—coupled with a shortage of programming personnel with the needed training and technical expertise. New approaches such as structured programming and design promise to be helpful in engineering computer programs and managing their design and implementation.

On the hardware side, microtechnology is making possible enormous increases in computational power through the creation of new hardware structures from clusters of small computer chips. Although these new configurations hold great potential, using them effectively will require corresponding advances in programming.

The Auditor and Technology

To the extent that these trends change the ways in which significant organizational information is handled, the CIS auditor will be affected directly. The prospect in this challenging field is for constant, perhaps continuous, technological and organizational change. Specifically, electronic transaction processing and digital communication techniques will change information flows in major ways.

THE TRAINING OF FUTURE CIS AUDITORS

Although the basic concepts of CIS auditing have been around since the 1960s (or since the 1950s, according to some authorities), CIS auditing as a profession came into its own in the 1970s. Today, as business and classified advertisements in many newspapers indicate, demand is strong for CIS auditors, internal auditors with CIS audit experience, or accountants with CIS knowledge and qualifications.

Demand for CIS auditors has grown recently due to headlines that have startled the business and financial community. News accounts of the Equity Funding fraud, the Stanley Rifkin Security Pacific incident, the Wells Fargo banking fraud—to name just a few—have caused general concern. Legal issues have been brought into focus by the passage of the Foreign Corrupt Practices Act, and the Counterfeit Access Device and Computer Fraud and Abuse Act.

The average dollar loss per crime or abuse of computer-based systems now is estimated at between $500,000 and $1 million. Managers in both private industry and in government are realizing that vulnerabilities exist in their information systems due to computer technology.

Levels of concern can only increase. Demand for competent CIS auditors will rise accordingly. To meet this need, CIS audit professionals and educators will have to turn their attention to the special areas of competency that must be emphasized.

Where Is CIS Auditing Going?

Many observers speculate that, before the turn of the century, there will be a revolution in thinking about and attacking CIS-related problems. CIS auditors will have to broaden their competencies to include all types of information systems.

Today's CIS auditors, especially those with international organizations, are feeling the pressure of advancing technology. Traditional installation reviews are not sufficient for approaching audits of systems that involve distributed processing, database architecture, local area networks, and other advanced techniques. Further, the gap between technology and the auditor's methods of dealing with it may widen as the limits are pushed beyond what today is considered possible or achievable.

Dramatic changes and as yet unanswered challenges can be expected in the areas of:

- Telecommunication and teleprocessing
- Firmware, microcircuitry, and embedded technology.

Telecommunication and teleprocessing.   The state of CIS technology is such that on-line, real-time financial information systems are on the horizon. Such systems will be made possible by developments in the fields of telecommunication and teleprocessing. The speed and efficiency of digital communication should increase by a factor of 100 within a few years. Some CIS auditors in the banking industry already are involved in the planning of on-line, real-time financial information systems. Within such a system, if a transaction occurs in a California subsidiary, the transaction will appear almost immediately on the financial books of the holding company in New York.

Telecommunication and teleprocessing involve a host of subtopics that the CIS auditor of the future must be able to review adequately and capably. Examining the controls in such a system requires a high level of technical expertise and a knowledge in such areas as telemetric transfer of data, cryptographics, and the security of telecommunication and teleprocessing.

Firmware, microcircuitry, and embedded technology.   Another area of technology's virtual explosion is in the packaging of computer instructions in microchips. Use of this technology already is far advanced in aerospace and weapon systems. More recently, applications within information systems in business have been tried. What is emerging are highly compact systems that can be self-contained or shared in distributed architecture. The orientation of such systems is toward total integration of multiple processing and communication channels.

To deal with these advancements, the CIS auditor must be able to conduct audits and examinations of the microcircuitry itself to assure that processing yields valid, reliable, and secure information for management decision making.

Legal Requirements

Besides facing challenges on the technical front, CIS auditors will have to deal with a host of changing legal issues. For example, public concern over information privacy and security has been felt particularly in some of the European countries. Public opinion in Luxembourg, Austria, and West Germany has recognized computerized data as a potentially harmful weapon in the wrong hands. These governments have enacted strong laws to assure that individual data and access to the dissemination of information are controlled and protection guaranteed.

The federal government in the United States also has become increasingly concerned about computer crimes. As discussed previously in this text, in November, 1983, public testimony before the Civil and Constitutional Rights Subcommittee and the House Judiciary Committee placed estimates of losses due to abuse of computers by white-collar criminals at $40 billion annually. Public concern resulted in the passage of the Counterfeit Access Device and Computer Fraud and Abuse Act in October, 1984. The act outlaws unauthorized access to the Federal government's computers and certain financial databases protected under the Right to Financial Privacy Act (1978) and the Fair Credit Reporting Act of 1971.

At this writing, in addition to the 1984 computer crime law, there are a number of initiatives before the U.S. Congress. These bills seek to protect computers and data in the private sector. (The private sector is not covered by the prior legislation.) The bills, which are similar to the ones introduced in 1984, include:

- H.R. 930, sponsored by Representative Bill Nelson (Democrat, FL), would outlaw unauthorized access to computers used in interstate commerce or in financial institutions.

- H.R. 995, sponsored by Representative Ron Wyden (Democrat, OR), would penalize the unauthorized access to or alteration of individual medical records through a telecommunication device.

- H.R. 1001, sponsored by Representative William J. Hughes (Democrat, NJ), would establish felony and misdemeanor charges for unauthorized access to computers used in interstate commerce if the defendant reaps $5,000 or more in the crime.

Clearly, the Privacy Act of 1974, the Foreign Corrupt Practices Act of 1977, and other legislation are stepping stones to more comprehensive security and protection legislation. The CIS auditor will need to understand these laws clearly and apply them in evaluation of automated systems.

A Centralized Future?

It seems possible that, one day, the knowledge, experiences, and the capabilities in the CIS audit field will be shared and communicated through some centralized resource. Advanced networks and integrated information systems could make this type of sharing feasible.

The concept of a centralized resource for CIS auditors might take the form of a learning center. Through such a learning center, professionals could exchange knowledge and develop the CIS audit discipline to its fullest potential. Figure 18-2 shows the possible elements of such a learning center.

Through such a learning center, international and national professional associations and government audit functions could contribute the valuable knowledge and experience of their members. Participating groups might include:

- American Institute of Certified Public Accountants
- Institute of Internal Auditors
- EDP Auditors Association (and its foundation)
- The National Association of Accountants
- Data Processing Management Association
- Quality Assurance Institute
- Association of Systems Management
- Association for Computing Machinery, Special Interest Group on Security, Audit, and Control
- Federal, state, county, and city audit organizations
- University and audit education societies
- International organizations such as Canadian Institute of Chartered Accountants and the International Federation of Accountants.

In addition, groups in related professional fields might contribute valuable information to such a center to help the CIS auditor of the future cope with the demands of a changing environment. The prospect is that professional societies, educational institutions, government agencies, and public accounting firms all will be instrumental in contributing to such a valued resource.

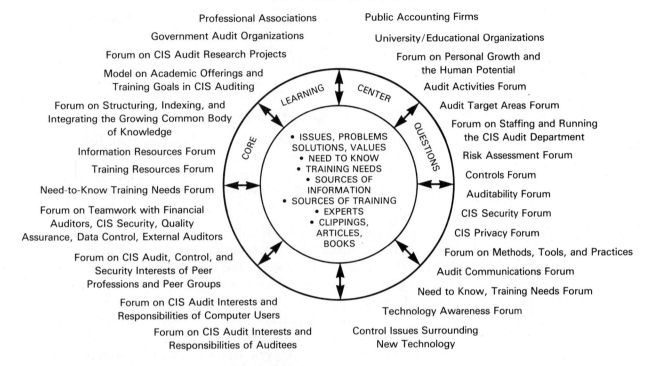

LEARNING CENTER ELEMENTS

Forum on CIS Audit Professional

Professional Associations

Government Audit Organizations

Forum on CIS Audit Research Projects

Model on Academic Offerings and Training Goals in CIS Auditing

Forum on Structuring, Indexing, and Integrating the Growing Common Body of Knowledge

Information Resources Forum

Training Resources Forum

Need-to-Know Training Needs Forum

Forum on Teamwork with Financial Auditors, CIS Security, Quality Assurance, Data Control, External Auditors

Forum on CIS Audit, Control, and Security Interests of Peer Professions and Peer Groups

Forum on CIS Audit Interests and Responsibilities of Computer Users

Forum on CIS Audit Interests and Responsibilities of Auditees

Public Accounting Firms

University/Educational Organizations

Forum on Personal Growth and the Human Potential

Audit Activities Forum

Audit Target Areas Forum

Forum on Staffing and Running the CIS Audit Department

Risk Assessment Forum

Controls Forum

Auditability Forum

CIS Security Forum

CIS Privacy Forum

Forum on Methods, Tools, and Practices

Audit Communications Forum

Need to Know, Training Needs Forum

Technology Awareness Forum

Control Issues Surrounding New Technology

LEARNING CENTER
CORE
QUESTIONS

- ISSUES, PROBLEMS SOLUTIONS, VALUES
- NEED TO KNOW
- TRAINING NEEDS
- SOURCES OF INFORMATION
- SOURCES OF TRAINING
- EXPERTS
- CLIPPINGS, ARTICLES, BOOKS

Figure 18-2.

This diagram presents a hypothetical information sharing network for the CIS auditors of the future. (Adapted from "The Need for a Better Trained EDP Auditor." GAO Review, Winter 1982, pp. 49–51.)

MICROCOMPUTERS AS AUDIT TOOLS

A significant change that already is having an impact is the adoption of microcomputers as automated support for CIS auditors. The need for this type of support is rooted in the auditor's role.

The Auditor's Role

Auditing is a complex and iterative investigative process under which data must be collected from a variety of sources. Tests and reviews are performed to establish patterns or conditions that suggest steps for further data gathering. The methodology is exploratory. That is, each step in the process could trigger an unanticipated, new direction. The objective is to come to some decision regarding the relevance of the data, signs of incorrectness, and observations in making recommendations for improvement.

The auditor is part of an investigative team whose place of work is highly transient. Mobility is a key job characteristic; typically, auditors must spend 40 to 60 percent of their working time in the field. This situation immediately suggests the need for a portable computer.

The problem of mobility, however, is much more complex than just moving about from place to place. Client circumstances and audit requirements change from one location or engagement to another. These types of challenges are illustrated in the scenario below.

Scenario: Challenges of Microcomputer-Assisted Auditing

Alice Nguyen, an audit manager with a public accounting firm in Los Angeles, must plan CIS audit support for an engagement at a client site in Fresno, which is a little more than 200 miles away. Her challenge is to identify requirements for portable audit computers in support of the engagement in Fresno.

In planning for CIS support, how will the auditors decide what software to take along for the expected work? Nguyen's first step is to think through all the systems resources and access methods that the team will be likely to need. Although many details of the audit environment are known to her, she also knows from experience that there will be inevitable surprises once the team is on site. She knows that it is virtually impossible to predict all such contingencies. Ideally, some form of ad hoc access to centralized software files will have to be available. Nguyen determines that the team must have dial-up access to the firm's computerized audit packages. With the entry of predetermined access codes, they should be able to download desired programs to portable computers over the telephone line.

Nguyen also knows that there may be a need to access a foreign computer system, such as the computer facility in the client's Dallas headquarters. If this contingency does arise, Nguyen knows that the team should not depend on the availability of the client's terminals or upon the availability of relatively "unfriendly" host software. However, she is not sure whether it will be possible for the team to obtain their own software for host operation. Even if they can identify such resources, how can they gain the cooperation of management of the local installation? Might not setting up the desired operating environment interfere with ongoing processing? Or, should she consider bringing the firm's computer system to bear on the problem?

On further reflection, Nguyen also realizes that working papers the team will need may be dispersed physically throughout the site of investigation. Inspecting these documents may require access to different client officers, perhaps in different buildings. There may be files or equipment that the auditors will need to inspect in person, and there will be people that they must interview. In thinking about this degree of mobility, Nguyen realizes that some small computers are too bulky to be truly portable; these microcomputers are designed to be transportable—to be moved from one place to another occasionally rather than constantly. She is convinced, then, that the audit team would be better served by units that are both more compact and more rugged.

Nguyen also feels that, once on-site and faced with an abundance of data, the team should have the tools for getting at the crux of the matter quickly and efficiently. Rather than building a vast database for subsequent analysis in the privacy of the home office, it should be more cost-effective to hone in on the pertinent data and derive insights from the situation on site. She concludes that the auditors will need computer support not just for data entry, data selection, or sampling, but also for sorting, comparing, formatting, and producing both tabular and graphic outputs. These requirements mean that the portable computer must have both high internal capacities and the ability to interface easily with large, external systems. Software also must be fully integrated. For example, the final report should be written as soon as possible following the examination with a word processing package, preferably one that can accept inputs from the team's computer-generated spreadsheets and graphics.

To make all this happen, Nguyen knows that the field computers will require a versatile communication facility. Since the auditors operate in a team, they will need to share data as well as to communicate with other members of the group. Also, the portable audit computer may have to operate as a terminal to a host computer; yet, it must have all of the capability of a dedicated, desk-top processor. Thus, there is the need to have the necessary computer hardware components and protocol handlers, a variety of terminal software emulators, and a high-speed modem.

Given these requirements, there is another major concern: The auditors are trained analysts but are not computer professionals. Hence, there is a requirement for providing a suitable user interface that is both easily learned and functionally useful.

Findings of Microcomputer Studies

Numerous studies that have assessed the usefulness of microcomputers within the audit function have been conducted by:

- Public accounting firms
- Federal government.

Public accounting firms.   A study performed by Arthur Young & Co. identified several potential benefits of microtechnology. The study found that, if auditors have their own microcomputers, there are fewer disruptions of the client's CIS operations. Also, the audit staff can do the work themselves rather than having to rely on client personnel to provide computer support. With microcomputers, the auditors have state-of-the-art technology to match the technology used by the client. For example, they no longer have 14- or 21-column manual spreadsheets, but can generate printouts in a full width of 132 characters. Accordingly, audit independence is increased. The auditors can determine more readily whether the data supplied by the client are accurate, appropriate to their request, and supported adequately.

Other major public accounting firms also have reported similar benefits and productivity gains. Some firms even have stated that microtechnology has enhanced audit effectiveness and efficiency by approximately 15 to 25 percent. Overall, the consensus of opinion has been highly favorable. Specific benefits that have been cited include the following:

- Spreadsheet software helps avoid extended delays when modifications to spreadsheets are necessary. The ability to edit quickly or to modify a given product is enhanced greatly. "What if?" questions can be posed and answered promptly.

- Manual handling, sorting, calculation, and recalculation of data can be eliminated or reduced greatly.

- With microcomputers, data are more accurate, timely, and readily accessible than under manual methods.

- Cumulative recording of data decreases work on later cycles.

- Electronic calendars and tickler files reduce the number of missed due dates.

- Word processing that is accessible to professional employees reduces turnaround time for drafts, revisions, and final documents.

- Graphic display of information contained in databases or spreadsheets promotes clarity of data presentation.

- Morale is improved as a result of working with state-of-the-art technology. Employees appreciate that management has recognized a need for productivity tools that help build effectiveness and morale.

Federal government.   The offices of the Inspector General (IG) are taking similar, progressive steps aimed at understanding more precisely how microcomputers can be used within the audit environment. In 1983, the

Computer Audit Committee under the President's Council on Integrity and Efficiency launched an aggressive program to train several thousand auditors and investigators to use portable microcomputers capably. The goal was to increase the efficiency and effectiveness of the IG's work. The following benefits have been realized in ongoing IG work:

- Auditors from the Department of Interior (DOI) used microtechnology to analyze data on royalty payments made to the DOI by oil and gas companies. The analysis uncovered underpayments amounting to $1.5 million.

- An official from the Computer Audit Committee reported that savings in work hours from using microcomputers in performing certain types of audits range from 24 to 75 percent.

- A former Department of Transportation (DOT) official cited startling results achieved by DOT auditors—including 318 indictments, 272 convictions and $40 million in fines—in activities supported by portable microtechnology. These tools helped auditors to uncover widespread rigging of bids in federal construction projects. DOT auditors experienced a 25 percent improvement in productivity, based on test results.

The U.S. General Accounting Office (GAO), the watchdog of Congressional spending, has conducted similar studies within its own agency that concur with the benefits cited by other agencies and firms. In addition, the GAO found that microcomputers can help auditors to:

- Access agency data directly from centralized systems for use in audit analyses.

- Share analyses and findings for comparisions with those of other government agencies, including the Congressional Budget Office (CBO) and Congressional Relations Office (CRS).

- Share applications and develop templates, or data formats, for ease of data transcription and analysis.

In its internal studies of the use of microtechnology, GAO cited productivity gains in the neighborhood of 25 to 35 percent. However, the study was realistic in noting that some of the productivity gains could be measured in staff-hours or dollars. In other instances, additional productivity was seen in that the offices were able to take on both more work and work not previously possible with existing resources.

Thus, microtechnology not only helps the agency's auditors to perform their tasks more efficiently and effectively, but also helps in the performance of collateral responsibilities such as budgeting, management reporting, and accounting, as well as audit and financial reporting.

Other federal, state, county, and city audit organizations are beginning to integrate microtechnology into their audit operations. Federal agencies that are involved actively include: NASA, Department of Agriculture, Department of Transportation, Department of Education, Department of Defense, Air Force Audit Agency, Defense Contract Audit Agency, and Naval Audit Service. Similar uses of these tools are being reported by state and local audit organizations, including the California State Auditor General's Office, the County of San Bernardino Auditor-Controller Office, and the City of New York Auditor's Office.

PREPARING AN AUDIT ORGANIZATION FOR MICROTECHNOLOGY

Change can be introduced into an organization either suddenly or in a planned, orderly manner. Microcomputers can represent significant organizational resources. Not only is there significant potential for productivity from this investment, but there is also the chance of waste and lost opportunity. For auditors and other business people alike, there is a growing need to develop an organizational view for managing rapidly changing technology. Major questions should be addressed in the areas of:

- Planning

- Pace of introduction

- Organizational impacts.

The ultimate goal of this process is successful integration of new technology into the workplace.

Planning

Determining the role and focus of microcomputers is a key planning step. Questions to be asked in assessing the potential application of this technology within the organization include:

- What role will this technology have in the organization?

- What level of skill does the organization have in place to accept this technology?

- How will this technology be used, now and over the next five years or so?

Figures 18-3 and 18-4 present specific functions that have been identified for microcomputer support within an audit organization that has multiple

- SCHEDULES
  Setting up formats (spreadsheets)
  Performing calculations
  Verifying data
  Summarizing

- MATHEMATICAL CALCULATIONS

- STATISTICAL FUNCTIONS

- WORKPAPER INDEXING AND CROSS-REFERENCING

- REPORT DRAFTS

- COMMUNICATIONS
  Transferring all or any of the above from one audit site to another or from
  an audit site to headquarters.

Figure 18-3.

This table lists audit tasks that can be performed using microcomputers.

USE OF MICROTECHNOLOGY

SUPPORT FIELD AUDITOR NEEDS	Data Capturing Word Processing Data Management Statistical Manipulation
SUPPORT REQUIREMENTS INVOLVING COMPREHENSIVE ANALYSIS	Modeling Uploading to Larger Resources Use of SPSS, SAS or Other Analytical Package
SUPPORT THE CAPABILITY TO TRANSFER APPLICATIONS TO OTHER AUDIT SITES	Data Files (ASCII) Applications • Higher Level Language • Family Software

Figure 18-4.

This table correlates uses of microtechnology with the types of support needed by CIS auditors.

offices. The identification of these functions is part of a needs assessment process in an attempt to integrate microcomputers with the organization's mission and goals.

Another area, assessment of existing skills in the organization, can help to determine how much training and preparation of staff will be needed before microcomputers can be brought successfully into an organization. Skills assessment can be supported by staff interviews or questionnaires during the needs assessment process. Types of skills to be identified include:

- Prior knowledge of or exposure to data processing and/or micro-computers

- Analytical skills, such as mathematics, logic, and qualitative methods

- Attitudes of staff toward automated tools such as the microcomputer.

Pace of Introduction

The introduction of microcomputer technology must be done so as to:

- Facilitate its use

- Minimize disruption

- Support an orderly transition to the new environment.

A phased introduction approach that can achieve these objectives is the *pilot project.* A pilot project is an initial, trial implementation within a relatively small work group. Such projects can help to determine appropriate support activities and effective ways of providing that support. Further, a pilot project can help an organization determine the policies and guidelines to be established for facilitating and controlling the application of microcomputers.

For example, a successful pilot project undertaken by a national public accounting firm covered a period of six months. The project confirmed specific areas in which microcomputers could be used. Figure 18-5 presents the audit areas in which microcomputers were found to be useful.

The pilot project provided organization-specific examples of how this technology could be used productively. The limited implementation permitted users to experiment with the technology in a routine work setting. In addition, the pilot group was able to identify reasonable goals for integration of specific applications. (See Figure 18-6).

Organizational Impacts

New technology, including microcomputers, is potentially disruptive to an organization that has not done sufficient planning. Changes in work roles and

AUDIT AREAS

- PLANNING
- ANALYTICAL PROCEDURES
- WORKPAPER FILING SYSTEM
- NARRATIVES
- FINANCIAL STATEMENTS

Figure 18-5.

Shown here are the audit areas in which microcomputers were found to be useful in a pilot study.

USE OF THE MICROCOMPUTER AS AN AUDIT TOOL

APPLICATIONS	GOALS AND OBJECTIVES
Education Phase:	
Client accounting data	Overall audit efficiency
Time and budget data	Automation of time-consuming activities
Trial balances and working papers	Improved time and budget control
Memo and report generation	Improved documentation
Adjusting and updating financial data	Reporting efficiency
Complete documentation	
Drafting final documents	
Familiarization Phase:	
Spreadsheet analysis	Improved basic auditing effectiveness
Designing audit programs	Improved audit programs
Simple analytical review procedures	Evidence collection efficiency
Sampling and results analysis	Improved evidence analysis
Controls analysis worksheet	
Application Phase:	
Sophisticated analytical review procedures	Sophisticated computerized functions
Access client files and remote databases	Improved auditor decision making
Generalized audit software functions	Audit scope enhancement
Modeling and decision support functions	Improved CIS audit skills
Audit-file collection	Decision support systems
Continuous monitoring	Standalone collection
	Independent audit files

Figure 18-6.

This table summarizes some goals and objectives for using the micro-computer as an audit tool in a three-phase approach that includes education, familiarization, and application.

work patterns have been observed; and, unless the organization is prepared to accept these changes, the transition can be difficult. With new technology, an organization typically goes through the following transitional phases:

- Education

- Familiarization

- Application.

Education.   The education phase involves training and initial orientation on how to use the equipment. In this process, it is important to begin by building an understanding of computer concepts. Physical components of the microcomputer, including the keyboard, processing unit, monitor, and disk drives, should be related to input, processing, output, and storage functions. Then, preliminary hands-on training can involve using the microcomputer to solve small case problems under the watchful eye of an instructor. Or, the auditor may learn through available tutorials or texts. In such cases, self-prompting, self-documenting software can be extremely helpful. The pace of learning and the ease of application will depend on the individual's skill, aptitude, and initiative.

Familiarization.   The objective of the next phase is helping the individual become comfortable with the microcomputer. Uses can be explored through experimentation and creativity. Also during this phase, microcomputer applications become useful in day-to-day operations. As individuals come to see potential applications, they can begin to incorporate new tools into their audit methodology. Management should be patient and understanding during this phase: The individual, through practice and learning from errors as well as successes, will begin to gain competency, as well as achieving levels of acceptance and comfort that promote productive, routine use.

Application.   In the application phase, the auditor gains proficiency. As proficiency is built, the auditor also begins to develop innovative approaches to problem solving, thus enhancing the audit methodology.

From an organizational viewpoint, these three phases are continuous and concurrent. That is, implementation is continuous in that people are trained as they enter the organization. The process is concurrent in that all three phases are interdependent. Phases become, in effect, building blocks for staff members at different levels of skill and development.

MICROCOMPUTER-BASED TOOLS FOR THE CIS AUDITOR

The term *audit automation* is used to describe the application of general-purpose microcomputers to such tasks as audit planning, data testing, analytical review, preparation of workpapers, reporting, and so on. Note that there is a basic distinction between audit automation and computer, or CIS, auditing. In computer auditing, a computer system is used to perform tests on computer-maintained data. The process of reviewing and evaluating a CIS also is encompassed by this term. By contrast, audit automation involves using computer technology to enhance all auditors' effectiveness and productivity. Thus, a general-purpose microcomputer may be equipped with application-software tools that potentially can support all types of audits—of manual or automated systems.

Such microcomputer-based tools for auditors fall generally into categories that include:

- Standalone application packages

- Integrated audit-support systems.

Standalone Application Packages

Microcomputer software in this category includes application packages for specific audit tasks. These packages, in turn, are available for different system configurations, including the most popular microcomputer hardware units and operating systems.

An example of this type of product is FAST, an application software package for assisting the auditor in preparing trial balances and financial statements. This package contains a set of application programs that have been written in a high-level database-management language.

Another approach is to adapt electronic spreadsheet software to support specific auditing and accounting formats. These formats, called *templates,* contain columns and rows corresponding with those of manual workpapers for specific types of analysis. Also embedded within the template are *macros,* or callable subroutines, for performing calculations that correspond with mathematical relationships. A format and set of mathematical relationships is called a *spreadsheet model.* Such macro-driven spreadsheet models may be used for financial-ratio analyses, listing and control of accounts receivable confirmations, and preparation of other types of audit schedules.

Integrated Audit-Support Systems

An integrated audit-support system is an attempt to implement a multipurpose, automated environment that can support many of the auditor's routine tasks. This is a system of integrated software modules for handling different aspects of planning, controlling, and performing audits, as well as managing data and workpapers in electronic form. Integration of the modules means that they all can reside on a single microcomputer, can share a common database, and are accessible by a common set of commands.

An example of such a system is AY/ASQ™ (Audit Smarter, Quicker), which has been developed by Arthur Young & Company. A diagram of the application modules within the system is shown in Figure 18-7. The five modules are:

- System control

- Communication

- Data testing

- Audit administration

- Decision support.

System control.   The system-control module provides the high-level interface that links the auditor (user), application programs, the microcomputer operating system, and the electronic database. To enter the system, the user must key in identification and security-access codes. The system-control module then authenticates these codes before access to programs or data is permitted.

Communication.   The communication module is composed of terminal-emulation and data-transfer software utilities. These utilities enable the system to be *connectable* with, rather than *compatible* with, other types of computer systems. Data transfers may involve downloading records from client mainframe computer systems or moving files from one microcomputer system to another, as in transferring workpapers, data, or reports from one auditor to another or from a remote location to the office. In an audit environment that includes diverse and potentially incompatible client systems, the ability of the auditor's microcomputer to operate under different communication modes and protocols is essential. Also, the concept of an "electronic office" for auditors would be meaningless if it were not possible to transfer data among microcomputers that might have different operating systems, microprocessors, and data storage formats.

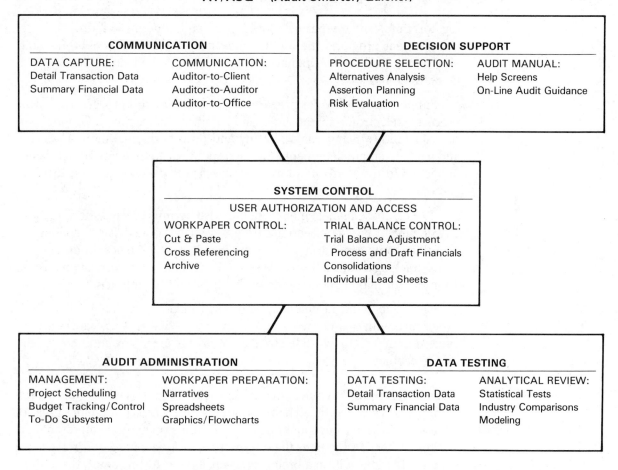

AY/ASQ™ (Audit Smarter, Quicker)

COMMUNICATION

DATA CAPTURE:	COMMUNICATION:
Detail Transaction Data	Auditor-to-Client
Summary Financial Data	Auditor-to-Auditor
	Auditor-to-Office

DECISION SUPPORT

PROCEDURE SELECTION:	AUDIT MANUAL:
Alternatives Analysis	Help Screens
Assertion Planning	On-Line Audit Guidance
Risk Evaluation	

SYSTEM CONTROL

USER AUTHORIZATION AND ACCESS

WORKPAPER CONTROL:	TRIAL BALANCE CONTROL:
Cut & Paste	Trial Balance Adjustment
Cross Referencing	Process and Draft Financials
Archive	Consolidations
	Individual Lead Sheets

AUDIT ADMINISTRATION

MANAGEMENT:	WORKPAPER PREPARATION:
Project Scheduling	Narratives
Budget Tracking/Control	Spreadsheets
To-Do Subsystem	Graphics/Flowcharts

DATA TESTING

DATA TESTING:	ANALYTICAL REVIEW:
Detail Transaction Data	Statistical Tests
Summary Financial Data	Industry Comparisons
	Modeling

Figure 18-7.

The five modules of the AY/ASQ™ integrated audit-support system are shown here.

Data testing. This module includes application programs for performing statistical sampling or analyses on client data, which may be downloaded under the communication module described above. Specific capabilities include applying regression analysis to identify irregularities or abnormalities within a given population of items. By obtaining input data from third-party sources or from the firm's audit database, comparisons may be made within the client's industry. Mathematical models also may be applied. Routines are available for generating random numbers, as well as for stratifying accounting transaction populations, evaluating the results of detail testing of statistical samples, and projecting account balances within given confidence levels.

Audit administration. Programs within this module assist the auditor in managing audit engagements, preparing schedules and budgets, accounting for time, and preparing workpapers and reports. Within the time-management program, the auditor may keep track of charged-time (staff hours) and audit fees. A management module also helps the auditor maintain a to-do list.

Support for workpaper preparation includes a word processor, a forms processor, electronic spreadsheet, and database management. Graphic output capabilities include data plotting and flowchart generation. Thus, the auditor may create documents for correspondence, create or edit standard or custom forms, perform numeric analyses, and generate graphic displays and outputs.

The database-management function also permits the auditor to retrieve any document based on searches for given strings of text. This capability is useful for composing form letters from prior correspondence, finding precedents, tracking confirmations, and so on. Performing such correlations within large files of manual documents probably would be impractical.

The database-management system is similar conceptually to the auditor's experience with manual workpapers and files. That is, workpapers are organized as though they resided in manual storage areas—by audit binder and by file cabinet.

Decision support.   Under this module, the auditor may develop overall audit plans, as well as detail audit programs for each account. Once areas of audit attention have been identified, the planning program then presents the auditor with a list of options that represent appropriate procedures, based on similar situations within a broad experience base. At this point, the auditor also may develop customized procedures for a specific industry, client, and situation. In presenting key options in the decision making process, the planning module functions as an expert system.

The output of the planning module is a textual description of the selected audit procedures. This text then may be input to the audit administration module for word processing, as in drafting workpapers and reports. These documents may be filed electronically with the audit workpapers for the account.

This type of integrated audit-support system, in effect, can serve as an electronic tool-kit or workbench for the auditor, whether the system under examination is manual or computer-based.

Looking to a Microcomputer-Based Future

The microcomputer holds prospects for being a universal work tool found on almost every desk in every office of every modern business. Combined with advanced digital communication and networking capabilities, electronic work stations will be integrated with all types of information systems on a global scale.

The challenge to auditors generally, and to CIS auditors in particular, is not to follow this trend, but to lead it. Because the auditors' mission is tied inextricably to the information flows in their organizations, assuring adequate controls in new, automated office environments means mastery of information processing and communication technologies.

D I S C U S S I O N   Q U E S T I O N S

1. In the Life Line scenario, what might be the nature of the controls within the company's financial reporting systems?

2. How does the level of integration of CIS resources affect the potential complexity of audit involvement?

3. What future developments might help remove the limitations that have resulted from a shortage of experienced computer programmers?

4. To what extent can microcircuitry and firmware be treated as "black boxes" for audit purposes?

5. How might future legal requirements on the private sector parallel recent legislation in the public sector?

6. Based on Alice Nguyen's evaluation in the case study, do you believe that use of portable audit computers would be practical with current technology?

7. What might be some organizational and behavioral impacts of introducing microcomputer technology to an internal audit department?

APPENDIX A
Case Study:
WhyMe Corporation

Project 1: Overview of Controls

This project is the suggested case assignment for Chapter 6.

CASE BACKGROUND

WhyMe Corporation, a multi-location retailing concern with stores and warehouses throughout the United States, presently is in the process of designing a new, integrated, computer-based information system. This new information system will process all company records, which include sales, purchase, financial, budget, customer, creditor, and personal information. This new system will permit data to be transmitted to a network of remote terminals. Accordingly, top management has expressed great concern over the potential for unauthorized use of system data. Also of concern is the prevention of physical threats to the new system, including sabotage, water damage, power failure, or magnetic radiation.

As a control procedure, the system routinely creates backup records for reconstructing information in the event of loss. However, such events would prove highly costly to normal company operations. WhyMe Corporation has requested the firm's internal auditors to identify possible control problems within the new system. Based on their findings, the auditors also may recommend control measures for safeguarding physical security for CIS facilities, equipment, and files and preventing unauthorized access to information. The directives of WhyMe management to the firm's internal auditors are listed in Figure A-1.

System Description

The Board of Directors of WhyMe has approved the acquisition of new computer hardware and system software to support the proposed system. Due

---

INTERNAL AUDITORS' TASKS

1. Identify and explain possible problems in relation to the confidentiality of information and records.
2. Recommend measures that would assure confidentiality of information and records.
3. Identify and describe safeguards that WhyMe could develop to provide physical security for:
    a. computer equipment
    b. files
    c. CIS facilities.

Figure A-1.

to the large scale of this system (see Figure A-2), management viewed hardware availability and maintenance, as well as software compatibility and support, as being the most important selection criteria. Thus, the decision to lease IBM hardware, along with the chosen system supports (see Figure A-3), was based upon management's perspective that such a large vendor was best able to meet these criteria.

WhyMe also approved a new data communication network for the system, as shown in Figure A-4. Presently, the central corporate office is in Los Angeles, while the three distribution centers are in Los Angeles, St. Louis, and New York City. Each of the three centers are equipped with a host processor (IBM 370). All of the store and warehouse terminals are connected to the host through several communication controllers (3705). In the event that one host processor fails, the other host processors have the responsibility to provide backup. If all three fail, a compatible system must be brought on-line.

The structure of the security function within WhyMe is diagrammed in Figure A-5. This documentation is critical to the auditor's job of identifying the controls necessary to meet management's requirements for system data protection.

Protection Against Exposures

Management has gone to great lengths to acquire nearly ideal system components for WhyMe's processing requirements. However, the new system

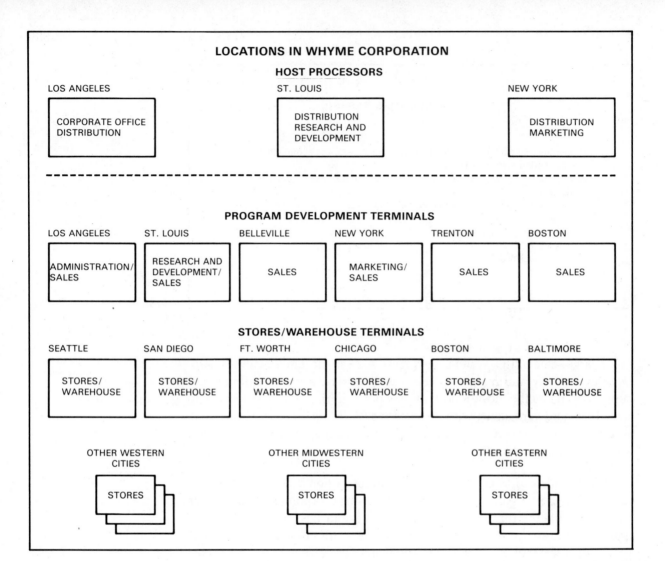

LOCATIONS IN WHYME CORPORATION

HOST PROCESSORS

LOS ANGELES

> CORPORATE OFFICE
> DISTRIBUTION

ST. LOUIS

> DISTRIBUTION
> RESEARCH AND
> DEVELOPMENT

NEW YORK

> DISTRIBUTION
> MARKETING

PROGRAM DEVELOPMENT TERMINALS

LOS ANGELES

> ADMINISTRATION/
> SALES

ST. LOUIS

> RESEARCH AND
> DEVELOPMENT/
> SALES

BELLEVILLE

> SALES

NEW YORK

> MARKETING/
> SALES

TRENTON

> SALES

BOSTON

> SALES

STORES/WAREHOUSE TERMINALS

SEATTLE

> STORES/
> WAREHOUSE

SAN DIEGO

> STORES/
> WAREHOUSE

FT. WORTH

> STORES/
> WAREHOUSE

CHICAGO

> STORES/
> WAREHOUSE

BOSTON

> STORES/
> WAREHOUSE

BALTIMORE

> STORES/
> WAREHOUSE

OTHER WESTERN
CITIES

> STORES

OTHER MIDWESTERN
CITIES

> STORES

OTHER EASTERN
CITIES

> STORES

Figure A-2.

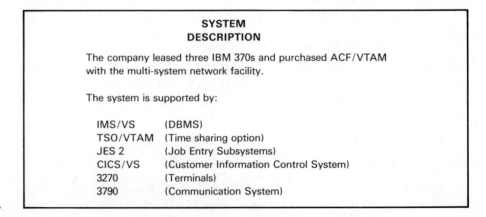

**SYSTEM
DESCRIPTION**

The company leased three IBM 370s and purchased ACF/VTAM with the multi-system network facility.

The system is supported by:

IMS/VS	(DBMS)
TSO/VTAM	(Time sharing option)
JES 2	(Job Entry Subsystems)
CICS/VS	(Customer Information Control System)
3270	(Terminals)
3790	(Communication System)

Figure A-3.

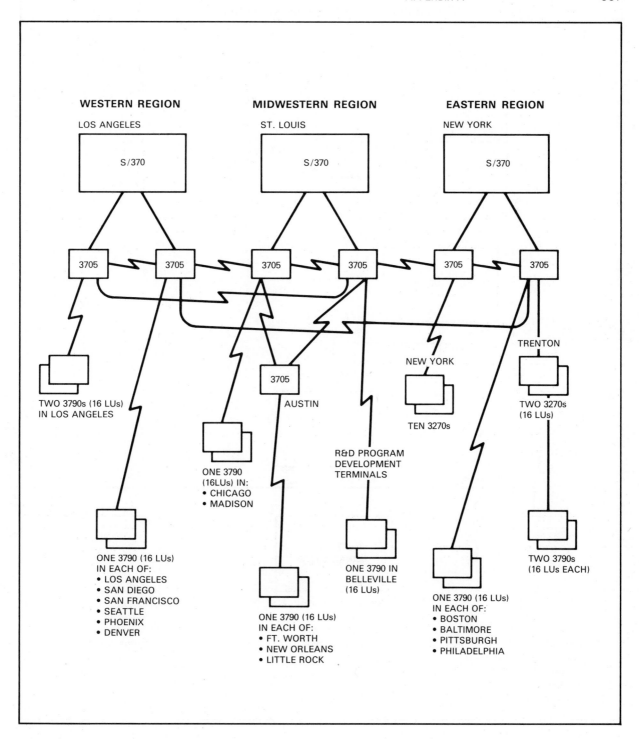

WESTERN REGION

LOS ANGELES

S/370

MIDWESTERN REGION

ST. LOUIS

S/370

EASTERN REGION

NEW YORK

S/370

3705 3705 3705 3705 3705 3705

3705

AUSTIN

TRENTON

NEW YORK

TWO 3790s (16 LUs)
IN LOS ANGELES

ONE 3790
(16LUs) IN:
• CHICAGO
• MADISON

R&D PROGRAM
DEVELOPMENT
TERMINALS

TEN 3270s

TWO 3270s
(16 LUs)

ONE 3790 (16 LUs)
IN EACH OF:
• LOS ANGELES
• SAN DIEGO
• SAN FRANCISCO
• SEATTLE
• PHOENIX
• DENVER

ONE 3790 (16 LUs)
IN EACH OF:
• FT. WORTH
• NEW ORLEANS
• LITTLE ROCK

ONE 3790 IN
BELLEVILLE
(16 LUs)

ONE 3790 (16 LUs)
IN EACH OF:
• BOSTON
• BALTIMORE
• PITTSBURGH
• PHILADELPHIA

TWO 3790s
(16 LUs EACH)

Figure A-4.

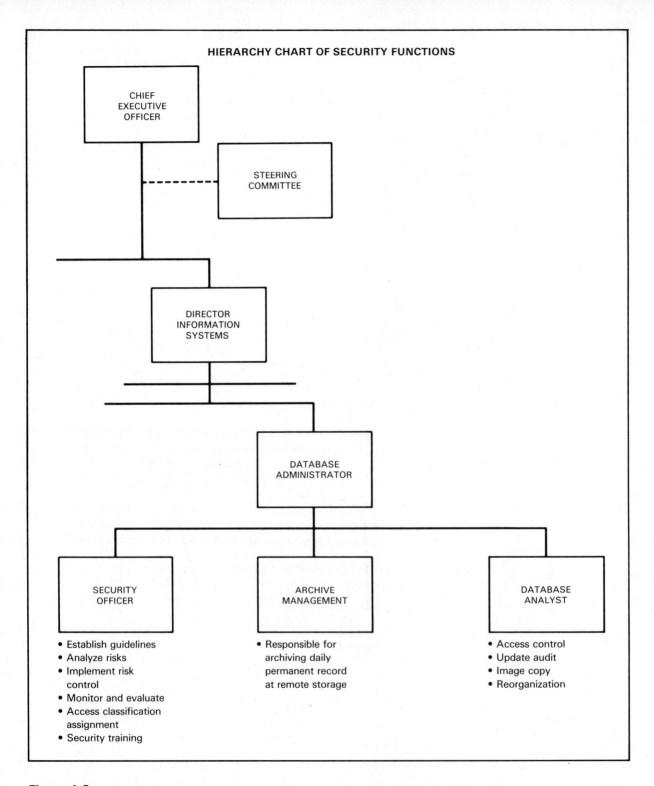

Figure A-5.

will have to be supported by numerous security measures to assure the reliability and security of its information resources. Physical damage or unauthorized access to WhyMe's computerized information system could result in the following adverse business effects, or exposures:

- Erroneous record keeping
- Unacceptable accounting
- Business interruption
- Erroneous management decision
- Fraud and embezzlement
- Statutory sanctions
- Excessive costs/deficient revenues
- Loss or destruction of assets
- Competitive disadvantage.

Realistically, it would be impossible to avoid completely all of these exposures. A balance must be struck between the cost of avoiding an exposure and the cost of having to absorb it. Thus, it is necessary to identify the security controls that would be cost-effective. The best means of identifying needed controls is by examining the system for unsatisfactory control points and predicting the types of threats to which the system remains vulnerable.

CASE ASSIGNMENT

Identify and describe controls that should be included within WhyMe's new information system to protect it against natural threats or unauthorized access. Include the specific application, input, programmed, output, and transmission controls—both manual and electronic—that would be appropriate for this system.

Project 2: Systems Development Controls

This project is the suggested case assignment for Chapter 9.

THE SYSTEM DEVELOPMENT TEAM'S REPORT

The WhyMe Corporation discussed in Project 1 has decided upon several objectives that it would like to meet over the next few years. Achieving these targets means making improvements in the company's present information systems. The following report was presented to the board of directors by a systems development team assigned to address WhyMe's information processing needs.

Short-Range Objectives

Five short-range objectives have been identified by management to improve the business position of WhyMe:

- Maximize profit centers.

- Develop a solid management foundation.

- Acquire or merge with at least two token companies in the next two years.

- Achieve a corporate profit of $400 million.

- Implement a new management information system (MIS).

Meeting these objectives calls for extensive changes in the present computer information systems at WhyMe. Perhaps the most important short-range objective in this regard is the implementation of a corporate MIS.

Long-Range Goals

Four long-range corporate goals also have been identified that will affect WhyMe Corporation's information systems:

- Achieve a corporate profit of $800 million by 1991.

- Acquire at least eight companies through merger.

- Develop a cadre of management capable of developing and supporting WhyMe's growth.

- Operate under a management-by-objectives philosophy.

For WhyMe, the determining factor in successful achievement of these long-range goals will be the ability to collect, process, and analyze information.

A well-designed MIS, identified as one of WhyMe's short-range objectives, will assist the company in meeting its information-processing goals.

Features of the Management Information System

The short- and long-range objectives listed above, and the responses of WhyMe's management to systems analysis interviews, have helped the development team to specify requirements for the new MIS. These requirements include providing the following to WhyMe management:

- Availability of financial status information on all corporate holdings within 48 hours
- Simulation, modeling, and decision support capabilities
- A user-friendly interface
- System accessibility to subsidiary management.

By providing status information on all corporate holdings on a 48-hour turnaround, management will be able to monitor its subsidiaries more effectively for planning and control purposes. The simulation and modeling capability will enable management to assess financial impacts on WhyMe that result from changing environmental conditions or from planned changes within WhyMe. A user-friendly interface will encourage use of the new system. A system that is accessible to subsidiary managers will not only assist them in performing management functions, but also will help enhance their knowledge about computer systems.

Moreover, the system needs to be flexible and expandable, and it must be operational within the next year or two. A flexible, expandable system will permit information systems of future subsidiaries to be incorporated into the corporate system more easily and efficiently, and will accommodate future procedural refinements. Finally, the system should be designed so that it can be implemented as quickly as possible. A system that is state of the art and has all the best features, but that might not be ready to use until 1991, would be of little value in helping to meet WhyMe's objectives.

Functions of the Management Information System

To provide the features and capabilities identified above, and to help WhyMe meet its corporate objectives, the company's new MIS must perform four functions:

1. The system must provide an interface with and gather data from WhyMe's subsidiaries.
2. The data gathered from the subsidiaries must be processed and stored.

3. The system must distribute summary information for control purposes to appropriate managers.

4. The system must provide decision support capabilities to assist top management in strategic planning.

Alternative information systems were investigated and evaluated by the team based upon the management and functional requirements identified above. Two systems were qualified as feasible alternatives for WhyMe Corporation. These alternatives and the team's recommendation are discussed below.

Alternative A

Alternative A is based on a database management computer or processor dedicated to the database management function. This processor will provide high-speed on-line access to the database by as many as 64 host computers. This would allow each WhyMe manager to interface with the system through a personal computer. Each personal computer would run application programs selected specifically for the user's needs. Similarly, the subsidiary computers would be linked directly to the database management computer. This system would provide the option of having a central database for all of the subsidiaries, or at least a second database for backup purposes. A major disadvantage of this alternative is the cost involved in providing a personal computer to every member of WhyMe's management group.

Alternative B

Alternative B involves the use of a general-purpose processor that uses database management software. This processor would interface with a second host processor that runs all of the application programs. The host processor would be connected to remote terminals for each of WhyMe's managers and its subsidiaries. The database management processor would collect data from the subsidiaries through translation software, as shown in Figure A-6. All of the information subsystems' software (finance, marketing, manufacturing, personnel) would reside in the applications processor, and would be available to all of the managers. The finance subsystem functionally provides a decision support system (DSS), as well as summaries and management control reports.

Alternative B is the system recommended by the systems development team.

THE TWO-PHASE APPROACH

To meet WhyMe's objective of implementing a management information system within a relatively short time, the study team recommends a two-phase

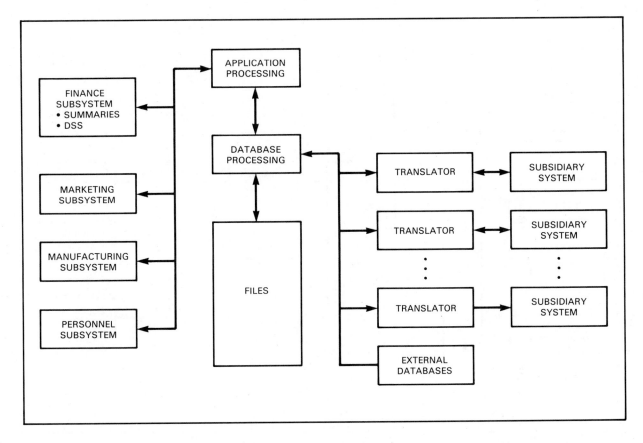

Figure A-6.

approach to the design and implementation of the new system. Phase 1 will consist of designing and installing the corporate hardware and software, but not the translation software, as shown in Figure A-7. At this stage, the subsidiaries will be required to enter data manually through keyboarding at a remote terminal until Phase 2 is implemented.

During Phase 2, the translation software needed to link the subsidiary computers with the corporate host computer will be designed and installed. The subsidiaries will be brought on-line one at a time. The estimated completion date is 42 months after the project has started. The exact completion date will depend upon the number of subsidiaries within WhyMe at that time.

There are two major advantages of this two-phase approach to design and implementation: First, WhyMe will receive benefits from the system relatively soon. By delaying the effort needed to develop the translation software, it becomes possible to implement Phase 2 in 24 months. At this point, the management information system will provide all four functions identified

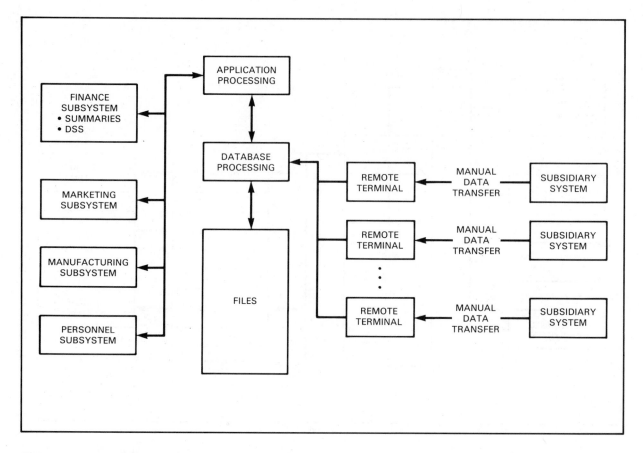

Figure A-7.

above. By comparison, a single-phase system design and implementation plan would require a 36-month implementation schedule (Figure A-8).

The second advantage of the two-phase approach is that the end of the first phase will provide WhyMe with a natural evaluation point before the full system is implemented. If any changes are needed in the data received from the subsidiaries, or in the time required to update the database, these changes can be made during Phase 2 with only a minor impact on the project.

CASE ASSIGNMENT

After reviewing the information presented in the systems development team report, what would be your plan for auditing the development project? What are some control issues you would identify? What are some apparent weaknesses you would note?

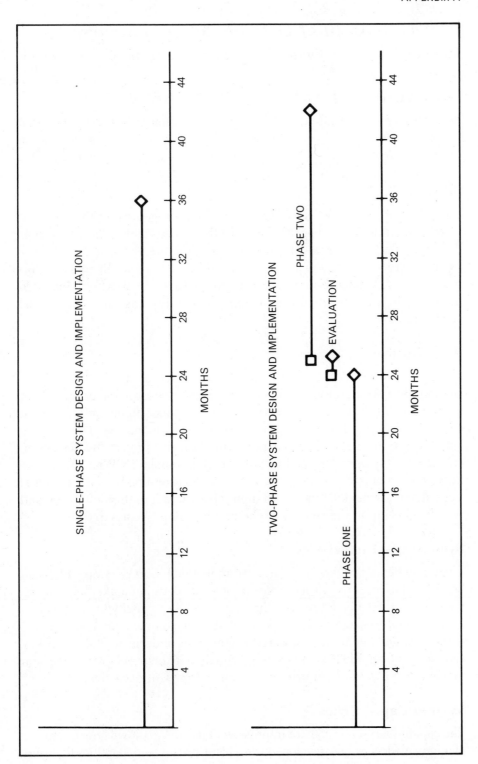

SINGLE-PHASE SYSTEM DESIGN AND IMPLEMENTATION

TWO-PHASE SYSTEM DESIGN AND IMPLEMENTATION

MONTHS

MONTHS

PHASE ONE

PHASE TWO

EVALUATION

Figure A-8.

Project 3: Audit of Decision Support System

This project is one of the suggested case assignments for Chapter 13.

AN EXECUTIVE INFORMATION SYSTEM

Below is a report submitted to the Executive Committee and to the Board of Directors at WhyMe Corporation about a decision support system, known within the company as an Executive Information Support System (EISS).

Summary

The intent of this report is to advise WhyMe management of the potential benefits of an EISS that is geared toward their needs and goals. This report deals with these executive information needs, requirements, and objectives, as they were identified during an initial survey. The requirements of a corporate planning model and decision support system are discussed. Included in this report are recommendations, software implications, and other special considerations.

Assumptions

This system will be designed with the corporate strategy of growth and diversity in mind. Management has expressed active interest in the development of this system. The success of this system depends upon the continued cooperation and assistance of WhyMe's top-level managers. Their knowledge, requirements, and needs are essential for this project. By definition, an EISS is a system designed to answer management's "What if?" questions, and to support, assist, and improve decision-making effectiveness. User-aided design and managerial input are inherent in this definition, and without this input, the success of the project cannot be assured.

System Characteristics

The many benefits of an EISS derive from its flexibility. WhyMe's EISS can be tailored to meet the varied needs of both the decision maker and the situation. The EISS will not replace the decision maker's ability to handle complex or poorly structured problems, but will complement and support managerial judgment, as well as reduce the risks of decision making. A key capability of an EISS is forecasting, which will help WhyMe's decision makers to evaluate the future implications of present decisions.

System Capabilities

The capabilities of an EISS are impressive. Figure A-9 shows how corporate planning models can be developed from historic data, and identifies the users

APPLICATIONS OF CORPORATE MODELS

APPLICATIONS	PERCENTAGE
Cash Flow Analysis	65
Financial Forecasting	65
Balance Sheet Projections	64
Financial Analysis	60
Pro Forma Financial Reports	55
Profit Planning	53
Long-term Forecasts	50
Budgeting	47
Sales Forecast	41
Investment Analysis	35
Marketing Planning	33
Short-term Forecast	33

PEOPLE RECEIVING AND USING OUTPUT FROM THE CORPORATE PLANNING MODEL

USER	PERCENTAGE
Vice President of Finance	55
President	46
Controller	46
Executive Vice President	32
Treasurer	30
Other Vice Presidents	30
Vice President of Marketing	29
Chairman of the Board	23

Figure A-9.

of outputs from the model. The capabilities that could be incorporated into WhyMe's EISS include the following:

- Simulate different strategies by projecting their impact on profits.

- Quantify and help establish corporate and divisional goals through simulation.

- Determine the feasibility of projects by applying discounted-cash-flow and return-on-investment analyses.

- Develop financial projections over any time period, based on the organization's goals and strategies.

- Measure the interactive effect of parts within a whole organization using a program that models the interrelationships of variables among those parts.

- Extend the reasoning capabilities of planning executives.

- Display "What if?" analyses in graphic form.

- Create consolidations from multiple charts of account.

- Evaluate critically the assumptions underlying environmental constraints by making these assumptions inputs to the model.

- Perform economic analysis using outside sources of data, such as economic variables derived from third-party information services.

- Adapt financial modeling capabilities to the specific characteristics of a particular organization, process or situation.

- Evaluate investment alternatives.

- In cash management, examine the impact of prime, loan and deposit mix and volumes, opening of new locations, and the profit impact of offering new services.

- Test the effects of alternative branching strategies, alternative liquidity strategies, changes in regulatory requirements, and the impact of the growth rate on profitability and capital adequacy.

- Analyze and evaluate new ventures, mergers, and acquisitions, as well as lease-versus-buy decisions.

- Upload or download to micro work stations.

This is just a small list of capabilities available to WhyMe. An EISS is a powerful decision and planning tool if used appropriately.

Subsystems of the EISS

The subsystems and programs within the EISS include:

- Information

- Econometric

- Risk analysis

- Simulation

- Optimization.

Information.   This subsystem controls all information flows in the planning system. It contains an executive program, input editors, output generator, data-editing routines, and the system database. The executive program organizes the flow of information and controls the interactive, time-sharing mode of operation. The input editors organize data inputs from WhyMe's divisions and place them in the database. The output generator handles report preparation and includes a graphics option.

Econometric.   This subsystem generates projections for the economy as a whole and for the specific industry segments, including those in which WhyMe is operating or plans to operate. This subsystem is composed of national and industry models, which include economic forecasting models and financial planning data for companies that are being considered for acquisition. (Acquisition data would come from outside sources.)

Risk analysis.   This subsystem uses the database information and shows the variability that exists in management's estimates. That is, this program shows how sensitive the outcomes are to slight changes in the input.

Simulation.   This subsystem performs for repetitive execution of a financial model with different inputs. This subsystem would permit WhyMe management to combine "What if?" questions with a particular modeling process. This process would continue until the best strategy or alternative was identified.

Optimization.   This subsystem would be used to help maximize WhyMe's corporate performance. The optimization subsystem would permit a manager to select an optimal set of strategies while considering a complex set of financial, legal, and operational limitations at both the corporate and the divisional levels.

The relationship of these subsystems to the entire EISS is shown in Figure A-10.

Implications

Due to the varied capabilities of an EISS, basic implications concerning design and cost include:

- The necessity of an on-line system
- The need for complex hardware and software
- The potentially expensive cost of development and maintenance.

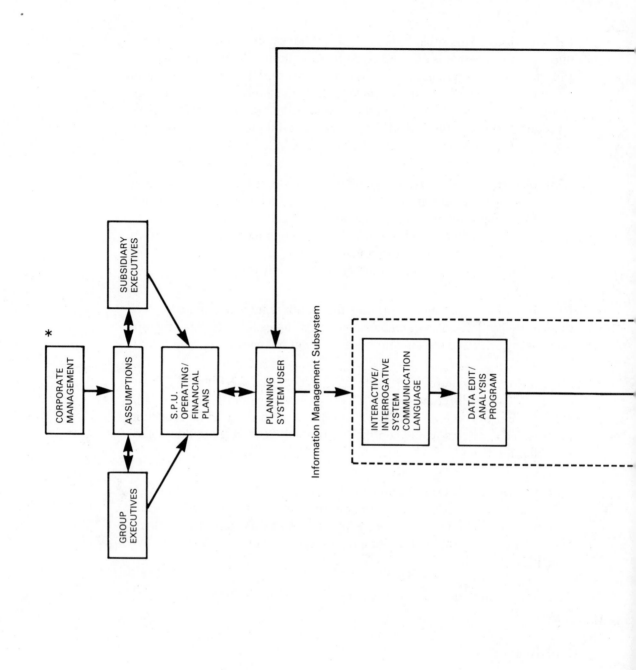

SUBSIDIARY
EXECUTIVES

*

CORPORATE
MANAGEMENT

ASSUMPTIONS

S.P.U.
OPERATING/
FINANCIAL
PLANS

GROUP
EXECUTIVES

PLANNING
SYSTEM USER

Information Management Subsystem

INTERACTIVE/
INTERROGATIVE
SYSTEM
COMMUNICATION
LANGUAGE

DATA EDIT/
ANALYSIS
PROGRAM

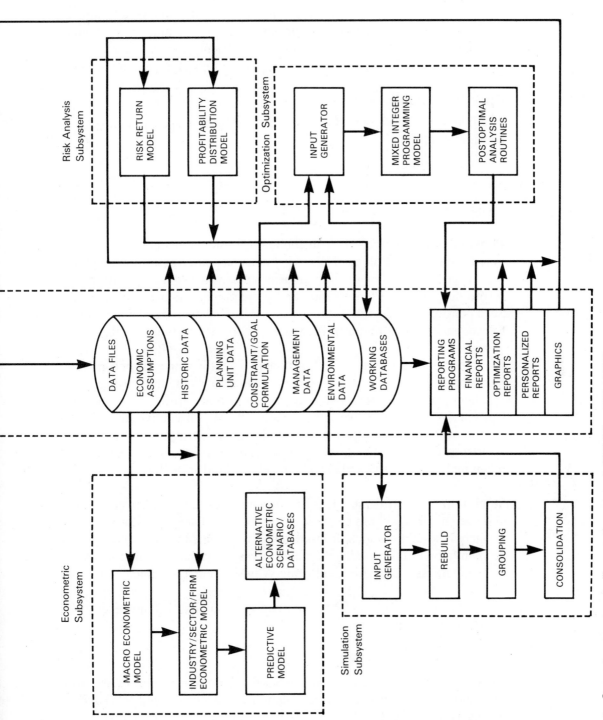

*Note: Corporate management will access the system via 3270-PC or IBM-AT/XT

Figure A-10.

The hardware requirements for such a system include intelligent terminals, minicomputers, microcomputers, time-sharing systems, and a data communication network. The software requirements encompass a database management system, model-oriented languages, and multiple application packages.

Special Considerations

The initial survey identified three areas that deserve special management consideration:

- Pension maintenance
- Portfolio management
- Stockholder accounting.

Pension maintenance.   The function of pension maintenance involves the monitoring and controlling of WhyMe's pension plan. Application programs would permit evaluation of different pension plans through plan illustrations, record keeping, report generation and preparation, and actuarial analysis. Such pension analysis software can assist WhyMe's managers in monitoring the company's pension portfolio while meeting government regulations.

Portfolio management.   This function involves the managing of corporate-held stocks, bonds, and cash resources as a means of obtaining higher yields that later can be used for capital investment or other growth opportunities. Current software technology could enable WhyMe's executives to make decisions on investments from the portfolio by analyzing the growth characteristics of stocks, bonds, and money market funds and by generating recommendations on whether to buy, sell, or hold securities.

Stockholder accounting.   This function involves the complete accounting of ownership in WhyMe's common stock. All record keeping associated with publicly held corporations, from dividend payments to stock splits, would be maintained on-line. WhyMe's executives could have on-line access to these details as a basis for monitoring WhyMe's current value.

These above opportunities represent items of additional cost; however, their benefits merit consideration.

CASE ASSIGNMENT

Based on the information presented, what risks and control issues commonly associated with a decision support system (DSS) can you identify? What control measures should be built into WhyMe Corporation's Executive Information Support System?

Project 4: Data Communication Controls

This project is the suggested case assignment for Chapter 14.

CASE ASSIGNMENT

Based on the descriptions of WhyMe's current system in Project 1 and the EISS in Project 3, identify the organization and system controls that would be necessary to assure the security and reliability of data communications within the new system.

Project 5: Security and Privacy

This project is the suggested case assignment for Chapter 16.

CASE ASSIGNMENT

Based on the description of the EISS in Project 3, identify and evaluate the security and privacy threats inherent in the system. Discuss several control measures that would help protect against these threats.

APPENDIX B
Case Study: Wedco

Project 1: Review of General Controls

This project is the suggested case assignment for Chapter 7.

CIS DEPARTMENT BI-WEEKLY PAYROLL PROCESSING

Processing of payroll and updating of the payroll master file is handled by the CIS department at Wedco. The complete payroll system within Wedco is illustrated in Figure B-1. As this diagram shows, the biweekly payroll processing is executed in two phases: off-week processing and pay-week processing.

OFF-WEEK PAYROLL PROCESSING

Off-week payroll processing consists of maintaining employee master files and generating time cards and payroll transmittals for the next payroll period.

Updating Employee Master Files

The payroll department initiates master file-maintenance transactions themselves or in response to requests made by employee supervisors on the form entitled Notice for Payroll Action. In each case, the payroll department sends altered or new employee master-file input records to the CIS department. Key-entry clerks in the CIS department capture the data for processing.

Off-week processing programs edit and process the master-file changes and print updated employee-master-file records for distribution to the payroll department.

Typical payroll changes that affect the master file include terminations, new hires, wage rate changes, reclassifications, and permanent transfers.

Generating Payroll Transmittals and Time Cards

At the close of each payroll period, off-week payroll processing programs generate the payroll transmittals and time cards to be used during the next pay period. These transmittals and time cards are generated from the payroll department master file.

One payroll transmittal is generated, in triplicate, for each department. Each payroll transmittal lists all employees in the department, their payroll numbers, job titles, and the payroll ending date. There are columns on the payroll transmittal form for the employee supervisor to enter the number of regular hours worked, number of overtime hours worked, and comments concerning changes in employee job status during the week (such as terminated, new hire/manual time card, leave of absence, etc.). Additional space is provided for payroll departmental review and entry of batch contol totals on each transmittal.

A single time card is generated for each employee listed on a payroll transmittal. In addition to employee name and number, each time card has entries for:

- Regular and overtime (time in and out) for each of the 14 days in a payroll period
- Number of regular and overtime hours worked each day
- Total hours worked during the payroll period
- Shift worked each day
- Classification of hours not worked during the period (sick leave, vacation, holiday, jury duty, other)
- Comments column for pertinent remarks.

There also are spaces for employee and supervisor signatures. The time cards, listed in employee-number order on each payroll transmittal, are sent with the payroll transmittals to the payroll department. From there, the time cards are distributed to the corresponding departments.

PAY-WEEK PROCESSING

Each employee supervisor is responsible for sending the transmittal and associated time cards to the payroll department at the end of each pay period. The payroll department checks and logs the transmittals and time cards, then forwards them to the CIS department. Each payroll transmittal sheet is wrapped around the batch of time cards that are listed on it. Written on the payroll transmittal sheet are the batch-control totals (number of cards, number of regular and overtime hours, etc.).

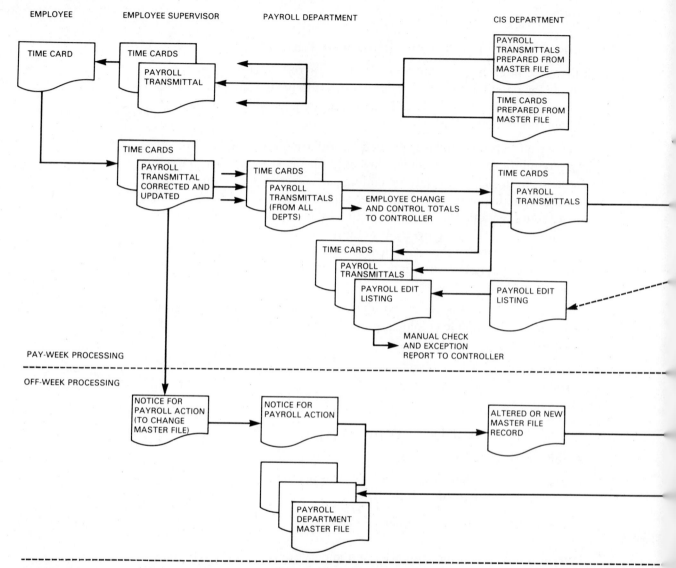

EMPLOYEE   EMPLOYEE SUPERVISOR   PAYROLL DEPARTMENT   CIS DEPARTMENT

TIME CARD

TIME CARDS
PAYROLL TRANSMITTAL

PAYROLL TRANSMITTALS PREPARED FROM MASTER FILE

TIME CARDS PREPARED FROM MASTER FILE

TIME CARDS
PAYROLL TRANSMITTAL CORRECTED AND UPDATED

TIME CARDS
PAYROLL TRANSMITTALS (FROM ALL DEPTS)

EMPLOYEE CHANGE AND CONTROL TOTALS TO CONTROLLER

TIME CARDS
PAYROLL TRANSMITTALS

TIME CARDS
PAYROLL TRANSMITTALS
PAYROLL EDIT LISTING

PAYROLL EDIT LISTING

MANUAL CHECK AND EXCEPTION REPORT TO CONTROLLER

PAY-WEEK PROCESSING

OFF-WEEK PROCESSING

NOTICE FOR PAYROLL ACTION (TO CHANGE MASTER FILE)

NOTICE FOR PAYROLL ACTION

ALTERED OR NEW MASTER FILE RECORD

PAYROLL DEPARTMENT MASTER FILE

Employee fills out and signs time cards.

Reviews and corrects payroll transmittal. Lines off terminated employee(s) and writes termination time card(s). Adds new hires or transferred transmittal and issues new manual time cards.

Reviews and signs approval of time cards.

Initiates changes to master files for new hires, terminations, permanent transfers, salary changes, qualifications.

Distributes payroll transmittal and time cards by location and department.

Receives all transmittals and time cards and computes, saves, and sends to controller, control totals for payroll (number of cards, regular hours, overtime hours).

Reviews CIS payroll edit listing and reports exceptions to controller dept. When necessary, can issue manual checks to controller.

Sends master file updates to data processing dept. Verifies master file update and inserts updated employee record in dept. master file for reference.

Control clerk logs in transmittals and checks input/output control totals for the time cards.

Figure B-1.

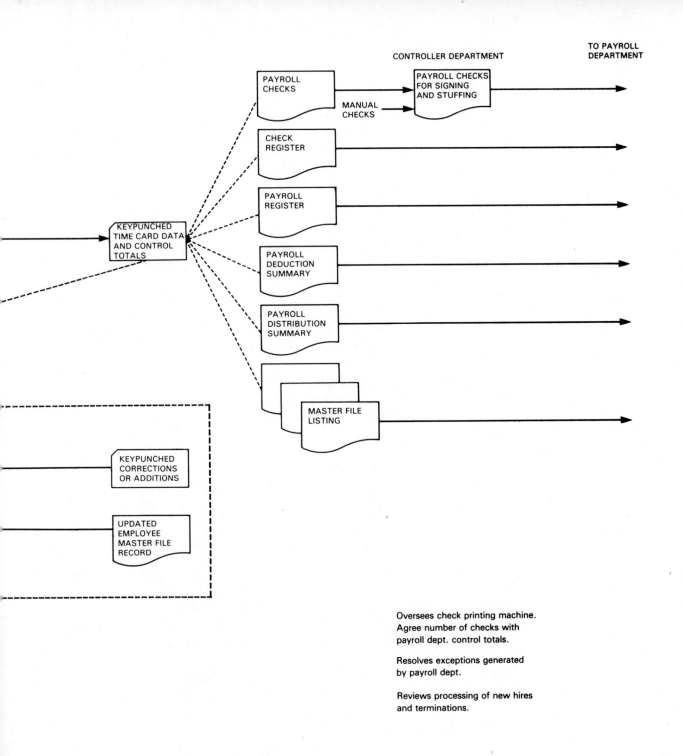

CONTROLLER DEPARTMENT

TO PAYROLL
DEPARTMENT

PAYROLL
CHECKS

PAYROLL CHECKS
FOR SIGNING
AND STUFFING

MANUAL
CHECKS

CHECK
REGISTER

PAYROLL
REGISTER

KEYPUNCHED
TIME CARD DATA
AND CONTROL
TOTALS

PAYROLL
DEDUCTION
SUMMARY

PAYROLL
DISTRIBUTION
SUMMARY

MASTER FILE
LISTING

KEYPUNCHED
CORRECTIONS
OR ADDITIONS

UPDATED
EMPLOYEE
MASTER FILE
RECORD

Oversees check printing machine.
Agree number of checks with
payroll dept. control totals.

Resolves exceptions generated
by payroll dept.

Reviews processing of new hires
and terminations.

607

For each batch of time cards and its payroll transmittal, employee-payroll-number and hours-worked data are captured for processing, along with the appropriate batch-control totals. The payroll transmittals, associated time cards, and an edit listing of the keyed data are sent to the payroll department for batch-control total verification.

In addition to generating payroll checks, the application program generates several payroll and management reports, all of which are forwarded to the payroll department. These reports include:

Check Register.   The check register is a list of all current-period-payroll checks in check number order. The check register is forwarded to the payroll department.

Payroll Register.   The payroll register is a list, in Social Security number order, of all detailed payroll-check items for the current pay period. These items include gross pay, net pay, FICA, SDI, and other deductions.

Payroll Distribution Summary.   The payroll distribution summary is an account distribution, in account number order, for current period payroll expenses. These expenses include salary administration, clerical work, maintenance expenses, etc.

Payroll Deduction Summary.   The payroll deduction summary is the current-pay-period listing of all employee voluntary and mandatory deductions. The listing is organized first by receiving organization and then by employee Social Security number. Typical deductions include FICA, SDI, credit union, pension plan, savings bonds, etc.

Payroll Master File.   The payroll master file provides a summary of employee data, current period earnings, and year-to-date earnings. The master file lists employees in payroll-number order and includes such data as name, address, Social Security number, starting date, classification, salary grade, department, location, current and year-to-date payroll information, etc.

A list of the subprograms within the payroll processing system is presented in Figure B-2, along with descriptions of these programs.

CASE ASSIGNMENT

Based on the information given, what general controls can you identify within this system? Explain the importance of these controls. Are there any major weaknesses within this system? If so, what control measures would you recommend to correct these weaknesses?

USER ORGANIZATION: PAYROLL DEPARTMENT
Name of Application: Bi-Weekly Payroll Processing
Topic: Subprogram Descriptions (Pay-Week Processing)

PR 01 Edit and store payroll-run control data, and branch to appropriate program.

PR 10 Edit time-card input data for valid field entries and for batch-control total correctness, and print edit listing.

PR 20 Sort payroll-card input data by employee payroll number.

PR 40 Retrieve current employee data from payroll master file and store current-payroll-period file to be used as a working file (such as employee name, number, classification, Social Security number, department, location, wage rate, etc.). Using these data:

- Compute gross pay using time-card hours and master-file regular and overtime pay rates.
- Compute mandatory payroll deductions including FICA, SDI, FUI, SUI.
- Compute voluntary payroll deductions including pension, credit union, savings bonds, and health insurance.
- Compute current payroll distributions to expense accounts by referencing employee classifications with corresponding expense account code classifications.
- Print unmatched employee records.

PR 50 Update master file with all current-payroll-period computations. Write current-payroll-period data and computation results to a current-payroll-period file for further processing.

PR 60 Sort current-payroll-period file data by employee location and write to work file.

PR 70 Sort data from current-payroll-period file by employee Social Security number; arrange data in payroll-register format; write to work file.

PR 80 Sort data from current-payroll-period file by organization receiving payroll deductions and then by employee Social Security number, and write to work file.

PR 90 Sort current-payroll-period file by account distribution sequence; rearrange data in payroll-distribution summary format; write to work file.

PR 100 Print sequentially numbered checks, check register, payroll register, payroll deduction summary, payroll distribution summary, and updated master file.

Topic: Subprogram Descriptions (Off-Week Processing)

PR 01 Edit and store run-control cards and branch to appropriate program.

PR 210 Access master file and sort employee time-card data (by location) into payroll transmittal formats. Print time cards.

PR 300 Edit update inputs to master file. Also, generate master-file records for new hires; transfer master file content for terminated employees to current-year-terminations file for year-end processing, and alter master file content in accordance with update data for wage change, reclassification, address change, vacation, leave of absence, etc. Also, print new or updated master file content for each altered employee master file.

Figure B-2.

Project 2: Design of Audit Tests

This project is the suggested case assignment for Chapter 8.

BACKGROUND

Refer to the case narrative on Wedco in Project 1. The payroll-processing pro-gram's master-file update is used to generate a current summary of employee data. The input format and field details for inputting new information to up-date the master file are shown in Figure B-3. This documentation was given to the auditors.

The internal auditor of Wedco has been charged with testing the control of erroneous input to the payroll application program's master-file update. To do this, the auditor intends to create a test deck.

CASE ASSIGNMENT

From the information in Figure B-3, prepare the specification for a test deck. See Figure B-4 for a suggested approach to creating files of test transactions and documenting the type of transaction data being used. (The format shown in Figure B-4 is one used in developing a test deck for a shipping application.) Be sure to include both valid and invalid conditions in the test deck.

Note: If there are any questions regarding the file specifications provided, the auditor should resolve them before developing the test data.

PROGRAM	EDIT	NEW EMPLOYEE	CREATE
		Character Length	Data Type
Input Format	Employee Number	5	A
	Name	15	A
	Address	20	A
	Department	2	N
	Date of Employment	6	N
	Payroll Rate	4	N
	Internal Telephone No.	4	N
	Spouse's Name	10	A
	Title	15	A
	Pension Plan	1	A
	Status	1	A
	Deduction	2	N
Field Details	Employee Number: 00000 to 05000 Department: 06-24, 30-71, 94-422 Date of Employment: MMDDYY Pension Plan: 1 = married > 3 children 2 = married 1-3 children 3 = married 0 children 4 = single Status: M = married, S = single Data Type: A = Alphanumeric, N = Numeric		

Figure B-3.

FIELDS

Comments	Customer No.	Item No.	Price	Quantity	Expected Results
	Blank	3004	2.00	3	
	Blank	Blank	2.00	3	
	Blank	Blank	Blank	3	
	Blank	Blank	Blank	Blank	
Check Digit Wrong	69144	3004	2	3	
OK	69146	A324	2	3	
Price Wrong	69146	3324	−2	3	

Figure B-4.

APPENDIX C
Case Study: Computer-Assisted Audit Procedures

Project 1: Sleepwell Memorial Hospital

This project is one of the suggested case assignments for Chapter 10.

BACKGROUND

Sleepwell Corporation is a large health-care services company that has decided to integrate its business vertically. As part of this process, Sleepwell Corporation acquired an acute-care hospital during the past year. Sleepwell Memorial Hospital is a large facility with a typically long collection cycle for its patient accounts receivable. During the annual audit, the computer auditors supplied a year-end aged accounts-receivable trial balance to the audit team. Now, ten weeks later, the audit team needs to determine subsequent collections on the 15,000 patient accounts.

CASE ASSIGNMENT

Complete the following tasks:

1. State the audit objective in determining subsequent collections, and discuss two functions in which use of a computer would be helpful to the auditors in meeting that objective.

2. Assuming transaction files also are available, describe the process required to summarize subsequent activity on each account. This can be done either in a narrative or graphically in a flow diagram, but be sure to indicate which tasks can be completed with computer assistance.

Project 2: Honest Bob's Insurance Company

This project is one of the suggested case assignments for Chapter 10.

BACKGROUND

Bob Fortune, president of Honest Bob's Insurance Company, has been asked to submit to an audit by the State Insurance Commissioner for the first time. The Commissioner's audit team would like to verify the company's total revenue from policy premiums by direct confirmation with policyholders. However, the company's computer-produced records do not show cumulative premiums by customer; moreover, Bob does not want his employees to use their valuable work time to generate these data.

The company's data processing department retains all transactions for the year on an IBM 370/158 computer. Each transaction is recorded individually, one per record, in an ISAM (Indexed Sequential Access Method) file, indexed by customer number. There are over two million records in the file, and backup copies of the records are made in random order on tape. The insurance company also keeps another file that contains name, address, and customer number for each policyholder. The senior auditor would like you to assist in obtaining the transaction data for a sample of policyholders and in preparing the confirmation. The client will make a small amount of time on its IBM computer available to the audit team.

CASE ASSIGNMENT

Describe the steps you would take to generate the transaction data and to produce the desired confirmations. You may either write a narrative or use a flow diagram for your description.

Project 3: Gotham City, Part I

This is one of the suggested case assignments for Chapter 10.

BACKGROUND

The computerized payroll system of Gotham City is undergoing an audit. Jill Fernandez is the audit senior of the team reviewing Gotham's payroll system. Jill has heard how helpful computer-assisted audit procedures (CAAPs) can be, and she has asked you to suggest how some of these procedures can be applied in this audit.

Gotham has two types of payroll disbursements: employee and welfare. Jill has been informed by the data processing manager, Fusako Endo, that the transactions for the year are available. However, the payroll programmer was terminated recently, and there are no funds budgeted for a replacement.

CASE ASSIGNMENT

Identify and describe potential CAAP applications for use in this situation.

Project 4: Gotham City, Part II

BACKGROUND

Jill is enthusiastic about the applications you suggested to her. The partner and manager of your audit firm have allowed you to proceed, and you have met personally with Fusako Endo to obtain the necessary details.

Unfortunately, you now have found that no transaction files are retained for either welfare or employee payroll. However, updated employee master files are available for each pay period during the last six months. Master files for prior periods may be available on multi-file backup tapes retained by the IRS under a record-retention agreement. The record layout was last revised in July 1976, and Fusako does not know anything about it. The only information available about welfare payments is contained in a print file that is used to print the actual checks.

CASE ASSIGNMENT

What do you do now?

APPENDIX D
Case Study:
Exotic Electronics, Inc.

Project: Advanced Computer-Assisted Audit Techniques

This project is the suggested case assignment for Chapter 11.

BACKGROUND

Exotic Electronics is a manufacturer of electronic equipment. The company's inventory consists of thousands of components and subassemblies that are distributed throughout the company's plant. To record this inventory, a computer application system is used that involves three-part inventory tags (see Figure D-1). The first part of the tag is used by the accounting department to adjust the perpetual inventory to reflect actual inventory. The second part is pulled by the auditors of a public accounting firm that has been hired by Exotic Electronics to review the company's inventory system. The third part of each tag remains with the piece of equipment that it describes.

Due to the rapid growth of the company last year, control procedures dealing with the inventory tags were not established thoroughly. A large number of tags (over 8,000) were used, and the auditors now are concerned about the possibility of fictitious tags having been entered into the client's computer system. Under the current audit program, many hours will be required in performing procedures to assure that the large book-to-physical write-up has not been affected by erroneous or fictitious inventory information. The audit team also will need to spend many hours on other routine inventory procedures.

The team has requested that a computer auditor review the situation to determine if computer-assisted audit procedures can improve the efficiency of the audit task. File layouts obtained during last year's CIS application audit are shown in Figure D-2.

SAMPLE INVENTORY TAGS

DESCRIPTION						CONSEC. NO.
ITEM NO.			POCKET LOCATION			
KARDEX BALANCE			KARDEX COST			
RECORD				STOCK CODE	165000	
NO. PCS.	SHORTAGES	TOTAL	NO. PCS.	SHORTAGES	TOTAL	
TOTAL THIS CARD			TOTAL OTHER CARDS			
TOTAL OTHER CARDS			TOTAL THIS CARD			
GRAND TOTAL			GRAND TOTAL			
RECOUNTED BY _____			COUNTED BY _____			
ACCOUNTING COPY _____						

DESCRIPTION						CONSEC. NO.
ITEM NO.			POCKET LOCATION			
KARDEX BALANCE			KARDEX COST			
RECORD				STOCK CODE	582500	
NO. PCS.	SHORTAGES	TOTAL	NO. PCS.	SHORTAGES	TOTAL	
TOTAL THIS CARD			TOTAL OTHER CARDS			
TOTAL OTHER CARDS			TOTAL THIS CARD			
GRAND TOTAL			GRAND TOTAL			
RECOUNTED BY			COUNTED BY			

Figure D-1. *Note in this illustration that the third part of the tag is missing, as it is with the piece of equipment that it inventories.*

FILE LAYOUTS

COUNTFILE—ITEM NUMBER SEQUENCE

FIELD	LENGTH	POSITION	TYPE	COMMENTS
Item number*	10	1	N	
Pocket location	6	11	CH	
Description	25	17	CH	
Quantity	10	60	4N	
Unit of measure	2	72	CH	
Tag number	6	75	N	

PRICE FILE—ITEM NUMBER SEQUENCE

FIELD	LENGTH	POSITION	TYPE	COMMENTS
Item number*	10	1	N	
Unit price	8	11	4P	
Unit of measure	2	21	CH	

JOB COST—GENERAL LEDGER SEQUENCE

FIELD	LENGTH	POSITION	TYPE	COMMENTS
G/L account number	8	1	N	
Job number	6	9	CH	
Input date	3	15	P	
Item number*	10	18	N	
Labor bonus	8	28	1P	
Labor dollars	8	36	2P	
Materials	8	44	2P	
Other	8	52	2P	
G & A applied	8	60	2P	

SALES—INVOICE NUMBER SEQUENCE

FIELD	LENGTH	POSITION	TYPE	COMMENTS
Invoice number	5	6	P	
Customer number	5	1	P	
Invoice date	4	11	P	
Item number*	6	15	P	
Job number	6	21	CH	
Quantity	5	27	P	
Value	8	32	2P	
Description	25	40	CH	

BILL OF MATERIALS—ITEM NUMBER WHERE USED SEQUENCE

FIELD	LENGTH	POSITION	TYPE	COMMENTS
Item number*	10	1	N	where used
Item number*	10	11	N	required
Quantity required	10	21	4N	
Last updated	4	31	P	
Document number	8	35	N	

* Item number prefixes

00-19	Finished Goods	50-99	Raw Materials
20-49	Subassemblies		

Figure D-2.

CASE ASSIGNMENT

Complete the following tasks:

1. Determine what computer-assisted audit procedures would be advisable in this situation.

2. Prepare a CAAP system flowchart that will implement the procedures that you identified in the assignment above. Your flowchart should show all necessary sorts and other programs, as well as all intermediate data files and reports. In a supporting narrative, briefly describe the function of each program.

APPENDIX E
Case Study: Abcor Facilities Audit

Project 1: Review of Operations

This project is the suggested case assignment for Chapter 12.

INTRODUCTION

During a recent audit of a computer information center, the CIS auditors found several exposures in operations. The Computer Information System Audit Group has submitted its recommendations (Figure E-1) to Computer Operations Management. The reply from Operations Management to the Audit Group is shown in Figure E-2.

CASE ASSIGNMENT

Review Figures E-1 and E-2. What is your reaction to the response of Computer Operations Management? Prepare a reply to their comments.

DATE: June 6, 198X

  TO: Vera Wilson, Computer Operations Management
         Dan Yoguchi, CIS Management

FROM: Joseph Rodriguez, Senior CIS Auditor
         Computer Information Systems Audit Group

SUBJECT: Programmers' access to the computer room

FINDINGS -- RECOMMENDATIONS

Upon reviewing Abcor's computer information center, the CIS Audit Group
has noted several exposures in operations and submits the following
findings and recommendations:

At present, all programmers have been issued a key-badge that apparently
gives them unrestricted access to the computer room. This situation
contradicts management's intent as established per policy memo dated
March 31, 1981, "Programmers' Access and Action Regarding the Computer
Room."
     On various occasions, we have noted the unchecked manner in
which the programmers enter the computer room. Good internal control
procedures require that access to the computer room be restricted, not
only to safeguard against intentional or unintentional misuse of computer
hardware and/or software, but also to minimize the disturbance to
computer operations personnel while they are performing their scheduled
assignments.
     We recommend that CIS management establish adherence to the policy
as noted in the memo of March 31. Further, we recommend that management
consider additional procedures to strengthen the controls regarding
access to the computer room. For example, certain designated, pre-
authorized programmers (Operation Systems Programmers) could be issued
a key-badge with access times controlled and/or approved by Computer
Operations Management. When programmers occasionally need access to the
computer room, they would be required to obtain written authorization
from senior CIS management.

Figure E-1.

DATE: June 22, 198X

  TO: Joseph Rodriguez, Senior CIS Auditor
         Computer Information Systems Audit Group

FROM: Vera Wilson, Computer Operations Management
         Dan Yoguchi, CIS Management

SUBJECT: Programmers' access to the computer room

In following through on the recommendations in your memo of June 6, we
have established adherence to the policy (3/31/81) by re-emphasizing to
the programmers that they are not to enter the computer room unless they
receive prior authorization from CIS/Computer Operations Management. In
addition, we have procured six separate badges that have a distinctive
color and pattern--yellow with orange dots. These badges will be held by
Computer Operations Management, and when deemed necessary, Computer
Operations Management will issue a "computer-room" badge that authorizes
the programmer to enter the computer room.
     The use of separate badges is not applicable to weekends or night
hours, as existing policy dictates that prior written authorization must
be granted to those wanting to enter the service center on a scheduled
basis during these periods; or, in the event of an emergency, the
security officer must obtain verbal authorization from CIS before
entrance can be granted.
     During the last four or five months, it may have appeared that
programmers had unrestricted access to the computer room; however, this
was not the case, as there has been a great deal of effort devoted to the
development of the Property Management system, as well as to several
conversions that required the presence of programmers in the computer
room. Computer Operations Management was aware of these situations.
     There is an exception to the above procedure: The Systems
Programmer has access to the computer room at all times.

Figure E-2.

Project 2: Review of Microcomputer Policies and Procedures

This is the suggested case assignment for Chapter 13.

INTRODUCTION

The document in Figure E-3 describes the policies and procedures at Abcor, Inc., relating to control and use of microcomputer equipment, software, and supplies. Review this document and complete the case assignment that follows.

CASE ASSIGNMENT

Complete the following tasks:

1. Assess the adequacy of corporate control over these resources.

2. What additional audit procedures, if any, might be necessary to determine the adequacy of controls in this area?

Figure E-3.

ABCOR
CIS STANDARDS AND PROCEDURES

Approved by: _____
                                        Date

Approved by: _____
                                        Date

Date First Issued: _____ JULY 6, 198X _____

TITLE:
    Security of Personal Computers and Equipment

PURPOSE:
    As required by corporate policy, the following establishes the appropriate approval, control, and use of microcomputer equipment, software, and supplies.

POLICY:
1. Abcor will secure its computer equipment. This policy specifies actions be taken to assure that appropriate security measures are taken to safeguard company property.

2. Strict enforcement of this policy will be expected. Appropriate controls are to be administered in the following departments: Accounting, Finance, Purchasing, Plant Security, Personnel and CIS.

SCOPE:
1. The scope of this policy includes all company-owned hardware, whether purchased through Capital Planning or Accounts Payable. As such, it is designed to include *all* computer-related equipment that is borrowed and removed from company premises to any outside location.

2. This policy also applies to software and supplies that are purchased through Accounts Payable and Purchasing.

ENVIRONMENT AND NESESSARY SAFEGUARDS:

1. Provision should be made for appropriate personnel to work at home using company terminals.

2. Company property must be secured against theft or illegal use of copyright as well as other poor management practices.

3. The company should minimize its hardware investment by encouraging the sharing of personal computers, peripheral devices, and other equipment, wherever possible.

ACQUISITION OF EQUIPMENT:

1. This section includes safeguards and controls to assure appropriate acquisition procedures.

1.1 All computer equipment or systems purchased as Capital items or intangible assets over $1,000 will be controlled by this policy. Where peripheral equipment of less than $1,000 is involved for home use, this equipment, regardless of cost, also will be covered by this policy.

1.2 Accounts Payable, Capital Planning, or Division Purchasing, as appropriate, will review all requisitions, expense reports, RCIs, and Purchase Orders to assure compliance with this policy.

1.3 Prior to approval of any such document, a review of all equipment specifications is mandatory. In particular, if another piece of comparable equipment (personal computer, I/O terminal, etc.) is available for use by the requesting department, appropriate need must be established.

NOTE: Audits will be performed that will determine usage. If the equipment is used for other than the designated purpose, it will be removed, pending justification of the new usage.

1.4 If home use is specified as the primary purpose for the equipment, such use must be verified. In addition, appropriate controls will be established to monitor said home use.

1.5 Division Accounting will record inventory of the equipment or system. After its purchase an appropriate Fixed Asset designation (sticker) and notations will be affixed thereto.

1.6 All equipment will be shipped to Abcor premises for control and inventory purposes. No equipment will be drop-shipped to an individual's home for any reason. A receiving document is required for each piece of equipment so ordered.

HOME USE:

1. Inventory of all equipment will be kept by Capital Planning. Logged information includes: the equipment Fixed Asset number, RCI number, responsible manager, appropriate software, description of equipment, and serial number.

2. All equipment to be taken from company premises will require a Property Pass duly executed by the Director of CIS, Personnel, and Plant Security.

NOTE: When the Director of CIS is not available, two signatures—that of Manager of Decision Support Services and Manager of Operations will be necessary for final approval. The signature of the Manager of Scientific Systems will be required in lieu of either of these for equipment related to that department. Appropriate signatures are on file.

3. Following signatures on the Property Pass by the appropriate Manager of CIS, a copy of the Property Pass will be placed in the individual's personnel file. Prior to payment of the final payroll check, the appropriate individual will return said property and receive the Personnel copy of the Property Pass.

4. All equipment leaving company premises will be verified by Plant Security. Equipment will not be taken from the Abcor Lobby.

5. Appropriate audits are required by the respective department manager to assure that equipment is returned by the due date. Otherwise, notification will be provided by the Director of CIS to the functional manager for follow-up.

COMPANY USE:

This section designates appropriate measures required to safeguard equipment left in uncontrolled areas.

1. Wherever possible, personal computers and other attractive items of computer equipment will be kept under lock and key during non-working hours.

624

2. Wherever possible, controlled areas (such as information centers) will be established to monitor use of personal computers, peripheral devices, etc., within designated areas.

3. All RCI's requesting approval will include the cost for an appropriate locking mechanism. This mechanism will secure the personal computer to an appropriate desk or permanent fixture. It is the responsibility of the functional manager to assure security of personal computers and associated supplies/software.

4. At least annually, audits will be performed by the Managers of Capital Planning and Consulting (CIS) on all personal computer equipment. These audits will assure:
- Compliance with these procedures
- Safeguards over physical inventory
- Appropriate continued need for the equipment—especially for continual off-site use
- All uses of the personal computer not covered under the original RCI.

5. The responsibility to assure continued dedicated use of the equipment is the burden of the user department. In all cases, if continued use cannot be supported, the personal computer may be removed to provide the next justified requestor of this equipment.

Figure E-3.

Concluded.

APPENDIX F
Standards for Audit of Governmental Organizations, Programs, Activities and Functions

The following is an excerpt from standards promulgated by the Comptroller General of the United States. The portions of the document presented below deal with computer-based information systems. Although these standards apply primarily to agencies of the federal government, they also may serve as a model for private organizations. The relevant portions of the document are:

- Auditing Computer-Based Systems (Section E)
- The Auditor's Role During System Design and Development (Appendix I).

AUDITING COMPUTER-BASED SYSTEMS

The fifth examination and evaluation standard for government economy and efficiency audits and programs results audits is:

The auditors shall:

1. Review general controls in data processing systems to determine whether (a) the controls have been designed according to management direction and known legal requirements and (b) the controls are operating effectively to provide reliability of, and security over, the data being processed.

2. Review application controls of installed data processing applications upon which the auditor is relying to assess their reliability in processing data in a timely, accurate, and complete manner.

In addition to reviewing general and application controls, the auditor should have a role in the design and development of new data processing systems or applications and significant modifications thereto.

It is possible to develop a data processing system with such poor controls that neither the manager nor the auditor can rely on its integrity. Thus, the auditor's review during the design and development of these systems has become crucial if management is to have reasonable assurance that auditable and properly controlled systems are being developed. Compliance with this objective may not always be feasible because audit organizations may not have the resources or staff skills to review the design and development of these systems. However, such review should be an auditing goal.

The role of the auditor in the review and design and development of data processing systems is discussed in Appendix I [below].

Review of General Controls in Computer-Based Systems

The transition from mechanical data processing to automatic data processing occasions the need for revision of traditional audit approaches. The complexity and scope of such systems requires that the auditor give greater attention to both the system that processes data and the data itself. If the system is reasonably secure and adequately controlled, the auditor can rely on the data processed and reported.

The auditor should distinguish between general and application controls. General controls are normally applicable to the majority of data processing being carried out within the installation, while application controls may vary among applications and are therefore reviewed on an individual basis. (See computer audit standard 2—not reprinted here—for application controls audit review.) The auditor is to consider the effectiveness of these general controls applicable to the system under review in performing the review of individual application controls.

Organizational controls.   Authority and responsibility must be delegated in such a manner that the organizational objectives can be met efficiently and effectively. The auditor should review the organization, delegation of authority, responsibilities, and separation of duties in the entity. The goal is to determine whether the separation of duties provides for strong internal control. For example, whenever feasible, separation of duties should provide for separation among program and systems development functions, computer operations, controls over input of data, and the control groups that maintain application controls. The "total system" must be considered.

In reviewing separation of duties, the auditor should evaluate the control strengths and report on weaknesses resulting from inadequate separation. Policies of periodic rotation of employees and mandatory vacation scheduling may help management maintain adequate separation of duties. The auditor should determine whether such policies are being followed.

Physical facilities, personnel, and security controls.   Adequate physical facilities and other resources (such as adequately trained personnel and supplies) are necessary for the entity to meet its data processing objectives. The auditor should determine whether the entity has adequate resources to meet its needs.

Personnel management, including supervision, motivation, and professional development of personnel, is integral to successful data processing. The auditor should evaluate management policies and practices to ascertain whether the necessary policies exist and determine whether they are properly followed. For example, since the entire field of computers is rapidly evolving, an organization's personnel management office needs to develop, in conjunction with the data processing staff, an education and training program. This program should keep employees abreast of current developments so that they may perform their duties most efficiently and economically and be able to use new methods whenever they are demonstrably cost effective. Inadequate personnel training and development programs in data processing can hinder accomplishment of the organization's mission.

The auditor should determine whether provisions for security of the computer hardware, computer programs, data files, data transmission, input and output material, and personnel have been adequately considered. This review should include not only the computer equipment in the central processing facility but also minicomputers, computer terminals, communications operations, and other peripheral equipment regardless of location.

In reviewing physical security of computer hardware, the auditor should consider the adequacy of a contingency plan for continued processing of critical applications in the event of a disruption of normal processing. This should include provisions for emergency power and hardware backup as well as detailed plans for using the backup equipment and transporting personnel, programs, forms, and data files to an alternate processing location. The auditor should also consider the extent to which this plan has been tested to determine the probability of continuing data processing support in the event of a real emergency.

The auditor should also review the physical security of data files. This review should ensure that, whenever feasible, data and program file libraries are kept by personnel who do not have access to computers and computer programs; the file libraries are secure; computer operators and other personnel do not have unlimited access to the libraries; and provisions have been made for backup of files (including offsite backup). When files are normally kept on-line, the auditor should consider whether they are protected by adequate access authorization controls and whether backup copies of files are kept regularly. Also, the auditor should verify whether data backup files are properly identified and labeled. The auditor should also check the contents to ensure that the files are complete and accurate. Similar stringent controls should exist for program backup files.

Operating systems controls.   Computer systems are often controlled by operating systems (usually referred to as systems software). Since these operating systems usually provide data handling and multiprogramming capabilities, file label checking, and many other authorization controls, they are integral to the general controls over computer processing. The auditor should be aware of the controls the operating systems can exercise and should ascertain the extent to which they have been implemented, as well as how they can be bypassed or overridden. The auditor should be aware that personnel who maintain the operating systems, and other persons with the ability to modify them, may either intentionally or accidentally cause specific controls within the operating systems to become ineffective.

Hardware controls.   Computer hardware frequently can detect errors related to hardware malfunctions (as contrasted with program malfunctions). The auditor should be aware of how (1) the installation relies on these hardware controls, (2) the operating systems use them, and (3) the detected hardware errors are reported within the installation, as well as the procedures for taking corrective action.

Review of Application Controls in Computer-Based Systems

Before any assessment of processing reliability or integrity in any application can be complete, both the specific application controls and the general controls must be evaluated in their entirety.

Audit work done in adhering to this standard has two objectives. Both are discussed below.

Conformance with standards and approved design.   The first objective is to determine whether the installed applications/systems conform to applicable standards and the latest approved design specifications.

Auditor compliance with this standard provides reasonable assurance that the approved specifications, with all built-in internal controls (such as input, processing, output), have been installed as intended, properly documented, and adequately tested.

When the auditor tests data reliability, the test should include examining documentation for selected transactions, testing the clerical accuracy of the entry and summarizing of transactions, and testing compliance with control procedures. In addition, the auditor may wish to test selected data files to identify possible exception conditions and accuracy of data conversion or capture. If the data files are kept in machine-readable condition, the auditor should, where appropriate, use computer-assisted audit techniques in testing them.

Tests for control weaknesses. The second objective is to test internal controls and the reliability of the data produced. In addition to evaluating adequacy of controls, such tests may disclose possible weaknesses in the installed applications/systems.

These audits should probe the installed applications/systems for adequacy as well as for weaknesses, changed circumstances affecting risk exposure, and so forth. Where such weaknesses are found, the auditor's work should stimulate corrective modifications and improve the applications. Also, the auditor must be mindful, when conducting tests, that there are no guarantees that the application systems will continue to operate in accordance with the latest approved specifications. Therefore, adequacy of controls over program changes, program documentation, and operating procedures is most important.

Although auditing for fraud is not the primary objective of audits, the auditor must be alert to the possiblity of fraud or other irregularities in computer systems (see discussion of fraud, abuse, and illegal acts in standard G [not included in this Appendix]).

THE AUDITOR'S ROLE DURING SYSTEM DESIGN AND DEVELOPMENT

With the computer becoming more complex through the development of sophisticated multiprogramming capacity, the growing number of telecommunications links, and the wide variety of new input and output devices, another dimension has been added to the auditor's role. Auditors must now be able to perform a wide variety of tasks which, until recently, did not exist or were not considered part of their role.

For example, when manual systems were audited, a wide variety of approaches were generally available and the most appropriate was selected for the circumstances. If there were control weaknesses, corrective changes were easily formulated and suggested. However, it is now possible to develop a data processing system with such poor controls that neither the manager nor the auditor can rely on its integrity.

The auditor's role during the design and development processes of automated systems has become crucial if management is to have reasonable assurance that auditable and properly controlled systems are being developed. Thus, it should be the objective of all audit organizations and auditors [both internal and external] to:

> "Review the design and development of new data processing systems or applications, and significant modifications thereto" [including software matters as well as hardware configuration decisions].

Compliance with this objective may not always be feasible because auditor organizations may not have the resources or staff skills to review the design and development of automated systems. Also, internal auditors may require additional specific managerial authorization or direction to perform this work, and external auditors such as public accountants may need a special engagement. However, compliance with this objective should be an auditing goal.

Whenever top management direction to perform such work has not already been given, the auditor must alert management to the potential results of such restriction. The auditor should formally communicate to management information on the possible adverse effects of not requiring audit review and evaluation of automated systems design and development processes. Such communication should point out that without effective audit of these processes, the systems

- may not possess the built-in controls necessary to provide reasonable assurance of proper operation;

- may not provide the capability to track events through the systems and thus impede, if not completely frustrate, audit review of the systems in operation; and

- (for financial systems) may not permit a classification of transactions in a manner that allows the preparation of financial statements in accordance with generally accepted accounting principles and may result in qualifications of the auditor's opinion on the financial statements.

Both the auditor and management have an interest in ensuring that system design, development, and overall operations achieve the objectives of adequate internal controls and effective auditability. (Because the engagement of public accountants has unique conditions, it is unlikely that public accountants will be able to comply fully with this objective. However, they may partially comply by determining the extent and effectiveness of the work of the company's internal auditors or outside accountants in the design and development phases.) For systems already in existence when audits are made, the auditor should determine whether the objectives of the system are being achieved.

Systems and applications of computer-based information systems have become more complex and interrelated. Initially, there were separate applications for personnel, payroll, and labor cost accounting. Each application or system was processed independently of the other, and its input material was generated from separate and distinct sources and then processed against separate data files.

With the integration of application systems now being encountered, the payroll, personnel, and labor-cost-accounting applications can be interrelated subsystems of a far larger on-line system, and the outputs of one subsystem can now be the inputs for another without any human review. Thus, a control weakness in one segment of the system may have completely unanticipated effects on other segments, with a cascading of unanticipated effects causing catastrophic results. Such mistakes, waste, and confusion may even adversely affect the entity's viability.

The objectives of requiring auditor review of system design, development, and modification are set forth below, with comments on each.

Management policies.

Objective 1: To provide reasonable assurance that systems/applications carry out the policies management has prescribed for them.

Policies on what is expected of automated systems should be established by management, and the auditor should determine whether they are being adhered to in design. The auditor should ascertain whether an appropriate approval process is being followed, both in developing new systems and in modifying existing systems. The auditor should consider the need for approval of a system's design by data processing management, user groups, and other groups whose data and reports may be affected. Also, the auditor should review the provisions for security required by management to protect data and programs against unauthorized access and modification.

If management's requirements are not being met, or have not been clearly articulated, the auditor must report such shortcomings to officials who can take corrective action. Frequently in the past, efforts to make new systems/applications operational by scheduled dates have resulted in some elements or controls—that were desired by management—being set aside by designers for later consideration. Auditors, in retaining their independence during the design and development processes, should report such actions to top management for resolution.

Audit trail.

> Objective 2: To provide reasonable assurance that systems/applications provide the controls and audit trails needed for management, auditor, and operational review.

In financial applications, a transaction must be capable of being traced from its initiation, through all the intermediate processing steps, to the resulting financial statements. Similarly, information in the financial statements must be traceable to its origin. Such capability is referred to by various terms—such as audit trail, management trail, transaction trail—and is also highly essential in nonfinancial systems/applications. The reliability of the output can be properly assessed when the transaction processing flow can be traced and the controls over it (both manual and automated) can be evaluated.

During the design and development process, the auditor may provide, through formal correspondence, suggested audit trails or other controls to the design/development team. By doing so through formal correspondence, the auditor will remain independent.

Audit of the systems design and development processes can help assure management that this capability is in fact being built into the systems/applications.

Controls.

> Objective 3: To provide reasonable assurance to management that systems/applications include the controls necessary to protect against loss or serious error.

The system design and development processes include (1) defining the processing to be done by a computer, (2) designing the processing steps, (3) determining the data input and files that will be required, and (4) specifying each individual program's input data and output. Each area must be properly controlled, in consonance with good management practices, and the auditor's review of these matters is designed to provide reasonable assurance to management that the systems/applications, once placed in operation, will be protected against loss or serious error.

Properly designed systems, with excellent control mechanisms built in, might have these controls bypassed or overridden by management direction. (This area is addressed under standards in chapter VI for computer-related auditing [not included in this Appendix].) This has occurred in systems that were recently implemented and put into operation. Many times the designers and developers override such controls to get the system operational and then forget to activate the controls after the system errors have been corrected.

Almost every system has manual aspects (for example, input origination, output disposition), and these, together with the electronic data processing controls, are considered when the auditor is reviewing system controls for adequacy.

Efficiency and economy.

Objective 4: To provide reasonable assurance that systems/applications will be efficient and economical in operation.

Determining whether an organization is managing and using its resources (such as personnel, property, space) efficiently and economically and reporting on the causes of inefficiencies or uneconomical practices, including inadequacies in management information systems, administrative procedures, or organizational structures, is considered here as a basic characteristic of government program audits. With the development of complex systems/applications, the auditor's review should also focus on whether the system has been developed in such a way that operations will produce desired results at a minimum cost. For example, early in a system's development, the auditor should review the adequacy of the (1) statement of mission needs and system objectives, (2) feasibility study and evaluation of alternative designs to meet those needs and objectives, and (3) cost-benefit analysis which attributes specific benefits and costs to system alternatives.

Legal requirements.

Objective 5: To provide reasonable assurance that systems/applications conform with legal requirements.

Legal requirements applicable to systems/applications may originate from various sources. One such requirement is compliance with State and Federal privacy statutes, which restrict collection and use of certain types of information about individuals. Safeguards are obviously necessary in such systems. Conversely, organizations subject to the Freedom of Information Act should have systems/applications designed so that appropriate and timely response can be made to legitimate requests. The applicability of the Federal

Information Processing Standards (required by Public Law 87-306, Oct. 1965) program to the system involved should also be considered by the auditor. If such standards apply, they should be included in the auditor's review.

Once again, auditor review of the design and development processes can help assure management that these requirements have been considered and satisfied.

Documentation.

Objective 6: To provide reasonable assurance that systems/applications are documented in a manner that will provide the understanding of the system required for appropriate maintenance and auditing.

The auditor should determine whether the design, development, and modification procedures produce documentation sufficient to define (1) the processing that must be done by programs in the system, (2) the data files to be processed, (3) the reports to be prepared, (4) the instructions to be used by computer operators, and (5) the instructions to user groups for preparation and control of data. The auditor should also ascertain whether management policy provides for evaluation of documentation and adequate testing of the system before it is made operational. These steps are taken to ensure that the system and its controls can be relied on.

The methods of achieving these six objectives are determined by the circumstances of each situation. Generally, audit work covers reviewing the adequacy of management policies—examining approvals, documentation, test results, cost studies, and other data to see whether management policies are followed and legal requirements met—and determining whether the systems/applications have the necessary controls and trails.

The auditor should not become part of the system design/development team to perform work under this objective. Auditor involvement should be limited to reviewing the team's work as it occurs and reporting to management an objective evaluation of the work.

At the completion of the design and development processes, and during final system testing phases, the auditor should verify that the implemented system conforms with these six objectives.

On all audits of programs, activities, and functions supported by existing computer-based systems, the auditor shall follow the general and application standards for computer-related auditing. If, during an audit, the auditor finds indications that the system objectives—as set forth in this objective—are not being met or have changed, this should be reported to appropriate officials.

APPENDIX G
The Effects of Computer Processing on the Examination of Financial Statements

Note: This statement supersedes SAS No. 3, *The Effects of EDP on the Auditor's Study and Evaluation of Internal Control,* AICPA, *Professional Standards,* vol. 1, AU sec. 321 (Commerce Clearing House). The amendments to other sections as presented in this Statement integrate guidance concerning the effects of computer processing on audits of financial statements with other existing auditing guidance, because auditors consider the methods of data processing, including the use of computers, in essentially the same way, and at the same time, they consider other factors that may affect their examination.

In this Statement, superseding paragraphs are introduced by a dual reference indicating their location in both the individual SASs and in AICPA, *Professional Standards,* vol. 1.

PLANNING AND SUPERVISION

(Amends Statement on Auditing Standards No. 22, AICPA, *Professional Standards,* vol. 1, AU sec. 311.03, .09, and .10.)

1. This amendment adds to the list of required planning considerations in paragraph 3 (as new item c) the methods used by the entity to process significant accounting information. It also adds a new paragraph 9, summarizing those aspects of computer processing that may have an effect on planning

an examination of financial statements. Furthermore, it adds a new paragraph 10 that describes how the auditor might consider the need for using a professional possessing specialized skills to determine the effect of computer processing on the examination. Existing paragraphs 9 through 13 are renumbered 11 through 15.

Planning

.03c. The methods used by the entity to process significant accounting information (see paragraph .09), including the use of service organizations, such as outside service centers.

[c through g are redesignated d through h]

.09 The auditor should consider the methods the entity uses to process accounting information in planning the audit because such methods influence the design of the accounting system and the nature of the internal accounting control procedures. The extent to which computer processing is used in significant accounting applications,[1] as well as the complexity of that processing, may also influence the nature, timing, and extent of audit procedures. Accordingly, in evaluating the effect of an entity's computer processing on an examination of financial statements, the auditor should consider matters such as:

a. The extent to which the computer is used in each significant accounting application.

b. The complexity of the entity's computer operations, including the use of an outside service center.[2]

c. The organizational structure of the computer processing activities.

d. The availability of data. Documents that are used to enter information into the computer for processing, certain computer files, and other evidential matter that may be required by the auditor may exist only for a short period or only in computer-readable form. In some computer systems, input documents may not exist at all because information is directly entered into the system. An entity's data retention policies may require the auditor to request retention of some information for his review or to perform audit procedures at a time when the information is available. In addition, certain information generated by the computer for management's internal purposes may be useful in performing substantive tests (particularly analytical review procedures).[3]

e. The use of computer-assisted audit techniques to increase the efficiency of performing audit procedures.[4] Using computer-assisted audit techniques may also provide the auditor with an opportunity to apply certain procedures to an entire population of accounts or transactions. In addition, in some accounting systems, it may be difficult or impossible for the auditor to analyze certain data or test specific control procedures without computer assistance.

.10. The auditor should consider whether specialized skills are needed to consider the effect of computer processing on the audit, to understand the flow of transactions, to understand the nature of internal accounting control procedures, or to design and perform audit procedures. If specialized skills are needed, the auditor should seek the assistance of a professional possessing such skills, who may be either on the auditor's staff or an outside professional. If the use of such a professional is planned, the auditor should have sufficient computer-related knowledge to communicate the objectives of the other professional's work; to evaluate whether the specified procedures will meet the auditor's objectives; and to evaluate the results of the procedures applied as they relate to the nature, timing, and extent of other planned audit procedures. The auditor's responsibilities with respect to using such a professional are equivalent to those for other assistants.[5]

ANALYTICAL REVIEW PROCEDURES

(Amends Statement on Auditing Standards No. 23, AICPA, *Professional Standards*, vol. 1, AU sec. 318.07.)

2. This amendment adds to the list of factors in paragraph 7 that the auditor should consider when planning and performing analytical review procedures. The additional factor is the effect (if any) that increased availability of computer-generated data may have on the auditor's decision in planning to perform analytical review procedures.

.07e. *The increased availability of data prepared for management's use when computer processing is used.* Computer systems have created an ability (which may not be practical in manual systems) to store, retrieve, and analyze data for use in achieving broader management objectives. These data and analyses, although not necessarily part of the basic accounting records, may be valuable sources of information for the auditor for use in applying analytical review procedures, other substantive tests, or compliance testing.

[e and f are redesignated f and g]

THE AUDITOR'S STUDY AND EVALUATION OF INTERNAL CONTROL

[Amends Statement on Auditing Standards No. 1, AICPA, *Professional Standards*, vol. 1, AU sec. 320.03, .33, .34, .37, .57, .58, and .65-.68 [as amended].]

3. This amendment (a) deletes paragraph 3, an introductory paragraph describing the use of computer processing, since it is no longer necessary; (b) adds a new paragraph 33 (under "Methods of Data Processing"), describing characteristics of computer processing that may have an effect on the system of internal accounting control; and (c) adds a new paragraph 34 (under "Methods of Data Processing"), which recognizes that classifying controls into general and application controls has no effect on the objective of internal accounting control. That objective is to provide reasonable, but not absolute, assurance (a) that assets are safeguarded and (b) that financial records are reliable for the preparation of financial statements.

4. This amendment also adds examples related to the use of computer processing. Examples are added to renumbered paragraph 37, which deals with the segregation of functions; and to renumbered paragraph 65, new paragraph 66, renumbered paragraph 67, and new paragraph 68, all of which discuss the nature of tests.

5. In addition, this amendment adds new paragraphs 57 and 58 (under "Review of System"), which discuss the interdependence of control procedures and their effect on the auditor's study and evaluation of internal control, explaining why it may be more efficient to review the design of general control procedures that have an effect on the performance of application control procedures before reviewing those application control procedures. Other existing paragraphs are renumbered as appropriate.

.33 The methods an entity uses to process significant accounting applications may influence the control procedures designed to achieve the objectives of internal accounting control. Those characteristics that distinguish computer processing from manual processing include:

a. *Transaction trails.*[6] Some computer systems are designed so that a complete transaction trail that is useful for audit purposes might exist for only a short period of time or only in computer-readable form.

b. *Uniform processing of transactions.* Computer processing uniformly subjects like transactions to the same processing instructions. Consequently, computer processing virtually eliminates the occurrence of clerical error normally associated with manual processing. Conversely, programming errors (or other similar systematic errors in either the computer hardware or software) will result in all like transactions being processed incorrectly when those transactions are processed under the same conditions.

c. *Segregation of functions.* Many internal accounting control procedures once performed by separate individuals in manual systems may be concentrated in systems that use computer processing. Therefore, an individual who has access to the computer may be in a position to perform incompatible functions. As a result, other control procedures may be necessary in computer systems to achieve the control objectives ordinarily accomplished by segregation of functions in manual systems. Other controls may include, for example, adequate segregation of incompatible functions within the computer processing activities, establishment of a control group to prevent or detect processing errors or irregularities, or use of password control procedures to prevent incompatible functions from being performed by individuals who have access to assets and access to records through an on-line terminal.

d. *Potential for errors and irregularities.* The potential for individuals, including those performing control procedures, to gain unauthorized access to data or alter data without visible evidence, as well as to gain access (direct or indirect) to assets, may be greater in computerized accounting systems than in manual systems. Decreased human involvement in handling transactions processed by computers can reduce the potential for observing errors and irregularities. Errors or irregularities occurring during the design or changing of application programs can remain undetected for long periods of time.

e. *Potential for increased management supervision.* Computer systems offer management a wide variety of analytical tools that may be used to review and supervise the operations of the company. The availability of these additional controls may serve to enhance the entire system of internal accounting control on which the auditor may wish to place reliance. For example, traditional comparisons of actual operating ratios with those budgeted, as well as reconciliation of accounts, are frequently available for management review on a more timely basis if such information is computerized. Additionally, some programmed applications provide statistics regarding computer operations that may be used to monitor the actual processing of transactions.

f. *Initiation or subsequent execution of transactions by computer.* Certain transactions may be automatically initiated or certain procedures required to execute a transaction may be automatically performed by a computer system. The authorization of these transactions may be implicit in its acceptance of the design of the computer system.[7]

g. *Dependence of other controls on controls over computer processing.* Computer processing may produce reports and other output that are used in performing manual control procedures. The effectiveness of these manual control procedures can be dependent on the effectiveness of controls over the completeness and accuracy of computer processing. For example, the effectiveness of a control procedure that includes a manual review of a computer-produced exception listing is dependent on the controls over the production of the listing.

.34 Where computer processing is used in significant accounting applications, internal accounting procedures are sometimes defined by classifying control procedures into two types: general and application control procedures.[8] Whether the control procedures are classified by the auditor into general and application controls, the objective of the system of internal accounting control remains the same: to provide reasonable, but not absolute, assurance that assets are safeguarded from unauthorized use or disposition and that financial records are reliable to permit the preparation of financial statements.

.37 Incompatible functions for accounting control purposes are those that place any person in a position to both perpetuate and conceal errors or irregularities in the normal course of his duties. Anyone who records transactions or has access to assets ordinarily is in a position to perpetrate errors or irregularities. Accordingly, accounting control necessarily depends largely on the elimination of opportunities for concealment. For example, anyone who records disbursements could omit the recording of a check, either unintentionally or intentionally. If the same person also reconciles the bank account, the failure to record the check could be concealed through an improper reconciliation. In an accounting system using a computer to print checks and record disbursements, the computer may also generate information used to reconcile the account balance. If the same person entering information into the computer to execute the payment process also receives the output for the reconciliation process, a similar failure could be concealed. These examples illustrate the concept that procedures designed to detect errors and irregularities should be performed by persons other than those who are in a position to perpetrate them; that is, these procedures should be performed by persons having no incompatible functions. Procedures performed by such persons are described hereinafter as being performed independently.

.57 Control procedures that achieve or contribute to the achievement of one or more specific control objectives are often interdependent. Some control procedures may be essential to the operation of other control procedures that meet specific control objectives (that is, they need to be functioning adequately for the achievement of those specific control objectives). In an accounting system that uses computer processing, the auditor's concern over the interdependence of control procedures may be greater than in a manual system because of the increased concentration of functions within the operations of computer processing.

.58 Control procedures that are designed to contribute to the achievement of specific control objectives, through their interdependence with specific control procedures, may be classified as general control procedures. Control procedures that are designed to achieve specific control objectives may be classified as application control procedures. Application controls are often dependent on general controls. For example, if an application control procedure, such as matching shipping information with billing information, were to be performed by a customer-billing computer program, the auditor might review the controls over the access to and changing of computer programs before reviewing this programmed control procedure or other programmed application control procedures. The adequacy of this programmed application control procedure is dependent on the adequacy of control procedures that ensure unauthorized changes have not been made to the computer program performing those procedures during the period under review. Accordingly, it may be more efficient to review the design of internal accounting control procedures that are essential to the operation of several specific control procedures before reviewing those specific control procedures.

.65 Some aspects of accounting control require procedures that are not necessarily required for the execution of transactions. This class of procedures includes the approval or independent review of documents evidencing transactions. In a manual processing system the evidence of performing those procedures may be supported by those transaction documents because the individual assigned to perform that control procedure is normally required to indicate approval (for example, by initialing the document). If an accounting application is processed by computer, however, those procedures performed by an application program frequently will not provide visible evidence of those procedures and may not be performed independently of the original processing of transactions.

.66 Tests of such procedures performed manually require inspection of the related documents (a) to obtain evidence in the form of signatures, initials, audit stamps, and the like; (b) to indicate whether the procedures were performed, and by whom; and (c) to permit an evaluation of the propriety of their performance. Tests of such procedures performed by a computer may be made in a similar manner, provided that the computer produces visible evidence (a) to verify that the procedures were in operation and (b) to evaluate the propriety of their performance. For example, a computer-generated error list may provide such evidence if the list is tested by comparison to a list of the transaction file used by the same application program. If such evidence is not generated by the computer, those control procedures may be tested by using computer-assisted audit techniques to reperform the processing of the relevant information and then comparing the results of reperformance with the actual results. Another method may be submission of test data to the same computer process. It is important to understand that tests designed to verify the operation of programmed control procedures can be effective only if the auditor can obtain reasonable assurance of the consistency of their operation throughout the period under examination. Reasonable assurance may be obtained by testing controls over the maintenance and processing of those programs or from alternative procedures such as testing the programmed control procedures throughout the period.

.67 Other aspects of accounting control require a segregation of duties so that certain procedures are performed independently, as discussed in paragraph .37 (as amended above). The performance of these procedures is largely self-evident from the operation of the business or the existence of its essential records; consequently, tests of compliance with such procedures are primarily to determine whether the procedures were performed by persons having no incompatible functions. This is true for both manual and computerized accounting systems. Examples of this class of procedures may include (a) the receiving, depositing, and disbursing of cash; (b) the recording of transactions; and (c) the posting of customers' accounts. Since such procedures frequently leave no audit trail of who performed them, tests of compliance in these situations are necessarily limited to inquiries of different personnel and observation of office personnel and routines to corroborate the information obtained during the review of the system. While reconciliations, confirmations, or other audit tests performed in accordance with the auditing standards relating to evidential matter may substantiate the accuracy of the underlying records, these tests frequently provide no affirmative evidence of segregation of duties because the records may be accurate even though maintained by persons having incompatible functions.

.68 In a computerized accounting system, functions that would be incompatible in a manual system are often performed by computer. Individuals who have access to computer operations may then be in a position to perpetrate or conceal errors or irregularities. This need not be a weakness if there are control procedures that prevent such an individual from performing incompatible functions within the accounting system. These control procedures might include (a) adequate segregation of incompatible functions within the data processing department, (b) segregation between data processing and user department personnel performing review procedures, and (c) adequate control over access to data and computer programs.

EVIDENTIAL MATTER

(Amends Statement on Auditing Standards No. 31, AICPA, *Professional Standards*, vol. 1, AU sec. 326.12.)

6. This amendment adds a new paragraph 12, making it clear that audit evidence is not affected by the use of computer processing. Only the method by which the auditor gathers that evidence can be affected. Existing paragraphs 12 through 23 are renumbered 13 through 24.

.12 The auditor's specific audit objectives do not change whether accounting data is processed manually or by computer. However, the methods of applying audit procedures to gather evidence may be influenced by the method of data processing. The auditor can use either manual audit procedures, computer-assisted audit techniques, or a combination of both to obtain sufficient, competent evidential matter. However, in some accounting systems that use a computer for processing significant accounting applications, it may be difficult or impossible for the auditor to obtain certain data for inspection, inquiry, or confirmation without computer assistance.

EFFECTIVE DATE

7. The amendments in this Statement are effective for examinations of financial statements for periods beginning after August 31, 1984. Earlier application is encouraged.

The Statement entitled *The Effects of Computer Processing on the Examination of Financial Statements* was adopted unanimously by the fifteen members of the board.

ENDNOTES

Note: These endnotes include all of the footnotes that are contained in the original SAS No. 48 published by the AICPA. However, the numbering of these notes is slightly different from those in the original publication.

[1] Significant accounting applications are those that relate to accounting information that can materially affect the financial statements the auditor is examining.

[2] See SAS No. 44, *Special-Purpose Reports on Internal Accounting Control at Service Organizations*, and the related AICPA Audit Guide *Audits of Service-Center-Produced Records* for guidance concerning the use of a service center for computer processing of significant accounting applications.

[3] SAS No. 23, *Analytical Review Procedures*, describes the usefulness of and guidance pertaining to such procedures.

[4] See the AICPA Audit and Accounting Guide *Computer-Assisted Audit Techniques* for guidance relating to this specialized area.

[5] Since the use of a specialist who is effectively functioning as a member of the audit team is not covered by SAS No. 11, *Using the Work of a Specialist,* a computer audit specialist requires the same supervision and review as any assistant.

[6] A transaction trail is a chain of evidence provided through coding, cross references, and documentation connecting account balances and other summary results with original transactions and calculations.

[7] To the extent that the computer is used to initiate transactions or execute procedures, the application program usually includes procedures designed to assure that the steps are executed in conformity with specific or general authorizations issued by management acting within the scope of its authority. Those procedures might include checks to recognize data that fall outside predetermined limits and tests for overall reasonableness.

[8] General controls are those controls that relate to all or many computerized accounting activities and often include control over the development, modification, and maintenance of computer programs, and control over the use of and changes to data maintained on computer files. Application controls relate to individual computerized accounting applications, for example, programmed edit controls for verifying customers' account numbers and credit limits.

Glossary

A

abend   Abnormal termination of a computer job due to a failure, error, or exception condition that causes a program halt. The term is derived from *ab*normal *end*ing.

AC   *See* audit comfort.

acceptable confidence level   In sampling, the degree of certainty, or statement of probabilities, that a conclusion is correct. Acceptable confidence level is expressed as a percentage of certainty.

access   The ability and the means necessary to approach, store, or retrieve data, or to communicate with or make use of any resource within a CIS.

access category   A classification to which a user, program, or process within a CIS may be assigned to indicate the resources or groups of resources that the user, program, or process is authorized to use.

access control   The process of limiting access to the resources of a CIS only to authorized users, programs, or processes, or to other computer information systems, as in computer networks. *Synonym:* controlled accessibility.

access control label   Within a CIS network, an identification for each object, or system resource, that specifies its security class and modes of access.

access control mechanism   Hardware or software feature, operating procedure, or management procedure—applied separately or in combination—that is designed to detect and prevent unauthorized access and to permit authorized access to a CIS.

access list   A catalog of users, programs, or processes, as well as the specifications of access categories to which each is assigned.

access period   A segment of time, generally expressed on a daily or weekly basis, during which access rights prevail.

access type   The nature of an access right to a particular device, program, or file: read, write, execute, append, modify, delete, create, etc.

accountability   The quality or state that permits violations or attempted violations of CIS security to be traced to individuals who then may be held responsible.

accounting   (1) The function of recording, classifying, and posting transactions and producing financial reports to management, owners, and to regulatory agencies of government. (2) One of the three basic objectives set forth in SAS No. 1 and subsequently incorporated in the Foreign Corrupt Practices Act of 1977.

accounting and audit department   Within public accounting firms, the combination of accounting and audit functions within a single administrative and service staff.

accounting model   A type of model-oriented decision support system (DSS) used for short-term planning within functional departments.

accreditation   The authorization and approval, granted to a CIS or network, to process sensitive data in an operational environment. Accreditation is made on the basis of a certification by designated technical personnel of the extent to which design and implementation of the system meet specified technical requirements for achieving adequate data security.

active wiretapping   (1) In accessing digital communication channels, the unauthorized deletion, addition, or alteration of intercepted data. (2) The attachment of an unauthorized device, such as a computer terminal, to a communication circuit for the purpose of obtaining access to data through the generation of false messages or control signals, or by altering the communications of legitimate users.

add-on security   The retrofitting of protection mechanisms, implemented by hardware or software, after a CIS has become operational.

administrative security   The management constraints, operational procedures, accountability procedures, and supplemental controls established to provide an acceptable level of protection for sensitive data. *See also* procedural security.

advanced office systems (AOS)   Information systems that incorporate office automation technology, usually for administrative support functions such as word processing.

aggregated file   A special file version in which personal identifiers have been stripped away and data relevant to a particular study have been placed in statistical data clusters.

aging   Indentification, by date, of unprocessed or retained items in files. Aging, usually by date of transaction, classifies items according to ranges of data.

AI   *See* audit interval.

ALE   *See* annualized loss expectancy.

amount control total   Total of homogeneous amounts, usually dollars or quantities, for a group of transactions or records.

analysis   *See* cost-risk analysis, cryptanalysis, risk analysis.

analysis information system   A type of data-oriented decision support system (DSS) that uses a model to simulate policy or to forecast the future.

annualized loss expectancy (ALE)   In risk assessment, the average monetary value of losses per year.

anticipation   The expectation of a given transaction or event at a particular time.

antistatic mat   A special floor covering made of conductive material that shunts charges of static electricity away from equipment and operators to an electrical ground.

application audit   Review by computer auditors of production systems, complex systems, program maintenance, or production of computer audit routines.

application control   Control that governs a specific, individual information system and that usually is applied to input, processing, or output.

application programmer   Within a CIS department, a person who does the actual coding of programs for new or enhanced application systems.

applications advisory committee   An adjunct to the CIS steering committee and systems planning functions in which a consultative group is composed of user department representatives and the head of the CIS function. The purposes of the committee involve resolving contention for limited systems development resources and coordinating overlapping interests of different user departments.

approval   The acceptance of a transaction for processing after it has been initiated.

approved circuit   *See* protected wireline distribution system.

AOS *See* advanced office systems.

AOS plan A set of corporate policies and procedures for guiding the implementation of advanced office systems and the building of microcomputer-based information networks throughout the organization.

asset safeguarding (1) Provision of reasonable assurance that the assets of an organization are protected against loss or damage. (2) One of the three basic objectives set forth in SAS No. 1 and subsequently incorporated in the Foreign Corrupt Practices Act of 1977.

attest Auditor's function encompassing all activities and responsibilities associated with the rendering of an opinion on the fairness of financial statements.

audit (1) To conduct the independent review and examination of system records and activities to test for adequacy of system controls, to assure compliance with established policy and operational procedures, and to recommend any indicated changes in controls, policy, or procedures. (2) The independent review and examination of system activities and records as in (1). (3) Within the context of technical security, a review of a CIS to determine whether unauthorized acts have occurred. *See also* external security audit, internal security audit, security audit.

audit automation The application of general-purpose microcomputers to such tasks as audit planning, data testing, analytical review, preparation of workpapers, reporting, and so on. (This term is not a synonym for computer auditing. *See also* computer auditing.)

audit charter *See* computer audit charter.

audit comfort (AC) In quantitative risk assessment, the auditor's subjective evaluation of an activity or entity.

audit committee Oversight group for internal and external audit functions composed of top managers and often constituted as a committee of the board of directors.

audit data flow diagram Graphic representation and analysis of data movement, processing functions (transformations), and the files (data stores) that are used to support processing in an information system. Unlike the data flow diagrams (DFDs) developed by systems analysts, the audit data flow diagram is prepared during the auditor's evaluation of an application, with particular attention to control weaknesses, and encompassing all information flows within the system, from source documents to final outputs, whether automated or manual.

audit interval (AI) In quantitative risk assessment, a factor that encompasses the length of time between audits, as well as the number and importance of prior audit recommendations.

audit of auxiliary operations Specific, repetitive functions of computer audit review surrounding CIS facilities and management services, encompassing related operations that are performed remotely from the central facility but that have significance to overall information resource management.

audit risk The probable unfavorable monetary effect associated with the occurrence of an undesirable event or condition. *See also* exposure.

audit risk prioritization scheme A four-step methodology for assessing the audit risk to the assets of an organization. Steps include: identifying risk dimensions, identifying risk characteristics, analyzing audit risk characteristics, and assessing audit risk.

audit risk profile In the assessment of audit risk, a graphic representation of the different risk characteristics measured.

audit risk score In the assessment of audit risk, the sum of assigned point values corresponding with the magnitude of each identified risk characteristic.

audit support In the context of computer auditing, the use of the computer itself to perform audit tests. In this support function, the computer carries out specific analyses and tests that provide the basis for evaluation by auditors. *See also* audit tool.

audit tool In the context of computer auditing, any computer-assisted technique that implements specific analyses or tests. *See also* audit support.

audit trail A chronological record of system activities that is sufficient to permit the reconstruction, review, and examination of the sequence of environments and activities surrounding or leading to each event in the path of a transaction, from its inception to output of final results. *See also* transaction trail.

audit work station A secure, microcomputer-based system that permits CIS auditors to download data from corporate databases for audit tests.

authentication (1) The process of verifying the eligibility of a station, originator, or individual to access specific categories of information or to enter areas of a CIS installation. This process often involves the matching of machine-readable code to a predetermined list of authorized users. (2) A measure designed to provide protection against fraudulent transmissions by establishing the validity of a transmission, message, station, or originator.

authenticator (1) The means used to identify or verify the eligibility of a station, originator, or individual to access specific categories of information. (2) A symbol, a sequence of symbols, or a series of bits that are arranged in a predetermined manner and that usually are inserted at a predetermined point within a message or transmission for the purpose of assuring the integrity of the message or transmission.

authorization (1) The granting to a user, a program, or a process the right of access. (2) Limiting the initiation of a transaction or performance of a process to designated individuals. (3) One of the three basic objectives set forth in SAS No. 1 and subsequently incorporated in the Foreign Corrupt Practices Act of 1977.

automated error correction Initiation, under program control, of actions that compensate for abnormal inputs in transactions or records that violate detective controls.

automated security monitoring The use of computerized procedures to assure that the security controls implemented within a CIS are not circumvented.

available balance hold Within a computer-based financial system, a control that restricts the processing of withdrawals from accounts with insufficient funds.

B

back entry Penetration of a CIS by way of access methods normally reserved for system maintenance or testing.

backup and recovery The ability to recreate current master files and reports using appropriate prior master records and transactions.

backup procedure A provision made for the recovery of data files and program libraries, or for restart or replacement of CIS equipment after the occurrence of a system failure or disaster.

balancing A test for equality between the values of two equivalent sets of items, or between one set of items and a control total. Any difference would indicate that an error has occurred.

batch balancing Comparison of the items or documents actually processed in a batch, with a predetermined control total.

batch control *See* batch total.

batch control log *See* control register.

batch control ticket *See* transmittal document.

batch sequence Order of transaction documents as indicated by batch serial numbers.

batch serial number Result of consecutive numbering and accounting for batches of transaction documents.

batch total Any type of control total or count applied to a specific number of transaction documents or to the transaction documents that are submitted for input within a specific period of time.

between-the-lines entry Access, obtained through the use of active wiretapping by an unauthorized user, to the momentarily inactive terminal of a legitimate user that is assigned to a communication channel.

black box A process for which the internal instructions and details are not known or are regarded as hidden, requiring analysis to be performed solely on the basis of comparing outputs with corresponding inputs.

block sampling Testing by auditors of all transactions that took place during selected periods, such as specific weeks or months. *See also* judgmental sampling.

bounds checking Testing of computer program results for access to storage locations outside of authorized limits. *Synonym:* memory bounds checking.

bounds register A hardware register that holds an address specifying a storage boundary for access control.

brevity list A code system that reduces data transmission time by substituting a few characters for long, commonly used phrases.

browsing Searching through computer storage to locate or acquire information, without necessarily knowing of the existence or the format of the information being sought.

C

calculated control Within a CIS, a control for which the parameters cannot be predetermined and must be computed during each processing run based on circumstances or inputs unique to that run.

call-back A procedure established for positively identifying a terminal dialing into a computer system. Upon receiving a request for access, the operator or system disconnects the calling terminal and re-establishes the connection by dialing the telephone number of the calling terminal.

cancellation Identification of transaction documents to prevent their further or repeated use after they have performed their function.

capacity planning Information resource management (IRM) function that attempts to match the expansion of CIS facilities to projected growth in demand for each type of resource.

career development plan A documented agreement between an employee and management that sets specific objectives for individual career progression and professional growth.

CDM *See* chief decision maker.

CDP *See* Certified Data Processor.

certification The technical evaluation, made as part of and in support of the accreditation process, that establishes the extent to which the design and implementation of a particular CIS or network meet a specified set of security requirements; also, the status conferred on an individual practitioner by a duly recognized professional society or organization, usually after a comprehensive examination and other demonstration of professional competency.

Certified Data Processor (CDP) Professional designation initiated by the Data Processing Management Association and currently administered by the Institute of Certified Computer Professionals (ICCP).

Certified Information Systems Auditor (CISA) Professional designation conferred by the EDP Auditors Association.

Certified Internal Auditor (CIA) Professional designation conferred by the Institute of Internal Auditors.

Certified Management Accountant (CMA) Professional designation conferred by the National Association of Accountants (NAA).

Certified Public Accountant (CPA) Independent auditors charged with the responsibility of attesting to the fairness of financial statements issued by companies, and particularly those companies that report to the Securities and Exchange Commission (SEC).

Certified Quality Assurance Analyst (CQAA) Professional designation conferred by the Quality Assurance Institute (QAI).

Certified Systems Professional (CSP) Professional designation conferred by the Association for Systems Management (ASM).

check bit *See* parity bit.

check digit One digit, usually the last, of an identifying field. This digit is a mathematical function of all of the other digits in the field. A value can be calculated from the other digits in the field and compared with the check digit to check the validity of the whole field.

chief decision maker (CDM) The manager who has direct authority over a specific function.

CIA *See* Certified Internal Auditor.

cipher Within cryptographic systems, a data encryption key, or algorithm that is used to scramble data messages.

cipher system A cryptographic system in which cryptography is applied to encode plain-text elements of equal length.

cipher text Unintelligible text or signals produced through the use of cipher systems.

CIS auditor Within a CIS department but usually reporting to the internal audit function, a person who is responsible for evaluating existing standards of control and audit trails that should be incorporated into system and program designs. The CIS auditor also reviews design documents and completed systems to assure that they adhere to the standards, develops standards for administration and operational controls, and conducts periodic reviews of the CIS operation to verify adherence to standards. *See also* computer auditor.

CIS operations review A formal evaluation by computer auditors of the efficiency with which a CIS department is being run.

CIS security All of the technological safeguards and managerial procedures established and applied to computer hardware, software, and data to assure the protection of organizational assets and individual privacy.

CIS steering committee *See* steering committee.

CISA *See* Certified Information Systems Auditor.

clearing account An amount that results from the processing of independent items of equivalent total value. The net control value should equal zero.

CMA *See* Certified Management Accountant.

code system (1) Any system of communication in which groups of symbols are used to represent plain text elements of varying length. (2) In the broadest sense, a means of converting information into a form suitable for communication or encryption: *e.g.*, coded speech, Morse Code, teletypewriter codes. (3) A cryptographic system in which cryptographic equivalents—usually called *code groups* and typically composed of letters, digits, or both—are substituted in meaningless combinations for plain-text elements, which may be words, phrases, or sentences. (4) *See also* brevity list.

collusion Collaborative effort for improper purposes.

Commission on Auditor's Responsibilities Review body created in 1974 by the American Institute of Certified Public Accountants (AICPA) to evaluate auditing standards, especially regarding computer-based financial information systems.

communication security Protection that assures the authenticity of telecommunication. Communication security results from applying measures that deny access by unauthorized persons to information of value carried over telecommunication channels.

comparison testing Selection of unusual items for audit examination by comparing items in financial records with corresponding items in prior periods.

compartmentalization (1) The isolation of the operating system, user programs, and data files from one another in main storage to protect against unauthorized or concurrent access by other users or programs. (2) The breaking down of sensitive data into small, isolated blocks for the purpose of reducing risk to the data.

compatible Term used to describe computer systems that use the same or very similar operating systems, microprocessors, and data storage formats. These similarities allow the systems to use the same software programs and to share data files. See also *connectable*.

competence of personnel Ability of persons assigned to processing or supervisory roles within a CIS, as determined by the technical knowledge necessary to perform their functions.

completeness check A test that data entries are made in fields that cannot be processed in a blank state.

complex systems audit Review and examination by computer auditors of systems that employ relatively advanced technologies.

compliance audit Audit engagement for which the objective is to attest to compliance of the system under study with generally accepted auditing standards (GAAS).

compliance test Audit procedure for testing individual transactions that generally is performed on a selective basis following a review and preliminary evaluation of internal control. Compliance testing probes for specific strengths and weaknesses of control.

compromise An unauthorized disclosure or loss of sensitive information.

compromising emanation Electromagnetic signals that may convey data and that, if intercepted and analyzed, might violate the integrity of sensitive information being processed by a CIS.

computer audit charter Documented authority for the involvement of an internal audit department in the evaluation of CIS systems, practices, and operations. The charter provides a way to communicate to the entire organization the scope and purposes of the internal audit/computer audit function.

computer auditing The evaluation of computer information systems, practices, and operations to assure the integrity of an entity's information.

computer auditor A specialist in examining and evaluating computer information systems and in using "through-the-computer" audit techniques. *See also* CIS auditor.

computer dependent Referring to organizations for which there virtually is no effective alternative to computer-assisted functions.

computer equipment feasibility study Investigation by computer auditors to determine management requirements for computer hardware. This type of audit can encompass criteria of performance, cost, acquisition procedures, and terms of purchase or lease, as well as provision for maintenance and support.

computer operator Within a CIS operations center, a person who oversees the actual running of both in-house and user jobs.

computer-assisted audit procedures Automated audit routines that are incorporated into the programs of operational computer information systems.

concealment system A method of achieving confidentiality in which the existence of sensitive information is hidden by embedding it in irrelevant data.

condition To maintain and monitor a communication channel so that noise and distortion are minimized.

confidentiality Status of and degree of protection that must be provided for sensitive data that describe individuals or organizations.

connectable Term that describes noncompatible computer systems that are linked through the use of special utility programs. See also *compatible*.

control clerk Within a CIS operations center, a person who logs jobs in and out of production.

control register A log or register indicating the disposition and control values of batches or transactions. *Synonym:* batch control log.

control zone The space, expressed in feet of radius, that surrounds equipment that is used to process sensitive information and that is under sufficient physical and technical control to preclude an unauthorized entry or compromise. *Synonym:* security perimeter.

controllable isolation Controlled sharing of system resources, under which the scope or domain of authorization can be reduced to an arbitrarily small sphere of activity.

controlled accessibility *See* access control.

controlled sharing The condition that exists if access control is applied to all users of a resource-sharing CIS.

corrective control Control implemented within a CIS that can detect errors or exception conditions and also can apply appropriate corrective action while processing is under way. *See also* detective control, preventive control.

correctness proof   An ideal, formal test by which it is demonstrated that a program performs its intended function and nothing more.

cost-risk analysis   The assessment of the costs of potential risk of loss or compromise of data in an unprotected CIS versus the cost of providing data protection.

CPA   *See* Certified Public Accountant.

criticality   A measure of the permissible delay in processing for a given system.

crosstalk   An unwanted transfer of energy from one communication channel to another.

cryptanalysis   The steps and operations performed in converting encrypted messages into plain text, without initial knowledge of the key employed in the encryption algorithm.

cryptographic system   The documents, devices, equipment, and associated techniques that are used as a unit to provide a single means of encryption (enciphering or encoding).

cryptography   The principles, means, and methods for rendering plain text unintelligible and for converting encrypted messages into intelligible form.

cryptology   The field that encompasses both cryptography and cryptanalysis.

crypto-operation   *See* off-line crypto-operation, online crypto-operation.

cryogenic   Referring to technologies that rely on supercold temperatures (on the order of -450 degrees F).

custody   Responsibility delegated by data owners for the maintenance and safeguarding of data resources.

D

data analysis system   A type of data-oriented decision support system (DSS) that answers questions dealing with cost controls.

data contamination   A deliberate or accidental process or act that results in a change in the integrity of the original data.

data bit   A binary digit within a byte that has informational value rather than being used as a status flag or error-checking code, such as a control bit or a parity bit. In vertical parity checking, summation of the values of all data bits within a byte determines the value of the parity bit (odd or even).

data dictionary   A document that lists and defines all elements within a database and that provides correlations among user inquiries and those elements.

data element   (1) A unit of data that has meaning in an application. (2) A unit of data within a database management system (DBMS).

data element check   Input control under which bits, characters, or character sequences within a unit of data are validated prior to processing.

data entry fraud   The destruction, alteration, or disclosure of items presented to a computer information system for processing.

data entry operator   Within a CIS operations center, a person who keys and/or verifies data inputs from source documents. Data entry operators also may enter and verify batch totals and batch counts.

data integrity   The state that exists if computerized data are the same as those in the source documents and if the data have not been exposed to accidental or malicious alteration or destruction.

data librarian   Within a CIS operations center, a person who is the custodian of all data resources and who has responsibility for logging data media in and out of the data library, as well as for assuring that both on-site and off-site backup copies are maintained.

data link layer   Within the seven-layer ISO model of a LAN, the network level that provides node-to-node control of data flowing across a communication circuit.

data preparation control   Within a CIS, a control that governs the creation of source documents or transaction media used by the system.

data protection engineering The methodology and tools used for designing and implementing mechanisms for safeguarding data.

data security The protection of data from accidental or malicious modification, destruction, or disclosure.

data type One of many categories of data, including: alphabetic, numeric, alphanumeric (string), integer, real, Boolean, and so on.

database administrator (DBA) The person responsible for defining and managing the content of a database. The DBA develops procedures for the operations of organizational databases and DBMS and also is responsible for assuring that access follows established procedures.

database management system (DBMS) System software that integrates data storage and access so that the user need not be concerned with the details of physical storage location and the characteristics of specific data storage devices.

database system A CIS that uses a database management system.

data-dependent protection Protection of data at a level commensurate with the sensitivity of individual data elements, rather than with the sensitivity of an entire file that contains the data elements.

data-oriented Within a decision support system (DSS), referring to a process that focuses on responses for specific inquiries. *See also* model-oriented.

dating The recording of calendar dates for purposes of later comparison or testing for expiration.

decipher To convert, by applying the appropriate key, enciphered text into its equivalent plain text.

decision support system (DSS) A database creation and manipulation capability that assists managers and executives in identifying and selecting decision alternatives on the basis of quantitative evaluations.

decision tree Graphic representation of successive alternatives to be addressed in solving a problem or reaching a conclusion. Choices between alternatives, when presented in diagram form, resemble the branches on a tree.

decrypt To convert, by applying the appropriate key, encrypted (encoded or enciphered) text into its equivalent plain text.

dedicated mode The operation of a CIS so that the central computer facility, its connected peripheral devices, its communication facilities, and all remote terminals are used and controlled exclusively by specific users or groups of users for the processing of particular types and categories of information.

default option The automatic input of a predefined value if the corresponding field in an input transaction has been left blank.

definition of responsibilities Description of tasks for each job function within an information processing system. Such descriptions indicate clear beginning and termination points for each job function. Also covered are the relationships among job functions.

degauss (1) To apply a variable, alternating current (AC) electrical field to demagnetize recording media, such as magnetic tapes. The process involves increasing the AC field gradually from zero to some maximum value and back to zero, which leaves a low residue of magnetic induction on the media. (2) In practical (but not technical) terms, to erase.

design review audit An in-process systems development review by computer auditors that is conducted at the ends of the preliminary design and detailed design phases. The objectives of this audit are to determine whether designs meet requirements and to examine control interfaces.

detection Within the context of technical security, catching an unauthorized procedure when it is attempted and preventing its completion. *See also* prevention.

detective control Control implemented within a CIS that identifies actual errors or exceptions that already have taken place. *See also* corrective control, preventive control.

determinant In risk assessment, the causal factor for a given risk.

disable In data processing terms, a command that removes a computer device from service.

discrepancy report A listing of items that have violated some detective control and require further investigation.

distributed processing The decentralization and coordination of computer processing and storage capabilities among devices that share a data communication network.

distribution list List describing the nature, the recipient(s), and the timing of each report or document produced by an application.

document control total A count of the number of individual documents in a batch or group of transactions.

documentation Written records for the purpose of communication and ongoing reference.

documentation specialist Job title for technical specialists within a CIS department who are charged with the responsibility of writing and organizing systems documentation, including program documentation, reference manuals, and users' manuals.

documented recovery procedure Step-by-step instructions for recovering from all disruptions—minor to major—including all resources needed, such as operating instructions and files.

dollar risk (1) In quantitative risk assessment, the monetary value of the loss that would occur if a given threat were realized. (2) In mathematical terms, the product of multiplying, for each risk characteristic, its frequency of occurrence by the expected loss (in dollars) per occurrence. *See* annualized loss expectancy.

dollar volume The monetary total of all transactions processed on an average day. In quantitative risk assessment, dollar volume is used as a factor in determining performance sensitivity.

dollar-value estimation In substantive testing, the stratification of accounting record populations according to criteria based on monetary amounts.

download Transfer of files or data from a mainframe computer facility or corporate network to local data storage in an intelligent terminal or microcomputer.

drum card Device for automatic spacing and format shifting of data fields on a keypunch machine.

DSS *See* decision support system.

dual access *See* dual controls.

dual controls Two independent, simultaneous actions or conditions that are required before processing is permitted.

E

eavesdropping The unauthorized interception, by methods other than wiretapping, of information-bearing emanations.

echo check Data transmission control under which characters are displayed and verified at the originating terminal as they are entered.

edit loop In on-line entry mode, a program module that performs acceptance edit checks of data prior to actual processing.

edit run Prior to processing, an application of programmed input controls to batches submitted to a CIS.

edited data check A logical test performed by an input edit routine on the content of data items presented to a system for processing.

EDP Auditors Foundation for Education and Research (EDPAF) Professional association for CIS auditors and computer audit specialists.

educational and standards audit An examination by computer auditors of the compliance of a new system with CIS development, organizational, and operational standards, as well as the assessment of user training efforts.

EFT *See* electronic funds transfer.

electromagnetic emanation Signals transmitted as radiation through space or as impulses through conductors.

electromagnetic interference (EMI) Disruptions to computer operations or digital communications, often caused by electric motors or magnetic devices.

electronic funds transfer (EFT) Computer process within which bits of data actually represent cash assets, or constitute the medium of monetary exchange.

electronic sweep Inspection of a facility with specialized equipment to detect electronic bugs or eavesdropping devices.

emanation *See* compromising emanation, electromagnetic emanation.

emanation security The protection that results from all measures designed to deny unauthorized persons information of value that might be derived from interception and analysis of compromising emanations.

EMI *See* electromagnetic interference.

enable In data processing terms, a command that activates a computer device for service.

encipher To convert plain text into unintelligible form by means of a cipher code.

encode To convert plain text into unintelligible form by means of a code system.

encrypt To convert plain text into unintelligible form by means of cryptographic systems.

encryption *See* end-to-end encryption, link encryption.

encryption algorithm A set of mathematically expressed rules for rendering information unintelligible by performing a series of transformations with variable elements that are controlled by a key. *Synonym:* privacy transformation.

endorsement The marking of a form or document to direct or restrict its further use in processing.

end-to-end encryption (1) Within a communication network, encrypting information at the point of origin and postponing decryption to the point of destination. *See also* link encryption.

entrapment The deliberate planting of apparent flaws in a system for the purpose of detecting attempted penetrations or confusing an intruder about which flaws to exploit.

entry *See* back entry, between-the-lines entry.

entry source analysis Computer-assisted technique for the selection of unusual items for audit examination by testing for errors of accounting entries within income statement or balance sheet accounts.

environmental control *See* general control.

error source statistics Accumulation of such details as type of error, department, and originator. This information is used to determine the nature of remedial training needed to reduce the number of errors.

evidential matter Documentary evidence upon which audit findings are based.

exception input Internally initiated processing in a predefined manner, unless specific input transactions are received that specify processing with different values or in a different manner.

executive state One of two generally possible states in which a CIS may operate. Specific, privileged instructions may be executed if the system is in the executive state. *Synonym:* supervisor state.

exit interview Activity at the completion of an audit engagement in which the auditor discusses suggestions for change with the responsible CIS manager.

expected loss In risk assessment, projected losses to organizational assets due to the pairing of threats and vulnerabilities. *See also* annualized loss expectancy (ALE).

expected rate of error In random attribute sampling, the estimated percentage of exception transactions in specified attributes within the local transaction population. *See also* random attribute sampling.

expiration A limit check based on a comparison of the current date with the date recorded in a transaction, record, or file.

exposure In risk analysis, the combination of a threat, an asset, and a vulnerability.

extent One of the three key criteria for designing audit tests, the others being nature and timing. Extent is the scope or depth of an examination and is governed by the degree of audit reliance on the controls within the system under study. *See also* nature, timing.

external security audit A security audit by an organization independent of the one being audited. *See also* security audit.

F

fail safe The automatic termination and protection of programs or other processing operations if a hardware or software failure is detected within a CIS.

fail soft The selective termination of affected nonessential processing if a hardware or software failure is detected within a CIS.

failure access An unauthorized—and usually inadvertent—access to data, resulting from a hardware or software failure within a CIS.

failure control The measures used to detect and provide fail-safe or fail-soft recovery from hardware and software failures with a CIS.

fairness Conformity of financial statements with generally accepted accounting principles applied on a consistent basis.

FASB *See* Financial Accounting Standards Board.

fault *See* loophole.

Federal Information Processing Standards (FIPS) Guidelines for computer installations within the federal government published by the National Bureau of Standards (NBS), a division of the U. S. Department of Commerce.

Federal Register Publication of the U. S. government that documents official business.

feeder system A CIS that supplies information to financial systems but that is not connected directly to the organization's financial records. *See also* financial system.

fetch protection A system-provided restriction that prevents a program from accessing data in another user's segment of storage.

field work standard One of the generally accepted auditing standards (GAAS) promulgated by the AICPA. The standard encompasses the planning, study, and evaluation of internal control, as well as the sufficiency of evidential matter.

file drawer A metaphor for DSS techniques under which specific data are retrieved from a database in response to an inquiry, just as a particular file folder can be removed from a file drawer containing many individual files.

file protection The aggregate of all processes and procedures established within a CIS and designed to inhibit unauthorized access, contamination, or elimination of a file.

final risk score (FRS) For a given audit entity, the result of quantitative risk assessment that correlates specific risks and pervasive risks.

Financial Accounting Standards Board (FASB) Governing body within the American Institute of Certified Public Accountants (AICPA) responsible for promulgating generally accepted accounting principles (GAAP).

financial system A CIS that either creates and maintains an organization's financial records or that posts information directly to those records.

FIPS *See* Federal Information Processing Standards.

firmware Computer instructions that reside permanently or semipermanently within integrated circuits such as read-only memory (ROM) chips.

flag (1) To segregate processed items on the basis of information content. (2) The setting of a data value or switch to indicate a specific status condition.

flaw *See* loophole. *See also* pseudo-flaw.

flowcharting software Computer utility programs that derive system flowcharts from the source code for application programs.

format check Determination that data are entered in proper mode—numeric, alphabetic, or alphanumeric—within designated fields.

forms design Methods under which forms are constructed to be self-explanatory, understandable, and concise, as well as to gather all necessary data with a minimum of effort by providers.

formulary   Permitting the decision to grant or to deny access to be determined dynamically at access time, rather than at the time of creation of the access list.

forward error correction   In synchronous data communication, the use of redundancy codes to detect, report, and correct errors.

fourth-generation, nonprocedural language   A programming language that produces program code based on nonprocedural specifications for inputs and outputs. Some packages that use fourth-generation programming techniques are called *application generators. See also* nonprocedural language.

frequency division multiplexing   Data communication technique in which a single broadband channel is partitioned into multiple subchannels, each capable of carrying a separate data stream.

frequency of occurrence   In risk assessment, the frequency with which a particular vulnerability, or system flaw, may combine with a possible threat, or exploitation of the vulnerability. *Synonym:* occurrence rate.

front end   An auxiliary computer, usually a minicomputer, that performs preprocessing and housekeeping tasks for a mainframe processor.

G

GAAP   *See* generally accepted accounting principles.

GAAS   *See* generally accepted auditing standards.

GAO   *See* United States General Accounting Office.

gateway   A data communication link within a computer-based network that connects microcomputers to a mainframe computer.

General Accounting Office (GAO)   *See* United States General Accounting Office.

general control   Controls that are universal, or that apply to all jobs run in a given CIS facility. *Synonym:* environmental control.

general integrity (GI)   In quantitative risk assessment, a factor that measures the overall environment of integrity of an information system, as well as the general attitude within an organization toward security and internal controls.

general standards   Within generally accepted auditing standards (GAAS), guidelines that relate to professional and technical competence of auditors, independence, and due professional care.

generally accepted accounting principles (GAAP)   Consistent guidelines for financial reporting by corporate managers. Such standards currently are promulgated by the Financial Accounting Standards Board (FASB) of the American Institute of Certified Public Accountants (AICPA).

generally accepted auditing standards (GAAS)   Standards promulgated by the American Institute of Certified Public Accountants (AICPA) for the conduct of audits, including general standards, field work standards, and reporting standards.

geosynchronous   Referring to the orbits of communication satellites that revolve at a rate that keeps pace exactly with the earth's rotation. The result is that the satellite maintains a fixed position in the sky.

GI   *See* general integrity.

global   Describing a factor that has universal, or pervasive, effect throughout an entire system.

ground station   Microwave transmitting/receiving facility that communicates with satellites.

H

handshaking procedure   A dialog between a user and a computer, a computer and another computer, or a program and another program for the purpose of identifying a user and authenticating his or her identity, through a sequence of questions and answers based on information either previously stored in the computer or supplied to the computer by the initiator of the dialog. *Synonym:* password dialog.

hash total   A meaningless total used for checking and developed from the accumulated numeric amounts of nonmonetary data.

help desk   A function, usually within a CIS department, that provides technical and consultative assistance to users of microcomputers within the organization.

high-level language   Programming language that uses English-like symbols to stand for computer operations and memory addresses, and in which a single instruction stands for multiple machine instructions.

histogram   (1) In general terms, any graph that plots variations in the magnitude of some parameter over time. (2) In computer auditing, a chart showing frequency distributions of records within data files.

housekeeping   Processing associated with getting jobs ready for main processing, as well as the handling of output functions after main processing has been performed.

HR/MR card   *See* human readable/machine readable card.

human readable/machine readable (HR/MR) card   A type of fiche that holds information in a digitized format that can be retrieved and read by computers as well as by humans.

I

identification   Within CIS security, the process that establishes a claim of access to a system by a user. This process often involves entering machine-readable code or physical objects into a security access system.

IIA   *See* Institute of Internal Auditors.

impersonation   An attempt to gain access to a CIS by posing as an authorized user. *Synonyms:* masquerade, mimic.

incomplete parameter checking   A condition that exists if all parameters have not been checked fully for correctness and consistency by the operating system, thus making the system vulnerable to penetration.

information center   A function that coordinates access to corporate information resources by individual users of microcomputers or work stations.

information resource management (IRM)   A coordinated approach to planning for CIS services that recognizes all information within an organization as an important asset to be managed by an authorized oversight function.

information system audit approach   A nine-phase methodology for CIS auditing that has been promulgated by the EDP Auditors Foundation (EDPAF).

information systems (IS)   (1) Computer-based systems, encompassing computer information systems (CIS), distributed data processing (DDP) systems, and advanced office systems (AOS). (2) Computer information systems that supply information for use by a department, branch, or function within an organization.

input control   Within a CIS, a control that governs authorization, conversion, completeness of data, or procedures for rejection or re-entry of data.

input screen   A computerized input editing routine that controls access to system resources according to predetermined authorization and security criteria.

Institute of Internal Auditors (IIA)   Professional association devoted primarily to the activities of staff auditors within organizations.

integrated system   The automated coordination of multiple computer hardware devices, software programs, and/or information systems.

integrated test facility   Within a large-scale CIS that serves multiple divisions of an organization, a fictitious corporation or branch that is modeled within the system and that accepts routine inputs as if it were a real entity. For this scheme to be effective, the existence of integrated test facilities must be a secret that is known only to key members of audit and management functions.

integrity *See* data integrity, system integrity.

intelligent terminal Computer entry and display device with limited electronic processing and memory capabilities.

interactive computing Availability of computer resources so that the user is in control and may enter data or make other demands on the system, which responds by processing user requests and returning appropriate replies to these requests, with a minimum of delay.

interactive database inquiry system A type of decision support system (DSS) that supports on-line data retrieval by interpreting inquiries, as well as gathering and presenting the desired data.

interdiction The act of impeding or denying system resources to a potential user.

intermittent testing The timing of audit tests on a random basis, spread over a representative period of operations. The rationale is to assure that variations in general controls or operating conditions are not influencing test results.

internal security audit A security audit conducted by personnel responsible to the management of the organization being audited.

IRM *See* information resource management.

IS *See* information systems.

isolation The containment of users and resources within a CIS so that users and processes are separate from one another, as well as from the protection controls of the operating system.

J

judgmental sampling Use of the auditor's judgment in the selection of specific time periods, such as weeks or months, for which blocks of transactions or items will be examined. *See also* block sampling.

K

key In cryptography, a sequence of symbols that controls the operations of encryption and decryption.

key generation *See* password.

key management Network security measure in which cryptographic keys are maintained on a separate microcomputer tied to the network, and users are authenticated by request.

key verification Input control technique that uses at least partial clerical redundancy to validate the accuracy of data entered into machine-sensible form through keyboarding.

keystroke verification The redundant keyboard entry of data to verify the accuracy of a prior entry. Differences between the data recorded previously and the data entered in verification signals an error condition.

keyword *See* password.

L

label check Function implemented in system software to assure that the correct data file is being processed by the appropriate application program. Under this approach, the computer compares the file name specified by the user program with a field containing a label code at the head of the data file to be processed.

laser card Plastic card that uses optical patterns to hold machine-readable identification information.

library control Within a CIS, a control that monitors a computer's files automatically to keep track of the application programs stored at any given moment. This control also requires the user to specify program names and versions to be executed.

limit check   Test of specified amount fields against stipulated high or low limits of acceptability. If both high and low values are used, the test may be called a *range check.*

line control count   A count of the individual line items on one or more documents.

line of sight   Path of microwave radio transmissions, which must pass unobstructed from one relay antenna to another along a straight line.

linguistic   Relating to variables that are expressed in generalized levels, such as zero, low, medium, or high, as opposed to expressing those variables with numerical weights.

link encryption   (1) The application of on-line crypto-operations to link a communication system so that all information passing over the link is encrypted in its entirety. (2) End-to-end encryption within each link in a communication network.

linkage   (1) The purposeful combination of data from one information system with those from another system with the aim of deriving additional information. (2) Specifically, the combination of computer files from two or more sources.

liquidity   (1) The speed with which an asset may be converted into cash. (2) The usefulness of an asset to an individual or an organization in gaining unfair competitive advantage. (3) In risk assessment, an element of performance sensitivity that measures the speed with which an asset can be put to use for an unauthorized purpose.

local area network (LAN)   Linking of microcomputers, peripherals, and office machines by hard-wiring within a limited area, such as within a single building or office floor.

lock-and-key protection system   An identification and authentication system that involves matching a key or password with a specified access requirement.

lock-out hold   Within a computer-based financial system, a control that restricts processing of specific accounts.

logging   (1) The process of a user signing on (logging in) or signing off (logging out) to/from a computer time-sharing network. (2) Maintaining an ongoing, chronological record of system access, transaction postings, or file usage. (3) In a security context, the process of auditing the accesses made to a database by all users.

logical comparison   Testing of two data items to see if one value is less than, equal to, greater than, less than or equal to, greater than or equal to, or not equal to the second value.

logical completeness measure   A means of assessing the effectiveness and degree to which security and access control mechanisms meet security specifications.

longitudinal parity check   Testing of a check byte, or block check character, the bits of which indicate the parity of all bits at a given character position in a group of bytes; a check on the validity of a sequence of characters or bytes. *Synonym:* longitudinal redundancy check. *See also* parity, vertical parity check.

loop-back   Data transmission test under which a modem sends a stream of test data through the communication channel and back to its own receiving circuits.

loophole   An error of omission or oversight in software or hardware that allows access controls to be circumvented. *See also* fault, flaw.

loss per occurrence   In risk assessment, the monetary value of the negative impact resulting from the pairing of a threat and a vulnerability.

loss potential   In quantitative risk assessment, the monetary value of a worst-case loss triggered by the threat to an asset.

M

MAC   *See* message authentication code.

machine-applied control   Preventive control exercised by a computer to abort the processing of either individual items or entire transaction streams.

macro   In programming, a subroutine that may be activated, or called, by a single command.

macroscheduling Preparing a calendar for all processing within a CIS center. This scheduling is done at an overview level that focuses on meeting user commitments and allocating resources so that data center capacities are utilized efficiently. *See also* microscheduling.

magnetic card Machine-sensible, plastic identification card that is coated with a magnetic stripe for data retention.

management information system (MIS) (1) Type of computer information system that provides information to support management control functions and tactical planning. (2) A CIS that supplies information for the use of an organization as a whole.

manual processing control *See* operating control.

masquerade *See* impersonation.

matching Comparison of items from the processing stream of an application with another independently developed application for the purpose of identifying unprocessed items.

mean time between failures (MTBF) Projected up-time for a component of computer hardware.

mechanization Consistency processing provided by mechanical or electronic means.

memory bounds The limits in the range of storage addresses for a protected region in memory.

memory bounds checking An application control that assures the integrity of protected regions of memory by testing memory bounds.

memory protection control Within a CIS, a control that governs the allocation of computer memory and storage to application programs.

message authentication code (MAC) A known digital value that is encrypted and included within a data transmission as a detective control on the integrity of the transmission.

message intercept A data communication function that receives transmissions that have been directed to inoperable or unauthorized terminals or devices.

microcomputer/mainframe linkage Interfacing of microcomputers with one or more mainframe systems, or centralized, large-scale computer facilities.

microprocessor card A plastic identification card composed of multiple layers in which microcircuitry is embedded. *Synonym:* smart card.

microscheduling Preparing a calendar for jobs in a CIS center that focuses on the details of computer operations. *See also* macroscheduling.

microwave Radio frequencies in the gigaHertz band, having billions of cycles per second.

mimic *See* impersonation.

MIS *See* management information system.

modeling (1) Mathematical or logical representation of a system that can be manipulated intellectually to assess hypothetical changes. (2) Graphic or written representation of an information system and its functions to aid in understanding that system. (3) Computer-assisted technique for selection of unusual items for audit examination by comparing the current income statement with a pattern of ratios, or model, developed from income statements for prior years.

model-oriented Within a decision support system (DSS), referring to a process that makes comparisons and performs analyses based on a model, or a coordinated set of parameters or conditions and their relationships. *See also* data-oriented.

monitoring *See* automated security monitoring, threat monitoring.

monitoring audit A systems development audit conducted at specific checkpoints within the systems development life cycle, coinciding with milestones and reviews that are built into the methodology, and focusing on outputs for phase reviews.

MTBF *See* mean time between failures.

multidisciplinary audit team Group of practitioners assembled for a specific audit engagement and comprising all of the skills and experience needed for the successful conduct of that audit.

multiple access rights terminal A terminal that may be used by more than one class of users, such as individuals with different access rights to data.

multiprocessing   Techniques under which two or more computer processors operate on an integrated basis to share work entered into any of the connected units.

multiprogramming   A method for using automatic, operating-system software to control allocation of memory to multiple jobs and to establish processing queues for execution of those jobs.

mutually suspicious   Relationship between two interactive processes (subsystems or programs), each of which contains sensitive data and is assumed to be designed to extract data from the other while protecting its own data.

N

nak attack   A penetration technique that capitalizes on a potential weakness in an operating system: The software does not handle asynchronous interrupts properly and thus leaves the system in an unprotected state during such interrupts. The term *nak* is derived from the ASCII control code NAK, which stands for Negative AcKnowledge, which is sent from a receiving device back to a transmitting device when errors in transmission have been detected.

National Bureau of Standards (NBS)   A division of the U. S. Department of Commerce that publishes Federal Information Processing Standards (FIPS) that govern computer installations within the federal government.

nature   One of the three key criteria for designing audit tests, the others being timing and extent. The nature of audit tests might include manual examination of audit trail documentation produced by a CIS, a combination of manual examination of computer-generated documents and computer-assisted procedures, or fully automated sampling and examination techniques. *See also* extent, timing.

NBS   *See* National Bureau of Standards.

network layer   Within the seven-layer ISO model of a LAN, the level that controls the routing of data packets within the network, as well as to other networks.

new systems review audit   Examination by computer auditors of a new system after it has been developed, but prior to turnover for production.

nonprocedural language   A programming language in which strict, formal syntax is not required. Typically, users enter specifications for inputs and outputs, which are translated into program statements that implement the required transformations. Some packages that use this approach are called *application generators. See also* fourth-generation language.

O

object   A system resource within a CIS network. *See also* subject.

occurrence rate   *See* frequency of occurrence.

off-line crypto-operation   Encryption or decryption performed as a self-contained operation distinct from the transmission of encrypted text, as in performing the operations by hand or by machines that are not connected electrically to a transmission line.

on-line crypto-operation   The use of cryptographic equipment that is connected directly to a transmission line. Under this approach, encryption and transmission, or reception and decryption, are performed in a continuous process.

on-line file inquiry and updating   Techniques under which users at terminals can gain immediate access to computer-based information, retrieve a desired record or data element on command, and write changes directly to master files.

operational audit   Special engagements or activities under which auditors study and report on the effectiveness and economies of data processing operations in areas beyond the scope of their attest function.

operating control Within a CIS department, a manual procedure that is aimed at assuring reliability of results from computer processing. *Synonym:* manual processing control.

optimization model A type of model-oriented decision support system (DSS) that provides objectives for a functional operation based on economic constraints.

organization management control Documentation or mechanism that establishes relationships between a CIS department and other entities, as well as defines the structure and principles applied to the CIS department itself.

output control Within a CIS, a control that governs the completeness and reasonableness of processing results, as well as the distribution of computer output only to authorized users.

overall corporate environment In quantitative risk assessment, a factor that identifies the type and structure of work being performed by a CIS.

overflow checks A limit check based upon the capacity of a memory or file area to hold additional data.

overwriting The obliteration of recorded data by subsequent recording of different data at the same location.

ownership Responsibility and authority of the creators and users of data to control the ultimate disposition and use of those data.

P

packet In digital communication, a unit of information created by subdividing a data message through time-division multiplexing (TDM).

parallel simulation The maintenance of two presumably identical sets of programs. One set is placed in production and is subject to change under normal authorization procedures. The other set, which is placed under the custody of auditors, also is updated independently based on the same change authorizations. Subsequent execution of corresponding versions of the programs with the same test data should yield identical results. If discrepancies are noted, the occurrence of unauthorized changes in the production version must be suspected.

parity For a given binary data element, the validity of its bit format.

parity bit Within a byte of data, a bit that is set to indicate whether the count of 1-bits in the byte is even or odd. *Synonym:* check bit.

passive wiretapping The monitoring and/or recording of data while the data are being transmitted over a communication link.

password (1) A protected word or string of characters that identifies or authenticates a user, a specific resource, or an access type. (2) The authorization to allow access to data by providing a signal known only to authorized individuals. *Synonyms:* key generation, keyword.

password dialog *See* handshaking procedure.

patch A machine-language instruction entered at the operator's console or through a peripheral device to modify the machine-language version of the program resident in computer memory. Patching is considered poor practice and generally results in loss of control over security of application programs.

PBX *See* private branch exchange.

PC *See* present cost.

penetration A successful, unauthorized access to a CIS.

penetration signature (1) The description of a situation or set of conditions under which an unauthorized access could occur. (2) The description of usual and unusual system events that—in conjunction—might indicate that a penetration is in progress.

penetration testing The use of special programmer/analyst teams to attempt unauthorized access to a system for the purpose of identifying any security weaknesses.

people-oriented tasks In quantitative risk assessment, one of two factors determining the security impact of a pervasive risk. People-oriented tasks include programming enhancements, troubleshooting fixes, and manual procedural changes.

performance audit   Review conducted by CIS auditors to provide current, raw data and a historical information base on computer resource usage and performance for forecasting and long-range planning.

performance sensitivity (PS)   In quantitative risk assessment, a measure of the relative impact of a given audit entity on the overall performance of the organization.

perimeter control   Control that governs physical access to a computer facility.

periodic audit   A verification of a file or of a phase of processing that is conducted on a regular basis and that is intended to check problems and to encourage future compliance with controls.

personnel security   Procedures to assure that all personnel who have access to sensitive information have both the authority and the appropriate clearances for such access.

pervasive risk (PR)   In risk assessment, a general risk that applies to all types of corporate activity. *See also* specific risk.

physical security   (1) Techniques that isolate computer systems physically from access by unauthorized persons. (2) The use of locks, guards, badges, and similar administrative measures to control access to a CIS and its related equipment. (3) The measures designed to protect the physical plant that houses a CIS, its related equipment, and storage media from damage by accident, fire, and environmental hazards.

physical site control   A physical security measure or a device for providing such security.

piggyback entry   Unauthorized access to a CIS through another user's legitimate connection.

pilot project   An initial, trial implementation of a CIS application, of limited scope and within a relatively small work group.

pin register   A computer-based facility for monitoring telephone traffic.

plain text   Intelligible text or signals that have meaning and that can be read or acted upon without the application of any decryption.

point estimate   In statistical sampling, an estimated mean value for the accounting record population from which the sample was drawn.

policy needs   Security requirements that derive from the principles and practices a CIS application is obligated to pursue.

poll list reconfiguration   Authorization of specific terminals within a network to access the system only at designated times during a business day.

post-implementation audit   A review by computer auditors of a new CIS, performed approximately three months after implementation and consisting of a thorough examination that assumes no previous audit participation in development or any prior audit examinations.

PR   *See* pervasive risk.

precoded forms   Input documents on which fixed elements of information are entered in advance, often in a format that permits direct machine processing, to prevent errors in entry of repetitive data.

prenumbered forms   Preprinted, sequential reference or serial numbers on individual forms. The numbers permit subsequent detection of loss or misplacement of any forms.

present cost (PC)   In cost/benefit analysis, the monetary cost figure obtained by adding historical maintenance and operating costs to installation cost, and subtracting projected salvage value.

present value (PV)   In cost/benefit analysis, the monetary value of benefits received from an investment. In quantitative risk assessment, the present value of a security measure is equal to the reduction in annualized loss expectancy, or ALE.

presentation layer   Within the seven-layer ISO model of a LAN, the network level at which data are transformed to be readable or accessible by users.

prevention   Within the context of technical security, the keeping of unauthorized persons from gaining access to a CIS, as well as keeping authorized persons from using the system wrongly. *See also* detection.

preventive control   Control implemented within a CIS that halts processing when an error or exception condition is identified. *See also* corrective control, detective control.

principle of least privilege   The granting of the minimum access authorization for the performance of required tasks.

print suppress   To eliminate the printing of characters to preserve their secrecy. The characters of a password might be suppressed on a display as they are keyed by a user at an input terminal.

privacy   (1) The right of an individual to control the sharing of information about himself/herself that may be compromised by unauthorized exchange among other individuals or organizations.

privacy protection   The establishment of appropriate administrative, technical, and physical safeguards to assure the security and confidentiality of data records and to protect such records against any anticipated threats or hazards that could result in substantial harm, embarrassment, inconvenience, or unfairness to any individual described in those records.

privacy transformation   *See* encryption algorithm.

private branch exchange (PBX)   Electronic switching equipment used to control connections within an organization's internal telephone network.

private key   Within a public key encryption scheme, an encryption code that is associated with a specific individual and that is known only to that individual.

privileged instructions   (1) A set of computer instructions or code that generally is executable only when a CIS is operating in the executive state (*e.g.*, the handling of interrupts). (2) Special computer instructions designed to control the protection features of a CIS (*e.g.*, storage protection features).

procedural security   The set of rules by which a system operator manages system personnel and the flow of work in an organization. *See also* administrative security.

procedure   *See* backup procedure, handshaking procedure, recovery procedure, system integrity procedure, unidentified report procedure.

procedures evaluation   The aspect of an operational audit that focuses on tests of controls.

processing control   *See* programmed control.

production systems audit   Periodic audit of routine applications, such as payroll, inventory, payments, accounts receivable, accounts payable, fixed assets, or other processing performed in the course of normal organizational activities.

program maintenance audit   Review by computer auditors that is implemented by obtaining control of a copy of the source-code instructions of all production programs from a computer information center or media library. Current versions of production programs then are compared with these original versions, and changes are noted and investigated for proper authorization.

programmed control   Within a CIS, control that governs processing and that is applied directly by equipment and/or software. *Synonym:* processing control.

programmer/analyst   Within a CIS department, a person who performs the functions of both a systems analyst and an application programmer. *See also* application programmer, systems analyst.

protected wireline distribution system   A telecommunication system that has been approved by a legally designated authority and to which electromagnetic and physical safeguards have been applied to permit safe electrical transmission of unencrypted sensitive information. *Synonym:* approved circuit.

protection   *See* data-dependent protection, fetch protection, file protection, lock-and-key protection system, privacy protection.

protection ring   One of a hierarchy of privileged modes of a CIS that gives specific access rights to the users, programs, and processes authorized to operate in a given mode.

PS *See* performance sensitivity.

pseudo-flaw An apparent loophole that is implanted deliberately in an operating system program as a trap for intruders.

public key Within a public key encryption scheme, an encryption code that is associated with a specific individual and that is known to all parties within a communication network.

public key encryption A security technique within a LAN for coding and decoding data transmissions in which each party to the communication has a public, or generally known, key and a private, or secret, key.

purging (1) The orderly review of storage and removal of inactive or obsolete data files. (2) The removal of obsolete data by erasure, by overwriting, or by resetting of registers.

PV *See* present value.

Q

QRA *See* quantitative risk assessment.

quality control specialist Job title within a CIS facility for personnel charged with responsibility for quality assurance and monitoring of systems development efforts for conformity with established standards and procedures.

quantitative risk assessment (QRA) An approach to selecting controls and security measures by estimating future losses through construction of an accurate model of threats, assets, and vulnerabilities.

R

RA *See* risk analysis.

radio frequency interference (RFI) Disruptions to computer operations or digital communications, caused by electrical disturbances or by radio or television transmissions.

random attribute sampling Statistical technique for selection of transactions or items for audit examination. This technique tests for specific, predefined attributes, or characteristics, of transactions selected on a random basis from an application file. *See also* statistical sampling.

range check *See* limit check.

ratio analysis Selection of unusual items for audit examination by computer-assisted analysis of mathematical relationships between sales figures and a number of other accounts on an income statement.

ratio modeling Computer-assisted audit procedure that develops and compares key mathematical relationships among current and past income statements.

read-only memory (ROM) A type of integrated computer circuit that provides relatively permanent storage of machine-code programs or binary data. *See also* firmware.

real-time processing Computer processing in which output occurs fast enough to fit within the normal cycle of the activity being performed, as in obtaining a credit authorization while a purchase transaction is being completed.

real-time reaction A response to a penetration attempt that is detected and diagnosed in time to prevent the actual penetration.

reasonable assurance Justifiable, but not absolute, confidence that data or other assets are being protected and that financial records are reliable.

reasonableness check Test applied to fields of data by comparing them with other data of known validity within transaction or master records.

reconciliation An identification and analysis of differences between the values contained in two substantially identical files or between a detail and a control total. Under this technique, errors are identified by the nature of the reconciled items rather than by the existence of a difference between the balances.

recovery procedure One of the actions necessary to restore a system's computational capability and data files after a system failure or penetration.

reduction in future losses In quantitative risk assessment, the difference between ALEs calculated for a system with and without safeguards.

redundancy (1) A positive attribute of a system that serves as a preventive control by duplicating a key resource or process so that errors or failures will be less likely to disrupt reliable operation. (2) Within a file or database, the instance of a data element in more than one location. Redundancy in this case can be either a positive or a negative attribute. In a positive sense, data redundancy can provide backup in case errors or accidental erasures corrupt one of the data copies. In a negative sense, redundancy creates the possibility that more than one version of the same data element will exist within the system at a given time.

redundancy code In data communication, a binary coding scheme used to perform checks on entire blocks of data that are being transmitted in synchronous mode.

regression analysis Statistical technique that correlates risk characteristics with actual performance.

relative materiality index (RMI) In quantitative risk assessment, an element of performance sensitivity. It is a value indicating the significance of an activity/cycle in relation to overall corporate performance.

relevance Materiality of a given item, transaction, or application to an organization's financial statements, as well as the justification for the degree of audit interest in that area.

reliability of personnel Characteristic of individuals who, in the performance of processing responsibilities, can be counted on to treat data in a prescribed, consistent manner.

remanence The residual magnetism that remains on magnetic storage media after degaussing.

remote source data capture The recording of data in machine-sensible form at the point of transaction.

repeater Within a digital communication network, a node that receives signals, amplifies or reprocesses them, and relays them to the next node.

reporting standards Within generally accepted auditing standards (GAAS), guidelines that stipulate compliance with GAAS, consistency with previous accounting periods, adequacy of disclosure, and, in the event that an opinion cannot be reached, the requirement to state the assertion explicitly.

representation model A type of model-oriented decision support system (DSS) that focuses on corporate or divisional goals in strategic planning.

request for quotation (RFQ) Document prepared for vendors that solicits bids and proposals based on specific system requirements.

required precision In random attribute sampling, the degree of accuracy desired, expressed as a tolerable percentage of error in results of a given sample. *See also* random attribute sampling.

residue Data left in storage after processing operations, and before degaussing or rewriting has taken place.

resource Within a CIS, any function, device, or collection of data that may be made available to users or programs.

resource sharing Within a CIS, the concurrent use of a resource by more than one user, job, or program.

retinal scanning Computerized techniques for distinguishing individuals by sensing patterns of blood vessels in the retina of the eye.

retry count In synchronous data communication, the number of times that retransmission is attempted if an error is detected. When the retry count reaches a predetermined limit, the communication program terminates the connection.

return on investment (ROI) For the result of any expenditure, the ratio of present value realized to present cost. *See also* present cost, present value.

RFI *See* radio frequency interference.

RFQ *See* request for quotation.

risk analysis (RA) Within the discipline of risk management, the identification of risks and risk characteristics.

risk assessment The evaluation of system assets and vulnerabilities to establish an expected loss from specific events, based on estimated probabilities of occurrence for those events.

risk characteristic In the assessment of audit risk, a system attribute that is known to create exposures.

risk dimension In the assessment of audit risk, a factor such as project size, experience with technology, or project structure. The identification of risk dimension helps to categorize an audit risk by causal factor.

risk management (RM) The entire process of identifying and controlling risks to an organization's assets. RM encompasses risk analysis, as well as costs and benefits of corresponding safeguards. *See also* risk analysis.

risk significancy value In risk assessment, a relative measure of risk, usually expressed as a linguistic variable: zero, low, medium, or high.

RM *See* risk management.

RMI *See* relative materiality index.

ROI *See* return on investment.

rotation of duties Procedure under which job assignments of personnel involved in key processing functions are changed routinely—at irregularly scheduled times, if possible.

run-to-run totals Output control totals from one process that are used as input control totals over subsequent processing. These control totals are used as links in a chain, in effect, that ties one process to another in a sequence of processes, or one cycle to another over a period of time.

S

sabotage Within the context of CIS auditing, the abuse, destruction, or theft of computer equipment.

sanitize To degauss or overwrite sensitive information held in magnetic or other storage media. *Synonym:* scrub.

SAS *See* Statements on Auditing Standards.

scan before distribution The visual review of output, before distribution, for general propriety and legibility.

scavenge To search through residue on magnetic media for the purpose of unauthorized data acquisition.

schema Within a database management system (DBMS), a model that provides a set of relations among data elements for use by a specific application.

scratch To erase or overwrite a data storage area used as a temporary register for holding intermediate results.

scrub *See* sanitize.

SDLC *See* systems development life cycle.

SEC *See* Securities and Exchange Commission.

secure configuration management The use of procedures for controlling changes to a system's hardware and software to assure that such changes will not lead to decreased data security.

secure operating system System software that controls effectively the programs and equipment within a CIS to provide a level of protection appropriate to the value of the data and resources maintained by the system.

Securities and Exchange Commission (SEC) Independent agency of the federal government that oversees the trading of stocks, bonds, and other forms of financial securities in public corporations.

security *See* add-on security, administrative security, CIS security, communication security, data security, emanation security, personnel security, procedural security, technical security, teleprocessing security, traffic flow security.

security administrator A person who is responsible for assigning, changing, and controlling passwords that permit access to system resources. The security adminstrator also assures that data are encrypted as necessary and that password tables are secure.

security audit An examination of procedures and measures for safeguarding data. The purpose of such audits is to evaluate the adequacy of the safeguards and their compliance with established policy.

security certification Within the scope of FIPS 102, the technical evaluation of CIS facilities and operations for accreditation, or management approval to operate a CIS application.

security filter A set of software routines and techniques implemented within a CIS to prevent automatic forwarding of specified data over unprotected wires or to unauthorized persons.

security impact (SI) In quantitative risk assessment, a measure of the potential impact of specific activities or cycles that are or could be detrimental to an organization.

security impact statement (SIS) A report by CIS auditors that assesses control opportunities early in the development of a new system.

security kernel The central part of a computer system, encompassing software and hardware, that implements the fundamental procedures for controlling access to system resources.

security perimeter *See* control zone.

security safeguard evaluation A review by CIS auditors of the extent to which an organization's assets are being protected from unauthorized access.

seepage The accidental flow to unauthorized individuals of information or information access, which is presumed to be controlled by computer security measures.

segregation of duties Separation, between job functions and individuals, of responsibility for custody of data and accountability for handling and processing of the same data.

sensitive information Any information that requires a degree of protection and that should not be made available generally.

sensitivity The magnitude of potential impacts on the security of an information system from disclosure of specific information.

separation of duties A type of control achieved by partitioning a system so that no one individual can have access to complete processes or operating cycles.

sequence checking Verification of the numeric order of keys, or sequential control fields, in items to be processed.

SI *See* security impact.

SIAS *See* Statements on Internal Auditing Standards.

single occurrence loss (SOL) In quantitative risk assessment, the monetary loss resulting from a single incidence of a threat against an asset.

SIS *See* security impact statement.

situational needs Security requirements that derive from a particular CIS application's characteristics and environment.

software analysis tool A computer utility program that may be applied to a variety of audit tasks, as in making comparisons, measuring complexity, measuring coverage, analyzing path flow, and performing formal verifications.

SOL *See* single occurrence loss.

specific risk (SR) In risk assessment, a risk that is identified for a specific type of activity or audit entity. *See also* pervasive risk.

spoof To induce deliberately a user or a resource to take an incorrect action.

spreadsheet model A numeric presentation format, or template, composed of columns and rows, and a set of mathematical relationships among its elements.

spurious connection initiation An attack of active wiretapping in which an intruder attempts either to violate identification security at terminals or at other equipment, or to violate time-integrity checks on the connection to a local area network.

SR *See* specific risk.

standardization Establishment of uniform, structured, and consistent procedures for all processing.

Statements on Auditing Standards (SAS) Pronouncements by the American Institute of Certified Public Accountants (AICPA) on generally accepted auditing standards (GAAS) that provide procedural guidance relating to many aspects of auditing.

Statements on Internal Auditing Standards (SIAS) Professional guidelines promulgated by the Institute of Internal Auditors (IIA).

statistical sampling Selection of transactions or items for audit examination based on mathematical principles of probability.

steering committee Management review group with oversight responsibility for systems projects. The committee is responsible for enforcing standards of quality and assuring that anticipated organizational benefits are derived from development efforts.

store-and-forward Data communication technique under which data are held in a buffer prior to being routed to a designated storage address or device.

stratification Segregation or subdivision of accounting record populations into levels corresponding with specific criteria or ranges, such as dollar amounts.

subject Within a CIS network, a user of system resources. *See also* object.

substantive test An audit procedure that verifies summarized, quantitative amounts in financial records, usually through outside references such as verification requests.

suggestion model A type of model-oriented decision support system (DSS) that poses options for the decision maker.

summary calculation A redundant process using an accumulated total. The summary calculation is compared for equality with a control total from the processing of detailed items.

supervisor state *See* executive state.

susceptibility to misappropriation or loss In quantitative risk assessment, an element of performance sensitivity. It is a measure of loss potential by area of activity.

suspense account A control total for items that are awaiting further processing; a temporary account that must be cleared before a trial balance or financial statements can be produced.

suspense file A file containing unprocessed or partially processed items that are awaiting further action.

system *See* cipher system, code system, concealment system, cryptographic system, lock-and-key protection system, protected wireline distribution system, secure operating system.

system fraud Unauthorized use of a computer information system, including the destruction, alteration, or disclosure of application programs, system programs, or databases.

system integrity The state that exists if there is complete assurance that, under all conditions, a CIS produces reliable information that is not subject to unauthorized alteration. System integrity is based on the logical correctness and reliability of the operating system, the logical completeness of the hardware and software that implement protection mechanisms, and the integrity of the data held within or maintained by the system.

system integrity procedure Administrative control for assuring that the hardware, software, and data within a CIS are maintained as intended and are not altered in unauthorized ways.

systems analyst A CIS professional who works with users in identifying and designing new or enhanced applications.

systems audit A formal engagement for the examination and evaluation of the effectiveness of systems controls.

systems communication log A record of all connections to a computer network.

systems control One of the measures for assuring the accuracy, completeness, and reliability of information.

systems development life cycle (SDLC) Policies and standards that apply to the design, development, testing, implementation, and maintenance of CIS application programs and subsystems. Specifically, an SDLC methodology implies a formal approach that subdivides development efforts into a mandated sequence of project phases and activities.

systems planning Administrative CIS function operating under direction of top management to set priorities and plan resource expenditures for proposed systems development projects.

systems programmer Within a CIS department, a person responsible for maintaining and implementing enhancements for all systems-level and technical software and utilities and who also must make appropriate changes in systems documentation.

T

TDM *See* time-division multiplexing.

technical security The software, firmware, and hardware controls set up within a CIS to protect against unauthorized access to or violations of the system.

technological attack A penetration attempt that is perpetrated by circumventing or nullifying hardware and software control access mechanisms, rather than by subverting system personnel or authorized users.

telecommunication Any transmission, emission, or reception of signs, writing, images, sounds, or other information via electrical, visual, optical, or electromagnetic means.

teleprocessing A system of information transmission that combines telecommunication, computer information systems, and human-machine interfaces for the purpose of interacting and functioning as an integrated whole.

teleprocessing security The protection that results from all measures designed to prevent deliberate, inadvertent, or unauthorized disclosure, acquisition, manipulation, or modification of information in a teleprocessing system.

teller alert message Within computer-based financial systems, a flag within an account that notifies the teller of a need for extra caution. The flag might indicate that the passbook for the account has been lost or stolen, or that two signatures are required for the completion of any transaction.

template A spreadsheet format, composed of columns and rows, for a specific application.

terminal identification The means used within a CIS for the automated recognition of specific terminals or input devices.

test deck Computer-assisted audit examination technique under which files of test transactions are input to application programs used for routine production. The reference to decks stems from the first applications of this technique that used decks of punched cards as input media.

test support software Computer programs that are designed to perform mathematical and clerical portions of specific audit tasks, such as generation of test data, data reduction, and statistical data collection.

threat A specific set of circumstances that may result in loss of or damage to computer or data resources and corresponding financial loss to the organization.

threat assessment The process of evaluating the probability of occurrence of particular types of threats to a CIS and identifying the security procedures that will be most effective against such threats.

threat monitoring The analysis, assessment, and review of audit trails and other data, for the purpose of searching out system events that might constitute violations of the system or that might precipitate incidents that could compromise the privacy of data.

tickler file A control file containing items ordered by age for purposes of follow-up. Such files usually are manual.

time-dependent password A password, or keyword, that is valid only at a specified time of day or during a specified interval.

time-division multiplexing (TDM) In digital communication, a technique that subdivides data transmissions into separate, discrete packets and transmits them in interleaved fashion within a single communication channel.

timing One of the three key criteria for designing audit tests, the others being nature and extent. The timing of audit tests involves scheduling those tests with careful consideration of data retention cycles and/or reporting requirements. *See also* extent, nature.

topology The structure and manner in which switching nodes, user devices, and transmission links are interconnected within a data communication network.

traffic flow security The protection that results from those features in some crypto-equipment that conceal the presence of valid messages on a communication circuit, usually by causing the circuit to appear busy at all times, or by encrypting the source and destination addresses of valid messages.

trailer label A record containing a control total used for comparison with accumulated counts or values of records processed.

training Procedure under which personnel are provided explicit instructions and tested for their understanding before being assigned new duties.

transaction control system A type of CIS that retrieves descriptions and current price information from a central database; a point-of-sale system.

transaction trail The availability of a manual or machine-readable means of tracing the status and content of an individual transaction record backward or forward, between output processing and source. *See also* audit trail.

transmission control Within a CIS, a control that governs the sending of data and information over communication channels.

transmittal document The medium for communicating control totals over movement of data, particularly from source to processing

point or between processing points. *Synonym:* batch control ticket.

transport layer Within the seven-layer ISO model of a LAN, the network level that provides end-to-end transfer of data messages from one network node to another.

trap door A breach created intentionally in a CIS for the purpose of collecting, altering, or destroying data.

Trojan horse A computer program that is apparently or actually useful and that contains a trap door.

tuning The modification of system software to enhance overall performance and/or responsiveness.

turnaround document Source medium generated by computer and reused for input of new transactions.

type of system In quantitative risk assessment, an element of performance sensitivity. It is a set of categories used to indicate which systems hold the greatest potential for fraud.

U

unidentified report procedure Action to be taken if a report or document that is not shown on the distribution list is produced by an application.

United States General Accounting Office (GAO) Independent agency of the federal government that may be directed by Congress to investigate practices within government agencies or their contractors.

upload Transfer of data generated locally with an intelligent terminal or microcomputer to a data storage area in a mainframe computer or corporate network.

upstream resubmission Step-by-step instructions for recovering from all processing disruptions—from minor to major—and including all resources needed for recovery, such as operating instructions and files.

use rule   In matters of privacy, a rule of law that stipulates that data only can be given to third parties for purposes that are compatible with those for which the data were collected originally.

user-defined needs   Specifications written by the user for the recovery of an application. Often, needs are expressed as the maximum delay that can be tolerated for each report produced by the user's application.

V

validation   The performance of tests to determine compliance with security specifications and requirements.

validity check   Under this control technique, the characters in a coded field are either matched to an acceptable set of values in a table or are examined, using logic and arithmetic rather than tables, for predefined patterns.

verification request   A form sent by the auditor to a company's customers to determine whether amounts owed are recorded accurately, are valid, and that accounts receivable are stated fairly.

vertical parity check   Testing of the last, or parity, bit within a given byte to determine the validity of the data bits within that byte. *Synonym:* vertical redundancy check. *See also* longitudinal parity check.

visual verification   The scanning of documents by a human supervisor for general reasonableness and propriety.

voice recognition   Computerized techniques for distinguishing individuals by their patterns of speech.

vulnerability area   In quantitative risk assessment, an area under study in which safeguards may be absent.

vulnerability factor   In quantitative risk assessment, the ratio of the actual loss from a single occurrence to the total loss potential of an asset.

W

white box   A process for which the internal instructions and details are known or are regarded as transparent for purposes of analysis.

wiretapping   *See* active wiretapping, passive wiretapping.

work factor   An estimate of the effort or time that would be required to overcome a protective measure by a would-be penetrator with specified expertise and resources.

work-load statistic   Quantitative measure of CIS technical performance, such as contention for resources, jobs processed, total response time, transaction rate, and so on.

writedown   Devaluation of inventory based on obsolescence of items remaining in stock from prior periods.

Bibliography

PURPOSE

This bibliography of selected references has been prepared to help the student interested in CIS auditing to identify sources of information in this fast-changing field. Many of the publications listed below also should become permanent additions to the libraries of CIS managers and audit staff.

Sources in the listing below have been organized according to the following categories:

- Government agencies

- Professional associations

- Commercial publishers.

GOVERNMENT AGENCIES

Government organizations that have published studies and reports on topics related to CIS auditing include:

- U.S. General Accounting Office (GAO)

- Office of Management and Budget (OMB)

- Congressional Research Service

- National Bureau of Standards (NBS)

- National Aeronautics and Space Administration (NASA)

- U.S. Department of Justice

- Office of Technology Assessment (OTA).

U.S. General Accounting Office (GAO)

GAO is an independent agency of the federal government. The agency is headed by the Comptroller General of the United States, who reports to Congress. GAO has published audit standards and guides, as well as numerous reports on CIS audit/security issues.

Besides providing individual copies of documents, GAO also will conduct bibliographic searches upon request. To obtain documents in this category, or to request a search, contact the agency at:

Document Handling and Information Service (DHIS)
U.S. General Accounting Office
Box 6015
Gaithersburg, MD 20877
(202) 275-6241

GAO Report, *Assessing Reliability of Computer Output,* Audit Guide, June, 1981, #AFMD-81-91.
GAO Report, *Bibliography of Documents Issued by the GAO on Matters Related to ADP,* #AFMD-81-85, #AFMD-82-50, #AFMD-83-53.
GAO Report, *Bibliography of Documents Issued by the GAO on Matters Related to: ADP, IRM and Telecommunications,* #IMTEC-84-9.
GAO Report, *Evaluating Internal Controls in Computer-Based Systems,* Audit Guide, June, 1981, #AFMD-81-76.
Standards for Audit of Governmental Operations, Program, Activities and Functions, Second Edition, 1981, GPO Stock #020-000-00205-1.
Standards for Internal Control in the Federal Government, First Edition, 1983.
Using Microcomputers in GAO Audits: Improving Quality and Productivity, March, 1986, Technical Guideline No. 1, Information Management and Technology Division.

Office of Management and Budget (OMB)

OMB is an executive agency that reports directly to the President. You may request documents from:

Office of Management and Budget
Old Executive Office Building
Washington, DC 20503

Internal Control Systems, OMB Circular A-123, October, 1981.
Security of Federal Automated Information Systems, OMB Circular A-71 Transmittal #1, effective July 27, 1978.

Congressional Research Service

The Congressional Research Service is a part of the Library of Congress. Its address is:

Congressional Research Service
Library of Congress
10 First Street SE
Washington, DC 20540

Becker, L. G., *Computer Security: An Overview of National Concerns and Challenges,* Report #83-135, February, 1983.

National Bureau of Standards (NBS)

NBS is part of the U.S. Department of Commerce. Of particular interest to auditors are its Federal Information Processing Standards (FIPS). Other relevant studies have been published by the Institute of Computer Science and Technology within NBS. Documents listed below may be ordered from:

U.S. Department of Commerce
National Technical Information Service
5285 Port Royal Road
Springfield, Virginia 22161
(703) 487-4650

Audit and Evaluation of Computer Security, ed. Zella Ruthberg and Robert McKenzie, NBS Spec. Pub. 500-19, October, 1977, SN 003-003-01848-1.

Audit and Evaluation of Computer Security II: System Vulnerabilities and Controls, ed. Zella G. Ruthberg, NBS Spec. Pub. 500-57, May, 1980, SN 003-003-02178-4.

Cole, Gerald D., and Heinrich, Frank, *Design Alternatives for Computer Network Security (vol. 1),* and *The Network Security Center: A System Level Approach to Computer Network Security (vol. 2),* NBS Spec. Pub. 500-21, January, 1978, SN 003-003-01881-3.

Computer Security and the Data Encryption Standard, ed. Dennis Branstad, NBS Spec. Pub. 500-27, February, 1978, SN 003-003-01891-1.

FIPS 31, *Guidelines for Automatic Data Processing Physical Security and Risk Management,* June, 1974.

FIPS 38, *Guidelines for Documentation of Computer Programs and Automated Data Systems,* February, 1976.

FIPS 39, *Glossary for Computer Systems Security,* February, 1976.

FIPS 41, *Computer Security Guidelines for Implementing the Privacy Act of 1974*, May, 1977.

FIPS 46, *Data Encryption Standard*, January, 1977.

FIPS 48, *Guidelines on Evaluation of Techniques for Automated Personal Identification*, April, 1977.

FIPS 65, *Guideline for Automatic Data Processing Risk Analysis*, August, 1979.

FIPS 73, *Guideline for Security of Computer Applications*, June, 1980.

FIPS 74, *Guidelines for Implementing and Using the NBS Data Encryption Standard*, April, 1981.

FIPS 81, *Data Encryption Standard*, December 1980.

FIPS 83, *Guidelines on User Authentication Techniques for Computer Network Access Control*, September, 1980.

FIPS 87, *Guidelines for ADP Contingency Planning*, March, 1981.

FIPS 88, *Guideline on Integrity Assurance and Control in Database Administration*, August, 1981.

FIPS 101, *Guideline for Life Cycle Validation, Verification, and Testing of Computer Software*, June, 1983.

FIPS 102, *Guideline for Computer Security Certification and Accreditation*, October, 1983.

FIPS 106, *Guideline on Software Maintenance*, June, 1984.

FIPS 107, *Local Area Networks*, November, 1984.

FIPS 112, *Standard on Password Usage*, September, 1985.

FIPS 113, *Standard on Computer Data Authentication*, December, 1985.

Gait, Jason, *Maintenance Testing for the Data Encryption Standard*, NBS Spec. Pub. 500-61, August, 1980, SN 003-003-02225-0.

Gait, Jason, *Validating the Correctness of Hardware Implementations of the NBS Data Encryption Standard*, NBS Spec. Pub. 500-20, November, 1977, SN 003-003-01861-9.

Levitt, Karl N., Neumann, Peter, and Robinson, Lawrence, *The SRI Hierarchical Development Methodology (HDM) and its Application to the Development of Secure Software*, NBS Spec. Pub. 500-67, October, 1980, SN 003-003-02258-6.

Neugent, William, Gilligan, John, Hoffman, Lance, and Ruthberg, Zella G., *Technology Assessment: Methods for Measuring the Level of Computer Security*. NBS Special Publication 500-133, October, 1985.

Neumann, Albrecht J., *Features of Seven Audit Software Packages—Principles and Capabilities*, NBS Spec. Pub. 500-13, July, 1977, SN 003-0903-01807-4.

Overview of Computer Security Certification and Accreditation, NBS Spec. Pub. 500-109, April, 1984.

Ruder, Brian and Madden, J. D., *An Analysis of Computer Security Safeguards for Detecting and Preventing Intentional Computer Misuse*, ed. Robert P. Blanc, NBS Spec. Pub. 500-25, January, 1978, SN 003-003-01871-6.

Security of Personal Computer Systems: A Management Guide, ed. Dennis Steinauer, NBS Spec. Pub. 500-120, January, 1985.

Shaw, James K. and Katzke, Stuart W., *Executive Guide to Contingency Planning,* NBS Spec. Pub. 500-85, January, 1982, PB 82-165226.

Smid, Miles E., *A Key Notarization System for Computer Networks,* NBS Spec. Pub. 500-54, October, 1979, SN 003-003-03130-0.

Wood, Helen, *The Use of Passwords for Controlled Access to Computer Resources,* NBS Spec. Pub. 500-9, May, 1977, SN 003-003-01770-1.

National Aeronautics and Space Administration (NASA)

For information regarding publications of this government agency, contact:

National Aeronautics and Space Administration
400 Maryland Avenue, SW
Washington, DC 20546

Documents designated NTIS may be ordered by number from:

National Technical Information Service
5285 Port Royal Road
Springfield, Virginia 22161
(703) 487-4650

Giragosian, Paul A., Mastbrook, David W., and Tompkins, Frederick G., *Guidelines for Certification of Existing Sensitive Systems,* NTIS, July, 1982, MTR-82W18 (NASA), PB84-22312-2.

Mastbrook, David W. and Tompkins, Frederick G., *Guidelines for Contingency Planning,* NTIS, January, 1984, MTR-82W203, PB84-189836.

President's Council for Integrity and Efficiency, *Microcomputer Audit Guidelines,* NASA-IG, April, 1985.

President's Council for Integrity and Efficiency, *Statistical Analysis of the Effects of Using a Microcomputer System for Field Audits and Investigations,* NASA-IG, August, 1984.

Tompkins, Frederick G., *Guidelines for Developing NASA's ADP Security Risk Management Plans,* NTIS, August, 1983, MTR-83W123, PB84-171321.

Tompkins, Frederick G., *Guidelines for Development of National Aeronautics and Space Administration Computer Security Training Programs,* NTIS, May, 1983, MTR-83W68, PB84-171339.

Tompkins, Frederick G., *NASA Guidelines for Assuring the Adequacy and Appropriateness of Security Safeguards in Sensitive Applications,* September, 1984, NTIS, MTR-84W179, PB85-14900-3.

U.S. Department of Justice

The following publication is a valuable resource for CIS auditors:

Computer Crime, Criminal Justice Resource Manual, Bureau of Justice Statistics, U.S. Dept. of Justice, Washington, DC, 1979.

The address is:

Bureau of Justice Statistics
U.S. Department of Justice
Constitution Ave. & 10th St. NW
Washington, DC 20530

Office of Technology Assessment (OTA)

OTA reports to the Congress and studies impacts of science and technology on government policy. A key report is:

Computer-Based National Information Systems—Technology and Public Policy Issues, September, 1981.

This report is available from:

U.S. Congress
Office of Technology Assessment
Publishing Office
Washington, D.C. 20510

PROFESSIONAL ASSOCIATIONS

CIS audit studies, reports, and guides are available from professional associations, including:

- The American Institute of Certified Public Accountants (AICPA)
- Institute of Internal Auditors (IIA)
- EDP Auditors Foundation
- Quality Assurance Institute (QAI).

American Institute of Certified Public Accountants (AICPA)

The AICPA influences many aspects of auditing by governing the professional conduct of certified public accountants. Its Statements on Auditing Standards (SAS) are issued by the Auditing Standards Board, the senior technical body of the Institute designated to issue pronouncements on auditing matters. Rule 202 of the Institute's Code of Professional Ethics requires adherence to the applicable generally accepted auditing standards promulgated by the Institute. It recognizes Statements on Auditing Standards as interpretations of generally accepted auditing standards and requires that members be prepared to justify departures from such statements.

SAS and other publications of the Institute may be requested from:

> American Institute of Certified Public Accountants (AICPA)
> 1211 Avenue of the Americas
> New York, NY 10036

Audit and Control Considerations in a Minicomputer or Small Business Computer Environment, 1981.

Audit Approaches for a Computerized Inventory System, 1980.

Audit Considerations in Electronic Funds Transfer System, 1979.

The Auditor's Study and Evaluation of Internal Control In EDP Systems, 1977.

Computer Assisted Audit Techniques, 1979.

Controls Over Using and Changing Computer Programs, 1979.

Davis, Gordon B., Adams, Donald L., and Schaller, Carol A., *Auditing and EDP*, 1983.

EDP Engagements: System Planning and General Design, 1982.

Management, Control and Audit of Advanced EDP Systems, 1977.

Perry, William E., *EDP Administration and Control*, 1984.

Report of the Joint Database Task Force, AICPA/CICA/IIA, 1983.

Report on the Study of EDP-Related Fraud in the Banking and Insurance Industries, 1984.

Statements on Auditing Standards, 1972–1984.

Study and Evaluation of Internal Control In EDP Systems, 1981.

Institute of Internal Auditors (IIA)

The Institute of Internal Auditors, Inc., offers a wide variety of operational, management, and financial auditing publications. Materials listed below may be ordered from:

> Institute of Internal Auditors, Inc.
> P.O. Box 1119
> 249 Maitland Ave.
> Altamonte Springs, FL 32701

Bakay, *A Guide for Auditing of Maintainability and Maintenance,* 1982.

Berry, *Coordinating Total Audit Coverage: Trends and Practices,* 1984.

Boritz, *Planning for the Internal Audit Function,* 1983.

Brink, *Evaluating Internal/External Audit Services and Relationships,* Research Report No. 24, 1980.

Brown, *Concepts of Government Auditing,* 1978.

Casler and Crockett, *Operational Auditing: An Introduction,* 1982.

Duff, Larry J., *Audit and Control of Distributed Data Processing Systems,* 1983.

Fergusson, *The Internal Audit Training Program,* Research Report No. 23, 1980.

Garner, *Corporate Audit Costs and Staffing: 1980–1982,* 1983.

Glazer and Jaenicke, *A Framework for Evaluating an Internal Audit Function,* 1980.

Guidelines to Controls for Data Processing Environments, 1983.

Hostrum, Collins, *Operational Auditing of Production Control,* Research Report No. 20, 1978.

How to Acquire and Use Generalized Audit Software, 1979.

Leathers, Ritts, and Ross, *A Guide for Evaluating Energy Management,* 1983.

Mair, Wood, and Davis, *Computer Control and Audit,* 1976.

Mints, *Bibliography of Internal Auditing, 1969–1979,* 1980.

1983 EDP Audit Forum Proceedings, Institute of Internal Auditors Research Foundation, 1983.

Patton, Evans, and Lewis, *A Framework for Evaluating Internal Audit Risk,* 1982.

Paz, *Integrating the Internal Auditor Into EDP,* 1983.

Rittenberg, Larry E., *Auditor Independence and Systems Design,* 1977.

Sawyer, *Elements of Management-Oriented Auditing,* 1984.

Sawyer, *The Practice of Modern Internal Auditing,* 1981.

Smith, *Management of the Information Systems Audit: A Case Study,* 1980.

Sorkin and Ricketts, *Quantitative Techniques for Internal Auditing,* 1983.

Standards for the Professional Practice of Internal Auditing, 1978.

Stanford Research Institute, *System Auditability and Control Study,* Data Processing Audit Practices Report, 1977.

Stanford Research Institute, *System Auditability and Control Study,* Executive Report, 1977.

Survey of Internal Auditing—1979, 1979.

Ward, Marshall, *Recommended Codes and Practices for the Audit of Data Processing Activities,* 1980.

Wilkins, *The Internal Auditor's Information Security Handbook,* 1979.

EDP Auditors Foundation

The EDP Auditors Foundation for Education and Research has promulgated numerous audit guides, as well as other publications on CIS control issues. These publications are available from:

EDP Auditors Foundation, Inc.
373 South Schmale Road
Carol Stream, IL 60188

Controls in a Computer Environment: Objectives, Guidelines, and Audit Procedures, 1983 Edition.
Perry, William E., *Auditing Hardware and Software Contracts*, Audit Guide, 1983.
Perry, William E., *Auditing the Information System*, Audit Guide, 1983.
Perry, William E., *Auditing the Integrity of Computer Programs*, Audit Guide, 1983.
Perry, William E., *Auditing the Small Business Computer*, Audit Guide, 1983.
Perry, William E., *EDP Audit Planning*, Audit Guide, 1982.
Perry, William E., *EDP Audit Workpapers*, Audit Guide, 1981.
Perry, William E., *Selecting EDP Audit Areas*, Audit Guide, 1982.
Svanks, Maija I., *Integrity Analysis: A Methodology for EDP Audit and Data Quality Assurance*, 1984.

Quality Assurance Institute (QAI)

Publications from the QAI may be obtained from:

Quality Assurance Institute
9222 Bay Point Drive
Orlando, FL 32811

Database Control Guidelines, 1984.
Hatching the EDP Quality Assurance Function, 1984.
Modern Project Management, 1984.
Quality Assurance Survey, 1984.
Quality Assurance System Development Reviews, 1984.
Quality Data Processing—The Profit Potential for the 80s, 1984.
Report Writing for Quality Assurance Analysts, 1984.

COMMERCIAL PUBLISHERS

Books, reports, and other publications of interest to CIS auditors are listed below, grouped by subject area:

- Hardware

- Software

- Management

- CIS Auditing

- Computer Security and Privacy

- Quality Assurance

- Statistics and Probability

- Legal Issues.

Hardware

Enockson, *A Guide for Selecting Computers and Software*, Reston Publishing Company, Inc., 1983.

Isshiki, *Small Business Computers: Selection*, Prentice-Hall, Inc., 1982.

Perry, *Microcomputer Software Selection Guide*, QED Information Sciences, Inc., 1983.

Segal, Berst, *How to Manage Your Small Computer*, Prentice-Hall, Inc., 1983.

Veit, *Using Microcomputers in Business*, Hayden Book Company, 1983.

Software

Atre, S., *Database: Structured Techniques for Design, Performance, and Management*, 1980.

Dunn, Robert, *Quality Assurance for Computer Software*, McGraw-Hill Book Company, 1982.

Fernandez, et al., *Database Security and Integrity*, Addison-Wesley Publishing Company, 1981.

Glasson, B.C., *EDP System Development Guidelines*, QED Information Sciences, Inc., 1984.

Hansen, H. Dines, *Upland Running: The Case Study of a Successful EDP Systems Development Project*, Yourdon, 1984.

Hong-Leong, Balkis W. and Plagman, Bernard K., *Data Dictionary/Directory Systems: Administration, Implementation and Usage*, 1982.

Microcomputer Educational Software, San Jose, CA: 1983.

Perry, *Ensuring Database Integrity*, John Wiley & Sons, Inc., 1983.

Wolberg, John R., *Conversion of Computer Software*, Prentice-Hall, Inc., 1983.

Management

Axelrod, C. Warren, *Computer Productivity: A Planning Guide for Cost Effective Management*, John Wiley & Sons, 1982.

Cortada, James W., *EDP Costs and Charges*, Prentice-Hall, Inc., 1980.

Cortada, James W., *Managing DP Hardware*, Prentice-Hall, Inc., 1983.

Dawson, Peter P., *Fundamentals of Organizational Behavior: An Experiential Approach,* Prentice-Hall, Inc., 1985.

EDP Performance Management, Applied Computer Research, 1978.

EDP Performance Management Handbook, (vols. 1, 2), Applied Computer Research, 1979.

Fried, Louis, *Practical Data Processing Management,* Reston Publishing Company, Inc., 1979.

Inmon, William H., *Management Control of Data Processing,* Prentice-Hall, Inc., 1983.

Jackson, Barbara B., *Computer Models in Management,* Homewood, IL: 1979.

Norton, David P., *A Guide to EDP Performance Management,* QED Information Sciences, Inc., 1978.

A Practical Guide to Data Center Operations Management, Auerbach Publishers, Inc., 1982.

A Practical Guide to Data Processing Management, Auerbach Publishers, Inc., 1982.

A Practical Guide to Distributed Processing Management, Auerbach Publishers, Inc., 1982.

A Practical Guide to Systems Development Management, Auerbach Publishers, Inc., 1982.

Reifer, *Software Management,* The Institute of Electrical and Electronics Engineers, Inc. (IEEE), 1981.

Schweitzer, James A., *Protecting Information in the Electronic Workplace—A Guide for Managers,* Reston Publishing Company, Inc., 1983.

Singer, Larry M., *The Data Processing Manager's Survival Manual,* John Wiley & Sons, Inc., 1982.

Stevens, Barry A., *Management Control of EDP Performance,* (vol. 1), Applied Computer Research, 1980.

CIS Auditing

Auditing Computer Systems, FTD Technical Library, 1981.

Backe, Steve, *The EDP Internal Audit Function: A Research Study on the Role of the EDP Internal Auditor,* University Microfilms, Inc., 1982.

Cornick, *Auditing in the Electronic Environment,* Lomond Publications, Inc., 1981.

Davis and Perry, *Auditing Computer Applications,* John Wiley & Sons, Inc., 1982.

Davis and Weber, *Auditing Advanced EDP Systems,* The Management Information Systems Research Center, 1983.

Fitzgerald, Jerry, *Designing Controls Into Computerized Systems,* Jerry Fitzgerald and Associates, 1981.

Fitzgerald, Jerry, *Internal Controls for Computerized Systems*, Jerry Fitzgerald and Associates, 1978.

Halper, Stanley, et al., *Handbook of EDP Auditing*, Warren, Gorham and Lamont, 1985.

Jancura and Boos, *Establishing Controls and Auditing the Computerized Accounting System*, Van Nostrand Reinhold Company, 1980.

Kuong, *How to Train, Develop, and Manage the EDP Audit and Control Resource*, Management Advisory Publications, 1982.

Macchiaverna, Paul R., *Auditing Corporate Data Processing Activities*, The Conference Board, 1980.

Porter and Perry, *EDP, Controls and Auditing*, XVII, Kent Publishing Company, 1984.

Roberts, Martin B., *EDP Controls: A Guide for Auditors and Accountants*, John Wiley & Sons, Inc., 1983.

Rothberg, Gabriel B., *Structured EDP Auditing*, Lifetime Learning, 1983.

Sardinas, Joseph L., *EDP Auditing: A Primer*, John Wiley & Sons, Inc., 1981.

Taylor, Donald H., *Auditing Integrated Concepts and Procedures*, John Wiley & Sons, Inc., 1982.

Watne and Turney, *Auditing EDP Systems*, Prentice-Hall, Inc., 1984.

Weber, Ron, *EDP Auditing: Conceptual Foundations and Practice*, McGraw-Hill Book Company, 1982.

Computer Security and Privacy

Beitman, Lawrence, *The Computer Security Dictionary*, Secureware, 1983.

Buck, *Introduction to Data Security and Controls*, QED Information Sciences, Inc., 1982.

Carroll, John M., *Controlling White Collar Crime*, Butterworth Publishers, 1982.

Computer Security Risk Analysis, Advent Group, 1983.

Cooper, James A., *Computer-Security Technology*, Lexington Books, 1984.

Denning, *Cryptography and Data Security*, Addison-Wesley Publishing Company, 1982.

Engel, Howerton, *Computer Security: A Management Audit Approach*, Amacom, 1980.

Enger, Normal L., *Computer Security*, Amacom, 1980.

Finch, *Computer Security: A Global Challenge*, Elservier, 1985.

Fisher, Royal P., *Information Systems Security*, Prentice-Hall, Inc., 1984.

Hsiao, David K., *Computer Security*, Academic Press, 1979.

Knauss, Leonard I. and Macgaher, Ailleen, *Computer Fraud and Countermeasures*, Prentice-Hall, Inc., 1979.

Knauss, Leonard I., *SAFE: Security Audit and Field Evaluation for Computer Facilities and Information Systems*, American Management, 1981.

Leiss, *Principles of Data Security*, Plenum Press, 1982.

Lord, Kenniston W., Jr., *The Data Center Disaster Consultant*, QED Information Sciences, Inc., 1981.

Norman, *Computer Insecurity*, Chapman and Hall, Ltd., 1983.

Novotny, Eric, *Computer Security Guide for Financial Institutions*, American Bankers Association, 1978.

Parker, *Computer Security Management*, Reston Publishing Company, Inc., 1981.

Perry, *Computer Control and Security*, John Wiley & Sons, Inc., 1981.

Perry, William E., *Management Strategies for Computer Security*, Butterworth Publishers, 1985.

Schabeck, Timothy A., *Managing Microcomputer Security*, Computer Protection Systems, 1983.

Schweitzer, James A., *Managing Information Security—A Program for the Electronic Information Age*, Butterworth Publishers, 1982.

Talbot, *Computer Security*, Halsted Press, 1981.

Walker, Bruce J., *Computer Security and Protection Structures*, Halsted Press, 1977.

Quality Assurance

Dunn, Robert H. and Ullman, R., *Quality Assurance for Computer Software*, McGraw-Hill, 1982.

Goetz, Victor J., *Quality Assurance*, Amacom, 1978.

Perry, William E., *Effective Methods of EDP Quality Assurance*, QED Information Sciences, Inc, 1981.

Statistics and Probability

Andrews, Frank M., *Guide for Selecting Statistical Techniques*, Institute for Social Research, University of Michigan, 1981.

Arkin, H., *Handbook of Sampling for Auditing and Accounting*, McGraw-Hill, 1984.

Arkin, H., *Sampling Methods for the Auditor*, McGraw-Hill, 1982.

Legal Issues

Auer, Harris, *Computer Contracts Negotiations*, Van Nostrand Reinhold Company, 1981.

Bigelow, *Computers and the Law*, Commerce Clearing House, 1981.

Gemignani, *Law and the Computer*, CBI Publishing Co., 1981.

Hoffman, *The Software Legal Book*, Carnegie Press, 1981.

Smith, *Products Liability: Are You Vulnerable?*, Prentice-Hall, Inc., 1981.

Westermeier, *DP and the Law*, Data Processing Management Association, 1981.

Index

Page numbers in *italics* refer to figures in the text.

A

Abuse/misuse of computers, 3, 56, 68, 259, 328, 565, 567–568. *See also* Fraud
  exposures associated with, 328, *331*
  by hackers (case study), 432–436
  increase in, 65
  legislation affecting, 89–90
  losses due to, 4, 95
  microcomputers and, 386
  minimizing, 255

Access
  audit trails of, 350
  clearances for, 182
  to decision support systems, 405
  logging, 395, 405
  operating systems and, 340–344, 351
  unauthorized, 68, 90, 117, 120, 123–124

Access control labels, 513

Access controls, 6, 12, 405

Accidental exposures, 68, 96, 329

Account numbers, self-checking, 167

Accountability, 12, 14

Accountants. *See* Certified public accountants

Accounting and audit departments, 76

Accounting and Auditing Act of 1950, 85

Accounting models, 399. *See also* Models/modeling

Accounting standards manuals, 44

Accounts payable, 291, 294
  controls involved in, 139, *146–147*, 148–149
  steps in processing, 139

Accreditation, 77–78, 500–501

Accuracy, 168–169, 185, 222

Active threats, 509

Active wiretapping, 416

Advanced office systems (AOS), 380–392
  CIS center and, 385–386
  defined, 380
  organizational policy for, 389–390
  projections, 382, *383*
  top management and, 381–382

Advanced systems/advanced systems technology
  applied to audit (case study), 558–561
  exposures associated with, 328, *330*

AICPA. *See* American Institute of Certified Public Accountants

Air conditioners, 198

ALE. *See* Annualized loss expectancy

American Accounting Association, Committee on Basic Auditing Concepts, 22

B

Backup, 130, 152, 197, 199–200, 251, 336, 385, 424, 499, 508, 520
  of microcomputer files, 391–392
  restart and, 432

Badges, magnetically coded, 405

Balance sheet accounts, 228

Balancing, 518

Batch processing, 159, 322, 518
  controls, 156, 157–158
  data control records, 338

Benchmarks, 345, 356, 368

"Black box," 13, 49

Block sampling, 221

Boards of directors, 100–101

Bottlenecks, 56, 119

Browsers, 10, 68

Budgets, 254, 313, 453, 534
  for computer audit (case study), 542

C

Calculated controls, 167

Call-back systems, 424

Cambridge Analyzer, 57

Canadian Institute of Chartered Accountants (CICA), 67

Capacity planning, 356

Career development, 533, 542, 543–544, 545, 546–549

Carter, Jimmy, 86

Case studies
  Abcor, 526–556, 619–624
  Discount Distributors, Inc., 292–298

Exotic Electronics, Inc., 615–617
Federal Home Loan Mortgage Corp., General Risk Analysis, 458–467
Gotham City, 614
Honest Bob's Insurance Company, 613
Sleepwell Memorial Hospital, 612
Wedco, 604–611
WhyMe Corporation, 584–603

CDP. *See* Certified Data Processor

Centralization, 10–11. *See also* Decentralization
  of computer auditing resources, 568
  of control, 382–384, 392–395
  decision support systems and, 404
  errors and, 177
  through information centers, 393

Certification, 75–76, 77–78, 547, 549

Certified Data Processor (CDP), 75

Certified Internal Auditors (CIA), 75

Certified Management Accountant (CMA), 75

Certified public accountant (CPA) firms, 8, 31, 32–33, 63, 572

Certified public accountants, 23, 250

Certified Information Systems Auditors (CISA), 76

Certified Quality Assurance Analyst (CQAA), 75

Certified Systems Professional (CSP), 75

Changes
  in computer auditing, 558–561
  to databases, 352
  in financial position, 228
  minimizing after implementation, 126
  to systems, 220–221, 253
  unauthorized, 519

Characters, counting, 166

Check bits, 430

Check digit verification, 430

Cipher text, defined, 495

Ciphers, defined, 375

CIS audit charters, 269–270, 371, 526

E

F

Firmware, 374, 495–496

Flagging, defined, 151

Flexibility, 109, 185
  high-level languages and, 407, *408*
  of IST/RAMP, 450

Flow diagrams. *See* Audit data flow diagrams; Data flow diagrams

Flowchart Symbols and Their Usage in Information Processing (NBS), 53

Flowcharting, 46, 47–49, 53, 56, 57, *58–59*

Flowcharts, 34–35, 44, 45, 46, 57, 193, 207, 248, 313, 517
  software generation of, 278–279
  symbols, 53

FOCUS, 274, 278, *279*, 365, 407

Follow-up phase, 268, 282

Footings, 286

Forecasts, of work-load demands, 359

Foreign Corrupt Practices Act (1977), 88–89, 568

Forms, 157, 248

FORTRAN, 368

Forward error correction, 173

Fourth-generation languages, 274, 278
  trends, 407–410

Fraud, 3–7, 95, 206, 259, 326, 386, 565. *See also* Abuse/misuse of computers
  computer-assisted auditing techniques and, 283
  elements required for, 197
  legislation on, 89–90
  losses due to, 95
  minimizing, 255
  responses of AICPA to, 24–25

Freedom of Information Act, 633

Front-end processors, 161, *346*, 358

Functional specifications, 240

Fundamentals of Organizational Behavior: An Experiential Approach (Dawson), 525

Future of computer auditing, 558–583. *See also* Trends

G

GAAP. *See* Generally accepted accounting principles

GAAS. *See* Generally accepted auditing standards

GAMMA, 124, 365

Gantt charts, *554*

GAO. *See* United States General Accounting Office

GAS. *See* Generalized audit software

General controls, 176–200. *See also* Environmental controls
  review and evaluation of, 34, 625, 626–628

General design phase (of SDLC), 240

General integrity (GRA model), 463–464, *465*

General ledger, 34, 35, 36, 167

General Risk Analysis (GRA)
  case study, 458–467
  final risk score calculation, 467, 468, *468*
  inputs and outputs, *470–475*
  pervasive risk factors, 460–467
  specific risk factors, 459

General standards, defined, 23

Generalized audit software (GAS), 113, 119, 307, 312, 365, 408

Generalized audit software languages, 124

Generally accepted accounting principles (GAAP), 23

Generally accepted auditing standards (GAAS), 23–24, 25, 26

Generation-control feature, 164

Geosynchronous orbits, defined, 414

Global, defined, 177

Glossary for Computer System Security (FIPS PUB 39), 513

Government. *See* Federal government; Legislation

GRA. *See* General Risk Analysis

Ground stations, 414

N